CRIMINAL JUSTICE *in* *A*MERICA

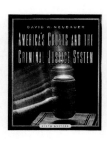

From Wadsworth's Criminal Justice series . . .

The Criminal Event:
An Introduction to Criminology
by Vincent F. Sacco and Leslie W. Kennedy
(ISBN: 0-534-26448-4)

Contemporary Criminology
by Walter S. DeKeseredy and Martin D. Schwartz
(ISBN: 0-534-19764-7)

Criminal Justice Organizations: Administration and Management, 2/E
by John Klofas, Stan Stojkovic, and David Kalinich
(ISBN: 0-534-21414-2)

America's Courts and the Criminal Justice System, 5/E
by David W. Neubauer
(ISBN: 0-534-23952-8)

Trusted Criminals: White Collar Crime in Contemporary Society
by David O. Friedrichs
(ISBN: 0-534-50517-1)

Also available from Wadsworth's Contemporary Issues in Crime and Justice Series . . .

Hard Time: Understanding and Reforming the Prison, 2/E
by Robert Johnson
(ISBN: 0-534-18750-1)

The Color of Justice: Race and Crime in America
by Samuel Walker
(ISBN: 0-534-26226-0)

The Invisible Woman: Gender, Crime, and Justice
by Joanne Belknap
(ISBN: 0-534-15870-6)

Crime Victims: An Introduction to Victimology, 3/E
by Andrew Karmen
(ISBN: 0-534-23772-X)

To order your copy of any of these titles, please visit your local bookseller.

CRIMINAL JUSTICE in AMERICA

George F. Cole
University of Connecticut

Christopher E. Smith
Michigan State University

Wadsworth Publishing Company
I(T)P® An International Thomson Publishing Company

Belmont • Albany • Bonn • Boston • Cincinnati • Detroit • London • Madrid • Melbourne
Mexico City • New York • Paris • San Francisco • Singapore • Tokyo • Toronto • Washington

Criminal Justice Editor: Sabra Horne

Assistant Editor: Claire Masson

Development Editor: Alan Venable

Editorial Assistant: Louise Mendelson

Production Editor: Deborah Cogan

Managing Designer: Carolyn Deacy

Text and Cover Designer: Ellen Pettengell

Print Buyer: Karen Hunt

Art Editor: Kevin Berry

Permissions Editor: Jeanne Bosschart

Copy Editor: Thomas Briggs

Illustrator: Precision Graphics

Cover Photograph: © Spencer Grant/Gamma Liaison

Compositor: Thompson Type

Printer: Von Hoffmann Press

1 2 3 4 5 6 7 8 9 10

Library of Congress Cataloging-in-Publication Data

Cole, George F., 1935–
    Criminal justice in America / George F. Cole,
Christopher E. Smith.
        p.   cm.
    Includes bibliographical references (p.   ) and index.
    ISBN 0-534-24420-3 (pbk.)
    1. Criminal justice, Administration of—United
States.   I. Smith, Christopher E.   II. Title.
HV9950.C6   1996
364.973—dc20   95-12626

For more information, contact:

Wadsworth Publishing Company
10 Davis Drive
Belmont, California 94002, USA

International Thomson Publishing Europe
Berkshire House 168-173
High Holborn
London, WC1V 7AA, England

Thomas Nelson Australia
102 Dodds Street
South Melbourne 3205
Victoria, Australia

Nelson Canada
1120 Birchmount Road
Scarborough, Ontario
Canada M1K 5G4

International Thomson Editores
Campos Eliseos 385, Piso 7
Col. Polanco
11560 México D.F. México

International Thomson Publishing GmbH
Königswinterer Strasse 418
53227 Bonn, Germany

International Thomson Publishing Asia
221 Henderson Road
#05-10 Henderson Building
Singapore 0315

International Thomson Publishing Japan
Hirakawacho Kyowa Building, 3F
2-2-1 Hirakawacho
Chiyoda-ku, Tokyo 102, Japan

BRIEF CONTENTS

DETAILED CONTENTS

PART II *Police*

PART III *Courts*

PART IV *Corrections*

PART V *The Juvenile Justice System*

PREFACE

Criminal Justice in America is designed to serve those instructors who want a textbook that introduces students to the dynamics of the American system of criminal justice without overwhelming them. This need was brought to our attention by faculty who reviewed the proposal, who participated in a focus group at the meetings of the Academy of Criminal Justice Sciences, and who told us that they wanted a briefer introductory book than was currently available. Instructors told us that they were unable to cover all of the material presented in the major texts, that they wanted to be able to supplement a core text with other readings, and that they wanted a book that was user-friendly to them and to their students.

Criminal Justice in America is an offspring of The American System of Criminal Justice, now in its seventh edition. However, it has not been created by merely dropping chapters, combining others, and limiting the graphic elements so as to reduce the page count. Criminal Justice in America relies on the research and the conceptual foundation of the larger text, but the material has been completely rewritten in a style that is descriptive and informative, without being overly theoretical. Throughout the book examples are used to link the concepts and information to real-life criminal justice situations.

Twin themes run throughout the book:

- *Criminal justice involves public policies* that are developed within the political framework of the democratic process.
- *The concept of social system* is an essential tool for explaining and analyzing the way criminal justice is administered in practice.

This approach has met with a high degree of acceptance and might be called the dominant paradigm in criminal justice education. Criminal justice is interdisciplinary, with criminology, sociology, law, history, psychology, and political science contributing to the field. The twin themes of public policy and social system help to place the research contributions of these disciplines in a context that allows students to better understand the dynamics of criminal justice.

Instructors of criminal justice enjoy an advantage that many of their colleagues in other disciplines might envy. Most students come to the introductory course intrigued by the prospect of learning about crime and the operation of the criminal justice system. Many of them are optimistic about the role they may one day play in allocating justice, either as citizens or in a career with the police, courts, or corrections. All have been exposed to a great deal of information—and misinformation—about criminal justice through the news and entertainment media. Whatever their views, few are indifferent to the subject they are about to explore.

Like all newcomers to a field, however, introductory students in criminal justice need, first, *a solid foundation* of valid information about the subject and, second, *a way to think about* this information. They need conceptual tools that enable them not only to absorb a large body of factual content but also to process that information critically, reflect on it, and extend their learning beyond the classroom. Providing both the essential content and the critical tools is the dual aim of this text.

SUPPLEMENTS

An extensive package of supplemental aids accompanies the text.

Instructor's Resource Manual and Computerized Test Bank. A full-fledged Instructor's Resource Manual has been developed by the authors. In it will be found lists of resources, lecture outlines, and testing suggestions that will help time-pressed teachers to more effectively communicate to their students. Each chapter has multiple-choice and true-false test items, as well as sample essay questions. To bring the graphic portions of the text to the classroom, transparency masters for overhead projection are provided. These transparencies help each instructor to fully discuss concepts and research findings with students. The instructor's manual is backed up with a computerized test bank suitable for IBM or Macintosh personal computers.

Study Guide. An extensive study guide has been developed for this book. Because students learn in different ways, a variety of pedagogical aids are included in the guide to help them. Each chapter is outlined, major terms are defined, summaries are given, and sample tests are provided. Featured in the study guide are worksheets so that students can confront hypothetical criminal justice situations where decisions must be made.

A Group Effort. It is not possible to be expert about all portions of the criminal justice system. Authors need help in covering new developments and ensuring that research findings are correctly interpreted. We have greatly benefited from the advice of two sets of scholars. Each read the manuscript from a different perspective. One group was asked to comment on the entire manuscript, with an emphasis on its organization and pedagogical usefulness. These reviewers were chosen from a wide range of colleges and universities throughout the country, so their comments were especially useful with regard to presentation, levels of student abilities, and the requirements of the introductory courses at their institutions.

A second group of reviewers was composed of scholars who are nationally recognized experts in the field, and they focused on the areas in which they specialize. Their many comments helped us avoid errors and drew our attention to points in the literature that had been neglected.

We have also been assisted in writing this edition by a diverse group of associates, chief among them development editor Alan Venable. The project has also benefited much from the attention and support of Sabra Horne, criminal justice editor at Wadsworth, whose encouragement and enthusiasm have been crucial, and from the careful work of Deborah Cogan, production editor. Ellen Pettengell designed the interior of the book; Carolyn Deacy managed the overall design process and worked with art editor Kevin Berry to develop the extensive photographic and art programs. And the following reviewers contributed valuable comments: Jerry Armor, Calhoun Community College; W. H. Copley, College of Denver; John Dempsey, Suffolk Community College; Daniel Doyle, University of Montana; Robert M. Hurley, Sacramento State University; Tim Jones, Athens State College; Thomas D. McDonald, North Dakota State University; Nicholas Meier, Kalamazoo Valley Community College; Patrick Patterson, Mohawk Valley Community College; Patricia Payne, Middlesex County College; Tim Perry, Shoreline Community College; Rudy K. Prine, Valdosta State University; Walter F. Ruger, Nassau Community College; Angelo Triniti, Passaic County Community College; Melvin Wallace, McHenry County College; Bob Walsh, University of Houston, Downtown; Vincent J. Webb, University of Nebraska, Omaha. Ultimately, however, the full responsibility for the book is ours alone.

George F. Cole

Christopher E. Smith

POLICE

PROSECUTION/DEFENSE

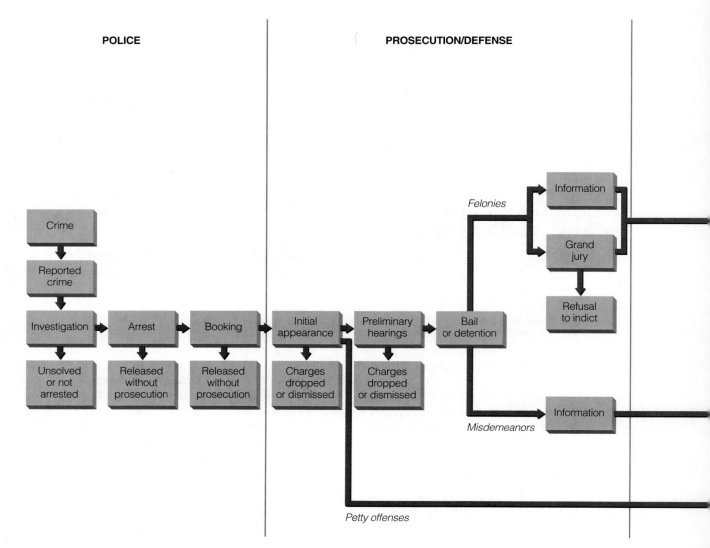

**The Sequence of Events in the American
Criminal Justice System**
This flowchart provides an overview of the criminal
justice system as it will be described in this book. It is
important to recognize that the system portrayed here is
a *social system*. Each event depicted represents a complex
interaction of people, politics, and procedures.

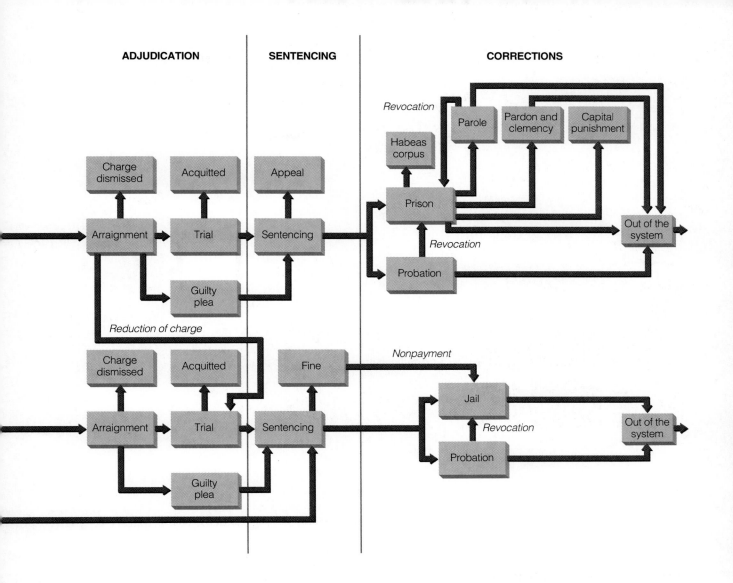

ADJUDICATION　　　**SENTENCING**　　　**CORRECTIONS**

Charge dismissed

Acquitted

Appeal

Revocation

Parole

Pardon and clemency

Capital punishment

Habeas corpus

Arraignment

Trial

Sentencing

Prison

Out of the system

Guilty plea

Revocation

Probation

Reduction of charge

Charge dismissed

Acquitted

Fine

Nonpayment

Arraignment

Trial

Sentencing

Jail

Out of the system

Guilty plea

Revocation

Probation

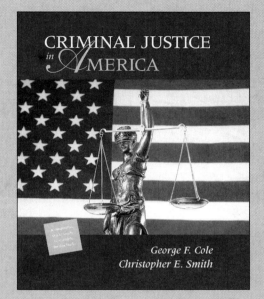

Welcome to the fascinating study of crime and justice. If you're like most Americans, you've already been exposed to a barrage of information about crime. Newpapers, novels, television, and films guarantee a steady dose. And yet, the crime problem is vastly more complex than what we see in the movies or read in the morning headlines. In this book you will explore criminal justice in all of its complexity.

Criminal Justice in America presents you with a completely *realistic* picture of crime and justice in the United States. You will receive a solid base of empirical information, drawn from scholarly research, government documents, popular media, and other sources. You will also receive a set of conceptual skills for analyzing what you read and hear about criminal justice. In this book we have tried to provide you with both the information and an approach for thinking about that information.

Whether you are considering a career related to criminal justice or simply want to become more informed on the subject, the reality is that *all of us* have a stake in the way criminal justice is administered. In our democratic society, the need for freedom and the need for order sometimes conflict, creating both problems and opportunities. *Now* is the time for a new generation of criminal justice practitioners, scholars, and concerned citizens to provide the insight and leadership that will bring long-overdue improvements to the control of crime.

To make this introduction to American criminal justice informative, stimulating, and fully understandable, we have designed a number of special features to guide you in the learning process. These features are illustrated on the following seven pages.

George F. Cole

Christopher E. Smith

To organize your study effectively, take advantage of the consistent format of each chapter.

CHAPTER 6
Policing: Issues and Trends

128

CHAPTER OUTLINES

present an overview of the topics to be covered that you can use as a framework for study and review.

CHAPTER INTRODUCTIONS

open each chapter with a real-life story that sets the stage for the content that follows.

CHAPTER QUESTIONS

focus your attention on the key points to be explored in the chapter.

PAYING THE PRICE FOR POLICE CORRUPTION

On Monday, July 11, 1994, former New York City police officer Michael Dowd stood before Judge Kimba Wood in a federal courtroom. Dowd was about to be sentenced for a variety of crimes in which he used his authority as a police officer to abuse people, steal money and goods, and obtain cocaine. His crimes ranged from stealing food intended for the needy from a church to plotting a kidnapping on behalf of drug dealers. Dowd had been the star witness in the city's Mollen Commission investigation, which uncovered the worst police corruption scandal in New York City in two decades. Dowd had hoped that his cooperation with authorities would lead to a lenient sentence, but prosecutors found many of his statements about illegal activities within the police department to be false or misleading. When Judge Wood sentenced him to fifteen years in prison, a sentence just short of the maximum possible, Dowd was stunned and mumbled, "Oh, my God. Oh, my God." In issuing her sentence, Judge Wood said to Dowd, "You did not just fall prey to temptation and steal what was in front of you and take kickbacks or sell confidential law enforcement information. You also continually searched for new ways to abuse your position and at times you recruited fellow officers to join in your crimes."

Dowd's case illustrates a problem that surfaces regularly in law enforcement. How can we make sure that the people who possess authority do not use their power for personal gain? Police have sworn an oath to protect society against illegal activities; thus, we are especially shocked and disappointed when they, of all people, violate public trust.

In this chapter, we will discuss a number of important issues concerning the police and their relationship with society. We will look at recruitment and training of the police and examine the unique subculture that develops from the environment, socialization, and pressures that the police experience. We will also explore the enduring problem of the abuse of power by the police and what is being done about it. Finally, we will look at two trends—unionism and private policing—that affect police operations. ★

129

criminal justice system serve? Although difficult to specify ex-

ment and Administration an apparatus society to protect individuals of our discussion of much debate about: (1) doing justice,

rules, procedures, system founded on between criminal justice Fairness is an essential investigate, adjudicate, the rights of individuals the goal of doing justice... offenders will be held persons who have like offenses will be relevant differences

to identify situations processes fall short of which criminal justice clearly serves the interests of those who hold political power, in a democracy people can aspire to improve the capacity of their institutions to do justice. Thus, however imperfect they may be, criminal justice institutions and processes in the United States can enjoy the support of the public as responsive agencies of government. In a democracy, a system that makes doing justice a paramount goal is viewed by citizens as legitimate and is thus able to pursue the secondary goals of controlling and preventing crime.

CONTROLLING CRIME

The criminal justice system is designed to control crime by apprehending, prosecuting, convicting, and punishing those members of the community who disobey the law. An important constraint on the system, however, is that efforts to control crime must be carried out within the framework of law. The criminal law not only defines what is illegal but also outlines the rights of citizens and prescribes the procedures that officials must use to achieve the system's goals.

27

RUNNING GLOSSARY

conveniently defines the terminology of the field. Because criminal justice is interdisciplinary, a number of terms used in criminology, sociology, law, history, psychology, and political science are fully defined in the margin, next to their first, bold-faced, appearance in the text. These terms are also defined at the end of the book in a complete Index/Glossary.

CHAPTER SUMMARIES

offer a capsulized version of each chapter's main ideas.

---

legal sufficiency model
Prosecution policy that asks whether sufficient evidence exists to provide a basis for prosecution of a case.

system efficiency model
Operation of the prosecutor's office that encourages speedy and early disposition of cases in response to caseload pressures in the system.

trial sufficiency model
Prosecution policy that asks whether sufficient legal elements exist to ensure successful prosecution of a case.

Under this **legal sufficiency model**, prosecutors are merely asking whether sufficient evidence exists to provide a basis for prosecuting the defendant. Some prosecutors believe that they have a responsibility to pursue any case for which they believe they can prove that the minimum legal elements of the charge are met. Prosecutors who use this policy may decide to prosecute a great many cases. As a result, they must employ strategies to avoid overloading the system and draining their own resources. Thus, assistant prosecutors, especially those assigned to misdemeanor courts, must use plea bargaining to the utmost, and they must expect many judicial dismissals and acquittals in court.

System Efficiency Model. In the **system efficiency model**, each case is evaluated in light of the caseload pressures affecting the prosecutor's office, with the underlying goal of attaining quick, early dispositions to stretch prosecution resources. If there are questions in the prosecutor's mind about the adequacy of evidence in a particular case, the case may simply be dismissed. If there is adequate evidence, the prosecutor may file felony charges but agree to reduce to misdemeanor charges in exchange for a quick guilty plea. According to Jacoby's research, the system efficiency model is usually followed when the trial court is backlogged and the prosecutor has limited resources.

Trial Sufficiency Model. According to the **trial sufficiency model**, a case is accepted and charges are made only when sufficient legal elements exist to ensure successful prosecution. The prosecutor asks, "Will this case result in a conviction?" Although the prosecutor does not pursue only sure convictions, the cases pursued have the appropriate facts and sufficient evidence to support a conviction, and the prosecutor makes every effort to obtain that outcome. This model requires good police work, a prosecution staff that is experienced in trial work, and sufficient court resources to handle trials.

Obviously, the different models lead to different results. While a suspect's case may be dismissed for insufficient evidence in a "trial sufficiency" [court, it] be prosecuted, and the suspect eventually pressured to enter a [plea in] a "legal sufficiency" court.

[### Deci]sion

[The charging process] is the series of events from the arrest and booking [of a suspect to] the filing of formal charges with the court. Throughout the [process, a pro]secutor must evaluate various considerations in order to de[cide whether t]o press charges and what charges to file. A prosecutor's deci[sions are s]tructured by whichever of the three models his or her office [uses. The]se models cannot, however, be applied automatically. Each [involve]s an evaluation of the quality and quantity of evidence for a [case]. In addition, each model may include assessments of the re[sources availab]le in the prosecutor's office and trial court. For example, if the [court is] crowded and the prosecutor has few resources, then the prose[cutor is] forced to use the system efficiency model even if he or she ide[ally prefers] to use another approach.

[Prosecuto]rs may decide pragmatically in individual cases that the accused [and society w]ould benefit from a particular course of action. In this sense, [they at]tempt to individualize justice according to their own assess[ment of] and beneficial outcomes. For example, a young, first-time of[fende]r offender with substance abuse problems may be placed in a [pro]gram rather than prosecuted in the criminal justice system.

SUMMARY

Prosecutors and defense attorneys are key figures in the processing of criminal cases. Both actors become involved in the early stages of cases and interact together at successive stages of the justice process until, in most cases, the charges are dropped or a negotiated plea bargain produces a guilty plea. Prosecutors have significant discretion to establish the framework for each case by determining which defendants will actually face charges and what charges they will face. Such decisions are shaped by a variety of factors, including the prosecutor's conception of his or her role, interactions with other actors, caseload pressures, and policies established within a particular prosecutor's office. There are no higher authorities who can overrule a prosecutor's decision to pursue specific charges or to drop all charges. Because most prosecutors are elected officials, they are primarily accountable only to a voting public that has little knowledge of their daily decisions.

Defense attorneys' actions and decisions are influenced by their relationships with other courthouse actors, their motivations as privately paid or publicly financed counsel, and the degree of cooperation that they can obtain from their clients. Defense attorneys have important responsibilities for protecting defendants' constitutional rights, yet serious questions exist about whether private attorneys and public defenders adequately fulfill these duties. There are risks that limited resources and attorneys' self-interest may contribute to inadequate representation.

As we will see in the next two chapters concerning pretrial and trial processes, the outcome of a case depends on many complex factors. Always central to the process are fallible human beings who, in their roles as prosecutors, defense attorneys, and judges, possess discretionary powers and cooperate with other courthouse actors.

QUESTIONS FOR REVIEW

1. How can prosecutors' decisions be made more visible, and what effect would increased visibility have on the system?
2. How do prosecutors' relationships with other criminal justice system actors affect their decisions?
3. Should we require that lawyers possess special qualifications or certification before they are allowed to handle criminal cases?
4. How can we create a system in which the defense lawyers' interests and attention are focused on providing the best possible representation for clients?
5. Should we make it easier for defendants to succeed in filing "ineffective assistance of counsel" claims, and if so, how?

NOTES

1. U.S. Department of Justice, *Principles of Federal Prosecution* (Washington, DC: Government Printing Office, 1980), p. 7.
2. Barbara Boland, Elizabeth Brady, Herbert Tyson, and John Bassler, *The Prosecution of Felony Arrests*, U.S. Department of Justice, Bureau of Justice Statistics (Washington, DC: Government Printing Office, 1983), p. 9.

QUESTIONS FOR REVIEW

allow you to test your understanding of specific material and express what *you* think about aspects of the criminal justice system.

GRAPHICS

are an essential component of this book. The many flowcharts, graphs, tables, and other visual aids are carefully designed and captioned to focus and enliven information so that it can be accurately perceived and easily understood.

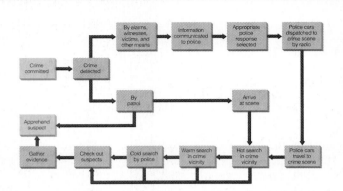

FIGURE 5.4
The Felony Apprehension Process
Apprehension of a felony suspect may result from a sequence of actions taken in response to the crime by patrol officers and detectives. Coordination of police response is important in solving major crimes.

search and may apprehend a suspect. This initial work is crucial. The officer must gather the basic facts, including the identity of the victim, a description of the suspect, and the names of witnesses. After the information is collected, it is transmitted to the investigation unit.

3. *Follow-up investigation.* After a crime has been brought to the attention of the police and a preliminary investigation has been made, the detective will determine what course of action to pursue. In the typical big-city department, incident reports from the previous day are analyzed the first thing in the morning. Assignments are distributed to individual investigators in accordance with their specialties. These investigators study the information, weigh each informational factor, and determine whether the factors are sufficient to indicate that the crime can be solved.

Some departments have developed formulas for guiding the disposition of cases so that resources will be used most efficiently. If the detectives determine tha[t] efforts m[...]

Whe[...] wider se[...] dertaken [...]

PHOTOGRAPHS

bring a captivating, realistic element to the text. Although a picture may be worth a thousand words, it takes the right picture set in the right place to enhance the idea communicated through words.

During the political era the officer on a neighborhood beat dealt with crime and disorder as it arose. Police also performed various social services.

80
Part II Police

South and West. Even if these descriptions of history are somewhat flawed, however, they provide a useful basis for noting the general changes in the organization of the police, the focus of their work, and the particular strategies of operation over the course of American history.

The Political Era: 1840–1920
The period 1840–1920 is called the Political Era because of the close ties that developed between the police and urban political leaders. In many cities, the police department appeared to work for the mayor or the political party in power rather than for the citizens in general. In some places, guns and badges were issued to white males who supported the mayor or the ruling political machine. These police officers would then help their political patrons stay in power by working to get out the vote on election day. Ranks in the force were often for sale to the highest bidder, and many police officers were "on the take."

In the United States, as in England, the growth of cities led to pressures for modernization of law enforcement. Social relations in the cities of the nineteenth century were quite different from those in the towns and countryside. In fact, from 1830 to 1870, there was unprecedented civil disorder in America's major cities. Ethnic conflict as a consequence of massive immigration from Europe, hostility toward nonslave blacks and abolitionists, mob actions against banks and other institutions of property during economic declines, and violence in settling questions of morality—all these factors contributed to fears that a stable democratic society would not survive.

Around 1840, the large cities began to take steps to create constabularies. Boston and Philadelphia were the first to add a daytime police force to supplement the night watchmen; other cities quickly followed suit. Soon, however, people recognized the inefficiency of separate day and night forces. In 1844, the New York state legislature passed a law to create a unified force for cities under the command of a chief appointed by the mayor and city council. By the 1850s, most major American cities had adopted this pattern.

Early police practices focused on watchman duties and reactive patrols. In effect, they sought to prevent crimes and keep order through the use of foot patrols. The officer on the beat dealt with crime, disorder, and other problems as they arose. The following Close-Up by Edward H. Savage, a fifteen-year veteran of the Boston Police Department, summarizes the role of the urban police officer during this period.

In addition to foot patrols, the police performed a number of service functions such as caring for derelicts, operating soup kitchens, regulating public health, and handling medical and social emergencies. In cities across the country, the police provided beds and food to homeless people. In station houses, these "lodgers" found overnight accommodations ranging from the floor to clean bunkrooms.[3] Because they were part of the only governmental agency with an organization and network on the streets of the city, the police became general public servants as well as crime control officers. Because of their close connections and service to the community during this era, they enjoyed citizen support.

Police in the South developed differently due to slavery and the rural, agricultural nature of that

community. Aggressive patrol takes a wide variety of forms, from programs that encourage citizens to identify their valuables, to "sting" operations, to repeat offender programs. James Q. Wilson and Barbara Boland have shown that patrol tactics that increase the risk of arrest are associated with crime reduction. They argue that the effect of the police on crime depends less on how many officers are deployed in a particular area than on what they do while they are there.[16]

An aggressive patrol strategy does not mean that officers are encouraged to patrol in a hostile manner; rather, they frequently stop and question people about what they are doing. In San Diego, an aggressive patrol strategy of field interrogations and street stops was associated with a significant decrease in certain "suppressible" crimes: robbery, burglary, theft, auto theft, assault, sex crimes, malicious mischief, and disturbances. It was concluded that field interrogations deterred potential offenders, especially young opportunists.[17] Officers in an "anticrime patrol" in New York worked the streets of high-crime areas in civilian clothes. Although these officers represented only 5 percent of the men and women assigned to each precinct, during one year they made over 18 percent of the felony arrests, including more than half of the arrests for robbery and about 40 percent of the arrests for burglary and auto theft.

In several cities, repeat offender programs have been successful in arresting career criminals. Using proactive tactics, the Washington, DC, repeat offender program targeted individuals with long criminal records who were believed to be engaged in criminal activity. Efforts were made to track down those for whom arrest warrants had been issued, and investigations were launched to close a large number of open cases and to recover stolen property. The program proved to be effective in removing repeat offenders from the streets, but it was also costly because it took officers away from their usual duties.[18]

The most cost-effective strategy for aggressive patrol seems to be to create incentives so that officers will increase the number of field interrogations and traffic stops that they initiate during each shift. In order to implement an aggressive patrol strategy, a police executive must recruit certain kinds of officers, train them in certain ways, and devise requirements and reward systems (traffic ticket quotas, field interrogation obligations, promotional opportunities) to encourage these officers to follow the strategy.[19]

Community-Oriented Policing. As discussed in Chapter 4, the new concept of community-oriented policing has taken hold in many cities. To a great extent, it has emerged because of perceived deficiencies in the crime fighter stance that most urban police departments took during the Professional Era.[20] Although a somewhat general term, community-oriented policing is most commonly associated with attempts by the police to involve the residents in making their own neighborhoods safe. This concept recognizes that citizens may be concerned about local disorder as well as crime in general. It emphasizes the need for collaboration between the police and citizens to identify community needs and determine the best ways to make improvements.[21]

Community-oriented policing may be carried out, for example, by patrol officers assigned to walk neighborhood beats so that they can cultivate better

Research indicates that although foot patrol does not greatly reduce crime, it does reduce the fear of crime.

111

REAL-LIFE EXAMPLES

—both historical and contemporary—are included throughout the text to help you identify with the human implications of criminal justice policy.

"IDEAS IN PRACTICE"

ask you to apply important ideas discussed in the chapter to criminal justice practice.

"CLOSE-UPS"

complement the text discussion with provocative perspectives from journalists, police officers, prisoners, judges, attorneys, and others.

IDEAS IN PRACTICE

Looking out the window of your room, you notice a young couple rolling on the ground beneath a large pine tree. You see books and a woman's purse scattered nearby. It is a beautiful spring day. You think, *Isn't love wonderful!* But a second thought enters your mind: *Are these two lovers or is that woman in trouble?* You stand up to get a better view. *The woman's clothes seem disheveled. Is she being assaulted? Should I dial 911? No, I think I'd better call Jim; he'd know what to do since he's ridden with the campus police.*

"Jim, there's a guy and girl rolling on the ground beneath my window. I can't make out if she's in trouble. Should I dial 911?"

"Of course. It can't do any harm and you may prevent a rape," replies Jim.

"O.K. I'll do it right now."

When the police arrive, they find a distraught young woman sobbing uncontrollably, her clothes torn and bloodied.

Are there any ways to shorten police response time to incidents such as this?

However, many citizens as well as some researchers claim that patrol officers in squad cars have become remote from the people they protect and less attentive to the needs and problems in specific neighborhoods. As Lawrence W. Sherman points out, the rise of motorized patrols and telephone dispatching has changed the older strategy of "watching to prevent crime" to "waiting to respond to crime."[12] Because officers rarely leave the patrol car, citizens have few chances to tell them what is going on in the community. Without information about problems and suspicious activities within neighborhoods, patrol officers cannot mediate disputes, investigate suspected criminal activity, and make residents feel that they personally care about their well-being. When officers are distant and aloof from the citizens they serve, the citizens may be less inclined to call for assistance or provide information.

By contrast, officers on foot are at home in the neighborhood. They are close to the daily life of the beat and in a better position to detect criminal activity and apprehend those who have violated the law. Further, when patrol officers are familiar to citizens, they are less likely to be perceived as symbols of oppression by poor or minority residents. In large cities, personal contact may help to reduce racial suspicion and conflict.

In the past decade, interest in foot patrol has revived primarily from citizens' demands for a familiar figure walking through their neighborhoods. Experiments in a number of cities have studied the cost and impact of foot patrol.[13] In general, these studies have shown that foot patrols do not greatly reduce crime but that citizens are less fearful of crime.[14]

One-Person versus Two-Person Patrol Units. The debate over one-person versus two-person patrol units has raged in police circles for years. A 1991 study of large cities revealed that 70 percent of patrol cars are staffed by one [officer, but the]re is much variation. For example, Los Angeles uses one-person [units for about] half of its units during the day, but only 9 percent at night. [___, h]owever, uses only one-officer cars.[15]

[___ ___]d their union leaders support the two-person squad car, argu[ing that a se]cond officer is required for safety's sake. They claim that police [are safe]r and more effective when two officers work together in dan[gerous or diffic]ult situations. However, police administrators contend that the [one-officer squ]ad car is significantly more cost-effective and permits them to [deploy more c]ars on each shift. With more cars to deploy, each can be as[signed to a smalle]r geographic sector, and response time can be decreased. Ad[ministrators fu]rther contend that an officer operating alone is more alert and [careful in his wo]rk because he or she cannot be distracted by idle conversation [with a colleag]ue.

[*Aggressive Pat*]***rol.*** **Aggressive patrol** is a proactive patrol strategy designed [to maximize t]he number of police interventions and observations in the

---

CLOSE-UP
Jeffrey Dahmer: The Insanity Plea That Didn't Work

The veteran Milwaukee police officers were understandably shocked when, in August 1991, they entered Jeffrey Dahmer's apartment and found two human heads in a refrigerator, two in a freezer, and seven others boiled clean. In the basement, they found an acid-filled barrel of body parts. Investigators soon learned the full extent of Dahmer's crimes. The thirty-one-year-old laborer confessed to the police how he lured young men and boys from gay bars to his apartment where he drugged and killed them, had sex with their corpses, and dissected and cannibalized the bodies.

Jeffrey Dahmer was charged with killing and dismembering fifteen young men and boys. Dahmer thus joined that small fraternity of killers such as Charles Manson, "Son of Sam" David Berkowitz, and John Wayne Gacy. All were serial killers whose behavior almost rivaled that of Hannibal (the Cannibal) Lecter in the movie *Silence of the Lambs*. Although the facts in these cases were not in doubt, given the horrific aspects of their crimes, the defendants' legal responsibility for their actions became an issue. Were they sane when they committed their crimes? Were their rights protected as they proceeded from arrest to trial? What is an appropriate punishment for such individuals?

At trial, Jeffrey Dahmer changed his plea to guilty by reason of insanity. Under Wisconsin law, he was given a two-part trial. During the first part, lasting three weeks, the jury heard the evidence from police investigators and determined that

---

Then it turns out that they are cultivating marijuana. You were not aware of this because you have no idea what a marijuana plant looks like. Should you be subject to a criminal conviction for growing an illegal drug on your property? The answer depends on the specific knowledge and intent requirements that the prosecution must prove for particular criminal offenses. Moreover, the success of such a defense may depend on the extent to which jurors understand and sympathize with your mistake.

Intoxication

People cannot usually claim to lack knowledge and intent when they voluntarily become intoxicated. However, if someone has been tricked into consuming intoxicating or mind-altering substances, then an intoxication defense may be raised. Intoxication may be argued to reduce the seriousness of a charge if the defendant can claim that his or her condition precluded the existence of the specific intent necessary for some crimes. Someone charged with theft may claim, for example, that she was too drunk to realize that she had left the restaurant without paying her bill.

Insanity

A claim of insanity can be used to negate the *mens rea* element of crimes. The insanity defense is rarely successful, yet it has raised significant public controversy.

In a highly publicized case in January 1994, Lorena Bobbitt was acquitted of the charge of malicious wounding when a jury found that she was temporarily insane when she cut off her husband's penis after being victimized by spousal abuse. In another example, John Hinckley shot former President Ronald Reagan in an assassination attempt. Despite the fact that Hinckley was apprehended on the spot with the gun in his hand, he was found not guilty by reason of insanity. Yet, as the Close-Up of the Jeffrey

TWO GUIDING THEMES

are integrated in this text to take you beyond mastering factual content to a more critical appreciation of criminal justice in American society.

CRIMINAL JUSTICE INEVITABLY INVOLVES ISSUES OF PUBLIC POLICY AND THEREFORE POLITICS.

In our democratic society, many issues involving criminal justice, such as crime rates, victims' rights, and the merits of the death penalty, are political by nature. By the same token, the fact that some officials of the criminal justice system, such as judges and district attorneys, are *elected* to their offices means their roles are inescapably political.

CLOSE-UP

A Three-Strike Penal Law Shows It's Not As Simple As It Seems

In the fight against violent crime, perhaps no idea is more popular than "three strikes and you're out"—locking up repeat offenders for life without parole. . . . But only one state, Washington, has any experience with it. Two months after a law went on the books requiring criminals to spend life in prison without parole if they are convicted of three felonies, the first cases of "three strikes" are emerging. And they present a more complicated picture than does the baseball slogan that inspired 76 percent of Washington State voters to back the measure.

Prosecutors and police officers say the law has had some unintended side effects. With nothing to lose, some criminals are showing a tendency to be more violent or desperate when officers try to arrest them. And prosecutors say first- and second-time felony offenders are less willing to plea bargain, when it means pleading guilty, to a first or second "strike." These offenders are instead forcing full trials in a court system that has neither the manpower nor the space to take on the extra load.

Among the first candidates for life in prison under the three-strikes law, several seem to fit the profile of violent predators with long criminal histories. But other cases may not be what voters here had in mind. One man has led a life of small-time crime. His third-strike offense was robbing a sandwich shop of $151 while pretending a concealed finger was a gun. . . .

The case most troubling to the law's critics is that of Larry Lee Fisher, 35, who has been in and out of jail since he was a teenager. His first strike was in 1986 when he was convicted of robbery in the second degree—pushing his grandfather down and taking $390 from him. Mr. Fisher served four months in jail. Two years later came his second strike, a $100 robbery of a pizza parlor in which he concealed his finger and said it was a gun. He served 17 months on a work farm.

Last month Mr. Fisher was arrested for holding up a sandwich shop in Everett, again without a gun but pretending he had one by pointing a finger inside his coat pocket. The police found him an hour after the holdup drinking beer in a nearby tavern. Normally, he would face about 22 months in jail. But now, if convicted, he will spend the rest of his life in prison. . . .

Dave LaCourse, a leader of the three-strikes initiative, said Mr. Fisher's case was unusual but not unintended. "Here's a guy with 10 misdemeanors on his record, he's 35 years old and he hasn't learned his lesson yet," Mr. LaCourse said. "What's it going to take? He seems to be one of those people who's making crime a career." . . .

Washington prosecutors said states now considering three-strikes laws would do well not to put too many crimes in the mix of what qualifies. Because of cases like Larry Lee Fisher's, Washington's law may have to be refined, they said.

"Don't assume this will have a dramatic effect on crime," said John Ladenburg, Pierce County Prosecutor. "This is not a cure-all. This is not going to fix crime. What it will do is get some of the worst offenders off of the street forever."

SOURCE: Adapted from Timothy Egan, "A 3-Strike Penal Law Shows It's Not as Simple as It Seems," *New York Times*, 15 February 1994, p. 1

...on may still be thwarted by the deci-...mple, the Massachusetts law de-...g an unregistered firearm *must* spend ...eterrent or incapacitative effects be-...duce charges when they do not be-...hing a particular individual.[6] When ...thments for drug dealers, the draco-...erely raised the stakes for the defen-...to reduce charges in order to obtain ...rikes" law in the state of Washington

235

JUDGE RELEASES ACCUSED RAPIST ON BAIL

Charles Hamlin was arrested for the rape of a twelve-year-old girl in Akron, Ohio. In his initial court appearance, a judge set a $2,500 cash bond for his release. He provided the money and was released on bail. His next scheduled preliminary hearing was in the court of Municipal Judge Jane Bond. Hamlin appeared at the hearing as required, and Judge Bond continued his $2,500 cash bond and permitted him to remain free on bail. A few days later, a husband and wife were shot and killed, and Hamlin was arrested for their murders. At the time of the murders, the local elections for municipal court judgeships were only a few weeks away. Judge Bond's opponent in the election, an attorney named Maureen O'Connor, mailed a flyer to voters throughout Akron that read:

> The AKRON FRATERNAL ORDER OF POLICE wants you to know about **LOW BOND, JANE BOND.**
> **FACT**: August 4, 1989, Charles Hamlin was **ARRESTED** for the **RAPE** of a **12 YEAR OLD GIRL.**
> **FACT**: Charles Hamlin had a prior **CONVICTION** for **GROSS SEXUAL IMPOSITION.**
> **FACT**: **JANE BOND** allowed **ONLY** a **$2,500 CASH BOND** at Charles Hamlin's **RAPE** Hearing.
> **FACT**: While out of **JAIL** on **ONLY** a **$2,500 CASH BOND**, Charles Hamlin **SHOT** and **KILLED TWO PEOPLE**, a **MINISTER** and his **WIFE**.

> **FACT**: The Akron Municipal Court needs TOUGH JUDGES that will PROTECT the VICTIMS, NOT the CRIMINALS! The AKRON FRATERNAL ORDER OF POLICE HAS **ENDORSED O'CONNOR** for **JUDGE.**

Judge Bond's supporters responded with radio commercials defending the judge, and she ultimately won the election. However, this election issue raised questions about the role of bail in the criminal justice system. Who should be released on bail? Was O'Connor correct in asserting that Judge Bond should not have permitted Hamlin to be released on bail? Was Judge Bond protecting criminals instead of victims by not setting a much higher amount for bail? How would this situation and this flyer have affected your choice if you had voted in the judicial election?

The decision regarding the release of an accused person on bail is one of several important stages in the pretrial process. Each stage relies on discretionary decisions by prosecutors, defense attorneys, bail bondsmen, judges, and others. Through their interactions, these actors determine what will happen to the vast majority of defendants. Very few defendants have their cases decided by a trial. Most leave the system by having their cases dismissed or by entering guilty pleas during the pretrial process. In this chapter, we will examine the pretrial stages to see how various decision makers use their power of discretion. ★

180

Behind the formally adversarial system, courtroom workgroup participants must constantly interact, negotiate, and cooperate.

Other officials may influence the smooth operation of the workgroup. For example, depending on the organization of the courthouse, a chief judge, prosecuting attorney, or chief public defender may limit the range of discretionary decision making undertaken by subordinates in the workgroup. Probation officers may work closely with the workgroup as they prepare presentence reports on which sentencing decisions may be based.

As the members of the workgroup interact, they must also ensure that their decisions and agreements do not harm their important relationships with actors outside the workgroup. The prosecutor, for example, needs to maintain good relations with the police in order to ensure cooperation during criminal investigations. This may limit the prosecutor's ability to "go easy" on a particular defendant, even if the prosecutor believes that the young first-offender deserves a break. Judges must be careful about how their sentencing decisions will be received and reported by news media, especially in states in which they will eventually face political opposition in a re-election campaign. Defense attorneys know that defendants and their families expect to see a vigorous defense, so they may take care to give the appearance that they are not too friendly with the prosecutor, even if they engage in highly cooperative plea bargaining. Indeed, the members of the workgroup may even cooperate with one another in "staging" an adversarial hearing to give the audience of police, defendants and their families, and the news media the impression that members of the workgroup are *not* cooperating with one another but are playing their stereotypical roles in an adversarial process.

Judges can be leaders in the courtroom context both for workgroups and for groupings that may never develop into workgroups. Judges who are passive or detached may find themselves confronted with messy personal conflicts between prosecutors and defense attorneys that hamper the efficiency of criminal case processing. Judges who actively take the lead in setting the tone for cooperative plea negotiations, establishing expectations for professional behavior, and facilitating the development of a consensus can anticipate problems and thereby increase the effectiveness of the courtroom actors in resolving cases.

THE IMPACT OF COURTROOM WORKGROUPS

James Eisenstein and Herbert Jaco[b] workgroups on felony cases in Balti[more] and Detroit, stable workgroups incre[ased] The shared understandings of these [members helped] cases effectively in order to dismiss th[e] and to reach prompt plea agreement[s] workgroups in Baltimore produced f[ewer cases] to be forwarded to the grand jury an[d]

Workgroups are more or less eff[ective] employed in each jurisdiction and cha[racteristics of court-] houses. For example, in Chicago and [other cities a prelimi-] nary hearing before they went to t[he] stage was usually omitted. This reduc[ed]

214

THE CONCEPT OF SYSTEM IS AN ESSENTIAL TOOL FOR UNDERSTANDING HOW CRIMINAL JUSTICE IS ADMINISTERED IN PRACTICE.

Throughout the text, a systems perspective illuminates how decisions related to crime and justice are *actually made.* As you discover how our interconnected *system* of criminal justice operates, you will better understand the hard realities of the system including why suspects are arrested or let go, convicted or acquitted at trial, kept in prison or released on probation or parole.

"A QUESTION OF ETHICS" BOXES

explore the ethical dilemmas that arise within the administration of justice and allow you to consider chapter topics on a personal, *more critical* level. After all, in the criminal justice system, decisions must not only be made within the framework of the law, but they must also be consistent with the ethical norms of society.

A QUESTION OF ETHICS

Assistant Prosecutor Debra McCoy looked at the case file. The police had arrested Leslie Wiggins, a prominent local businessman, for drunken driving. It seemed that Wiggins had been stopped after weaving on the highway at a high rate of speed. From the moment Officer Tompkins asked Wiggins to get out of the car, he knew he was very drunk. A breathalizer test revealed that Wiggins was well above the legal limit for sobriety. There was no question that this was an open-and-shut case. McCoy noted that Wiggins had been previously arrested, but the DWI (driving while intoxicated) charge had been dropped by her chief, Prosecutor Marc Gould.

"I don't know what happened last time," she thought, "but there is no question now." She recorded the charge of "driving while intoxicated" in the case file and forwarded it for review.

When the file had not yet returned for arraignment several days later, McCoy went to Gould's office.

"What happened to the Wiggins case?" she asked.

"Wiggins? Oh, that. Seems that the breathalizer wasn't reading right that night."

"Gee, I'm surprised. Tompkins didn't say anything about that when I talked with him yesterday. In fact, he was wondering when the case was coming up."

"Well, let's just not worry about this. I'm sure that Tompkins has other things to concern him. Don't think anything more about Wiggins."

McCoy left the office and wondered, "What's going on here?"

What *is* going on here? Will Gould's statement influence the cases of other drivers who were tested on the breathalizer the same evening that Wiggins was? How would dropping this case reflect on Gould or McCoy if, the next time Wiggins was stopped, it was at the scene of a fatal car accident? Is the fact that Wiggins is a prominent local businessman a factor?

Fortunately for prosecutors, most cases do not attract sustained public attention. After an arrest is announced, the public frequently pays little attention to the ultimate outcome in a criminal case. This low public visibility enhances the prosecutor's discretionary power. For example, discussions in which a prosecutor may agree to drop several charges against a defendant in exchange for a guilty plea take place behind closed doors. The accompanying Question of Ethics presents an example of the use of discretion as a factor in prosecutorial decisions.

Despite the fact that they make many decisions behind closed doors, prosecutors may be sensitive to public opinion. If the community favors or opposes strict enforcement of certain laws, especially victimless crimes such as marijuana smoking, petty gambling, or prostitution, then the prosecutors' decisions are likely to reflect that view.

ROLES OF THE PROSECUTOR

The description of the O. J. Simpson case at the beginning of this chapter conveyed the image of lawyers clashing in court as representatives of two competing sides. Defense attorney Robert Shapiro was seeking to cast doubt on the trustworthiness and admissibility of evidence that might be used against his client. Marcia Clark was seeking to overcome questions about the legality of the search of Simpson's home so as to gain court approval for charging Simpson with murder. While Shapiro sought only to advance his client's interests, Clark bore the additional responsibility of making sure that justice was achieved. Protecting the rights of defendants and ensuring that justice prevails are inherent duties of a prosecutor. Many prosecutors come to view themselves as instruments of law enforcement since they work closely with the police to obtain convictions. An underlying risk is that prosecutors may work toward obtaining convictions without adequately assessing whether the police respected the rights of the accused and whether the evidence clearly points only to the suspect rather than to someone else.

Social scientists use the concept of *role* to describe how people in a certain position may decide what to do according to the expectations both that they have for themselves and that others have for them. Various prosecutors may hold different ideas about the best role to play. Differing expectations from essential outsiders (judges, police officers, defense attorneys, and the public) can influence the

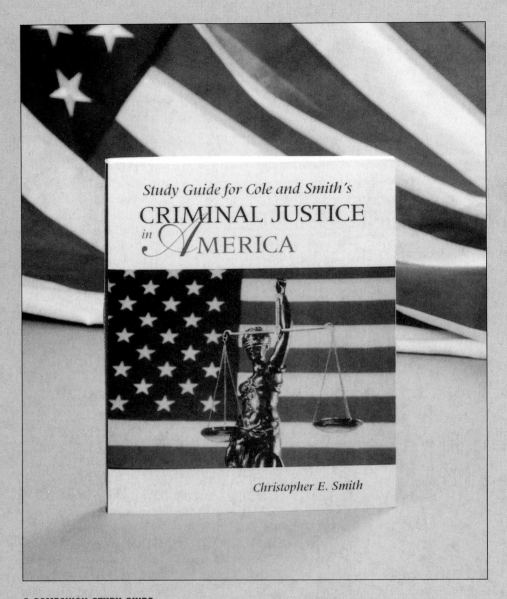

Study Guide for Cole and Smith's
CRIMINAL JUSTICE *in* AMERICA

Christopher E. Smith

A COMPANION STUDY GUIDE

is available with this text. Because students learn in different ways, a variety of features are included in the Study Guide to help you. Each chapter is outlined, major terms are defined, summaries are given, and sample tests are provided. Additionally, worksheets are designed to encourage your critical response to various criminal justice situations. Using this guide in conjunction with the text should help ensure your complete understanding of the material.

To order a copy of the Study Guide, contact your local bookseller.

PART I *The Criminal Justice Process*

1 *Crime and Justice in America*

2 *The Criminal Justice System*

3 *Criminal Law and Procedure*

The American system of criminal justice is a response to a problem that has required attention in all societies from time immemorial: crime. In order to understand how the system works and why crime persists in spite of our best efforts to control it, we need to examine both the nature of criminal behavior and the functioning of the justice system itself. As you will see, the reality of crime and justice involves much more than "cops and robbers," the details of legal codes, and the penalties prescribed for lawbreaking. From defining what behavior counts as criminal to determining the fate of those offenders who are caught, the process of criminal justice is a *social* process that is subject to many influences besides written law.

Part I introduces you to the study of this process and provides a broad framework within which to analyze the way our society—through its police, courts, and corrections—attempts to deal with the age-old problem of crime.

CHAPTER 1
Crime and Justice in America

HERE, THERE, AND EVERYWHERE?
CRIME IN AMERICAN DAILY LIFE

Pick up a newspaper. Today's, yesterday's, last week's—it does not matter. You know that stories about crime in American society will be prominently featured. The stories will simultaneously numb you to the violence that occurs every day and infuriate you that people can commit such harmful acts. Pick a day, any day. On the day we chose, Chicago mourned a five-year-old boy who was pushed from the four-teenth floor of a housing project for refusing to steal candy for two older boys. The perpetrators, ages ten and eleven, faced a maximum sentence of only five years' probation for committing such a terrible mur-der. In Connecticut, a two-year-old girl, caked with blood from head to toe, was found sleeping next to the body of her father, a convicted drug dealer killed execution-style in his own kitchen. In Washington, DC, a former bank executive was sentenced to eight years in prison and ordered to pay $255.4 million in restitution for bank fraud. The paper contained addi-tional stories about carjacking, sexual assault, rob-bery, and murder. In short, the paper's pages convey a sense of shocking numbers of terrible crimes that deprive people of their money, possessions, and even lives and that stem from problems often not adequately addressed by the law.

Criminal justice is a fascinating and crucial sub-ject. A major challenge facing any democracy is the development of policies that will promote security and safety by dealing with crime while preserving the ideals of law, justice, and freedom. In response to that challenge, two basic themes pervade this book: (1) that crime and justice are public policy issues and (2) that criminal justice can best be analyzed as a so-cial system.

To begin our study, in this chapter we examine the nature of crime; the ways in which it is defined, categorized, and measured; and the characteristics of victims. These subjects are important because they affect the policies pursued by government in seeking to control crime and punish lawbreakers. Therefore, we will also examine how public policies are devel-oped to deal with crime. ★

CHAPTER QUESTIONS

How are crimes defined and who defines them?

What are the major categories of crimes?

How much crime is there and how is crime measured?

Who are the victims of crime?

How are government crime policies shaped in the United States?

High levels of crime aren't new to the United States. "War on crime" is a frequent refrain in American political life.

CRIME IN AMERICA

Crime is hardly unique to the late twentieth century. Virtually every generation of Americans since the founding of the country has felt threatened by crime and believed that there was too much crime. Nor was crime in previous eras limited to the robberies, thefts, and assaults that have always been present in the United States. There have also been incidents of extreme, large-scale violence that threatened the social order. For example, farmers and others openly rebelled in the earliest years of the republic. Military policies produced significant draft riots during the Civil War. In the early twentieth century, mobs of whites set upon and murdered African-Americans in cities throughout the United States, including St. Louis, Kansas City, and Chicago. In other decades, police officers battled labor union organizers, veterans seeking payment of benefits, war protestors, and civil rights advocates. Thus, when riots erupted in Los Angeles in 1992 in the aftermath of the acquittal of police officers who were videotaped beating African-American motorist Rodney King, the country was not witnessing a new kind of event.

Nor is the total amount of crime in the United States necessarily increasing. Beginning in the 1980s, rates for many crimes that had been rising since the mid-1960s peaked and remained fairly stable. However, the public's perception is that crime is ever increasing, in part because of the influx of drug cases brought about by the "War on Drugs." Drug usage in the United States peaked in the late 1970s, yet arrests and prosecutions for such offenses increased dramatically in the late 1980s. Thus, perceptions and fears about the "crime problem" respond not only to the actual number of people committing illegal acts but also to the government's decisions about which crimes to target, publicize, and pursue.

What is most striking about crime in the United States, however, is that the problem is so much greater here than it is in other industrialized countries. In per capita terms, about ten American men die by criminal violence for every Japanese, Austrian, German, or Swedish man; about fifteen American men die for every Swiss or English man; and over twenty die for every Dane.[1] More than 150 countries, both developed and less or undeveloped, have lower murder rates than the United States.

When we examine robbery rates, the data are even more troubling. The robbery rate in New York City is 5 times greater than that in London and, incredibly, 125 times higher than that in Tokyo.[2] Apparently, the historical and social factors that shape societies have affected the United States differently than comparable countries with democratic systems of government and free enterprise economic systems. Crime has always posed a major challenge for our country.

DEFINING CRIME

In order to understand the nature of crime, we must first consider how crime is defined and what categories of crime exist in American society. In legal terms, a **crime** is a specific act of commission or omission in violation of the law, for which punishment is prescribed. Note, however, that not all behavior that is considered offensive or deviant is criminal behavior. Only behaviors banned by the criminal code are illegal. We must also recognize that in different times and places, different behaviors have been defined as criminal. Although there is broad consensus that certain behaviors are rightly defined as criminal, there are also outlawed behaviors that many believe should not be illegal.

crime
A specific act of commission or omission in violation of the law, for which punishment is prescribed.

SOURCES OF CRIME DEFINITIONS

Why does the law declare some types of behavior criminal and not others? It is legislators who write the criminal codes that specify which behaviors are illegal. For some behaviors, the legislators' job is not too difficult because they share the same values as the citizens who elected them. For example, most Americans agree that intentionally killing another human being or using a weapon to forcibly take money or property should be labeled crimes. As a result, every state has laws against murder and armed robbery. But is there a consensus on all behaviors that are defined as criminal?

Evidence from a national public opinion survey on the perceived severity of various crimes sheds some light on this question.[3] Survey respondents were asked to rank the seriousness of 204 illegal events. As Table 1.1 shows, there was generally broad agreement on the severity of specific crimes. However, crime victims rated the acts as more severe than did nonvictims, and the severity ratings assigned by African-Americans and other minority group members were generally lower than those assigned by whites. As the survey results suggest, there is a consensus for certain crimes, but not for others.

If, as the survey indicates, many Americans believe that some behaviors specified in the criminal code should not be illegal, why are they crimes? One view is that those who hold political power determine the definitions of crimes and the appropriate punishments. Their own feelings aside, legislators also respond to public opinion in making decisions about crime and justice. As elected officials, they try to enact laws that will please their constituents and lead to their reelection.

In 1994, politicians reacted immediately to several highly publicized incidents of carjacking in which car thieves pulled motorists from their cars, assaulted or killed them, and then fled in the vehicles. Members of the U.S. Congress loudly proclaimed that carjacking should be a federal crime. By overwhelming majorities, Congress passed, and President Clinton signed, legislation

TABLE 1.1

Ranking the Severity of Crimes

Survey respondents were asked to rank 204 illegal events from playing hookey from school to planting a bomb that killed twenty people in a public building. Severity scores were developed through mathematical techniques from the survey responses. For example, a severity score of 40 indicates that people believe that the crime is twice as bad as one with a severity score of 20.

SOURCE: U.S. Department of Justice, Bureau of Justice Statistics, *Report to the Nation on Crime and Justice*, 2nd ed. (Washington, DC: Government Printing Office, 1988), p. 16.

Severity Score	Ten Most Serious Offenses	Severity Score	Ten Least Serious Offenses
72.1	Planting a bomb in a public building. The bomb explodes and twenty people are killed.	1.3	Two persons willingly engage in a homosexual act.
52.8	A man forcibly rapes a woman. As a result of physical injuries, she dies.	1.1	Disturbing the neighborhood with loud, noisy behavior.
43.2	Robbing a victim at gunpoint. The victim struggles and is shot to death.	1.1	Taking bets on the numbers.
39.2	A man stabs his wife. As a result, she dies.	1.1	A group continues to hang around a corner after being told to break up by a police officer.
35.7	Stabbing a victim to death.	0.9	A youngster under sixteen runs away from home.
35.6	Intentionally injuring a victim. As a result, the victim dies.	0.8	Being drunk in public.
33.8	Running a narcotics ring.	0.7	A youngster under sixteen breaks a curfew law by being on the street after the hour permitted by law.
27.9	A woman stabs her husband. As a result, he dies.	0.6	Trespassing in the backyard of a private home.
26.3	An armed person skyjacks an airplane and demands to be flown to another country.	0.3	A person is a vagrant. That is, he has no home and no visible means of support.
25.8	A man forcibly rapes a woman. No other physical injury occurs.	0.2	A youngster under sixteen is truant from school.

adding carjacking to the federal criminal code. In reality, defining carjacking as a federal crime provides no greater protection for citizens than that which they had already under existing state laws against assault, robbery, and auto theft. The legislation was enacted in an effort to show the public that the legislators were taking action against crime. Members of Congress had little reason to think about whether their actions would actually reduce carjacking or increase our ability to apprehend carjackers.

As you can see, harmful behaviors are not automatically defined as crimes. Laws that define crimes are shaped by the values of government decision makers, especially legislators, and by the values that those decision makers believe are being expressed in public opinion polls and elections.

TYPES OF CRIMES

Criminal acts can be categorized in various ways. One way is to distinguish between a crime that is legally defined as a felony and one that is legally defined as a misdemeanor. **Felonies** are crimes punishable by one year or more of imprisonment or by death. **Misdemeanors** are crimes punishable by one year or less of imprisonment and by community punishments such as probation, fines, and/or community service.

Criminologists have developed a second scheme that categorizes crimes according to the nature of the behavior and the type of person most likely to commit specific offenses. This scheme distinguishes five categories of crime: occupational, organized, visible, victimless, and political. Each type has its

felony

A serious crime punishable by one year or more of imprisonment or by death.

misdemeanor

An offense less serious than a felony and usually punishable by one year or less of imprisonment or by probation, fines, and/or community service.

6

own level of risk and profitability, each arouses varying degrees of public disapproval, and each has its own types of offenders.

Occupational crime, sometimes called "white-collar crime," is committed by individuals in the course of a legal business or profession. Often viewed as shrewd business practices rather than as illegal offenses, these are crimes that, if done "correctly," may never be discovered. Such crimes include price fixing, embezzlement, fraud, employee theft, and tax evasion. Although highly profitable, most categories of occupational crime do not come to public attention. Regulatory agencies, such as the Federal Trade Commission and the Securities and Exchange Commission, are often ineffective in their enforcement of the law. Many business and professional organizations "police" themselves, dropping employees or members who commit offenses.

The low level of enforcement of occupational crimes may also result from the fact that the general public does not view these crimes as serious. Such crimes usually do not involve violence or threats to public safety, although some may involve selling unsafe food or defective products. Many members of the public may not realize, however, the tremendous financial costs to society of occupational crimes.

Organized crime refers to a social framework for the perpetration of criminal acts rather than specific types of offenses. Organized criminals tend to engage in illegal activities that minimize risk and maximize profit. Thus, organized crime involves a network of enterprises, usually crossing state and national borders, that range from legitimate businesses to shady involvement with labor unions to activities that cater to desires for illegal "goods" such as drugs, prostitutes, and pornography.

Although the public often associates organized crime with Americans of Italian ancestry, other ethnic groups have dominated this type of activity at various times. Members of ethnic groups may resort to illegal activities if American society does not grant them full access to good schools, jobs, and professions. This process may be particularly true for some new immigrant groups. The Irish were the first group to organize criminal activity on a large scale in the United States, followed by Jews who dominated gambling and labor racketeering at the turn of the century and then by Italians in the early twentieth century. Today, African-Americans, Hispanics, and Asians increasingly are beginning to manage organized crime enterprises in some cities. Drug trafficking has brought Colombian and Mexican crime groups to U.S. shores, and reports from California document the emergence of Vietnamese-, Chinese-, and Japanese-led organizations.

Visible crime, often referred to as "street crime" or "ordinary crime," refers to offenses against persons and property committed primarily by members of the lower classes. These crimes, ranging from shoplifting and robbery to rape and homicide, are viewed as the most upsetting by the American public because they threaten individuals' security and safety. Although they are the least profitable crimes, they receive the most attention from law enforcement officials because they captivate the news media and heighten the public's fears, and because they often involve violence. Certain crimes, such as drunk driving and domestic violence, involve perpetrators from all social classes. These crimes generate many arrests, but relatively few drunk drivers and abusive spouses receive harsh punishments. This has led some theorists to argue that the decidedly lower-class characteristics of the inhabitants of American correctional institutions reflect the class bias of a society that focuses only on certain types of criminal activity. They note that we do not prosecute white-collar crimes such as embezzlement or fraud with the same

occupational crime
Offenses committed by individuals in the course of a legal business or profession; sometimes called "white-collar crime."

organized crime
A social framework for the perpetration of criminal acts rather than specific types of offenses, usually in such fields as gambling, drugs, and prostitution, in which illegal services that are in great demand are provided.

visible crime
Offenses against persons and property committed primarily by members of the lower class. Often referred to as "street crimes" or "ordinary crimes," these are the offenses most upsetting to the public.

Should prostitution be defined as criminal? Some places allow it. Is it "victimless"?

victimless crime
Offenses involving a willing and private exchange of illegal goods or services for which there is a strong demand. Although participants do not feel that they are being harmed, prosecution is justified on the grounds that society as a whole is being injured by the act.

political crime
Acts such as treason, sedition, and espionage that constitute threats to the government.

intensity as we do such street crimes as drug trafficking and larceny. Perpetrators of visible crimes generally come from the more impoverished segments in society.

Victimless crime consists of offenses involving a willing and private but illegal exchange of goods or services for which there is a strong demand. These crimes are often considered to be offenses against morality. For example, prostitution, gambling, pornography, and illegal drug use are viewed as "wrong" by many people, yet many others view them as merely the private affairs of people in a free society. These crimes are termed *victimless* because the participants in the exchange do not feel that they are being harmed. Prosecution of these offenses is justified on the grounds that society as a whole is being injured since the moral fabric of the community is endangered. However, the use of the criminal justice system to enforce standards of morality is costly. These cases can flood the courts while placing police officers in difficult and dangerous positions through the use of informers, decoys, and undercover operations. There is also a risk that the criminalization of such activities merely provides opportunities for organized crime groups to prosper.

There is a lack of consensus in American society as to whether all of these activities should be crimes. At the same time, there is disagreement as to whether these crimes should be regarded as "victimless." Although some people argue that adults should have the freedom to harm their bodies with drugs or their financial situation through gambling, this argument seems to ignore the impact of these activities on family members and others.

Political crime includes activities, such as treason, sedition (rebellion), and espionage, that are viewed as threats to the government. Political freedom is never absolute, and the United States historically has enacted many restrictive laws in response to perceived threats. The Sedition Act of 1789, for instance, provided for the punishment of individuals uttering or publishing statements critical of the government. More recently, during the turmoil surrounding the Vietnam War in the late 1960s, the federal government filed charges of criminal conspiracy against citizens who opposed the administration's policies.

In Western democracies today, there is virtually no political crime except for rare cases of treason. Many illegal acts that are politically motivated, such as the 1992 bombing of New York's World Trade Center, are essentially prosecuted as visible crimes because we have laws against bombing, arson, and murder.

Which one of the five categories of crime is of greatest concern to you? If you are like most people, your concerns about the crime problem in the United States focus on visible crimes. Thus, as a nation, we devote most of our criminal justice resources and energy toward dealing with such crimes. In order to evaluate how we can best develop public policies to address the crime problem, we need to know more about the amount and types of crimes that occur in the United States.

HOW MUCH CRIME IS THERE?

In 1994, Americans watched Congress and the president trying to prove that the federal government is "tough on crime." The Violent Crime Control and Law Enforcement Act enacted by Congress that year reflected politicians' recognition that the voters are increasingly concerned about crime, especially visible crimes. Because over 60 percent of Americans polled in 1993 believed that the crime rate had increased in the preceding five-year period,[4] Republicans and Democrats each tried to show that the opposing party was soft on crime by adding new crimes and stiffer punishments to existing federal laws. When President Clinton signed the new legislation that, among other things, expanded the application of the death penalty to sixty additional offenses, he said the bill would "roll back this awful tide of violence in America." By characterizing the crime problem as a "tide," Clinton mirrored the public's view that crime is continually growing. In fact, however, crime generally is *not* increasing. For example, crime rates for offenses such as rape, robbery, larceny, and burglary all peaked in the early 1980s and then declined thereafter.[5] The 1994 legislation thus demonstrated that criminal justice policies do not necessarily address actual trends in crime rates.

In order to evaluate accurately the crime problem in the United States, we need to consider a number of important questions. How do we know that crime is not increasing steadily? Why is the public so fearful if they are actually less threatened by crime than they were in the 1980s? What is the nature and extent of crime in the United States? By examining these questions, we can gain a better understanding of the influences of the crime problem itself and the public's beliefs about the problem.

SOURCES OF CRIME DATA

It is not easy to measure the amount of crime. Our knowledge depends on the reports of victims and witnesses, yet many people do not report crimes to the police. Although it may seem odd that victims often do not call the police, there are reasons for this. For example, many people know who victimized them. If the offender is from their neighborhood, they may not wish to run the risk of retaliation by filing a police report. If it is a member of their own family, they may not wish to see their son, daughter, father, mother, or other relative sentenced to prison. Many drug addicts steal continuously from their relatives without ever being reported to the police. Many people who assault their spouses enjoy the same luxury of having their victims quietly suffer. Some victims of rape and assault fear the embarrassment of public disclosure and interrogation by the police. In cases of larceny, robbery, or burglary, victims may believe that it is not worth the trouble to file a police report that is unlikely to result in their property being returned. Many citizens are also deterred from reporting crimes because they are unwilling to become "involved" by going to the station house to fill out papers or perhaps appearing in court.

As these examples suggest, many people feel that the costs of reporting crimes outweigh the gains. Criminal justice scholars speak about the **dark figure of crime** as the unknown amount of crime that is never reported to the police. It is estimated that the number of unreported crimes far exceeds the number of crimes reported to the police. Figure 1.1 draws from national survey results to show the percentage of various victimizations not reported to the police.

How can we measure the extent of crime if we know from the outset that our analysis will never be completely accurate? All we can do is use the tools that are available to us. Until the 1970s, crime data consisted of those incidents that made their way via police reports into the Federal Bureau of Investigation's *Uniform Crime Reports*. Since 1972, however, the Department of Justice has

dark figure of crime
The unknown amount of crime that is never reported to the police.

FIGURE 1.1

Percentage of Victimizations Not Reported to the Police

Why do some people not report their victimizations to the police? What can be done to encourage reporting?

SOURCE: U.S. Department of Justice, Bureau of Justice Statistics, *Report to the Nation on Crime and Justice*, 2nd ed. (Washington, DC: Government Printing Office, 1988), p. 34.

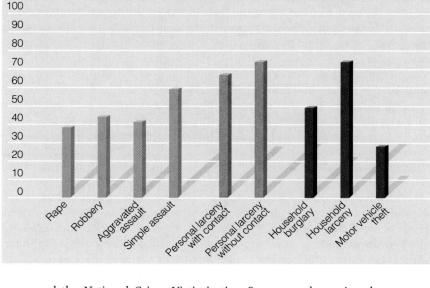

sponsored the National Crime Victimization Survey to determine the amount of victimization. Although these sources permit us to evaluate the nature and extent of crime from two approaches, each approach has its limitations.

Uniform Crime Reports

Uniform Crime Reports
An annually published statistical summary of crimes reported to the police based on voluntary reports to the FBI by individual police departments.

Published annually by the FBI, the **Uniform Crime Reports (UCR)** are a statistical summary of crimes reported to the police based on voluntary reports to the FBI by individual police departments. At the urging of the International Association of Chiefs of Police, Congress created this national system of compiling crime data in 1930. The *UCR* data come from a voluntary national network of some 16,000 local, state, and federal law enforcement agencies, policing 95 percent of the U.S. population. The *UCR* presents information about the twenty-nine types of offenses listed in Table 1.2. For eight major crimes—"index offenses"—the collected data show such factors as age, race, and number of reported crimes solved; for the twenty-one other offense categories, the data are not so complete.

The *UCR* permit us to monitor the number of *reported* crimes each year for the listed categories, the annual percentage changes in these reported crimes, and the rates of crimes per 100,000 people for each offense.

The *UCR* provide a useful but incomplete picture of crime levels. Because the *UCR* only cover reported crimes in certain categories, they cannot detect the extent to which people fail to call the police and they cannot measure occupational crimes and other offenses not included in the designated categories. In addition, these reports focus only on the most serious offense when several crimes are committed in a single incident. Further, since reporting is voluntary, there are always questions about whether police departments are taking the time to make complete and careful reports. Also, events that produce criminal reports are subject to interpretation and definition by the police officers who are called to the scene. What an officer classifies as a felonious assault in one situation might be classified as a misdemeanor by another officer in a different city. These differences in classification, which affect the ultimate portrait of crime painted by the *UCR*, can stem from individual officers' interpretations or from different policies followed by various police

Part I (Index Offenses)	Part II (Other Offenses)
1. Criminal homicide	9. Simple assaults
2. Forcible rape	10. Forgery and counterfeiting
3. Robbery	11. Fraud
4. Aggravated assault	12. Embezzlement
5. Burglary	13. Buying, receiving, or possessing stolen property
6. Larceny-theft	14. Vandalism
7. Auto theft	15. Weapons (carrying, possession, etc.)
8. Arson	16. Prostitution and commercialized vice
	17. Sex offenses
	18. Violation of narcotic drug laws
	19. Gambling
	20. Offenses against the family and children
	21. Driving under the influence
	22. Violation of liquor laws
	23. Drunkenness
	24. Disorderly conduct
	25. Vagrancy
	26. All other offenses (excluding traffic)
	27. Suspicion
	28. Curfew and loitering (juvenile)
	29. Runaway (juvenile)

TABLE 1.2
Uniform Crime Report **Offenses**
The *UCR* present extensive data on eight index offenses and twenty-one other offenses for which there is less information. An important limitation of the *UCR* is that they tabulate only crimes reported to the police.
SOURCE: U.S. Department of Justice, Federal Bureau of Investigation, *Crime in the United States* (Washington, DC: Government Printing Office, 1994).

departments. For example, domestic violence may still be treated as a family quarrel in some locations rather than as a criminal assault.

There are, however, two crimes for which the *UCR* can provide relatively accurate information: homicide and auto theft. In homicide cases, a body is discovered, and authorities are required to investigate the cause of death. In motor vehicle thefts, people report the crimes because insurance companies require police reports before making payments. Unfortunately, many other crimes, including serious offenses such as rape and assault, are not reported to police at similar levels. Thus, *UCR* data must be interpreted with care.

In response to some of the criticisms of the *UCR*, changes will be implemented nationwide during the late 1990s. Some offenses are being redefined, and police agencies are being asked to report more details about crime events. Using the **National Incident-Based Reporting System** (NIBRS), police agencies will report all crimes committed during an incident, not just the most serious one, as well as data on offenders, victims, and the environments in which they interact. While the *UCR* currently count incidents and arrests for the eight index offenses and count arrests for other offenses, the NIBRS will provide detailed incident information on forty-six offenses in twenty-two crime categories. Unlike the *UCR*, NIBRS also will make a distinction between attempted and completed crimes.[6]

National Crime Victimization Surveys

A second source for information about crime in the United States is the **National Crime Victimization Surveys (NCVS)**. Since 1972, the Bureau of the Census has surveyed large segments of the public to determine the extent and nature of crime victimization and thus the extent of unreported as well as reported crime. Interviews are conducted with a national probability sample of approximately 100,000 people representing 50,000 households.

National Incident-Based Reporting System

System in which the police will report each offense in a crime incident as well as data on offenders, victims, and the environments in which they interact.

National Crime Victimization Surveys

Interviews of samples of the U.S. population conducted for the Bureau of Justice Statistics to determine the number and types of criminal victimizations and thus the extent of unreported as well as reported crime.

	Uniform Crime Reports	National Crime Victimization Surveys
Offenses Measured	Homicide	
	Rape	Rape
	Robbery (personal and commercial)	Robbery (Personal)
	Assault (aggravated)	Assault (aggravated and simple)
	Burglary (commercial and household)	Household burglary
	Larceny (commercial and household)	Larceny (personal and household)
	Motor vehicle theft	Motor vehicle theft
	Arson	
Scope	Crimes reported to the police in most jurisdictions; considerable flexibility in developing small-area data	Crimes both reported and not reported to police; all data are for the nation as a whole; some data are available for a few large geographic areas
Collection method	Police department reports to FBI	Survey interviews: periodically measures the total number of crimes committed by asking a national sample of **49,000** households representing **101,000** people over the age of twelve about their experiences as victims of crime during a specific period
Kinds of information	In addition to offense counts, provides information on crime clearances, persons arrested, persons charged, law enforcement officers killed and assaulted, and characteristics of homicide victims	Provides details about victims (such as age, race, sex, education, income, and whether the victim and offender were related) and about crimes (such as time and place of occurrence, whether or not reported to police, use of weapons, occurrence of injury, and economic consequences)
Sponsor	Department of Justice Federal Bureau of Investigation	Department of Justice Bureau of Justice Statistics

TABLE 1.3

The *UCR* and NCVS Compare these data sources. Remember that the *UCR* tabulate only crimes reported to the police, whereas the NCVS are based on interviews with victims.

SOURCE: U.S. Department of Justice, Bureau of Justice Statistics, *Report to the Nation on Crime and Justice*, 2nd ed. (Washington, DC: Government Printing Office, 1988), p. 11.

The same people are interviewed twice a year for three years and asked questions about whether they have been victimized in the previous six months. Questions are then asked to elicit specific facts about the event, characteristics of the offender, and resulting financial losses or physical disabilities. In addition to the household interviews, specialized surveys focus on the nation's twenty-six largest cities, and separate studies are conducted concerning the victimization of businesses.

These surveys are designed to generate nationwide estimates of quarterly and yearly victimization rates for all index offenses except homicide and arson. The data are used to show offender trends and demographic patterns of crime. Because the victims are interviewed, the NCVS data include crimes that were never reported to the police. As a result, the NCVS document more criminal offenses than do the *UCR*.

Although the NCVS help to provide a more complete picture of the nature and extent of crime, they, too, have flaws. Because the survey workers are government employees, interviewees are unlikely to report crimes in which they or members of their family participated. They also may not want to admit that a family member engages in criminal activities, or they may be too embarrassed to admit that they have permitted themselves to be victimized repeatedly.

The NCVS also are imperfect because they focus on the victim's *perception* of an incident. The theft of a child's lunch money by a schoolyard bully may be reported as a crime by one person, yet never be mentioned by another who considers such behavior merely a normal event of childhood. People may tell interviewers that their property was stolen when in fact they unknowingly lost it. Moreover, people's memories of dates may fade, and they may misreport the year in which a crime occurred, even though the feelings of victimization remain fresh in their minds.[7]

Next time you hear or read about increased amounts of crime, consider the source of the data and its possible limitations. Table 1.3 compares the *UCR* and NCVS.

CRIME TRENDS

Perceptions versus Reality

Criminal justice specialists generally agree that, contrary to public opinion and statements by politicians, crime rates have not been steadily increasing (see Figure 1.2). In fact, the rates for many crimes have dropped since the early 1980s.

The National Crime Victimization Surveys show that the victimization rates peaked in the late 1970s and early 1980s and subsequently fell. For example, the personal theft victimization rate climbed to 95 per 1,000 persons in 1974 and remained at this level through 1978 before beginning to decline. By 1992, the rate had reached a twenty-year low of 59 theft victims per 1,000 persons. With respect to violent crimes, the category most feared by many members of the public, the victimization rate peaked in 1981 at 35 per 1,000 persons, declined to new lows in the late 1980s, and then increased in 1992 to 32 per 1,000 persons.[8] Thus, although the rate of violent crimes increased in the early 1990s, the rates were still lower than they had been a decade earlier.

The *Uniform Crime Reports* show somewhat similar results. They detected a dramatic rise in crime rates beginning in 1964 and continuing increases for most categories until 1980, when the rates began to stabilize or decline. Only the rates for violent crimes have continued to rise.[9] The inconsistencies between the *UCR* and the NCVS are explainable in terms of the changes in citizen reporting habits. For example, the continual increases in violent crimes in

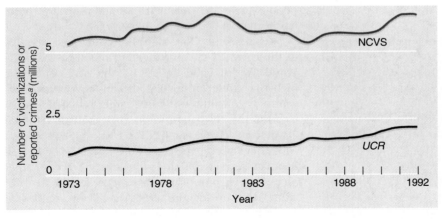

FIGURE 1.2

Violent Crime Trends As Measured by the *UCR* and NCVS

Note that these data are for the *number* of violent victimizations reported, not for victimization rates for 1973–1992.

SOURCE: U.S. Department of Justice, Bureau of Justice Statistics, *Highlights from Twenty Years of Surveying Crime Victims* (August 1993), p. 4.

[a]Includes NCVS violent crimes of rape, robbery, aggravated assault, and simple assault, and *UCR* violent crimes of murder and nonnegligent manslaughter, forcible rape, robbery, and aggravated assault.

the *UCR* are attributed to a greater willingness by citizens to report criminal behavior to police. The introduction of "911" emergency phone numbers has made it easier for citizens to contact the authorities directly, even when they are upset or frightened after witnessing or being victimized by a violent crime. In addition, the introduction of policing strategies that place patrol officers in closer contact with the communities they serve can encourage greater citizen cooperation with police and more complete reporting of crimes.

However, we cannot make predictions about crime trends simply by gathering information about how many crimes were committed or how many people were victimized. We must also look carefully at social factors that accompany changes in the crime rates. These factors may be causes of crime that future projections must consider. What kinds of factors might lead to more crime? You can probably think of several that have intrigued criminologists over the years, such as levels of unemployment, poverty, education, and substance abuse. Although these and other factors have been associated with, and perhaps seen as causing changes in, crime rates, in fact, these particular factors have *not* provided the best basis for making predictions about crime. Instead, two demographic factors—age distribution and urbanization—are most productive in calculating crime trends. First, let's explore the connection between age distribution and crime trends. We will examine the factor of urbanization when we discuss crime victims.

Age and Crime

Criminologists have demonstrated a close association between crime, especially the visible crime that the public fears most, and the age distribution within American society. Persons in the fourteen-to-twenty-four age category are the most crime-prone group. The larger the number of persons in this age category, the greater the number of visible crimes such as robberies, thefts, and assaults. In 1993, for example, the *UCR* disclosed that 29 percent of those arrested for serious crimes were under the age of eighteen. Almost half of those arrested for violent crimes and 60 percent of those arrested for property crimes were under twenty-five.[10] The disproportionate participation of young people, especially males, in violent crimes and property crimes has been documented for many years.

Should we expect more visible crime just after the year 2000? There are now more children in grade school, and they will enter their crime-prone years at the beginning of the new century.

Crime rates for many offenses rose rapidly in the early 1970s, a change attributed to the post–World War II baby boom. By the mid-1970s, the high-risk crime group of fourteen- to twenty-four-year-olds constituted a much larger proportion than usual of the U.S. population. Thus, between 40 and 50 percent of the total arrests during that period could have been expected as the result of the overall population increase and the size of the "crime-prone" age group. The subsequent decline in most crime rates during the 1980s has been ascribed to the maturing of the post–World War II generation. Scholars now predict that the United States can expect an increase in crime at the dawn of the twenty-first century as more of those baby boomers' children—the grandchildren of the World War II veterans—reach their crime-prone years and comprise an unusually large proportion of the population.

Social Policy and Crime

Some researchers argue that age alone has not shaped our crime rates. During the 1980s, legislatures throughout the United States increased the severity of sentences and imposed mandatory sentences for many crimes, which doubled the number of people in prison. According to this argument, these tough policies counteracted the rehabilitative policies of the 1960s that had contributed to the rise in crime. As crime control policies were made more punitive, the probability of arrest and incarceration increased. In short, it was the tougher stance that caused crime rates to drop.

Although this alternative explanation suggests that we can control crime by being tough on offenders, it cannot easily be proved that it was punishment rather than changes in the age distribution that caused the drop in crime rates. Neither can this alternative explanation readily explain the rise in violent crimes in the early 1990s despite the implementation of tough crime control policies. Until we have a better understanding of the causes of change in criminal behavior, it is premature to assign either blame or credit to governmental policies for shifts in crime rates.

Crime is a complex social problem, and its causes are difficult to understand. This difficulty stems, in part, from the near impossibility of fully understanding human behavior. Why do people do what they do? Why do some people do things that most us would never do?

We also face difficulties in determining the "cause" of crime because, as a concept, crime has so many different meanings. Do serial killers who repeatedly commit murder violate the law for the same reasons that an accountant embezzles money from a bank? Both acts are crimes, yet surely they are committed for very different reasons. Criminologists must look for complex causes rather than simple explanations, and they must be very specific in identifying the kinds of crimes that they are trying to explain.

We also face challenges in understanding why crime in the United States is so much more prevalent than in other industrialized democracies. Certainly, much of our history differs. Our frontier traditions, the legacy of slavery and racial discrimination, the unequal distribution of wealth, and private ownership of firearms all distinguish us from Europe and Japan. Yet none of these factors provides a ready explanation for the nature and extent of crime.

It was once thought that with the proper tools the crime problem could be analyzed and solved. As we have recognized the great complexity of crime and its causes, it has become more difficult to believe that we can control crime. We can manage aspects of our crime problem through decisions about how we will enforce laws and punish lawbreakers, but broad "solutions" are beyond our current understanding and control.

CRIME VICTIMIZATION

Who are the victims of crimes? What happens to them after a crime has been committed? These important questions historically have been neglected by researchers who, until recent decades, devoted most of their attention to who offenders were and how the criminal justice system dealt with them. It was not until the 1950s that **victimology**—the study of crime victims, including their role in precipitating crimes—emerged as an important research subject. By examining the victims of crime, we gain a better understanding of when and where certain kinds of crimes are committed. We can also evaluate the extent to which criminal justice officials and institutions are responsive to the individuals who have suffered the greatest harms.

VICTIM CHARACTERISTICS

The National Crime Victimization Surveys provide a good source of information about crime victims. Table 1.4 lists actual victimization rates for violent crimes according to a number of personal and demographic characteristics. Data from the NCVS have been used to create a series of estimates of the chances that a given person over the age of twelve will become a victim of the violent crimes of rape, robbery, and assault. Such data help us to see the links between sex, age, race, and so on and the occurrence of victimization.

With the exception of rape and personal robbery with contact (purse snatching), men are more likely than women to be victims of crime. In any given year, the victimization rate is about 40 per 1,000 persons for males and 23 per 1,000 for females. Because these figures exclude such crimes as murder, kidnapping, and harm from a drunken driver, the actual victimization rates are a bit higher. Moreover, these data show rates for a single year. Obviously, the occurrence of victimization is more frequent over the course of a lifetime.[11]

Most victims are between the ages of twelve to twenty-four. Youths aged twelve to fifteen are most likely to be the victims of personal larceny without contact, robbery, and simple assault. Despite concern about crimes against the elderly, most crime is directed against the young.

Race is also an important factor, with African-Americans and lower-class minority group members being more likely than whites to be raped, robbed, and assaulted. Although many white Americans fear being victimized by members of minority groups, three of every four victims of a violent crime are of the same race as the attacker. Property crimes are also more likely to occur among people of the same race and socioeconomic status than across groups. Because social and economic factors largely determine where people live, work, and seek recreation, Americans often do not have sustained contacts with people who are ethnically or socioeconomically different from themselves. Moreover, many people who commit crimes act on the opportunities that are most easily and regularly available to them. Thus, robberies tend to occur near the residence of robbers; assaults tend to occur in bars and workplaces where people congregate with others like themselves; and burglaries tend to occur in neighborhoods that are familiar to the burglar. In rural areas and small towns that are predominantly white, victims and lawbreakers are both likely to be white. Minority group members will bear a disproportionate risk of being victimized in poor urban neighborhoods in which their demographic group is predominant.

Violent crime is primarily a phenomenon of large cities. Of the 14 million index offenses known to the police in 1992, more than 13 million occurred in cities. Overall, studies have shown that crime rates invariably rise in proportion to proximity to the center of an urban area. The neighborhoods closest to the city's core are likely to have higher crime rates than outlying areas.

It is in the inner cities, where drug use and trafficking are rampant, that

	Victims	Violence	Theft		Victims	Violence	Theft
Sex	Male	40	65	**Family income**	Less than $7,500	59	62
	Female	23	58		$7,500–$9,999	42	61
Age	12–15	63	101		$10,000–$14,999	43	60
	16–19	91	94		$15,000–$24,999	31	57
	20–24	75	115		$25,000–$29,999	32	57
	25–34	35	71		$30,000–$49,999	25	60
	35–49	20	56		$50,000 or more	20	66
	50–64	10	35	**Education**	0–4 years	18	16
	65 and older	4	20		5–7 years	45	67
Race	White	30	61		8 years	28	49
	Black	44	61		9–11 years	49	62
	Other	28	52		High school graduate	28	49
Ethnicity	Hispanic	36	59		1–3 years college	36	83
	Non-Hispanic	31	61		College graduate	18	68
Marital status by sex	Males			**Residence**	Central city	44	75
	Never married	80	97		1,000,000 or more	39	76
	Divorced/separated	44	95		500,000–999,999	50	80
	Married	19	43		250,000–499,999	54	70
	Widowed	[a]	23		50,000–249,999	38	74
	Females				Suburban	26	61
	Never married	43	90		Rural	25	44
	Divorced/separated	45	74				
	Married	11	44				
	Widowed	6	22				

murder rates have skyrocketed. Many of those slain, like their killers, tend to be young African-Americans. The homicide rate among African-American males aged twenty to twenty-nine is 100 per 100,000 population, about six times that for the same age bracket in the general population.

We cannot conclude, however, that urbanization and poverty automatically create an environment for high crime rates. Some poor neighborhoods have more crime than others. The differences between neighborhoods' crime rates may be affected by other factors, such as the physical conditions of the neighborhoods, the residents' attitudes toward society and the law, the extent of opportunities for crime, and the effectiveness of social control by families and government agencies.[12] As noted previously, crime is such a complex problem that it cannot be reduced to a single primary cause.

THE IMPACT OF CRIME

Financial Costs

Crime affects not only its immediate victims but the rest of society as well. Put another way, we are all victims of crime because we live in a society that is affected by serious crime problems in many cities. The precise impact of crime is difficult to estimate. Researchers have estimated, for example, that

TABLE 1.4
Who Are the Victims of Personal Crime? NCVS data help clarify the characteristics of crime victims.

SOURCE: U.S. Department of Justice, Bureau of Justice Statistics, *Highlights from Twenty Years of Surveying Crime Victims* (Washington, DC: Government Printing Office, 1993), p. 18.

[a]Based on ten or fewer cases.

receipts from criminal activity total somewhere between $26.9 billion and $136.9 billion.[13] This broad range reflects the difficulties of trying to calculate precise figures for the costs imposed on society by crime. The Bureau of Justice Statistics has estimated that American households lost over $19 billion in stolen property, cash losses, and medical expenses to crime in 1991.[14] The cost of operating the criminal justice system is over $70 billion per year.

As large as these figures are, they still fail to reflect the full cost of crime. They do not include such additional costs as the increased cost to consumers of organized crime activity. For example, when owners of small businesses have to pay "protection money" to criminal organizations, those businesses must raise their prices to cover the costs. Thus, law-abiding citizens must pay a price for the activities of organized crime. In addition, estimates of the costs of crime do not place any value on the pain and suffering of victims and their families. Nor are purchases of expensive private security devices and services, such as burglar alarms and private security guards, taken into account. We know that crime exacts staggering economic, personal, and psychological costs on Americans, but we can never place an accurate value on the costs.

Fear as an Impact of Crime

Fear of crime is a powerful force that shapes Americans' daily behavior. For example, it limits their freedom to leave their houses whenever they wish and narrows their choice of places to go. Fear also creates unmeasurable anxieties that affect people's physiological and psychological well-being.

The fear is not limited to people who have been victimized or who live in neighborhoods with high crime rates. Violent crime is a pervasive subject in print and electronic media—on the evening news, in television dramas, and in real-life "cop" shows in which the camera takes the viewer directly to the scene of drug busts, car chases, and assaults. Ironically, if not surprisingly, people who have the least chance of being victimized by crime are often the most fearful.

Since 1965, public opinion organizations—Gallup, Harris, and others—have been asking Americans about their reactions to crime to determine whether they "feel more uneasy" or "fear to walk the streets at night." More than 40 percent of respondents say that the fear of crime limits their freedom. In large cities, more than 60 percent of residents say that they are afraid to walk through their neighborhoods at night, while in small towns and rural areas fewer than 30 percent express this concern. High levels of fear are found among nonwhites and low-income individuals, who are in fact the most likely to be victimized. However, women, the elderly, and upper-income suburbanites, groups that generally have low rates of victimization, are also more frightened than the average citizen.

Even so, among *all* groups, the fear of crime outstrips the reality. People do not have an accurate sense of the actual risk of crime as it affects their lives. They see crime all around them and behave accordingly, even though they are "seeing" crime that is not actually there.

Researchers point to vicarious or indirect victimization as an explanation for unrealistic fears; that is, people permit fear to guide their behavior merely from reading, hearing, or seeing shows about crime. It may not be the news media and television shows alone that create this effect. Some researchers believe that personal communication networks report and magnify the apparent volume of violent crime. The most frightening aspects of particular crimes may be increasingly accentuated as the stories are passed from person to person. Crimes against women and the elderly, in particular, may receive extra attention in both news reports and neighborhood conversations. Accounts about old, frail, or otherwise defenseless victims seem to heighten perceptions that violent criminals lurk everywhere.

Unfortunately, actions that might reduce one's fear of crime are costly. Ironically, those least threatened by crime are in the best position to defend themselves. Some responses to the perceived risk of crime may not seem costly, such as staying at home after dark. Yet, even such a simple measure is often far easier for the rich than the poor. Affluent people are more likely to work during the day and to have control over their working hours. By contrast, poorer people are more likely to work evenings and nights in manufacturing, custodial, and service jobs (for example, as waitresses, security guards, or convenience store clerks). Other defenses, such as moving to the suburbs, installing home security systems, and hiring private security companies, are also most available to the affluent people who are least at risk of becoming victims.

CRIME VICTIMS AND THE CRIMINAL JUSTICE SYSTEM

After a crime, the victim is often forgotten or even mistreated. Victims may have suffered physical, psychological, and economic losses, yet the criminal justice system focuses almost exclusively on investigating, prosecuting, adjudicating, and punishing offenders. Thus, the system is sometimes insensitive to the feelings of victims. For example, defense attorneys often target crime victims for vigorous, hostile questioning on behalf of their clients, frequently attempting to paint the victim as the guilty party. Rape victims in particular have historically found themselves accused of immoral behavior and of having invited the sexual contact with the offender. Likewise, while victims are an essential source of evidence for the police and prosecutors, police may interrogate victims suspiciously as they try to determine whether the truth is being told. Often, the police and prosecutor talk with the victim immediately after the crime, but the victim never hears from them again. The offender may even remain free in the community on bail or on probation. To come face to face with one's assailant can be quite a shock, especially if one erroneously assumed that the offender was sitting in prison.

Only during the past two decades have justice agencies become sensitive to the plight of crime victims. In many cases victims still feel that they are the ones on trial.

The victim may also be forced to miss work and forfeit pay in order to appear at various judicial proceedings. Further, victims may be repeatedly summoned to court, only to learn that the arraignment or trial has been postponed. Any recovered property that was stolen by the offender may be held by court for months in order to keep evidence available as the case winds its way through the system. Thus, the initial suffering imposed on the victim by the criminal may simply be compounded by the various steps in the justice process. In short, after cases have been completed, victims may feel that they have been victimized twice, once by the offender and once by the criminal justice system.

During the past two decades, criminal justice agencies have become increasingly sensitive to the needs and interests of crime victims. This sensitivity has resulted, in part, from the recognition that victims are often the only witnesses to the crime and that their cooperation is necessary for a conviction. If police and prosecutors do not consider the victim's feelings or if they force the victim to absorb unnecessary psychological and financial costs by having to show up for canceled court dates, some victims will eventually refuse to cooperate.

Advocates have proposed adoption of a "Crime Victims' Bill of Rights" that would grant victims the right to be informed about plea bargains, the right to be "made whole" through restitution, and the right to prevent offenders from profiting from books and films about their criminal activities.[15] Although victims have gained few such legal guarantees, there are increasing efforts to provide assistance to victims. For example, in some states, the investigating officer hands the victim a booklet containing information about the steps that will be taken and telephone numbers that can be called should questions arise. Other kinds of programs provide crisis assistance, including counseling, medical and financial help, and even a safe place to stay.

THE ROLE OF VICTIMS IN CRIMINALITY

Increasingly, criminologists have studied the role played by victims in criminal incidents. By analyzing the characteristics of a variety of victims, researchers have advanced the idea that many victims behave in ways that invite the acts committed against them. This is not necessarily to say that it is the victim's fault that the crime occurred. It is merely to recognize that the victim's behavior may have brought about commission of a crime through consent, provocation, enticement, unnecessary risk taking, or carelessness with property.

The phrase *victim precipitation* refers to the idea that people may do things that make them more likely to become victims. First, people sometimes do not take proper precautions to protect themselves. Although we like to believe that we are free to act as we wish, in reality we must use common sense and take precautions in order to minimize our risk of victimization. Second, under certain circumstances, victims, by some action, may provoke or entice someone to commit a criminal act. For instance, yelling at the wrong person after a traffic altercation may trigger an assault. Third, victims in certain types of nonstranger crimes are often unwilling to assist official agencies in investigation and prosecution. As we saw previously, victims do not always report crimes to the police. When the offender is a member of the family or a friend, this inaction may encourage additional criminal actions against the victim. Again, such actions do not make the victim *responsible* for the crime. They merely help us to understand the contexts in which crimes occur and the reasons that some people are more likely than others to become victims.

CRIME AND JUSTICE AS PUBLIC POLICY ISSUES

Crime and justice are crucial public policy issues. We struggle to strike the appropriate balance between maintaining public order and protecting individual freedom. We could impose policies that make us feel safer from crime, such as placing a police officer on every street corner and summarily executing suspected criminals. Such severe practices have been used elsewhere in the world. While they may reduce crime, however, they also greatly damage cherished democratic values. If we gave the government and law enforcement officers a free hand to work their will on the public, we would be surrendering individual freedom, due process, and our conception of justice.

CRIME CONTROL AND AMERICAN IDEALS

The way we control crime represents a basic test of our ideals. The administration of justice in a democracy can be distinguished from that in an authoritarian state by the extent and form of protections provided for the accused as guilt is determined and punishment is imposed.

Our laws begin with the premise that all people have rights, the guilty as well as the innocent. Moreover, unlike in some other countries, our laws reflect our concern that we avoid unnecessarily depriving people of liberty, either by permitting police to search people at will or by mistakenly punishing an innocent person for a crime that he or she did not commit. Our greatest challenge may be to find ways to remain true to these legal principles supporting fair treatment and justice while also operating a system that can effectively protect, investigate, and punish. There are significant divisions, especially between liberals and conservatives, about policies to deal with crime within our democratic framework.

Conservatives believe that the answer lies in stricter enforcement of the law through the expansion of police forces and the enactment of punitive measures that will result in the swift and certain punishment of criminals. The holders of this conservative view have remained politically dominant since the early 1980s. They argue that we must strengthen crime control, which they assert has been hurt by decisions of the U.S. Supreme Court and by liberal programs that have weakened traditional values of responsibility and family. In contrast, liberals argue that the strengthening of crime control has endangered our cherished values of due process and justice. They claim that strict approaches are ineffective in reducing crime because the answer lies in reshaping the lives of individual offenders and changing the social and economic conditions from which, they believe, criminal behavior springs.

As you encounter these arguments, think about how they relate to actual crime trends. Crime increased in the 1960s when we were trying the liberal approach of rehabilitating offenders. Does this mean that the approach does not work? Perhaps the liberal approach was merely overwhelmed by the number of people in their crime-prone years at that time. Perhaps there would have been even more crime if not for the efforts to rehabilitate. On the other hand, crime rates diminished when tough policies were implemented in the 1980s. But was that because of the conservative policies or because of the shrinking size of the crime-prone age group? If conservative policies are effective, then why did violent crime rates move upward in the early 1990s when tough policies were still in force? Obviously, there are no easy answers, yet we cannot avoid making choices about how to use our police, our courts, and our corrections system most effectively.

THE POLITICS OF CRIME AND JUSTICE

As we examine alternative criminal justice policies, we need to remember that such policies are developed in national, state, and local political arenas. Because the public is so deeply concerned about crime, there is always a risk

Controlling and preventing crime cannot depend solely on the police, courts, and corrections. All citizens must be involved.

that politicians will simply say what they believe the voters want to hear rather than think seriously about whether the policies will achieve their goals. The crime bill passed by Congress in 1994 expanded the death penalty to sixty additional crimes, including murder of members of Congress, the Supreme Court, and the president's staff. These are tough provisions, but do they actually accomplish anything relevant to crime in America or to people's fear of crime? Politicians may claim that they "got tough on crime," but the public has little knowledge of the specific provisions of most legislation.

The most visible connection between politics and criminal justice is in the arguments and posturing by Republicans and Democrats who attempt to outdo each other in showing the voters how tough they can be. Equally important are the more "routine" linkages between politics and the justice system. Penal codes and the budgets of criminal justice agencies are passed by legislators who are responsive to the voters. Congress appropriates millions of dollars to assist states and cities in waging the "war on drugs" but prohibits any expenditures for legal counsel for poor defendants. At the state and local level, many criminal justice authorities, including sheriffs, prosecutors, and judges, are also elected officials. Thus, their decisions will be influenced by the community's concerns and values.

As you learn about each part of the criminal justice system, keep in mind the ways in which decision makers and institutions are connected to politics and government. Criminal justice is intimately connected to society and its institutions, and to fully understand it we must recognize those connections.

SUMMARY

Crime and justice pose fundamental challenges to a democratic society like the United States: How do we control and punish harmful behavior without unnecessarily undermining freedom and fairness? The tension between stopping criminal behavior and protecting individual freedom also confronts us when we consider the policies we will develop to investigate, process, adjudicate, and punish offenders.

Our understanding of the nature and extent of crime can help inform our decisions about which policies will be most appropriate. Although we lack the ability to measure crime precisely, we have gained useful knowledge through such tools as the *Uniform Crime Reports* and the National Crime Victimization Surveys.

If we recognize the links between crime and such factors as age distribution, urbanization, and victim behavior, we have the opportunity to limit our policy choices to those that will best respond to crime without surrendering more freedom than is necessary. Our ability to maximize the effectiveness of our policy choices is limited, however, because political pressures frequently cause policymakers to lose sight of the causes of crime and the effects of policy choices. Instead, they often undertake strong actions that cater to the public's fears but have little impact on actual crime trends.

Criminal justice represents a fascinating, ongoing challenge in the task of making policy choices to control complex and harmful forms of human behavior while maintaining the democratic traditions upon which the country was founded.

QUESTIONS FOR REVIEW

1. Which categories of crime are most difficult to investigate and prosecute?
2. What factors affect changes in the crime rate and cause American crime rates to differ from those in other countries?
3. What are the positive and negative attributes of the two major sources of crime data?
4. What role do victims play in crime incidents, and how does the criminal justice system treat those victims?
5. How does politics affect criminal justice?

NOTES

1. Elliot Currie, *Confronting Crime* (New York: Pantheon, 1985), p. 25.
2. Dane Archer and Rosemary Gartner, *Violence and Crime in Cross-National Perspective* (New Haven, CT: Yale University Press, 1984).
3. U.S. Department of Justice, Bureau of Justice Statistics, *Report to the Nation on Crime and Justice*, 2nd ed. (Washington, DC: Government Printing Office, 1988), p. 16.
4. Jill Smolowe, "Danger in the Safety Zone," *Time*, 23 August 1993, p. 30.
5. Bureau of Justice Statistics, *Criminal Victimization in the United States: 1973–1992* (Washington, DC: U.S. Department of Justice, 1994), p. 5.
6. U.S. Department of Justice, Bureau of Justice Statistics, *Bulletin* (October 1993).
7. Ronet Bachman and Bruce Taylor, "The Measurement of Family Violence and Rape by the Redesigned National Crime Victimization Survey," *Justice Quarterly* 11 (September 1994), pp. 499–512.
8. Bureau of Justice Statistics, *Criminal Victimization in the United States: 1973–1992 Trends* (Washington, DC: U.S. Department of Justice, 1994), p. 1.
9. U.S. Department of Justice, *Crime in the United States 1992* (Washington, DC: Government Printing Office, 1993), p. 58.
10. Ibid., p. 216.

11. U.S. Department of Justice, Bureau of Justice Statistics, *Highlights from 20 Years of Surveying Crime Victims* (Washington, DC: Government Printing Office, 1993), p. 18.

12. Rodney Stark, "Decent Places: A Theory of the Ecology of Crime," *Criminology* 25 (1987), pp. 893–909.

13. U.S. Department of Justice, *Report to the Nation*, p. 114.

14. U.S. Department of Justice, *Highlights*, p. 16.

15. *Victimology: An International Journal* 5 (1980), pp. 428–437.

CHAPTER 2
The Criminal Justice System

FEDERAL AND STATE FORCES ASSAULT TEXAS CULT

In the early morning hours of February 28, 1993, nearly one hundred agents of the U.S. Bureau of Alcohol, Tobacco, and Firearms (ATF) approached the compound of the Branch Davidian religious cult outside Waco, Texas. Officers were attempting to serve search and arrest warrants, alleging that the compound contained illegal weapons. A burst of gunfire suddenly emanated from the buildings, which housed more than one hundred cult members. The federal agents returned fire. A ferocious forty-five-minute gun battle ensued during which four ATF officers were killed, sixteen others were injured, and at least three members of the cult perished. For the next fifty-one days, Americans watched the standoff between the government and the cult. On April 19, agents of the FBI and ATF, supported by a U.S. Army medical team, members of the McLennan County sheriff's office, and the Texas Rangers, battered the fortified walls of the compound using tanks and tear gas. As the tear gas entered the buildings, they suddenly exploded in flames. Within an hour, only the

charred ruins of the complex remained. The death toll was an estimated eighty cult members, including seventeen children.

The events at Waco gave Americans an elementary education in the complexity of criminal justice in the United States. Before the confrontation, few had ever heard of the Bureau of Alcohol, Tobacco, and Firearms of the U.S. Treasury Department—let alone suspected what actions it might take in such circumstances. The fact that the final assault involved not only the ATF but also the FBI and Texas law enforcement agencies further illustrated the complex relationships among national, state, and local police forces. The arrest and prosecution of four Branch Davidian members and their ultimate trial in federal courts further added to the complexity.

The event in Waco was only one of countless encounters between American citizens and their agents of criminal justice. Crime and justice is a major governmental function employing 1.7 million employees in over 60,000 agencies of the police, prosecution, courts, and corrections at an annual cost of more than $74 billion. In this chapter, we will examine how the criminal justice system really works. In many important respects, the manner in which the system operates is different from the idealistic image of law and justice that we learned in eighth-grade civics classes. Criminal justice is a system with certain important characteristics that shape the processing of cases and determine the fates of individual defendants. Throughout this process, formal rules of law have less impact on case outcomes than many people believe. ★

THE GOALS OF CRIMINAL JUSTICE

Before we begin our examination of the reality of the criminal justice system, we must first ask, What goals does the system serve? Although these goals may seem straightforward, it can be difficult to specify exactly what they mean in practice.

In 1967, the President's Commission on Law Enforcement and Administration of Justice described the criminal justice system as an apparatus society uses to "enforce the standards of conduct necessary to protect individuals and the community."[1] This statement serves as the basis of our discussion of the goals of the criminal justice system. Although there is much debate about the purposes of criminal justice, three goals are prominent: (1) doing justice, (2) controlling crime, and (3) preventing crime.

DOING JUSTICE

We must first recognize that doing justice is the basis for the rules, procedures, and institutions of American criminal justice. Without a system founded on the principle of justice, there would be little difference between criminal justice in the United States and that in authoritarian countries. Fairness is an essential element. We want to have fair laws. We want to investigate, adjudicate, and punish fairly. Doing justice also requires upholding the rights of individuals and punishing persons who violate the law. Thus, the goal of doing justice embodies several underlying principles: (1) that offenders will be held fully accountable for their actions, (2) that the rights of persons who have contact with the system will be protected, and (3) that like offenses will be treated alike and that officials will take into account relevant differences among offenders and offenses.[2]

Successfully doing justice is a tall order, and it is easy to identify situations in which American criminal justice agencies and processes fall short of achieving this ideal. Unlike in authoritarian systems in which criminal justice clearly serves the interests of those who hold political power, in a democracy people can aspire to improve the capacity of their institutions to do justice. Thus, however imperfect they may be, criminal justice institutions and processes in the United States can enjoy the support of the public as responsive agencies of government. In a democracy, a system that makes doing justice a paramount goal is viewed by citizens as legitimate and is thus able to pursue the secondary goals of controlling and preventing crime.

CONTROLLING CRIME

The criminal justice system is designed to control crime by apprehending, prosecuting, convicting, and punishing those members of the community who disobey the law. An important constraint on the system, however, is that efforts to control crime must be carried out within the framework of law. The criminal law not only defines what is illegal but also outlines the rights of citizens and prescribes the procedures that officials must use to achieve the system's goals.

CHAPTER QUESTIONS

What are the goals of the criminal justice system?

How is criminal justice pursued in a federal system of government such as the United States?

What are the major characteristics of criminal justice as a social system?

What is the flow of decision making from arrest and prosecution through sentencing and release from corrections?

How do the crime control and due process models of criminal justice help us understand the reality of the system?

A QUESTION OF ETHICS

After his jewelry store had been burglarized for the third time in less than six months, Tom Henderson was frustrated. The police were of little help, merely telling him that they would have a patrol officer keep watch during nightly rounds. Tom had added new locks and an electronic security system. When he unlocked his shop one morning, he saw that he had been cleaned out again. He looked around the store to see how the thief had entered, since the door was locked and the security alarm evidently had not sounded. Suddenly, he noticed that the glass in a skylight was broken.

"Damn, I'll fix him this time," cursed Henderson.

That evening, after replacing the glass, he stripped the insulation from an electric cord and strung it around and across the frame of the skylight. He plugged the cord into a socket, locked the store, and went home.

Two weeks later, when he entered the store and flipped the light switch, nothing happened. He walked toward the fuse box. It was then that he noticed the burned body lying on the floor below the skylight.

To what extent can someone freely choose the methods to "protect his castle"? If the police are unable to solve a crime problem, is it ethical for individuals to take matters into their own hands?

In any city or town, we can see the goal of crime control being actively pursued: police officers walking a beat, patrol cars racing down darkened streets, lawyers advocating points of law before a judge, probation officers visiting clients, and the maximum security prison looming tall and forbidding. Taking actions against wrongdoers helps to control crime, but the system must also employ strategies to prevent crimes from happening.

PREVENTING CRIME

Crime can be prevented in various ways. Perhaps most important is the deterrent effect of both the justice and crime control goals. The actions of the police, courts, and corrections officials not only punish those individuals who violate the law but, in so doing, also provide examples that are likely to deter others from committing wrongful acts. For example, a racing patrol car is both responding to a crime situation and serving as a warning that law enforcement is at hand.

Crime prevention depends on the actions of criminal justice officials and citizens. Unfortunately, many Americans do not take the often simple steps necessary to protect themselves and their property. For example, many people leave homes and vehicles unlocked, do not use alarm systems, and walk in dangerous unlighted areas.

Citizens do not have the authority to enforce the law; society has given that responsibility to the criminal justice system. Thus, citizens must rely upon the police to stop criminals; they cannot take the law into their own hand. Still, they can and must be actively engaged in preventing crime.

CRIMINAL JUSTICE IN A FEDERAL SYSTEM: PARALLEL SYSTEMS

federalism
A system of government in which power is divided between a central (national) government and regional (state) governments.

Criminal justice, like other aspects of American government, is based on the concept of **federalism**, whereby power is divided between a central (national) government and regional (state) governments. States have significant authority over their own affairs, but an overarching federal government handles certain matters of national concern. Because of federalism, no single level of government is solely responsible for administration of criminal justice.

The American governmental structure was created in 1789 with the ratification of the U.S. Constitution. The Constitution created a delicate political agreement. The national government was given certain powers—to raise an army, to coin money, to make treaties with foreign countries—but all other powers, including police power, were retained by the states. No national police force with broad enforcement powers may be established in the United States.

There are no specific references in the Constitution to criminal justice among the federal government's powers. However, the contemporary federal government is involved in criminal justice in many ways. We all are familiar with the Federal Bureau of Investigation (FBI), a national law enforcement agency. You may also recognize that criminal cases are often tried in U.S. district courts, which are federal courts, and know that the Federal Bureau of Prisons operates institutions from coast to coast. All of these agencies are busily operating despite the fact that most criminal justice activity is at the state, rather than the national level.

Both the national and the state systems of criminal justice are involved in enforcing laws, trying criminal cases, and punishing offenders, but they do so on different authority, and their activities differ in scope and purpose. The vast majority of criminal laws are written by state legislatures and enforced by state agencies. However, a variety of national criminal laws have been enacted by Congress and are enforced by the FBI, the Drug Enforcement Administration, the Secret Service, and other federal agencies. With the exception of federal drug offenses, relatively few offenders break federal criminal laws in comparison to the large numbers who break state criminal laws. For example, only small numbers of people violate the federal law against counterfeiting and espionage, while large numbers of people violate state laws covering assault, larceny, drunk driving, and other visible crimes. Even in the case of drug offenses, which during the 1980s and 1990s swept large numbers of offenders into federal prisons, many additional violators of drug laws also ended up in state corrections systems because such crimes violate both state and federal laws.

The role of criminal justice agencies following the assassination of President John F. Kennedy in November 1963 further illustrates the federal-state division of jurisdiction. Because Congress had not made killing the president of the United States a federal offense, the suspect, Lee Harvey Oswald, would have been charged under Texas laws had he lived (Oswald was shot to death by nightclub owner Jack Ruby shortly after his arrest). The U.S. Secret Service had the job of protecting the president, but apprehension of the killer was the formal responsibility of the Dallas police and other Texas law enforcement agencies.

Over time, federal involvement in the criminal justice system has slowly expanded. Because many criminal enterprises and activities span state borders, we no longer think of some crimes as being committed at a single location within a single state. In organized crime, for example, crime syndicates and gangs deal with drugs, pornography, and gambling on a national basis. Thus, Congress has expanded the powers of the FBI and other federal agencies to pursue criminal activities of national concern that previously were considered the responsibility of the states.

Congress has also passed laws designed to allow the FBI to investigate situations in which local police forces are likely to be less effective. Under the National Stolen Property Act, for example, the FBI is authorized to investigate thefts exceeding $5,000 in value when the stolen property is likely to have been transported across state lines. Because the FBI is a national organization, it is better able than any state agency to pursue criminal investigations across state borders. In such circumstances, disputes over jurisdiction may occur because the offense is a violation of both state and federal laws. If the FBI and local law enforcement agencies do not cooperate with one another, they may each be seeking independently to apprehend the same criminals. The court to which a case is brought may be determined by the law enforcement agency that makes the arrest. Usually, law enforcement and judicial officials at all levels of government seek to cooperate and coordinate their efforts.

Because of the existence of parallel systems, criminal justice in the United States is highly decentralized. As Figure 2.1 shows, two-thirds of all criminal justice employees work for local units of government. With the exception of corrections employees, the majority of workers in all of the subunits of the criminal justice system—police, judiciary, prosecution, public defense—are tied to local government. Likewise, the costs of criminal justice are distributed in varying proportions among the federal, state, and local governments, as shown in Figure 2.2.

Laws are enforced and violators are brought to justice primarily in the states, counties, and municipalities. As a result, local traditions, values, and

FIGURE 2.1

Percentage (rounded) of Criminal Justice Employees at Each Level of Government
The administration of criminal justice in the United States is very much a local affair as these employment figures show. It is only in corrections that states employ a greater percentage of workers than do municipalities.

SOURCE: U.S. Department of Justice, Bureau of Justice Statistics, *Bulletin* (September 1993).

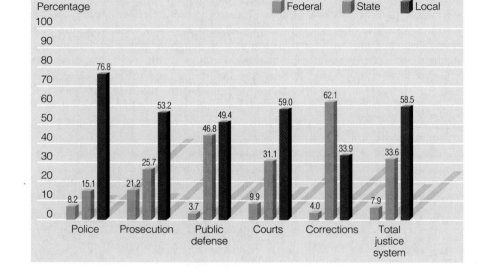

FIGURE 2.2

Who Pays for Criminal Justice Services?
State and local governments bear the brunt of the costs.

SOURCE: U.S. Department of Justice, Bureau of Justice Statistics, *Bulletin* (September 1992), p. 3.

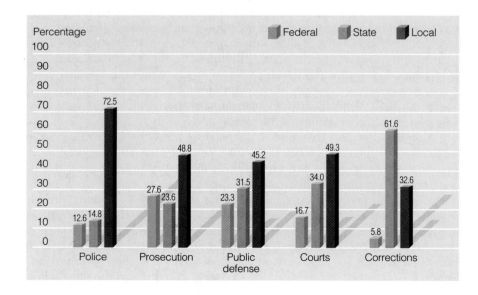

practices shape the way in which criminal justice agencies are organized and operate. Local leaders, whether members of city council or influential citizens, can help to set law enforcement priorities by applying pressure on the police. Will the city's police officers crack down on illegal gambling? Will juvenile offenders be turned over to their parents with stern warnings, or will they be sent away to state institutions? The answers to these and other important questions vary from city to city.

CRIMINAL JUSTICE AS A SYSTEM

To achieve the goals of criminal justice, many organizational subunits—police, prosecution, courts, corrections—have been developed. Each of these organizations has its own personnel, functions, and responsibilities. If we were to construct an organizational chart, we might assume that criminal justice is an orderly process in which a variety of professionals act on the accused's case in the interests of society. To understand how the system really works, however, we must look beyond the formal organizational chart. To assist in this task, we can use the social science concept of **system**: a complex whole consisting of interdependent parts whose operations are directed toward goals and are influenced by the environment within which they function.

CRIMINAL JUSTICE FROM A SYSTEM PERSPECTIVE

Criminal justice is a system made up of a number of parts or subsystems—police, courts, corrections. The subsystems have their own goals and needs but are also interdependent. When one unit changes its policies, practices, or resources, other units will be affected. An increase in the number of people arrested by the police on felony charges, for example, will affect the work not only of the judicial subsystem but also of the probation and correctional subsystems. For criminal justice to achieve its goals, each part must make its own distinctive contribution; each part must also have at least minimal contact with at least one other component of the system.

Although it is important to understand the characteristics and operations of the entire criminal justice system and its individual subsystems, we must also see how individual actors play their roles. The criminal justice system is made up of a great many persons performing specific tasks. Some, such as police officers and judges, are well known to the public. Other important actors, such as bail bondsmen and probation officers, are less visible and less well known.

A key concept for analysis of the relationships among individual decision makers is exchange. In this context, **exchange** refers to a mutual transfer of resources among individual decision makers, each of whom has interests and goals that he or she cannot readily accomplish alone. Therefore, each needs to gain cooperation and assistance from other actors by contributing to their interests and goals. The concept of exchange allows us to see interpersonal behavior as the result of individual decisions about the values and costs of alternative courses of action.

There are a variety of exchange relationships in the criminal justice system, some of which are more visible than others. Probably the most obvious example of an exchange relationship is **plea bargaining**. Here, a defendant's

system
A complex whole consisting of interdependent parts whose operations are directed toward goals and are influenced by the environment within which they function.

exchange
A mutual transfer of resources among individual decision makers, each of whom has interests and goals that he or she cannot readily accomplish alone.

plea bargaining
Process in which a defendant's fate is determined not through a trial, but rather through an agreement between the defense attorney and the prosecutor whereby the defendant agrees to plead guilty in exchange for a reduction of charges or a specific sentence recommendation.

FIGURE 2.3
Exchange Relationships Between Prosecutors and Others
The prosecutor's decisions are influenced by the relationships that are maintained with other criminal justice agencies, governmental units, and influential community members.

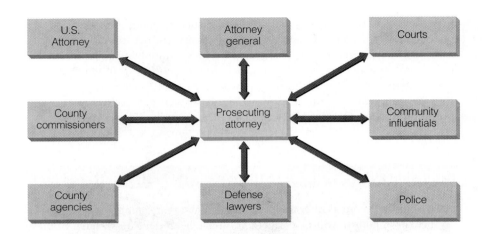

TABLE 2.1

Who Exercises Discretion?

Discretion is exercised by various individuals throughout the criminal justice system.

SOURCE: U.S. Department of Justice, Bureau of Justice Statistics, *Report to the Nation on Crime and Justice*, 2nd ed. (Washington, DC: Government Printing Office, 1988), p. 59.

Criminal Justice Officials	Discretionary Tasks
Police	Enforce specific laws
	Investigate specific crimes
	Search people, vicinities, buildings
	Arrest or detain people
Prosecutors	File charges or petitions for adjudication
	Seek indictments
	Drop cases
	Reduce charges
Judges or magistrates	Set bail or conditions for release
	Accept pleas
	Determine delinquency
	Dismiss charges
	Impose sentence
	Revoke probation
Correctional officials	Assign to type of correctional facility
	Award privileges
	Punish for infractions of discipline
	Determine date and conditions of parole
	Revoke parole

fate is determined not through a trial, but rather through an agreement between the defense attorney and the prosecutor in which the defendant agrees to plead guilty in exchange for a reduction of charges or a specific sentence recommendation. As a result of this exchange, the defendant achieves a shorter sentence, the prosecutor secures a quick, sure conviction, and the defense attorney can move on to the next case. Thus, the cooperation underlying the exchange promotes the goals of each participant.

The concept of exchange reminds us that decisions are the products of interactions among individuals and that the major subsystems—police, court, and corrections—are tied together by the actions of individual decision makers. Figure 2.3 presents selected exchange relationships between a prosecuting attorney and other individuals and agencies involved in the criminal justice process.

The concepts of system and exchange are closely linked, and their value as tools for the analysis of criminal justice cannot be overemphasized. In this book, these concepts serve as the organizing framework to describe individual subsystems and actors and to help us understand how the justice process really works. However, several additional characteristics of the criminal justice system shape the decisions that determine the fates of individual defendants.

CHARACTERISTICS OF THE CRIMINAL JUSTICE SYSTEM

Four important attributes characterize the workings of the criminal justice system: (1) discretion, (2) resource dependence, (3) sequential tasks, and (4) filtering.

Discretion

At all levels of the justice process, there is a high degree of **discretion**—the ability of officials to act according to their own judgment and conscience (see Table 2.1). For example, police officers decide how to handle a crime situation, prosecutors decide what charges to file against the accused, judges decide how long a sentence will be, and parole boards decide when an offender should be released from prison.

Police officers have the discretion to consider the circumstances of a situation before they act. Can the exercise of discretion be consistent with the rule of law?

The fact that discretion exists throughout the criminal justice system may seem odd given that our country is ruled by law and has created procedures to ensure that decisions are made in accordance with that law. However, instead of a mechanical system in which law preempts human decision making, criminal justice is a system in which the participants may consider a wide variety of circumstances and exercise many options as they dispose of a case.

Two primary arguments are frequently used to justify discretion in the criminal justice system. First, discretion is needed because the system lacks the resources to treat every case in the same fashion. If every violation of the law were pursued through trial, the costs would be staggering. Second, many officials in the system believe that their discretionary authority permits them to achieve greater justice than rigid rules would produce.

Resource Dependence

Criminal justice agencies generally do not generate their own resources—for example, budgets, staff, and equipment—but depend on others for them. Therefore, criminal justice actors (police chiefs, prosecutors, judges) frequently must cultivate and maintain good relationships with people responsible for the allocation of resources—that is, the political decision makers (legislators, mayors, city council members, and so on). Some police departments gain revenue through traffic enforcement and property forfeiture, but these sources cannot sustain their budgets.

Because the budgetary decision makers are elected officials who seek to please the public, criminal justice officials must also maintain a positive image and good relations with the voters. If the police enjoy strong public support, for example, then the mayor will be reluctant to reduce the law enforcement budget. In maintaining positive public relations, criminal justice officials inevitably seek favorable coverage from local news media. Since the media often provide a crucial link between government agencies and the public, criminal justice officials may publicize notable achievements while simultaneously seeking to limit or control publicity about controversial cases and decisions.

discretion
The ability of officials to act according to their own judgment or conscience.

33

Sequential Tasks

Decisions in the criminal justice system are made in a particular sequence. The police must make an arrest before defendants are passed to the prosecutor, whose decisions ultimately determine the nature of the workload for courts and corrections. Officials cannot achieve their objectives by acting out of sequence. For example, prosecutors and judges cannot bypass the police by making arrests on their own, and corrections officials cannot punish anyone who has not already passed through the decision-making stages administered by the police, prosecution, and courts. Obviously, the sequential nature of the system is a key element in the exchange relationships that characterize the interactions of decision makers who depend on each other to achieve their respective goals. Thus, the system is highly interdependent.

FIGURE 2.4

Criminal Justice as a Filtering Process
Decisions made at each point of the criminal justice system result in some cases being dropped and others being passed on to the next decision point. Are you surprised by the small number of cases that actually go to trial?

SOURCE: Data drawn from many sources, including U.S. Department of Justice, *Sourcebook of Criminal Justice Statistics, 1992* (Washington, DC: Government Printing Office, 1993), and Bureau of Justice Statistics, *Bulletin* (January 1988, February 1989).

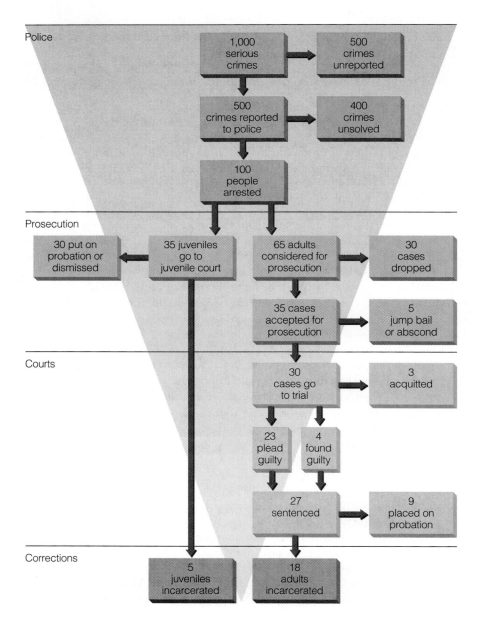

Filtering

The criminal justice system may be viewed as a **filtering process** through which cases are screened. At each stage, some defendants are sent on to the next stage of decision making while others are either released or processed under changed conditions. As shown in Figure 2.4, persons who have been arrested may be filtered out of the system at various points. Note that very few suspects arrested by the police are prosecuted, tried, and convicted. Some go free because the police decide that a crime has not been committed or that the evidence is not sound. The prosecutor may drop charges by deciding that justice would be better served by diverting the suspect to a substance abuse clinic. Large numbers of defendants will plead guilty, the judge may dismiss charges against others, and the jury may acquit a few defendants. Most of the offenders who are actually tried, however, will be convicted. Thus, the criminal justice system is often described as a "funnel" into which many cases enter but only a few result in conviction and punishment.

filtering process
A screening operation in which some defendants are sent on to the next stage of decision making while others are either released or processed under changed conditions.

OPERATIONS OF CRIMINAL JUSTICE AGENCIES

The criminal justice system encompasses a major commitment on the part of American society to deal with persons who are accused of criminal law violations. As discussed previously, the police, courts, and corrections are the primary subsystems of criminal justice in the United States. Each subsystem is linked to the other two subsystems, and the exchange relations of each has an impact on the others. These linkages are related to the system characteristics that we examined earlier, including discretion, resource dependence, sequential tasks, and filtering.

POLICE

We usually think of the police as the officials who bear "frontline" responsibilities for controlling crime. When we use the term *police*, however, we are referring not to a single agency or type of agency, but to many agencies at each level of government. The complexity and fragmentation of the criminal justice system is demonstrated by the large number of public organizations in the United States engaged in law enforcement. Of the 17,000 agencies in total, only 50 are federal and another 49 state. Thus, the remaining 16,901 agencies are dispersed throughout counties, cities, and towns, reflecting the fact that the police function is dominated by local governments. At the state and local level, these agencies have over 840,000 employees and a total annual budget in excess of $41 billion.[3]

Police organizations have four general responsibilities:

1. *Keeping the peace.* This broad and most important mandate involves the protection of rights and persons in a wide variety of situations, ranging from street-corner brawls to domestic quarrels.
2. *Apprehending law violators and combating crime.* This is the responsibility the public most often associates with police work, although it accounts for only a small proportion of law enforcement agencies' time and resources.
3. *Engaging in crime prevention.* By educating the public about the threat of crime and by reducing the number of situations in which crimes are most likely to be committed, the police can lower the incidence of crime.

4. *Providing a variety of social services.* For example, police officers may recover stolen property, direct traffic, provide emergency medical aid, or help people who have locked themselves out of their apartments.

COURTS

dual court system
A system consisting of a separate judicial structure for each state in addition to a national structure.

Although we may talk about *the* judiciary, the United States has a **dual court system**, consisting of a separate judicial structure for each state in addition to a national structure. Each system has its own series of courts, while the U.S. Supreme Court has overriding responsibility for correcting certain errors made in all other court systems. Although the U.S. Supreme Court can review cases from both the state and federal courts, it will hear only cases involving a federal law or those involving claims that a constitutional right was denied.

With a dual court system, interpretation of the law can vary from state to state. Although states may have laws that are similarly worded, none of the state courts interpret the law exactly the same. To some extent, these variations reflect different social and political conditions. The dominant values of citizens and judges may differ from region to region. Differences may also represent attempts by state courts to solve similar problems by different means. For example, before the U.S. Supreme Court ruled that evidence illegally obtained by the police should be excluded from use at trials, some states had already enacted rules prohibiting the use of such evidence.

adjudication
The process of determining the guilt or innocence of a defendant.

Courts have primary responsibility for **adjudication**—the process of determining the guilt or innocence of a defendant. In so doing, they must use fair procedures that will produce just, reliable decisions. Courts must also impose appropriate sentences that hold individuals accountable for their behavior.

CORRECTIONS

The public often equates corrections with prisons, but only about a third of convicted offenders are incarcerated. Two thirds are on probation or parole in the community.

On any given day, approximately 4 million Americans are under the supervision of state and federal corrections systems. There is no "typical" corrections agency or official, but rather a great variety of correctional institutions and programs provided by public and private organizations, including federal, state, and local governments, and carried out in many different community and closed settings.

While the average citizen probably equates corrections with prisons, only about a third of convicted offenders are actually incarcerated; the remainder are under supervision in the community. Probation and parole have long been important components of corrections, as have community-based halfway houses, work release programs, and supervised activities.

The federal government, all the states, most counties, and all but the smallest cities are engaged in the corrections enterprise. Increasingly, nonprofit private organizations such as the YMCA have contracted with governments to perform correctional services. In recent years, for-profit businesses have undertaken the construction and administration of institutions through contracts with governments.

The relationships between the justice subsystems can be seen more clearly when we examine the flow of decision making within the criminal justice system.

FACTORS IN DECISION MAKING

The disposition of cases in the criminal justice system involves a series of decisions made by officials, including police officers, prosecutors, judges, probation officers, wardens, and parole board members. At each stage in the process, they decide whether a case will move on to the next point or be dropped from the system. Although the flowchart shown in Figure 2.5 appears streamlined, with cases entering at the top and moving swiftly through thirteen steps toward their disposition at the bottom, the route may actually be quite long and involve many detours. At each step, officials have the discretion to decide what happens next. Many cases are filtered out of the system, others are forwarded to the next decision maker, and still others are dealt with through informal processes.

Moreover, the flowchart does not show the influences of the social relations of the actors or the political environment within which the system operates. For example, in September 1994, Eric Metcalf, a running back for the Cleveland Browns, was sentenced to probation for racing his car in excess of 100 miles per hour on a public highway and for having a gun in his car. Would another defendant have received probation for illegally possessing a firearm? Would an elected state judge risk arousing the public by jailing a star football player in the middle of the team's most successful season in years? Such factors may influence decisions in ways that are not reflected in a simple description of decision-making steps. As we follow the thirteen steps of the criminal justice system, remember that the formal procedures do not always hold for individual cases. The application of discretion, political pressures from the public or from prominent citizens, and other factors may alter outcomes for different defendants.

THE THIRTEEN STEPS IN THE DECISION-MAKING PROCESS

The criminal justice system can be viewed as consisting of thirteen major steps covering the stages of law enforcement, adjudication, and corrections. The system looks like an assembly line in which decisions are made about defendants—the raw material of the process. As these steps are described, keep in mind the concepts discussed earlier in the chapter: system, discretion, sequential tasks, filtering, and exchange. Be aware that the terms used for different stages in criminal proceedings may differ from state to state and that the precise sequence of the steps may vary in some parts of the country. However, the flow of decision making generally follows this pattern.

1. *Investigation.* The flow of decision making begins when the police believe that a crime has been committed. At this point, an investigation is initiated. The police are normally dependent on a member of the community to report the offense. Except for traffic and public order offenses, it is relatively

FIGURE 2.5

The Flow of Decision Making in the Criminal Justice System
Each criminal justice agency is responsible for a portion of the decision-making system. Thus, the police, prosecution, courts, and corrections are bound together through a series of exchange relationships.

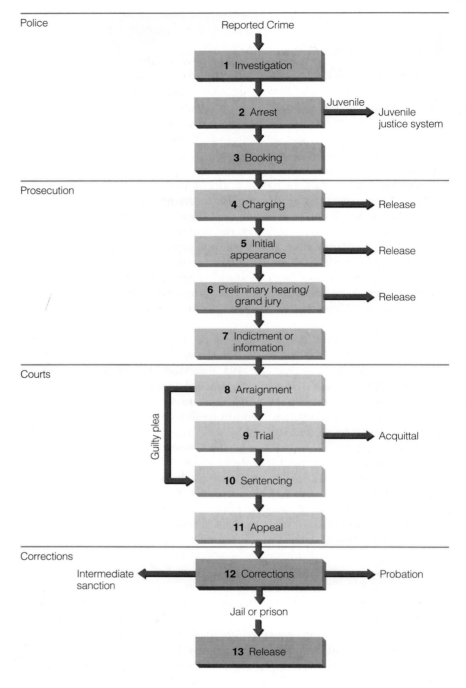

arrest
Physically taking a person into custody, based on evidence indicating that he or she has committed a crime, and holding the accused pending a court proceeding.

unusual for the police to observe illegal behavior themselves. Since most crimes have already been committed and the perpetrators have left the scene before the police arrive, law enforcement is at an initial disadvantage in achieving its goal of quickly apprehending lawbreakers.

2. *Arrest.* If the police find enough evidence indicating that a particular person has committed a crime, an arrest may be made. **Arrest** involves physi-

cally taking a person into custody pending a court proceeding. This action not only restricts the suspect's freedom, it also constitutes the initial step toward prosecution.

Under some conditions, arrests may be made on the basis of a **warrant**—that is, a court order issued by a judge authorizing police officers to take certain actions, such as arresting suspects or searching premises. In practice, most arrests are made without warrants. In some states, police officers may issue a summons or citation that orders a person to appear in court on a particular date, thus eliminating the need to hold the suspect physically until decisions are made about the case.

3. *Booking.* The immediate effect of arrest is that the suspect is usually transported to a police station for booking, the procedure by which an administrative record is made of the arrest. When booked, the suspect may be fingerprinted, photographed, interrogated, and placed in a lineup for identification by the victim or witnesses. All suspects must also be warned that they have the right to counsel, that they may remain silent, and that any statement they make may later be used against them. Bail may be set so that the suspect learns what amount of money must be advanced or what other conditions must be fulfilled in order to gain release from custody until the case is processed.

4. *Charging.* Prosecuting attorneys provide the key link between the police and the courts. They must take the facts of the situation as provided by the police and determine whether there is reasonable cause to believe that an offense was committed and that the suspect committed the offense. The decision to charge is crucial because it sets in motion the adjudication of the case.

5. *Initial appearance.* Within a reasonable time after arrest, suspects must be brought for an initial appearance before a judge. When in court, the suspects are given formal notice of the charge(s) for which they are being held, advised of their rights, and, if approved by the judge, given the opportunity to post bail. At this stage, the judge determines if there is sufficient evidence to hold the suspect for further criminal processing. If sufficient evidence has not been produced, the judge will dismiss the case.

The purpose of bail is to permit the accused to be released while awaiting trial while at the same time ensuring that he or she will show up in court at the appointed time. Bail requires the accused to provide or arrange a surety (or pledge), usually in the form of money or a bond. The amount of bail is based primarily on the judge's perception of the seriousness of the crime and the defendant's prior criminal record. Suspects may also be released on their own recognizance—a promise to appear in court at a later date. In a limited number of cases, bail may be denied and the accused detained because he or she is viewed as a threat to the community.

6. *Preliminary hearing/grand jury.* After suspects have been arrested, booked, and brought to court to be

warrant
A court order issued by a judge authorizing police officers to take certain actions, such as arresting suspects or searching premises.

After arrest suspects are usually taken to the stationhouse for booking, a process during which key information and fingerprints are taken.

notified of the charge and advised of their rights, the evidence and the probability of conviction must be evaluated before a decision is made that they should be held for prosecution. The preliminary hearing, used in about half the states, allows a judge to determine whether **probable cause** exists to believe a crime has been committed and that the accused committed the offense. If the judge does not find probable cause, the case is dismissed. If there is sufficient evidence, the accused is bound over for arraignment on an **information**—a document charging an individual with a specific crime. In the federal system and in states with grand juries, the prosecutor appears before this body of laypersons who decide if there is enough evidence for the prosecutor to file an **indictment** or "true bill" charging the individual with a specific crime. The preliminary hearing and grand jury deliberations are designed to prevent hasty and malicious prosecutions, to protect persons from mistakenly being humiliated in public, and to discover whether substantial grounds exist for a prosecution.

7. *Indictment/information.* If the preliminary hearing produces an information or the grand jury vote produces an indictment, the prosecutor prepares the formal charging document and enters it before the court.

8. *Arraignment.* The accused person appears before a judge to hear the indictment or information read and to enter a plea. Defendants may plead guilty or not guilty or, in some states, stand mute. If an accused pleads guilty, the judge must determine whether the plea is made voluntarily and whether the person has full knowledge of the possible consequences of the plea. When a guilty plea is accepted as knowing and voluntary, a trial becomes unnecessary and sentencing follows. Plea bargaining may take place at any time throughout the steps in the criminal justice process, but it is likely to be completed prior to or after arraignment. Very few criminal cases proceed to trial. Most move from the entry of the guilty plea to the sentencing phase.

9. *Trial.* For the relatively small percentage of defendants who plead not guilty, the right to a trial by an impartial jury is guaranteed by the Sixth Amendment if the charges are sufficiently serious to raise the possibility of imprisonment for more than six months. In many jurisdictions, lesser charges do not entail a right to a jury trial. Most trials are summary or bench trials—that is, they are conducted before a judge without a jury. Because the outcomes of most criminal cases are determined by guilty pleas, it is estimated that only about 10–15 percent of cases go to trial and only about 5 percent are heard by juries. Whether a criminal trial is held before a judge alone or before a judge and jury, the procedures are similar and are set out by state law and Supreme Court rulings. A defendant may be found guilty only if the evidence proves beyond a reasonable doubt that he or she committed the offense.

10. *Sentencing.* Judges have the responsibility of imposing sentences. At this stage, attention is focused on the offender. In seeking to do justice and control crime, the intent is to make the sentence suitable to the particular offender and offense within the requirements of the law. Although criminal codes place limitations on sentences, the judge still has leeway. Options may include suspension of the sentence, probation, imprisonment, or other sanctions such as fines and community service.

---

probable cause
The evidentiary criteria necessary to uphold an arrest or to support issuance of an arrest or search warrant. Also, facts upholding the belief that a crime has been committed and that the accused committed the offense.

information
A document prepared by a prosecuting attorney and presented to a court at a preliminary hearing charging an individual with a specific crime.

indictment
A "true bill" charging an individual with a specific crime on the basis of a determination of probable cause as presented by a prosecuting attorney.

11. *Appeal.* Defendants found guilty may appeal their convictions to a higher court. An appeal may be based on the claim that the trial court failed to follow the proper procedures or that misconduct or errors by police, prosecutors, defense attorneys, and judges violated the defendants' constitutional rights. The number of criminal trial verdicts appealed is small in comparison with the total number of convictions, and in most such appeals (about 80 percent), trial judges and other criminal justice officials are ruled to have acted properly. Further, even defendants who win appeals do not generally go free. An appellate victory normally provides the defendant with a second trial, which may result in an acquittal, a second conviction, or a plea bargain to lesser charges.

12. *Corrections.* Execution of the court's sentence is the responsibility of the correctional subsystem. Probation, intermediate sanctions such as fines and community service, and incarceration are the sanctions most often imposed.

Probation allows convicted offenders to serve their sentences in the community while under supervision. Youthful offenders, first offenders, and offenders convicted of minor violations are most likely to be sentenced to probation rather than incarceration. The conditions of probation may require offenders to observe certain rules—be employed, maintain an orderly life, attend school—and to report to their supervising officer periodically. Violations of the conditions of probation may result in its cancellation by the judge and the imposition of a prison sentence.

Many intermediate sanctions have been developed and expanded in recent years. These are viewed as more restrictive than probation but less restrictive than incarceration. Intensive probation supervision, boot camp, home confinement, and community service are common types of intermediate sanctions.

Whatever the reasons used to justify incarceration, prisons exist mainly to segregate the criminal from the rest of society. Offenders convicted of misdemeanors usually serve their time in city or county jails, while felons serve their time in state prisons. Isolation from the community is one of the most painful aspects of incarceration. Not only are visits from family members and correspondence restricted, but supervision and censorship are ever-present. In order to maintain internal security, prison officials make unannounced searches of and apply rigid discipline to inmates.

13. *Release.* Upon completion of the sentence, the offender will be released. Release may be accomplished through serving the full sentence imposed by the court or by returning to the community under the supervision of a parole officer. Parolees remain under supervision until the length of time represented by their maximum sentence has expired or for a period as specified by law. Parole may be revoked and the person returned to prison if the conditions of parole are not fulfilled or if the parolee commits another crime.

To give a real-life example of the system in operation, the following Close-Up describes the experience of Donald Payne, a young man from Chicago who is processed through the system for charges incurred when he attempted to hold up a liquor store.

CLOSE-UP

The People versus *Donald Payne*

An 18-year-old named Donald Payne came hand-cuffed and sullen into the Chicago courthouse—a tall, spidery, black, school dropout charged with the attempted armed robbery and attempted murder of a white liquor-store owner, Joe Castelli, in a "changing" fringe neighborhood. The police report told it simply: ". . . victim stated that two male Negroes entered his store and the taller of the two came out with a gun and announced that this is a holdup, 'give me all of your money.' With this the victim . . . walked away from the area of the cash register. When he did this, the smaller offender shouted 'shoot him.' The taller offender aimed the pistol at him and pulled the trigger about two or three times. The weapon failed to fire. The offenders then fled. . . ."

Investigation

Patrolman Joe Higgins nosed his unmarked squad car through the night places of [Chicago's] Gresham police district, watching the alleys and storefronts slide past, half-listening to the low staccato of the radio, exchanging shorthand grunts with his partner, Tom Cullen, slouched low in the seat beside him. They had been riding for three humdrum hours when, shortly after 9 P.M., they picked up the call: gunfire in the street up in the north reaches of the district. The two cops glanced at one another. Cullen got the mike out of the glove compartment and radioed: "Six-sixty going in." Higgins hit the accelerator and snaked through the sluggish night traffic toward Shop-Rite Liquors—and the middle of his own neighborhood. . . .

It was near first light when they spotted the car, parked in a deserted industrial area with two runaways, 13 and 17 years old, curled up asleep inside. The two patrolmen rousted the boys, searched the car—and found the blue-steel .25 under a jacket in the front seat. One of the boys, thoroughly scared, led them to a 17-year-old named James Hamilton who admitted having driven the car but not having gone into the store. Hamilton led them to his kid cousin, Frank, who admitted having gone into the store but not having

handled the gun or clicked the trigger. And Frank Hamilton led them to Donald Payne.

Arrest

And so, red-eyed and bone-weary, Higgins and Cullen, along with a district sergeant and two robbery detectives, went to the little green-and-white frame house in Roseland at 9 A.M. and rang the bell. Payne's sister let them in and pointed the way upstairs.

Payne was sleeping when the cops crowded into his little attic bedroom and he came awake cool and mean. "Get moving," someone said. "You're under arrest." . . .

They marched him out in handcuffs past his mother, took him to the district station and shackled him to a chair while one of the officers started tapping out an arrest report. . . . The cops put Payne into a little back room. Castelli [the liquor store owner] picked him out—and that, for the cops, was enough.

Booking

Payne was taken to the South Side branch police headquarters to be booked, then led before a magistrate who set bond [bail] at $10,000. The bond is a paper figure: the Chicago courts require only 10 percent cash. But Payne didn't have it, and by mid-afternoon he was on his way by police van to the Cook County Jail. . . .

The Defender

Public Defender Connie Xinos disliked Donald Payne from the beginning. They met in the prisoners' lockup behind Judge Fitzgerald's courtroom, and all Xinos had to go on then was the police report and Payne's public-defender questionnaire ("All I know is I was arrested for attempted murder on August 5") and that insinuating half smile. *He did it*, Xinos thought; all of them except the scared children and the street-wise old pros swear they are innocent, but you get a feeling. . . .

The Jail

He clambered out of the van with the rest of the day's catch and was marched through a tunnel into a white-tiled basement receiving area. He was questioned, lectured, classified, stripped, showered, photographed, fingerprinted, X-rayed for TB, bloodtested for VD and handed a mimeographed sheet of rules of the Cook County jail. He was issued a wristband, an ID card, led upstairs and checked into a tiny 4-by-8 cell with an open toilet, a double bunk, two sheets, a blanket and a roommate. The door slammed shut, and Donald Payne—charged with but still presumed innocent of attempted robbery and attempted murder—began nearly four and a half months behind bars waiting for his trial. . . .

Preliminary Hearing/Grand Jury
Waiting naturally comes easier to a man out on bail than to one behind bars, but Payne sat and waited. On August 24, nineteen days after his arrest, he went . . . to the basement tunnel to the courthouse, stripped naked for a search, then dressed and was led upstairs for a hearing in Room 402—Violence Court. . . . Payne waited in the lockup until a clerk bellowed his name, then stood before Judge John Hechinger in a ragged semicircle with his mother, the cops, the victims, Assistant State's Attorney Walter Parrish and Assistant Public Defender Connie Xinos, and listened to the prosecution briefly rehearse the facts of the case. . . .

Judge Hechinger ordered Payne held for the grand jury. The day in court lasted a matter of minutes; Payne was shuffled back through the lockup, the nude search, the basement tunnel and into [the jail] again.

Indictment
On September 18, word came over that the grand jury had indicted him for attempted armed robbery (gun) and attempted murder, and the case shortly thereafter was assigned to Circuit Judge Richard Fitzgerald for trial. . . .

Arraignment
Everybody kept trying to talk him out of his trial. "Plead guilty, jackass, you could get ten to twenty for this," Xinos whispered when they finally got to trial. *Ain't no need for that*, said Payne. "You really want a jury?" the assistant state's attorney, Walter Parrish, teased him. "Or you want to plead?" *I want my trial*, said Payne. Everything in the building says cop out, make a deal, take the short time. . . .

The pressures to plead are sometimes cruel, the risks of going to trial high and well-advertised. . . . Still, Payne insisted, and Xinos painstakingly put a defense together. He opened with a pair of preliminary motions, one arguing that the pistol was inadmissible because the evidence tying it to Payne was

hearsay, the other contending that the police should have offered Payne a lawyer at the line-up but didn't. The witnesses straggled in for a hearing on December 1. Joe Castelli took the stand, and Patrolman Cullen, and, for a few monosyllabic moments, Payne himself. Had anyone advised him of his rights to a lawyer? "No." Or let him make a phone call? "No." But another of the arresting officers, Robert Krueger, said that Payne had been told of his rights—and such swearing contests almost always are decided in favor of the police. Everybody admired Xinos's energy and craftsmanship. Nevertheless, Fitzgerald denied both of the defense motions and docketed the case for trial on December 14.

Trial
And so they all gathered that wintry Monday in Fitzgerald's sixth-floor courtroom, a great dim cave with marbled and oak-paneled walls, pitted linoleum floors and judge, jury, lawyers, defendant and a gallery so widely separated that nobody could hear anything without microphones.

Jury Selection. Choosing a jury took two hours that day, two the next morning. Parrish [the state's attorney] worked without a shopping list. "I know some lawyers say fat people are jolly and Germans are strict," he says, "but none of that's true in my experience. If you get twelve people who say they'll listen, you're all right."

But Xinos is a hunch player. He got two blacks on the jury and was particularly pleased with one of them, a light-skinned Urban League member who looked as if she might be sympathetic. And he deliberately let one hard hat sit on the panel. Xinos had a point to make about the pistol—you couldn't click it more than once without pulling back the slide to cock it—and the hard hat looked as if he knew guns.

Presentation of the State's Case. That afternoon, slowly and methodically, Parrish began to put on his case. He opened with the victims, and Castelli laid the story on the record: "About ten after 9, the gentleman walked in. . . . He had a small-caliber pistol. . . . I edged away. . . . The other lad came up to me and he said, 'Shoot him, shoot him, shoot him.' . . . The first youth pointed the gun at me and fired three times or four—at least I heard three clicks." And the gunman—did Castelli see him in court?

"Yes I do, sir."

"And would you point him out, please?"

Castelli gestured toward the single table shared by the prosecution and defense. "That," he said, "is Donald Payne."

Presentation of the Defense's Case. But Xinos, in his opening argument, had promised to alibi Payne—his mother was prepared to testify for him—and now, on cross-examination, he picked skillfully at Parrish's case. Playing to his hard hat on the jury, he asked Castelli whether the stick-up man had one or two hands on the gun. "Only one, sir," said Castelli. "And was that trigger pulled in rapid succession—click—click—click?" Xinos pressed. "Yes, sir," said Castelli, and Xinos had his point: it takes two hands to keep pulling the slide and clicking the trigger.

Next came Patrolman Joe Higgins, who remembered, under Xinos's pointed cross-examination, that Castelli had described the gunman as weighing 185 pounds—30 more than Payne carries on his spindly 6-foot-1 frame. Payne had nearly botched that point by wearing a billowy, cape-shaped jacket to court, but Xinos persuaded him to fold it up and sit on it so the jurors could see how bony he really was. The 30-pound misunderstanding undercut Castelli's identification of Payne—and suddenly the People and their lawyer, Walter Parrish, were in trouble. . . .

What [Parrish] had in *People* vs. *Payne* was the Hamilton boys, the two cousins through whom the police had tracked Payne. Parrish had hoped he wouldn't have to put them on the stand. "It was a risk," he said later. "They could have hurt us. They could have got up there and suddenly said Donald wasn't there." But he was behind and knew it. He needed Frank Hamilton to place Payne inside the store, James to connect him with the car and the pistol. So, that afternoon, he ordered up subpoenas for the Hamiltons. "We know how to scramble," said his young assistant, Joe Poduska. "That's the name of the game."

Plea Bargaining. The subpoenas were being typed when Connie Xinos happened into the state's attorney's office to socialize—*it's like a family*—and saw them in the typewriter. Xinos went cold. He had

talked to the mother of one of the Hamiltons; he knew their testimony could hurt. So, next morning, he headed first thing to Parrish's austere second-floor cubicle—and found the Hamiltons there. "We're going to testify," they told Xinos, "and we're going to tell the truth."

Xinos took Parrish aside. "Let's get rid of this case," he said.

"It's Christmas," Parrish said amiably. "I'm a reasonable man."

"What do you want?" Xinos asked.

"I was thinking about three to eight."

"One to five," said Xinos.

"You got it."

It's an absolute gift, Xinos thought, and he took it to Payne in the lockup. "I can get you one to five," he said. Payne said no. Xinos thought fast. It was a dead-bang case—the kind Clarence Darrow couldn't pull out—and it was good for a big rattle, maybe ten to twenty years. Xinos went back downstairs, got the Hamiltons and sat them down with Payne in [Judge] Fitzgerald's library. "They rapped," he remembers, "and one of them said, 'Donald—you mean you told them you weren't *there*?' I told him again I could get him one to five. They said, 'Maybe you ought to take it, Donald.' I said, 'You may get ten to twenty going on with the trial.' And he said, 'Well, even if I take one to five, I'm not guilty.' That's when I knew he would go."

But would Fitzgerald buy it? Xinos was worried. The judge is a handsome 57, with a pink Irish face rimmed with silver hair and creased to smile. "He looks like God would look and acts like God would act if God were a judge," says Xinos. "He doesn't take any [expletive]." . . . So Xinos fretted. "The judge is the judge," he told Payne while they waited for an audience with Fitzgerald. "He might give you three to eight. You better think about that."

But Fitzgerald agreed to talk, and the ritual began to unfold. Xinos led Payne to the bench and announced for the record that they wanted to discuss pleading—"Is that correct, Donald?" Payne mumbled, "Correct," and, while he went back to the lockup to wait, the lawyers followed the judge into chambers. A bailiff closed the door behind them. Fitzgerald sat at his desk and pulled a 4-by-6 index card out of a box; he likes to keep his own notes. Parrish dropped into a deep, leathery sofa, his knees coming up almost to his chin. Xinos sat in a green guest chair in a row along the wall. . . .

Fitzgerald scanned Parrish's prep sheet, outlining the state case. Xinos told him glumly about the Hamiltons. "We look beat," he conceded.

"Walter," asked the judge, "what do you want?"

"I don't want to hurt the kid," Parrish said. "I talked to Connie, and we thought one to five."

They talked about Payne's record—his jobs, his family, his old gas-station burglary rap. "Two years' probation," Xinos put in hopefully. "That's nothing." Fitzgerald pondered it all. He had no probation report . . . and no psychological workup; sentencing in most American courts comes down to a matter of instinct. Fitzgerald's instincts told him one to five was a long time for Payne to serve—and a wide enough spread to encourage him to reform and get out early. . . .

"Will he take it?" the judge asked Xinos.

"I'll go back and see," Xinos replied. He ducked out to the lockup and put the offer to Payne.

"Let's do it," Payne said. "Right now."

Sentencing

A light snow was falling when they brought him back into court, grinning slightly, walking his diddybop walk. A bailiff led him to a table below Fitzgerald's high bench. His mother slipped into place beside him. The judge led him through the prescribed catechism establishing that he understood what he was doing and that no one had forced him to do it. Payne's "yesses" were barely audible in the cavernous room. [Judge Fitzgerald then imposed the sentence agreed to as part of the plea agreement.] . . .

And then it was over. Fitzgerald called the jurors in and dismissed them. They knew nothing of the events that had buried Donald; they sat there for a moment looking stunned. . . .

Prison

You can write to your lawyer, your preacher and six other people, the sergeant was saying. . . . No. 69656, born Donald Payne, sat half listening in the front row in his gray prison coveralls, his eyes idling over the chapel wall from the flag to the sunny poster—GOOD MORNING WORLD. . . .

Payne had been marched aboard a sheriff's bus by early light only a few days before and had been shipped with sixteen other County Jail inmates to Joliet Prison, a 112-year-old yellow-stone fortress on the Des Plaines River forty miles southwest of Chicago. . . . And so, on February 5, he checked into Joliet's diagnostic center, drew his number and his baggy coveralls, was stripped, showered and shorn and began four to six weeks of testing to see which prison he would fit into best and what if anything it could do for him. Coveralls aren't much, but Payne, sharp, flipped the collar rakishly up in back and left the front unbuttoned halfway down his chest. Cool. Good morning, world. . . .

Joliet is a way station for Payne. He may wind up at Pontiac, where most younger offenders do their time; he would prefer the company of older men at Stateville. . . . He says that in either event he will stick to his cell and go for early parole. "When I get out," he told his mother once in jail, "I'll be in church every day." Yet the odds do not necessarily favor this outcome: though the Illinois prisons have made progress toward cutting down on recidivism, a fifth to a third of their alumni get in trouble again before they have been out even a year. "Well," said Payne, smiling that half-smile at a visitor during his first days as No. 69656, "I'm startin' my time now and I'm on my way home."

Afterword
Donald Payne was released on parole from Joliet after serving eighteen months of the one-to-five-year sentence ordered by Judge Fitzgerald. Available records indicate that he was free for the next eleven years until he was convicted and incarcerated in California for possession of controlled substances. Fourteen months later he was released on parole to be served in Illinois. Upon discharge from parole he was again convicted and sentenced to five years for possession of cocaine and heroin. He served his time in the Vandalia Correctional Center in Illinois and was released in April 1993.

SOURCE: Excerpted from Peter Goldman and Don Holt, "How Justice Works: The People vs. Donald Payne," *Newsweek*, 8 March 1971, pp. 20–37. Copyright © 1971 by Newsweek, Inc. All rights reserved. Reprinted by permission. Afterword information provided in a letter from Nic Howell, Chief Public Information Officer, Illinois Department of Corrections.

THE CRIMINAL JUSTICE WEDDING CAKE

amuel Walker has suggested that although the flowchart of criminal justice decisions shown in Figure 2.5 is a notable aid to our understanding, we must recognize that not all cases are treated equally.[4] The nature of the process applied to a particular case, as well as its outcome, is shaped by the importance of the case to decision makers, the seriousness of the charge, and the defendant's resources.

Some cases achieve a high level of visibility either because of the notoriety of the defendant or victim or because of the heinous nature of the crime. At the other extreme are those "run-of-the-mill cases" involving unknown persons who are charged with committing minor crimes. Walker suggests that we look at the criminal justice process as a cake with tapered layers, like those of a wedding cake, in order to understand how different cases receive different kinds of treatment in the justice process. Figure 2.6 illustrates Walker's model of the criminal justice process.

Layer 1 consists of those very few "celebrated" cases that are exceptional, get great public attention, result in a jury trial, and often drag on through extended appeals. These cases embody the ideal of an adversary system of justice in which each side battles the other vigorously, either because the defendant faces a stiff sentence or because the defendant possesses the wealth to pay for a vigorous defense. The cases of mass murderer Charles Manson, would-be presidential assassin John Hinckley, serial killer Jeffrey Dahmer, and former football star O.J. Simpson fit this category. Not all cases in Layer 1 achieve national notoriety. From time to time, local crimes, especially cases of murder and rape, are treated in this manner. These celebrated cases are like morality plays. The carefully crafted arguments by the prosecution and defense are analyzed by commentators as expressing fundamental issues or problems in our society. Too often, however, the public erroneously concludes that all criminal cases follow this model.

Layer 2 consists of felonies that are deemed to be serious by officials: crimes of violence committed by persons with long criminal records against victims unknown to them. These are the cases that the police and the prosecutors consider important from the perspective of crime control and that usually result in "tough" sentences. Because the prosecutors and police are seeking stiff sentences, there are fewer incentives put forth for the defendant to plead guilty. Thus, the defense attorney must face the prospect of preparing for trial in many cases.

Layer 3 also consists of felonies, but the crimes and the offenders are seen as less important than those in Layer 2. They may involve the same offenses as in Layer 2, but the offender may have no record, and the victim may have had a prior relationship with the accused. The primary goal of criminal justice officials is to dispose of such cases quickly. For this reason, many are filtered out of the system, and plea bargaining is encouraged.

Layer 4 is made up of misdemeanors. About 90 percent of all cases handled in the criminal justice system fit this category. They concern such offenses

FIGURE 2.6

The Criminal Justice Wedding Cake
Different criminal cases are treated in different ways. Only a very few cases are played out in the full, dramatic "O. J. Simpson" style; the greatest number are handled administratively through plea bargaining and dismissals.

SOURCE: Based on Samuel Walker, *Sense and Nonsense About Crime Policy*, 2nd ed. (Pacific Grove, CA: Brooks/Cole, 1989), pp. 22–27.

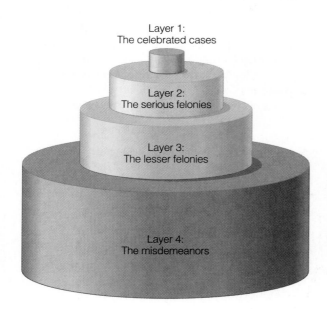

Layer 1:
The celebrated cases

Layer 2:
The serious felonies

Layer 3:
The lesser felonies

Layer 4:
The misdemeanors

as public drunkenness, shoplifting, prostitution, disturbing the peace, and motor vehicle violations. Looked upon by officials as the "garbage" of the system, these cases are adjudicated in the lower courts, where speed is essential. Prosecutors make discretionary judgments about reducing charges or recommending probation as a means of encouraging defendants to plead guilty quickly. Trials are rare, processes are informal, and fines, probation, or short jail sentences result. Assembly-line justice reigns.

Walker's model is a useful corrective to the flow-chart perception of the system. Cases are not treated equally; some are viewed as very important by criminal justice officials, others as merely part of a mass that must be processed. When one knows the nature of a case, one can predict fairly well how it will be handled and what its outcome will be.

The Menendez brothers were tried for the murder of their wealthy parents in 1994. Highly visible cases like theirs do not give an accurate picture of the criminal justice system as a whole.

CRIME CONTROL VERSUS DUE PROCESS

Keep the "wedding cake" model in mind as we consider other models that give us a more complete and accurate picture of how the criminal justice system really operates. Scholars often use models to organize their thinking about a subject and to guide their research. **Models** are representations of something that cannot be visualized, permitting generalized statements to be made about it and evaluations of its strengths and weaknesses.

In one of the most important contributions to systematic thought on the administration of criminal justice, Herbert Packer describes two competing schemes: the Crime Control Model and the Due Process Model.[5] Packer's models present two ways of looking at the goals and procedures of the criminal justice system. They represent opposing views of how the criminal law *ought* to operate. The Crime Control Model is much like an assembly line while the Due Process Model is much like an obstacle course. In reality, no one actor or law enforcement subsystem functions totally in accordance with either model. Elements of both are found throughout the system. However, the opposing values of the two models underlie key tensions within the criminal justice process as well as the gap between idealized descriptions of the system and the way that most cases are actually processed. Table 2.2 compares the major elements of each model.

model
A representation of something that cannot be visualized, permitting generalized statements to be made about it and evaluations of its strengths and weaknesses.

	Goal	Value	Process	Major Decision Point	Basis of Decision Making
Due Process Model	Preserve individual liberties	Reliability	Adversarial	Courtroom	Law
Crime Control Model	Repress crime	Efficiency	Administrative	Police, pretrial processes	Discretion

TABLE 2.2
Due Process Model and Crime Control Model Compared
What other comparisons can be made between the two models?

CRIME CONTROL: ORDER AS A VALUE

Crime Control Model
A model of the criminal justice system that assumes that freedom is so important that every effort must be made to repress crime; it emphasizes efficiency and the capacity to apprehend, try, convict, and dispose of a high proportion of offenders, and it also stresses speed and finality.

Underlying the **Crime Control Model** is the assumption that every effort must be made to repress crime. It emphasizes efficiency and the capacity to apprehend, try, convict, and dispose of a high proportion of offenders, and it also stresses speed and finality. In relation to our previous discussion of the goals of criminal justice, this model places the goal of controlling crime uppermost and emphasizes only one aspect of doing justice: holding people accountable. It minimizes the other aspect of doing justice, namely the protection of individuals' rights. As Packer points out, to achieve liberty for all citizens to interact freely as members of society, the Crime Control Model requires that primary attention be paid to efficiency in screening suspects, determining guilt, and applying appropriate sanctions to the convicted. Because of the high incidence of criminal behavior and the limited resources given to law enforcement agencies, emphasis must be placed on speed and finality. All of these elements depend on informality, uniformity, and the minimizing of occasions for challenge by a defense attorney or defendant.

Thus, on the basis of police investigation alone, police and prosecutors make an early decision about how probable it is that the suspect will be found guilty. Those cases unlikely to end in conviction are filtered out through discretionary decisions by prosecutors to drop charges. At each successive stage, from arrest to preliminary hearing, arraignment, and trial, a series of routinized procedures is used by various judicial actors to determine whether the accused should be passed on to the next stage. Rather than stressing the combative elements of the courtroom, this model highlights bargaining between the state and the accused at several points. Nearly all cases are disposed of through negotiations over the charges, and they typically end with defendants entering guilty pleas. Packer's characterization of this model as an assembly-line process conveys the idea of quick, steady, efficient decisions by system actors standing at fixed stations that turn out the intended product—guilty pleas and closed cases.

DUE PROCESS: LAW AS A VALUE

Due Process Model
A model of the criminal justice system that assumes that freedom is so important that every effort must be made to ensure that criminal justice decisions are based on reliable information; it emphasizes the adversarial process, the rights of defendants, and formal decision-making procedures.

If the Crime Control Model looks like an assembly line, the Due Process Model resembles an obstacle course. The **Due Process Model** assumes that freedom is so important that every effort must be made to ensure that criminal justice decisions are based on reliable information. It emphasizes the adversarial process, the rights of defendants, and formal decision-making procedures. For example, because people are notoriously poor observers of disturbing events, the possibility is great that police and prosecutors can be wrong in presuming the guilt of defendants. Thus, people should be labeled as criminals and deprived of their freedom only on the basis of conclusive evidence. To minimize error, hurdles must be erected to force the government to prove beyond doubt that the defendant is guilty of the crime. The model assumes that persons are innocent until proved guilty. Therefore, the process must provide the opportunity to discredit the evidence presented against the defendant, and an impartial judge and jury must decide the outcome. According to Packer, the assumption that the defendant is innocent until proved guilty has a far-reaching impact on the criminal justice system.

In the Due Process Model, the state must prove in a procedurally sound manner that the person is guilty of the crime as charged. Prosecutors must prove their cases while obeying various rules regarding the admissibility of evidence, the burden of proof, the requirement that guilt be proven beyond a reasonable doubt, and respect for defendants' constitutional rights. Forcing the state to prove its case in an adversarial proceeding serves to protect citizens from wrongful convictions and punishments. Thus, the Due Process Model emphasizes particular aspects of the goal of doing justice. The model provides protection for the rights of individuals and takes special care to reserve punishment for those who unquestionably deserve it. These values are emphasized even though these careful processes mean that some guilty defendants will go free because the evidence against them is not sufficiently conclusive. By contrast, the Crime Control Model values efficient case processing and imposition of punishment over the possibility that innocent people might be swept up in the process.

REALITY: CRIME CONTROL OR DUE PROCESS?

Which model provides the best picture of criminal justice in the United States? The public's idealistic views of law and justice in a democracy correspond with the Due Process Model, in which principles, not personal discretion, control the actions of police officers, judges, and prosecutors. Criminal justice is thus seen as an ongoing, mechanical process in which violations of laws are discovered, defendants are indicted, and punishments are imposed, according to clearly defined rules and neutral principles of justice. This perspective takes little notice of the importance of discretion and other system characteristics.

However, the reality of criminal justice in America more closely resembles the Crime Control Model. In most cases, guilt is determined administratively early in the process and cases are disposed of through negotiation. Decision makers act as if they assume that those arrested by the police have committed *some* criminal act. Accordingly, efforts are made to select a charge that the accused will plead guilty to and that will result in an appropriate sentence.

SUMMARY

As schoolchildren, we are taught that the American system of justice involves prosecution of criminal offenders through the enforcement of neutral rules of justice and the protection of individual rights. This vision reflects the ideals of justice that we associate with law and courts in a democracy. However, the idealistic vision of neutral justice in an adversarial system does not accurately describe the manner in which most cases are processed. The idealistic vision fits Packer's Due Process Model and applies, to some extent, to those few cases at the top of the "wedding cake" model. In reality, most criminal cases are processed through means that more closely resemble the assembly-line procedures of the Crime Control Model.

What makes the American justice process operate so differently from its idealized version? Quite simply, it is the justice process's "system" characteristics that cause it to deviate from pure adversarial trials and decision making strictly according to the "law." The system characteristics, including discretion, resource dependence, sequential tasks, and filtering, link criminal justice actors and provide them with opportunities to shape case outcomes quickly and efficiently. The system characteristics of the justice process are not a form of corruption in which actors are seeking to torpedo the ideals of justice. Instead, they reflect natural responses by human beings who must undertake difficult tasks in a challenging environment. When the environment of criminal justice is recognized and understood, it should not be surprising that the human decision makers work together through informal means to do their best to pursue the objectives of doing justice, controlling crime, and preventing crime.

QUESTIONS FOR REVIEW

1. What are the goals of the criminal justice system?
2. What is meant by the concept of system? How is the administration of criminal justice a system?
3. What are the thirteen steps in the criminal justice decision-making process?
4. Why does Walker suggest that the criminal justice "wedding cake" model is a better depiction of reality than a linear model of the system?
5. What are the major elements of the Due Process Model and Crime Control Model?

NOTES

1. U.S. President's Commission on Law Enforcement and Administration of Justice, *The Challenge of Crime in a Free Society* (Washington, DC: Government Printing Office, 1967).
2. John J. DiIulio, Jr., "Rethinking the Criminal Justice System: Toward a New Paradigm," *Performance Measures for the Criminal Justice System* (Washington: Bureau of Justice Statistics, 1993), p. 10.
3. U.S. Department of Justice, Bureau of Justice Statistics, *Bulletin* (July 1993).
4. Samuel Walker, *Sense and Nonsense About Crime: A Policy Guide*, 2nd ed. (Pacific Grove, CA: Brooks/Cole, 1989), p. 22. Walker bases his analysis on Lawrence M. Friedman and Robert V. Percival, *The Roots of Justice: Crime and Punishment in Alameda County, California, 1870–1910* (Chapel Hill: University of North Carolina Press, 1981), and Michael R. Gottfredson and Don M. Gottfredson, *Decision Making in Criminal Justice: Toward the Rational Exercise of Discretion* (Cambridge, MA: Ballinger, 1980).
5. Herbert L. Packer, *The Limits of the Criminal Sanction* (Stanford, CA: Stanford University Press, 1968). For alternative models, see John Griffiths, "Ideology in Criminal Procedures or a 'Third Model' of the Criminal Process," *Yale Law Journal* 79 (1970), p. 359, and Thomas E. Reed and Larry K. Gaines, "Criminal Justice Models as a Function of Ideological Images: A Social Learning Alternative to Packer," *International Journal of Comparative and Applied Criminal Justice* (Winter 1982), p. 213.

CHAPTER 3
Criminal Law and Procedure

ENTITLED TO A CHRISTIAN BURIAL

Ten-year-old Pamela Powers disappeared from a YMCA on Christmas Eve in Des Moines, Iowa, while attending her brother's wrestling tournament. A boy told police that he saw a man carrying a large bundle out of the building and that he thought he saw some legs sticking out of the bundle. The police learned that Robert Williams, the man who carried the bundle, had recently escaped from a mental hospital. The following day, Williams' car was found abandoned 160 miles away in Davenport, Iowa. The next morning, Henry McKnight, an attorney who represented Williams, arrived at the Des Moines police station and said that the suspect was going to turn himself in to the Davenport police. Detective Leaming and his partner were about to depart for Davenport to bring Williams back to Des Moines when McKnight stopped them and insisted that they could not question Williams until he consulted with the suspect. The police officers agreed that Williams would not be questioned during the trip back to Des Moines.

Upon arriving in Davenport, another lawyer representing the suspect reiterated that no questions be asked until Williams met with Attorney McKnight. The lawyer asked to ride in the car to make sure that there was no improper questioning, but Detective Leaming told him that would not be necessary.

During the trip to Des Moines, Williams said several times, "When I get to Des Moines and see Mr. McKnight, I am going to tell you the whole story," but he never agreed to submit to questioning. However, Detective Leaming, who knew from Williams' psychological history that he was deeply religious, addressed Williams as "Reverend" and began to talk to him. Leaming said, "I feel that you yourself are the only person that knows where this little girl's body is, . . . and snow gets on top of it, you may be unable to find it. I feel that we could stop and locate the body, that the parents of this little girl should be entitled to a Christian burial for the little girl who was snatched away from them on Christmas and murdered." In response to Leaming's comment, Williams directed the police to the body of the girl alongside a nearby highway.

After Williams was convicted of first-degree murder, he took his case to the U.S. Supreme Court claiming that Detective Leaming violated his constitutional rights by questioning him without his attorney being present. This case highlighted in very stark terms the tension that exists between ensuring that lawbreakers are punished and that police officers and other government officials follow proper rules in criminal cases. In the case of *Brewer* v. *Williams* (1977), the justices were deeply divided. By a five-to-four vote, they decided that Detective Leaming had violated Williams' rights by questioning him without his attorneys present. Williams was granted a new trial, and his statements, including those that led to the discovery of the girl's body, were ruled inadmissible.[1]

Before we return to this case later in the chapter, ask yourself whether you agree with this decision. Should we be proud that we value the law so highly that we are willing to risk freeing criminals in order to preserve our rules of law? Should we be ashamed of this decision because it shows that we would rather protect an abstract rule than vindicate an unfortunate victim's life?

Criminal laws define which behaviors will be subject to punishment and what procedures officials must use in arresting, prosecuting, and sentencing offenders. In this chapter, we will examine the origins and fundamental elements of the laws that tell us which forbidden actions are "crimes." We will also discuss the various provisions of the U.S. Constitution that spell out both rights for criminal defendants and rules for criminal justice officials. ★

FOUNDATIONS OF CRIMINAL LAW

Whether or not you agree with the Supreme Court's decision in *Brewer* v. *Williams*, like most Americans, you undoubtedly recognize that law and legal procedures are central elements of our criminal justice system. Americans are fond of saying that "we have a government of laws, not of men (and women)." We do not have a system that operates entirely on the whims of a king or dictator. No president, governor, or mayor can simply choose to punish people whom they dislike.

Laws tell citizens what they can and cannot do. Laws also tell government officials when they can seek to punish citizens for violations and how they must go about it. Government officials are not supposed to do whatever they want. They are supposed to follow and enforce the law. Thus, in a democracy, laws are a primary tool to prevent government officials from seizing too much power or using power improperly.

CRIMINAL VERSUS CIVIL LAW

Criminal law is only one of two important categories of laws. Citizens' lives and behavior are also affected by *civil law*, which governs business transactions, contracts, real estate, and other aspects of citizens' relationships with one another. For example, if you negligently damage someone's property or accidentally injure them, they may use the civil law to sue you in order to get compensation for the damage or injury. By contrast, the distinguishing feature of criminal law is the government's power to punish people. Criminal laws define special categories of behavior that are so harmful or undesirable that they deserve the application of the government's power to levy fines, require meetings with probation officers, deprive people of freedom through imprisonment, or even take lawbreakers' lives. Legislatures must decide which kinds of harmful behaviors can be remedied by compensation between citizens or corporations under civil law and which kinds require the government to prosecute and punish individuals.

SUBSTANTIVE AND PROCEDURAL CRIMINAL LAW

Criminal law is divided into two categories, substantive and procedural. **Substantive criminal law** defines the behaviors that are subject to punishment by the government and the sanctions for such offenses. Often referred to as the penal code, substantive law answers the question, *What* is illegal? By contrast, **procedural criminal law** defines the rules that govern enforcement

CHAPTER QUESTIONS

What are the foundations and sources of American criminal law?

How does the substantive criminal law define punishable behavior?

What elements must exist for someone to be found guilty of a crime?

How does the procedural criminal law define the rights of the accused and the processes that must be observed in dealing with a case?

What are the major interpretations by the U.S. Supreme Court of the criminal justice amendments to the Constitution?

substantive criminal law
Law defining the behaviors that are subject to punishment by the government and the sanctions for such offenses.

procedural criminal law
Law defining the rules that officials must follow in the enforcement, adjudication, and corrections portions of the criminal justice system.

of the substantive law. It protects the constitutional rights of criminal defendants and stipulates the procedures that officials must follow in the enforcement, adjudication, and corrections portions of the criminal justice system.

SUBSTANTIVE CRIMINAL LAW

Can you shoot someone who is attempting to break into your house? The
substantive criminal law specifies whether such a shooting is regarded as
a crime (for example, felonious assault) or as justifiable protection of
person and property.

It is a basic principle of law that people must know in advance what is
required of them, but that is more easily said than done because legal language is often confusing and ambiguous. In such instances of ambiguity, the
judiciary is responsible for interpeting the criminal law so that its intended
meaning can be understood.

SEVEN PRINCIPLES OF CRIMINAL LAW

Seven major principles of Western criminal law have been neatly summarized in a single statement by the legal scholar Jerome Hall.[2] These seven in-
terlocking legal requirements are summarized in Figure 3.1. In order to
convict a defendant of a crime, prosecutors must prove the fulfillment of all
seven principles.

1. *Legality.* A law must exist defining the specified action as a crime. Offensive and harmful behavior is not illegal unless it has been prohibited by law
before it has been committed. The U.S. Constitution specifically forbids *ex
post facto* laws, or laws written and applied after the fact. Thus, when the legislature defines a new crime, people can be prosecuted only for violations
that occur after enactment of the new criminal statute. In 1993, for instance,
the state of Michigan enacted legislation to bar people from assisting others
in committing suicide. However, it could not use this law to prosecute the
prior deeds of Dr. Jack Kervorkian, the controversial "suicide" doctor whose
actions spurred the legislation.

2. *Actus reus.* Criminal laws are aimed at human conduct, including actions
an individual undertook or failed to undertake. The Supreme Court has ruled
that people may not be convicted of a crime simply because of their status.
Thus, according to **actus reus**, there must be behavior of either commission
or omission by the accused to constitute a crime.
In *Robinson* v. *California* (1962), for example, the
Supreme Court invalidated a California statute that
made it a crime to be addicted to drugs. States can
prosecute people for using, possessing, selling, or
transporting drugs when they catch them undertaking these *actions*, but states cannot prosecute them
merely for their *status* of being addicted to drugs.[3]

3. *Causation.* For a crime to have been committed,
a causal relationship must exist between an act and

---

actus reus
Behavior of either com-
mission or omission by
the accused that consti-
tutes the violation of the
criminal law.

FIGURE 3.1
**The Seven Principles
of Criminal Law**
These principles under-
girding Western law
provide the basis for
defining behaviors that
may be criminalized and
the conditions that must
be met for successful
prosecution.

A crime is	
1 legally proscribed	(legality)
2 human conduct	(*actus reus*)
3 causative	(causation)
4 of a given harm	(harm)
5 which conduct coincides	(concurrence)
6 with a blameworthy frame of mind	(*mens rea*)
7 and is subject to punishment	(punishment)

whatever harm has been suffered. In Ohio, for example, a prosecutor attempted to convict a burglary suspect on a manslaughter charge when an innocent person, asleep in his house, was killed by a stray bullet as officers fired at the unarmed, fleeing suspect. The burglar was acquitted on the homicide charge because his actions in committing the burglary and running away from the police were not the direct cause of death for the sleeping person.

4. *Harm.* To be criminal, an act must cause damage or harm to some legally protected value. The harm can be to a person, property, or some other objective that a legislature deems sufficiently valuable to deserve protection through the government's power to punish.

An act can also be considered criminal if it has potential to do harm that the law seeks to prevent; this is an **inchoate offense**. Thus, the criminal law includes conspiracies and attempts, even when the lawbreakers do not succeed in completing their intended crime. For example, people can be prosecuted for planning to murder someone or hiring a "hit man" to undertake a killing. The potential for grave harm from such activities justifies the application of the government's power to punish.

In some instances, such as prostitution, the use of illegal drugs, or failure to wear a motorcycle helmet, people may believe that they are not causing any harm to other people. However, legislatures have decided that such actions are harmful to others, such as the children of heroin users, and to community values.

5. *Concurrence.* To be considered a crime, there must be a simultaneous occurrence of the intention and the act. For example, if you hire an electrician to fix your wiring, and while in your house he commits a crime, he cannot be prosecuted for trespassing. The intent and the conduct are not fused.

6. *Mens rea.* The commission of an act is not criminal unless accompanied by a guilty state of mind. This concept is related to *intent*. This element seeks to distinguish between harm-causing *accidents*, which are generally not subject to criminal punishment, and harm-causing *crimes* in which some level of intention is present. Certain crimes require a specific level of intent, such as first-degree murder, which is normally a planned, intentional killing, and larceny, which involves the intent to permanently and unlawfully deprive an owner of his or her property. Later in this chapter, we will examine several defenses, such as necessity and insanity, that defendants can use to assert that they did not have the necessary *mens rea*—"guilty mind" or blameworthy state of mind—to be held responsible for a criminal offense.

Exceptions to the concept of *mens rea* are **strict liability** offenses involving health and safety in which no demonstration of intent is required. In order to protect the public, legislatures have criminalized regulatory offenses whereby, for example, a business owner may be held responsible for violations of a toxic waste law whether or not the owner actually knew what the company's employees were doing with the wastes. Other laws may apply strict liability to the sale of alcoholic beverages to minors. The purpose of strict liability offenses is to pressure executives to make certain that their employees obey government regulations designed to protect the health and safety of the public. Thus, courts frequently limit the application of such laws to situations in which recklessness or indifference is present.

inchoate offense
An act considered criminal if it has the potential to do harm that the law seeks to prevent, even if it does not produce the harm.

mens rea
"Guilty mind," or blameworthy state of mind, necessary to be held responsible for a criminal offense.

strict liability
Offenses involving health and safety in which no demonstration of *mens rea* is required.

7. *Punishment.* There must be a provision in the law mandating punishment for people found guilty of violating the criminal law. The punishment is enforced by the government and may carry with it the loss of freedom, social stigma, criminal record, loss of rights, and other attendant consequences of criminal penalties.

ELEMENTS OF A CRIME

Legislatures define certain acts as crimes when they are committed in accordance with the seven principles just outlined, in the presence of certain "attendant circumstances," and while the offender is in a certain state of mind. These three factors—the act (*actus reus*), the attendant circumstances, and the state of mind (*mens rea*)—are called the *elements of the crime*. All three elements must be present to constitute a crime. These elements can be seen in the section of one penal code dealing with burglary, which reads as follows:

> **Section 3502. Burglary**
> 1. Offense defined: A person is guilty of burglary if he enters a building or occupied structure, or separately secured or occupied portion thereof [*actus reus*], with intent to commit a crime therein [*mens rea*], unless the premises are at the time open to the public or the actor is licensed or privileged to enter [attendant circumstances].

Defendants accused of crimes can attempt to avoid conviction by challenging any of the three elements. If they can defeat the prosecution's efforts to prove any of these elements, they can gain dismissal of the charges or acquittal.

STATUTORY DEFINITIONS OF CRIMES

The Federal code and individual state codes often define criminal acts somewhat differently. To find out how a state defines an offense, one must read its penal code; this document will give a general idea of which acts are illegal. To fully understand the special interpretations of the code, however, one must also analyze the judicial rulings that have sought to clarify the code's legal language.

To further understand the substantive criminal law, consider the definition of homicide, one of the eight index crimes of the *Uniform Crime Reports* (see Table 3.1). Its elements are interpreted somewhat differently in individual states. One of the problems of categorizing criminal behavior that has brought about death is that legislatures have subdivided the definition of homicide into degrees of murder and voluntary and involuntary manslaughter. Thus, the categories of homicide in some states range from planned, intentional killings (with "malice aforethought"), frequently called "first-degree murder," to "vehicular homicide" involving unintentional deaths that result from automobile accidents. In between these two categories may be a variety of other homicides (for example, "second-degree murder") reflecting less planning and intention underlying the killing, or various levels of "manslaughter," usually unplanned killings that result from reckless, impulsive, or negligent behavior. Other kinds of homicide offenses may be based on the simultaneous commission of a separate felony.

In summary, the substantive criminal law contains the basic conditions that must be met before a person can be convicted of an offense. The seven

1. **Criminal homicide:**
   a. Murder and nonnegligent manslaughter: the willful (nonnegligent) killing of one human being by another. Deaths caused by negligence, attempts to kill, assaults to kill, suicides, accidental deaths and justifiable homicides are excluded. Justifiable homicides are limited to:
      (1) the killing of a felon by a law enforcement officer in the line of duty; and
      (2) the killing of a felon by a private citizen.
   b. Manslaughter by negligence: the killing of another person through gross negligence. Excludes traffic fatalities. While manslaughter by negligence is a Part 1 crime, it is not included in the Crime Index.

2. **Forcible rape:**
   The carnal knowledge of a female forcibly and against her will. Included are rapes by force and attempts or assaults to rape. Statutory offenses (no force used—victim under age of consent) are excluded.

3. **Robbery:**
   The taking or attempting to take anything of value from the care, custody, or control of a person or persons by force or threat of force of violence and/or by putting the victim in fear.

4. **Aggravated assault:**
   An unlawful attack by one person upon another for the purpose of inflicting severe or aggravated bodily injury. This type of assault usually is accompanied by the use of a weapon or by means likely to produce **death** or great bodily harm. Simple assaults are excluded.

5. **Burglary—breaking or entering:**
   The unlawful entry of a structure to commit a felony or a theft. Attempted forcible entry is included.

6. **Larceny-theft (except motor vehicle theft):**
   The unlawful taking, carrying, leading, or riding away of property from the possession or constructive possession of another. Examples are thefts of bicycles or automobile accessories, shoplifting, pocket-picking, or the stealing of any property or article which is not taken by force and violence or by fraud. Attempted larcenies are included. Embezzlement, "con" games, forgery, worthless checks, and so on, are excluded.

7. **Motor vehicle theft:**
   The theft or attempted theft of a motor vehicle. A motor vehicle is self-propelled and runs on the surface and not on rails. Specifically excluded from this category are motorboats, construction equipment, airplanes, and farming equipment.

8. **Arson:**
   Any willful or malicious burning or attempt to burn, with or without intent to defraud, a dwelling house, public building, motor vehicle or aircraft, personal property of another, and so on.

TABLE 3.1

Definition of the Eight Index Offenses in the *Uniform Crime Reports* **(Part 1)**

States differ as to the exact descriptions of offenses, but these *UCR* definitions provide a national standard that helps us distinguish the substantive criminal law.

SOURCE: U.S. Department of Justice, Federal Bureau of Investigation, *Uniform Crime Reports* (Washington, DC: Government Printing Office, 1994).

principles of Western law undergird these definitions, and each state's penal code as well as U.S. laws explicitly define offenses.

RESPONSIBILITY FOR CRIMINAL ACTS

Thus far, we have examined the elements of crime and the statutory definition of offenses; we now need to look further into the question of responsibility. We would recognize that someone should not be charged with committing a crime if the event was an accident or if the perpetrator did not intend to violate the law. Among the seven principles of criminal law, that of *mens rea* is crucial in establishing that the accused is responsible for the act committed. In the absence of *mens rea*, eight defenses are recognized in

IDEAS IN PRACTICE

The New York Penal Code provides that a person is guilty of murder when, "under circumstances evincing a depraved indifference to human life, [he or she] recklessly engages in conduct that creates a grave risk of death to another person, and thereby causes the death of that person."

You are counsel for Richard Kane, who is charged with murder. Kane spent a cold, winter evening drinking in a tavern with George Telling. The bartender told the police that Telling was in an intoxicated condition and was flashing a wad of hundred-dollar bills when he left the bar in Kane's company at approximately 9:00 P.M.

Your client admits that he drove Telling out of town, robbed him, took his trousers, shirt, and glasses, and left him on a rural dirt road. The temperature was near zero, and visibility was obscured by blowing snow.

At about 10:00 P.M. Michael Brose was traveling in his pickup truck down the road at approximately 50 miles per hour. As he drove over a rise, he spotted a naked man standing in the middle of the road but "didn't have time to react" before his vehicle struck Telling. The medical examiner ruled that Telling died of massive head injuries and that his blood alcohol level was proof of a high degree of intoxication.

What will be your defense to the murder charge?

appropriate circumstances: (1) entrapment, (2) self-defense, (3) necessity, (4) duress (coercion), (5) immaturity, (6) mistake, (7) intoxication, and (8) insanity.

Entrapment

Individuals are excused from criminal liability for their actions when they can show that government officials induced them to commit an offense. Police may use undercover agents and "sting" operations, but they must not cross the admittedly blurred line between creating opportunities for individuals to commit crimes and actually inducing individuals to violate the law. While the government can use deception to catch citizens who are inclined to break the law, the government is not supposed to implant the idea of committing a crime into the minds of its citizens.

In a 1992 case, the Supreme Court reversed the conviction of a Nebraska farmer for possessing child pornography because the farmer had been entrapped by federal agents.[4] Posing as pornography distributors, the agents repeatedly sent advertisements and solicitations to the farmer. When he finally ordered some magazines, they arrested him. A majority of justices believed that the federal officials had gone too far in encouraging the farmer to commit a crime when he had shown no inclination on his own to break the law.

Self-Defense

People are entitled to use reasonable force to protect themselves against bodily harm. However, the level of force cannot exceed the person's reasonable perception of the threat being faced. Thus, a person may be justified in shooting a robber who is holding a gun to her head and threatening to kill her, but homeowners are generally not justified in shooting an unarmed burglar who has left the house and is running away across the lawn.

Bernhard Goetz, the "subway vigilante" in New York City, successfully argued that he was justified in shooting four youths who approached him in a threatening manner and asked for money. The focus of the case was not on whether the youths brandished lethal weapons (they did not), but on whether Goetz's belief in the necessity of using deadly force in that situation was reasonable. Goetz did not escape conviction on all counts, however; he was convicted on a lesser weapons-possession charge.

Necessity

Unlike self-defense, in which a defendant reasonably feels required to harm an aggressor, the necessity defense is used when people break the law in order to save themselves or prevent some greater harm. The person who speeds through a red light to get an injured child to the hospital or who breaks into a building to seek refuge from a snowstorm could claim to be violating the law out of necessity.

entrapment
The defense that the individual was induced by the police to commit the criminal act.

The English case *The Queen* v. *Dudley and Stephens* (1884) is a famous example of necessity. After their ship sank, four sailors were adrift in the Atlantic without food or water. Twenty days later, two of the sailors, Thomas Dudley and Edwin Stephens, killed the cabin boy and ate his flesh. Four days later, they were rescued by a passing ship. When they returned to England, Dudley and Stephens were tried for murder. The court did not accept their defense of necessity, and they were convicted and sentenced to death; the Crown later commuted the sentence to six months imprisonment.[5]

Duress (Coercion)

The defense of duress arises when someone commits a crime because he or she is coerced by another person. During a bank robbery, for instance, if an armed robber forces one of the bank's customers at gunpoint to drive the getaway car, the customer would be able to avoid conviction by claiming duress. However, courts are generally unwilling to accept the defense if people do not seize opportunities to escape from their situation. When heiress Patty Hearst was kidnapped and held for many months by a radical political group, she eventually participated in some of the group's armed robberies. She could not successfully claim the defense of duress because she participated in these crimes without being under the direct force and supervision of her captors.

Immaturity

Traditionally, criminal behavior by children under the age of seven has been excused because young children are presumed to be unable to understand and be held responsible for their actions. This premise has carried over into the American juvenile justice system, in which children who commit criminal offenses are treated differently than adults who commit the same acts. Teenagers who are repeat offenders or who commit violent crimes, however, may be tried and punished as adults when prosecutors ask judges to permit these offenders to be processed through the regular criminal justice system.

Mistake

While the general rule is that ignorance of the law is no excuse, if an accused person has made a mistake regarding some crucial fact, that may provide him or her with a defense. For example, suppose some neighborhood teenagers asked for your permission to grow sunflowers in a vacant lot that you own behind your home. You help them weed the garden and water the plants.

The veteran Milwaukee police officers were understandably shocked when, in August 1991, they entered Jeffrey Dahmer's apartment and found two human heads in a refrigerator, two in a freezer, and seven others boiled clean. In the basement, they found an acid-filled barrel of body parts. Investigators soon learned the full extent of Dahmer's crimes. The thirty-one-year-old laborer confessed to the police how he lured young men and boys from gay bars to his apartment where he drugged and killed them, had sex with their corpses, and dissected and cannibalized the bodies.

Jeffrey Dahmer was charged with killing and dismembering fifteen young men and boys. Dahmer thus joined that small fraternity of killers such as Charles Manson, "Son of Sam" David Berkowitz, and John Wayne Gacy. All were serial killers whose behavior almost rivaled that of Hannibal (the Cannibal) Lecter in the movie *Silence of the Lambs*. Although the facts in these cases were not in doubt, given the horrific aspects of their crimes, the defendants' legal responsibility for their actions became an issue. Were they sane when they committed their crimes? Were their rights protected as they proceeded from arrest to trial? What is an appropriate punishment for such individuals?

At trial, Jeffrey Dahmer changed his plea to guilty by reason of insanity. Under Wisconsin law, he was given a two-part trial. During the first part, lasting three weeks, the jury heard the evidence from police investigators and determined that

Then it turns out that they are cultivating marijuana. You were not aware of this because you have no idea what a marijuana plant looks like. Should you be subject to a criminal conviction for growing an illegal drug on your property? The answer depends on the specific knowledge and intent requirements that the prosecution must prove for particular criminal offenses. Moreover, the success of such a defense may depend on the extent to which jurors understand and sympathize with your mistake.

Intoxication

People cannot usually claim to lack knowledge and intent when they voluntarily become intoxicated. However, if someone has been tricked into consuming intoxicating or mind-altering substances, then an intoxication defense may be raised. Intoxication may be argued to reduce the seriousness of a charge if the defendant can claim that his or her condition precluded the existence of the specific intent necessary for some crimes. Someone charged with theft may claim, for example, that she was too drunk to realize that she had left the restaurant without paying her bill.

Insanity

A claim of insanity can be used to negate the *mens rea* element of crimes. The insanity defense is rarely successful, yet it has raised significant public controversy.

In a highly publicized case in January 1994, Lorena Bobbitt was acquitted of the charge of malicious wounding when a jury found that she was temporarily insane when she cut off her husband's penis after being victimized by spousal abuse. In another example, John Hinckley shot former President Ronald Reagan in an assassination attempt. Despite the fact that Hinckley was apprehended on the spot with the gun in his hand, he was found not guilty by reason of insanity. Yet, as the Close-Up of the Jeffrey

Dahmer committed the crimes. During the second part, known as the penalty stage, the jury was asked by Judge Lawrence Gram, Jr., to decide whether, "as a result of mental disease or defect, [Jeffrey Dahmer] lacked substantial capacity to appreciate the wrongfulness of his conduct or to conform his conduct to the requirements of the law."

Most people would agree that Dahmer was insane when he committed the crimes. As journalist Richard Moran noted before the trial, "All the defense really has to do is describe the contents of his refrigerator and freezer. Normal murderers do not mutilate their victims, nor do they display their heads or hearts. Cannibalism is not an alternative lifestyle, nor is necrophilia just some odd sexual preference." However, public concerns were raised as early as the pretrial phase that Dahmer would be "let off" and released to the community. This alarm stemmed from that part of Wisconsin

law that gives insanity acquittees the right to petition the court every six months for conditional release. Little credence seems to have been given to the distinction between the right to petition for release and actual release.

It was perhaps this concern that led the Wisconsin jury not to accept Dahmer's insanity defense. Judge Gram gave him the maximum sentence, fifteen consecutive life terms in prison. [Dahmer was murdered in prison in December 1994.]

SOURCES: Adapted from Richard Moran, "His Insanity Plea Can't Free Jeffrey Dahmer," *The Boston Globe*, 2 February 1992, p. 60, and Tom Mathews, "Secrets of a Serial Killer," *Newsweek*, 3 February 1992, pp. 44–49.

Dahmer case shows, juries often find defendants guilty of behavior that many would call insane.

Public outrage over Hinckley's acquittal, notwithstanding the fact that he is incarcerated in a mental hospital, led several states to enact statutes to permit verdicts of "guilty but mentally ill." Under such laws, people who were insane at the time that they committed crimes receive sentences that fit their crimes. They serve their sentences in mental institutions or receive treatment in the prison system, but they cannot be released prior to fulfilling their sentences even if they recover their sanity.

Over time, American courts have followed five different tests for determining whether a defendant should be found not guilty by reason of insanity. These tests are summarized in Table 3.2.

M'Naghten Rule. More than a dozen American states use this rule, which was developed in England in 1843. Daniel M'Naghten killed a man who he mistakenly thought was the prime minister of Great Britain. M'Naghten was acquitted because he claimed that he was delusional at the time of the killing. In developing the M'Naghten Rule, the British court established a standard for determining criminal responsibility known as the "right-from-wrong test." It asks whether "at the time of the committing of the act, the party accused was laboring under such a defect of reason, from disease of the mind, as not to know the nature and quality of the act he was doing, or if he did know it that he did not know he was doing what was wrong."[6]

Irresistible Impulse Test. Four states have supplemented the M'Naghten Rule with the Irresistible Impulse Test. Because psychiatrists argue that some people can feel compelled by their mental illness to commit criminal actions even though they recognize the wrongfulness of their conduct, the Irresistible Impulse Test is designed to bring the M'Naghten Rule in line with modern

The public was outraged when John B. Hinckley was found not guilty by reason of insanity of the attempted assassination of President Ronald Reagan. At the time, federal rules required that once the insanity defense was offered, the prosecution must prove that the accused was sane at the time of the event.

Test	Legal Standard Because of Mental Illness	Final Burden of Proof	Who Bears Burden of Proof
M'Naghten (1843)	"didn't know what he was doing or didn't know it was wrong"	Varies from proof by a balance of probabilities on the defense to proof beyond a reasonable doubt on the prosecutor	
Irresistible Impulse (1897)	"could not control his conduct"		
Durham (1954)	"the criminal act was caused by his mental illness"	Beyond reasonable doubt	Prosecutor
Model Penal Code (1972)	"lacks substantial capacity to appreciate the wrongfulness of his conduct or to control it"	Beyond reasonable doubt	Prosecutor
Present federal law	"lacks capacity to appreciate the wrongfulness of his conduct"	Clear and convincing evidence	Defense

TABLE 3.2
Insanity Defense Standards
The evolution of the standards for the insanity defense can be traced in this table.
SOURCE: U.S. Department of Justice, National Institute of Justice, *Crime File: "Insanity Defense,"* by Norval Morris (Washington, DC: Government Printing Office, n.d.).

psychiatry. Thus, the Irresistible Impulse Test permits defendants to avoid criminal culpability when a mental disease controlled their behavior, even if they knew that what they were doing was wrong.

Durham Rule. New Hampshire developed and still applies the rule that took its name from a federal court case (*Durham* v. *United States*, 1954). Under this rule, an accused is not criminally responsible if his or her actions were "the product of mental disease or defect."[7]

Model Penal Code's Substantial Capacity Test. Because the Durham Rule lacks precise definition, half of the states have adopted the Substantial Capacity Test from the Model Penal Code. This rule states that a defendant cannot be held culpable "if at the time of such conduct as a result of mental disease or defect he lacks substantial capacity either to appreciate the criminality of his conduct or to conform his conduct to the requirements of the law." This test essentially combines and broadens the M'Naghten Rule and the Irresistible Impulse Test.

Comprehensive Crime Control Act of 1984. Congress changed the federal rules on the insanity defense by limiting it to persons who are unable to appreciate the nature and quality or the wrongfulness of their acts as a result of severe mental disease or defect. Congress also shifted the burden of proof from the prosecutor to the defendant. Instead of prosecutors having to prove that defendants are sane, as in most insanity tests, defendants have to establish that they are insane. The statute also provides for automatic commitment to a mental hospital for people found innocent by reason of insanity. They must be confined to the hospital until it is determined that they no longer present a danger to society.

In practice, the outcomes of the various insanity tests frequently depend on jurors' reactions to the opinions of opposing psychiatrists presented as expert witnesses by the prosecution and defense. For example, the prosecution's psychiatrist will testify that the defendant does not meet the relevant criteria for insanity, while the defendant's psychiatrist will testify that the defendant does. The psychiatrists themselves do not make the determination about whether criminal responsibility applies to the defendant. Instead, the jurors decide the defendant's fate based on their understanding of and reaction to the psychiatrists' testimony and other factors, such as the seriousness of the crime and their own skepticism about the desirability or applicability of the insanity defense.

PROCEDURAL CRIMINAL LAW

Procedural law defines how the state must process defendants' cases. According to **procedural due process**, accused persons in criminal cases must be tried in accordance with legally established procedures. That is, defendants must be accorded certain rights as protections in keeping with the adversarial nature of the proceedings. As Chapter 2 explained, the Due Process Model is based on the premise that freedom is so valuable that efforts must be made to prevent erroneous decisions that would result in an innocent person's being deprived of it. The state may act against accused persons only when it follows due process procedures, thus ensuring that the rights of all are maintained.

procedural due process
The constitutional requirement that accused persons in criminal cases be tried in accordance with legally established procedures.

Some procedural rules, such as the right to a jury trial, may advance the truth-seeking goals of the criminal justice process. Other rules, however, such as the prohibition against unreasonable searches and seizures, are designed to protect individuals, including guilty people, from heavy-handed actions by government officials. American history contains many examples of police officers and prosecutors improperly using their investigative powers to harass and victimize people who lacked political power, including poor people, racial and ethnic minorities, and unpopular religious groups. The development of procedural safeguards for individuals through the decisions of the U.S. Supreme Court has helped to protect citizens from abusive actions by government officials.

In the case of *Brewer* v. *Williams*, discussed at the beginning of the chapter, the defendant gained a new trial and key pieces of evidence were thrown out because the detectives violated the rule against questioning in isolation suspects who are already represented by attorneys. Is adherence to procedural rules worth the risk that guilty people will go free because the rules may sometimes prevent police and prosecutors from gathering legally acceptable evidence? As we shall see later in the chapter, many people throughout American society, including justices on the U.S. Supreme Court, disagree about the answer to this question.

THE PRINCIPLES OF PROCEDURAL CRIMINAL LAW

Unlike substantive criminal law, which is defined by legislatures through statutes, procedural criminal law is defined by appellate courts through judicial decisions. Judges interpret the provisions of the U.S. Constitution and state constitutions, and their interpretations establish the procedures that government officials must follow.

Because it possesses the authority to review cases from state supreme courts as well as all federal courts, the U.S. Supreme Court has been especially influential in defining procedural criminal law. As illustrated by the case at the beginning of the chapter, procedural rules generate controversy because they frequently favor the goal of protecting individuals' rights over the goal of ensuring that guilty people are convicted and punished for their crimes. Both of these goals are important for American society, but many people disagree about the circumstances in which one should take precedence over the other.

THE BILL OF RIGHTS AND THE HISTORY OF DEFENDANTS' RIGHTS

The U.S. Constitution contained few references to criminal justice when it was ratified in 1789. Because many people were concerned that the document did not specify the rights of individuals to protection against infringement by the national government, amendments were added to the Constitution in 1791. The first ten amendments, commonly known as the Bill of Rights, contain a list of protections for individuals, and four of them directly bear on criminal justice issues. The Fourth Amendment bars unreasonable searches and seizures. The Fifth Amendment outlines basic due process rights in criminal cases. For example, consistent with the assumption that the state must prove the defendant's guilt, the right to protection against **self-incrimination** means that persons cannot be forced to answer questions that may tend to incriminate them. The protection against **double jeopardy** means that a person may be subjected to only one prosecution or punishment for an offense in the same jurisdiction. The Sixth Amendment provides for the right to a speedy, fair, and public trial by an impartial jury as well as the right to counsel. The Eighth Amendment bars excessive bail, excessive fines, and cruel and unusual punishments.

However, for most of our history, the Bill of Rights has had little applicability to most criminal cases because it was drafted to protect people from abusive actions by the *federal* government. It did not seek to protect people from state and local officials who handled nearly all criminal cases. This view was upheld by the U.S. Supreme Court in the 1833 case of ***Barron v. Baltimore***.[8] The following discussion explains how the view gradually changed through the late nineteenth and into the twentieth centuries.

The Fourteenth Amendment:
Rights Applied Against the States

After the Civil War, three amendments were added to the Constitution that intended to protect individuals' rights against infringement by state and local government officials. One of these, the **Fourteenth Amendment**, ratified in 1868, forbade states from violating people's right to due process of law. The amendment states that "no State shall . . . deprive any person of life, liberty, or property without due process of law; nor deny to any person within its jurisdiction the equal protection of the laws." These rights to due process and equal protection provided a basis for protecting individuals from abusive actions by local criminal justice officials. However, the terms *due process* and *equal protection* are so vague that it was left entirely up to justices on the U.S. Supreme Court to determine if and how these new rights applied to the criminal justice process.

The effort to convince the Supreme Court to declare that the Fourteenth Amendment provides specific protections for individuals spanned several decades and met with very limited success. It was not until the 1920s that the Supreme Court first began to identify specific personal rights that were protected by the Fourteenth Amendment.

---

self-incrimination
Provision of the Fifth Amendment that one cannot be forced to answer questions that may tend to incriminate oneself.

double jeopardy
Provision of the Fifth Amendment that a person cannot be prosecuted or punished more than once for the same offense.

Barron **v.** *Baltimore* **(1833)**
The Bill of Rights applies only to actions of the national government.

Fourteenth Amendment
Constitutional amendment forbidding states from violating people's right to due process of law and thereby nationalizing the application of many provisions of the Bill of Rights.

Initially, the Supreme Court reacted against convictions obtained by prosecutors under conditions that were obviously unfair. In 1923, the justices overturned the convictions of five African-American men who, after a forty-five-minute trial featuring a howling lynch mob outside the courthouse, were quickly sentenced to death (*Moore* v. *Dempsey*).[9]

A few years later, in **Powell v. Alabama (1932)**, the Supreme Court ruled that the Due Process Clause required that defense attorneys be provided to represent poor people facing the death penalty.[10] This decision stemmed from a notorious case in Alabama in which nine African-American men, known as the "Scottsboro boys," were quickly convicted and condemned to death for allegedly raping two white women, even though one of the alleged victims later admitted that she had lied about the rape.

The Supreme Court also overturned convictions of African-American defendants in Mississippi who had been hung from trees by ropes and beaten with metal-studded belts until they confessed (*Brown* v. *Mississippi*, 1936). The Supreme Court's description of the actions of the Mississippi sheriff's deputies clearly illustrated why the justices believed that such brutality violated the right to due process of law:

*The Scottsboro case (*Powell v. Alabama, 1932) grew out of the quick conviction and sentence to death of nine young African-American men accused of rape, even though one of the alleged victims later admitted she had lied about the rape.*

> [The deputies] hanged [the defendant] by a rope to the limb of a tree, and having let him down, they hung him again, and when he . . . still protested his innocence, he was tied to a tree and whipped . . . signs of the rope on his neck were plainly visible. . . . [Other defendants] were made to strip and they were laid over chairs and their backs were cut to pieces with a leather strap with buckles on it. . . ."[11]

In these early cases, the justices had not developed clear rules for determining which specific rights applied to state and local officials as components of the Due Process Clause of the Fourteenth Amendment. The justices simply reacted against brutal individual situations that shocked their consciences.

The Due Process Revolution

Changes in the Supreme Court's composition during the 1950s and 1960s created what has become known as the "Due Process Revolution." Under the leadership of Chief Justice Earl Warren, a majority of justices gradually applied the individual provisions of the Bill of Rights to the states. During the Warren Court era (1953–1969), the Supreme Court greatly expanded the number of rights protected by the Constitution and the application of those rights throughout the country. The justices did this through **incorporation** of various constitutional rights into the Due Process Clause of the Fourteenth Amendment so as to "nationalize" the Bill of Rights by making state and local officials adhere to the same Fourth, Fifth, Sixth, and Eighth Amendment rights that already applied to federal officials. By the dawn of the 1970s, the Supreme Court had extended most criminal justice safeguards to the states. Figure 3.2 shows the relationship of the Bill of Rights and the Fourteenth Amendment to the constitutional rights of the accused.

Powell v. Alabama (1932)
Counsel must be provided to defendants in capital cases.

incorporation
The extension of the due process clause of the Fourteenth Amendment to make binding on state governments many of the rights guaranteed in the first ten amendments to the U.S. Constitution (Bill of Rights).

FIGURE 3.2

Relationship of the
Bill of Rights and
the Fourteenth
Amendment to the
Constitutional Rights
of the Accused
For most of U.S. history,
the Bill of Rights pro-
tected citizens only against
violations by the federal
government. The Warren
Court began the process
of interpreting portions
of the Fourteenth Amend-
ment (incorporation) to
protect citizens from un-
lawful actions by state
officials.

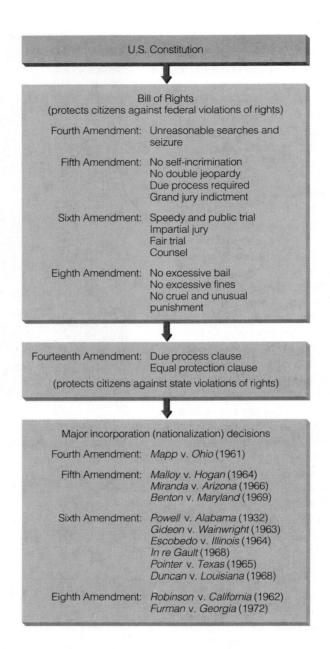

The Fourth Amendment: Protection Against Unreasonable Searches and Seizures

The right of the people to be secure in their persons, houses, papers, and effects, against unreasonable searches and seizures, shall not be violated, and no Warrants shall issue, but upon probable cause, supported by Oath or affirmation, and particularly describing the place to be searched, and the persons or things to be seized.

The Fourth Amendment recognizes the right to privacy and limits the ability of law enforcement officers to search a person or property in order to obtain evidence of criminal activity. The Fourth Amendment does not prevent the police from conducting searches; it merely bars "unreasonable" searches. It is up to the Supreme Court to define the situations in which a search is "reasonable" or "unreasonable."

It is apparent from the phrasing of the Fourth Amendment that the authors of the Bill of Rights did not believe that law enforcement officials should be given the authority to pursue criminals at all costs. The Fourth Amendment's protections are not limited to law-abiding citizens. Police officers are supposed to follow the rules for obtaining search warrants, and they may not conduct unreasonable searches even when they are trying to catch dangerous criminals.

In 1914, the Supreme Court declared, in *Weeks* v. *United States*, that federal courts must exclude any evidence obtained as the result of an improper search by federal law enforcement agents.[12] With this **exclusionary rule** the justices created the principle that illegally obtained evidence would be excluded from a trial, on the assumption that this would cause law officers to follow the dictates of the Fourth Amendment.

In 1961, in *Mapp* **v.** *Ohio* the Warren Court incorporated the Fourth Amendment into the Due Process Clause by declaring that state and local law enforcement officials also could not use evidence that they had obtained improperly. Many politicians and law enforcement officials criticized this decision and complained that the Court was creating rules that favored the rights of criminals over the control of crime. However, the justices saw themselves as upholding constitutionally protected rights even if some guilty parties would be freed because of illegal searches.

After being expanded during the Warren Court era, Fourth Amendment rights were narrowed during the chief justiceships of Warren Burger (1969–1986) and William Rehnquist (1986–present). With a new conservative majority on the court, a number of recent decisions have limited the use of the exclusionary rule to protect against illegal searches.

In *United States* v. *Leon* (1984), the Court created a "good faith" exception to the exclusionary rule.[13] In this case, police officers had relied on outdated information from an informant of unproven reliability in obtaining a warrant to conduct a search for narcotics. Using what later proved to be a defective warrant, the police discovered illegal drugs in the course of their search. Under the rule established in *Mapp* v. *Ohio*, the drugs should have been excluded as the product of an improper search. However, the new conservative majority on the Court created an exception to the exclusionary rule. Because the police officers had tried to follow proper procedures and a judge rather than the police had made the error in issuing the improper warrant, the Supreme Court declared that the evidence could be used against the defendant. Justice Byron White justified the Court's decision by writing that the

A QUESTION OF ETHICS

The short, muscular black man strode through the Los Angeles International Airport carrying an attaché case and a small piece of luggage. He abruptly set down the bag and walked to a row of pay phones. His telephone conversation was interrupted by two Drug Enforcement Administration (DEA) agents, who grabbed the phone and started asking the man a series of questions. When the suspected "drug smuggler" did not respond, he fell or was thrown to the floor and was then handcuffed and led off for questioning. Only after his protestation that they had stopped the wrong person was Joe Morgan—Hall of Fame second baseman and ESPN broadcaster—released.

Los Angeles narcotics detective Clayton Searle and DEA agent Bill Woessner claimed that they did nothing wrong; they merely responded to a DEA-developed profile of the characteristics of persons likely to be drug couriers. The fact that race is a major element of this profile has been justified as conforming to reality. Blacks and Hispanics, it is argued, are more likely to be involved in this aspect of the drug trade. Others have said that this is merely an expression of institutional racism—the darker your skin, the more likely that you will be stopped for questioning.

Is it ethical to base law enforcement actions on physical characteristics? Or should government agents stop and question only those whose behavior indicates they are committing or are about to commit a crime?

exclusionary rule
The principle that illegally obtained evidence must be excluded from a trial.

Mapp **v.** *Ohio* **(1961)**
Evidence obtained through unreasonable searches and seizures by state and local law enforcement officers must be excluded.

The exclusionary rule requires that evidence illegally seized not be used in a prosecution. Should the guilty go free if the police do not follow due process?

social costs of excluding evidence outweighed the social benefits of deterring improper police searches. White's claim is debatable because detailed studies on the effects of the exclusionary rule have shown that evidence is excluded in very few cases and the police often have other evidence to support a conviction even when some evidence is barred by the rule.[14]

This and related decisions have made it easier for law enforcement officials to use the evidence obtained through questionable searches, but the Court has also made the exclusionary rule less clear. The creation of exceptions makes it more difficult for police officers to know beforehand whether evidence obtained from a questionable search will be admissible.

The Burger and Rehnquist Courts did not abolish the exclusionary rule but limited its applicability, giving the police greater flexibility in investigating criminal cases. For example, the Rehnquist Court made it much easier for police officers to conduct warrantless searches of automobiles and closed containers found inside automobiles.[15]

The Supreme Court will undoubtedly continue to face new cases that force it to interpret the "reasonableness" of searches and the Fourth Amendment's warrant requirements. Technological advances and new situations have led the Court in recent years to consider whether helicopter surveillance of property constitutes a search that requires a warrant (the justices ruled that it does not) and whether the Fourth Amendment applies to the search and seizure by U.S. government agents of a noncitizen outside of the country (again, the justices said no). Other new issues will likely include electronic surveillance and prosecutors' efforts to gain access to computer files. Even with the new moderate members of the Court appointed by President Clinton, the Court likely will continue to tilt in favor of law enforcement officials and will not establish new, broader Fourth Amendment rights for criminal defendants.

The Fifth Amendment: Protection Against Self-Incrimination and Double Jeopardy

No person shall be held to answer for a capital, or otherwise infamous crime, unless on a presentment or indictment of a Grand Jury, except in cases arising in the land or naval forces, or in the Militia, when in actual service in time of War or public danger; nor shall any person be subject for the same offence to be twice put in jeopardy of life or limb; nor shall be compelled in any criminal case to be a witness against himself, nor be deprived of life, liberty, or property without due process of law; nor shall private property be taken for public use, without just compensation.

The two Fifth Amendment rights applied to the states by the Warren Court are the right against compelled self-incrimination and the right against double jeopardy.

Self-Incrimination. Two Warren Court decisions generated outrage among politicians, law enforcement officers, and members of the public. In ***Escobedo v. Illinois* (1964)** and ***Miranda v. Arizona* (1966)**, the justices decided that, prior to questioning criminal suspects, the police must inform suspects of their right to remain silent and their right to have an attorney present.[16] In response to these decisions, many police officers argued that they depended on interrogations and confessions as the primary means of solving crimes. However, nearly three decades after the two rulings, many suspects continue to confess for a variety of reasons, including feelings of guilt, inability to understand their rights, and the desire to gain a favorable plea bargain.

The Warren Court justices were not seeking to interfere with the ability of police officers to investigate crimes when they ordered the police to read suspects the "Miranda warnings." They were attempting to fulfill the Fifth Amendment's prohibition on compelled self-incrimination. In addition, they knew that suspects' confessions can be notoriously unreliable, especially if there are no rules limiting police questioning. The justices were aware that law enforcement officials often "solve" crimes when they are allowed to badger, intimidate, or otherwise coerce defendants into confessing. This may mean that the crime is "solved," but it is unclear whether the person who confessed is actually the one who committed the crime.

The Warren Court had made the exclusionary rule applicable to violations of Fifth Amendment rights as well as the Fourth Amendment. You will recall how the improper police questioning described in the "Christian Burial" case at the beginning of the chapter resulted in a Supreme Court decision ordering a second trial at which the suspect's incriminating statements and the body found as a result of those statements could not be used as evidence. In that example, the exclusionary rule was being applied in relation to a violation of the Fifth Amendment right against compelled self-incrimination. The new trial in that case did not, however, result in the suspect going free.

Just as the Burger Court created the "good faith" exception in a Fourth Amendment case, other new exceptions to the exclusionary rule were created in Fifth Amendment cases. For example, in the second Williams trial, the prosecution used the little girl's body as evidence based on the claim that the police would have found the body eventually even if the suspect had never led the police to it as a result of improper questioning. When the introduction of this evidence was challenged in a second appeal to the U.S. Supreme Court, the Burger Court justices created an "inevitable discovery"

IDEAS IN PRACTICE

While on patrol, police officers stop a car being driven at a high rate of speed. As they write the ticket, they notice tools and metal objects in the back seat and realize that the driver and his passenger resemble persons wanted for stealing auto parts. The officers call for assistance, arrest the occupants, and search the vehicle, including the trunk.

Back at the station, their sergeant says that the search was improper and that they should have gotten a warrant before opening the trunk. Is he correct?

***Escobedo* v. *Illinois* (1964)**
Suspects are entitled to representation by counsel during questioning in police custody.

***Miranda* v. *Arizona* (1966)**
Confessions made by suspects who have not been informed by police about their due process rights cannot be admitted as evidence.

exception to the exclusionary rule.[17] A majority of justices endorsed the prosecutor's claim that illegally obtained evidence may be admitted at trial if the police would have inevitably discovered the evidence by legal means.

The day after the Burger Court announced the creation of the "inevitable discovery" exception to the exclusionary rule, it announced another exception. In *New York* v. *Quarles* (1984), the court created a "public safety" exception permitting police to use evidence obtained when a situation presenting an immediate threat to public safety requires them to question a suspect before reading the Miranda warnings.[18]

These decisions illustrate how, in the 1980s and 1990s, the Burger and Rehnquist Courts weakened the clarity and impact of the Miranda precedent, although they never overturned Miranda.

Double Jeopardy.   Because of the limitations imposed by the Fifth Amendment, a person charged with a criminal act may be subjected to only one prosecution or punishment for that offense in the same jurisdiction. As previously noted, illegal acts often violate both state and federal laws, so the prohibition against double jeopardy does not necessarily rule out prosecution in successive jurisdictions. For example, the Los Angeles police officers accused of using excessive force in the arrest of Rodney King were first acquitted by a California jury and then prosecuted under federal civil rights laws by the U.S. government.

At what point in the criminal process does double jeopardy come into force? It has generally been held that if a case is dismissed before trial, a subsequent prosecution for the offense is permissible.

The Sixth Amendment: The Right to Counsel and a Fair Trial

> In all criminal prosecutions, the accused shall enjoy the right to a speedy and public trial, by an impartial jury of the State and district wherein the crime shall have been committed, which district shall have been previously ascertained by law, and to be informed of the nature and cause of the accusation; to be confronted with the witnesses against him; to have compulsory process for obtaining witnesses in his favor, and to have the Assistance of Counsel for his defence.

Gideon v. *Wainwright*
(1963)

Defendants have a right to counsel in felony cases, and the state must provide attorneys for defendants who are too poor to hire their own.

Argersinger v. *Hamlin*
(1972)

Defendants have a right to counsel when conviction may result in incarceration.

In 1963, in **Gideon v. Wainwright**, the Warren Court ruled that in all felony cases, states must provide attorneys to criminal defendants who are too poor to hire their own attorneys.[19] This decision had little immediate impact because by 1963 all but a few states were already providing attorneys for indigent felony defendants. However, the Gideon decision was the first of a number of decisions by both the Warren and Burger Courts on the right to counsel at various points in the criminal justice process. For example, defendants gained the right to appointed counsel for the initial appeal filed in state court after a conviction (*Douglas* v. *California*, 1963).[20] Subsequently, in **Argersinger v. Hamlin (1972)** defendants gained the right to counsel when conviction might result in imprisonment.[21] Convicted offenders have no right to counsel for subsequent appeals to state supreme courts or petitions filed in federal courts alleging constitutional violations in the investigation and adjudication of their state court cases. Thus, many prisoners, including those on death row awaiting execution, must attempt to present their own cases in court or hope that an attorney will volunteer to represent them if they lack the funds to hire a lawyer.

In ***Duncan* v. *Louisiana* (1968)**, the Warren Court nationalized the Sixth Amendment right to trial by jury when the defendant faces six months or more of imprisonment.[22] When defendants face lesser charges, state law determines whether a jury trial is available.

The composition of juries has also been a focus of Supreme Court decisions. Although the laws of many states require twelve-member, unanimous juries, the Burger Court in ***Apodaca* v. *Oregon* (1972)** established that twelve-member juries could issue nonunanimous verdicts and that criminal juries could have as few as six members if they were required by state law to reach unanimous verdicts.[23]

The case of Clarence Gideon resulted in a 1963 decision that states must provide defense counsel in felony cases for those who cannot pay for it.

***Duncan* v. *Louisiana* (1968)**
States must provide a jury trial for defendants charged with serious offenses.

***Apodaca* v. *Oregon* (1972)**
If states choose to use twelve-person juries for criminal cases, unlike six-member juries, the large juries need not reach unanimous verdicts in order to convict.

The Eighth Amendment: Protection Against Excessive Bail, Excessive Fines, and Cruel and Unusual Punishment

> Excessive bail shall not be required, nor excessive fines imposed, nor cruel and unusual punishments inflicted.

Most of the Supreme Court's attention in Eighth Amendment cases has been focused on questions about cruel and unusual punishments. Relatively few Supreme Court decisions concern the issues of bail and excessive fines.

Bail permits defendants awaiting trial to be freed from jail until their cases are decided. However, the Eighth Amendment does not require that bail be granted to all defendants, and the Supreme Court has endorsed the Bail Reform Act of 1984, which authorizes federal judges to keep suspects in jail if there is evidence that they might flee or might present a danger to the community if released (*United States* v. *Salerno*, 1987).[24]

With respect to excessive fines, the Rehnquist Court declared that federal judges must make sure that government seizures of money and property from drug dealers do not violate the Eighth Amendment by constituting "excessive fines" (*Austin* v. *United States*, 1993).[25]

The Warren Court established the standard for judging issues of cruel and unusual punishment in a case concerning a former soldier who was punished by loss of U.S. citizenship for deserting his post during World War II (*Trop* v. *Dulles*, 1958).[26] In that case, Chief Justice Warren declared that judges must use the values of contemporary society to determine whether a specific criminal punishment is cruel and unusual. This test has been applied in death penalty cases, but the justices have strongly disagreed with one another about American society's current values. For example, only Justices William Brennan, Thurgood Marshall, and, later, Harry Blackmun, insisted that the death penalty violates the Eighth Amendment's ban on cruel and unusual punishment.

In 1972, a majority of justices decided that the death penalty was being applied in an arbitrary and discriminatory manner (*Furman* v. *Georgia*, 1972).[27] When many state legislatures wrote new statutes that specified more careful decision-making procedures for death penalty cases, a majority of justices in ***Gregg* v. *Georgia* (1976)** endorsed reactivating the death penalty.[28] Under the new procedures, there is a trial to consider the defendant's guilt and then a separate hearing to consider whether the defendant deserves the death penalty. In the sentencing hearing, the jury or judge is required to examine any factors that make this defendant especially deserving of the most severe

***Gregg* v. *Georgia* (1976)**
Capital punishment statutes are permissible if they provide careful procedures to guide decision making by judges and juries.

punishment—for example, "aggravating factors" such as the commission of a particularly gruesome killing. They must also examine any "mitigating factors" that make this defendant less deserving, such as youthfulness or mental retardation.

In the 1980s, lawyers who wanted to abolish the death penalty brought new cases to the Supreme Court in unsuccessful efforts to persuade the justices to declare that capital punishment violates the Constitution. For example, *McCleskey* v. *Kemp* (1987) presented elaborate statistics showing that racial discrimination exists in Georgia's death penalty decision making.[29] In Georgia, murderers who kill white victims, especially if those murderers are African-Americans, are significantly more likely to be sentenced to death than white killers of African-Americans. A narrow majority on the Rehnquist Court rejected the use of statistics to prove such discrimination and insisted that defendants must show clear evidence of racial bias in their own specific cases, not just in the Georgia criminal justice system generally, in order to challenge a conviction.

CONSTITUTIONAL RIGHTS AND CRIMINAL JUSTICE PROFESSIONALS

As a result of the Supreme Court's decisions, people in all states now enjoy the same basic protections against illegal searches, improper police interrogations, and other violations of constitutional rights related to the criminal justice process.

In response to these decisions, police, prosecution, and corrections offices have had to develop policies and guidelines to inform criminal justice professionals about what they are and are not permitted to do while undertaking responsibilities for investigation, prosecution, and punishment.

If you were a police officer, prosecutor, or correctional officer, how would you feel about the Supreme Court's decisions defining the rights that benefit criminal defendants? While you would recognize the desirability of upholding constitutional rights in order to maintain democratic freedoms, you might also feel frustrated when court decisions excluded relevant evidence indicating that someone was guilty of a crime or granted new trials to guilty defendants because of errors made by officers investigating a case.

As you read about the individual rights possessed by criminal defendants, think about the policy outcomes produced by the Supreme Court's recognition of these rights. Has the Court made it too difficult for police to investigate cases? Has the Court failed to provide sufficient protection for individuals? Or has the Court struck an appropriate balance between protecting individuals' rights and permitting criminal justice officials to do their jobs?

As a criminal justice professional, you must be concerned as to whether the Supreme Court's decisions are giving you clear guidance about what you are supposed to do. You do not want to make an inadvertent error that will result in a new trial or the exclusion of evidence. Think back to the Williams case concerning the officer's comments to the suspect in the back of the police car. The detective knew he was not supposed to question the suspect without an attorney present, but did he know that his comments directed to the suspect would be considered improper "questioning"? Perhaps he knew, perhaps not.

Substantive criminal law tells the public which actions are illegal and subject to punishment by the government. Legislatures have primary responsibility for defining substantive criminal law and punishments. Police officers and prosecutors must be keenly aware of the principles of criminal law. These officials are responsible for deciding which charges to bring against defendants. They must also gather and present sufficient evidence to fulfill the elements of the crime in order to gain a conviction. Among other things, defense attorneys often look closely at the prosecution's proof concerning the defendant's intent to commit the crime.

Procedural criminal law defines the rights of individuals and provides rules for criminal justice officials' actions in investigating, prosecuting, and adjudicating cases. The Supreme Court bears primary responsibility for interpreting the Bill of Rights and defining criminal defendants' rights. During the Warren Court era (1953–1969), the Supreme Court made many major decisions that expanded the definition of defendants' rights and required all states to follow common procedural rules in order to protect constitutional rights. Many of these decisions were criticized by law enforcement officials and politicians as favoring the rights of criminals over society's need to catch and punish lawbreakers. Conservative presidents appointed new justices to the Supreme Court in the 1970s, 1980s, and early 1990s who made decisions that reduced the scope of criminal defendants' rights granted by the Burger and Rehnquist Courts.

QUESTIONS FOR REVIEW

1. How is substantive criminal law different from procedural criminal law?
2. What are the seven underlying principles of substantive criminal law?
3. Which provisions of the Bill of Rights provide protections for criminal defendants?
4. How have the Supreme Court's interpretations of criminal defendants' rights changed over the years?

NOTES

1. *Brewer* v. *Williams*, 430 U.S. 387 (1977).
2. Jerome Hall, *General Principles of Criminal Law*, 2nd ed. (Indianapolis, IN: Bobbs-Merrill, 1947), p. 18.
3. *Robinson* v. *California*, 370 U.S. 660 (1962).
4. *Jacobson* v. *United States*, 112 S.Ct. (1992).
5. *The Queen* v. *Dudley and Stephens*, 14 Q.B.D. 273 (1884).
6. *M'Naghten's Case*, 8 Eng. Rep. 718 (H.I. 1843).
7. *Durham* v. *United States*, 94 U.S. App. D.C. 228, 214 F. 2nd 862 (1954).
8. *Barron* v. *Baltimore*, 32 U.S. 243 (1833).
9. *Moore* v. *Dempsey*, 261 U.S. 86 (1923).
10. *Powell* v. *Alabama*, 287 U.S. 45 (1932).
11. *Brown* v. *Mississippi*, 297 U.S. at 281–282 (1936).
12. *Weeks* v. *United States*, 232 U.S. 383, (1914).
13. *United States* v. *Leon*, 468 U.S. 897 (1984).

14. Peter F. Nardulli, "The Societal Costs of the Exclusionary Rule: An Empirical Assessment," *American Bar Foundation Research Journal* (1983), pp. 585–690, and Craig Uchida and Timothy Bynum, "Search Warrants, Motions to Suppress and 'Lost Cases': The Effects of the Exclusionary Rule in Seven Jurisdictions," *Journal of Criminal Law and Criminology* 81 (1991), pp. 1034–1066.

15. *California* v. *Acevedo,* 111 S.Ct. 1982 (1991).

16. *Escobedo* v. *Illinois,* 378 U.S. 478 (1964), and *Miranda* v. *Arizona,* 384 U.S. 436 (1966).

17. *Nix* v. *Williams,* 467 U.S. 431 (1984).

18. *New York* v. *Quarles,* 467 U.S. 649 (1984).

19. *Gideon* v. *Wainwright,* 372 U.S. 335 (1963).

20. *Douglas* v. *California,* 372 U.S. 353 (1963).

21. *Argersinger* v. *Hamlin,* 407 U.S. 25 (1972).

22. *Duncan* v. *Louisiana,* 391 U.S. 145 (1968).

23. *Apodaca* v. *Oregon,* 406 U.S. 404 (1972).

24. *United States* v. *Salerno,* 481 U.S. 739 (1987).

25. *Austin* v. *United States,* 61 L.W. 4811 (1993).

26. *Trop* v. *Dulles,* 356 U.S. 86 (1958).

27. *Furman* v. *Georgia,* 408 U.S. 238 (1972).

28. *Gregg* v. *Georgia,* 428 U.S. 153 (1976).

29. *McClesky* v. *Kemp,* 478 U.S. 1019 (1986).

PART II *Police*

4 *Policing America*   **5** *Police Operations*   **6** *Policing: Issues and Trends*

Most of us have gained an image of the police from movies and television; but the reality of law enforcement differs greatly from the dramatic exploits of the cops in *The Fugitive* or on "Miami Vice." In some ways, it is curious that our images come from fiction and fictionalized accounts, because the police are the most visible agents of the criminal justice system in American society.

In Part II, we deal with the role of the police as the critical subunit of the system that confronts crime at the community level. Chapter 4 traces the history of policing and looks at its function and organization. Chapter 5 examines the daily operations of the police, and Chapter 6 analyzes some of the current issues and trends in law enforcement. As we will see, police work often takes place in a hostile environment with crucial issues of life and death, honor and dishonor at stake. Officers are given discretion to deal with these situations; how they use that discretion has an important effect on the way society views policing.

CHAPTER 4
Policing America

MANHUNT FOR MENACING YOUTH

On Sunday, August 28, 1994, shots were fired at two groups of children playing on the south side of Chicago. Two boys were wounded and a fourteen-year-old girl, Shavon Dean, was killed as she stood a few feet away from her house. She had come out of the house to tell her brother, one of the boys who was fired upon, that it was time to stop playing and come inside. At that moment, a seemingly random shooting cut short her young life.

Using descriptions from witnesses, the police mounted a citywide manhunt for Robert "Yummy" Sandifur. It was believed that Sandifur chose the boys as random targets as part of a gang initiation.

Although any homicide is disturbing, the national news media had little interest in the story of yet another inner-city youngster gunned down in senseless violence until they learned that the suspect was only *eleven years old* and that he had been prosecuted for eight felonies including robbery, car theft, arson, and burglary, committed between the ages of nine and eleven. He was not yet five feet tall and weighed less than seventy pounds.

Robert had been the victim of serious child abuse as a three-year-old. An investigation by the Illinois Department of Children and Family Services had found scars on his face, cordlike marks on his abdomen, and cigarette burns on his buttocks. At the time of the shooting, he was in temporary custody of his grandmother while the state tried to find a place for him in a secure juvenile detention center.

With the national news media following their every move, the Chicago police looked for Robert for several days. On Thursday, September 1, 1994, they found him—lying dead in a pool of blood beneath a railroad overpass with two bullets in his head. It was believed that he had been executed by older members of his own gang for generating too much "heat" from the police. The police arrested sixteen-year-old Cragg Hardaway and an unnamed juvenile for the killing of Robert Sandifur.

As the most visible representatives of government, the police inevitably face criticism and public scrutiny. Although their day-to-day accomplishments may go unnoticed and unrewarded when neighborhoods remain calm and society functions smoothly, at other times, when crimes are committed or people are injured, police may become the focus of disappointment and anger. "Where were you when this crime was being committed?" "How come we can never find a cop when we need one, but they're always around to hand out traffic tickets?" In view of the high expectations placed on it by the public, policing is, in many respects, "mission impossible." In the final analysis, no matter how intimately linked they are to the society that they serve, the police do not control the conditions that produce the Robert Sandifurs of America.

In a free society, the police are required to maintain order. In carrying out this responsibility, police officers are given significant authority. Using their powers to detain, search, arrest, and use force, they can interfere with the personal freedom of any citizen. If they use such powers excessively, they can harm the underlying goal of a stable, democratic society.

To understand the role of police in American society, we will examine several aspects of policing in this chapter. A brief history of the police will demonstrate their evolution from our English past. Discussions of the functions and policies of American police will show how police officers carry out their duties and how law enforcement decisions are made. ★

frankpledge

A system in medieval England whereby members of a tithing, a group of ten families, agreed to maintain order, uphold the law, and commit violators to a court.

THE HISTORICAL DEVELOPMENT OF THE POLICE IN THE UNITED STATES

Law and order is not a new concept; it has been a focus of discussion since the first police force was formed in metropolitan London in 1829. Looking back even further to the Magna Carta of 1215, we see that limitations were placed on the constables and bailiffs of thirteenth-century England. We can read between the lines of this historic document to surmise that problems of police abuse, the maintenance of order, and the rule of law have challenged societies throughout history.

THE ENGLISH ROOTS OF THE AMERICAN POLICE

The roots of American policing lie in our European, and particularly our English, heritage. Before it developed an organized police force, England relied on local residents to uphold the law. For example, in the thirteenth century, the **frankpledge** system required that groups of ten families, called tithings, agree to maintain order, uphold the law, and commit violators to a court. By custom, every male above the age of twelve was part of the system. When an individual became aware that a crime had occurred, he was obliged to raise a "hue and cry" and to join others in his tithing to track down the offender. The tithing was fined if members did not perform its duties.

Eventually, England developed a system in which individuals were selected within each community to take responsibility for catching criminals. The Statute of Winchester, enacted in 1285, set up a parish constable system. The citizens of the community were still required to pursue criminals, just as they had been under the frankpledge, but now a constable supervised law enforcement efforts. The constable was a man selected from the parish to serve without pay as its law enforcement officer for one year. Watchmen were appointed to assist the constable, and the constable retained the additional power, if need be, to call the entire community into action.

It was not until the eighteenth century that an organized police force evolved in England. With the development of commerce and industry, cities grew while farming declined as the major source of employment and the focus of community life. In the larger cities, these changes to the traditional patterns of life produced social disorder.

In the mid-eighteenth century, novelist Henry Fielding and his brother, Sir John Fielding, led efforts to improve law enforcement in London. They wrote newspaper articles to educate the public on the problem of increased crime and published fliers carrying descriptions of known offenders. Henry Fielding became a magistrate of London in 1748. He organized a small group of experienced constables as "thief-takers," who worked together to pursue and arrest lawbreakers. The government was impressed with Fielding's Bow Street Amateur Volunteer Force (known as the "Bow Street Runners"). It paid the volunteers and attempted to develop such law enforcement groups in other parts of London.

After Henry Fielding's death in 1754, however, these efforts fell by the wayside. As the decades passed, it became clear to many people that the government needed to assert itself in enforcing laws and maintaining order because London, in particular, had become a dangerous place where the streets were periodically controlled by unruly mobs.

In the early 1800s, several attempts were made to create a centralized police force for London. While people generally recognized the need to maintain social order, some opposed the creation of a centralized police force by the government. They feared that such a force would interfere with the freedom of citizens and engender tyranny. Finally, in 1829, Sir Robert Peel, Home Secretary in the British cabinet, pushed Parliament to establish the Metropolitan Constabulary for London. This agency was organized like a military unit with a 1,000-man force commanded by two magistrates, later called "commissioners." The officers were called "bobbies" in reference to Sir Robert Peel, who not only promoted the idea in Parliament but ultimately controlled the agency, since the Home Department was responsible for domestic affairs. In the British system, members of the cabinet who oversee the departments of government are selected from among the elected members of Parliament. Thus, by being under Peel's supervision, the first official police force was under the control of democratically elected officials.

During the early part of the nineteenth century, the English police had a four-part mandate:

1. To prevent crime without the use of repressive force and to avoid the necessity of intervention by the military in community disturbances
2. To manage public order nonviolently, using force to obtain compliance only as a last resort
3. To minimize and reduce conflict between the police and the public
4. To demonstrate efficiency by the absence of crime and disorder rather than by visible evidence of police actions in dealing with problems[1]

In effect, the mandate meant keeping a low profile while maintaining order. Because there were fears that a national police force would threaten civil liberties, political leaders made every effort to focus police activities at the local level.

AMERICAN POLICING

The American colonists brought with them to the New World the English concern about the possible threats of an organized police force. As a result, American policing followed several English traditions: (1) limited authority, (2) local control, and (3) organizational fragmentation. Like the British police, and unlike those in continental Europe, the U.S. police have limited authority. Statutes passed by legislatures inform the American police about the extent of their powers. Court decisions limit the ways in which those powers are exercised. Also, the United States has no nationwide police force; except for a few specialized agencies within the federal government, each American law enforcement unit is under state or local control. Further, policing in the United States is fragmented. There are many types of agencies, each with its own special jurisdiction and responsibilities—sheriff, city and town police, state police, the FBI, and so on.

While both the English and American police developed in response to changing social conditions such as increased urbanization and industrialization, American policing was also shaped by such additional factors as ethnic and racial diversity, local political control, regional differences, and the violent frontier tradition.

American police history is often divided into three periods: (1) the Political Era (1840–1920), (2) the Professional Era (1920–1970), and (3) the Community Policing Era (1970–present).[2] This division has been criticized as describing policing only in the urban areas of the Northeast without taking into account the very different development of the police in rural areas of the

South and West. Even if these descriptions of history are somewhat flawed, however, they provide a useful basis for noting the general changes in the organization of the police, the focus of their work, and the particular strategies of operation over the course of American history.

The Political Era: 1840–1920

The period 1840–1920 is called the Political Era because of the close ties that developed between the police and urban political leaders. In many cities, the police department appeared to work for the mayor or the political party in power rather than for the citizens in general. In some places, guns and badges were issued to white males who supported the mayor or the ruling political machine. These police officers would then help their political patrons stay in power by working to get out the vote on election day. Ranks in the force were often for sale to the highest bidder, and many police officers were "on the take."

In the United States, as in England, the growth of cities led to pressures for modernization of law enforcement. Social relations in the cities of the nineteenth century were quite different from those in the towns and countryside. In fact, from 1830 to 1870, there was unprecedented civil disorder in America's major cities. Ethnic conflict as a consequence of massive immigration from Europe, hostility toward nonslave blacks and abolitionists, mob actions against banks and other institutions of property during economic declines, and violence in settling questions of morality—all these factors contributed to fears that a stable democratic society would not survive.

Around 1840, the large cities began to take steps to create constabularies. Boston and Philadelphia were the first to add a daytime police force to supplement the night watchmen; other cities quickly followed suit. Soon, however, people recognized the inefficiency of separate day and night forces. In 1844, the New York state legislature passed a law to create a unified force for cities under the command of a chief appointed by the mayor and city council. By the 1850s, most major American cities had adopted this pattern.

Early police practices focused on watchman duties and reactive patrols. In effect, they sought to prevent crimes and keep order through the use of foot patrols. The officer on the beat dealt with crime, disorder, and other problems as they arose. The following Close-Up by Edward H. Savage, a fifteen-year veteran of the Boston Police Department, summarizes the role of the urban police officer during this period.

During the political era the officer on a neighborhood beat dealt with crime and disorder as it arose. Police also performed various social services.

In addition to foot patrols, the police performed a number of service functions such as caring for derelicts, operating soup kitchens, regulating public health, and handling medical and social emergencies. In cities across the country, the police provided beds and food to homeless people. In station houses, these "lodgers" found overnight accommodations ranging from the floor to clean bunkrooms.[3] Because they were part of the only governmental agency with an organization and network on the streets of the city, the police became general public servants as well as crime control officers. Because of their close connections and service to the community during this era, they enjoyed citizen support.

Police in the South developed differently due to slavery and the rural, agricultural nature of that

CLOSE-UP
Advice to a Young Policeman

MY FRIEND: You have recently been appointed, and are about to assume the responsibilities of an office the duties of which are much more varied and difficult, and the trust of which is of much more importance to the public and to yourself, than is generally admitted.

Do not forget that in this business your character is your capital. Deal honorably with all persons, and hold your word sacred. . . . Make it your business to know what is doing on every part of [your beat]; let no person or circumstance escape your notice. Learn the people residing or doing business on your beat; protect their property; make yourself useful, and aid them in all their lawful pursuits, and by an upright and straightforward course, and a close attention to duty, endeavor to merit the good will of all good citizens. You know not how soon you may need their aid, and their favor will add much to your power and influence to do good. But in the pursuance of your duties, as much as possible avoid laying yourself under special obligations to any one; let your services rather place others under an obligation to you.

Lend a willing ear to all complaints made to you in your official capacity; the most unworthy have a right to be heard, and a word of comfort to the afflicted, or an advice to the erring, costs you nothing, and may do much good.

Remember that in your official duties, you are continually and eminently exposed to the ten thousand snares and temptations in city life. Treat all persons kindly; avoid discussion in politics; . . . I might say more, but should I, you would still have to go out and *learn* your duty.

SOURCE: Edward H. Savage, *A Chronological History of the Boston Watch and Police from 1631 to 1865*, 2nd ed. (Boston: J. E. Farwell, 1865), p. 127.

---

region. Historians have noted that the first police agencies in the South with full-time officers developed in those cities with large slave populations (Charleston, New Orleans, Savannah, and Richmond) where the white masters lived in fear of possible uprisings.[4] "Slave patrols" were organized by the white owners as a means of dealing with runaways. The patrols had full power to break into the homes of African-Americans suspected of keeping arms, to whip those who did not obey their orders, and to assist slave owners by arresting and returning runaway slaves.

The westward expansion of the United States during the nineteenth century presented circumstances quite different from those in the urbanizing East and the agricultural South. Settlements formed before order could be established. Thus, the citizens who wanted to enforce law and order often had to take matters into their own hands through vigilante groups.[5]

One of the first official positions to be created in rural areas was that of sheriff. Although the sheriff had responsibilities similar to those of his counterpart in seventeenth-century England, the American officer was chosen by popular election and had broad powers to enforce the law. Elections meant that sheriffs were closely connected to local politics. They depended on the men of the community for assistance, and the **posse comitatus** (Latin for "power of the county"), borrowed from fifteenth-century Europe, came into being. This institution required local men above the age of fifteen to respond to the sheriff's call for assistance.

In the period following the Civil War, the federal government appointed U.S. marshals to help enforce the law in the western territories. Some of the best-known folk heroes of American policing were U.S. marshals such as Wyatt Earp, Bat Masterson, and Wild Bill Hickock, who attempted to bring law to the

posse comitatus
Latin for "power of the county"; the requirement that able-bodied men above the age of fifteen aid the sheriff when required.

"Wild West." While some federal marshals carried out extensive law enforcement activities, most of them had primarily judicial responsibilities, such as maintaining order in the courtroom and holding prisoners for trial.

The twentieth century brought increasing urbanization to all parts of the country. This social change reduced some of the distinctive regional differences that had helped to define policing. In addition, growing criticism of the influence of politics on the police in eastern and midwestern cities resulted in efforts to reform the nature and organization of the police. Reformers sought to make police into law enforcement professionals and reduce their connection to local politics.

The Professional Era: 1920–1970

Policing was greatly influenced by the Progressive reform movement in the early twentieth century. The Progressives were mostly upper-middle-class, educated Americans interested in two primary goals: (1) efficient government and (2) the provision of governmental services to improve the conditions of the less fortunate. A related goal was the removal of undesirable political influences, such as party politics and patronage, on government. When the Progressives applied these goals to the police, they envisioned professional law enforcement officials who would use modern technology to benefit the entire society, not just the local politicians.

August Vollmer, chief of police of Berkeley, California, from 1909 to 1932, was one of the leading advocates of professional policing. Vollmer initiated the use of motorcycle units, handwriting analysis, and fingerprinting. He and other police reformers, such as Leonhard Fuld, Raymond Fosdic, Bruce Smith, and O. W. Wilson, argued that the police should be a professional force, a nonpartisan agency of government committed to the highest ideals of public service. Six essential elements comprise this model of professional policing:

1. The force should stay out of politics.
2. Members should be well trained, disciplined, and tightly organized.
3. Laws should be equally enforced.
4. The force should take advantage of technological developments.
5. Personnel procedures should be based on merit.
6. The crime-fighting role should be prominent.

The refocusing of police attention on crime control and away from maintaining order probably did more than anything else to change the nature of American policing. This narrow focus on crime fighting severed many of the ties that the police had developed with the communities they served. By the end of World War I, police departments had significantly reduced their involvement in the social service functions they had performed previously. Instead, for the most part, cops became crime fighters.[6]

O. W. Wilson, a student of Vollmer's, was a leading advocate of professionalism in the period from 1929 to 1960 and a proponent of the use of motorized patrols, efficient radio communication, and rapid response to facilitate effective crime fighting. He believed that one-officer patrols were the best way to utilize personnel. When combined with the use of two-way radios, police commanders could effectively supervise the officers on the streets and policing could become especially efficient. Wilson emphasized the importance of rotating beat assignments so that officers on patrol would not become

The rise of civil rights movements in the 1960s challenged some of the assumptions of the Professional Era. While police saw themselves as crime fighters, many inner-city residents saw them as an occupying force.

too familiar with individuals in their community and thus prone to police corruption. Such rotations were intended to remove officers from close contact and communication with the neighborhoods and citizens that they were supposed to serve. Advocates of professionalism sought to instill in officers a strong commitment to the supremacy of the law and the importance of equal treatment for all citizens.

By the 1930s, with their new orientation toward fighting crime, the police were adopting modern technologies and methods in order to combat serious crimes. Effectiveness in fighting serious crimes like murder, rape, and robbery was especially important for gaining citizen support. By contrast, efforts to control victimless offenses and to strictly maintain order often aroused citizen opposition. As emphasized by Mark Moore and George Kelling, "The clean, bureaucratic model of policing put forth by the reformers could be sustained only if the scope of police responsibility was narrowed to 'crime fighting'."[7]

In the 1960s, the civil rights and antiwar movements, urban riots, and rising crime rates challenged many assumptions of the professional model. In their attempts to maintain order during public demonstrations, the police in many cities appeared to be primarily concerned with maintaining the status quo. Thus, police officers found themselves enforcing laws that had severe discriminatory impacts on African-Americans and the poor. With American cities increasingly populated by low-income members of racial minorities, the professional style isolated officers from the communities they served. In the eyes of many inner-city residents, the police were an occupying army keeping them at the bottom of society rather than public servants providing help to all citizens. Although the police continued to portray themselves to the public as crime fighters, citizens became increasingly aware that the police were often ineffective in this role. Crime rates rose for many offenses, and the police were unable to change the perception that the quality of urban life was diminishing.

The Community Policing Era: 1970–Present

Beginning in the 1970s, there were calls for movement away from the overriding crime-fighting focus and toward greater emphasis on maintaining order and providing services to the community. Major research studies were published showing the complexities of police work and the extent to which day-to-day practices deviated from the ideals of the professional model. The research also questioned the effectiveness of the police in catching and deterring criminals. It indicated that increasing the number of patrol officers in a neighborhood had little effect on the crime rate and that it was difficult, if not impossible, to improve rates for solving crimes. Such findings undermined the underlying principles of the professional crime-fighter model.

Critics argued that the professional style isolated the police from the community and reduced their knowledge about and accountability to the neighborhoods that they served. Motorized patrols encapsulated officers inside their patrol cars so that they had few personal contacts with citizens. As an alternative, it was argued that police officers should get out of their cars and spend more time directly meeting and assisting citizens. This new approach would permit police to help people with a range of problems and place officers in the position of preventing some problems from developing or from escalating. For example, if police officers know about disagreements between individuals within a neighborhood, they can mediate and possibly prevent the conflict from growing into a criminal assault or other more serious problem. It was hoped that closer contact with citizens would not only permit the police to help neighborhood residents in new ways but also make those residents feel safer knowing that officers were available and interested in neighborhood problems.

In a provocative article, "Broken Windows: The Police and Neighborhood Safety," published in 1982, James Q. Wilson and George L. Kelling argued for a reorientation of policing to emphasize "little problems" such as the maintenance of order, provision of services to those in need, and adoption of strategies to reduce the fear of crime. They based their approach on three assumptions:

1. Neighborhood disorder creates fear. Areas with street people, youth gangs, prostitution, and drunks are high-crime areas.
2. Just as unrepaired broken windows are a signal that nobody cares and lead to more serious vandalism, untended disorderly behavior is a signal that the community does not care. This encourages more serious disorder and crime.
3. If the police are to deal with disorder to reduce fear and crime, they must rely on citizens for legitimacy and assistance.[8]

Advocates of the community policing approach urged a greater emphasis on foot patrols so that officers would become known to the citizens whom they served. Personal relationships and closer contact could lead citizens to cooperate more with police. Through a problem-oriented approach to policing, officers could be prepared to handle a range of problems for which citizens seek police help. In dealing with noisy teenagers, battered spouses, accident victims, and other problems, police could be encouraged to identify and address the underlying causes of problems within a community. By addressing various problems, small or large, within neighborhoods, the police could reduce disorder and the fear of crime. It was hoped that closer contacts between the police and the community would eliminate the adversarial relationships that had developed between officers and residents in many urban neighborhoods.

Although current reformers have argued for a greater focus on the order maintenance and service functions of the police, they do not advocate dropping the crime fighter role. Instead, they have called for a rearrangement of priorities. The police should pay greater attention to community needs and seek to better understand problems underlying crime, disorder, and incivility. These proposals have been adopted by police executives in many cities and by such influential bodies as the Police Foundation and the Police Executive Research Forum.

Questions still remain about community policing and whether it can or should be implemented throughout the nation. The populations in some cities, especially in the West, are too dispersed to permit a switch from motorized to foot patrols. In addition, some critics of community policing question whether the professional model really disconnected police from community residents and whether Americans actually want their police to be something other than crime fighters.

Whichever policy direction the police take—professional, crime fighter, or community policing—it must be implemented through a bureaucratic structure. We now turn to an examination of police organization in the United States.

Community policing emphasizes the need for officers to be in close contact with citizens so as to deal with problems and service needs as they arise.

THE ORGANIZATION OF THE POLICE IN THE UNITED STATES

As discussed in Chapter 2, the United States is a federal system with separate national and state structures each having authority over certain governmental functions. Most of the 17,500 police agencies at the national, state, county, and municipal levels are general-purpose agencies responsible for carrying out three functions: (1) law enforcement, (2) order maintenance, and (3) service to the community. They employ a total of more than 800,000 people, sworn and unsworn. The agencies include the following:

- 12,502 municipal police departments
- 3,086 sheriffs' departments
- 1,721 special police agencies (limited jurisdictions to transit systems, parks, schools, and so on)
- 49 state police departments (every state except Hawaii)
- 50 federal law enforcement agencies[9]

This list shows both the fragmentation and the local orientation of American police. The local nature of law enforcement is further illustrated by the fact that only 12 percent of the funds for police work are spent by the national government, 15 percent by state governments, and 73 percent by municipal and county governments. Each level of the governing system undertakes different kinds of responsibilities, either for different kinds of crimes, such as the federal authority over counterfeiting, or for different geographic locations, such as state police authority over major highways. Broadest authority tends to lie with local units that bear general responsibility for all policing tasks.

FEDERAL AGENCIES

Federal police organizations are part of the executive branch of the national government. They investigate a specific list of crimes defined by Congress. Recent federal efforts against drug trafficking, organized crime, insider stock trading, and environmental pollution have drawn significant public attention to these agencies even though they employ few agents and handle relatively few crimes.

The Federal Bureau of Investigation is an investigative agency with broad jurisdiction over all federal crimes not specifically placed under the responsibility of other agencies. Established as the Bureau of Investigation in 1908, it achieved national prominence under J. Edgar Hoover, its director from 1924 until his death in 1972. Hoover instituted major changes to increase the professionalism of the agency. He sought to remove political considerations from the selection of agents, instituted the national fingerprint filing system, and oversaw development of the Uniform Crime Reporting System. Although Hoover has been criticized for many aspects of his career, such as FBI spying on civil rights activists and antiwar protestors during the 1960s, his contributions to improved police work and the FBI's effectiveness are widely recognized.

Other federal agencies are concerned with specific kinds of crimes. Within the FBI is the semi-autonomous Drug Enforcement Administration (DEA). As part of the Treasury Department, the Internal Revenue Service pursues violations of laws related to the collection of taxes; the Bureau of Alcohol, Tobacco, and Firearms deals with alcohol, tobacco, and gun control; and the Customs Service deals with customs violations. Additional federal agencies concerned with specific areas of law enforcement include the Secret Service Division of the Treasury (counterfeiting, forgery, and protection of the president), the Bureau of Postal Inspection of the Postal Service (mail offenses), and the Border Patrol of the Department of Justice's Immigration and Naturalization Service. Some other departments of the executive branch, such as the U.S. Coast Guard, the National Parks Service, and the Postal Service, have police powers related to their specific duties.

STATE AGENCIES

Every state except Hawaii has its own police force with statewide jurisdiction. These agencies are typically small and do not handle the bulk of police work. The American reluctance to centralize police power has generally kept state forces from replacing local officials. State police forces were first established after the turn of the century, primarily as a wing of the executive branch of state government that would enforce the law when local officials did not. The Pennsylvania State Constabulary, established in 1905, was the first such force. By 1925, almost all of the states had an agency with some level of enforcement power.

All state forces regulate traffic on the main highways, and two-thirds of the states have also given them general police powers. In only about a dozen populous states, however, are state forces adequate to the task of general law enforcement outside the cities. Where the state police are well developed—as in Pennsylvania, New York, New Jersey, Massachusetts, and Michigan—they tend to fill a void in rural law enforcement. For the most part, however, they operate only in areas where no other form of police protection exists or where local officers request their expertise or the use of their facilities. In many states, for example, the crime laboratory is operated by the state police as a means of assisting all local law enforcement agencies.

COUNTY AGENCIES

Sheriffs are found in almost every one of the 3,100 counties in the United States. They are responsible for policing rural areas, but over time, particularly in the Northeast, many of their criminal justice functions have been assumed by the state or local police. In parts of the South and West, however, the sheriff's department remains a well-organized force. In thirty-three states, sheriffs have broad authority, are elected, and occupy the position of chief law enforcement officer in the county. Even when the sheriff's office is well organized, however, it may lack jurisdiction over cities and towns. In these situations, the sheriff and his or her deputies patrol unincorporated areas within the county or small towns that do not have adequate law enforcement personnel of their own.

In addition to having law enforcement responsibilities, the sheriff is often an officer of the court and is responsible for operating jails, serving court orders, and providing the bailiffs who must maintain order in courtrooms. In many counties, sheriffs can appoint their political supporters to be deputies and bailiffs; here, politics mixes with law enforcement. In other places, such as Los Angeles County and Oregon's Multnomah County, the sheriff's department is staffed by trained professionals.

MUNICIPAL AGENCIES

The police departments of cities and towns are vested by state law with general law enforcement authority. The sizes of city police forces range from more than 35,000 employees in the New York Police Department to only one sworn officer in 1,602 small towns. Nationally, nearly 90 percent of local police agencies serve populations of 25,000 or less, but half of all sworn officers are employed in cities of at least 100,000.[10]

In a metropolitan area composed of a central city and a number of independent suburbs, the policing function is usually divided among agencies at all governmental levels, and jurisdictional conflict may inhibit the efficient use of resources. The city and each suburb purchases its own equipment and deploys its officers without coordinating efforts with the neighboring jurisdictions. In some large-population areas, agreements have been made to facilitate cross-jurisdiction cooperation.

In essence, the United States is a nation of small police forces, each of which is authorized, funded, and operated independently within the limits of its jurisdiction. This is in direct contrast to the centralized organization of the police in other countries. For example, in France, the police are a national force divided between the Ministry of Interior and the Ministry of Defense. All police officers report directly to these national governmental departments in Paris.

Because of the fragmentation of police agencies in the United States, each jurisdiction develops its own enforcement priorities and policies. Each agency must make choices about how to organize and employ its resources to achieve its main objectives.

Criminal laws make a variety of behaviors punishable, and the police bear primary responsibility for apprehending lawbreakers. The police cannot, however, enforce every law and catch every lawbreaker. Legal rules limit the ways in which officers can investigate and pursue lawbreakers. For example, the constitutional prohibition against unreasonable searches and seizures prevents police from investigating many situations without search warrants.

Because the police have limited resources, they cannot have officers on every street during every minute of the day and night. This means that officials must make choices about how to deploy their resources by setting priorities as to which offenses will receive primary attention and which tactics will be employed. Police chiefs must decide, for example, whether to have officers patrol neighborhoods in cars or on foot. Changes in enforcement policy—for example, increasing the size of the night patrol or tolerating prostitution and other vice crimes—influence the amount of crime that comes to official attention and the system's ability to deal with offenders.

IDEAS IN PRACTICE

Soon after his appointment as chief of the Ledgecrest Police Department, Hal Lewis learned that he could not use the same tactics as when he was a captain in the Millbridge Police Department. In Millbridge, an industrial town of 150,000, youths arrested for stealing cars were taken to the station, booked, and usually given a night in jail.

Warned by Ledgecrest's assistant chief John Manning that in this upper-income suburban community the residents expected their delinquent sons and daughters to be brought home, not to the stationhouse, by the arresting officer, Lewis exploded, saying, "I'm no babysitter, I'm going to enforce the law, and that may mean that some of these snobby kids will learn what it's like to break the law!"

After seventeen-year-old Chip Lawson told his parents that he had been mistreated while awaiting their arrival at the stationhouse to post bond, the *Ledgecrest Ledger* editorialized that perhaps the "heavy-handed policies" of the new chief were not for the community. The editorial commented, "Perhaps that style worked in Millbridge, which has a crime problem, but in Ledgecrest we expect more from our police department."

If you were in Chief Lewis's position, what style of policing would you adopt for the Ledgecrest department?

As previously discussed, the police have emphasized their crime-fighting role for most of the past half-century. As a result, police in most communities focus on the categories of crimes documented in the FBI's *Uniform Crime Reports*. These are the crimes that make headlines and that politicians highlight when advocating increases in the police budget. They are also the crimes generally committed by the poor. Other crimes, such as white-collar crimes like forgery, embezzlement, or tax fraud, generally are viewed as less threatening by the public and thus receive less police attention. Voters pressure politicians and the police to emphasize enforcement of laws that help them to feel personally safe and secure in their daily lives.

Decisions about how police resources will be deployed influence the types of people arrested and processed through the criminal justice system. Place yourself in the position of a police chief and imagine the difficult choices you must make. Should a disproportionate number of officers be sent into high-crime areas? Should the police presence in the central business district be increased during shopping hours? What should be the mix between traffic control and crime fighting? These questions have no easy or automatic responses. Police officials must answer them according to their values and priorities.

American cities differ in their governmental, economic, and racial/ethnic characteristics, as well as their degree of urbanization. These factors can influence the style of policing expected by the community. In a now classic study, James Q. Wilson discovered that citizen expectations regarding police behavior are brought to bear through the political process in the choice of the top police executive. Not

Style	Defining Characteristics	Community Type
Watchman	Emphasis on maintaining order	Declining industrial city, mixed racial/ethnic composition, "blue collar"
Legalistic	Emphasis on law enforcement	Reform-minded city government, mixed socioeconomic composition
Service	Emphasis on service with balance between law enforcement and order maintenance	Middle-class suburban communities

TABLE 4.1

Styles of Policing
Wilson found three distinct styles of policing in the communities he studied. Each style places emphasis on different police functions, and each is associated with the particular characteristics of the community.

SOURCE: Based on James Q. Wilson, *Varieties of Police Behavior* (Cambridge, MA: Harvard University Press, 1968).

surprisingly, chiefs whose departments are run in ways that antagonize the community are likely to have their jobs for only a short time. Wilson's key finding was that the political culture, reflecting the socioeconomic characteristics of a city and its organization of government, exerted a major influence on whether a city's police force acted in accordance with one of three different styles of operation—watchman, legalistic, or service.[11] Table 4.1 documents these styles of policing and the types of communities in which they are found.

Departments with a **watchman style** emphasize order maintenance. Police administrators allow officers to ignore minor violations of the law, especially those involving traffic and juveniles, provided that there is general order. The police exercise discretion and deal informally with many infractions. Officers make arrests only for flagrant breaches of the law and when order cannot be maintained. The broad discretion exercised by officers can produce discrimination because officers do not treat members of different racial and ethnic groups in a uniform fashion.

In departments with a **legalistic style**, police work is marked by professionalism and an emphasis on law enforcement. Officers are expected to detain a high proportion of juvenile offenders, act vigorously against illicit enterprises, issue traffic tickets, and make a large number of misdemeanor arrests. They act as if there is a single standard of community conduct—that which the law prescribes—rather than different standards for juveniles, minorities, drunks, and other groups. Thus, although the officers may not discriminate in making arrests and issuing citations, the strict enforcement of laws, including traffic laws, can seem overly harsh to some segments of the community.

In suburban middle-class communities, a **service style** often predominates. Residents expect police work to be oriented toward providing service and feel they deserve individualizd treatment. Burglaries and assaults are taken seriously, while minor infractions tend to be addressed by informal, nonarrest sanctions, such as stern warnings.

Regardless of the style, even before police officers investigate crimes or make arrests, each police chief formulates policies that will influence the level and type of enforcement within a given community. Since the police are the entry point to the criminal justice system, developments in all segments of the system are shaped to a large extent by the decisions made by police officials. As community expectations shape decisions about enforcement priorities and the allocation of police resources, they simultaneously shape the cases that will ultimately be handled by prosecutors and corrections officials.

watchman style
A style of policing that emphasizes order maintenance whereby officers exercise discretion and deal informally with many infractions.

legalistic style
A style of policing that emphasizes professionalism and law enforcement whereby officers are expected to act against all infractions of the law and to employ a single standard of community conduct treating all groups the same.

service style
A style of policing that emphasizes the provision of services to the community and individualized treatment at the hands of the police.

Police work can be divided into three functional categories: order maintenance, law enforcement, and service.

POLICE FUNCTIONS

The police are expected to maintain the peace, prevent crime, and serve and protect the community. However, their day-to-day responsibilities include other tasks as well, many of them having little to do with crime and justice. Officers must direct traffic, handle accidents and illnesses, stop noisy gatherings, find missing persons, administer licensing regulations, provide ambulance services, take disturbed or inebriated people into protective custody, and so on. The list is long and varies from place to place. Some researchers have even suggested that the police have more in common with agencies of municipal social service than with the criminal justice system.

The American Bar Association has developed a list of police objectives and functions as a first step toward understanding how many different expectations they confront. The police are expected to serve at least eight functions:

1. Prevent and control conduct widely recognized as threatening to life and property (serious crime).
2. Aid individuals who are in danger of physical harm, such as the victim of a criminal attack.
3. Protect constitutional guarantees, such as the right of free speech and assembly.
4. Facilitate the movement of people and vehicles.
5. Assist those who cannot care for themselves: the intoxicated, the addicted, the mentally ill, the physically disabled, the old, and the young.
6. Resolve conflict, whether it be between individuals, groups of individuals, or individuals and their government.
7. Identify problems that have the potential for becoming more serious problems for the individual citizen, for the police, or for government.
8. Create and maintain a feeling of security in the community.[12]

It is easy to understand how the police gained such broad responsibilities. In many places, the police are the only public agency that is available seven days a week and twenty-four hours a day to respond to citizens' calls for help. They are also best able to perform the initial investigations for many kinds of problems. Moreover, the police ability to use force when necessary lets them intervene in problem situations and produce either voluntary or involuntary citizen compliance.

The functions of the police can be categorized into three main groups: (1) order maintenance, (2) law enforcement, and (3) service. Police agencies allocate their resources among these three primary functions and other activities according to community need, citizen requests, and departmental policy.

ORDER MAINTENANCE

order maintenance
The police function of preventing behavior that disturbs or threatens to disturb the public peace or that involves face-to-face conflict among two or more persons. In such situations the police exercise discretion in deciding whether a law has been broken.

The **order maintenance** function is a broad mandate to prevent behavior that either disturbs or threatens to disturb the public peace or that involves face-to-face conflict among two or more persons. A domestic quarrel, a noisy drunk, loud music in the night, a panhandler soliciting on the street, a tavern brawl—all represent disorder that may require the peacekeeping efforts of police. Unlike most criminal laws defining specific acts as illegal, laws regulating disorderly conduct deal with ambiguous situations that may be interpreted differently in light of the values and perceptions of individual police officers. For many crimes, it is obvious when the law has been broken. By contrast, order maintenance activities require the officer to make judgments not only about whether a law has been broken, but about whether any action should be taken, and if so, who should be blamed. In a bar fight, for example, the officer must decide who started the fight, whether an arrest should be made for assault, and whether to arrest other participants as well as the initiator of the conflict.

When we study the work of patrol officers, we can see that they are concerned primarily with behavior that either disturbs or threatens to disturb the peace. In these situations, they confront the public in ambiguous circumstances and have wide discretion in matters that affect people's lives. If an officer decides to arrest someone for disorderly conduct, that person may spend time in jail and possibly lose his or her job even if never convicted for the crime.

Officers find themselves in many situations that require discretionary judgments about order maintenance. They may be required to help persons in trouble, to manage crowds, to supervise a variety of services, and to assist people who are not fully accountable for what they do. The officers have significant discretion and control over how situations will develop. Patrol officers are not subject to direct external control. They have the power to arrest, but they also have the authority to decide against making an arrest. The order maintenance function is further complicated by the fact that the patrol officer is normally expected to "handle" a situation rather than to enforce the law, usually in an emotionally charged atmosphere. In controlling a crowd outside a rock concert, for example, the arrest of an unruly person may restore order by removing a troublemaker and serve as a warning to others that they could be arrested if they do not cooperate. On the other hand, an arrest may incite the crowd to hostility against the officers, making matters worse. It can be very difficult for officers to predict precisely how their discretionary decisions may promote or hinder order maintenance.

LAW ENFORCEMENT

The **law enforcement** function applies to situations in which the law has been violated, the identity or whereabouts of the violator needs to be determined, and the suspect must be apprehended. Police officers whose jobs focus exclusively on law enforcement are in the specialized branches of modern departments, such as the vice squad and the burglary detail. Although the patrol officer may be the first officer on the scene of a crime, in serious cases a detective usually prepares the case for prosecution by bringing together all the evidence for the prosecuting attorney. When the offender is identified but not located, the detective conducts the search. Alternatively, if the offender is not identified, the detective has the responsibility of analyzing clues to determine who committed the crime.

Although the police often portray themselves primarily as enforcers of the law, their effectiveness at this function has been questioned. For example, when a property crime is committed, the perpetrator usually has a time advantage over the police, which can limit the officers' ability to identify, locate, and arrest a suspect. Burglaries, for instance, usually occur when people are away from home. Thus, the crime may not be discovered until hours or days after the burglar has disappeared. The effectiveness of the police is further decreased when assault or robbery victims are unable to identify the offender. Victims frequently delay calling the police, reducing the likelihood that someone will be apprehended.

law enforcement
The police function of determining the identity or whereabouts of the violator and apprehending the suspect.

service

The police function of providing assistance to the public, usually in matters unrelated to crime.

SERVICE

Police are increasingly called on to perform a broad range of services for the general population, particularly lower-income citizens, in matters unrelated to crime. This **service** function—providing first aid, rescuing animals, extending social welfare, and so on—has become the dominant area of police activity especially at night and on weekends. Analysis of more than 26,000 calls to twenty-one police departments confirms the long-held belief that about 80 percent of citizens' requests for police intervention involve matters unrelated to crime; in fact, the largest percentage of calls, 21 percent, were requests for information.[13] Because the police department is readily accessible twenty-four hours a day, this is the agency to which people turn in times of trouble. Many departments provide information, operate ambulance services, locate missing persons, check locks on vacationers' homes, and intervene in suicide attempts.

It may appear that valuable resources are being diverted from law enforcement to service activities. However, performing service functions can help police in controlling crime. Through the service function, officers gain knowledge of the community, and citizens come to trust the police. Checking the security of buildings is the service that most obviously helps prevent crime, but other activities, such as dealing with runaways, drunks, and public quarrels, may help solve problems before they lead to criminal behavior.

Studies demonstrate that although the public may depend most heavily on the order maintenance and service functions of the police, they may *act* as though law enforcement—the catching of lawbreakers—is the most important function. According to public opinion polls, the crime-stopping image of the police is firmly rooted in citizens' minds and is a primary reason given by recruits for joining the force. Police administrators have learned that public support can be gained for budgets when the crime-fighting law enforcement function is stressed. This emphasis is demonstrated by the internal organization of metropolitan departments, wherein high status is accorded the officers, such as detectives, who perform this function. This focus leads to the creation of specialized units within the detective division to deal with such crimes as homicide, burglary, and auto theft. The assumption of police executives seems to be that all other requirements of the citizenry will be handled by the patrol division. In some departments, this pattern may create morale problems because extra resources are allocated and prestige devoted to a function that is concerned with a minority of the problems brought to the police. In essence, police are public servants occupied with peacekeeping, but they reinforce their own law enforcement image and the public's preoccupation with crime fighting.

POLICE ACTIONS

We have examined the organization of the police and the three functions of policing—law enforcement, order maintenance, and service. Now let us look at the everyday actions of the police as they deal with citizens in various—often highly discretionary—ways. We will then examine domestic violence as an example of the response of the police to one of many serious problems.

Police depend on the public to assist them in identifying crime and in carrying out investigations. Although most people are willing to assist the police, fear, self-interest, and other factors may keep some citizens from cooperating fully. Many people fail to call the police because they think it is not worth the effort and cost. They do not want to spend time filling out papers at the station, appearing as a witness, or confronting a neighbor or relative in court. In some low-income neighborhoods, citizens are reluctant to assist the police since past experience has shown that contact with law enforcement "only brings trouble." Without information about a crime, the police may decide not to pursue an investigation.

As indicated previously, the discretionary decisions of police officers determine which crimes will be targeted and which suspects will be arrested. Patrol officers—the most numerous, the lowest-ranking, the newest to police work—are vested with the greatest amount of discretion. This is necessary because patrol officers are out on the streets dealing with ambiguous situations. If they chase a young thief into an alley, they can decide outside of the view of the public whether to make an arrest or merely to recover the stolen property and give the offender a stern warning. It is patrol officers who are primarily responsible for maintaining order and enforcing such ambiguous laws as those concerning disorderly conduct, public drunkenness, breach of the peace, and other situations in which it is unclear if a law has been broken, which person committed the offense, and whether an arrest should be made. Wilson has caught the essence of the patrol officer's role when he describes it as "unlike that of any other occupation . . . one in which subprofessionals, working alone, exercise wide discretion in matters of utmost importance (life and death, honor and dishonor) in an environment that is apprehensive and perhaps hostile."[14]

In the final analysis, it is the individual officer on the scene who must define the situation, decide how it is to be handled, and determine whether and how the law should be applied. Four factors seem particularly influential with regard to police discretionary action:

1. *Characteristics of the crime.* The less serious a crime is to the public, the more freedom officers have to ignore it.
2. *The relationship between the alleged criminal and the victim.* The closer the personal relationship, the more variable the exercise of discretion. Family squabbles may not be as grave as they appear, and police are wary of making arrests since a spouse may, on reflection, decline to press charges.
3. *The relationship between the police and the criminal or victim.* A respectful complainant will be taken more seriously than an antagonistic one. Likewise, a respectful alleged wrongdoer is less likely to be arrested.
4. *Departmental policies.* The leadership of the chief and the city administration as reflected in the policy style will promote more or less discretion.[15]

In encounters between citizens and police, the matter of fairness is often intertwined with departmental

Police officers often encounter ambiguous situations, which they must resolve by employing discretion.

policy. When should the patrol officer frisk? When should a deal be made with the addict–informer? Which disputes should be mediated on the spot and which left to adjudicatory personnel? Surprisingly, these conflicts between the demands of justice and policy are seldom decided by heads of departments but are left largely to the discretion of the officer on the scene. In fact, departmental control over police actions is lacking in many types of activities.

Although some people advocate the development of detailed instructions to guide the police officer, such an exercise would probably be futile. No matter how detailed the formal instructions, the officer will still have to make judgments about how to apply the rules in each situation. At best, police administrators can develop guidelines and training that, one hopes, will give officers shared values and a common outlook to make decisions more consistent.

DOMESTIC VIOLENCE

By looking at police actions with respect to domestic violence, we can see the links between police–citizen encounters, the exercise of discretion, and actions taken (or not taken) by officers. Domestic violence, also called "battering" and "spouse abuse," has been defined as assaultive behavior involving adults who are married or who have an ongoing or prior intimate relationship. In the overwhelming number of cases, domestic violence is perpetrated by men against women and is not limited to specific socioeconomic groups. In fact, a national survey of two thousand families led researchers to estimate that during any one year 1.7 million Americans had faced a spouse wielding a knife or gun and that well over 2 million had experienced a severe beating at the hands of a spouse.[16] Once a woman is victimized by domestic violence, she faces a high risk of being victimized again. *Uniform Crime Reports* data have also shown that 30 percent of all female murder victims were killed by their husbands or boyfriends.[17]

Despite the prevalence of domestic violence (or perhaps because of it), American society has tended in the past not to do very much about it. As recently as 1970, most citizens and criminal justice agencies largely regarded domestic violence as a "private" affair best settled within the family. Concern was often expressed that police involvement would only make the situation more difficult for the victim, because she faced the possibility of reprisal.

From the viewpoint of most police departments, domestic violence was thought to be a "no-win" situation in which officers responding to calls for help were often set upon by one or both disputants. If an arrest was made, the police found that the victim often refused to cooperate with a prosecution. In addition, entering a residence to handle such an emotion-laden incident was thought to be more dangerous than answering calls to investigate "real" criminal behavior. Many officers believed that intervention in family disputes was a leading cause of officer deaths and injury.

Police response to an instance of domestic violence is an excellent example of a highly charged, uncertain, and potentially dangerous encounter with citizens in which officers must exercise discretion. In such a situation, how does an officer maintain order and enforce the law in accordance with the criminal law, departmental policies, and the needs of the victim?

In the past, most departments advised officers to try to calm the parties and to make referrals to social service agencies rather than to arrest the attacker. Police departments began to reconsider their policies when research in Minneapolis and other cities indicated that abusive spouses who are arrested and jailed briefly are much less likely to commit acts of domestic violence again. Although these studies did not produce identical results, the research led some departments to order their officers to make arrests in every case in which there was evidence of an assault. Other departments developed arrest policies in response to lawsuits against police by injured women who claimed that the police ignored evidence of criminal assaults and effectively permitted the abusive spouse to inflict serious injuries. In addition, because there is a growing sense that domestic violence situations can no longer be left to the discretionary judgments of individual patrol officers, training programs on the dynamics of domestic violence have been developed in most large departments and police academies to educate officers about the important problem.

Even though we can point to a number of policy changes with respect to domestic violence, the fact remains that it is the officer in the field who must handle these situations. As with most law enforcement situations, laws, guidelines, and training help; but, as is often true in police work, the discretionary judgment of the officer inevitably determines what actions will be taken.

SUMMARY

Policing in the United States has been shaped by the English practices brought by British colonists and by changing social conditions that affected each region of the country. The organization of American police is decentralized and fragmented because of the federal system of government. Police agencies throughout the country embody limited authority and local control because of concerns that law enforcement agencies remain accountable to and controlled by elected officials and the local community.

The historical eras of American policing are the Political Era, the Professional Era, and the Community Policing Era. Changing values and conditions within each era determined how the police would prioritize and carry out their functions for law enforcement, order maintenance, and service. Inevitably, individual police administrators must make choices about which functions to emphasize, and these choices are often affected by the political dynamics of the local community. The watchman, legalistic, and service styles of policing each reflect different needs and values expressed by people within the communities served by the police.

In their daily duties, the police have often been occupied mainly by service and order maintenance tasks requested by the public in calls for assistance. However, the police still portray themselves primarily as crime fighters because politicians and the public as well as many officers themselves view the police mandate as primarily concerned with crime and justice.

Police officers are dependent on the public for providing assistance and information that will facilitate effective fulfillment of each police function. In

IDEAS IN PRACTICE

Once more, the police were called to the Trembley apartment. At the door, a distraught Janet Trembley met Officers Kendall and Park. She was crying, and there was a red swelling on her face. The two Trembley children, also crying, clutched at their mother's legs.

"This time I want him arrested," she told the officers.

"Are you sure? The last time this happened you were at the station the next morning pleading for his release," responded Officer Kendall.

"I know. But this time, I mean it. We can't go on like this," said Janet.

"Are you going to let him back into this apartment when he is released?" queried Officer Park.

"I'm going to have to face that when the time comes. I have nowhere to go, and we need his earnings. But he can't continue to act like that."

"All right. Do you know where we can find him?"

"Yes, he's probably at the Tip Top Bar, down the street."

What should Officers Kendall and Park do? Can this problem be solved by an arrest and prosecution?

any given situation, however, the discretionary decisions of individual officers largely determine what will happen to the suspects, victims, and witnesses involved. Police departments may attempt to develop policies that will guide officers' discretion and facilitate effective communication and cooperation with the public, as in the case of domestic violence. Despite any efforts to develop clear policies, the authority of individual officers to make discretionary judgments remains central to everyday policing.

QUESTIONS FOR REVIEW

1. What principles borrowed from England still underlie policing in the United States?
2. What are the three eras of U.S. policing, and how are they characterized?
3. What are the functions of the police, and what styles of policing can departments employ as they seek to fulfill these functions for their communities?
4. How does the problem of domestic violence illustrate basic elements of police action?

NOTES

1. Peter Manning, *Police Work* (Cambridge, MA: MIT Press, 1977), p. 82.
2. George L. Kelling and Mark H. Moore, "The Evolving Strategy of Policing," *Perspectives on Policing*, National Institute of Justice (November 1988).
3. Eric H. Monkkonen, *Police in Urban America, 1860–1920* (Cambridge: Cambridge University Press, 1981), p. 127.
4. J. F. Richardson, *Urban Police in the United States* (Port Washington, NY: National University Publications, 1974), p. 19; Dennis C. Rousey, "Cops and Guns: Police Use of Deadly Force in Nineteenth Century New Orleans," *American Journal of Legal History* 28 (1984), pp. 41–66.
5. Roger McGrath, *Gunfighters, Highwaymen, and Vigilantes: Violence on the California Frontier* (Berkeley: University of California Press, 1984).
6. Monkkonen, *Police in Urban America, 1860–1920*, p. 127.
7. Mark H. Moore and George L. Kelling, "'To Serve and Protect': Learning from Police History," *Public Interest* (Winter 1983), p. 55.
8. James Q. Wilson and George L. Kelling, "Broken Windows: The Police and Neighborhood Safety," *Atlantic Monthly* (March 1982), pp. 29–38.
9. U.S. Bureau of Justice Statistics, *Bulletin* (July 1993), p. l.
10. U.S. Department of Justice, *Bulletin*, p. 9.
11. James Q. Wilson, *Varieties of Police Behavior* (Cambridge, MA: Harvard University Press, 1968).
12. Herman Goldstein, *Policing a Free Society* (Cambridge, MA: Ballinger, 1977), p. 35.
13. Eric J. Scott, *Calls for Service: Citizen Demand and Initial Police Response*, U.S. Department of Justice (Washington, DC: Government Printing Office, 1981), pp. 26–37.
14. Wilson, *Varieties of Police Behavior*, p. 30.
15. Herbert Jacob, *Urban Justice* (Boston: Little, Brown, 1973), p. 27.
16. Murray A. Straus, Richard J. Gelles, and Suzanne K. Steinmetz, *Behind Closed Doors: Violence in the American Family* (Garden City, NY: Anchor Press, 1980), pp. 25–26, 32–36.
17. U.S. Department of Justice, *Crime in the United States* (Washington, DC: Government Printing Office, 1990), p. 39.

CHAPTER 5
Police Operations

DANGEROUS PURSUIT IN THE PUBLIC SPOTLIGHT

On Friday, June 17, 1994, television screens in households across the country were filled with the spectacle of police cars and helicopters following a white Ford Bronco down the highways of Los Angeles. Inside the car, sports hero O. J. Simpson sat crouched in the back seat with a small gun pressed against his own chin while Simpson's former football teammate and childhood friend, Al Cowlings, drove. Helicopter camera crews provided live television coverage as national network news anchors described the police pursuit.

On the preceding Sunday, June 12, Simpson's former wife Nicole had been murdered on her own front steps in a vicious knife attack, along with a young restaurant waiter who had gone to her home to return some sunglasses. Throughout the intervening week, police had searched for evidence at Nicole's home and at O. J.'s home. By Friday, Los Angeles prosecutor Gil Garcetti had decided that sufficient evidence had been found to charge Simpson with murder. Defense attorney Robert Shapiro arranged for Simpson to be taken into custody at a friend's home where Simpson had been staying. However, when the police arrived, he and Cowlings had left.

Six hours later, police identified the location of Simpson's moving car by tracing his cellular phone calls. Simpson threatened to kill himself when he spoke on the phone as Cowlings drove him across Los Angeles. The police were faced with a difficult dilemma. If they stopped Simpson's car, he might kill himself or they might be forced to shoot him if he threatened officers with the gun. If they did not stop the car, however, there was nothing to stop Simpson from using the gun on himself or others. The police would then be criticized for not immediately apprehending a suspect whose location they knew.

Finally, Cowlings drove to Simpson's home where the police were waiting. While a SWAT team trained their guns on Simpson, he crouched in the car, gun in hand, talking by cellular phone to police a few feet away, inside the house. Police negotiator Pete Weireter talked to Simpson for forty-five minutes, trying to persuade him to surrender. When he finally agreed, the SWAT team was advised that he did not have a gun in his hands. Any false move might have resulted in a nationally televised shooting, but Simpson left the car and collapsed into the arms of officers.

The incident ended peacefully, but questions remained. Were the police overly cautious because they were dealing with a celebrity? Did they create extra danger by permitting him to drive back to his home in a residential neighborhood where he might have fired at officers and bystanders?

The police are expected to deal with some of the most difficult and controversial social problems such as crime, violence, racial tensions, and drugs. This is a tall order—especially since they must attempt to do so within the limits of the law. When highly publicized crimes occur, constant public scrutiny may make the task even harder.

In this chapter, we focus on police operations—the actual work of police agencies as they pursue offenders and prevent crimes. The police must be organized so that patrol efforts can be coordinated, investigations conducted, arrests made, evidence assembled, crimes solved, and violators prosecuted. ★

ORGANIZATION OF THE POLICE

CHAPTER QUESTIONS

How are the police organized?

What is the purpose of patrol, and how is it carried out?

What is the role of the detective?

What legal mandates guide police actions?

The police have traditionally been organized in a military manner. A structure of ranks from patrol officer to sergeant, lieutenant, captain, and up to chief helps designate the authority and responsibilities at each level in the organization. The superior–subordinate relationships in this organizational model emphasize discipline, control, and accountability, which are considered important for both efficiently mobilizing police resources and ensuring that civil liberties are protected. If police officers are accountable to their superiors, then they are less likely to abuse their authority by needlessly interfering with the personal freedom and rights of citizens.

The structure of a well-organized police department, such as the one shown in Figure 5.1, is designed to fulfill five functions:

1. Apportion the work load among members and units according to a logical plan.
2. Ensure that lines of authority and responsibility are as definite and direct as possible.
3. Specify a unity of command throughout so that there is no question as to which orders should be followed.
4. Link responsibilities with commensurate authority. If the authority is delegated, the user is held accountable.
5. Coordinate the efforts of members and units so that all will work harmoniously to accomplish their mission.

Large police departments divide the city into districts or precincts so that most operations affecting the districts can function within them. This may permit the police to allocate resources and supervise personnel with greater sensitivity to the needs and problems in particular neighborhoods. Although specialized units are frequently located in the centralized police headquarters for the city, patrol and traffic units may be dispersed to district stations.

Major police departments assign their officers to specialized units that emphasize specific functions: patrol, investigation, traffic, vice, and juvenile. These units perform the basic tasks of crime prevention and control. The patrol and investigation (detective) units are the core of the modern department. The patrol unit handles a wide range of functions, including preventing crime, apprehending offenders, mediating domestic quarrels, helping the ill, and providing assistance at accidents. The investigation unit specializes in the identification, apprehension, and conviction of lawbreakers who commit serious crimes. The separation of patrol and investigation can create difficulties because the units' responsibilities overlap. While the investigation unit usually concentrates on murder, rape, and major robberies, the patrol unit also investigates the much more numerous lesser crimes.

The extent to which departments create specialized internal units may depend on the size of the city and its police force. While many departments typically have traffic units, only police departments in midsized to large cities also maintain specialized vice and juvenile units. As a result of the war on drugs, some cities have specialized units working only on this problem. Large departments usually have an internal affairs section to investigate charges of

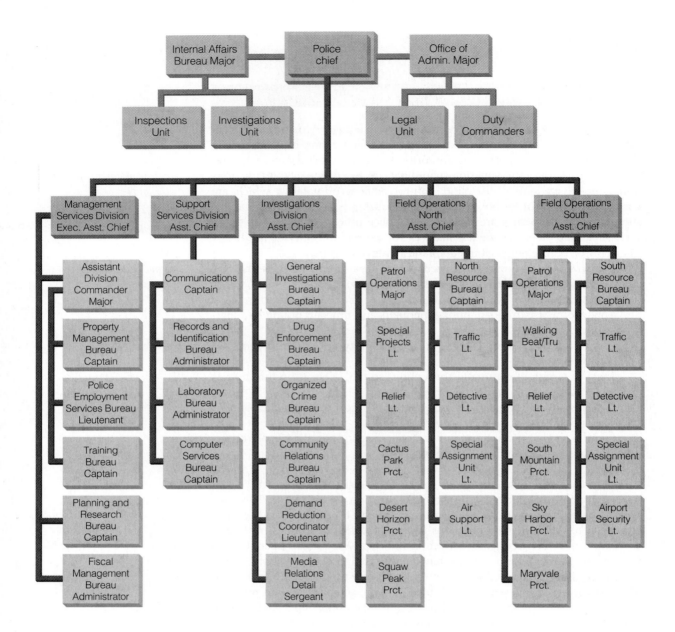

FIGURE 5.1

Structural Organization of the Phoenix, Arizona, Police Department
This is a typical police organization. Note the major divisions of patrol, special operations, investigation, and management and technical services. The administration of the internal affairs bureau is closely tied to the chief.

SOURCE: City of Phoenix, Arizona, Police Department, *Annual Report*, 1990.

corruption against officers and other disciplinary problems associated with the staff and officers. The juvenile unit is concerned primarily with crime prevention as it works with young people. All specialized units depend on the patrol officers for information and assistance.

In considering how police decisions are made, it is important to keep in mind the role of the police as a bureaucracy within the broader criminal justice system. Three points stand out. First, the police are the gateway to the justice system through which information and individuals enter to be processed. Based on their discretionary powers, police determine which suspects will be arrested and moved into the system. Those cases sent to the prosecutor for charging and then on to the courts for adjudication have their beginning with an individual officer's decision that probable cause exists to arrest. The care taken by the officer in making the arrest and collecting evidence has a significant impact on the ultimate success of the prosecution. The outcome of the case, whether through plea bargaining by lawyers or through a trial with a judge and jury, hinges on the police officer's decisions and information gathering that set the case in motion.

Second, the administrative decision making of the police is influenced by the fact that the ultimate outcome of a case is largely in the hands of others. The police officers introduce the suspects into the criminal justice process, but they cannot control the decisions made by prosecutors and judges after that point. In some cases, the police officers may feel that their efforts have been wasted if the prosecutor agrees to a plea bargain that does not, in the eyes of the officer, adequately punish the offender. The potential for conflict between police and other decision makers within the justice system is increased by the social status differences between lawyers, including judges, who have graduate degrees and elite status, and the police officers, many of whom do not have college degrees.

Third, as part of a bureaucracy, police officers are expected to observe rules and follow the orders of superiors while simultaneously exercising independent, discretionary judgments. They are duty-bound to stay in line within their chain of command, yet they are also responsible for independent choices in response to incidents occurring on the streets. To understand the impact of these organizational factors on the behavior of the police, let us examine two aspects of their daily activities—organizational response and productivity.

POLICE RESPONSE AND ACTION

In a democracy, people do not want police on every street corner questioning them about what they are doing. Such an atmosphere would reduce the feeling of individual freedom that Americans expect. Thus, the police are organized to be primarily **reactive** (responding to citizen calls for service) rather than **proactive** (initiating actions in the absence of citizen requests). Studies of police work indicate that 81 percent of actions result from citizen telephone calls, 5 percent are initiated by citizens who request service in the field by approaching an officer, and only 14 percent are initiated in the field by an officer. These facts influence the organization of departments and the way the police respond to a case.

Because they are primarily reactive, the police are usually able to arrive at the scene only after the crime has been committed and the perpetrator has fled. This means that the police are hampered by the time lapse and by inaccurate information given by witnesses. For example, crimes such as muggings may happen so quickly that victims and witnesses are not able to accurately describe what happened. In about a third of the calls to the police, no citizen is present when the police arrive on the scene. Citizens have come to expect that the police will respond quickly to *every* call, not discriminating among those that require immediate attention and those that can be handled in a more routine manner. The result is what is called "incident-driven policing."[1] To a large extent, then, reports by victims and observers define the boundaries of policing.

The police do employ proactive strategies such as surveillance and undercover work to combat some crimes. The police must rely on informers, stakeouts, wiretapping, stings, and raids when addressing crimes without direct victims. Because of society's current focus on drug offenses, police

reactive
Occurring in response to a stimulus, such as police activity in response to notification that a crime has been committed.

proactive
An active search for offenders on the part of the police in the absence of reports of violations of the law. Arrests for crimes without victims are usually proactive.

resources in many cities have been redistributed to emphasize proactive efforts to apprehend people who use or sell illegal drugs.

ORGANIZATIONAL RESPONSE

How the police respond to citizens' calls for assistance is greatly influenced by the organization of the police bureaucracy. Administrative factors that affect the response process include the separation of police into various functional groups (patrol, vice, investigation, and so on), the quasi-military command system, and the various incentives to induce patrol officers to respond in desired ways.

Police organizations are being reshaped by new communications technology, which has increasingly centralized decision making. The core of modern police departments is the communications center, where commands are given to activate officers. Patrol officers are expected to be in constant touch with headquarters and are required to report each of their actions. Two-way radio has become the primary means for police administrators to monitor the decisions of the officer in the field. Whereas in former times patrol officers might have administered their own version of on-the-spot justice to a mischievous juvenile, they may now be expected to file a report, take the delinquent into custody, and initiate formal proceedings. Because patrol officers must call headquarters with reports about each incident, police headquarters is better able to guide and control some elements of patrol officers' discretion and ensure that they comply with departmental policies.

In most cities, citizens can report crimes or call for information or assistance through the standardized "911" telephone number. Development of the 911 procedure has resulted in many departments being inundated with calls, many of which are not directly related to police responsibilities. The Close-Up box shows how emotionally draining the work of a 911 operator often is.

differential response
A patrol strategy that prioritizes calls for service and assigns various response options.

To improve efficiency, police departments use a strategy of **differential response** that prioritizes calls for service and assigns various response options. The strategy assumes that it is not always necessary to rush a patrol car to the scene when a call is received. The most appropriate response to a call depends on several factors—such as whether the incident is in progress, has just occurred, or occurred some time ago; and whether anyone is or could be injured. A dispatcher receives the calls and asks for certain facts about the crime or need for service. The dispatcher may send an officer or other personnel immediately to the scene, may give a lower priority so that the response is delayed, or may refer the caller to another agency. Differential police response saves resources because patrol units are not diverted to nonemergency situations.

The centralization of communications and decision making has been criticized by some experts. Many advocates of community policing believe that advancements in technology tend to isolate the police from the citizens they serve. As we discussed in Chapter 4, the extensive use of motorized patrols has meant that residents have only a fleeting glimpse of officers as they cruise through their neighborhoods. Community-oriented policing represents one attempt to overcome some of the negative aspects of centralized response.

PRODUCTIVITY

The police have great difficulty measuring the quantity and quality of their work, partly because of the wide variety of responsibilities and day-to-day tasks of officers. Traditionally, the crime rate and the clearance rate have been

CLOSE-UP
Holding the 911 Line

It's a new day. I walk down to the basement of the public-safety building, pass through a secured entrance and walk slowly down a long, quiet corridor. My stomach tightens a bit as I approach a final locked door. . . . I'm in the Phoenix Police Communications Center, known as "911." . . .

It's 0800 hours. I take a deep breath, say a little prayer and hope that I don't make any mistakes that might get me on the 6 o'clock news. This will be my not-so-happy home for the next 10 hours.

"911, what is your emergency?" It's my first call of the day. The woman is crying but calm. She has tried to wake her elderly husband. With the push of a button I connect her to the fire department. They ask if she wants to attempt CPR, but she says, "No, he's cold and blue . . . I'm sure he's dead." I leave the sobbing widow in the hands of the fire dispatcher. I'm feeling sad, but I just move on. I have more incoming calls to take. It's busy this morning. The orange lights in each corner of the room are shining brightly, a constant reminder that nonemergency calls have been holding more than 90 seconds. My phone console appears to be glowing, covered with blinking red lights. It's almost hypnotic, like when you sit in the dark and stare at a lit Christmas tree, or gaze into a flickering fireplace. But then I remember that each light represents a person—a person with a problem, someone in crisis.

A loud bell is ringing. It means an emergency call is trying to get through but the lines are jammed. All operators are already on a call. I quickly put my caller on hold. He's just reporting a burglary that occurred over the weekend. . . .

"911, what is your emergency?" This one's serious. A bad traffic accident, head-on collision.

"Yes, sir, we'll get right out there." I get officers started and advise the fire department. Now everyone in the vicinity of the accident is calling. "Yes, ma'am, we're on the way." "We'll be out shortly, sir, thanks for calling." My supervisor comes out of his office to advise us of something. He always looks serious, but this time it's different. He looks worried and upset. He tells us that two of our detectives were involved in the collision. He doesn't know who they are or how badly they're injured. My heart stops momentarily because my husband is a detective. I quickly call the office and confirm that he is safe. I'm relieved but still stunned. . . . But there's not much time for sentiment. There are more calls to take, more decisions to make and more pressures needing attention. . . .

"911, what is your emergency?" It's just a boy on a phone getting his kicks by calling me vulgar names. He hangs up before I have a chance to educate him on correct 911 usage. We get a lot of trivial calls, pranksters, hang-ups, citizens complaining to us about a noncrime situation, something they should handle themselves. People call us because they don't know where to turn. Everyone must be treated fairly and with respect. It's a difficult balance to maintain.

My supervisor again comes out to advise us. His face shows a sadness I've never seen in him. "The officers were killed in the accident." A quietness descends over the room. I suppose the bells are still ringing and the lights flashing but I don't hear or see them. The typing stops; talking ceases. I just want to get out of here and cry, but I have to stay and do my job. I have to keep going. I can break down on my long drive home tonight; for now I have phones to answer, people to help.

SOURCE: Tracy Lorenzano, "Holding the 911 Line," *Newsweek*, 20 June 1994, p. 10. Copyright 1994 by Newsweek, Inc. All rights reserved. Reprinted by permission.

used as measures of "good" policing. A declining crime rate might be cited as evidence of an effective department, but critics can point to reasons unrelated to policing that affect this measure.

The **clearance rate**, one basic measure of police performance, refers to the percentage of crimes known to police that they believe they have solved through an arrest. The clearance rate varies with each category of offense. In situations such as burglary, in which the police learn about the crime hours or even days after its commission, the clearance rate is only about 14 percent. Police are much more successful handling violent crimes (46 percent), in which victims tend to know their assailants.[2] Proactive police operations have

clearance rate
The percentage of crimes known to the police that they believe they have solved through an arrest; a statistic used as a measure of a police department's productivity.

even higher clearance rates because the police catch offenders as they commit illegal acts.

These measures of productivity may be supplemented by data that reflect other actions taken during an officer's shift—the number of traffic citations issued, illegally parked cars ticketed, suspects stopped for questioning, and the value of stolen goods recovered. An officer may work hard for many hours yet have no arrests or other actions that fit the traditional measures of productivity.[3] Although difficult to measure, it may be more beneficial to society when officers spend their time calming disputes, becoming acquainted with citizens in neighborhoods, and providing services to people who need all kinds of help.

POLICE UNITS AND SERVICES

line functions
Police actions that directly involve field operations such as patrol, investigation, traffic control, vice and juvenile crimes, and so on.

staff functions
Police actions that supplement or support the line functions, based in the chief's office and the auxiliary services and staff inspection bureaus.

sworn officers
Police employees who have taken an oath and been given powers by the state to make arrests, apply necessary force, and so on in accordance with their duties.

Within service bureaucracies such as the police, a distinction is often made between line and staff functions. **Line functions** are those that directly involve field operations such as patrol, investigation, traffic control, vice and juvenile crimes, and so on. By contrast, **staff functions** supplement or support the line functions. Staff functions are based in the chief's office and the auxiliary services bureau as well as in the staff inspection bureau. The efficient police department has a proper balance between line and staff duties, coordinated into an effective crime control, order maintenance, and service force. Most officers are in line functions handling patrol, investigations, and special operations.

PATROL

Patrol is often called the backbone of police operations.[4] Every modern police department in the United States has a patrol unit. Even in large specialized departments, patrol officers constitute up to two-thirds of all **sworn officers**—police employees who have taken an oath and been given powers by the state to make arrests, apply necessary force, and so on in accordance with their duties. In small communities, police operations are not specialized, and the patrol force *is* the department. The patrol officer is the police generalist and must be prepared on any given day for any imaginable situation and many responsibilities.

Patrol Functions

Television has given citizens an image of the patrol officer as always on the go—rushing from one incident to another and making a number of arrests during the course of a shift. The patrol officer may indeed be called to deal with robberies in progress or to help rescue people from burning buildings. While these activities may represent the pinnacle of excitement and importance in police work, however, the patrol officer's life is not always exciting. The patrol officer may encounter challenging and satisfying tasks, but this same officer may also be called on to handle routine and even boring tasks such as directing traffic at accident scenes and road construction sites. Research has shown that most officers, on most shifts, do not make even one arrest.[5] To better understand patrol work, note the allocation of time for various patrol activities by the police of Wilmington, Delaware, as shown in Figure 5.2.

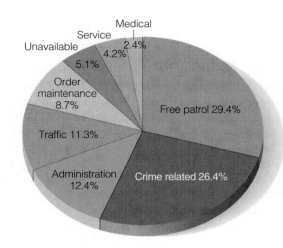

Free Patrol: park and walk

Crime related: officer in trouble, suspicious person/vehicle, crime in progress, alarm, investigate crime not in progress, service warrant/subpoena, assist other police

Administration: meal break, report writing, firearms training, police vehicle maintenance, at headquarters, court related

Traffic: accident investigation, parking problems, motor vehicle driving problems, traffic control, fire emergency

Order maintenance: order maintenance in progress, animal complaint, noise complaint

Service: service related

Medical: medical emergency, at local hospital

The patrol function has three components: (1) answering calls for assistance, (2) maintaining a police presence, and (3) probing suspicious circumstances. Patrol officers are well suited to answering calls, because they are usually near the scene and can render timely help or speedily move to apprehend a suspect. When not responding to calls, they engage in **preventive patrol**—that is, making the police presence known—on the assumption that doing so will both deter crime and make officers available to respond quickly to calls within neighborhoods. Either walking the streets of a neighborhood or cruising in a vehicle, the patrol officer is constantly on the lookout for suspicious people and behavior. With experience, officers come to believe in their own abilities to spot signs of suspicious activity that merit further investigation or intervention by questioning people on the street.

Patrol officers also perform the important function of helping to maintain smooth relations between police and community. As the most visible members of the criminal justice system, they can have a profound effect on the willingness of citizens to cooperate in an investigation. When police officers earn the trust and respect of the residents of the neighborhoods they patrol, people are much more willing to cooperate in providing information about crimes and suspicious activities. Effective work by patrol officers can also help reduce citizens' fear of crime and foster a sense of security among residents within a neighborhood.

When patrol officers' duties are described, they sound fairly straightforward, yet these officers often find themselves in complex situations requiring sound judgments and careful actions. As the first to arrive at a crime scene, the officer must simultaneously comfort and render aid to victims, identify and question witnesses, control crowds, and gather evidence. This requires effective communication and creativity.

Because the patrol officer has the most direct contact with members of the public, the police department's image in and relationship with the community derives from patrol officers' actions. Moreover, successful investigations and prosecutions frequently depend on patrol officers' actions in questioning witnesses and gathering evidence in the immediate aftermath of a crime. As you read the Close-Up "Saturday Night in a Squad Car," think of the variety of events that come to the attention of patrol officers. How would you handle these situations?

Because the patrol officer's job involves the most sensitive contact with the public, it is important that the best-qualified officers do this work.

FIGURE 5.2

Percentage of Time Allocated to Various Patrol Activities by the Police of Wilmington, Delaware
The time spent on various activities was accumulated by analyzing activity records for each police car unit. Note the range of activities and the time allocated for each.
SOURCE: Jack H. Green and Carl B. Klockars, "What Police Do," in *Thinking About Police*, 2nd ed., ed. Carl B. Klockars and Stephen D. Mastrofski (New York: McGraw-Hill, 1991), p. 279.

preventive patrol
Providing regular protection to an area while maintaining a mobile police presence to deter crime.

Saturday Night in a Squad Car

Car 120 covers an area one-half mile wide by one mile long in the heart of downtown Minneapolis. Bisecting the district along its long axis is Hennepin Avenue, a street lined with bars, nightclubs, and movie theaters. South of Hennepin Avenue lie the shopping and business areas of Minneapolis; north of Hennepin are warehouses and older office buildings. At the east end of the district lies the Mississippi River, and along it, just north of Hennepin Avenue, is the Burlington Northern Railway Station. That portion of the district is heavily populated with derelict alcoholics.

6:45: We saw some derelicts drinking wine, and the officers forced them to pour the wine out.

7:00: 9 West Franklin, Apt., unwanted guest. The caretakers of the apartment building advised us that the ex-husband of one of their tenants was threatening harm to the tenant and abduction of the tenant's child. He had also threatened the baby-sitter. We determined the kind of car that the ex-husband was driving. The tenant then returned with a friend and asked us to keep out of the area so that her husband would not be afraid to find her. She then hoped to tell him that the divorce was final and that he ought not to bother her any more.

7:50: Cassius Bar, fight. It had been settled by the time we arrived.

7:58: Cafe, domestic. A 20-year-old girl and her sister-in-law met us and advised us that the girl's stepfather, the proprietor of the cafe, had let the air out of the tires of the girl's car. He had also pulled loose some wires under the hood and then blocked their car with his. All of this had occurred in the cafe's parking lot. She also claimed that he had hit her. We talked to the stepfather and mother of the girl, and they said that they had taken this action in order to prevent the girl from driving to Wisconsin until she had cooled down. They claimed that she had had a fight with her husband, that she wanted to get away by driving to see her grandmother in Wisconsin, and that she was too emotionally upset to drive. This was apparently evidenced by the fact that she was willing to take her baby with her in only a short-sleeved shirt. The mother also told us that the girl was a bad driver with many arrests and that the car wasn't safe. The officers advised the girl that she call a tow truck and that, if she wished, she could sign a complaint against her parents in the morning. We then left.

8:28: Cafe, "settle it this time." The sister-in-law claimed that she had been verbally abused by the stepfather. The officers decided to wait until the tow truck arrived. The stepfather moved the car that was blocking. The parents of the girl began to criticize the officer in sarcastic terms, saying such things as "Isn't it a shame that the police have nothing better to do than to spend hours helping to start a car." They also threatened not to give half-price food to police officers any more. The tow truck arrived and reinflated the tires of the car. However, the tow truck driver was unable to start the car. The stepfather, although advised by one of the officers not to do so, tried to move his car in a position to block his daughter's car. The officer at that point booked him for reckless driving and fail-

---

Unfortunately, the low status of patrol assignments encourages officers to seek more prestigious positions such as that of detective. A major challenge facing policing is to accord status and rewards to patrol officers that reflect the function's importance to society and the criminal justice system.

Issues in Patrolling

In the last twenty years or so, much research has been done on methods of allocating patrol officers and choosing various means of transportation and communication. Though the results of these studies are not definitive, they have caused police specialists to rethink some traditional aspects of patrolling. However, patrol practices that may appear to researchers to be the most effective often run counter to the desires of departmental personnel. The issues now confronting police administrators include the following: (1) allocation of

ure to obey a lawful police order. The officer had the stepfather's car towed away. Another squad car came to sit on the situation until the tow truck had moved the girl's car to a service station. We took the stepfather to jail, where he immediately arranged to bail himself. The stepfather said that he was going right back. The officer replied, "We can book you more than you've got money." As soon as we left the police station, we went back to the parking lot and found that the girl's car had been started and that she had left town.

9:55: Spruce, Apt. unwanted guest. The tenant told us that she had been ill and that she had not opened the door when her landlady knocked. The landlady then had opened the door and walked in. The officers [told] the landlady, "You can't just walk in. You are invading her privacy." The landlady replied, "The hell I can't, you damned hippie-lover. I'm going to call the mayor." "Go ahead," the officer said. He then added, "The next time this happens, we will advise the tenant to use a citizen's arrest on you."

10:35: We saw a woman crying outside a downtown bar and a man with his hands on her. We stopped but were told by both that this was merely a domestic situation.

10:50: The officers saw a drunk in an alley, awakened him and sent him on his way.

10:55: We saw a door open in a downtown automobile dealership. When we checked, we learned that all the employees were there to carry out an inventory.

11:15: We noticed an elderly man in a car talking to a number of rather rough-looking motorcycle types. We stopped and learned from the motorcyclists that the man was very intoxicated. They offered to drive the car for him to a parking spot, and the officers allowed them to do this. The man was told by the officers to sleep off his drunk condition, and the officers took the keys from the car and threw them into the trunk so that he would be unable to drive further that evening.

11:45: 15th and Hawthorne, gang fight. When we arrived, the officers from two other squad cars were busy booking some young men. The officers believed that occupants of the top floor of the building adjoining this corner had been throwing things at them. When the landlord refused admittance to that building, the officers broke the door down. The apartment from which the objects had been thrown was locked, and the tenants refused admittance. Again, the officers broke down the door and booked the occupants.

12:25: Nicollet Hotel, blocked alley. By the time we arrived, the car which had blocked the alley had been driven away.

12:55: 11th and LaSalle, take a stolen [police radio slang]. We made a report of a stolen automobile.

1:22: We saw one woman and two men standing outside an apartment building. The men appeared to be fighting. One man and the woman said that the other man was bothering them. We sent him away. The couple then went into an apartment building. As we drove away, we saw the man who had been sent returning and trying to obtain entrance to the apartment building. We returned and booked him as a public drunk.

1:45: Continental Hotel, see a robbery victim. We took a report from a young man who had been robbed at knife point. We drove around the neighborhood looking, without success, for his assailant.

SOURCE: Joseph M. Livermore, "Policing," *Minnesota Law Review* 55 (1971), pp. 672–674. Reprinted by permission.

patrol personnel, (2) preventive patrol, (3) response time, (4) foot patrol versus motorized patrol, (5) one-person versus two-person patrol units, (6) aggressive patrol, (7) community-oriented policing, and (8) special populations.

Allocation of Patrol Personnel. It has traditionally been assumed that patrol officers should be assigned where and when they will be most effective in preventing crime, maintaining order, and serving the public. For the police administrator, the practical question becomes, Where should the troops be sent and in what numbers? There are no precise guidelines to answer this question, and most allocation decisions seem to be based on the assumption that patrols should be concentrated in areas where the crime is occurring or in "problem" neighborhoods. Thus, the distribution of police resources is determined by factors such as crime statistics, the degree of urbanization, pressures from businesspeople and community groups, ethnic composition, and socioeconomic conditions.

Many citizens victimized by crime believe that crime is distributed randomly and that no place is safe. Research indicates, however, that crime "hot spots" can be identified. Apparently, direct-contact predatory violations, such as muggings and robberies, will occur when three elements converge: (1) motivated offenders, (2) suitable targets, and (3) the absence of capable guardians against the violation.[6] In a study of crime in Minneapolis, researchers found that a relatively small number of "hot spot" streets and intersections produced most of the calls to the police. By analyzing the location of calls, it was possible to identify those places that produced the most crime.[7] With this knowledge, officers can be assigned to **directed patrol**—a proactive patrol strategy designed to direct resources to known high-crime areas. There is always a risk, however, that extra police attention to particular locations in the city will simply cause the predatory lawbreakers to move to new locations.

directed patrol
A proactive patrol strategy designed to direct resources to known high-crime areas.

Preventive Patrol. Preventive patrol has long been assumed to be an important deterrent to crime. Since the days of Sir Robert Peel, it has been argued that a patrol officer moving through an area will prevent criminals from carrying out illegal acts. When these assumptions were tested in Kansas City, Missouri, the results were surprising. A fifteen-beat area was divided into three sections, each with similar crime rates, population characteristics, income levels, and numbers of calls for police service. In one area, designated "reactive," all preventive patrol was withdrawn, and the police entered only in response to citizens' calls for service. In another section, labeled "proactive," preventive patrol was raised to as much as four times the normal level, and all other services were provided at the pre-experimental levels. The third section was used as a control, and the department maintained the usual level of services, including preventive patrol. After observing developments in the three sections, researchers concluded that the changes in patrol strategies produced no significant differences in the amount of crime reported, the amount of crime measured by citizen surveys, or the extent to which citizens feared criminal attack.[8] Neither a decrease nor an increase in patrol activity had any apparent effect on crime. These findings have led many departments to shift their focus to greater attention on maintaining order and serving the community. If the police have little ability to prevent crime by changing their patrol tactics, then they may be able to provide greater service to society by focusing patrol activities on other beneficial functions while continuing to fight crime as best they can.

Response Time. Modern patrol tactics are based on the system whereby calls for assistance come to a central section of the department, which then dispatches the nearest officers by radio to the site of the incident. Because most citizens have access to telephones and most officers today are in squad cars that are linked to their headquarters by two-way radios, police can respond quickly to calls.

Several studies have measured the impact of police response time on the ability of officers to intercept a crime in progress and arrest the criminal. In a famous study, William G. Spelman and Dale K. Brown found that the police were successful in only 29 of 1,000 cases. It made little difference whether they arrived two minutes or twenty minutes after the call. What did matter, however, was the speed with which citizens called the police.[9] Figure 5.3 presents these findings.

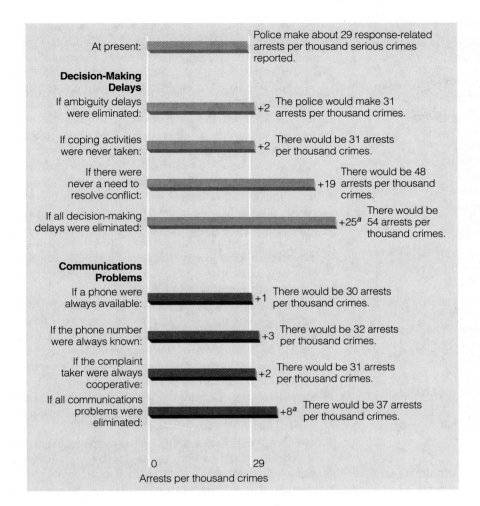

FIGURE 5.3

Potential Increases in Response-Related Arrests by Eliminating Key Causes of Delay Although emphasis has been on creating opportunities for citizens to call the police quickly (through 911 numbers), research has shown that a major factor in police response time is the observer's delay in recognizing that a crime has been committed and that the police should be called.

SOURCE: William G. Spelman and Dale K. Brown, *Calling the Police: Citizen Reporting of Serious Crime* (Washington, DC: Police Executive Research Forum, 1984), p. xxix.

NOTE: Even if all reporting delays could be eliminated, no more than 70 crimes per 1,000 would result in response-related arrests.

[a]The total is more than the sum of the individual savings because of the nonlinear nature of the relationship between reporting time and arrest.

Although delayed arrival of the police is frequently due to citizen slowness in calling, it seems unlikely that arrest rates would be improved merely by educating the public about their important role in stopping crime. As Spelman and Brown point out, there are three major reasons for delay in calling the police. Some people find the situation *ambiguous* and are undecided as to whether the police should be called. They might see an event but not be sure whether it is a robbery or two young males who are "horsing" around. Other people are so busily engaged in *coping activities*—taking care of the victim, directing traffic, and generally helping out—that they are unable to leave the scene in order to call the police. Still other people experience *conflicts* that they must first resolve before they call the police. For example, they may call someone else for advice on whether the authorities should be notified.[10]

Foot versus Motorized Patrol. One of the most frequent requests of citizens is that officers be put back on the beat. This was the dominant form of police patrol until the 1930s when motorized patrol came to be viewed as more effective. Squad cars increased the territory that officers could patrol, and two-way radios enabled officers to be quickly deployed where they were needed. A recent study of large cities shows that almost 94 percent of patrol time is taken by motorized patrol.[11]

However, many citizens as well as some researchers claim that patrol officers in squad cars have become remote from the people they protect and less attentive to the needs and problems in specific neighborhoods. As Lawrence W. Sherman points out, the rise of motorized patrols and telephone dispatching has changed the older strategy of "watching to prevent crime" to "waiting to respond to crime."[12] Because officers rarely leave the patrol car, citizens have few chances to tell them what is going on in the community. Without information about problems and suspicious activities within neighborhoods, patrol officers cannot mediate disputes, investigate suspected criminal activity, and make residents feel that they personally care about their well-being. When officers are distant and aloof from the citizens they serve, the citizens may be less inclined to call for assistance or provide information.

By contrast, officers on foot are at home in the neighborhood. They are close to the daily life of the beat and in a better position to detect criminal activity and apprehend those who have violated the law. Further, when patrol officers are familiar to citizens, they are less likely to be perceived as symbols of oppression by poor or minority residents. In large cities, personal contact may help to reduce racial suspicion and conflict.

In the past decade, interest in foot patrol has revived primarily from citizens' demands for a familiar figure walking through their neighborhoods. Experiments in a number of cities have studied the cost and impact of foot patrol.[13] In general, these studies have shown that foot patrols do not greatly reduce crime but that citizens are less fearful of crime.[14]

One-Person versus Two-Person Patrol Units.   The debate over one-person versus two-person patrol units has raged in police circles for years. A 1991 study of large cities revealed that 70 percent of patrol cars are staffed by one officer, but there is much variation. For example, Los Angeles uses one-person cars for about half of its units during the day, but only 9 percent at night. Philadelphia, however, uses only one-officer cars.[15]

Officers and their union leaders support the two-person squad car, arguing that the second officer is required for safety's sake. They claim that police officers are safer and more effective when two officers work together in dangerous or difficult situations. However, police administrators contend that the one-person squad car is significantly more cost-effective and permits them to deploy more cars on each shift. With more cars to deploy, each can be assigned a smaller geographic sector, and response time can be decreased. Administrators further contend that an officer operating alone is more alert and attentive to work because he or she cannot be distracted by idle conversation with a colleague.

Aggressive Patrol.   **Aggressive patrol** is a proactive patrol strategy designed to maximize the number of police interventions and observations in the

aggressive patrol
A proactive patrol strategy designed to maximize the number of police interventions and observations in the community.

community. Aggressive patrol takes a wide variety of forms, from programs that encourage citizens to identify their valuables, to "sting" operations, to repeat offender programs. James Q. Wilson and Barbara Boland have shown that patrol tactics that increase the risk of arrest are associated with crime reduction. They argue that the effect of the police on crime depends less on how many officers are deployed in a particular area than on what they do while they are there.[16]

Research indicates that although foot patrol does not greatly reduce crime, it does reduce the fear of crime.

An aggressive patrol strategy does not mean that officers are encouraged to patrol in a hostile manner; rather, they frequently stop and question people about what they are doing. In San Diego, an aggressive patrol strategy of field interrogations and street stops was associated with a significant decrease in certain "suppressible" crimes: robbery, burglary, theft, auto theft, assault, sex crimes, malicious mischief, and disturbances. It was concluded that field interrogations deterred potential offenders, especially young opportunists.[17] Officers in an "anticrime patrol" in New York worked the streets of high-crime areas in civilian clothes. Although these officers represented only 5 percent of the men and women assigned to each precinct, during one year they made over 18 percent of the felony arrests, including more than half of the arrests for robbery and about 40 percent of the arrests for burglary and auto theft.

In several cities, repeat offender programs have been successful in arresting career criminals. Using proactive tactics, the Washington, DC, repeat offender program targeted individuals with long criminal records who were believed to be engaged in criminal activity. Efforts were made to track down those for whom arrest warrants had been issued, and investigations were launched to close a large number of open cases and to recover stolen property. The program proved to be effective in removing repeat offenders from the streets, but it was also costly because it took officers away from their usual duties.[18]

The most cost-effective strategy for aggressive patrol seems to be to create incentives so that officers will increase the number of field interrogations and traffic stops that they initiate during each shift. In order to implement an aggressive patrol strategy, a police executive must recruit certain kinds of officers, train them in certain ways, and devise requirements and reward systems (traffic ticket quotas, field interrogation obligations, promotional opportunities) to encourage these officers to follow the strategy.[19]

Community-Oriented Policing. As discussed in Chapter 4, the new concept of community-oriented policing has taken hold in many cities. To a great extent, it has emerged because of perceived deficiencies in the crime fighter stance that most urban police departments took during the Professional Era.[20] Although a somewhat general term, community-oriented policing is most commonly associated with attempts by the police to involve the residents in making their own neighborhoods safe. This concept recognizes that citizens may be concerned about local disorder as well as crime in general. It emphasizes the need for collaboration between the police and citizens to identify community needs and determine the best ways to make improvements.[21]

Community-oriented policing may be carried out, for example, by patrol officers assigned to walk neighborhood beats so that they can cultivate better

problem-oriented policing
An approach to policing in which officers seek to identify, analyze, and respond, on a routine basis, to the underlying circumstances that create the incidents that prompt citizens to call the police.

relations with residents. It may entail creating mini–police stations in the community and police-sponsored youth and elderly activities. Police departments may also survey citizens to determine problems and needs within neighborhoods.

Problem-oriented policing is a strategy that is associated with community policing. In **problem-oriented policing**, officers seek to identify, analyze, and respond, on a routine basis, to the underlying circumstances that create the incidents that prompt citizens to call the police.[22] With knowledge of underlying problems, officers can then enlist community agencies and citizens to resolve them. With this approach, the police may not limit their attention to crime but also consider a wider array of problems that affect the quality of life within the community.

Although community-oriented policing has been embraced by the police executives of major cities, the Police Foundation, the Police Executive Research Forum, and nationally known researchers, there have been problems with implementing it. As with any reform, traditional ways are difficult to change. Police managers are accustomed to dealing with problems according to established procedures and may believe that their authority is diminished through the allocation of responsibility to precinct commanders.[23] In addition, community policing does not reduce costs; it requires either the infusion of new money or the redistribution of existing budgets. It is also difficult to measure its success in reducing the fear of crime, solving underlying problems, maintaining order, and serving the community. Finally, questions remain about the extent to which the police should extend their role beyond the problem of crime to other social problems.

Special Populations. In addition to the problems of crime, urban police forces must deal with a very complex population. City streets contain increasing numbers of the mentally ill, the homeless, runaways, public inebriates, drug addicts, and people infected with AIDS. Crowded jails, the deinstitutionalization of mental health services, the decriminalization of public drunkenness, economic dislocations, and reductions in public assistance programs—all have increased the number of "problem" people on the street. Most of these people are not involved in criminal activities, but their presence in the community is disturbing to residents, and they may contribute to disorder and fear of crime. However, the police must walk a very fine line with regard to their authority to require individuals to go to a homeless shelter, to obtain medical assistance, or to be taken to a mental health unit.[24]

Clearly, the handling of special populations is a major problem now confronting police in most cities. Each community must develop policies so that officers will know when and how they are to intervene in situations where an individual may not have violated the criminal law but is upsetting residents.

The Future of Patrol

Preventive patrol and a rapid response to calls for assistance have been the hallmarks of policing in the United States for the past half-century. However, the research conducted during the past twenty years has raised many questions about the most appropriate patrol strategies that police departments should employ. The rise of community policing has shifted law enforcement efforts in many cities to deal with criminals as well as problems that affect the quality of life of residents. Police forces need to consider a mix of patrol tactics that fit the needs of various neighborhoods. Neighborhoods with crime "hot spots" may require different patrol strategies than neighborhoods in which citizens are primarily concerned with order maintenance. Many researchers believe that traditional patrol operations have focused too narrowly on crime control, neglecting the order maintenance and service activities for which police departments were originally formed.

INVESTIGATION

Every city with a population over 250,000 and 90 percent of the smaller cities have officers specially assigned to investigative duties.[25] Traditionally, detectives have enjoyed a prestigious position in police departments. The pay is higher, the hours are more flexible, and the dectectives are supervised less closely than patrol officers. Detectives do not wear uniforms, and their work is considered more interesting than patrol officers'. In addition to these incentives, they are engaged solely in law enforcement rather than in order maintenance or service work; hence, their activities correspond more closely to the image of the police as crime fighters. Within the investigative unit, detectives are frequently organized according to the type of crime they investigate—homicide, robbery, forgery—or by geographical area. Reported crimes are automatically referred to the appropriate investigator. Investigative units are normally separated from the patrol chain of command. Many argue that this separation results in duplication of effort and lack of continuity in handling cases. It often means that vital pieces of information held by one branch are not known to the other.

Detectives are concerned primarily with law enforcement activities after a crime has been reported and a preliminary investigation held. Their activities depend on the circumstances of the case:

- When a serious crime occurs and the offender is immediately identified and apprehended, the detective prepares the case for presentation to the prosecuting attorney.
- When the offender is identified but not apprehended, the detective tries to locate the individual.
- When the offender is not identified but there are several suspects, the detective conducts investigations aimed at either confirming or disproving his or her suspicions.
- When there is no suspect, the detective starts from scratch to determine who committed the crime.[26]

In performing an investigation, detectives depend not only on their own experience but also on the technical expertise in their department or in a cooperating police force. Much of the information they need will come from criminal files, laboratory technicians, and forensic scientists. Many small departments turn to the state crime laboratory or the FBI for such information when serious crimes have been committed. Detectives are often pictured as working alone, but in fact they are members of a departmental team.

Although detectives focus their work on the investigation of serious crimes, they do not bear the sole responsibility for investigating crimes. Patrol, traffic, vice, and sometimes juvenile units contribute to this process. In small towns and rural areas, patrol officers must perform investigative duties because police departments are too small to have separate detective bureaus. In urban areas, because they are normally the first police at the scene of a crime, patrol officers must undertake much of the preliminary investigative work. The patrol unit's investigation can be crucial. Successful prosecution of

Much of the work of detectives involves the careful collection and documentation of evidence.

many kinds of cases, including robbery, larceny, and burglary, is closely linked to the speed with which a suspect is arrested. If patrol officers are not effective in eliciting needed information immediately from victims and witnesses, the likelihood of successfully apprehending and prosecuting the perpetrator may diminish.

The Apprehension Process

Discovery that a crime has been committed is likely to set off a chain of events leading to the capture of a suspect and the gathering of the evidence required for the suspect's conviction. Unfortunately, it may also lead to a number of dead ends, including an absence of clues pointing to a suspect or a lack of evidence linking the suspect to the crime.

Actions to apprehend a felon can be divided into three responses to commission of a crime: (1) crime detected, (2) preliminary investigation, and (3) follow-up investigation. Depending on the outcome of the investigation, a fourth response might be forthcoming: (4) clearance and arrest. As depicted in Figure 5.4, these actions are designed to mobilize the resources of criminal justice to bring about the arrest of a suspect and to assemble enough supporting evidence to substantiate a charge.

1. *Crime detected.* Information that a crime has been committed usually comes in the form of a telephone call by the victim or complainant to the police. The patrol officer on the beat may also come upon a crime, but usually the police are alerted by others. Alternatively, the police may be alerted to a crime on business premises by automatic security alarms connected to police headquarters. Such direct communications may help to shorten response time and thereby increase the likelihood of apprehending the perpetrator.

2. *Preliminary investigation.* The first law enforcement official on the scene is usually a patrol officer who has been dispatched by radio. The officer is immediately responsible for providing aid to the victim, for securing the crime scene for later investigation, and for beginning to document the facts of the crime. If a suspect is present or in the vicinity, the officer conducts a "hot"

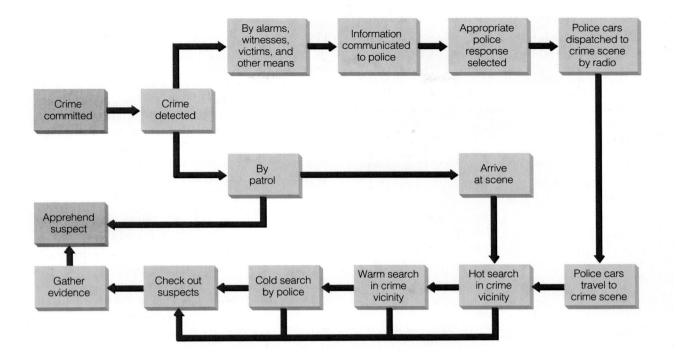

search and may apprehend a suspect. This initial work is crucial. The officer must gather the basic facts, including the identity of the victim, a description of the suspect, and the names of witnesses. After the information is collected, it is transmitted to the investigation unit.

3. *Follow-up investigation.* After a crime has been brought to the attention of the police and a preliminary investigation has been made, the detective will determine what course of action to pursue. In the typical big-city department, incident reports from the previous day are analyzed the first thing in the morning. Assignments are distributed to individual investigators in accordance with their specialties. These investigators study the information, weigh each informational factor, and determine whether the factors are sufficient to indicate that the crime can be solved.

Some departments have developed formulas for guiding the disposition of cases so that resources will be used most efficiently. If the detectives determine that there is little likelihood of solving the crime expeditiously, further efforts may be dropped in favor of a more promising investigation.

When detectives determine that a full-scale investigation is warranted, a wider search—referred to as a "cold" search—for evidence or weapons is undertaken. Witnesses may be reinterviewed, contact made with informants, and evidence assembled for analysis. The pressure of new cases, however, often requires an investigation in progress to be shelved so that resources may be directed toward "warmer" incidents.

4. *Clearance and arrest.* The decision to arrest is a key part of the apprehension process. In some cases, additional evidence or links between suspects and their associates are not discovered if arrests are premature. A crime is considered cleared when evidence supports the arrest of a suspect. If a suspect admits having committed other unsolved crimes in department files, those crimes are also "cleared." When a crime is cleared in police files, it does

FIGURE 5.4
The Felony Apprehension Process
Apprehension of a felony suspect may result from a sequence of actions taken in response to the crime by patrol officers and detectives. Coordination of police response is important in solving major crimes.

115

not necessarily mean that the suspect will eventually be found guilty.

Forensic Techniques

American police have long relied on science to aid investigators in gathering, identifying, and analyzing evidence. The scientific analysis of fingerprints, blood, semen, hair, textiles, and weapons has assisted the police in identifying perpetrators of crimes. It has also helped prosecutors convince jurors about the guilt of specific defendants. Forensic laboratories exist in all states, and many large cities have their own scientists to provide technical assistance.

The development of DNA "fingerprinting" techniques is the latest weapon for detectives to use in investigating many kinds of crimes. This technique is used to identify people through their distinctive gene patterns (also called "genotypic features"). DNA, or deoxyribonucleic acid, is the basic building code for all chromosomes and is the same for all of the cells in a person's body, including skin, blood, organs, and semen. The characteristics of certain segments of DNA vary from person to person and thus form a genetic "fingerprint" for each individual. It is thus possible to analyze, for example, hair samples and compare them to those of suspects. The full utilization of the DNA technique has been hampered by the scarcity of laboratories equipped to undertake the analysis. Moreover, many detectives and prosecutors do not take full advantage of the forensic resources that might assist them. In addition, there are concerns that the method is being used prematurely and that a sound scientific foundation for the approach is yet to be established.[27] Courts in a number of states have accepted DNA results as evidence, but in other courts, defense attorneys have successfully challenged the introduction of such evidence.

The use of DNA fingerprinting may have an important impact on future investigations. However, a recent case showed that jurors may not agree with scientists about what appears to be conclusive evidence. In a Connecticut rape trial, an FBI specialist testified that DNA analysis revealed that the accused had not committed the crime. Rather than rely on this statement, the jury chose to believe the victim since she seemed so certain in her identification of her assailant and gave a very detailed description of the car in which the rape occurred.

Evaluating Investigation

The results of several research studies have raised important questions about the value of investigations and the role detectives play in the apprehension process. This research suggests that the police have overrated the importance of investigation as a means of solving crimes and shows that most crimes are cleared because of arrests made by the patrol force at or near the scene. Response time—the time between commission of the crime and the arrival of the police—is an important factor in the apprehension process, as is the information given by the victim or witnesses to the responding patrol officer.

A Rand Corporation study of 153 large police departments found that the major determinant of success in solving crimes was information identifying the perpetrator supplied by the victim or witnesses at the scene. Of those cases not immediately solved but ultimately cleared, most were cleared by such routine procedures as fingerprint searches, receipt of tips from informants, and mug-shot "show-ups." The report emphasized that special actions by the investigating staff were important in very few cases. In summary, the study indicated that about 30 percent of the crimes were cleared by on-scene arrest and another 50 percent through an identification by victims or witnesses when the police arrived. Thus, only about 20 percent could have been solved by detective work. Even among this group, however, the study found that most crimes "were also solved by patrol officers, members of the public who spontaneously provide further information, or routine investigative practices."[28]

Does this research indicate that detectives are not important? No. The detective's role is important in at least two respects (apart from the ability to solve crimes). First, the prestigious rank of detective provides a goal to which the patrol officer may aspire and gives these officers an additional motivation to excel in their work. Second, citizens expect investigations to be carried out. Citizens may have greater confidence in the police or feel more willing to cooperate with them when they see investigations being conducted, even if those investigations are not essential or may not produce arrests efficiently.

DNA testing is becoming an important aspect of forensic science.

SPECIALIZED OPERATIONS

Patrol and investigation are the two largest and functionally most important units within a police department. In metropolitan areas, however, specialized units are set up to deal with specific types of problems. The most common specialized units are for traffic, vice, and juveniles. Some cities also have separate units to deal with organized crime and drugs. The existence of specialized units should not overshadow the fact that patrol officers and investigators also have a responsibility to deal with the same problems.

Traffic

Because almost everyone in the community is a pedestrian, passenger, or driver, almost everyone is affected by the problems associated with the use of the automobile. The police are required to regulate the flow of vehicles, to investigate accidents, and to enforce traffic laws. This work may not seem to fall within the category of crime fighting or maintenance of order, but certain dimensions of the task of traffic control further these objectives. In addition to contributing to the maintenance of order, the enforcement of traffic laws also educates the public in safe driving habits and provides a visible community service. Traffic duty can also contribute to the apprehension of criminals. As an enforcer of traffic laws, the patrol officer has an opportunity to stop vehicles and interrogate drivers. As a result, stolen property and suspects connected with other criminal acts are often discovered. Most departments can now automatically check automobile and operator license numbers against lists of wanted vehicles and suspects.

Enforcement of traffic regulations provides one of the best examples of police discretion. This work is essentially proactive, and the level of enforcement can be considered a direct result of departmental policies and norms. Officers target particular kinds of violations or particular highways according to departmental priorities. In addition, some departments expect officers to issue a certain number of citations during each shift. Although these expectations may be either explicit or informal, they serve as a means to monitor the traffic officers' productivity. For the most part, selective enforcement is the general policy, since the police have neither the desire nor the resources to enforce all traffic laws.

Vice

Enforcement of laws against vice is dependent on proactive police work often involving the use of undercover agents and informers. Most large city police departments include a specialized vice unit. Vigorous enforcement of these laws requires that officers be given wide discretion. They must often undertake degrading activities, such as posing as prostitutes or drug dealers, in order to apprehend lawbreakers. The special nature of vice work requires the members of the unit to be well trained in the legal procedures that must be followed if arrests are to lead to convictions. The potential for corruption in this type of police work presents a number of administrative dilemmas. Undercover officers are in a position to blackmail gamblers and drug dealers and may also be offered bribes to protect ongoing vice. In addition, officers are subject to transfer when their identities become known and their effectiveness is lost.

The expansion of undercover work and electronic surveillance troubles critics who believe that this is a departure from the traditional style of open policing. Critics fear that the use of these tactics violates civil liberties and can result in a greater intrusion of government into the private affairs of citizens, whether or not those citizens are engaged in criminal activities.

Drug Enforcement

Many large cities now have a separate bureau that deals only with drug law enforcement. Within these agencies, there may also be task forces dedicated to dealing with organized crime groups or gangs that are involved in drug dealing. Other sections may use sting operations to arrest drug sellers on the street or to provide community drug education.

Drug enforcement policies may reflect the goal of "aggressive law enforcement," allocating extensive police resources to attain a maximum number of arrests and to stop brazen street dealing. Police executives believe that it is important to demonstrate to dealers and to the community that drug laws are enforced. Various creative strategies have been employed to attack drug dealing, such as coordinated safety and building inspections of houses and apartment buildings used by drug dealers. Those that do not meet city standards can be boarded up in order to rid neighborhoods of dealers. Police leaders may flood particular streets where drugs are dealt openly with officers who engage in proactive stops and interrogations.

Although arrests for drug sale or possession have increased dramatically, some observers believe that the law enforcement approach will not be successful. As an alternative, many public officials now argue that drugs should be treated as a public health problem rather than as a crime problem. The critics of current policies believe society would derive greater benefits from devoting resources to drug treatment programs, which can sometimes succeed in getting people away from drug abuse, than from police actions that fill the prisons with convicted offenders without making a noticeable dent in drug activity.

As we saw in Chapter 3, the police must work within the framework of the law; they are not free to use any means necessary to attack crime. Three police practices—search and seizure, arrest, and interrogation—are specially structured to ensure that the rule of law is upheld and that the rights of citizens are protected.

The Supreme Court has emphasized two particular devices to make certain that police officers respect the rights of suspects. First, the exclusionary rule requires that illegally seized evidence or improperly obtained confessions be excluded from trials. Second, the Supreme Court has interpreted the Sixth Amendment's provision of the right to counsel to mean that the defendant may have a lawyer present during questioning by the police. Police departments develop policies and procedures for searches, arrests, and interrogations that officers learn during training. Police officers become keenly aware that their actions in the field or station house may jeopardize successful prosecution of a case if they do not follow proper procedures.

SEARCH AND SEIZURE

In *Mapp* v. *Ohio* (1961), the Supreme Court applied the exclusionary rule to all searches conducted by state and local police departments. Previously, it had applied only to federal law enforcement officials and to police within states that had their own rules about exclusion of improperly obtained evidence. Thus, all police officers had to conduct investigations and arrests in accordance with the Fourth Amendment's rules against *unreasonable* searches and seizures. As we shall see, there are circumstances, however, when searches are reasonable and evidence thus obtained is admissible in court even if a judge has not authorized the search.

When a **search warrant** has been issued by a judge, the police may search a designated place for specific persons or items to be seized. To obtain the warrant, the officer must fulfill two requirements. First, the officer must provide reliable information indicating that there is *probable cause* to believe that a crime has been or is being committed. Second, the *particular* premises and pieces of property to be seized must be identified, and the officer must swear under oath that the facts given are correct.

We will examine five kinds of searches that may be legally conducted without a warrant and still be in accord with the Fourth Amendment: (1) searches incident to a lawful arrest, (2) searches during field interrogation, (3) searches of automobiles under special conditions, (4) seizures of evidence that is in "plain view," and (5) searches when consent is given. Warrantless searches may also involve the inventory of property when vehicles are impounded and exigent circumstances when evidence may be destroyed if police do not conduct an immediate search.

1. *Incident to a lawful arrest.* When an officer has observed a crime or believes that one has been committed, an arrest may be made and a search conducted without a warrant. Such searches are justified by the need to prevent the loss of evidence and to protect the safety of officers and bystanders. In *Chimel* v. *California* (1969), the Supreme Court ruled that such a search is limited to the person of the arrestee and the area within the arrestee's

search warrant
An order issued by a judge that allows a police officer to search a designated place for specific persons or items to be seized.

A QUESTION OF ETHICS

Officer Mike Gorton knocked on the apartment door. He and fellow officer Howard Reece had gone to this rundown part of town to arrest Richard Watson on the basis of evidence from an informer that Watson was a drug seller. "Police officers, open up," said Gorton. The door opened slowly, and a small, tense woman peered into the hallway.

"Ma'am, we have a warrant for the arrest of Richard Watson. Is he here?"

"No, I don't know any Watson," was the answer.

"Well, let us in so that we can see for ourselves."

Gorton and Reece entered the apartment. Reece quickly proceeded to a back bedroom. The window leading to a fire escape was open and the bed looked as though someone had left in a rush. Reece started to poke around the room, opening bureau drawers and searching the closet. In the back of the closet he noticed a woman's pocketbook hanging on a hook. He opened it and found three glassine packets of a white powder.

"Hey Mike, look what I found," he called. Gorton came into the bedroom. "Looks like heroin to me," said Reece. "Too bad we can't use it."

"Why can't we use it? This is the place."

"But the warrant only specified the arrest of Watson. It didn't say anything about searching his closet."

"Let's just keep these packets. When we catch him we can 'find' it in his pocket."

What are the issues here? Can the officers keep the heroin packets? Is bending the rules acceptable in some circumstances? If so, do the circumstances warrant it? What should the officers do?

"immediate control," defined as that area "from within which he might [obtain] a weapon or something that could have been used as evidence against him" in order to destroy it.[29] Thus, if the police are holding a person in one room of a house, they are not authorized to search and seize property in another part of the house, away from the suspect's physical presence.

2. *Field interrogation.* The police often stop and interrogate persons without knowing any facts to justify an arrest. As a society, we want police to investigate people who behave suspiciously as well as those who are disrupting public order. Thus, police officers frequently stop people on the street to ask for their identification and inquire about what they are doing. These street encounters, often called "threshold inquiries," allow for brief questioning and frisking: patting down the outside of the suspect's clothing to ascertain whether there is a concealed weapon.

In the case of **Terry v. Ohio (1968)**, the Supreme Court upheld the stop-and-frisk procedure when a police officer stopped and patted down three men who had been looking repeatedly into store windows in a suspicious manner.[30] When the officer found handguns during the patdown search, the Court ruled that the frisk could be conducted for the officer's own safety or that of others because he reasonably believed that he was dealing with potentially dangerous individuals.

On the basis of *Terry* and subsequent decisions, it is now accepted that a police officer is justified in stopping and questioning an individual if it is reasonable to assume that a crime is being committed, is about to be committed, or has been committed. The individual may be frisked for a weapon if the officer fears for his or her life and the officer believes that the person's clothing harbors a weapon. The courts have concluded that an officer may conduct this form of field interrogation in order to investigate suspicious persons without first showing probable cause.

Terry v. *Ohio* (1968)
A police officer may stop and frisk an individual if it is reasonable to suspect that a crime has been or will be committed.

3. *Automobiles.* Warrantless searches may be conducted when there is probable cause to believe that an automobile contains criminal evidence. The Supreme Court permits officers to search automobiles more freely than houses because cars are mobile and evidence may disappear if officers were required to seek a warrant before conducting a search.

The Supreme Court has struggled with many cases in the course of attempting to define the circumstances in which an automobile may be searched. The court has concluded that the warrantless search of an automobile may extend to include containers within the automobile if there is probable cause to believe that they contain evidence of a crime. Because of the

importance of the automobile in American society, there will undoubtedly be additional interpretations of the Fourth Amendment with regard to unreasonable search and seizure, including cases concerning searches of people who are passengers and drivers.

4. *"Plain view."*   Items that are in "plain view" may be searched and seized without a warrant when officers have reason to believe that the items are connected with a crime. If an officer has a warrant to search a house for cocaine, for example, and during the course of the search comes upon firearms, the guns may also be seized. In order for the plain-view doctrine to apply, the officer must be legally entitled to be at the location, such as inside a house, and the item must be plainly visible. Moreover, the evidentiary value of the item must be readily apparent.

Two recent decisions have further defined permissible actions by police officers under the plain-view doctrine. In *New York* v. *Class* (1986), the Supreme Court ruled that a gun protruding from under a seat, seen by an officer when he entered the car to look for the vehicle identification number, was within the bounds of the doctrine.[31] However, in *Arizona* v. *Hicks* (1987), the Court ruled that an officer who moved a stereo system to find its identification number during a legal search for weapons had violated the Fourth Amendment ban against unreasonable search and seizure.[32] The serial number was not in plain view, and the police did not have probable cause to believe that the stereo had been stolen.

5. *Consent.*   A citizen may waive the rights granted by the Fourth Amendment and allow the police to conduct a search or to seize items without a warrant and in the absence of special circumstances. The prosecution must be able to prove, however, that the consent was given voluntarily by the correct person. In some circumstances, as when passengers' belongings are searched by security employees before they board a plane and by customs agents at international borders, consent is implied. In some circumstances, there are questions about who may give consent to search a particular location.

121

May consent be given, for example, by a landlord or parent of the defendant? In *Illinois* v. *Rodriguez* (1990), the Supreme Court permitted police to use evidence obtained when officers reasonably, but mistakenly, believed that a defendant's girlfriend lived at the defendant's apartment and therefore had the authority to grant permission for a search of the premises.[33]

ARREST

As noted previously, arrest is the seizure of an individual by a governmental official with authority to take the person into custody. Because the normal consequence of arrest is that the suspect is taken to the station house, it is more intrusive than a street stop and field interrogation. The law of arrest mixes the Fourth Amendment's protections and local rules regarding procedure. Generally, this means that the arresting officer must be able to show that there is probable cause to believe (1) that a crime has been committed and (2) that the person taken into custody is the perpetrator. Although courts generally prefer that officers seek arrest warrants before making felony arrests, such warrants have not been required. Officers frequently make arrests without a warrant even when they had time to obtain one.

INTERROGATION

Protection against self-incrimination is one of the most important rights guaranteed by the Fifth Amendment. People may not be compelled to be witnesses against themselves. Under our adversarial system, it is the responsibility of the government to prove the defendant's guilt. The prosecutor and police are not supposed to seek their proof by pressuring the defendant to provide evidence of his or her own guilt. Courts will exclude from evidence any confession obtained illegally through undue pressure. In addition, the Sixth Amendment right to counsel protects suspects by permitting them to have the advice and assistance of an attorney during questioning.

As discussed in Chapter 3, the Supreme Court ruled that as soon as the investigation of an unsolved crime begins to focus on a particular suspect and the suspect is taken into custody, the so-called Miranda warnings must be read aloud before interrogation can commence.[34] Suspects must be told four things:

1. They have the right to remain silent.
2. If they decide to make a statement, it can and will be used against them in court.
3. They have the right to have an attorney present during interrogation or to have an opportunity to consult with an attorney.
4. If they cannot afford an attorney, the state will provide one.

CONTROVERSY OVER THE EXCLUSION OF EVIDENCE

The Supreme Court's decisions in *Mapp* and *Miranda* generated criticism and controversy from the law enforcement community. It was argued that (1) confessions were essential for the apprehension and conviction of law violators,

(2) informing suspects of their rights would greatly reduce the ability of the police to secure confessions, (3) few police would actually give the required warnings, (4) remedies other than exclusion were available to punish those officers who failed to observe rules, and (5) instead of deterring police misconduct, the exclusion of evidence would punish the prosecutor and society by freeing guilty people.

All of these assumptions were later challenged by both law enforcement officials and social scientists studying the impact of the rulings. The most extensive of these studies focused on felony cases and found that fewer than 1 percent of the cases that reached the courts had been dismissed because of the exclusionary rule.[35] Similar findings were reported in a study of the rule's impact on the federal courts.[36] With some exceptions, the rule seems to be an issue primarily in drug cases. In 7,500 felony cases in nine counties in three states, only 46 cases (0.6 percent) were lost because of the exclusionary rule. Most of those involved offenses that might have resulted in incarceration for less than six months. Indeed, it can be argued that the exclusionary rule has had only a marginal impact on the criminal court system.[37]

In most cities, the police solve crimes either by catching the accused in the act or by locating witnesses who will testify. Because most departments have limited resources for scientific investigation, suspects are not usually arrested until the crime is solved and conviction is assured. Under these circumstances, interrogation is less essential than many critics of the *Miranda* rule originally believed. Instead of diminishing police officers' ability to catch lawbreakers, court decisions such as *Miranda* and *Mapp* seem to have improved the professionalism of many departments by making officers more conscious of the legal rules that govern their decisions and actions.

Through a series of retirements, the composition of the Supreme Court changed in the 1980s. However, the new conservative majority on the Court has not overturned the liberal rules establishd by the *Mapp* and *Miranda* decisions. Instead, the Court has created exceptions to these precedents or given them narrower applicability. Three of the most important exceptions affecting the exclusionary rule are (1) the "public safety" exception, (2) the inevitable discovery rule, and (3) the "good faith" exception.

In the case of *New York* v. *Quarles* (1984), a "public safety" exception to the Miranda warnings was established.[38] Thus, officers may ask arrested suspects questions prior to reading Miranda warnings if those questions concern an urgent situation affecting public safety. The suspect in the *Quarles* case had hidden a gun inside a grocery store as the police chased him and the police immediately asked him about the location of the gun when he was handcuffed. The police were concerned that someone else might find the gun if they did not question the suspect as quickly as possible.

The "inevitable discovery exception" was established by the Court in *Nix* v. *Williams* (1984).[39] This case, discussed in Chapter 3, concerned the discovery of the murder victim's body based on improper questioning of the suspect by the police. After the defendant's second trial, the Supreme Court accepted the prosecution's argument that the body would have been located eventually anyway even without the improper questioning of the defendant.

Under the "good-faith exception" to the exclusionary rule, the Supreme Court has declared that evidence may be used even though it has been obtained under a search warrant that later is proved to be technically invalid. In **United States v. Leon (1984)**, police presented evidence to a judge concerning an informant's tip about drug activity at a certain house. The judge made an error in issuing a search warrant. The Supreme Court approved the search, despite the defective warrant, because the real error had been made by the

United States v. *Leon* **(1984)**
Evidence seized using a warrant later found to be defective is valid if the officer was acting in good faith.

judge. The police followed proper procedures by presenting evidence to the judge that they believed supported their request for a warrant. The Court ruled that the costs of enforcing the exclusionary rule, namely the overturning of criminals' convictions, outweighed the benefits of seeking to deter police misconduct.

In large part, the Supreme Court decisions affecting the exclusionary rule reflect continuing debates in American society. Supporters of the decisions of the Warren Court argue that constitutional rights must protect all Americans, including criminal defendants, against the exercise of excessive power by police and prosecutors. Critics say that the Supreme Court has gone too far, so that too many guilty people have avoided prosecution and punishment. This debate likely will continue and the relationship of police actions to the rule of law will always be a subject of disagreement.

SUMMARY

The police in American society face, in Peter Manning's words, an "impossible mandate."[40] The public has high expectations about their crime-fighting capabilities, yet the police devote much of their effort to order maintenance and service problems. As the primary governmental agency that is available to the public around the clock, the police inevitably confront a greater array of problems and challenges than most citizens realize.

Police administrators are challenged to organize their departments and operations in ways that will gain maximum effectiveness from scarce resources. They must find ways to spread their patrol officers around the city or town while retaining the ability to monitor and supervise their activities. It is extremely difficult to measure police productivity for anything other than proactive traffic and vice enforcement. Thus, police administrators face significant dilemmas about how to convey realistic performance expectations to officers who undertake an array of unmeasurable tasks. Administrators must also find ways to persuade public officials and the public that the police are effective.

The police are organized along military lines. Operational units are responsible for various crime prevention and control activities, most often including patrol, investigation, traffic control, and vice and juvenile crimes. Police operations can be influenced by pressures from community businesspeople and political leaders who want law enforcement resources to be allocated in ways that will further their own interests. Other portions of the criminal justice system can also shape law enforcement activities. The police are the system's crucial entry point for the disposition of offenders, and law enforcement officers are under pressure to obtain the evidence the prosecution needs.

Police administrative organization and patrol strategies are being reassessed in light of studies of police effectiveness. Questions have emerged about the crime-fighting value of detectives' investigations and preventive patrol. However, effective crime fighting is merely one consideration in planning police operations, and the public may expect the police to undertake certain activities, such as detective work, even if those activities do not significantly enhance arrest rates. Contemporary police must question long-standing assumptions about the effectiveness of traditional methods and re-examine their operations in light of a broader understanding of the varied responsibilities imposed on them by society.

The police are not free to undertake any means necessary to obtain evidence. Their actions must abide by the rules and values imposed by their superiors as well as by the rights specified in the Fourth, Fifth, and Sixth Amendments to the U.S. Constitution. Decisions by the Supreme Court over the past quarter-century have interpreted the Bill of Rights with regard to search and seizure, arrest, and interrogation. The exclusionary rule requires that evidence illegally obtained must not be used in the prosecution of a suspect. In recent years, under the leadership of Chief Justice William Rehnquist and a conservative Court, interpretations of key elements in the Bill of Rights have been narrowed.

QUESTIONS FOR REVIEW

1. What are the purposes and consequences of the military-style organization of police departments?
2. What is the purpose of patrol? How is it carried out?
3. What has research shown about the effectiveness of patrol?
4. What is the role of detectives?
5. What specialized operations exist within police departments in major cities?
6. How do various amendments of the Bill of Rights affect police operations?

NOTES

1. John Eck, William Spelman, Diane Hill, Darrel W. Stephens, John Stedman, and Gerald R. Murphy, *Problem Solving: Problem-Oriented Policing in Newport News* (Washington, DC: Police Executive Research Forum, 1987), pp. 1–2.
2. U.S. Department of Justice, *Crime in the United States* (Washington, DC: Government Printing Office, 1990), p. 164.
3. George Kelling, "Measuring What Matters: A New Way of Thinking About Crime and Public Order," *The City Journal* (Spring 1992), p. 23.
4. Samuel G. Chapman, *Police Patrol Readings*, 2nd ed. (Springfield, IL: Charles C. Thomas, 1970), p. ix.
5. Albert Reiss, *The Police and the Public* (New Haven, CT: Yale University Press, 1971), p. 19; Egon Bittner, *The Functions of Police in Modern Society* (Cambridge, MA: Oelgeschlager, Gunn & Hain, 1980), p. 127.
6. Lawrence E. Cohen and Marcus Felson, "Social Change and Crime Rate Trends: A Routine Activity Approach," *American Sociological Review* 44 (1979), p. 589.
7. The results of this analysis were that 50 percent of the calls to the police were concentrated in 3 percent of all Minneapolis places; calls reporting all predatory crimes were found for robberies at 2.2 percent of places, for rapes at 1.2 percent of places, and for auto thefts at 2.7 percent of places. Lawrence W. Sherman, Patrick R. Gartin, and Michael E. Buerger, "Hot Spots of Predatory Crime: Routine Activities and the Criminology of Place," *Criminology* 27 (February 1989), p. 27.
8. George Kelling, Tony Pate, Duane Dieckman, and Charles E. Brown, *The Kansas City Preventive Patrol Experiments: A Summary Report* (Washington, DC: Police Foundation, 1974).
9. William G. Spelman and Dale K. Brown, *Calling the Police: Citizen Reporting of Serious Crime* (Washington, DC: Police Executive Research Forum, 1984), p. xxix.

10. Spelman and Brown, *Calling the Police*, p. 4.

11. Brian A. Reaves, *Police Departments in Large Cities* (Washington, DC: Bureau of Justice Statistics, 1989).

12. Sherman, "Patrol Strategies for Police," p. 149.

13. Lee A. Brown and Mary Ann Wycoff, "Policing Houston: Reducing Fear and Improving Service," *Crime and Delinquency* 33 (January 1987), p. 71; *The Newark Foot Patrol Experiment* (Washington, DC: Police Foundation, 1981); Robert C. Trojanowicz, *An Evaluation of the Neighborhood Foot Patrol Program in Flint, Michigan* (East Lansing: Michigan State University, n.d.).

14. Mark A. Cohen, Ted R. Miller, and Shelli B. Rossman, "The Costs and Consequences of Violent Behavior in the U.S." Paper prepared for the Panel on the Understanding and Control of Violent Behavior, National Research Council, National Academy of Science, Washington, DC, 1990, pp. 64–79.

15. Anthony Pate and Edwin H. Hamilton, *The Big Six: Policing America's Large Cities* (Washington, DC: Police Foundation, 1991).

16. James Q. Wilson and Barbara Boland, *The Effect of the Police on Crime*, U.S. Department of Justice (Washington, DC: Government Printing Office, 1979).

17. James Q. Wilson, *Thinking About Crime*, 2nd rev. ed. (New York: Basic Books, 1983), p. 71.

18. Susan E. Martin and Lawrence W. Sherman, "Selective Apprehension: A Police Strategy for Repeat Offenders," *Criminology* 24 (February 1986), pp. 155–173; Susan E. Martin, "Policing Career Criminals: An Examination of an Innovative Crime Control Program," *Journal of Criminal Law and Criminology* 77 (Winter 1986), pp. 1159–1182.

19. Wilson and Boland, *Effect of the Police*, p. 4.

20. Patrick V. Murphy, "Organizing for Community Policing," in *Issues in Policing: New Perspectives*, ed. John W. Bizzack (Lexington, KY: Autumn Press, 1992), pp. 113–128.

21. Mark Harrison Moore, "Problem-Solving and Community Policing," in *Modern Policing*, ed. Michael Tonry and Norval Morris (Chicago: University of Chicago Press, 1992), pp. 99–158.

22. Herman Goldstein, *Problem-Oriented Policing* (New York: McGraw-Hill, 1990).

23. George L. Kelling and William J. Bratton, "Implementing Community Policing: The Administrative Problem," *Perspectives on Policing* 17 (Washington, DC: National Institute of Justice, 1993).

24. Candace McCoy, "Policing the Homeless," *Criminal Law Bulletin* 22 (May/June 1986), p. 263; Barney Melekian, "Police and the Homeless," *FBI Law Enforcement Bulletin* 59 (1990), pp. 1–7.

25. Peter Greenwood and Joan Petersilia, *The Criminal Investigation Process*, Vol. l: *Summary and Policy Implications* (Santa Monica, CA: Rand Corporation, 1975).

26. Herman Goldstein, *Policing a Free Society* (Cambridge, MA: Ballinger, 1977), p. 55. See also James Q. Wilson, *The Investigators: Managing FBI and Narcotics Agents* (New York: Basic Books, 1978).

27. Peter J. Neufeld and Neville Colman, "When Science Takes the Witness Stand," *Scientific American* 262 (May 1990), p. 46.

28. Peter W. Greenwood, Jan M. Chaiken, and Joan Petersilia, *Criminal Investigation Process* (Lexington, MA: Lexington Books, 1977), p. 227.

29. *Chimel* v. *California*, 395 U.S. 752 (1969).

30. *Terry* v. *Ohio*, 392 U.S. l (1968).

31. *New York* v. *Class*, 475 U.S. 106 (1986).

32. *Arizona* v. *Hicks*, 480 U.S. 321 (1987). See also Kimberly Kingston, "Look But Don't Touch: The Plain View Doctrine," *FBI Law Enforcement Bulletin* (December 1987), p. 17.

33. 110 S.Ct. 2793 (1990).

34. *Escobedo* v. *Illinois*, 378 U.S. 478 (1964); *Miranda* v. *Arizona*, 384 U.S. 436 (1966).

35. U.S. Department of Justice, National Institute of Justice, *The Effects of the Exclusionary Rule: A Study in California* (Washington, DC: Government Printing Office, 1982).

36. U.S. Controller General, *Impact of the Exclusionary Rule on Federal Criminal Prosecutions*, Report GGD-79-45, 19 April 1979.

37. Peter Nardulli, "The Societal Cost of the Exclusionary Rule: An Empirical Assessment," *ABF Research Journal* (Summer 1983), pp. 585–609.

38. *New York* v. *Quarles*, 467 U.S. 649 (1984).

39. *Nix* v. *Williams*, 52 L.W. 4732 (1984).

40. Peter Manning, *Police Work* (Cambridge, MA: MIT Press, 1977).

CHAPTER 6
Policing: Issues and Trends

PAYING THE PRICE FOR POLICE CORRUPTION

On Monday, July 11, 1994, former New York City police officer Michael Dowd stood before Judge Kimba Wood in a federal courtroom. Dowd was about to be sentenced for a variety of crimes in which he used his authority as a police officer to abuse people, steal money and goods, and obtain cocaine. His crimes ranged from stealing food intended for the needy from a church to plotting a kidnapping on behalf of drug dealers. Dowd had been the star witness in the city's Mollen Commission investigation, which uncovered the worst police corruption scandal in New York City in two decades. Dowd had hoped that his cooperation with authorities would lead to a lenient sentence, but prosecutors found many of his statements about illegal activities within the police department to be false or misleading. When Judge Wood sentenced him to fifteen years in prison, a sentence just short of the maximum possible, Dowd was stunned and mumbled, "Oh, my God. Oh, my God." In issuing her sentence, Judge Wood said to Dowd, "You did not just fall prey to temptation and steal what was in front of you and take kickbacks or sell confidential law enforcement information. You also continually searched for new ways to abuse your position and at times you recruited fellow officers to join in your crimes."

Dowd's case illustrates a problem that surfaces regularly in law enforcement. How can we make sure that the people who possess authority do not use their power for personal gain? Police have sworn an oath to protect society against illegal activities; thus, we are especially shocked and disappointed when they, of all people, violate public trust.

In this chapter, we will discuss a number of important issues concerning the police and their relationship with society. We will look at recruitment and training of the police and examine the unique subculture that develops from the environment, socialization, and pressures that the police experience. We will also explore the enduring problem of the abuse of power by the police and what is being done about it. Finally, we will look at two trends—unionism and private policing—that affect police operations. ★

I f you or someone you know is planning to embark on a career in law enforcement, ask yourself what aspects of the job make it more appealing than other kinds of work. Some people might want the adventure and excitement of investigating crimes and apprehending lawbreakers. Others might be attracted to the satisfactions that come from being a public servant who is able to help people in various contexts. Still other people may be attracted to a civil service job with good benefits and a government retirement plan. Table 6.1 summarizes the reasons people offer for choosing police work as a career.

RECRUITMENT

How can departments recruit well-rounded, dedicated public servants? If pay scales are low, educational requirements minimal, and physical standards unrealistic, police work will attract only those who are unable to enter more attractive occupations. This was a problem in the past. However, a majority of departments now offer entrance salaries of over $20,000 with the possibility for extensive overtime. While many departments now expect a minimum of two years of college, most require new members to have only a high school education. Good physical condition and the absence of a criminal record are required by all departments. To widen the pool of recruits and avoid discriminating against women and some ethnic groups, height and weight requirements have been changed, and many departments even overlook a minor criminal record if it was acquired in the applicant's youth. In addition, many departments now use written and psychological tests as well as traditional physical fitness tests to identify the best candidates.

Increasingly, departments are attracting recruits with a college education, although officers in rural areas and small cities are more likely to have less education. In the past twenty years, the educational levels of American police officers has risen. Now, as shown in Figure 6.1, about 60 percent of sworn officers have more than two years of college education.[1]

TABLE 6.1

Reasons for Choosing Police Work as a Career
To what extent do the reasons for choosing police work differ from the reasons that might be given for choosing other careers? What is indicated by the different responses given by men and women?

SOURCE: Harold P. Slater and Martin Reiser, "A Comparative Study of Factors Influencing Police Recruitment," *Journal of Police Science and Administration* 16 (1988), p. 170.

Reason	Male	Female	Total
Variety	62.2%	92.1%	69.4%
Responsibility	50.4	55.3	51.6
Serve public	48.7	50.0	49.0
Adventure	49.6	39.5	47.1
Security	46.2	34.2	43.3
Pay	43.7	42.1	43.3
Benefits	36.1	31.6	35.0
Advancement	31.9	34.2	32.5
Retirement	27.7	5.3	22.3
Prestige	16.0	13.2	15.3

TRAINING

The performance of police officers is not based solely on the characteristics and values of the people recruited; it is also shaped by their training. Most states now require preservice training for all recruits. This is often a formal course of training at a police academy. Large departments generally run their own programs while state police academies train recruits from rural and small-town units. The courses range from two-week sessions that emphasize the handling of weapons to more academic four-month programs followed by fieldwork, such as those developed by the Los Angeles police and sheriff's departments. In the latter courses, recruits hear lectures on social relations, receive foreign language training, and learn emergency medical treatment.

Formal training is necessary for gaining an understanding of legal rules, weapons use, and other aspects of the job. However, the police officer's job demands a wide range of skills in dealing with people that cannot be learned from a lecture or a book. Much of the most important training for police officers takes place during a probationary period when new officers work with and learn from experienced officers. After finishing their classroom training and arriving for their first day of patrol duty, it is not unusual for experienced officers to tell their rookie partners, "Now, I want you to forget all that stuff you learned at the academy. You really learn your job on the streets."

The process of **socialization**—whereby members learn the symbols, beliefs, and values of a group or subculture—includes learning the informal aspects of law enforcement. New officers must learn how to appear "productive" to their superiors, how to take shortcuts in filling out paperwork, how to keep themselves safe in dangerous situations, how to analyze conflict situations in order to maintain order, and a host of other bits of wisdom, norms, and folklore that define the subculture of a particular department. Recruits learn that loyalty to fellow officers, professional esprit de corps, and respect for police authority are esteemed values.

In police organizations, the success of the group depends on the cooperation of its members. All patrol officers are under direct supervision and must recognize that their performance is measured by their contribution to the group's work. Supervisors are not, however, the only people who evaluate the officers' contribution. Officers are also influenced by pressures from their colleagues. Police officers within a department may develop strong, shared views on the proper way to "handle" the multitude of different situations they confront. The ways in which individual officers use their personal skills and judgment can mean the difference between defusing a conflict and escalating a situation so that it endangers citizens and other officers. In tackling their "impossible mandate," new recruits must learn the ways of the world from the other officers who depend on them and on whom they depend.

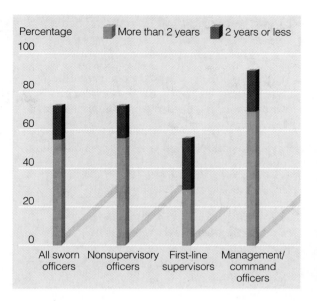

FIGURE 6.1

College Education of Police Officers
During the past two decades, the number of police officers with at least some college education has increased. However, about a quarter of all sworn officers have only a high school diploma.

SOURCE: David L. Carter, Allen D. Sapp, and Darrel W. Stephens, *The State of Police Education: Policy Direction for the Twenty-First Century* (Washington, DC: Police Executive Research Forum, 1989), p. 45.

socialization
The process by which the rules, symbols, and values of a group or subculture are learned by its members.

THE CHANGING PROFILE OF THE POLICE

The composition of American police has changed dramatically. For most of American history, virtually all police officers were male and white. In 1968, the National Advisory Commission on Civil Disorders identified police–minority relations as a major factor contributing to the ghetto riots of the 1960s. The Equal Employment Opportunity Act of 1972 prohibits state and local governments from discriminating in their hiring practices. Pressured by state and federal agencies as well as by discrimination lawsuits, most city police forces have undertaken extensive campaigns to recruit more minority and female officers. Figure 6.2 shows major changes in the profile of the American police officer.

Minority Police Officers

Prior to the 1970s, many police departments resisted hiring nonwhites. As discriminatory practices declined, new opportunities arose for people to serve as law enforcement officers. As a result, the composition of police departments has changed, especially in major cities. Samuel Walker's 1989 study of the country's fifty largest cities found substantial progress in opening doors for new people to become police officers. From 1983 to 1988, 28 percent of the departments reported an increase of 50 percent or more in the number of African-American officers, and 23 percent reported a similar increase in the number of Hispanic officers.[2]

However, because of the importance of seniority in layoff procedures during any financial crisis, minority officers may be the first to go, and the gains of the past decade may thus be lost.

Women on the Force

There have been female police officers since 1905, when Lola Baldwin was made an officer in Portland, Oregon. However, the number of women officers remained small for most of the twentieth century due to a widespread belief that policing was "men's work." As discriminatory barriers began to fall and social attitudes changed, the percentage of female officers nationwide went from 1.5 percent of sworn officers in 1970 to 8.6 percent in 1985. In some police departments, more than 10 percent of officers are women.[3] Despite the changes, about half of U.S. police agencies still employ no women.

Although some male police officers still question whether women can handle dangerous situations and physical confrontations, most policewomen have easily met the performance expectations of their superiors. Indeed, studies conducted by the Police Foundation and by other researchers point to a positive reception for women in law enforcement work. Research in Washington, DC, in which a group of female recruits was compared with a group of male recruits found that being male "is not a bona fide occupational qualification for doing police patrol work."[4] This study, whose findings were corroborated in other cities, found that most citizens had generally positive things to say about the work of policewomen.

Yet, despite positive reviews and increases in their numbers, women still have difficulty breaking into the traditionally male stronghold of police work.

Cultural expectations of women often conflict with ideas about behavior appropriate for officers as shown in the Close-Up describing Patrol Officer Cristina Murphy's confrontation with an inebriated citizen. Many people do not believe that women are tough enough to confront dangerous suspects. Moreover, as newcomers to the force, women have often found their upward mobility blocked and have had to contend with prejudice from their male colleagues. Relatively few women have been promoted to supervisory positions, so they generally are not yet positioned to combat remaining barriers to the recruitment, retention, and promotion of female officers. As citizens become accustomed to women on patrol and in other nontraditional roles, it will probably become less difficult for women officers to gain cooperation and support from citizens and their male colleagues.

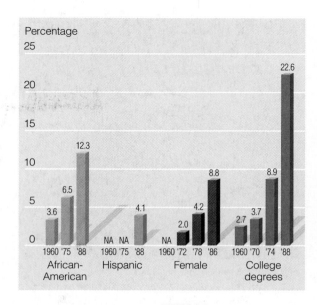

FIGURE 6.2
The Changing Profile of the American Police Officer
Since 1970, efforts have been made to increase the percentage of minority group members, women, and persons with college degrees on the force.
SOURCE: Samuel Walker, *The Police in America*, 2nd ed. (New York: McGraw-Hill, 1992), p. 303.

SUBCULTURE OF THE POLICE

A **subculture** is composed of the symbols, beliefs, values, and attitudes shared by members of a subgroup within the larger society. Like members of other occupational subcultures, police develop shared values that affect their interpretations of human behavior and their role within society. The police subculture produces a **working personality**—that is, a complex of emotional and behavioral characteristics developed by members of an occupational group in response to the work situation and environmental influences.

The formation of a close-knit, occupation-based social group is solidified by the strong bonding that commonly occurs among people who deal with violence. This solidarity "permits fallible men to perform an arduous and difficult task, and . . . places the highest value upon the obligation to back up and support a fellow officer."[5]

An increasing number of women have become officers. What are some of the problems they face? With the public? With their colleagues?

ELEMENTS OF THE WORKING PERSONALITY

The working personality of police is defined by two continual stresses of police work: (1) the threat of danger and (2) the need to establish and maintain one's authority.[6] Because they encounter dangerous situations, officers remain keenly aware of clues in people's behavior or in specific situations that indicate that violence and lawbreaking may be imminent. As officers drive the streets, they notice things that seem amiss—a broken window, a person hiding something under a coat, anything that looks suspicious. As sworn officers, they are never off duty. People who recognize them as police officers will call on them for help at any time, day or night. Throughout the socialization process, experienced officers warn

CLOSE-UP
Patrol Officer Cristina Murphy

Jim Dyer was drunk out of his mind when he called the Rochester Police Department on a recent Saturday night. He wanted to make a harassment complaint; a neighbor, he claimed, was trying to kill him with a chair. Officer Cristina Murphy, 27, a petite, dark-haired, soft-spoken three-year veteran of the Rochester P.D., took the call.

"What's the problem here?" she asked when she arrived at the scene. A crowd had gathered. Dyer's rage was good local fun.

"You're a *woman!*" Dyer complained as Murphy stepped from her squad car. "All they send me is *women*. I called earlier and they sent me a Puerto Rican and *she* didn't do nothing either."

"Mr. Dyer, what exactly is the problem?"

"Dickie Burroughs is the problem. He tried to kill me." Through a drunken haze, Dyer made certain things clear: He wanted Dickie Burroughs locked up. He wanted him sent to Attica for life. He wanted it done that night. Short of all that, Dyer hoped that the police might oblige him by roughing up his foe, just a little.

"We don't do that sort of thing," Murphy explained in the voice she uses with drunks and chil-

dren. "Mr. Dyer, I can do one of two things for you. I can go find Mr. Burroughs and get his side of the story; I can talk to him. The other thing I can do is take a report from you and advise you how to take out a warrant. You'll have to go downtown for that."

Later, in her squad car, Murphy would say that she isn't usually so curt to complaining citizens. "But it's important not to take crap about being a female. Most of the stuff I get, I just let slip by. This guy, though, he really did not want service on his complaint, he wanted retribution. When he saw a woman taking his call, he figured that I wouldn't give it to him; it never struck him that no male officer would either. You know, *everyone* has an opinion about women being police officers—even drunks. Some people are very threatened by it. They just can't stand getting orders from a woman. White males, I think, are the most threatened. Black males seem the least—they look at me and they just see blue. Now women, they sometimes just can't stand the idea that a woman exists who can have power over them. They feel powerless and expect all women to feel that way too. As I said, everyone has an opinion."

SOURCE: Claudia Driefus, "People Are Always Asking Me What I'm Trying to Prove," *Police Magazine* (March 1980).

---

subculture
The aggregate of symbols, beliefs, values, and attitudes shared by members of a subgroup within the larger society.

working personality
The complex of emotional and behavioral characteristics developed by members of an occupational group in response to the work situation and environmental influences.

new recruits to be suspicious and cautious. Rookies are told about fellow officers who were killed while trying to settle a family squabble or writing a traffic ticket.[7] The message is clear: Even seemingly minor offenses can suddenly escalate into extreme danger. Constantly pressured to recognize signs of crime and anticipate potentially violent situations, police officers may become suspicious of everyone and all situations. Thus, police officers remain in a perpetual state of "high alert," always on the lookout and never letting down their guard.

The constant sense that they are surrounded by risks of unexpected danger creates tension in officers' lives. They may feel constantly on edge and worried about the possibility of attack. This concern with danger may affect their interactions with citizens and suspects. Officers' caution and suspicion may be perceived as hostility by citizens who come into contact with them. This perceived hostility may generate counterhostility from criminal suspects. As a result, on-the-street interrogations and arrests may become confrontational.

The second element that defines the working personality is the need to exert authority. Unlike many professionals, such as doctors, psychiatrists, and lawyers, whose clients recognize and defer to their authority, a police officer must establish authority through his or her actions. The symbols of police authority—the uniform, badge, gun, and nightstick—help to signify the officer's position and power, but the officer's demeanor and behavior really determine whether people will cooperate and defer.

Unlike the law enforcement function in which victims are happy to see the police, the order maintenance function creates pressures on officers' assertions of authority. If police officers try too hard to establish their authority in the face of hostility, they may cross the line and use excessive force. For example, when officers are dispatched to investigate a report of a neighborhood disturbance or a victimless crime, they usually do not find a cooperative complainant. Instead, they must contend not only with the perpetrators but also with onlookers who may escalate the conflict. In these circumstances, officers must "handle the situation" by asserting authority without becoming emotionally involved. Even when verbally challenged by citizens on their personal conduct and right to enforce the law, the police are expected to react in a detached or neutral manner. For officers who feel constantly burdened with the twin pressures of danger and authority, this may not be easy to do. Thus, in the daily work of policing, the rules and procedures taught at the academy may have less impact on officers' actions than the perceived need to establish authority in the face of danger.

WORKING PERSONALITY, ISOLATION, AND COMMUNITY RELATIONS

Police officers' suspicion of people and their isolation from the public may be increased by their perception that the public is hostile to them. The police do not generally believe that the public regards their vocation as honorable or their work as just. Many officers feel that they are looked upon with suspicion, in part because they have the authority to use force to ensure compliance. Some scholars argue that this pessimistic attitude increases officers' desire to use force on citizens.[8] Yet, in public opinion polls, the overwhelming majority of Americans express a high opinion of the police. Even in economically depressed inner-city areas where the police may be viewed by some as the tools of an unjust society, most of the inhabitants see them as protectors of their persons and property.

Police officers' isolation from the public is enhanced by the fact that many officers primarily interact with the public during moments of conflict, emotion, and crisis. Victims of crimes and accidents are often too hurt or distraught to thank the police. Citizens who are told to cease some activity when the police attempt to maintain order may be angry that the police intervened. Even something as minor as telling someone to reduce the volume on a stereo may make the police the "bad guy" in the eyes of citizens who believe that the officers' authority limits their freedom. Ironically, these problems may be worst in the urban ghetto neighborhoods that most need and want effective policing. In these neighborhoods, citizens may fail to report crimes and refuse to cooperate with investigations because of pervasive mistrust of the police.

Why do some urban residents resent the police? Studies have shown that permissive law enforcement and brutality are the two basic reasons. In minority neighborhoods, the police are often accused of giving inadequate service and, as discussed more fully in the next section, with abusing residents physically or verbally. The police are seen as permissive when an officer treats an offense committed against a victim from the same ethnic group as the offender more lightly than a similar incident in which offender and victim are members of different groups. The police often explain such differential treatment as a result of working in a hostile environment. The white patrol officer may fear that breaking up a street fight among members of a minority group will provoke the wrath of onlookers, while community residents may in fact view such negligence as a further indication that the police do not care about their neighborhood.

Studies have documented the prejudices of many police officers toward the poor and racial minorities. These attitudes lead some officers to view all African-Americans and Hispanics as slum dwellers and thus as potential criminals. Likewise, many residents of urban ghettos feel that police mistreat them. If police and citizens view each other with intense hostility, personal encounters will be strained, and the potential for violent explosions will be great. Some people attribute the Los Angeles riots of 1992, in part, to a buildup of mistrust and hostility between central-city residents and governing officials, including the police. In such circumstances, it is little wonder that ghetto residents think of the police as an occupation army and that the police think of themselves as combat soldiers. As noted by Jerome Skolnick and James Fyfe, the military organization of the police and the "war on crime" mentality encourage police violence against citizens of the inner city, who are viewed as the enemy.[9]

JOB STRESS

The police officer's working personality can contribute to conflict and increase the stressfulness of situations faced by officers. This stress, stemming from the elements of danger and authority, may adversely affect not only the officer's treatment of the citizens whom he or she encounters but also the officer's personal health. Considering the fact that police officers are perpetually on alert, occasionally face grave dangers, and feel unappreciated by a public they perceive to be hostile, it's hardly surprising that their physical and mental health may suffer. Only since the late 1970s have law enforcement officials truly recognized the nature of these hazards. One study of 2,300 officers in twenty departments found that 37 percent had serious marital problems, 36 percent health problems, 23 percent alcohol problems, 20 percent problems with their children, and 10 percent drug problems.[10] Newspaper and magazine articles with such titles as "Time Bombs in Blue" discuss the effects of the pent-up emotions, regular confrontations with violence and human tragedy, and physical demands of the job.

Psychologists and other behavioral scientists have identified many of the factors that produce stress and have noted four general categories of stress to which officers are subject:

1. *External stress.* This is produced by real threats and dangers, such as the necessity of entering a dark and unfamiliar building, responding to a "man with a gun" alarm, and pursuing lawbreakers at high speeds.

2. *Organizational stress.* This is produced by the inherent characteristics of work within a paramilitary structure: constant adjustment to changing schedules, irregular working hours, and forced compliance with detailed rules and procedures.

3. *Personal stress.* This may be generated by an officer's racial or gender status among peers, with consequent difficulty in getting along with individual fellow officers and in adjusting to group-held values not in accordance with one's own, as well as perceptions of bias and social isolation.

4. *Operational stress.* This reflects the total effect of confronting daily the tragedies of urban life; dealing with thieves, derelicts, and the mentally deranged; being lied to so often that all citizens become suspect; being required to place oneself in dangerous situations to protect an apparently unappreciative public; and being constantly aware of the possibility of being held legally liable for one's actions.[11]

Officials have been slow to deal with the problems of police stress, but psychological and medical counseling has become more available for officers. Some departments have instituted stress prevention, group counseling, liability insurance, and family involvement programs. In addition, many state legislatures have instituted more liberal disability and retirement rules for police than for other public employees because their jobs are recognized to be more stressful and potentially debilitating.[12]

As we have seen in the foregoing discussion, police officers face special pressures that can affect their interactions with the public and even harm their physical and mental health. How would you react to the prospect of facing danger and being on the lookout for crime every moment outside your home, even when you were not actually working? It seems understandable that police officers become a close-knit group, yet such isolation from society may diminish their understanding of other human beings. It may also needlessly enhance their belief that the public is ungrateful and hostile. As a result, police officers' actions toward members of the public may be unnecessarily hostile, gruff, and sometimes violent.

POLICE ABUSE OF POWER

The example of Officer Dowd and police misconduct in New York City is not unique. The beating of Rodney King by Los Angeles police officers as described in the Close-Up attracted national attention. In addition, there have been periodic investigations of police corruption in various cities. Although such incidents have occurred throughout American history, only during the past quarter-century has an awakened citizenry focused attention on the problems of police misconduct, especially the illegal use of violence by law enforcement officers and criminal activities associated with police corruption. Although most officers do not engage in extreme misconduct, these problems deserve examination because they raise questions about the extent to which the public can control and trust law enforcement officers.

CLOSE-UP *The Beating of Rodney King*

A Sony camcorder owned by Los Angeles resident George Holliday may have been the instrument that had the most dramatic impact on the American police in the 1990s. Awakened late at night by sirens on March 3, 1991, Holliday looked out his apartment window to see a helicopter spotlight shining on a white Hyundai surrounded by police cars. Holliday grabbed his new camcorder and directed it at the scene. The videotape showed a large black man on his hands and knees being repeatedly beaten by two police officers using their two-foot metal truncheons, while a third officer stomped on him as others watched. The officers were seen striking the man on the ground, who attempted to rise, was beaten back down, and then beaten again.

Two days later, the ninety-second tape was shown on Los Angeles television and CNN broadcast it worldwide. The savage beating of Rodney King dominated the media for days, giving Americans some of the most explicit and shocking news footage of police misconduct ever seen on television. The videotape provided dramatic evidence of police actions that many had previously dismissed as unlikely to happen in America.

The arrest and trial of the LAPD officers set in motion an additional series of events that raised further questions about American justice. After a long trial, the four officers were acquitted by an all-white jury in suburban Simi Valley. News of that decision astounded most Americans. Many thought the evidence on the videotape was enough to convict the officers. The jury's decision confirmed the belief among African-Americans that the criminal justice system is racist. It led to massive rioting in the black and Hispanic areas of South Central Los Angeles, resulting in fifty-three fatalities, over a billion dollars in damage, and a city seething with racial fury. Only after a second, federal trial and the conviction of two of the officers on civil rights charges did many Americans believe that justice had finally been done.

SOURCE: Based on Jerome H. Skolnick and James J. Fyfe, *Above the Law: Police and the Excessive Use of Force* (New York: Free Press, 1993), Chapter 1.

POLICE BRUTALITY

Citizens use the term *police brutality* to describe a wide range of practices, from the use of profane or abusive language to physical force and violence. Stories of police brutality are not new. However, unlike the untrained officers of the early 1900s, today's officers are supposed to be professionals who know the rules and understand the need for proper conduct. Thus, the beating of Rodney King and other incidents of police brutality are deeply disturbing. Moreover, when abusive behavior by police comes to light, there is no way for the public to know how frequently police engage in such actions because the violence is often hidden from public view. If a citizen in a nearby window had not videotaped the beating of Rodney King, the officers could simply have rested on their claim that they did not use excessive force and King would have had no way to prove otherwise. How can we monitor and control such incidents, especially when many of them occur without witnesses present?

By law, the police have the right to use force if necessary to make an arrest, to keep the peace, or to maintain public order. But just how much force is necessary and under what circumstances it may be used are extraordinarily complicated and debatable questions. In particular, the use of deadly force in the apprehension of suspects has become a deeply emotional issue with a direct connection to community relations. When the police kill a suspect or bystander in the course of seeking an arrest, their actions can generate public outrage and hostility. Estimates of the number of citizens killed annually by the police range between 300 and 600, with about 1,500 more wounded.[13] That number has declined dramatically from the high level set in the 1970s. The drop in police killings of civilians, however, should not obscure the fact that "the typical victim of deadly force employed in police–civilian contact has been a young black male."[14]

Until the 1980s, the police had broad authority to use deadly force in pursuing suspected felons. The police in about half the states were previously guided by the common-law principle allowing the use of whatever force was necessary to arrest a fleeing felon. In 1985, the Supreme Court set a new standard for the police in *Tennessee v. Garner*, ruling that the police may not use deadly force in apprehending fleeing felons "unless it is necessary to prevent the escape and the officer has probable cause to believe that the suspect poses a significant threat of death or serious physical injury to the officer or others."[15] The events leading up to the killing of Edward Garner, a fifteen-year-old eighth-grader who was shot by a member of the Memphis Police Department, are examined in the accompanying Ideas in Practice.

The new standard presents problems because it can be difficult for the police to evaluate a suspect's dangerousness. Since officers must make quick decisions in highly stressful situations, it is impossible to create rules that will give clear guidance in all circumstances. The risk of significant lawsuits by victims of improper police shootings looms over contemporary police departments and creates an additional incentive for administrators to set and enforce standards for the use of force. However, as long as police officers carry weapons, some incidents will occur. Training, internal review of incidents, and disciplining or firing trigger-happy officers may help reduce the use of unnecessary force. Unfortunately, as long as police carry guns, such fatalities will occur and will drive a wedge between the community and the police.

POLICE CORRUPTION

Police corruption is not new to America. Early in the twentieth century, numerous city officials actively organized liquor and gambling businesses. In many cities, a link was maintained between politicians and police officials so that favored clients would be protected and competitors harassed. Much of the Progressive-Era movement to reform the police was designed to combat such corrupt relationships. Although political ties between police and politicians have been limited in most cities, corruption still exists.

Sometimes, corruption is defined so broadly that it ranges from accepting a free cup of coffee to robbing unlocked business establishments or beating suspects. Obviously, corruption is not easily defined, and there are many disagreements about what activities it should include. As a useful starting point, we can focus on concepts applied by criminal justice scholars who distinguish between corrupt officers who are "grass eaters" and those who are "meat eaters."

IDEAS IN PRACTICE

Officer Elton Hymon and his fellow officer, Leslie Wright, of the Memphis Police Department were dispatched to answer a "prowler-inside" call. Arriving at the scene, they saw a woman standing on her porch and gesturing toward the adjacent house. She told them she heard glass breaking and someone was inside next door. While Wright radioed for help, Hymon went to the back of the house, heard a door slam, and saw someone run across the backyard toward a six-foot chainlink fence. With his flashlight, Hymon was able to see that the fleeing young male was unarmed. The officer called out, "Police! Halt!" but the young man began to climb the fence. Convinced that if he made it over the fence he would escape, Hymon fired, hitting him in the back of the head. The fleeing suspect died on the operating table, the ten dollars he had stolen in his pocket. Hymon was acting under Tennessee law and Memphis Police Department policy.

Given the Supreme Court's decision in *Tennessee v. Garner*, what should police officers do in such situations? What if it is unclear whether the fleeing suspect is armed?

Tennessee v. Garner (1985)

Deadly force may not be used against an unarmed and fleeing suspect "unless it is necessary to prevent the escape and the officer has probable cause to believe that the suspect poses a significant threat of death or serious physical injury to the officer or others."

"Grass Eaters" and "Meat Eaters"

"Grass eaters" are officers who accept payoffs that the routines of police work bring their way. "Meat eaters" are officers who aggressively misuse their power for personal gain. Although meat eaters are few in number, their exploits make headlines when discovered. By contrast, because "grass eaters" are numerous, they make corruption seem acceptable and they encourage adherence to a code of secrecy among police officers that brands anyone who exposes corruption as a traitor. Grass eaters are the heart of the problem and are often much more difficult to detect.

In the past, poor salaries, politics, and the hiring of flawed recruits have been cited as factors behind corruption. While some claim that a few "rotten apples" should not taint an entire police force, corruption in some departments has been so rampant that the rotten-apple theory does not adequately explain the situation. An explanation based on organizational factors adds another dimension. Much police work involves the enforcement of laws in situations in which there is no complainant or it is unclear whether a law has actually been broken. Moreover, most police work is carried out at the officer's own discretion, without direct supervision. Thus, many opportunities may arise for police officers to gain benefits by using their discretion to favor people engaged in questionable or even illegal conduct.

The norms of a department may shield the corrupt cop from detection. Officer Dowd engaged in a wide range of criminal activities in New York City for many years without other police officers acting to stop him. If police administrators judge success merely by maintenance of order on the streets and a steady flow of arrests and traffic citations, then they may not have any idea what their officers actually do while on patrol. Officers therefore may learn that they can engage in improper conduct without worrying about investigations by supervisors as long as the streets remain in a normal state of order and they keep their activities out of the public spotlight. Officer Dowd's activities and those of other New York City police officers were investigated by the Mollen Commission in 1993. Another officer who testified before the Commission startled its members when he said that "no commanding officer ever asked how he and his colleagues were spending their days . . . or how well they were serving the residents they were supposed to protect."[16] Opportunities for corruption will always exist when police administrators make little or no effort to monitor the activities of their officers. Moreover, as the Knapp Commission discovered when it investigated widespread corruption among New York City police in 1972, patrol officers who are not involved in corruption often tolerate and ignore illegal activities that they see or suspect is conducted by their colleagues. Thus, informal practices throughout the police hierarchy create an environment in which corruption may flourish.

Enforcement of vice laws, especially those regarding drugs, creates formidable problems for police agencies. In many cities, the financial rewards to vice offenders are so high that they can easily afford to make lucrative payments to unethical officers to protect themselves against prosecution. Problems are compounded by the fact that police operations against victimless crimes are proactive. Unless drugs are being sold openly and thereby upsetting residents in a neighborhood, there are no victims to complain if police officers ignore or even profit from the activities of drug dealers.

Over time, illegal activity may become accepted as the normal way to do business. Ellwyn Stoddard, who studied "blue-coat crime," has said that it can become part of an "identifiable informal 'code.'"[17] He suggests that police officers can become socialized to the code early in their careers. Those who deviate by "snitching" on their fellow officers may be ostracized. When corruption comes to official attention because it exceeds the limits of the code, officers protect the code by distancing themselves from the known offender rather than stopping their own improper conduct. Activities under this blue-coat code may include the following:

*The enforcement of drug laws
creates situations in which
police corruption can occur.*

- *Mooching:* Accepting free coffee, cigarettes, meals, liquor, groceries, or other items, justified as compensation either for being in an underpaid profession or for providing future acts of favoritism to the donor.
- *Bribery:* Receiving cash or a "gift" in exchange for past or future help in avoiding prosecution. The officer may claim to be unable to positively identify a criminal, may deliberately be in the wrong place when a crime is to occur, or may take some other action that can be excused as carelessness and not used as proof of deliberate miscarriage of justice. Bribery is distinguished from mooching by the higher value of the gift and by the mutual understanding in regard to services to be performed.
- *Chiseling:* Demanding price discounts, free admission to places of entertainment whether in connection with police duty or not, and the like.
- *Extortion:* Demanding payment for an advertisement in a police magazine or purchase of tickets to a police function; holding a "street court" in which minor traffic tickets can be avoided by the payment of cash "bail" to the arresting officer, with no receipt given.
- *Shopping:* Picking up small items such as candy bars, gum, and cigarettes at a store where the door has been accidentally left unlocked at the close of business hours.
- *Shakedown:* Appropriating expensive items for personal use during an investigation of a break-in, burglary, or unlocked door and attributing their loss to criminal activity. Shakedown is distinguished from shopping by the value of the items taken and the ease with which former ownership of items may be determined if the officer is caught in the act of procurement.
- *Premeditated theft:* Carrying out planned burglaries involving the use of tools, keys, or other devices to force entry and steal property. Premeditated theft is distinguished from shakedown only by the previous arrangements made in regard to the theft, not by the value of the items taken.
- *Favoritism:* Issuing license tabs, window stickers, or courtesy cards that exempt users from arrest or citation for traffic offenses (sometimes extended to wives, families, and friends of recipients).
- *Perjury:* Lying to provide an alibi for fellow officers apprehended in unlawful activity approved by the "code" or otherwise failing to tell the truth so as to avoid sanctions.

- *Prejudice:* Treating minority groups in a manner less than impartial, neutral, and objective, especially members of groups that are unlikely to have sufficient political influence in City Hall to cause the arresting officer trouble.[18]

Police corruption has multiple effects on law enforcement: (1) Criminals are left free to pursue their illegal activities, (2) departmental morale and supervision drop, and (3) the image of the police suffers. The credibility of a police agency is extremely important in light of the need for citizens' cooperation. When the belief prevails that the police are not much different from the "crooks," effective crime control is impossible.

What is startling is that many people do not equate police corruption with other forms of criminal activity. Some citizens believe that police corruption is tolerable as long as the streets are safe. This unfortunate attitude ignores the underlying point that corrupt officers are serving only themselves and are not actually committed to serving the public.

Controlling Corruption

The public must be involved in stopping police corruption. All departments have policy statements about proper police behavior and mechanisms for dealing with complaints. Highly publicized scandals attract the attention of politicians and the news media, but it is up to individual citizens to initiate complaints about day-to-day improprieties. Once a member of the public makes a complaint, however, significant questions remain about how best to investigate and respond. Some police departments tend to sweep such complaints under the rug. The most successful departments often have strong leaders who make it clear to the public and to officers that corruption will not be tolerated and that complaints will be investigated and pursued seriously.

It is difficult to strike the appropriate balance between making a police department responsive to citizen complaints and possibly paralyzing law enforcement by a flood of citizen complaints. The fundamental challenge of developing civic accountability mechanisms is to use citizen input to force police to follow appropriate guidelines without limiting unnecessarily the ability of the police to carry out their legitimate functions. Unfortunately, no perfect means exist to control police and hold them accountable to the public. Currently, four less-than-perfect methods predominate: (1) internal affairs units, (2) civilian review boards, (3) standards and accreditation, and (4) civil liability suits.

internal affairs unit
A branch of a police department designated to receive and investigate complaints against officers alleging violation of rules and policies.

Internal Affairs Units. Depending on the size of the department, a single officer or an entire section may be designated an **internal affairs unit** to receive and investigate complaints against officers alleging violation of rules and policies. An officer who is charged with misconduct may face criminal prosecution or departmental disciplinary action that may lead to resignation, dismissal, or suspension. Officers assigned to the unit carry responsibilities similar to those of the inspector general's staff in the military. They have the unenviable task of investigating complaints against fellow officers. Hollywood films and television dramas may depict dramatic investigations of drug dealing and murder, but the more common investigations concern sexual harassment, alcohol or drug problems, misuse of physical force, and violations of departmental operational policies.

The internal affairs unit must be provided with sufficient investigative resources to carry out its mission and must have direct access to the chief.

Unfortunately, many departments have no formal complaint machinery, and when such machinery does exist, it often seems designed to discourage civilian input. Internal investigators on the force may assume that a citizen's grievance is an attack on the police as a whole and reflexively move to shield individual officers. Such situations deprive top administrators of information they need to correct a problem. The public, in turn, may come to believe that the questioned practices are expected or even condoned and that filing complaints is pointless. Moreover, even when the top administrator seeks to attack misconduct, it is often difficult to persuade police to testify against fellow officers. Internal affairs investigators find the work stressful since their status prevents them from maintaining close personal relationships with their fellow officers. A wall of silence arises around them. Such problems can be especially severe in smaller departments where the officers all know each other and regularly socialize together.

Civilian Review Boards. If a police department cannot demonstrate to the public that it effectively investigates and combats corrupt activities by officers, then the public likely will demand that the department submit to external investigations by civilian review boards. Police departments often resist such "interference" by "outsiders." However, because police departments are subject to regulations imposed by state legislatures and city councils, they may not be able to resist outside mechanisms for investigating corruption if the public doubts their ability to solve their own problems.

Civilian review boards are organized so that complaints can be channeled through a publicly constituted committee of persons who are not sworn police officers. These boards vary in their organization and powers, but all are charged with overseeing and reviewing how police departments dispose of citizen complaints. The boards may also recommend remedial action. They do not have the power to investigate or discipline individual officers.

Creation of the first civilian review boards in New York and Philadelphia in the 1960s led to major political battles. The Patrolman's Benevolent Association led a successful effort to have the voters reject the New York board in a referendum, and Mayor Frank Rizzo, a former police chief, dismantled Philadelphia's board. During the 1980s, with the growth of minority political power in major cities, there was a revival of civilian review boards. A 1991 survey of the fifty largest American cities found that thirty had some form of civilian review of the police.[19]

The primary police argument against civilian review boards is that persons outside law enforcement do not understand the problems of policing. The police contend that civilian oversight lowers morale and hinders performance and that officers will become ineffective in their duties if they must be concerned about possible disciplinary actions. In reality, however, the civilian review agencies have not been harsh in their recommendations about police conduct. As noted by Wayne Kerstetter, "The experience in New York, Philadelphia, and Berkeley suggests that civilian review is less likely than police internal review to find officers guilty of misconduct and is more lenient in its disciplinary recommendations when it does find them guilty."[20]

The review of police actions occurs after the incident has taken place and usually comes down to the officer's word against that of the complainant. Given the low visibility of the incidents that lead to complaints, a great many complaints are destined to be ruled unsubstantiated no matter how they are reviewed. For example, during 1990, only 8 percent of complaints against police officers in San Francisco were upheld by the civilian review board.[21]

Standards and Accreditation.   One way that communities can gain greater police accountability is to require that operations be conducted by nationally recognized standards. The movement to accredit departments that adhere to these standards has gained momentum during the past decade. This work has been supported by the Commission on Accreditation for Law Enforcement Agencies (CALEA), a private nonprofit corporation jointly developed by four major professional associations: the International Association of Chiefs of Police (IACP), the National Organization of Black Law Enforcement Executives (NOBLE), the National Sheriffs Association (NSA), and the Police Executive Research Forum (PERF).

The *Standards,* first published by CALEA in 1983, have been periodically updated. There are now nine hundred standards organized according to forty-eight topics. Each standard is a declarative statement, supplemented by an explanatory paragraph, that places clear-cut requirements on the agency. For example, under "Limits of Authority," Standard 1.2.2 requires that "a written directive governs the use of discretion by sworn officers." The commentary section states: "In many agencies, the exercise of discretion is defined by a combination of written enforcement policies, training and supervision. The written directive should define the limits of individual discretion and provide guidelines for exercising discretion within those limits."[22] Since police departments have been almost completely silent on their use of discretion, this requirement represents an enormous shift. However, the standard is not specific enough to define its own coverage. For example, does it cover stop and frisk, the handling of drunks, and the use of informants?

Police accreditation is voluntary. Organizations seeking accreditation contact CALEA, and personnel from that organization work with the department to meet the standards. This process involves self-evaluation by departmental executives, the development of management policies that meet the standards, and the training of officers with respect to the policies. CALEA personnel act like the inspector general within the military, visiting the department, examining the policies, and determining if the standards are met in daily operations. Certification is given to those departments that meet the criteria. The standards can be used as an important management tool, with officers trained to understand the standards and be held accountable for their actions.

Obviously, the standards do not guarantee that police officers within an accredited department will not engage in misconduct. However, they represent a significant effort to provide clear guidelines to officers about proper behavior. Moreover, accreditation can demonstrate to the public that the department is committed to ensuring that its officers perform their responsibilities in an ethical, professional manner.

Civil Liability Suits.   Civil suits against departments for their misconduct have potential for increasing civic accountability. Only recently has it been possible for citizens to sue public officials. In 1961, the U.S. Supreme Court ruled that Section 1983 of the Civil Rights Act of 1871 allows citizens to sue public officials for violations of their civil rights. This right was extended in 1978 when the Supreme Court ruled in *Monell* v. *Department of Social Services for the City of New York* that individual officials and the agency may be sued when an individual's civil rights are violated by the agency's "customs and usages." If an individual can demonstrate a harm caused by employees whose wrongful acts were the result of these "customs, practices, and policies, including poor training and supervision," then the individual can sue.[23]

Lawsuits charging brutality, false arrest, and negligence are increasingly being brought in both state and federal courts. Damages awards in the millions of dollars have been granted by courts to individuals in a number of states, and individual police departments have settled civil suits out of court. For example, a Michigan court awarded $5.7 million to the heirs of a man mistakenly shot by a Detroit officer, and the city of Boston paid a settlement of $500,000 to the parents of a teenager who was shot to death. The total payments made each year by city governments can be substantial. In 1990, Los Angeles paid $8 million in damages and Detroit paid $20 million.[24]

The courts have ruled that police work must follow generally accepted professional practices and standards. The potential for civil suits seems to have led to policy changes within departments. For instance, a $2-million judgment awarded to a Connecticut woman when police did nothing to stop her spouse from attempting to kill her led police departments throughout the country to re-evaluate their procedures for dealing with domestic violence complaints. Plaintiffs' victories in civil suits have helped spur accreditation because police executives believe that liability can be avoided or minimized if it can be demonstrated that their officers are complying with the highest professional standards. In fact, insurance companies providing civil liability protection now offer discounts to departments that achieve accreditation.

POLICE UNIONS

Like members of other occupational groups, the police have found that they can maximize their influence by organizing for collective action. Thus, police unions have become important players in shaping the working conditions, compensation rates, and procedural rules applied to law enforcement officers.

During much of this century, police employee organizations were mainly fraternal associations designed to provide opportunities for fellowship, to serve the welfare needs of police families (death benefits, insurance), and to promote charitable activities. In some cities, however, the police were organized for the purpose of collective bargaining, and by 1919, thirty-seven police locals had been chartered by the American Federation of Labor. The Boston police strike of 1919 was in fact triggered by the refusal of the city to recognize a local police union. However, it was not until the 1960s that the police, along with other public employees, began to join labor unions in large numbers. Today, nearly three-fourths of all U.S. police officers are members of unions. In some states, a police "union" is not recognized by the law, even though such an organization may have informal powers to meet with management and discuss the concerns of its membership.

The growth of police unionism has alarmed many law enforcement administrators and public officials. Police chiefs fear they will be unable to manage their departments effectively because various aspects of personnel administration (transfers, promotions) will become tied up in arbitration and grievance procedures. These administrators believe that unions interfere with their responsibilities for law enforcement policy and police administration. Meanwhile, public officials, recognizing the effectiveness of unions in gaining financial advantages for their members, are wary of their demands on government resources. They do not want the police unions to pressure them to

Police unions have become an active force in some cities.

raise taxes and thereby jeopardize their own prospects for re-election. There are also lingering questions about the implications of police participation in strikes, work slowdowns, and sickouts. Do such actions threaten the safety of the public? Do they undermine the legitimacy and image of police officers as persons dedicated to upholding the law and protecting the public?

Unlike with the steelworkers and other trade unionists, no national union represents all police. The localized employment relationship between police officers and local governments helps to explain why the relatively centralized national police organizations have failed to enroll large numbers of police officers as members.

Clearly, police officers are little different from other union members in that they are concerned primarily with wages, hours, and working conditions. Broader issues of changes in operating procedures have been touched on only when they affect these three traditional concerns. Unions in some localities have succeeded in having a "police officers' bill of rights" written into their contracts, specifying the procedures that will be followed when an officer must submit to an investigation that could lead to disciplinary action, demotion, or expulsion. In response to calls for increased recruitment of women and minorities, police unions also have tried to maintain the status quo. They have resisted affirmative action efforts, especially with regard to promotion, because such efforts threaten the prerogatives attached to seniority.

Police and other public employees have dramatically increased their collective bargaining since the 1970s. Police administrators have been challenged to deal with this new source of influence over many of the decisions traditionally made by police chiefs or commissioners. In addition, unions have added new dimensions to relationships between officers and their supervisors and thereby diminished aspects of the traditional strict, hierarchical military model of law enforcement organizations. New relationships between unions and police management have become all the more difficult during recent times of financial crisis as municipal governments have been forced to cut expenditures and personnel during periods of economic decline. State and local governments simply may not have the funds to increase police salaries to keep pace with inflation. In spite of concerns about their participation in shaping departmental policies, however, unions will continue to be an important vehicle through which officers attempt to voice their concerns and interests.

PRIVATE POLICING

In recent years, businesses have increasingly employed private security forces to deal with shoplifting, employee pilfering, robbery, and airplane hijacking. Today, retail and industrial establishments spend nearly as much for private protection as all localities spend for police protection. Many private groups of citizens, such as residents of affluent suburbs, have hired private police to patrol their neighborhoods.

ISSUES AND TRENDS IN PRIVATE POLICING

As Figure 6.3 shows, private policing has become a $52-billion-a-year enterprise and is a growth industry. An estimated four thousand such agencies employ a total of 1.5 million people in private security operations.[25] It has been

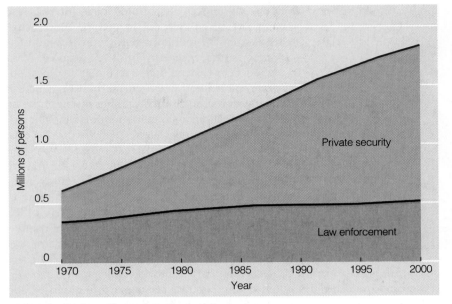

a Private security and law enforcement employment

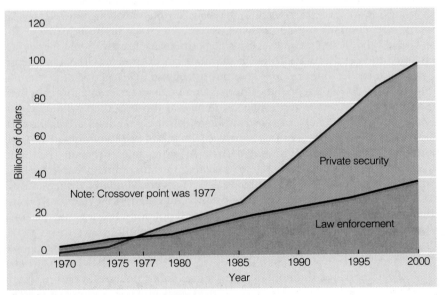

b Private security and law enforcement spending

FIGURE 6.3

Employment in Private and Public Protection, 1970–2000 (projected)
The number of people employed in the private security industry has surpassed the number employed by the public police and is growing. Such a large private force presents questions for the criminal justice system.

SOURCE: William Cunningham, John Strauchs, and Clifford Van Meter, *Private Security: Patterns and Trends* (Washington, DC: National Institute of Justice, 1991), p. 3.

estimated that by the year 2000 over $100 billion will be spent on private security in the United States, at which point the private policing field will be larger in terms of both personnel and resources than the federal, state, and local public police forces combined. A major concern of law enforcement officials and civil libertarians is the recruitment and training of private security personnel. Studies have shown that most such personnel are recruited from among persons with minimal education and training; because the pay is low, the work often attracts only people who cannot find other jobs or who seek only temporary work. Thus, most of the work is done by the young and the retired. Many security personnel carry firearms but have not been given any

Private security is assuming an increasingly large role in American society. However, questions have been raised about the training, tactics, and jurisdiction of these "rent-a-cops."

firearms training. As a result, some interests are strongly urging government to become more active in regulating and monitoring this growing industry.

In some states, security firms are licensed, often by the attorney general, while in others the local police have this authority. In general, however, there is little regulation of such firms, and many states have no hiring qualifications or training requirements for private policing personnel. The regulations that do exist tend to be focused on *contractual* rather than *proprietary* private policing services. Contractual services are those provided by private practitioners and agencies for a contracted fee. Proprietary services are those in which security personnel are actual employees of the organization that they protect. Contractual practitioners include individuals such as locksmiths, alarm specialists, and polygraph examiners as well as businesses such as Brink's, Burns, and Wackenhut, which provide guards and detectives. States and municipalities often require contract personnel to be licensed and bonded. Similar services are sometimes provided by proprietary security personnel employed by organizations such as retail stores, industrial plants, and hospitals. With the exception of individuals carrying weapons, proprietary security operations are not normally regulated by the state or municipality.

The activities of private security personnel vary greatly. Some merely act as watchmen and call the police at the first sign of trouble. Others are deputized by a public authority to carry out patrol and investigative duties as police officers do. Other private officers attempt to deter crime through their presence at businesses and other locations and through their willingness to make "citizens' arrests." In most instances, private personnel are authorized by law to make an arrest only when a felony has been committed in their presence. If private security agents or their companies overstep this limit, they face the possibility of being held civilly or even criminally liable for false arrest and the violation of an individual's civil rights. Similarly, if such officers conduct a search, the evidence might not be admitted into evidence in court and the officer might be subjected to a lawsuit for violating the person's rights. Some states, however, have passed antishoplifting laws to give civil immunity to store personnel who reasonably but mistakenly detain people suspected of larceny.

Private employers are often eager to hire public police officers on a part-time basis. These officers retain their full powers and status as police personnel even when working for a private employer while off duty. Although "moonlighting" is prohibited by 20 percent of American police departments, an estimated 150,000 police officers still work part-time for private firms.[26] While the use of off-duty police officers expands the number and visibility of law enforcement officers, it also raises concerns.

Police officers must avoid any appearance of conflict of interest when they accept private employment. They are barred from jobs that conflict with their public responsibilities. For example, they may not work as process servers, bill collectors, repossessors, or pre-employment investigators for industry. They are also banned from working as investigators for criminal defense attorneys or as bail bondsmen. Officers are also generally prohibited from working in places that profit from gambling, and many departments prohibit employment in bars or other places where regulated goods, such as alcohol, are sold. It is difficult to anticipate the complete range of situations in which an officer's private employment might harm the image of the police department or create a conflict with police responsibilities. Thus, departments need to be aware of new situations that might demand refinement of their regulations for private employment for off-duty officers.

An additional issue concerns the practical impact of private employment on the capabilities of the local police department. Private employment cannot be allowed to tire out police officers and impair their ability to protect the public when they are on duty. Late-night duties as a private security officer, for example, may compromise a sworn officer's ability to police effectively the following morning.

As a result of potential problems, departments require that officers request permission for outside work. Permission may be denied for a number of reasons, including work that lowers the dignity of the police, that is physically dangerous or unacceptably risky, that is not in the "home" jurisdiction and approval is not granted by the "outside" police jurisdiction, that requires more than eight hours of off-duty service, and that interferes with routine department schedules.

PUBLIC-PRIVATE INTERFACE

The relationship between public and private law enforcement is a concern for police officials. Private agents work for the people who employ them, and their goals may not always coincide with the public interest. Questions have been raised about the authority of private policing personnel to make arrests, to conduct searches, and to participate in undercover investigations. Of crucial importance is the issue of the boundary between the work of the police and that of private agencies. Lack of coordination and communication between public and private organizations has resulted in botched investigations, destruction of evidence, and overzealousness, all of which harm our ability to control crime.

Growing recognition of this problem has led to increased efforts in many locales for private security officials to work closely with police. However, many corporate security managers still tend to treat crimes by employees as internal matters that do not concern the police. Security managers have said that they generally report *UCR* index crimes to the police. However, incidents of employee theft, insurance fraud, industrial espionage, commercial bribery, and computer crime tend *not* to be reported to public authorities. In such situations, the chief concern of private companies is to prevent losses and protect assets. Although some such incidents are reported to the public prosecutor for action, the majority of them are resolved through internal procedures ("private justice") within the victimized company. When such offenses are discovered, the offender may be "convicted" within the company and punished by forced restitution through payroll deductions or the loss of the job and the dissemination of information about the incident throughout the industry. Private organizations often bypass the public criminal justice system in an effort to avoid the need to cope with changing prosecution policies, administrative delays in prosecution, discovery rules that would open the internal affairs of the company to public scrutiny, and bad publicity. Thus, an interesting question arises: To what extent does a parallel system of private justice exist with regard to some offenders and some crimes?[27]

The private policing industry arose and has grown in response to a perceived need. The need may have come from the growth of crime, but it may also have developed because of the perception that the public police could not effectively carry out particular tasks. It is important that citizens distinguish between the policing actions of the public and private sectors. It also is important that private policing not hamper the work of law enforcement or create new problems by recruiting unqualified personnel, misusing off-duty police officers as private employees, or failing to communicate with police departments.

SUMMARY

American policing is shaped by many forces. The people recruited to be police officers and the training that they receive provide the initial bases for the actions of law enforcement officers and their relationship with the public. The profile of the American police has changed dramatically as more women and minority group members have been recruited to the force. Although police departments control the recruitment and training of officers, these mechanisms do not completely determine how officers will make decisions and react to situations. Decisions and actions are also shaped by the norms and values of the police subculture, which are taught to new officers in informal ways through their socialization experiences on the streets with experienced officers. The stress of danger and the need to assert authority are powerful influences on the working personality of police officers interacting with the public on the streets. Some aspects of their informal training may give officers realistic tools for spotting suspicious activities and preventing disorder. Other aspects, however, may have detrimental consequences, isolating officers from others in society and fostering a sense of police solidarity that interferes with investigations of police corruption.

When police misconduct is reported, departments may face major challenges in gaining cooperation from officers who have relevant information and in avoiding a tendency to protect the department from scandal rather than seek the truth. If police departments, through their internal affairs units, do not seem able to investigate and correct wrongdoing, pressures will build from the public and politicians to employ other means to civil accountability. Civilian review boards are resisted by officers and their unions, but such boards actually have not been harsh on officers whose actions have been reviewed. Some departments have employed standards and accreditation, which can clarify departmental regulations but cannot control the actions of officers on the streets. Hovering over all contemporary departments is the threat of significant monetary damages awards from civil lawsuits against the police. This realistic threat has increased administrative concern about guiding, monitoring, and controlling the activities of police officers. In spite of departments' best efforts, however, there is no way to prevent occasional "bad apples" like Officer Dowd from seizing opportunities for self-enrichment through police work.

Two trends in policing—unionism and private policing—will influence the future of policing. The unionization of officers has challenged many practices of police executives. The expansion of private policing is a response to the need of organizations and individuals for order maintenance and crime prevention, but it also creates new issues and problems concerning the recruitment and training of private police, the powers of private police, and the relationship between private police and public police departments.

QUESTIONS FOR REVIEW

1. What is the importance of recruitment and training practices for policing?
2. What is meant by the police subculture, and how does it influence an officer's work?
3. How should police administrators attempt to combat the problems of police brutality and corruption?
4. How does the unionization of police officers affect police administration?
5. What are some problems associated with private policing?

NOTES

1. David L. Carter, Allen D. Sapp, and Darrel W. Stephens, *The State of Police Education: Policy Direction for the 21st Century* (Washington, DC: Police Executive Research Forum, 1989), p. 43.
2. Samuel Walker, "Employment of Black and Hispanic Police Officers, 1983–1988," Occasional Paper 89-1, Center for Applied Urban Research, University of Nebraska at Omaha, February 1989.
3. U.S. Department of Justice, *Crime in the United States* (Washington, DC, Government Printing Office, 1993), p. 217.
4. Peter Bloch and Deborah Anderson, *Policewomen on Patrol: First Report* (Washington, DC: Police Foundation, 1974), pp. 1–7.
5. Michael K. Brown, *Working the Street* (New York: Russell Sage Foundation, 1981), p. 82.
6. Jerome Skolnick, *Justice Without Trial: Law Enforcement in a Democratic Society* (New York: Wiley, 1966), p. 44.
7. U.S. Department of Justice, National Institute of Justice, Joel Garner and Elizabeth Clemmer, "Danger to Police in Domestic Disturbances—A New Look," *Research in Brief* (Washington, DC: Government Printing Office, 1986).
8. Robert M. Regoli, John P. Crank, and Robert G. Culbertson, "Rejoinder-Police Cynicism: Theory Development and Reconstruction," *Justice Quarterly* 4 (1987), pp. 281–286.
9. Jerome H. Skolnick and James J. Fyfe, *Above the Law: Police and the Excessive Use of Force* (New York: Free Press, 1993), p. 160.
10. John Blackmore, "Are Police Allowed to Have Problems of Their Own?" *Police Magazine* 1 (1978), pp. 47–55.
11. Robert J. McGuire, "The Human Dimension in Urban Policing: Dealing with Stress in the 1980s," *Police Chief* 46 (November 1979), p. 27. See also Francis Cullen, Terrence Leming, Bruce Link, and John Wozniak, "The Impact of Social Supports in Police Stress," *Criminology* 23 (1985), p. 503–522.
12. Gail A. Goolkasian, Ronald W. Geddes, and William DeJong, "Coping with Police Stress," in *Critical Issues in Policing*, ed. Roger G. Dunham and Geoffrey P. Alpert (Prospect Heights, IL: Waveland Press, 1989), pp. 498–507.

13. William Geller, "Deadly Force: What We Know," *Journal of Police Science and Administration* 10 (1982), pp. 151–177; Lori Fridell, "Justifiable Use of Measures in Research on Deadly Force," *Journal of Criminal Justice* 17 (1989), pp. 157–165.

14. James J. Fyfe, "Reducing the Use of Deadly Force: The New York Experience," in U.S. Department of Justice, *Police Use of Deadly Force* (Washington, DC: Government Printing Office, 1978), p. 28.

15. *Tennessee* v. *Garner*, 53 L.W. 4410 (1985).

16. Joseph P. Armao and Leslie U. Cornfeld, "Why Good Cops Turn Rotten," *The New York Times*, 1 November 1993, p. A12. The authors are chief counsel and deputy chief counsel to the Mollen Commission.

17. Ellwyn R. Stoddard, "The Informal 'Code' of Police Deviancy: A Group Approach to Blue-Coat Crime," *Journal of Criminal Law, Criminology, and Police Science* 59 (1968), p. 204.

18. Ibid., p. 205.

19. Samuel Walker and Vic W. Bumphus, "Civilian Review of the Police: A National Survey of the 50 Largest Cities, 1991," *Criminal Justice Policy Focus*, Criminal Justice Policy Research Group, Department of Criminal Justice, University of Nebraska at Omaha, 1991.

20. Wayne A. Kerstetter, "Who Disciplines the Police? Who Should?" in *Police Leadership in America*, ed. William Geller (New York: Praeger, 1985), p. 162.

21. Skolnick and Fyfe, *Above the Law*, p. 229.

22. *Standards for Law Enforcement Agencies* (Fairfax, VA: Commission on Accreditation for Law Enforcement Agencies, 1989), pp. 1–2.

23. Skolnick and Fyfe, *Above the Law*, p. 202.

24. Rolando del Carmen, *Civil Liabilities in American Policing* (Englewood Cliffs, NJ: Brady, 1991); Samuel Walker, *The Police in America*, 2nd ed. (New York: McGraw-Hill, 1992); Skolnick and Fyfe, *Above the Law*, p. 202.

25. William C. Cunningham, John H. Strauchs, and Clifford W. Van Meter, *Private Security Trends 1970 to the Year 2000: The Hallcrest Report II* (Boston: Butterworth-Heinemann, 1990).

26. U.S. Department of Justice, National Institute of Justice, *Private Employment of Public Police*, by Albert J. Reiss, Jr. (Washington, DC: Government Printing Office, 1988).

27. See Melissa Davis, Richard Lundman, and Ramiro Martinez, Jr.,"Private Corporate Justice: Store Police, Shoplifters, and Civil Recovery," *Social Problems* 38 (1991), pp. 395–408.

PART III *Courts*

The arrest of an individual in a democracy is only the first part of a complex process designed to separate the guilty from the innocent. Part III examines this process by which guilt is determined in accordance with the law's requirements. Here, we will look into the work of prosecutors, defense attorneys, bondsmen, and judges to understand the contribution each makes toward the ultimate decision. It is in the adjudicatory stage that the goals of an administrative system blunt the force of the adversarial process prescribed by law. Although we may focus on courtroom activities, most decisions relating to the disposition of a case are made in less public surroundings. After studying these chapters, we should ask ourselves whether justice is served by processes that are more akin to bargaining than to adversarial combat.

CHAPTER 7
Prosecution and Defense

The Prosecutorial System

The Defense Attorney: Image and Reality

PROSECUTING AND DEFENDING O. J.

Three weeks after the June 12, 1994, murder of Nicole Brown Simpson and Ronald Goldman, Los Angeles Assistant District Attorney Marcia Clark faced off against Robert Shapiro, O. J. Simpson's attorney, in a preliminary hearing to determine whether sufficient evidence existed to charge the former football star with the murders of his ex-wife and Goldman. The preliminary hearing was conducted in the Los Angeles Municipal Court. The case was later transferred to Superior Court for a trial supervised by Judge Lance Ito.

Prosecutor Clark presented evidence and methodically questioned witnesses, including the police officers who had searched O. J. Simpson's home on the morning following the murders. There they had found a bloody glove that appeared to match one found at the murder scene as well as blood on Simpson's car and outside his home.

The search had been conducted without a warrant. In her role as prosecutor, Marcia Clark questioned the police in ways that allowed them to explain that they had not obtained a warrant because

they had genuine concerns about public safety. The police claimed they had not obtained a warrant because they feared that the killer was targeting Simpson and his family and may have attacked other people in the home. Defense attorney Robert Shapiro focused his argument on the legality of the search. He asked why, if the officers entered the house to make sure no one was injured rather than to search for evidence, they did not ask Simpson's daughter and a houseguest whether everyone was okay.

Municipal Court Judge Kathleen Kennedy-Powell listened intently to the testimony and arguments for several days. The prosecutor bore the burden of showing that the state had enough evidence to file formal charges against Simpson. Through skillful questions and arguments, Clark and Shapiro battled each other over the issue of whether the evidence obtained in the warrantless search should be excluded from court because it had been obtained illegally. Ultimately, Judge Kennedy-Powell ruled that the emergency situation justified the warrantless search and that there was adequate evidence to charge O. J. Simpson with the murders of Mrs. Simpson and Goldman.

As we examine the roles of prosecutors and defense attorneys in this chapter, keep in mind your image of Clark and Shapiro as highly skilled combatants. The prosecutor must present evidence to justify pursuing criminal charges and then prove the defendant's guilt beyond a reasonable doubt. The defense attorney must zealously defend his or her client by challenging the validity and trustworthiness of the prosecutor's evidence. These are the formal responsibilities of opposing attorneys in criminal cases. Clark and Shapiro showed how these adversarial roles can lead to courtroom battles. ★

prosecuting attorney
Legal officer, representing the government, who brings criminal charges against the accused.

United States attorneys
Officials appointed by the president and responsible for the prosecution of crimes that violate federal laws; members of the Department of Justice.

attorney general
Chief legal officer of a state who, in most states, has the power to prosecute in certain circumstances.

THE PROSECUTORIAL SYSTEM

In the United States, it is the government, through the actions of the **prosecuting attorney**, that brings criminal charges against the accused. Prosecutors have been immortalized in novels and motion pictures and on radio and television, so that they have become virtual folk heroes, securing conviction of the guilty while upholding justice for the innocent.

Like other aspects of the criminal justice system, responsibility for prosecution is decentralized. There is no "chief prosecutor of the United States." Violations of federal laws are prosecuted by **United States attorneys**, who are appointed by the president and who are members of the Department of Justice. One U.S. attorney and a staff of assistant U.S. attorneys are responsible for prosecuting federal crimes in each of the ninety-four U.S. district courts. These federal prosecutors are heavily involved in cases concerning drugs, corruption, and white-collar crime.

Each state has an elected **attorney general** who, in most states, has the power to prosecute under certain circumstances. A state attorney general may, for example, handle a statewide consumer fraud case if a chain of auto repair shops is suspected of systematically overcharging customers.

However, the vast majority of criminal cases are handled in the 2,700 county-level offices of the prosecuting attorney—known in various states as district attorney, state's attorney, or commonwealth attorney. These offices may range in size from five hundred assistant prosecutors and investigators, as in Los Angeles, to a single prosecutor with a part-time assistant in sparsely populated rural counties. Many assistant prosecutors are young attorneys who use the position as a means to gain courtroom experience before seeking higher-paying positions in private law firms.

POLITICS AND PROSECUTION

In all states except Connecticut and New Jersey, prosecutors are elected. The position is a traditional stepping-stone to higher political office, and many members of Congress and other important political figures began their careers as local prosecutors. Senator Arlen Specter of Pennsylvania, for example, was previously the district attorney for Philadelphia. In most states, neither the governor nor the attorney general possesses the power to oversee the activities and decisions of county prosecutors; the prosecutors are accountable only to the voters at election time.

Prosecutors' actions may be affected by local partisan politics. They may pursue cases in ways that enhance their own political fortunes or those of their parties. Los Angeles District Attorney Gil Garcetti, for example, held several nationally televised press conferences during the early stages of the O. J. Simpson investigation. Many people speculated that he was seeking to take advantage of free publicity because he was coming up for re-election in two years and because his office had previously received adverse publicity for its failure to gain successful convictions in other highly publicized cases, such as the Reginald Denny beating case after the Los Angeles riots of 1992 (see Chapter 9). In other cases, political motivations may cause prosecutors to investigate wrongdoing by leaders of the opposing political party while overlooking questionable activities by members of their own party.

Prosecutors are exceptionally influential because they are involved with many stages of the criminal justice process. From the time of arrest until the case is resolved, the prosecutor makes a series of decisions that help to determine what will happen to each suspect (see Figure 7.1). The prosecutor decides which charges to file, what bail amount to recommend, whether to pursue a plea bargain, and what sentence to recommend to the judge. Prosecutors are also influential in that state laws do not generally guide or limit their powers to make discretionary decisions. Courts have upheld the view that the prosecutor has complete freedom in deciding whether to bring charges and what the charges should be. Thus, while the state penal code describes the elements to be proven for specific crimes, prosecutors choose their course of action. For example, the lack of sufficient evidence to persuade a jury about a key element of the crime may give the prosecutor strong reason to discuss a plea bargain. In general, however, neither laws nor higher officials tell prosecutors which cases to pursue, what charges to file, and which cases to plea bargain. Prosecutors make their own calculations and apply their own values in making these decisions.

However, there are limits to the power of the prosecutor, including outside influences on their choices. As we shall see later in more detail, throughout the process, prosecutors have links with the other actors in the system—police, defense attorneys, judges—and prosecutors' decisions are usually affected by their relationships with these officials. Prosecutors' decisions are also affected by the public's awareness of a particular case. For example, the Los Angeles prosecutors, Gil Garcetti and Marcia Clark, would have to think long and hard before agreeing to a plea bargain in a highly visible double-murder case like that of O. J. Simpson. They would be forced to explain their decision to the public and they would know that many voters might disagree with their decision.

FIGURE 7.1
Typical Actions of a Prosecuting Attorney in Processing a Felony Case
The prosecutor has certain responsibilities at various points in the criminal process. At each point, the prosecutor is an advocate for the state's case against the accused.

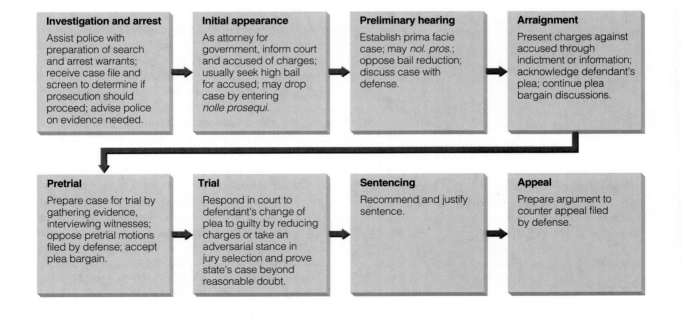

Investigation and arrest

Assist police with preparation of search and arrest warrants; receive case file and screen to determine if prosecution should proceed; advise police on evidence needed.

Initial appearance

As attorney for government, inform court and accused of charges; usually seek high bail for accused; may drop case by entering *nolle prosequi*.

Preliminary hearing

Establish prima facie case; may *nol. pros.*; oppose bail reduction; discuss case with defense.

Arraignment

Present charges against accused through indictment or information; acknowledge defendant's plea; continue plea bargain discussions.

Pretrial

Prepare case for trial by gathering evidence, interviewing witnesses; oppose pretrial motions filed by defense; accept plea bargain.

Trial

Respond in court to defendant's change of plea to guilty by reducing charges or take an adversarial stance in jury selection and prove state's case beyond reasonable doubt.

Sentencing

Recommend and justify sentence.

Appeal

Prepare argument to counter appeal filed by defense.

A QUESTION OF ETHICS

Assistant Prosecutor Debra McCoy looked at the case file. The police had arrested Leslie Wiggins, a prominent local businessman, for drunken driving. It seemed that Wiggins had been stopped after weaving on the highway at a high rate of speed. From the moment Officer Tompkins asked Wiggins to get out of the car, he knew he was very drunk. A breathalizer test revealed that Wiggins was well above the legal limit for sobriety. There was no question that this was an open-and-shut case. McCoy noted that Wiggins had been previously arrested, but the DWI (driving while intoxicated) charge had been dropped by her chief, Prosecutor Marc Gould.

"I don't know what happened last time," she thought, "but there is no question now." She recorded the charge of "driving while intoxicated" in the case file and forwarded it for review.

When the file had not yet returned for arraignment several days later, McCoy went to Gould's office.

"What happened to the Wiggins case?" she asked.

"Wiggins? Oh, that. Seems that the breathalizer wasn't reading right that night."

"Gee, I'm surprised. Tompkins didn't say anything about that when I talked with him yesterday. In fact, he was wondering when the case was coming up."

"Well, let's just not worry about this. I'm sure that Tompkins has other things to concern him. Don't think anything more about Wiggins."

McCoy left the office and wondered, "What's going on here?"

What *is* going on here? Will Gould's statement influence the cases of other drivers who were tested on the breathalizer the same evening that Wiggins was? How would dropping this case reflect on Gould or McCoy if, the next time Wiggins was stopped, it was at the scene of a fatal car accident? Is the fact that Wiggins is a prominent local businessman a factor?

Fortunately for prosecutors, most cases do not attract sustained public attention. After an arrest is announced, the public frequently pays little attention to the ultimate outcome in a criminal case. This low public visibility enhances the prosecutor's discretionary power. For example, discussions in which a prosecutor may agree to drop several charges against a defendant in exchange for a guilty plea take place behind closed doors. The accompanying Question of Ethics presents an example of the use of discretion as a factor in prosecutorial decisions.

Despite the fact that they make many decisions behind closed doors, prosecutors may be sensitive to public opinion. If the community favors or opposes strict enforcement of certain laws, especially victimless crimes such as marijuana smoking, petty gambling, or prostitution, then the prosecutors' decisions are likely to reflect that view.

ROLES OF THE PROSECUTOR

The description of the O. J. Simpson case at the beginning of this chapter conveyed the image of lawyers clashing in court as representatives of two competing sides. Defense attorney Robert Shapiro was seeking to cast doubt on the trustworthiness and admissibility of evidence that might be used against his client. Marcia Clark was seeking to overcome questions about the legality of the search of Simpson's home so as to gain court approval for charging Simpson with murder. While Shapiro sought only to advance his client's interests, Clark bore the additional responsibility of making sure that justice was achieved. Protecting the rights of defendants and ensuring that justice prevails are inherent duties of a prosecutor. Many prosecutors come to view themselves as instruments of law enforcement since they work closely with the police to obtain convictions. An underlying risk is that prosecutors may work toward obtaining convictions without adequately assessing whether the police respected the rights of the accused and whether the evidence clearly points only to the suspect rather than to someone else.

Social scientists use the concept of *role* to describe how people in a certain position may decide what to do according to the expectations both that they have for themselves and that others have for them. Various prosecutors may hold different ideas about the best role to play. Differing expectations from essential outsiders (judges, police officers, defense attorneys, and the public) can influence the ways in which prosecutors define the appropriateness of their own decisions and actions.

Prosecutors commonly hold one of four distinct conceptions about their role:

1. *Trial counsel for the police.* These prosecutors believe that they should reflect law enforcement views in the courtroom and take a crime fighter stance in public.
2. *House counsel for the police.* These prosecutors believe their primary function is to give legal advice so that arrests will stand up in court.
3. *Representative of the court.* These prosecutors consider their primary responsibility to be enforcement of the rules of due process to ensure that the police act in accordance with the law and uphold the rights of defendants.
4. *Elected official.* These prosecutors may be most responsive to community opinion, such that the possible political content of their decisions is one of their major concerns.

As lawyers for the state, prosecutors are expected to do everything to win each case, but they are also expected to see that justice is done.

Each of these roles involves a different conception of the prosecutor's responsibilities and primary clients. In the first two roles, prosecutors act as if the police are their primary clients and neglect their obligation to see that justice is done. By contrast, the third role may make the police unhappy if the prosecutor behaves as a supervising authority rather than as a member of a joint team intent on controlling crime and processing suspected wrongdoers toward punishment. In the fourth role, prosecutors may be less concerned about their own assessments of crime, justice, and punishment and more concerned with accommodating public opinion about whether to prosecute specific crimes and suspects.

THE DECISION TO PROSECUTE

The ultimate effectiveness of prosecutors depends on the cooperation of others (for example, police, judges, defense attorneys), because these actors are involved in gathering evidence, bargaining for plea agreements, and determining sentences. At the same time, prosecutors have complete discretion with respect to a crucial stage early in the process: the decision to prosecute. No case will move on to subsequent stages in the system unless the prosecutor decides to pursue charges. Even though the police may have made an arrest and gathered substantial evidence indicating that a person is guilty of a crime, the prosecutor makes the pivotal decision about whether to push that defendant further into the system or filter the defendant out.

Prosecutors may decide not to press charges because of factors related to a particular case or because they have established policies not to bring charges for certain offenses. For example, the U.S. Department of Justice provides its prosecuting attorneys with guidelines for determining whether a prosecution should be pursued or declined. The criteria include the following:

- Federal law enforcement priorities
- The nature and seriousness of the offense

- The deterrent effect of the prosecution
- The suspect's culpability in connection with the offense
- The suspect's history with respect to criminal activity
- The suspect's willingness to cooperate in the investigation or prosecution of others
- The probable sentence or other consequences if the suspect is convicted[1]

Along with deciding to prosecute a defendant, the prosecutor must also decide what charges to pursue. A defendant who commits a robbery, for example, may also be eligible to face charges for other actions committed during the robbery, such as assault and weapons possession. The prosecutor may charge this defendant only with robbery or may also include the other charges. For some offenses, such as armed robbery, a weapons possession charge is a **necessarily included offense**—that is, an offense committed for the purpose of committing another offense. In such cases, there may be a basis for conviction separately if the robbery charge is dropped during plea bargaining or if in a trial the jury chooses not to convict on the most serious charge. One important strategy for prosecutors is to charge defendants with several counts in order to create "bargaining chips" that can be used in working out a plea agreement. Each **count** is a separate offense of which a person is accused in an indictment or an information. For certain crimes, multicount indictments may be produced for the same criminal context, for example, when a forger cashes more than one check at a bank.

After deciding to bring charges, the prosecutor must disclose to the defense the facts and evidence to be introduced at trial, in a process called **discovery**. The defense must have the opportunity to see copies of any statements made by the defendant during questioning or reports on tests (for example: blood samples) conducted on the defendant, as well as the names and statements of witnesses. In O. J. Simpson's case, the prosecution assured the judge at the preliminary court appearance that medical tests on blood and hair samples would be made available to the defense as soon as they were received from the laboratory.

Discovery prevents the prosecution from surprising the defense with unexpected evidence and witnesses at trial. If the prosecutor's evidence is sufficient to convince the judge and jury, beyond a reasonable doubt, that the defendant committed the crime, revealing this information to the defense during discovery should not prevent the achievement of justice. If, however, the evidence is questionable or incomplete, then the defense needs the opportunity to challenge it so as to ensure that an innocent person is not convicted.

After a charge has been made, the prosecutor still possesses the discretion to reduce it in exchange for a guilty plea or to enter a notation of *nolle prosequi*, indicating that the charges will not be prosecuted and are therefore dismissed. In our system of public prosecution, there is no recourse to this decision since private citizens cannot institute a criminal action.

Key Relationships of the Prosecutor

Prosecutors' decisions are not determined solely by the formal policies and role conceptions within their office. Their decisions are also influenced informally by relationships with other actors in the system. Despite their independent authority, in reality prosecutors must take into consideration how the police, judges, and others will react.

necessarily included offense

An offense committed for the purpose of committing another offense, such as weapons possession for the purpose of committing robbery.

count

Each separate offense of which a person is accused in an indictment or an information.

discovery

A prosecutor's pretrial disclosure to the defense of the facts and evidence to be introduced at trial.

nolle prosequi

A notation entered by a prosecutor to indicate that the charges specified will not be prosecuted. In effect, the charges are thereby dismissed.

Police. Prosecutors depend on the police to handle the investigations, arrests, and evidence-gathering activities that make it possible to process criminal cases. Prosecutors cannot control which kinds of cases they will be able to pursue. They can only work with the cases that are brought to them by the police. If police are making many arrests simply to create an impressive crime clearance rate but those cases lack adequate evidence, the prosecutor will waste time identifying those cases that deserve to be pursued. Prosecutors may send some cases back to the police and request further evidence. Thus, there is a reciprocal exchange relationship between police and prosecutors. Each needs the other to achieve the joint goal of controlling crime, processing cases efficiently, and ensuring that lawbreakers are appropriately punished.

Prosecutors depend on the police for the information and evidence needed for successful indictment and conviction. Their exchange relationships with officers will influence the extent to which police cooperate.

Coordination between police officers and prosecuting attorneys has been a concern of many criminal justice officials because these two groups have different perspectives on crime and case processing. Police frequently believe that if they make an arrest, the prosecutor should pursue the case through to conviction. By contrast, prosecutors may be much more concerned with the quality of evidence in each case and therefore consider dropping charges in cases in which sufficient evidence is lacking. To remedy these problems, in many jurisdictions a deputy prosecutor and a police officer are assigned to form a cooperative link between police and prosecutors so that cases will flow more easily through the system.

Victims and Witnesses. Prosecutors also depend on the cooperation of victims and witnesses. Although a case can be prosecuted whether or not a victim wishes to press charges, many prosecutors will not bother pursuing cases in which an uncooperative victim must provide the key testimony and other necessary evidence. Similarly, prosecutors need cooperation from members of the public who have witnessed crimes.

The prosecutor's decision to prosecute is frequently based on an assessment of the victim's contribution to his or her own victimization and the victim's potential credibility as a witness. If a victim has a criminal record, the prosecutor may choose not to pursue the case because a jury would not consider the victim to be a credible witness. This judgment may be made despite the fact that the jury will never learn that the victim has a criminal record. In fact, the decision not to prosecute may actually reflect the prosecutor's belief, either explicit or unconscious, that someone with a criminal record is untrustworthy as a complainant or undeserving of the law's protection. In other words, the prosecutor's own biases in sizing up victims may determine which cases to pursue. Similarly, victims who are poorly dressed, uneducated, or inarticulate may find prosecutors more inclined to dismiss charges against the perpetrators based solely on the prosecutor's fear that a jury would find the victim unpersuasive as a witness.

Other victim characteristics may be factors. For example, prosecutors may not pursue cases involving prostitutes who are raped, drug abusers who are assaulted by drug dealers, and children who cannot stand up to the pressure of testifying in court.

161

Lt. Roger Cirella of the police drug task force of Northwest City entered the office of Chief Deputy Prosecutor Michael Ryan. Cirella reported that during questioning a well-known drug dealer intimated that he could provide evidence against a pharmacist suspected of illegally selling drugs. The officer wanted to transfer the case to the friendlier hands of a certain deputy prosecutor and to arrange for a reduction of charges and bail.

Cirella: Yesterday we got a break in the pharmacy case. We had arrested Sam Hanson after an undercover buy down on First Avenue. He says that a druggist at the Green Cross Pharmacy is selling out the back door. We thought that something like that was happening since we had seen these bums standing around there, but we've not been able to prove it. Hanson says he will cooperate if we'll go easy on him. Now, I'd like to get this case moved to Wadsworth, he's worked with us before, and that new guy who's on it now just doesn't understand our problems.

Ryan: O.K., but what's that going to accomplish?

Cirella: We also need to be able to fix it so Hanson gets out on bail without letting the druggies out there know he has become an informer. If we can get Judge Griffin to reduce bail, he can probably put up the bond. Now we also need to reduce the charges yet keep him on the string so that we can bring him right back if he doesn't play our game.

Ryan: I want to cooperate with you guys, but I can't let the boss get a lot of heat for letting a pusher out on the street. How are we going to know that he's not going to screw up?

Cirella: Believe me, we will keep tabs on him.

Ryan: O.K. But don't come here telling me we're going to get splashed with mud in the press.

What does this scenario tell us about the problem of enforcing drug laws?

Prosecutors may also base their decision to prosecute on whether or not the victim and the defendant had a prior relationship. Studies have shown that prosecutions are most successful when aimed at defendants accused of committing crimes against strangers.[2] When the victim is an acquaintance, friend, or even relative of the defendant, victims may refuse to cooperate as witnesses, and prosecutors and juries may regard the offense as less serious. Even if police officers make an arrest on the scene, a fight between spouses may strike a prosecutor as a weak case, especially if the complaining spouse begins to have second thoughts about prosecution. Fundamentally, many victims want to avoid the personal consequences of cooperating with the prosecutor to convict a spouse, family member, friend, or neighbor.

Judges. Prosecutors' decisions are also shaped by their knowledge of and relationships with judges. Knowing that a judge imposes exceptionally lenient sentences for particular offenses may discourage the prosecutor from pursuing such cases. For example, a judge in one major city announced that he believed that the only solution to America's drug problem was the legalization of drugs and a shift in governmental emphasis from law enforcement to treatment programs. As a result, the judge declared that every drug offender appearing before him who would be eligible for probation under state law could be assured of being sentenced to probation. In such situations, the prosecutor may begin dismissing cases rather than wasting resources in which strong penalties will not be gained. Other judges may adopt particular views about police practices, such as search and seizure or entrapment, which lead them to dismiss charges when evidence is obtained through questionable police conduct. When prosecutors can accurately anticipate such tendencies by judges, they become more likely to dismiss cases before they ever reach the judge.

Prosecutors also learn each judge's standards for sentencing. This enables the prosecutor to make effective decisions and sentencing recommendations during plea bargaining. In order for prosecutors to know whether they should reduce charges or drop counts in exchange for a plea bargain, they must be able to predict accurately what sentence the judge will agree to impose for a particular offense. If defense attorneys do not believe that the prosecutor is consulting with the judge or understands the judge's sentencing practices, then there is little incentive for the defense lawyer to encourage the defendant to plead guilty.

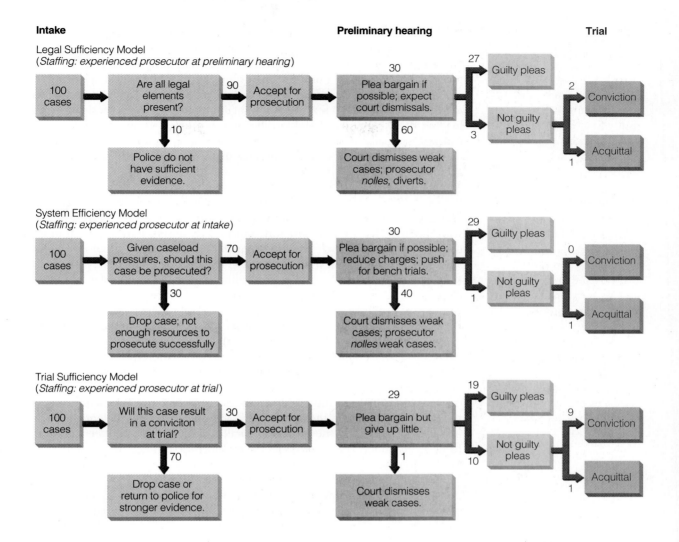

Intake　　　　　　　　　　**Preliminary hearing**　　　　　　　　**Trial**

Legal Sufficiency Model
(*Staffing: experienced prosecutor at preliminary hearing*)

100 cases → Are all legal elements present? → 90 → Accept for prosecution → Plea bargain if possible; expect court dismissals. → 27 → Guilty pleas → 2 → Conviction; 3 → Not guilty pleas → 1 → Acquittal

Are all legal elements present? → 10 → Police do not have sufficient evidence.

Plea bargain if possible; expect court dismissals. → 60 → Court dismisses weak cases; prosecutor *nolles*, diverts.

System Efficiency Model
(*Staffing: experienced prosecutor at intake*)

100 cases → Given caseload pressures, should this case be prosecuted? → 70 → Accept for prosecution → Plea bargain if possible; reduce charges; push for bench trials. → 29 → Guilty pleas → 0 → Conviction; 1 → Not guilty pleas → 1 → Acquittal

Given caseload pressures, should this case be prosecuted? → 30 → Drop case; not enough resources to prosecute successfully

Plea bargain if possible; reduce charges; push for bench trials. → 40 → Court dismisses weak cases; prosecutor *nolles* weak cases.

Trial Sufficiency Model
(*Staffing: experienced prosecutor at trial*)

100 cases → Will this case result in a conviciton at trial? → 30 → Accept for prosecution → Plea bargain but give up little. → 19 → Guilty pleas → 9 → Conviction; 10 → Not guilty pleas → 1 → Acquittal

Will this case result in a conviciton at trial? → 70 → Drop case or return to police for stronger evidence.

Plea bargain but give up little. → 1 → Court dismisses weak cases.

Decision-Making Policies

Guided by their role conceptions and by their exchange relations with actors in their respective courthouses, prosecutors develop their own policies on how to handle cases. These policies then serve to structure decision making, especially by guiding the decisions of assistant prosecutors about which cases to filter out of the system, which cases to terminate through plea bargaining, and which to push further along in the criminal justice process.

In a national study of prosecutors, Joan Jacoby identified three decision-making models: (1) the legal sufficiency model, (2) the system efficiency model, and (3) the trial sufficiency model.[3] As shown in Figure 7.2, the model adopted by a particular office affects decisions regarding the screening and disposing of cases. Within each model, the prosecutors select certain stages in the criminal justice process as the decision points for discretionary determinations that filter large numbers of cases out of the system.

Legal Sufficiency Model.　A case is initially screened merely to make sure that there are minimum legal elements to proceed with a preliminary hearing.

FIGURE 7.2
Three Policy Models of Prosecution Case Management and Allocation of Staff Resources
Prosecutors develop policies as to how their offices will manage cases. An assumption of all three models is that a portion of arrests will be dropped at some point in the system so that few

legal sufficiency model
Prosecution policy that asks whether sufficient evidence exists to provide a basis for prosecution of a case.

system efficiency model
Operation of the prosecutor's office that encourages speedy and early disposition of cases in response to caseload pressures in the system.

trial sufficiency model
Prosecution policy that asks whether sufficient legal elements exist to ensure successful prosecution of a case.

accusatory process
The series of events from the arrest and booking of a suspect to the filing of formal charges with the court.

diversion
An alternative to prosecution in the criminal justice system whereby a defendant is placed in a treatment, education, or community service program.

Under this **legal sufficiency model**, prosecutors are merely asking whether sufficient evidence exists to provide a basis for prosecuting the defendant. Some prosecutors believe that they have a responsibility to pursue any case for which they believe they can prove that the minimum legal elements of the charge are met. Prosecutors who use this policy may decide to prosecute a great many cases. As a result, they must employ strategies to avoid overloading the system and draining their own resources. Thus, assistant prosecutors, especially those assigned to misdemeanor courts, must use plea bargaining to the utmost, and they must expect many judicial dismissals and acquittals in court.

System Efficiency Model. In the **system efficiency model**, each case is evaluated in light of the caseload pressures affecting the prosecutor's office, with the underlying goal of attaining quick, early dispositions to stretch prosecution resources. If there are questions in the prosecutor's mind about the adequacy of evidence in a particular case, the case may simply be dismissed. If there is adequate evidence, the prosecutor may file felony charges but agree to reduce to misdemeanor charges in exchange for a quick guilty plea. According to Jacoby's research, the system efficiency model is usually followed when the trial court is backlogged and the prosecutor has limited resources.

Trial Sufficiency Model. According to the **trial sufficiency model**, a case is accepted and charges are made only when sufficient legal elements exist to ensure successful prosecution. The prosecutor asks, "Will this case result in a conviction?" Although the prosecutor does not pursue only sure convictions, the cases pursued have the appropriate facts and sufficient evidence to support a conviction, and the prosecutor makes every effort to obtain that outcome. This model requires good police work, a prosecution staff that is experienced in trial work, and sufficient court resources to handle trials.

Obviously, the different models lead to different results. While a suspect's case may be dismissed for insufficient evidence in a "trial sufficiency" court, it may be prosecuted, and the suspect eventually pressured to enter a guilty plea, in a "legal sufficiency" court.

Case Evaluation

The **accusatory process** is the series of events from the arrest and booking of a suspect to the filing of formal charges with the court. Throughout the process, the prosecutor must evaluate various considerations in order to decide whether to press charges and what charges to file. A prosecutor's decision will be structured by whichever of the three models his or her office employs. These models cannot, however, be applied automatically. Each model requires an evaluation of the quality and quantity of evidence for a particular case. In addition, each model may include assessments of the resources available in the prosecutor's office and trial court. For example, if the court is overcrowded and the prosecutor has few resources, then the prosecutor may be forced to use the system efficiency model even if he or she ideally would prefer to use another approach.

Prosecutors may decide pragmatically in individual cases that the accused and society would benefit from a particular course of action. In this sense, prosecutors attempt to individualize justice according to their own assessments of proper and beneficial outcomes. For example, a young, first-time offender or minor offender with substance abuse problems may be placed in a **diversion** program rather than prosecuted in the criminal justice system.

Some courts have programs that divert defendants to treatment, education, and community service programs, as well as to other alternatives to criminal conviction.

The preceding discussion may seem to suggest that prosecutors make rational calculations concerning each case. We must not forget, however, that prosecutors are human beings whose decisions are affected by attitudes, values, and opinions, some of which may be contrary to the ideals of law. Thus, improper considerations may also infect their decisions. For example, a study of 70,000 cases in the Los Angeles County district attorney's office found that men were more likely than women to be prosecuted and that Hispanics were prosecuted more often than African-Americans, who were prosecuted more often than Anglos. The researchers believe that in marginal cases—those that may be either rejected or prosecuted—the scale is often tipped against minorities.[4]

THE DEFENSE ATTORNEY: IMAGE AND REALITY

In an adversarial legal system, the **defense attorney** is the prosecutor's counterpart—the lawyer who represents accused and convicted offenders in their dealings with the criminal justice system. O. J. Simpson's attorney, Robert Shapiro, waged a vigorous battle against the police and prosecution in each stage of the criminal justice process. Remember, however, as we saw with the "wedding cake" model in Chapter 2, that only celebrated cases are decided through the adversarial processes that characterize the O. J. Simpson case. By contrast, most cases are processed through plea bargaining, discretionary judgments by prosecutors and other actors, and exchange relations among justice system personnel. Thus, in many cases, the defense attorney may seem less like the prosecutor's adversary and more like a partner in the goal of concluding cases as quickly and efficiently as possible through negotiation.

defense attorney
The lawyer who represents defendants and convicted offenders in their dealings with the criminal justice system.

THE ROLE OF THE DEFENSE ATTORNEY

Defense attorneys possess knowledge of law and procedure, investigative resources, advocacy skills, and, in many instances, relationships with prosecutors and judges that will help a defendant avoid an unjustified conviction or will produce a guilty plea with less than the maximum possible punishment. Under our constitutional legal system, the defense attorney fulfills the important function of ensuring that the prosecution proves its case in court or possesses substantial evidence of guilt before a trial or guilty plea leads to conviction and punishment.

As shown in Figure 7.3, the defense attorney is involved in advising the defendant and protecting the defendant's constitutional rights at each stage of the criminal justice process. The defense attorney advises the defendant during initial questioning by the police, represents the defendant at each arraignment and hearing, and continues to advocate for the defendant throughout the appeal process if he or she is convicted. Without the active involvement of a defense attorney, there would be a risk that prosecutors and judges would not respect the constitutional rights of defendants. While performing these functions, the defense also provides psychological support to the defendant and the defendant's family. Relatives are often bewildered, frightened, and confused about how the criminal justice process operates. The

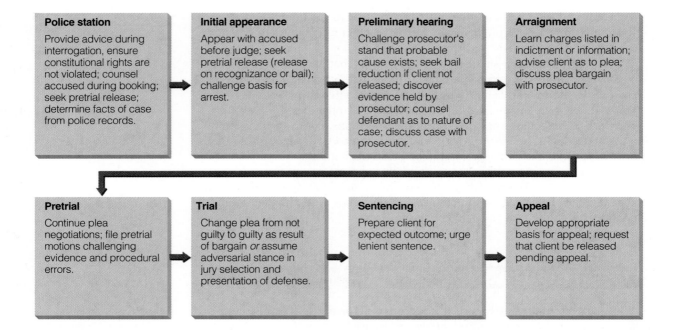

Police station	Initial appearance	Preliminary hearing	Arraignment
Provide advice during interrogation, ensure constitutional rights are not violated; counsel accused during booking; seek pretrial release; determine facts of case from police records.	Appear with accused before judge; seek pretrial release (release on recognizance or bail); challenge basis for arrest.	Challenge prosecutor's stand that probable cause exists; seek bail reduction if client not released; discover evidence held by prosecutor; counsel defendant as to nature of case; discuss case with prosecutor.	Learn charges listed in indictment or information; advise client as to plea; discuss plea bargain with prosecutor.

Pretrial	Trial	Sentencing	Appeal
Continue plea negotiations; file pretrial motions challenging evidence and procedural errors.	Change plea from not guilty to guilty as result of bargain *or* assume adversarial stance in jury selection and presentation of defense.	Prepare client for expected outcome; urge lenient sentence.	Develop appropriate basis for appeal; request that client be released pending appeal.

FIGURE 7.3

Typical Actions of a Defense Attorney Processing a Felony Case
Defense attorneys are advocates for the accused. They have an obligation to legally challenge the system at every stage of the criminal justice process and to advise clients of their rights.

defense attorney is the only person who can answer their repeated question, "What will happen next?" In short, the attorney's relationship with his or her client is extremely important—there must be respect, openness, and trust. If the defendant refuses to follow the attorney's advice, the lawyer may feel obliged to withdraw from the case in order to protect his or her own reputation.

THE REALITIES OF THE DEFENSE ATTORNEY

How good are various defense attorneys at advocating for their clients? Several factors are involved. Attorneys who are inexperienced, uncaring, or overburdened have difficulty in effectively representing their clients. In such cases, the attorney may quickly agree to a plea bargain and then work to persuade the defendant to accept the agreement. The attorney's self-interest in disposing of cases quickly, receiving payment, and moving on to other cases may cause the attorney, in effect, to work in conjunction with the prosecutor to pressure the defendant to plead guilty. Although the most skilled and dedicated defense attorneys will also consider the prospect of a plea bargain in the earliest stages of the case, their use of plea bargaining will be guided by their role as an advocate for the defendant. The effective defense attorney does not automatically try to take every case all the way to trial. In many instances, a negotiated plea with a predictable sentence will serve the defendant better than a trial spent fending off a larger number of more serious charges. As we will discuss more completely in Chapter 9, good defense attorneys seek to understand the facts of the case and to assess the nature of the prosecution's evidence in order to reach the best possible outcome for their client. Even in the plea-bargaining process, this level of advocacy requires more time, effort, knowledge, and commitment than some attorneys are willing to devote.

The defense attorney's job is made all the more difficult because neither the public nor criminal defendants fully understand the attorney's responsibilities and goals. The public often views defense attorneys as mere protectors of criminals. In fact, the attorney's fundamental responsibility is not to save criminals from punishment, but to protect constitutional rights, keep the prosecution honest in preparing and presenting cases, and prevent the conviction of innocent people. In performing these tasks, which ultimately benefit both the defendant and society, the attorney must evaluate and challenge the prosecution's evidence. However, defense attorneys rarely can arrange for guilty defendants to go free. When prosecutors decide to pursue serious charges, they have already filtered out those cases that appear questionable. Instead, the defense attorney is often negotiating the most appropriate punishment in light of the limited resources of the court system, the strength of the evidence, and the defendant's prior criminal record.

Criminal defendants who, like the general public, have watched hours of "L.A. Law," "Matlock," and "Perry Mason" on television, often expect that their attorneys should fight visible, vigorous battles against the prosecutor at every stage of the justice process. They do not realize that plea agreements that are negotiated in a friendly, cooperative fashion may actually advance their best interests. Public defenders, in particular, frequently are criticized by defendants and convicted offenders because the defendants did not have any choice in the selection of their legal representatives. The defendants often assume that if the state provided an attorney for them, the attorney must be working for the state rather than on behalf of the accused.

PRIVATE COUNSEL

Relatively few attorneys represent criminal defendants, and only a small portion of these are private defense attorneys. Of the estimated 800,000 practicing lawyers in the United States, an estimated 20,000 are criminal law specialists, and of these, 14,000 are employed as public defenders. The average criminal lawyer comes from a middle-class, nonprofessional background; graduated from a lesser law school; and practices alone. He or she (only 4 percent are women) enters private criminal practice after some experience as a public sector lawyer. In Paul Wice's study of criminal defense attorneys, 38 percent of the sample had been prosecutors and 24 percent had been public defenders, civil legal services attorneys, or other public sector lawyers.[5]

There is a status hierarchy of criminal defense attorneys. At the top are the nationally known specialists who charge substantial fees to handle celebrated cases. O. J. Simpson's defense team included two such attorneys who built their reputations by defending famous clients: F. Lee Bailey, who defended heiress Patty Hearst, and Alan Dershowitz, the Harvard professor who handled the appeal for boxer Mike Tyson. Each major city typically contains a small group of prominent defense attorneys who are the lawyers of choice for defendants who can afford to pay high fees. These attorneys can make handsome incomes representing white-collar criminals, drug dealers, and affluent people charged with criminal offenses. When business executives are charged with drunk driving, for example, they may be willing to pay top dollar to a specialist who can help them avoid losing their driver's licenses. Attorneys may join this group by succeeding in highly publicized cases, but there are usually too few clients who can pay the highest fees to permit very many criminal lawyers in one locale to make impressive amounts of money.

The largest group of private sector attorneys in full-time criminal practice are courthouse regulars who accept many cases for small fees and who participate every day in the criminal justice process as either retained counsel for paying clients or assigned counsel for indigent defendants. Rather than

Criminal defense requires attorneys to deal with their clients under conditions that are not always conducive to a successful outcome.

preparing cases for the possibility of trial, these attorneys make their profits by handling a large volume of cases quickly. They negotiate guilty pleas and then persuade their clients that the plea agreements constitute exceptionally attractive deals. These practitioners depend heavily on the cooperation of prosecutors, judges, and other courtroom actors, with whom they develop exchange relationships in order to facilitate quick plea agreements.

Other attorneys accept criminal cases as one part of a diversified practice. These attorneys may lack both trial experience and the necessary relationships with prosecutors and judges for the development of effective plea bargaining. In fact, their clients may be better served by the courthouse regulars, who have little interest in each individual case, but whose relationships with prosecutors and judges facilitate more favorable plea agreements.

Criminal defense lawyers face special difficulties in their work. Much of their time is spent preparing clients and their families for likely conviction. They may also be forced to pressure the defendants for advance payment of fees because, once a client pleads guilty or is convicted at trial, there is little incentive to pay. Although defense attorneys may have actual knowledge that their clients are guilty of a crime, they may become emotionally entangled in cases by being the only judicial actors who know the defendants as human beings and see the defendants in the context of social environment and family ties.

Most defense lawyers interact continually with lower-class clients whose lives and problems are depressing. These lawyers may also visit the local jail at all hours of the day and night. Thus, the work setting of the criminal lawyer is far removed from the fancy offices and expensive restaurants that comprise the world of corporate attorneys.

The fact that these attorneys are usually on the losing side of their cases may affect their personal self-esteem. No one likes to lose, yet defense attorneys must quickly adjust to the fact that most of their clients will be found guilty through plea bargains or, on occasion, trials. They must also face the possibility of "losing by winning." That is, if they mount a vigorous, effective defense and succeed in winning an acquittal for a defendant charged with a terrible crime, the community may blame them for using "technicalities" to defeat justice. In addition, a defense attorney who embarrasses the prosecutor or judge in the process of winning the case may harm the relationships that would be most useful in negotiating pleas in subsequent cases. In short, the criminal practice environment involves extensive social and psychological pressures. Many attorneys get "burned out" after only a few years of such practice; few criminal law specialists stay in the field past the age of fifty.

COUNSEL FOR INDIGENTS

As we learned in Chapter 3, the Supreme Court has established that indigent criminal defendants are entitled to have attorneys to represent them beginning at early stages in the criminal process. Table 7.1 traces the Court's major rulings on the right to counsel. As a result of these decisions, an increasing percentage of poor defendants who face the possible punishment of incarceration are represented by attorneys through publicly financed programs.

Case	Year	Ruling
Gideon v. *Wainwright*	1963	The Fourteenth Amendment gives defendants in state noncapital felony cases the right to counsel.
Escobedo v. *Illinois*	1964	The accused has the right to counsel during interrogation by the police.
Miranda v. *Arizona*	1966	The right to counsel begins when investigation of a crime focuses on a suspect. The suspect must be informed of the right to remain silent and to have counsel and be informed that any statement made may be used against him or her.
United States v. *Wade*	1967	The defendant has the right to be assisted by counsel during a police lineup (extended to state defendants in *Gilbert* v. *California* [1967]).
Coleman v. *Alabama*	1970	Counsel must be present at a preliminary hearing.
Argersinger v. *Hamlin*	1972	Whenever a criminal charge may result in a prison sentence, the accused has the right to counsel.
Ross v. *Moffitt*	1974	States are not required to provide counsel for indigents beyond one appeal.
Moore v. *Illinois*	1977	The defendant has the right to counsel at a preliminary court hearing at which he or she appears to be identified by a witness.
United States v. *Henry*	1980	Government agents may not solicit a statement from a defendant covertly and then introduce the statement at trial.
Strickland v. *Washington*	1984	The defendant has the right to the *effective* assistance of counsel, whether privately retained or publicly provided.

TABLE 7.1
The Right to Counsel: Major Supreme Court Rulings
Through judicial decisions in the second half of the twentieth century, the Supreme Court gradually gave meaning to the words "right to counsel" that were placed in the Constitution in 1791.

The Quality of Counsel

There is debate about the quality of representation provided for indigent defendants. Under ideal conditions, experienced, dedicated lawyers would be appointed soon after arrest to represent defendants zealously in each stage of the criminal justice process. In reality, however, lawyers are sometimes appointed during courtroom proceedings, and many resist calls from judges to assume certain types of cases.

Lacking the time and inclination to interview the client and investigate the case, the appointed counsel may simply persuade the defendant to plead guilty right there in the courtroom during their first and only brief conversation. When the lawyers responsible for advocating on behalf of poor defendants cooperate with the prosecutor so quickly and easily without even asking the defendant about his or her version of events, it is little wonder that convicted offenders often believe that their interests were not represented at all in the courtroom. This point was well illustrated during one famous study when a jail inmate was asked whether he had a lawyer when he went to court. The inmate replied, "No, I had a public defender." Not all publicly financed lawyers who represent poor defendants ignore their clients' interests. However, the nature of representation for indigent defendants may vary from courthouse to courthouse depending on the quality of attorneys, conditions of defense practice, and administrative pressures to reduce the caseload as quickly as possible.

Methods of Providing Indigents with Counsel

In the United States, there are three basic methods of providing counsel for indigent defendants: (1) the assigned counsel system, (2) the contract system, and (3) public defender programs, established as public or private nonprofit

assigned counsel

An attorney in private practice assigned by a court to represent an indigent defendant and whose fee is paid by the government that has jurisdiction over the case.

organizations with full-time or part-time salaried staff. Figure 7.4 shows the system in use in the majority of counties within each state.

Assigned Counsel. In the **assigned-counsel** system, the court appoints an attorney in private practice to represent an indigent defendant; the lawyer's fee is paid by the government that has jurisdiction over the case. The system is widely used in small cities and rural areas, but even some urban areas with public defender systems follow the practice of assigning counsel when a case has multiple defendants and the possibility of conflict of interest might result if one of the defendants is represented by a public lawyer. In other cities, such as Detroit, the private bar has been able to insist that its members receive a major share of the cases.

Assigned-counsel systems are organized in two ways: the ad hoc system and the coordinated system. In courthouses that employ the ad hoc system, private attorneys indicate to judges that they are willing to handle cases for indigent defendants. This usually merely involves placing the attorney's name on a list of available counsel. When an indigent defendant requires representation, the judge either appoints the next available lawyer on the list or selects from among the listed attorneys who are present in the courtroom. In coordinated-assignment systems, a court administrator oversees the appointment.[6]

A major problem for assigned-counsel systems is the lack of any particular qualifications for the attorneys who represent indigent defendants. In many cities, the attorneys who volunteer to take cases are inexperienced, recent law school graduates who have little interest in or knowledge of criminal law but who need the small, steady income provided by such cases until they can attract paying clients for more profitable civil cases. Because most jurisdictions pay low fees for criminal appointments, experienced or successful attorneys have little incentive to volunteer to accept assignments.

The low fees not only discourage participation by skilled attorneys but also encourage less skilled attorneys to pressure defendants to plead guilty quickly. Some assigned defenders find that they can make more money by collecting a preparation fee, perhaps fifty dollars, payable when the client pleads guilty, than by going to trial. Thus, by facilitating several quick guilty pleas each day, the attorney makes more money than with a single case and the attendant preparation and court time required for a trial. Obviously, this payment system creates risks that a defendant's constitutional right to counsel may be a sham. The attorney's interest may be very different from the client's, and attorneys may fail to fulfill their ethical responsibility to represent the defendant with full consideration of whether plea agreements advance defendants' interests.

A QUESTION OF ETHICS

The call to attorney Joy Chaplin came from Judge Henry.

"Joy, you're on the Bar Association's list for assigned counsel, and I want to assign an indigent defense case to you. It's going to be a hard case, but I hope you'll be willing to take it."

"Sure, Your Honor, what's the case?"

"Well, Joy, it's the Scott case. You've probably read about it in the papers. Alan Scott has been charged with ten counts of child molestation."

"Oh, no! Not that one. You want me to defend the guy accused of sexually abusing his two young stepdaughters? From what I've seen of him on TV, he's rotten to the core. Judge, as a woman I would have great difficulty dealing with him as a client."

"But you are also an attorney, and Scott has a right to a defense. I know it's going to be difficult, but just let me put you down as the counsel. You can pick up the case file from the D.A.'s office."

Does attorney Chaplin have an obligation to take Alan Scott's case? Since she already has an opinion about the case, should Judge Henry look for another defense lawyer? Given the nature of the case, does it make a difference if the defense attorney is a man or a woman? Does it matter if the defense attorney has children? Can Chaplin provide a full and vigorous defense?

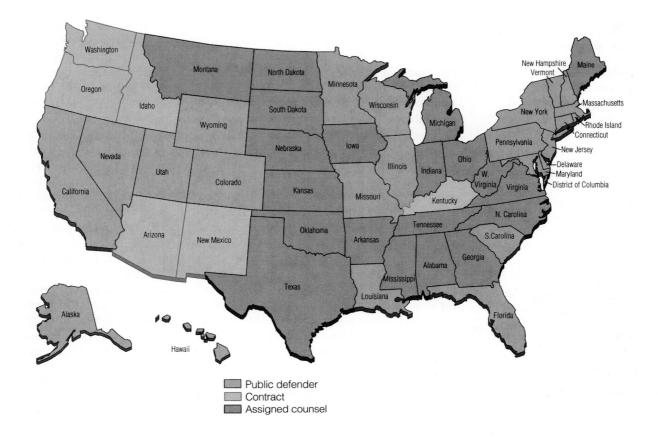

Public defender
Contract
Assigned counsel

Contract System. The contract system is used in a few counties, primarily in western states. Most counties that select this method are not heavily populated. In this system, the government contracts with an individual attorney, nonprofit association, or private law firm to handle all indigent cases. Some jurisdictions use public defenders for most cases but contract for services in multiple-defendant situations that might present conflicts of interest, in extraordinarily complex cases, or in cases that require more time than the government's salaried lawyers can provide.

There are several different kinds of contracts. The most common kind provides for a fixed yearly sum to be paid to the law firm that handles all cases. Some people fear that this fixed-payment method encourages attorneys to cut corners on cases in order to preserve their own profits, especially if there are more cases than anticipated for the year. Other contracts are based on a fixed price per case or per hour of work. Still other jurisdictions use a cost-plus contract in which a new contract is negotiated when the original estimated cost of representation is exceeded.

Public Defender. The public defender is the twentieth-century response to the legal needs of the indigent criminal defendant. The concept, which originated in Los Angeles in 1914, is now employed in many of the largest metropolitan areas and covers over 70 percent of the nation's population.[7] Use of this type of defense system continues to spread and is the dominant form of representation in forty-three states. Only two states, North Dakota and Maine, do not have public defenders.

FIGURE 7.4
Indigent Defense Systems Used in Each State by the Majority of Counties
These aggregate descriptions often mask the fact that some states use a combination of approaches to indigent defense.
SOURCE: U.S. Department of Justice, Bureau of Justice Statistics, *Bulletin* (September 1988).

171

public defender
An attorney employed on a full-time, salaried basis by the government to represent indigent defendants.

Public defenders are full-time, salaried government employees devoted to the representation of indigent defendants. Therefore, they are not susceptible to the same risks facing low-fee assigned counsel. Many public defenders are young and inexperienced because public sector salaries do not attract and retain veteran attorneys, but as young, energetic workers they quickly gain significant experience in criminal law. In addition, more than 81 percent of the public defender counties provide regular training for their attorneys, as opposed to only 21 percent of the assigned-counsel counties and 37 percent of the contract counties.[8] Thus, public defenders are more likely to stay abreast of recent legal developments and continually improve their knowledge and skills.

However, public defenders do experience disadvantages. First, they may have greater difficulty gaining the trust of indigent clients who presume that attorneys on the state payroll must literally work for the state rather than for the client. This difficulty can be exacerbated when the defendants see their lawyers chatting in a friendly manner with assistant prosecutors in court. The impression may hold despite the fact that the public defender's relationship with the members of the prosecutor's staff may assist the defendant in gaining a more favorable plea agreement. If attorneys are to be effective in their work, they need to achieve a degree of what is often called "client control." If trust is absent, the defendant will not listen to the attorney's advice. As a result, favorable plea agreements may be jeopardized, and defendants may make statements in court that weaken their position. For public defenders, many of whom work with very few resources, it can be difficult to establish adequate trust in brief meetings with a skeptical client. Yet, as described in the Close-Up, some public defenders are able to maintain a personal interest in their clients.

Second, public defenders may have such burdensome caseloads that they cannot give enough attention to each case. A set number of public defenders works in each office, and each public defender must handle his or her share of the work no matter how much the caseload unexpectedly increases during a given year. In New York City's public defender program, for example, Legal Aid lawyers may be responsible for as many as one hundred felony cases at any time. A public defender in Atlanta may be assigned as many as forty-five new cases *at a single arraignment*.[9] Such heavy caseloads make it difficult for attorneys to be thoroughly familiar with each case.[10] A public defender program can maximize its effectiveness when it has sufficient funds to keep caseloads at a manageable size. Because these programs do not control their own budgets and are not usually a high priority in local governmental budgets, however, it is difficult to achieve this ideal.

Some public defenders' offices attempt to make better use of limited resources by organizing assignments in more specialized and efficient ways. In some systems, each indigent defendant has several public defenders, each handling a different stage or "zone" in the criminal justice process. One attorney may handle all arraignments, another all preliminary hearings, and still another any trial work. No one attorney is responsible for handling the entire case of any specific defendant. Although the zone system may increase efficiency, there is a risk that cases will be processed routinely, disregarding special elements of any individual case. With only limited responsibility for a given case, the attorney is less able to counsel the defendant. The attorney is also unlikely to develop the level of trust necessary for the defendant to make complete contributions to the preparation of the most appropriate defense strategy.

CLOSE-UP

The Public Defender: Lawyer, Social Worker, Parent

Eddie, a nervous-looking heroin abuser with a three-page police record, isn't happy with his lawyer's news about his latest shoplifting arrest.

"The prosecutor feels you should be locked up for a long time," public defender William Paetzold tells Eddie in a closet-sized interview room in Superior Court. Barely big enough for a desk and two chairs, the room is known as "the pit."

Eddie, 34 and wide-eyed with a blond crew cut, twists a rolled-up newspaper in his hands. And as Paetzold goes over the evidence against him for the theft of $90.67 worth of meat from a supermarket, the paper gets tighter and tighter.

"So, you basically walked right through the doors with the shopping carriage?" Paetzold asks, scanning the police report.

"Well, there was another person involved and we really never got out of the store," Eddie replies quickly, now jingling a pocketful of change.

Eddie wants to take his case to trial. Paetzold doesn't like his chances with a jury.

"If you're going to base your whole case on that statement about not leaving the store, you're going to lose," he says. "If you lose, you're going to get five years."

Paetzold advises Eddie to consider pleading guilty in exchange for a lesser sentence.

Eddie rolls his eyes and grumbles. He thinks he deserves a break because he has been doing well in a methadone clinic designed to wean him from heroin.

"I'm not copping to no time," he says, shifting in his seat. "I'm not arguing the fact that I've been a drug addict my whole life, but I haven't been arrested since I've been in that program. I'm finally doing good and they want to bury me."

Paetzold says he will talk to the prosecutor and see what can be done.

"I'll be waiting upstairs," Eddie says, grabbing his newspaper and walking out past a small crowd of other clients waiting to see Paetzold or public defender Phillip N. Armentano.

Every client wants individual attention. Many expect Paetzold or Armentano to resolve their case with little or no punishment. And they don't care that the lawyers may have 25 other clients to see that morning demanding the same.

"A lot of what we do is almost like social work," says Armentano. "We have the homeless, the mentally ill, the drug addicts, and the alcoholics. Our job isn't just to try to find people not guilty, but to find appropriate punishment, whether that be counselling, community service or jail time."

"It's like being a parent," says Paetzold. "These clients are our responsibility and they all have problems and they want those problems solved now."

And like many parents, the lawyers often feel overwhelmed. Too many cases, not enough time or a big enough staff. Those obstacles contribute to another—the stigma that overworked public defenders are pushovers for prosecutors and judges.

"There's a perception that public defenders don't stand up for their clients," Armentano says. "We hear it all the time, 'Are you a public defender or a real lawyer?' There's a mistrust right from the beginning because they view us as part of the system that got them arrested."

With a caseload of more than a thousand clients a year, Paetzold and Armentano acknowledge that they cannot devote as much time to each client as a private lawyer can. But they insist that their clients get vigorous representation.

"Lawyers are competitors, whether you're a public defender or not," Paetzold says. "I think that under the conditions, we do a very good job for our clients."

SOURCE: Steve Jensen, "The Public Defender: He's One Part Lawyer, One Part Social Worker and One Part Parent," *The Hartford Courant*, 4 September 1994, p. H1. Reprinted with permission of *The Hartford Courant*.

With or without zone systems, overburdened public defenders find it difficult to avoid processing cases by routine decisions. Decisions are made quickly and with minimal resources. One case comes to be viewed as very much like the next, and the process can become routine and repetitive. When the routine goes too far, no attorney looks at individual cases to see if there are special facts or other circumstances that would justify a more vigorous defense or other options.

PRIVATE VERSUS PUBLIC DEFENSE

Publicly funded defense counsel now represent up to 85 percent of the defendants in many jurisdictions, and privately retained counsel has become more and more unusual in criminal courts. As noted previously, in some courthouses, private defense attorneys represent only white-collar crime defendants, organized crime figures, and drug dealers. This trend has made the question of the relative quality of representation increasingly important.

Do defendants who can hire their own counsel receive better legal services than those who cannot? Many convicted offenders apply the expression "you get what you pay for" to their public defenders, meaning that they would have received more skilled and vigorous representation if they had been able to pay for their own attorneys. At one time, researchers thought that public defenders entered more guilty pleas than did lawyers who had been either privately retained or assigned to cases. However, recent studies indicate little variation in ultimate case disposition by various types of defense attorney. For example, in a study of plea packages negotiated in nine medium-sized counties in Illinois, Michigan, and Pennsylvania, the type of attorney representing the client appeared to make no difference with respect to the particular plea agreement developed for the defendant.[11] Other studies have also found few differences among assigned counsel, contract counsel, public defenders, and privately retained counsel with respect to case disposition and length of sentence.[12] Table 7.2 lists data on the relationship between type of counsel and case disposition in four jurisdictions.

THE PERFORMANCE OF THE DEFENSE ATTORNEY

As we have seen, defense attorneys face many difficulties. They may work in difficult physical surroundings—crowded, dirty, noisy urban courtrooms and unpleasant jail visiting rooms. They must work with people who are angry,

TABLE 7.2

Case Disposition and Types of Defense Attorneys
Although the private-versus-public debate continues, the data show there are few variations in disposition among the defense systems within each jurisdiction. Why are there differences among the cities with regard to case outcomes?

SOURCE: Roger Hanson and Joy Chapper, *Indigent Defense Systems.* Report to the State Justice Institute. Copyright © 1991 by National Center for State Courts (Williamsburg, VA: National Center for State Courts, 1991).

Type of Disposition	Detroit, Michigan			Denver, Colorado		Norfolk, Virginia		Monterey, California		
	Public Defender	Assigned Counsel	Private Counsel	Public Defender	Private Counsel	Assigned Counsel	Private Counsel	Public Defender	Assigned Counsel	Private Counsel
Dismissals	11.9%	14.5%	12.8%	21.0%	24.3%	6.4%	10.4%	13.5%	8.9%	3.0%
Trial acquittals	9.5	5.7	10.3	1.8	0.0	3.3	5.2	1.7	1.3	0.0
Trial convictions	22.6	14.5	24.4	5.1	9.5	5.2	2.2	7.1	11.4	18.2
Guilty pleas	54.8	64.9	52.6	72.1	66.2	85.1	81.3	76.8	78.5	78.8
Diversion	1.2	.3	0.0	0.0	0.0	0.0	.7	1.0	0.0	0.0
	100.0%	99.9%	100.1%	100.0%	100.0%	100.0%	99.8%	100.1%	100.1%	100.0%
Total number of cases	84	296	78	276	74	329	134	294	79	33

frightened, and often troubled by untreated psychiatric and substance abuse problems. They may receive low pay, whether as assigned counsel handling many cases for low fees or as public defenders earning lower salaries than those of other attorneys including their counterparts in the prosecutor's office. They may face daunting caseloads that overwhelm their ability to give each case the attention that it needs and deserves. They must become accustomed to "losing" nearly all of their cases as a steady stream of clients enters guilty pleas and receives punishments imposed by the criminal justice system. And, to top it all off, their clients are frequently distrustful, hostile, and uncooperative, especially indigents who had no choice about which attorney would represent them in court. Anyone would like to feel appreciated for doing a good job, especially when coping with extraordinary burdens and pressures and unpleasant working conditions. Defense attorneys, however, must seek their own rewards and satisfactions; their clients are not likely to appreciate their feats when "victories" are measured in terms of time shaved off a prison sentence rather than vindication and freedom.

Attorney Goals and Actions

In light of the burdens and pressures facing defense attorneys, how should we judge their effectiveness? How do they accomplish their goals?

Different types of defense attorneys work for different goals. The privately retained attorney wants clients to believe that they are getting their money's worth. Sometimes, this may involve staging a dramatic performance at trial; other times, it may involve effective pretrial negotiations that lead to reduced charges. The assigned attorney wants to process a sufficient number of cases quickly enough to show a profit from the accumulation of small fees. The public defender wants to keep cases flowing smoothly because of continuous caseload pressures that can become overwhelming if any particular cases require extra time and attention.

Although attorneys may seek different goals, the context of immediate objectives for which they work leads them down a common path. In all instances, they require effective exchange relations with prosecutors and judges for plea bargaining and other steps in the process. Even privately retained attorneys use plea agreements to save their clients from the worst-case results of significant punishment for conviction on multiple serious charges. In fact, O. J. Simpson's primary attorney, Robert Shapiro, built his reputation as an elite attorney by obtaining favorable plea bargains for celebrity defendants, such as actor Marlon Brando's son, who avoided a possible first-degree murder conviction by pleading guilty to a lesser offense.

In effect, defense lawyers are selling their ability to influence other actors in the justice process in order to gain benefits for clients. Thus, they must cultivate and maintain cooperative relationships. Just as the prosecutor needs good relationships in order to achieve prosecutorial goals, the defense attorney needs the same kinds of relationships to gain favorable bail, charges, plea agreements, and sentences. The defense attorney can push the prosecutor to cooperate by threatening to invoke the adversarial model and take the case to trial. When faced with that time-consuming alternative, prosecutors and judges may work with the defense attorney to develop an acceptable plea bargain.

Lawyers who seek paying clients often develop relationships with other actors in the justice process. By gaining the cooperation of police officers, fellow attorneys, jailers, and bail bondsmen, the lawyer may receive referrals. In order to gain and keep these relationships, of course, the lawyer cannot maintain a thoroughly adversarial posture.

The need for cooperative interactions within the system will ultimately affect both the lawyer's relationships with and performances for defendants. The attorneys help to prepare the defendants for the eventual outcome, usually a guilty plea, and help to gain clients' cooperation in the processing of cases. In effect, attorneys help both defendants and the criminal justice system by guiding their clients to accept their fates. The smooth processing of cases depends, in part, on the cooperation of criminal defendants and the mediation of their attorneys.

Attorney Competence

The work of a defense attorney usually reflects a great deal of self-interest and compromise with other agents in the system. Since such behaviors do not necessarily focus on the best interests of the client, defendants may rightly question whether their attorneys are adequately and competently performing their duty to uphold constitutional rights and provide zealous, adversarial representation. The Sixth Amendment right to counsel has little meaning if the attorneys are not representing clients properly.

If paying clients are dissatisfied with their attorneys, they can, in theory, fire them and hire replacements. However, if the case has moved too far along toward trial, the judge may not permit them to change attorneys. Indigent criminal defendants, by contrast, have no choice about representation. They will be represented by the attorney that a judge or public defender's office assigns to the case and will have little opportunity to complain about the attorney's performance. Thus, both the paying client and the indigent criminal defendant can find themselves trapped in a relationship with an attorney whose actions and judgments they have reason to question. Sometimes, the client questions strategic actions taken by an attorney, such as declining to question specific witnesses or challenge potential jurors. Other times, attorneys may apparently fall short on knowledge and preparation, failing to conduct research or formulate arguments on relevant legal issues. In all these cases, the defendant will have little power to intervene.

One recourse for challenging a defense attorney's competence after the completion of a case is to pursue a postconviction legal action alleging "ineffective assistance of counsel." The Supreme Court has opened the door for defendants to seek new trials if they can demonstrate that their attorneys were incompetent. However, the level of proof that defendants need to establish is so strict that very few defendants can realistically expect to challenge even highly questionable actions. In two 1984 cases, *United States* v. *Cronic* and *Strickland* v. *Washington*,[13] the Supreme Court declared that a defense counsel's performance may be judged inadequate only if a reasonably competent attorney would not have acted as did the trial counsel. In addition, the defendant must establish that there is a reasonable probability that, but for the attorney's unprofessional errors, the outcome of the case would have been different. Because so many of an attorney's actions, such as failing to call or question a witness, can be attributed to trial strategy, judges are reluctant to second-guess attorneys' actions. Moreover, even if there is a serious issue of incompetence, it is extremely difficult to persuade judges that the outcome of the case would have been different if not for the attorney's actions. Thus, "ineffective assistance of counsel" claims are frequently filed by convicted offenders, but they rarely prevail. As a result, people sit in prison, and even on death row awaiting execution, whose cases were handled by lawyers who offered only minimal defense.

SUMMARY

Prosecutors and defense attorneys are key figures in the processing of criminal cases. Both actors become involved in the early stages of cases and interact together at successive stages of the justice process until, in most cases, the charges are dropped or a negotiated plea bargain produces a guilty plea. Prosecutors have significant discretion to establish the framework for each case by determining which defendants will actually face charges and what charges they will face. Such decisions are shaped by a variety of factors, including the prosecutor's conception of his or her role, interactions with other actors, caseload pressures, and policies established within a particular prosecutor's office. There are no higher authorities who can overrule a prosecutor's decision to pursue specific charges or to drop all charges. Because most prosecutors are elected officials, they are primarily accountable only to a voting public that has little knowledge of their daily decisions.

Defense attorneys' actions and decisions are influenced by their relationships with other courthouse actors, their motivations as privately paid or publicly financed counsel, and the degree of cooperation that they can obtain from their clients. Defense attorneys have important responsibilities for protecting defendants' constitutional rights, yet serious questions exist about whether private attorneys and public defenders adequately fulfill these duties. There are risks that limited resources and attorneys' self-interest may contribute to inadequate representation.

As we will see in the next two chapters concerning pretrial and trial processes, the outcome of a case depends on many complex factors. Always central to the process are fallible human beings who, in their roles as prosecutors, defense attorneys, and judges, possess discretionary powers and cooperate with other courthouse actors.

QUESTIONS FOR REVIEW

1. How can prosecutors' decisions be made more visible, and what effect would increased visibility have on the system?
2. How do prosecutors' relationships with other criminal justice system actors affect their decisions?
3. Should we require that lawyers possess special qualifications or certification before they are allowed to handle criminal cases?
4. How can we create a system in which the defense lawyers' interests and attention are focused on providing the best possible representation for clients?
5. Should we make it easier for defendants to succeed in filing "ineffective assistance of counsel" claims, and if so, how?

NOTES

1. U.S. Department of Justice, *Principles of Federal Prosecution* (Washington, DC: Government Printing Office, 1980), p. 7.
2. Barbara Boland, Elizabeth Brady, Herbert Tyson, and John Bassler, *The Prosecution of Felony Arrests*, U.S. Department of Justice, Bureau of Justice Statistics (Washington, DC: Government Printing Office, 1983), p. 9.

3. Joan E. Jacoby, "The Charging Policies of Prosecutors," in *The Prosecutor*, ed. William F. McDonald (Beverly Hills, CA: Sage, 1979), p. 75.

4. Cassia Spohn, John Gruhl, and Susan Welch, "The Impact of the Ethnicity and Gender of Defendants on the Decision to Reject or Dismiss Felony Charges," *Criminology* 25 (1987), p. 175.

5. Paul B. Wice, *Criminal Lawyers: An Endangered Species* (Beverly Hills, CA: Sage, 1978), p. 75.

6. Pauline Houlden and Steven Balkin, "Costs and Quality of Indigent Defense: Ad Hoc v. Coordinated Assignment of the Private Bar within a Mixed System," *Justice System Journal* 10 (1985), p. 159.

7. U.S. Department of Justice, Bureau of Justice Statistics, *Bulletin* (September 1988).

8. Robert L. Spangenberg, Beverly Lee, Michael Battaglia, Patricia Smith, and A. David Davis, *National Criminal Defense Systems Study* (Washington, DC: Bureau of Justice Statistics, 1986), p. 56.

9. Stephen B. Bright, "Counsel for the Poor: The Death Sentence Not for the Worst Crime but for the Worst Lawyer," *Yale Law Journal* 103 (1994), p. 1850.

10. Robert Hermann, Eric Single, and John Boston, *Counsel for the Poor: Criminal Defense in Urban America* (Lexington, MA: Lexington Books, 1977), p. 67.

11. Peter Nardulli, "Insider Justice: Defense Attorneys and the Handling of Felony Cases," *Journal of Criminal Law and Criminology* 79 (1986), p. 416.

12. Roger Hanson and Joy Chapper, *Indigent Defense Systems*, Report to the State Justice Institute (Williamsburg, VA: National Center for State Courts, 1991).

13. *United States* v. *Cronic*, 444 U.S. 654 (1984); *Strickland* v. *Washington*, 466 U.S. 686 (1984).

CHAPTER 8
Pretrial Processes

JUDGE RELEASES ACCUSED RAPIST ON BAIL

Charles Hamlin was arrested for the rape of a twelve-year-old girl in Akron, Ohio. In his initial court appearance, a judge set a $2,500 cash bond for his release. He provided the money and was released on bail. His next scheduled preliminary hearing was in the court of Municipal Judge Jane Bond. Hamlin appeared at the hearing as required, and Judge Bond continued his $2,500 cash bond and permitted him to remain free on bail. A few days later, a husband and wife were shot and killed, and Hamlin was arrested for their murders. At the time of the murders, the local elections for municipal court judgeships were only a few weeks away. Judge Bond's opponent in the election, an attorney named Maureen O'Connor, mailed a flyer to voters throughout Akron that read:

> The AKRON FRATERNAL ORDER OF POLICE wants you to know about **LOW BOND, JANE BOND**.
>
> **FACT**: August 4, 1989, Charles Hamlin was **ARRESTED** for the **RAPE** of a **12 YEAR OLD GIRL.**
>
> **FACT**: Charles Hamlin had a prior **CONVICTION** for **GROSS SEXUAL IMPOSITION**.
>
> **FACT**: **JANE BOND** allowed **ONLY** a **$2,500 CASH BOND** at Charles Hamlin's **RAPE** Hearing.
>
> **FACT**: While out of **JAIL** on **ONLY** a **$2,500 CASH BOND**, Charles Hamlin **SHOT** and **KILLED TWO PEOPLE,** a **MINISTER** and his **WIFE**.

> **FACT**: The Akron Municipal Court needs TOUGH JUDGES that will PROTECT the VICTIMS, NOT the CRIMINALS! The AKRON FRATERNAL ORDER OF POLICE HAS **ENDORSED O'CONNOR** for **JUDGE**.

Judge Bond's supporters responded with radio commercials defending the judge, and she ultimately won the election. However, this election issue raised questions about the role of bail in the criminal justice system. Who should be released on bail? Was O'Connor correct in asserting that Judge Bond should not have permitted Hamlin to be released on bail? Was Judge Bond protecting criminals instead of victims by not setting a much higher amount for bail? How would this situation and this flyer have affected your choice if you had voted in the judicial election?

The decision regarding the release of an accused person on bail is one of several important stages in the pretrial process. Each stage relies on discretionary decisions by prosecutors, defense attorneys, bail bondsmen, judges, and others. Through their interactions, these actors determine what will happen to the vast majority of defendants. Very few defendants have their cases decided by a trial. Most leave the system by having their cases dismissed or by entering guilty pleas during the pretrial process. In this chapter, we will examine the pretrial stages to see how various decision makers use their power of discretion. ★

THE PRETRIAL PROCESS: FROM ARREST TO TRIAL OR PLEA

A t each stage of the pretrial process, important decisions are made that move some defendants further along in the criminal justice system and filter others out of the system.

ARRAIGNMENT AND THE PROSECUTOR'S INITIAL DECISIONS

As we saw in Chapter 2, after an arrest the accused is booked at the police station. The booking process includes taking photographs and fingerprints, the basis of an administrative record of the case. Within forty-eight hours of a warrantless arrest, the defendant must be taken to court for the initial appearance to hear which charges are being pursued, be advised of his or her rights, and be given the opportunity to post bail. These initial steps set the pretrial process in motion as the prosecution and defense begin to prepare their cases.

Frequently, the first formal encounter between the prosecutor and the defense attorney representing the defendant is the **arraignment**: the formal court appearance in which the charges against the defendant are read and the defendant, advised by his or her lawyer, enters a plea of "Guilty" or "Not guilty." Normally, defendants will enter a plea of "Not guilty," even if they are likely to plead guilty at some later point. This is because, thus far, the prosecutor and defense attorney usually have had little time or opportunity to discuss a potential plea bargain.

At the time of the arraignment, prosecutors begin to evaluate the evidence concerning the defendant's potential guilt. This is the process of screening cases. If the prosecutor believes that the case against the defendant is weak, he or she may simply drop the charges. Prosecutors do not wish to waste their limited time and staff resources on cases that will not stand up in court. A prosecutor may also drop charges if the alleged crime is minor, if the defendant is a first offender, or if the prosecutor believes that the few days spent in jail prior to arraignment are a sufficient punishment for the defendant's alleged offense. Prosecutors' decisions to dismiss charges may also be influenced by jail overcrowding or the need to work on more serious cases.

As explained in Chapter 7, the prosecutor plays a pivotal role in the criminal justice process and is regarded by many observers as the most powerful decision maker in the system. As a result of the discretionary power of prosecutors, two defendants who have committed the same offense may receive completely different treatment. For example, imagine two eighteen-year-old high school dropouts who, as first offenders, each shoplift a Chicago Bulls jersey from a sporting goods store. One prosecutor may divert one defendant to an education program and subsequently drop the charges when the defendant begins to work seriously toward his or her high school diploma. Another prosecutor may pursue larceny charges against the other defendant that result in a short jail sentence. Individual prosecutors play a fundamental role in determining which defendants will be subjected to criminal punishment.

CHAPTER QUESTIONS

What are the important decision points in the criminal justice process prior to the trial stage?

What are the purposes of bail?

What are the effects of pretrial detention?

Who benefits from plea bargaining?

arraignment
The formal court appearance in which the charges against the defendant are read and the defendant enters a plea in response to those charges.

181

As Figure 8.1 shows, prosecutors use their decision-making authority to filter many cases out of the system. The one hundred cases illustrated represent typical felony cases that may confront a prosecutor. Obviously, the precise percentages of cases will vary from city to city depending on a number of factors, including the effectiveness of police investigations and the prosecutor's policies about which cases to pursue. For example, nearly half of the arrestees did not ultimately face felony prosecutions. A small number of defendants were steered toward diversion programs. A larger number had their cases dismissed by the prosecutor for reasons that we have discussed, including lack of evidence, the minor nature of the charges, or first-time-offender status. Other cases were dismissed by the courts because the police and prosecutors did not present enough evidence to a grand jury or a preliminary hearing to justify moving forward with a prosecution. As noted in Chapter 2, grand juries and preliminary hearings ensure that cases are pursued only if there is adequate evidence to suggest that the defendant may be guilty of the crime.

Preliminary hearings, in particular, present an opportunity for defense attorneys to challenge the prosecution's evidence and to make **motions** to the court requesting that an order be issued to bring about a specified action. For example, a motion might seek to have the judge exclude evidence that was obtained through illegal searches or improper interrogation of the suspect. The aggressive use of pretrial motions by defense attorneys can force the prosecution to "show its cards" early in the game. It can also plant in the judge's mind the "seeds" of arguments that the defense intends to make at trial. If the defense succeeds in persuading a judge to exclude important prosecution evidence before any plea bargaining or trial preparation can begin, the case may be dismissed.

Some people believe that the criminal justice system is failing to fulfill its necessary functions because as many as half of arrestees have their cases dismissed. This is not necessarily a logical conclusion. Some of the people arrested by the police may actually be innocent. Police may make arrests based on information provided by witnesses, for example, yet the witnesses may be incorrect in classifying people's behavior as criminal or they may make mistakes in identifying people whom they believe were involved in a particular crime. Witnesses may believe they observed someone on a street corner selling drugs to the driver of a car that stopped and then quickly pulled away. If this event occurs in a neighborhood where drug sales are frequent, the police

motion

An application to a court requesting that an order be issued to bring about a specified action.

FIGURE 8.1

Typical Outcome of One Hundred Urban Felony Cases

Crucial decisions are made by prosecutors and judges during the period before trial or plea. Once cases are bound over for disposition, guilty pleas are many, trials are few, and acquittals are rare.

SOURCE: Barbara Boland, Paul Mahanna, and Ronald Stones, *The Prosecution of Felony Arrests*, U.S. Department of Justice, Bureau of Justice Statistics (Washington, DC: Government Printing Office, 1992), p. 2.

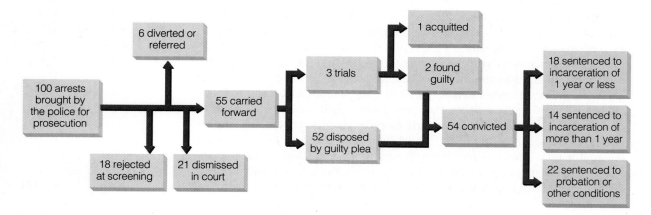

may regard the witness information as sufficient for making an arrest. Later, it may emerge that the person arrested was merely giving directions to a passing motorist. Alternatively, even if the person really was selling drugs, the police may be unable to discover drugs, money, or other evidence that would be needed to support a conviction.

Instead of assessing the effectiveness of the criminal justice system according to the percentage of people arrested who are released by the prosecutor or court, we might want to focus on the cases that the prosecutor decides to carry forward for prosecution. As shown in Figure 8.1, when there is sufficient evidence to move a case forward and when the prosecutor decides to prosecute, conviction rates are remarkably high. Of the 100 typical felony cases, 48 convictions emerge from the 49 cases prosecuted. Most of these cases (45 out of 49) end with guilty pleas that emerge from the plea-bargaining process. Only a small number go to trial (4 out of 49), and most of these (3) result in convictions. From the perspective of cases actually prosecuted, the criminal justice system appears remarkably effective in producing convictions when a prosecutor, with sufficient evidence, pursues a felony prosecution.

BAIL: PRETRIAL RELEASE

Under the principles that govern the American legal system, we frequently say that defendants are presumed innocent until proven guilty or until they enter a guilty plea. However, people who are arrested are taken to jail. They are deprived of their liberty and, in many cases, subjected to miserable living conditions while they await the processing of their cases. The notion that presumably innocent people can lose their liberty, potentially for many months as their cases work their way toward trial, clashes with the American ideal of individual freedom. This clash is inevitable because we must protect society by detaining people who are violent or who may flee from prosecution. We do not, however, need to detain everyone who is charged with a criminal offense. Thus, we use bail and other methods as the means of releasing defendants on the condition that they appear in court as required.

Bail is a sum of money or property specified by the judge that will be posted by the defendant as a condition of pretrial release and that will be forfeited if the defendant does not appear in court for scheduled hearings. The concept was originally developed in England as a convenience for sheriffs so that they would not have to fill their jail cells with people awaiting trial. There is no constitutional right to release on bail, nor even a right to have the court set an amount as the condition of release. The Eighth Amendment of the U.S. Constitution prohibits excessive bail, and state bail laws are usually intended to prevent discriminatory practices. They do not guarantee, however, that all presumably innocent defendants will actually have a realistic chance for pretrial release.

bail
A sum of money specified by a judge to be posted as a condition of pretrial release and that will be forfeited if the defendant does not appear in court for scheduled hearings.

THE PURPOSES OF BAIL

The fundamental purpose of bail is to ensure that accused persons return to court for their hearings and trials. Thus, the decision on an appropriate bail amount should be based on an amount of money and accompanying set of

Bail bondsmen often have the power to say whether a defendant will go free or remain in jail. The influence of this profitable business over individual justice process decisions raises serious policy issues.

conditions (for example, surrender of passport) that will make certain that the defendant returns to court. In setting bail, the judge should ideally assess, among other things, the wealth of the defendant in order to determine how much money placed at risk of forfeiture would prevent the defendant from disappearing. In reality, however, because bail must be determined within two days of arrest, bail decisions are based primarily on the seriousness of the pending charge and the defendant's prior criminal record. It is difficult to make a precise determination about an appropriate amount. Ideally, the amount should be enough to induce a defendant to return for hearings, but not so much as to require a defendant to remain in jail because, as we have seen, many defendants will ultimately have the charges against them dismissed and therefore should not be punished with pretrial incarceration.

In modern times, a second consideration that judges may use in determining whether bail will be granted and how much it should be is protection of the community. Thus, in federal and some state courts, the bail hearing may include consideration of evidence concerning whether the defendant poses a risk of harm to the community. Is the defendant likely to commit another crime while on bail? We will discuss this second purpose in detail when we consider the issue of preventive detention later in the section.

Given the twin mandates of bail—to ensure return of the defendant for court appearances and to protect the community from harm—let us return to the chapter-opening example of the controversy surrounding Judge Bond granting a $2,500 cash bail to a rape suspect who committed two murders while out on bail. The campaign flyer used against Judge Bond implied that she either should have set bail at an amount that would have prevented Hamlin from gaining release or should have denied bail altogether and required Hamlin to remain in jail until his case was completed. In reality, how did Judge Bond's actions fit with the underlying purposes of bail?

Recall that Judge Bond did not set the original $2,500 cash bond for Hamlin. That amount was set by another judge. Judge Bond continued bail at that amount *after Hamlin had returned for his hearings as required*. Thus, from the perspective of bail's first underlying purpose, Hamlin had proven that $2,500 was a bail amount that would lead him to appear for his hearings. Judge Bond fulfilled the first purpose of bail by continuing that amount because Hamlin had demonstrated that he did not intend to flee.

What about the second purpose of bail? Maureen O'Connor accused Judge Bond of failing to protect the community from harm by permitting Hamlin to gain pretrial release. Moreover, O'Connor strongly implied that if she were the judge, she would not let such people gain pretrial release. We should ask, however, whether O'Connor was accurately portraying the difficulties involved in setting bail. Could O'Connor, or anyone else, predict that a particular defendant was going to commit multiple murders if released on bail? Hamlin had never committed any murders before. Why should Judge Bond have predicted that he might commit murders in the future if released? Or was O'Connor claiming that all defendants like Hamlin who are accused of serious violent crimes or who have prior felony records should be denied the opportunity for pretrial release? How would this policy affect our so-called presumption of innocence? How would major cities, which have overcrowded jails and large numbers of defendants accused of violent crimes, ever find space to house all of the people detained pending trial? These are some of the difficult questions that judges face when they conduct bail hearings for people charged with serious offenses.

The controversy surrounding Judge Bond's handling of Hamlin's bail also illustrates another aspect of bail. If mistakes are made in setting bail, even if those mistakes were unexpected and perhaps even unavoidable, the people involved in the bail process will find themselves the focus of significant adverse publicity and controversy. For example, in one federal court, the U.S. attorney (the federal prosecutor) asked that a man accused of running an illegal nationwide gambling operation be denied bail. There was no evidence that the man had ever been violent, but the U.S. attorney feared that he would flee prosecution. The judge considered the available evidence and set the bail at $600,000, presuming that if the defendant could come up with that much money, he would not wish to forfeit it by failing to appear in court. After posting bail, the defendant promptly disappeared, and local newspapers harshly criticized the judge with editorials and even a political cartoon depicting the defendant sending a "thank-you" postcard to the federal judge from a tropical island.

Even though bail decisions rarely go awry, political and social pressures may lead judges to err on the side of caution and detain even some people that the judges actually believe are unlikely to cause any trouble. In addition, even though judges may have the authority to apply discretion in setting bail, they normally involve the prosecutor and the defense attorney in the process of establishing the amount and the conditions for release. When the prosecutor makes a bail recommendation and the defense attorney attempts to negotiate the amount and the release conditions, the judge can share the blame with others if the defendant disappears or commits a crime during pretrial release. Table 8.1 shows the median amount of bail set for felony offenders in the seventy-five largest counties nationwide.

Most Serious Arrest Charge	Median Bail Amount
All offenses	$ 5,000
Violent offenses	$10,000
Murder	75,000
Rape	23,500
Robbery	10,000
Assault	5,000
Other violent	10,000
Property offenses	$ 5,000
Burglary	5,000
Theft	4,000
Other property	4,000
Drug offenses	$ 5,000
Sales/trafficking	5,000
Other drug	5,000
Public-order offenses	$ 4,000
Weapons	3,000
Driving-related	2,000
Other public-order	5,000

TABLE 8.1

Median Bail Amounts for Felony Defendants in the Seventy-Five Largest Counties
The amount of bail varies according to the offense and the individual judge.
SOURCE: U.S. Department of Justice, Bureau of Justice Statistics, *Bulletin* (November 1994), p. 5.

THE BAIL BONDSMAN

A central figure in the bail process is the bail bondsman, who, despite the label, can be either a man or a woman. As profit-seeking businesspeople, these private actors are paid fees by defendants who lack the money to make bail. In exchange for the fee, which may be 5–10 percent of the bail amount, the bondsman will put up the necessary money (or property) to gain the defendant's release. Bondsmen are not obligated to provide bail money for every defendant who seeks to use their services. Rather, they decide which defendants are likely to return for court appearances. If the defendant skips town, it is the bondsman's money that is forfeited to the court.

Bondsmen may develop relationships with police officers and jailers in order to seek referrals. Many defendants may not know whom to call for help in making bail, and law enforcement officers can steer them to a particular bondsman. This creates risks of corruption if a bondsman is actually paying a jailer or police officer to make such referrals. Moreover, these relationships may create other kinds of improper cooperation, such as a bondsman refusing to help a particular defendant if the police would prefer to see that defendant remain in jail.

A suspect who can't make bail will probably have to enter the courtroom already looking like a prisoner. Is that likely to make any difference in the minds of judge or jury?

The role of the bondsman poses questions for the criminal justice system even beyond the issue of corrupt relationships. Most importantly, is it proper for a private, profit-seeking decision maker to determine who will gain pretrial release and profit from a person who is technically "presumed innocent" but is threatened by loss of liberty? If charges are dropped against a defendant or the defendant is acquitted, the bondsman still keeps the fee that was paid to make bail. This can be costly to a defendant, especially one who is poor. Although judges set the bail amount, it is the bondsmen who frequently determine whether particular defendants will actually gain pretrial release.

Despite the problems posed by bondsmen's activities, they provide benefits for the criminal justice system. Although bondsmen act in their own self-interest to make a profit, they do contribute to the smoother processing of cases. A major reason that defendants fail to appear for their scheduled court appearances is confusion and forgetfulness about when and where they must appear. Courthouses in large cities are huge bureaucracies in which changes in the times and locations of hearings may not always be communicated properly to the affected individuals. Bondsmen serve the system by reminding defendants about court dates, calling defendants' relatives to make sure that the defendant will arrive on time, and warning defendants about the penalties for failing to appear. In an informal way, they may act much like defense attorneys in helping to explain legal procedures to defendants and to advise them that the case might best be resolved through a negotiated guilty plea. Bondsmen may also benefit the court system by locating and returning defendants who have disappeared and therefore placed the bondsmen's money at risk. This scenario was illustrated in humorous fashion in the Hollywood film *Midnight Run* in which Robert DeNiro, a bounty hunter for a bail bondsman, chased Charles Grodin around the country in an effort to return him to court before the bail money was forfeited. There is, however, little reason to believe that the bondsmen can perform this function as effectively as law enforcement officers.

The criminal justice system may benefit in some ways from the activities of bondsmen, but federal judges have argued that bail bondsmen are not necessary to the federal courts. By using U.S. marshals and the staff of federal pretrial services offices, the courts could accomplish all of the tasks undertaken by the bondsmen, but without the risks of corruption and discrimination against the poor. In fact, several of the largest federal courts handle bail processing for all criminal cases without involving bail bondsmen at all.[1]

SETTING BAIL

Depending on the procedures used in individual cities, bail may be set at several different points in the pretrial process. For misdemeanors, in most places, bail is usually handled by a police officer according to a schedule established by the local judiciary. Since little is known about the accused at this time, a person facing a misdemeanor will be required to post the same amount of money as anyone else facing that same charge. For felony cases, bail will usually be set by a judge at an initial appearance or an arraignment. In these cases, the judge uses his or her discretion in determining both a bail amount and restrictive conditions as the terms for pretrial release. As the accompanying Question of Ethics illustrates, discretion can be a major ingredient in determining bail.

When a judge sets bail, the actual amount and conditions of release are generally determined by the perceptions and interactions of the judge, prosecutor, and defense attorney, especially with regard to the defendant's personal qualities and criminal history. The prosecutor frequently makes a bail recommendation to the judge. This recommendation is based not only on the seriousness of the crime and the defendant's prior record, but also on whether the defendant has a good job, is well liked by neighbors, or takes care of his or her family. Like other aspects of bail, consideration of such factors may produce decisions that favor affluent defendants over the poor, the unemployed, or people mired in an unstable family environment.

A classic study of bail in New York by Frederic Suffet found that the interactions of the judge, prosecutor, and defense attorney produced common understandings about what range of bail would be set according to the seriousness of offense, the defendant's prior record, and the defendant's ties to the community. The prosecutor tended to have more influence than the defense attorney in the process. In direct disagreements about bail, judges sided more frequently with prosecutors, in part because they tended to share similar conceptions of the appropriate level of bail. The defense attorney could attempt to negotiate with the prosecutor and persuade the judge to set a lower bail amount, but the commonly understood "rules of the game" established the boundaries in which bail would be set for a particular individual.[2] By practice, experience, and tradition, specific bail patterns become established and accepted by the lawyers and judges within a courthouse. An experienced defense attorney will know better than to risk conflict with the prosecutor and judge by seeking minimal bail for an offender charged with a very serious crime or one with a significant prior record.

Local political and legal culture can also affect bail patterns. In a study of Detroit and Baltimore, Roy Flemming found significant differences in the practices that determined pretrial release of defendants. In Detroit, nearly half of felony defendants were released on their own recognizance compared to only 12 percent in Baltimore. For those defendants required to provide money as surety, the average bail amount in Detroit was less than half that in Baltimore. As a result, in Detroit, less than 33 percent of defendants were kept in detention while in Baltimore more than 40 percent were detained. The numerical differences were caused by different political climates and criminal justice resources. Bail practices in Detroit had been reformed in light of historically

A QUESTION OF ETHICS

Jim Rourke stood in front of Desk Sergeant Jack Sweeney at the Redwood City Police Station. Rourke was handcuffed and waiting to be booked. He had been caught by Officers Davis and Timulty outside a building in a prestigious neighborhood soon after the police had received a frantic 911 call from a resident who reported that someone had entered her apartment. Rourke was seen loitering in the alley with a flashlight in his back pocket. He was known to the police because of his prior arrests for entering at night. As Timulty held Rourke, Davis went around behind the desk and spoke to Sergeant Sweeney in a soft voice.

"I know we don't have much on this guy, but he's a bad egg and I bet he was the one who was in that apartment. The least we can do is set the bail high enough so that he'll know we are on to him."

"Davis, you know I can't do that. You've got nothing on him," said Sweeney.

"But how's it going to look in the press if we just let him go? You know the type of people who live in Littleton Manor. There will be hell to pay if it gets out that this guy just walks."

"Well, he did have the flashlight . . . I suppose that's enough to indicate that he's a suspect. Let's make the bail $1,000. I know he can't make that."

What is the purpose of bail? Was the amount set appropriate in this instance? Should Rourke be held merely because of the suspicion that he might have burglarized the apartment? Do you think the case would have been handled in the same way if the call had come from a poorer section of town?

harsh and discriminatory treatment of African-American suspects. In addition, judges had been ordered to limit the number of people who could be held in Detroit's overcrowded jail. By contrast, the Baltimore jail had ample space. Moreover, bail was set in Baltimore by low-level court commissioners who lacked job security and therefore erred on the side of caution in order to prevent any public outcry if a defendant fled or committed a crime while out on bail.[3]

As the comparison of Detroit and Baltimore demonstrates, defendants face different bail conditions in different locales. In one city, a defendant accused of a violent crime may gain release on his or her own recognizance, while in another city, a defendant charged with a property crime may be unable to gain release because the judge has set a high bail.

REFORM OF THE BAIL SYSTEM

The unequal impact of bail, especially on poor people who lack the resources to gain release, was one motivating factor that contributed to efforts to reform bail practices. Five ideas for reform deserve special attention: (1) police citation, (2) ROR (release on own recognizance), (3) 10 percent cash bail, (4) bail guidelines, and (5) preventive detention.

citation
A written order issued by a law enforcement officer directing those accused of committing a minor offense to appear in court at a specified time rather than place them under arrest.

release on own recognizance (ROR)
Pretrial release without bail granted on the defendant's promise to appear in court.

1. *Police citation.* In many jurisdictions, law enforcement officers issue a **citation** directing those accused of committing a minor offense to appear in court at a specified time rather than place them under arrest. Experience has shown that relatively few people disobey the order contained in the citation, also known as a summons in some jurisdictions.

2. *ROR (release on own reognizance).* Most courts now grant pretrial release without bail on the defendant's promise to appear in court—a procedure generally referred to as **release on own recognizance (ROR)** but also known as "promise to appear" or "signature bond." Defendants are interviewed about their ties to the community, their job history, and their family stability to determine if they are likely to return to court without posting bail. Many of these defendants might otherwise remain in jail because they lack the money to make bail.

Studies indicate that closer evaluation of the defendants' community ties can permit larger numbers of pretrial releases while producing high rates of attendance at scheduled hearings. In fact, many courts use ROR without such detailed evaluations of defendants' backgrounds, sometimes because of jail overcrowding, and still have relatively few problems with defendants disappearing.[4] As the accompanying Ideas in Practice shows, the decision to grant ROR is not always an easy one.

3. *Ten percent cash bail.* Obviously, the use of citations and ROR not only reduces the risk that poor people will needlessly suffer from pretrial detention but also eliminates the role of the bail bondsman. In another reform, 10 percent cash bail, defendants must merely post 10 percent of the bail amount with the court in order to gain release. The court usually retains a small amount of this money as an administrative fee. In effect, the court replaces the bail bondsman by making the defendant pay only 10 percent. From the defendant's point of view, this arrangement is preferable because the defendant gets most of that 10 percent back when he or she returns for the scheduled court date.

4. *Bail guidelines*. Bail guidelines are intended to reduce discrimination in the discretionary bail decisions of judges. These guidelines require all judges in a jurisdiction to consider the same factors and set comparable bail for similarly situated defendants. Judges may use a worksheet to tally the number of "points" each defendant has "earned" based on the seriousness of the pending charge, prior record, and other factors. After totaling the points, the judge consults the bail guidelines to find the appropriate range of bail amounts, from ROR to several thousand dollars, to be imposed on defendants.

5. *Preventive detention*. One reform has been aimed at an entirely different problem: the risk of releasing defendants who pose a danger to the community. Some studies indicate that a notable percentage of defendants set free on bail commit additional crimes while on pretrial release. To address this problem, many states have instituted **preventive detention**, whereby defendants may be held in custody for trial based on a judge's finding that, if released on bail, they would pose a threat to society.

Federal preventive detention is based on the Bail Reform Act of 1984. It gives federal judges the power to detain defendants without bail after holding hearings in which the prosecution and defense present evidence and arguments about the suspect's dangerousness and likelihood of flight. Many federal judges believe that the act has permitted them to be more honest in their bail decision making. Previously, they often simply set extremely high bail if they did not want a defendant to gain pretrial release. Now, they can formally declare that the defendant cannot be released by holding a hearing and citing evidence that the offender is dangerous and/or likely to flee. Although civil libertarians complain that preventive detention improperly violates the right to liberty of people who should be presumed innocent until proven guilty, the U.S. Supreme Court has upheld the use of preventive detention for detaining both adults and juveniles. For instance, in *Schall v. Martin* (1984), the Court ruled that pretrial detention of a juvenile is constitutional to protect the welfare of a minor and the community.[5] In *United States v. Salerno* (1987), the Court upheld the preventive detention provisions of the Bail Reform Act of 1984 as a legitimate use of governmental power to prevent people from committing crimes while out on bail.[6]

THE IMPACT OF THE BAIL SYSTEM

The impact of bail is obviously harshest on those defendants who do not gain release. While in jail pending the processing of the criminal charges, the defendant may lose a job, be unable to provide expected financial support to his or her family, and sit helplessly behind bars while the family suffers hardships or even disintegrates. Moreover, the jailed suspect cannot help his or her defense attorney locate witnesses and prepare the best possible defense.

IDEAS IN PRACTICE

As judge of the District Court of Northampton, Massachusetts, you are responsible for setting bail. In the following cases, indicate whether you would order release on recognizance (ROR), set bail at some specific amount (state the amount), or deny bail and order preventive detention. Explain your decision.

Tony Smith is charged with possession of cocaine with intent to distribute. He has one prior conviction for misdemeanor assault. He is twenty years old, works at a grocery store, and supports his wife and one child. He is a life-long resident of Northampton.

Susan Claussen is charged with theft for ordering and consuming dinner at an expensive restaurant and then leaving without paying the bill. She has entered guilty pleas to this offense on five previous occasions over the past three years. She has been placed on probation several times and served one thirty-day jail sentence. She is unemployed, lives with her parents, and is a life-long resident.

preventive detention
The holding of a defendant for trial, based on a judge's finding that, if released on bail, the defender would pose a threat to society.

Schall v. Martin (1984)
Pretrial detention of a juvenile is constitutional to protect the welfare of the minor and the community.

United States v. Salerno (1987)
Preventive detention provisions of the Bail Reform Act of 1984 upheld as a legitimate use of governmental power to prevent people from committing crimes while out on bail.

CLOSE-UP
Justice Jailed

Bobby Jones was an 18-year-old New Haven [Connecticut] resident when he was arrested in a drug raid at an acquaintance's apartment in 1990. Though he had once been convicted of a minor offense, his personal appearance prompted a judge to remark that Jones "seems like a nice young gentleman."

His bond: $350,000.

Robert J. Conkling was a 29-year-old unemployed mechanic with a criminal record and no fixed address. After a manhunt by state, local and federal authorities, he was charged in New Haven court with kidnapping a 7-week-old girl.

So far as is known, no judge called him a nice young gentleman.

His bond: $175,000.

Conkling is white. Jones is black.

Conkling, whose relatives helped pay his bond, is free. Jones, who could not raise the money for his bail, is still in jail—seven months later.

Their cases are typical of the huge inequalities between minorities and whites in Connecticut's bail system as revealed in a computer-assisted review of about 150,000 cases.

Even if he has an apparently clean record, a black or Hispanic man will initially have to pay—on average—more than double what a white man will pay to get out of jail.

And although a judge may lower his bond later if the defendant can't get out of jail, a black man's average bond at arraignment will be 71 percent higher than a white man's. And a Hispanic man's will be 62 percent higher.

Some lawyers argue that blacks and Hispanics are charged with more serious crimes and usually have worse criminal records, meaning that higher bonds would be justified.

Indeed, the review found that the proportion of defendants charged with felonies was greater for blacks and Hispanics than it was for whites. About 48 percent of all Hispanic defendants were charged with felonies, as opposed to misdemeanors, compared with 45 percent of blacks and 33 percent of whites.

But the review also found about 36,400 cases in which the defendants had no records of convictions within five years of their arrest, were not on parole or probation, had no outstanding warrants against them, were not in jail for other crimes, had no pending cases, and had no records of failing to appear for court hearings while out on bail.

Comparing the bond amounts for those defendants when they were charged with the most frequent kind of felony—punishable by as much as five years in prison—the study found that getting out of jail is still substantially cheaper for whites. On average, judges set bonds 84 percent higher for black men and 69 percent higher for Hispanic men.

SOURCE: Brant Houston and Jack Ewing, "Justice Jailed," *The Hartford Courant*, 16 June 1991, p. 1. Reprinted with permission of *The Hartford Courant*.

These practical effects create a double whammy on top of the hardship of losing one's freedom and living in difficult and sometimes dangerous conditions in jail.

Poor defendants most often face these circumstances because they are least likely to be able to raise the necessary money for bail. In fact, because of the way in which the bail process operates, poor defendants may even find themselves in the tragically awkward position of having to decide whether to plead guilty based on the prospects for release rather than on their own guilt or innocence. For example, a defendant charged with a moderately serious crime may be told by the defense attorney that if he or she enters a quick "guilty" plea, the prosecutor and judge will agree to impose a sentence of probation. However, if the defendant enters a plea of "not guilty," bail will be set. If the defendant does not have any money, he or she will have to remain in jail until the case is resolved. What a choice! Plead guilty and go free, or assert your innocence and go to jail. Because the bail system has relied on the possession of money and property as the basis for surety, poor people may find themselves pressured to enter guilty pleas in order to have their cases processed quickly.

The bail system also tends to discriminate by race, as discussed in the Close-Up.

Although many jurisdictions have implemented reforms designed to address specific problems in the bail system, there are no standardized national procedures for setting bail and administering pretrial release. As a result, bondsmen remain important but problematic participants in the bail system in many cities, poor defendants still suffer special hardships, and discretionary decisions by judges and prosecutors still shape bail decisions in many courts.

PRETRIAL DETENTION

People who cannot obtain pretrial release must remain in jail. As we will discuss in greater detail in Chapter 11, jails, unlike prisons, hold persons awaiting trial and those sentenced to incarceration for less than one year. Conditions in jails are frequently much harsher and more difficult than those in prisons. People are often locked in large cells with a mixed group of pretrial detainees, people serving short misdemeanor sentences, and convicted felons awaiting transfer to prisons. The cell may also contain a changing population of people who need psychiatric help or who have substance abuse problems. Inmates may not be separated according to their status or the seriousness of their offenses. Thus, a "presumed innocent" pretrial detainee might spend weeks in the same confined space as people who have been convicted of felonies.

More than 450,000 people are confined in jails every day throughout the country, and approximately half of these people are pretrial detainees who are waiting for their cases to be processed.

PRETRIAL DETENTION AND EMOTIONAL HARDSHIP

In many instances, the period immediately following arrest is the most frightening and difficult time for criminal suspects. Imagine freely walking the streets one minute and being locked in a small space with a large number of troubled and potentially dangerous cellmates the next. Suddenly, you have lost all privacy and must share an open toilet with a multitude of hostile strangers. You have been fingerprinted, photographed, and questioned—treated like the "criminal" that the police and criminal justice system now regard you to be. You are alone in the company of people whose behavior you cannot predict. You are left to worry and wonder about what might happen both during the first night in jail and in the future if you are convicted of a serious crime. If you are female, you may very well be completely isolated in a cell by yourself. Given the stressful nature of arrest and jailing, it is little wonder that most jail suicides occur during the first hours of detention and that most psychotic episodes occur during or just after the intake procedures between arrest and incarceration.

The shock of arrest and detention can be exacerbated by other factors. Many people are arrested for offenses that they committed while under the influence of alcohol or some other substance. Such people may be less able to cope rationally with the emotional crisis of confronting and adapting to their new situation. Young arrestees who face the risk of violent victimization from older, more powerful cellmates may sink into debilitating depression. In addition, detainees face the stress of worrying about losing their jobs and about providing financial support for their families while they are held in jail without knowing precisely if or when they will be released.

Pretrial detention can last a long time. In some jurisdictions, the average time from arrest to trial is as long as six months. Thus, the personal, psychological, and economic hardships on pretrial detainees and their families can be both prolonged and substantial.

PRETRIAL DETENTION AND CASE PROCESSING

The period following arrest is the most stressful for a defendant. Most jail suicides take place during the first few hours of confinement. What might be going through your mind when you may not even yet know what charges are being brought against you?

Pretrial detention not only imposes personal stresses and hardships that may reach crisis proportions but also can affect the outcomes of defendants' cases. As we mentioned earlier, people who are held in jail can provide little assistance to their defense lawyers, and they may feel extra pressure to plead guilty because they want to get out of jail. In addition, their failure to make bail can increase the likelihood that a judge or jury will find them guilty when their case goes to trial. Defendants who make bail can return for the trial well-groomed and neatly dressed, escorted into the courtroom in the loving embrace of mothers or grandmothers who thereby subtly indicate to the jury that this "nice" boy or girl is not a blameworthy criminal. By contrast, pretrial detainees may be brought into the courtroom in handcuffs, unshaven and bedraggled, and wearing an orange jail jumpsuit. These contrasting images alone may affect, if only subconsciously, the judge's or jury's perceptions about the defendant, no matter how strong or weak the prosecution's evidence might be. One study indicated that defendants who failed to make bail were more likely to be convicted and received harsher sentences than those who obtained pretrial release.[7] Although another study questioned whether pretrial detention increased the likelihood of conviction, that study found a greater likelihood of imprisonment as an ultimate punishment.[8] It is difficult to know for certain if and how pretrial detention affects the final outcomes of cases, but clearly, money bail systems often keep poor people in jail and let wealthier people out. Therefore, whatever adverse consequences flow from failing to make bail, poor people suffer the most.

PLEA BARGAINING

For the vast majority of cases, plea bargaining is the most important step in the criminal justice process. Very few cases go to trial; instead, a negotiated guilty plea developed through the interactions of prosecutors, defense lawyers, and judges determines what will finally happen to most criminal defendants.

INCENTIVES TO PLEA BARGAIN

Thirty years ago, plea bargaining was not publicly acknowledged or discussed; it was the criminal justice system's "little secret." There were doubts about its constitutionality, and it clashed with the idealized image of the courtroom as a place where prosecutors and defense attorneys engaged in legal battles as the jury witnessed the emergence of the "truth" amid the "smoke and noise" of adversarial conflict. Yet the quick and quiet resolution of cases through negotiated guilty pleas historically has been common. Indeed, scholars have documented that guilty pleas have been a primary means of finalizing criminal cases at least since the late 1800s. Scholars began to shed light on plea bargaining in the 1960s, and the Supreme Court openly acknowledged and endorsed the process in the 1970s. In 1971, for example, in **Santobello v. New York**, Chief Justice Warren Burger described plea bargaining in very favorable terms in deciding that prosecutors are obligated to fulfill promises made during plea negotiations. According to Burger, "'Plea bargaining' is an essential component of the administration of justice. Properly administered, it is to be encouraged."[9] Burger also listed a number of reasons that plea bargaining was a "highly desirable" part of the criminal justice process:

Santobello v. New York
(1971)
Prosecutors are obligated
to fulfill promises made
during plea negotiations.

- If every case went to trial, federal and state governments would need many times more courts and judges than they currently have.
- Plea bargaining leads to the prompt and largely final disposition of most criminal cases.
- Plea bargaining reduces the time that pretrial detainees must spend in jail awaiting the resolution of their cases. If they plead guilty to serious charges, they can be moved to prisons that have recreational and educational programs instead of enduring the enforced idleness of jails.
- By disposing of cases more quickly, plea bargaining reduces the amount of time that other suspects spend released on bail, and therefore, the public is better protected from crimes that such suspects may commit while on pretrial release.
- Offenders who plead guilty to serious charges can begin their rehabilitation efforts more quickly by moving into prison counseling, training, and education designed to rehabilitate offenders.[10]

In 1976, former Justice Potter Stewart came much closer to revealing the heart and soul of plea bargaining when he wrote, in *Blackledge* v. *Allison*, that plea bargaining "can benefit all concerned" within a criminal case.[11] Plea bargaining exists because it creates advantages for defendants, prosecutors, defense attorneys, and judges.

Defendants have great incentives to plea bargain because they can have their cases completed more quickly and they can participate in establishing a definite punishment rather than facing the uncertainty of a judge's discretionary sentencing decision after a trial. Moreover, in exchange for pleading guilty, the defendant is likely to receive less than the maximum punishment that might have been imposed after a trial. Prosecutors are not being "soft on crime" when they plea bargain. Instead, they are gaining a relatively easy conviction, even in cases in which there may not have been enough evidence to convince a jury to convict the defendant. They also save time and resources by disposing of cases and recommending a punishment without the need for time-consuming trial preparations. As indicated in Chapter 7, private defense attorneys also benefit from plea bargaining by saving the time involved in trial preparation, earning their fees quickly, and moving on to the next income-producing case. Likewise, plea bargaining helps public

Largely kept out of the public mind until recent years, plea bargaining has become such an integral part of the system that judges frequently take part in negotiations.

explicit plea bargaining
Direct negotiations between the prosecution and defense, sometimes with the participation of judges, in which a defendant agrees to plead guilty in exchange for reduced charges or the recommendation of a lighter-than-maximum sentence.

implicit plea bargaining
The entry of a guilty plea by a defendant with the unspoken but reasonable expectation of a less harsh sentence for saving the court the time and expense of conducting a trial and for admitting responsibility and regret.

defenders cope with large and ever-growing caseloads. Judges, too, avoid time-consuming trials and are spared the difficult decision of deciding what sentence should be imposed on the defendant. Instead, they frequently merely adopt the sentence recommended by the prosecutor in consultation with the defense attorney, provided that the sentence fits within the range of sentences that the judge believes appropriate for a given crime and offender.

Because plea bargaining is beneficial to everyone involved, it is little wonder that it existed long before it was publicly acknowledged by the legal community and that it continues to exist even when prosecutors, legislators, or judges claim that they are seeking to abolish it. In California, for example, legislation was enacted to prohibit plea bargaining in serious felony cases. As Candace McCoy's research demonstrated, when plea bargaining was barred in the felony trial courts, such bargaining did not disappear. It simply occurred earlier in the criminal justice process, soon after arrest at the initial appearance in the lower-level municipal court.[12] In other contexts, efforts to abolish plea bargaining result in bargaining over *charges* instead of directly negotiating the sentence that will be recommended in exchange for a guilty plea. Alternatively, if a prosecutor forbids his or her staff to plea bargain, judges may become more directly involved in negotiating and facilitating guilty pleas that result in predictable punishments for offenders.

In the unlikely event that all prosecutors *and* judges in a court agreed that they would no longer engage in **explicit plea bargaining** by negotiating guilty pleas with defense attorneys in exchange for reduced charges or a lighter-than-maximum sentence, many defendants would still have powerful incentives to engage in **implicit plea bargaining**. In other words, they would enter guilty pleas to many charges with the unspoken but reasonable expectation that they would receive less harsh sentences from the judges. Lighter sentences could be expected because the defendants would have spared the court from the time and expense of conducting a trial and indicated their responsibility and regret by admitting guilt.

RELATIONSHIPS AND TACTICS IN PLEA BARGAINING

Plea bargaining is guided by the relationships and interactions of the decision makers directly involved in the case, namely the prosecutor, defense attorney, defendant, and judge. The prosecutor wants a quick, certain conviction. If the case goes to trial, the judge and jury make important decisions beyond the control of the prosecutor; but in the plea bargaining process, the prosecutor exerts maximum control over the ultimate sentence. He or she can recommend the punishment that would achieve his or her sense of justice, in exchange for a guilty plea. Although judges retain the formal authority to determine the sentence, they know that the effectiveness of the system depends on their acceptance of the prosecutor's recommendation.

A friendly, cooperative spirit often characterizes the bargaining between prosecutors and defense attorneys, even when they each are trying to gain an advantage for their side. Overt hostility and noncooperation during plea bargaining could poison the personal relationships between the attorneys involved and make it much more difficult for them to deal with each other in future cases. Conversations between attorneys tend to be frank and open. Both sides may freely discuss their evidence and even attempt to impress the other side by revealing planned strategies in the event of a trial. The openness of these conversations is guaranteed by the shared understanding that neither side will attempt to use in court the statements made during confidential negotiations.

Effective plea bargaining depends on the actors understanding the local legal culture and sharing perceptions of the "going rate" for certain offenses.

The prosecutor and defense attorney are often both members of a particular **local legal culture**—that is, they share norms as to case handling and participants' behavior in the judicial process. Thus, they have an understanding about how criminal cases should be processed, how attorneys should treat each other, and, most importantly, what the **"going rate,"** or the locally accepted view of the appropriate punishments for specific crimes based on seriousness of offense and offender's prior record, should be.

These shared understandings are important for several reasons. First, they facilitate effective plea bargaining since both sides understand which potential sentences apply to which cases. Instead of debating about whether burglary cases should be punishable by a short prison term, both sides will already know whether incarceration is a penalty that is part of the going rate for burglary. Thus, they can focus their attention on the facts of the case and the characteristics of the defendant in determining whether burglary is an appropriate charge according to the provable facts and whether this defendant merits incarceration. If the going rate is not applicable to these facts or this defendant, then both sides ought to be able to agree on a guilty plea to a lesser offense. Second, the shared understandings help to create a cooperative atmosphere in plea bargaining, even if bad feelings actually exist between the prosecutor and defense attorney. The norms of the local legal culture dictate how attorneys are expected to treat each other and thereby facilitate agreement. And, third, as already sugggested, the shared understandings about behavior help to preserve the future relationships between the attorneys.

The pervasiveness of cooperation and shared understandings makes "bargaining" a misleading term in discussing plea agreements in many courts. Instead of engaging in an exchange (for example, "If you plead guilty, we will recommend probation"), the two sides are simply attempting to "settle the facts." The attorneys already know from local practice that the going rate will determine the sentence for each particular crime and offender. Therefore, they are really seeking to establish the provable facts in an effort to arrive at a mutual decision about the appropriate criminal charge to be applied to the defendant for his or her actions.

The facts of a case are often the most difficult element to sort out because contradictory "facts" may be presented (for example, two witnesses disagree about what happened) and facts may be subject to interpretation. For example, whose actions precipitated the bar fight? Did the defendant intend to hurt

local legal culture
Norms shared by members of a court community as to case handling and participants' behavior in the judicial process.

"going rate"
Local view of the appropriate punishments for specific crimes based on the seriousness of offense and offender's prior record.

195

someone when he left his home that morning with a jackknife in his pocket? If no weapon was brandished, did the clerk at the convenience store really have a reasonable basis to believe that the defendant was armed when he told her to give him the money in the cash register? These are difficult questions to answer, yet they will determine which charge and which punishment are most appropriate in each case. Each side in the case may hope to persuade the other that its interpretation of the defendant's actions is supported by provable facts. The prosecution wants the defense to believe that strong evidence exists to prove its version of the defendant's crime. The defense attorney, by contrast, wants to persuade the prosecution that the evidence is not solid and that, in fact, there is a risk of acquittal if the case is heard by a jury. Once the prosecutor and defense attorney reach a consensus about the provable facts in a case, then the appropriate charge and the going-rate sentence are apparent to both of them, and the guilty plea can be entered without any formal exchange or bargain.

In other situations, bargaining may be vigorous and thereby provide the basis for formal exchanges. If the prosecution and defense cannot "settle the facts," then they have no choice but to bargain. Bargaining may also be necessary in a large city when multiple courthouses, dozens of judges, and personnel turnover in the prosecutor's and public defender's offices inhibit the development and maintenance of a generally recognized going rate for each offense.

A common tactic for prosecutors is to pursue a multicount indictment against a defendant. They enter the plea-bargaining process by charging the defendant with every conceivable offense that might be even remotely supported by the facts. When Congressman Dan Rostenkowski was charged with corruption and fraud in 1994, for example, his attorneys accused the government of producing a "kitchen sink" indictment containing seventeen felony charges that arguably overlapped one another. The prosecution may know that it cannot prove many of the charges, but it hopes to make the defendant fearful that the most serious charges might be provable. In addition, the long list of charges gives prosecutors room to negotiate. They can agree to trade away certain charges during the process of bargaining while knowing that they were unlikely to prove those charges anyway. By scaring the defendant into imagining the sentence he or she might face on the most serious charges, the prosecutor may gain a quick guilty plea by offering to charge the defendant only with a less serious offense.

A common tactic of defense attorneys is to threaten to take the case all the way to trial if the prosecutor does not compromise on charges or recommended sentences. In some cases, prosecutors may be especially reluctant to take a case to trial, either because they doubt the strength of their evidence or because they do not wish to expend the time and resources necessary for trial preparation. Defense attorneys can also increase the pressure on prosecutors by filing pretrial motions that require the expenditure of time and energy in order to prepare written responses. Defense attorneys may also seek to delay the case by requesting that pretrial hearings and other stages be rescheduled. If the defendant was unable to make bail and remains in jail, this strategy will place an extra burden on the defendant. However, because witnesses may move away, die, or forget, the passage of time can weaken a prosecutor's case and increase the likelihood of a compromise that favors the defendant.

Through the interactions of the prosecutor and the defense attorney, a plea agreement may be produced. This agreement will not automatically determine the outcome of the case, however, because neither the prosecutor nor the defense attorney possesses the authority to finalize a plea bargain. The prosecutor is dependent on the cooperation and agreement of the judge with respect to the sentence that will be imposed. Meanwhile, the defense attorney needs the approval of the defendant before an agreement can be finalized. For many defense attorneys, the defendants may seem like additional adversaries if they refuse to accept the idea that a particular plea agreement advances their best interests. Defendants may be reluctant, for example, to accept a plea bargain that calls for a period of incarceration because they do not fully recognize the possibility that conviction on more serious charges would produce an even longer sentence.

CRITICISMS OF PLEA BARGAINING

Although plea bargaining determines the outcomes for nearly all cases and advances the interests of all participants involved, the process is not without its problems. Criticisms of plea bargaining focus on two issues: (1) fairness to society and (2) fairness to defendants.

Fairness to Society

Does plea bargaining fulfill the goal of applying appropriately severe punishments to criminal offenders? This issue hovers like a dark cloud over the entire process. In the eyes of many members of the public, plea bargaining is simply an avenue through which offenders escape from the severe punishments that they deserve. Many publicized efforts by elected officials, including prosecutors, to "ban" plea bargaining stem from the perception that the public is unhappy that every offender is not given the maximum possible sentence.

Politicians may attempt to generate support from voters by opposing plea bargaining even though they are well aware that plea bargaining is acknowledged by members of the legal community, including conservative Supreme Court justices, to be a beneficial and essential component of the criminal justice system. In fact, attempts in Alaska and California to end plea bargaining were quickly thwarted by attorneys and judges who found ways to maneuver around the "ban."

It is easy to see why the public views plea bargaining with suspicion, especially when they observe offenders pleading guilty to reduced charges or fewer offenses than the substantial serious charges that were originally announced to the news media by the prosecutor's office. In part, the prosecution's own plea-bargaining tactics help to feed this negative image when prosecutors use multicount indictments as a bargaining tool, even though they would have little chance of gaining conviction on some of the charges.

Lawyers and judges respond to this criticism of plea bargaining by claiming that society benefits from the widespread use of negotiated guilty pleas. Plea bargaining allows decision makers within the criminal process to seek *individualized* justice. Although legislators enact statutes that might subject all thieves to the same punishment, lawyers and judges frequently believe that individual differences among people who commit theft justify different punishments. These differences may involve personal characteristics of the offender. For example, was it a poor seventeen-year-old from a broken home who gave in to the temptation to steal new basketball shoes, or was it someone who is part of an organized larceny operation that regularly steals selected items from department stores? Many decision makers within the court system believe that the motivations, circumstances, and rehabilitation potential of individual offenders must be taken into account in determining punishment. The need to individualize justice may also arise from the factual circumstances of a case. Although they may face identical assault charges, someone charged with assault while arguably defending himself in an altercation initiated by drunken fans at a football game may deserve different treatment than someone who beats up the paperboy for carelessly throwing a newspaper into the bushes. Lawyers and judges would argue that they can make the punishment fit the crime by looking carefully at both the crime and the offender.

Lawyers and judges also argue that plea bargaining benefits the public by saving the significant costs that the court system would incur if every case went to trial. However, even without explicit bargaining and agreements, defendants will enter guilty pleas in order to seek the expected benefits from admitting responsibility and sparing judges the time and trouble of holding trials.

Fairness to Defendants

The second primary criticism of plea bargaining focuses on whether the process is fair to criminal defendants. There are concerns that defendants do not benefit from their due process rights under the Constitution when they surrender their right to a jury trial by entering a guilty plea. This problem may be exacerbated when defense attorneys attempt to persuade defendants to accept plea bargains without seriously considering defendants' claims of innocence. The defense attorney's desire to terminate the case in order to receive payment and move on to the next revenue-producing case may clash with the defendant's interest in having a thorough, fair examination of the facts. One result is that some defendants may believe that they have been "sold out" by their attorneys.

Of great concern is the possibility that innocent defendants are persuaded to plead guilty in the plea-bargaining process, especially if those defendants lack the education and social status to give them the confidence to say no to an attorney who pressures them to plead guilty. Poor people, in particular, may feel helpless when drawn into the stressful chaos of the courthouse and jail, and they may be most susceptible to pressures to follow their attorneys' advice even if they believe that they are not guilty.

If the attorneys do not have the time or resources to examine and discuss the facts of the case and the offender's characteristics, plea bargains may fail to achieve anyone's sense of justice, individualized or not, by being finalized in a hurry. Because judges are often brought into the plea-bargaining process after the attorneys have already reached an agreement, busy judges have little opportunity or inclination to look closely at the case to see whether the attorneys have overlooked some important consideration in their haste to move on to the next batch of cases.

Plea bargaining, whether explicit or implicit, is based on the assumption that defendants will receive lighter punishments after pleading guilty than they would have received on being convicted at trial. This is inherently unfair, according to many critics, because it effectively punishes people for asserting their constitutional rights. Why should someone who pleads guilty to robbery receive a lighter sentence than someone convicted of the same crime after a trial? Figure 8.2 presents the results of a Bureau of Justice Statistics study that supports the view that offenders going to trial receive harsher sentences. These results should be viewed with caution, however, because it is

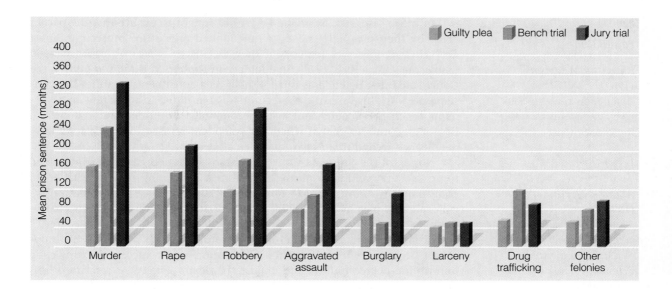

difficult to determine the strength of the evidence against a defendant and the reason a plea was not the method of disposition.

Questions remain about the extent to which people actually receive harsher punishment for taking their cases to trial. There is a widespread perception among defendants and their attorneys that plea bargains produce leniency. Because decision makers within the plea-bargaining process believe that they are advancing individualized justice, they may have few concerns about critics' claims that there should be greater consistency between sentences from trial verdicts and sentences from plea bargains.

In supervising the judicial system, the U.S. Supreme Court has been presented with opportunities to create rules for the plea-bargaining process. Some of these rules have been intended to protect defendants against unfairness in the plea-bargaining process. In ***Boykin v. Alabama (1969)***, for example, the Court ruled that the defendant must make an affirmative statement that a guilty plea was made voluntarily before a judge may accept the plea.[13] This does not guarantee that the plea is actually voluntary, but it provides the judge with an opportunity to detect instances in which the defendant seems especially hesitant or confused about events. In the typical **"copping out"** ceremony, as the courtroom procedure is called, the judge asks the defendant a series of questions to determine whether the plea is accurate and voluntary. Most defendants have been coached by their attorneys so that they answer the questions "correctly." They must answer yes to such questions as, "Are you admitting that you committed this crime?" and "Are you entering your plea voluntarily?" Some defendants, however, also answer yes when asked, "Were you promised anything that caused you to plead guilty?" The explicit acknowledgment of a promise, although honest and accurate, may convey the impression that the plea was not given voluntarily, so defense attorneys may ask the judge if they may speak to their clients for a moment. After the brief conference, the judge asks the question again, and the defendant, following the attorney's instructions, says, "No, I was not promised anything." In such situations, in which the courtroom actors pretend that a plea bargain did not take place, the judge may not accurately detect whether the defendant's guilty plea was both knowing and voluntary.

FIGURE 8.2

Conviction by Guilty Plea, Bench Trial, or Trial by Jury: A Comparison of Prison Sentences Although it appears to be in the offender's interest to plead guilty for most crimes, there is not enough information in this graph to support such a conclusion. What else would you need to know?

SOURCE: U.S. Department of Justice, Bureau of Justice Statistics, *Bulletin* (February 1990).

Boykin v. *Alabama* **(1969)**

Defendants must make an affirmative statement that they are voluntarily making a plea of guilty.

"copping out"

Courtroom procedure in which the judge asks the defendant a series of questions to determine whether a guilty plea is accurate and voluntary.

Ricketts v. Adamson
(1987)

Defendants must uphold plea agreements or suffer the consequences.

Alford v. North Carolina
(1970)

A plea of guilty may be accepted for the purpose of a lesser sentence by a defendant who nevertheless maintains his or her innocence.

Bordenkircher v. Hayes
(1978)

A defendant's rights are not violated by a prosecutor who warns that refusal to accept a guilty plea will result in a harsher sentence.

In other cases, the Supreme Court has sought to ensure that the parties abide by their plea agreements. As mentioned previously, prosecutors must keep their promises of leniency if they are made as part of a plea bargain (*Santobello* v. *New York*, 1971). In addition, in *Ricketts* **v.** *Adamson* **(1987)**, the Court ruled that defendants must uphold plea agreements or suffer the consequences. In this case, the prosecutor was permitted to withdraw an agreement to charge a defendant with second-degree murder and reimpose a first-degree murder charge when the defendant refused to testify at another defendant's second trial as part of a plea agreement.[14]

Not all of the Supreme Court's decisions have necessarily been designed to ensure that voluntary pleas result from a bargaining process with equal obligations. In *Alford* **v.** *North Carolina* **(1970)**, the Court approved, in principle, a guilty plea by a defendant who nevertheless said he was innocent but was pleading guilty rather than risk conviction on a more serious charge.[15] Alford pleaded guilty to second-degree murder, despite protesting his innocence, because he feared that the prosecution might succeed in convicting him of first-degree murder and impose the death penalty. As a result of this decision, some courts around the country routinely accept "Alford pleas" in which defendants enter guilty pleas while continuing to maintain their innocence. The existence of such pleas weakens the trial judge's ability to detect and reject involuntary guilty pleas.

In *Bordenkircher* **v.** *Hayes* **(1978)**, the Court approved the practice of prosecutors threatening defendants with more serious charges if they refuse to plead guilty and instead insist on jury trials. The Court claimed that this was merely a part of the "give and take" of plea bargaining, but such practices obviously create risks that prosecutors may be able to pressure reluctant and fearful defendants to enter guilty pleas that they otherwise would not make.[16]

One notable reform effort that accepts the importance and usefulness of plea bargaining is the preplea conference. This is a conference in which all parties—judge, victim, defendant, police, and prosecutor—meet to seek an agreement on an appropriate sentence that will be imposed if the defendant agrees to plead guilty. For purposes of the conference, the defendant's guilt is assumed, and the discussion focuses on issues that may contribute to the development of an agreement. The presence of the judge is intended to ensure that the agreement carefully considers the facts of the case and the defendant's characteristics and circumstances before determining an appropriate sentence. The use of such conferences presumes that plea bargaining will be more effective if a wider array of interested parties participate in the process.

The issues raised by plea bargaining's perceived impact on society and on defendants will continue to generate discussion and reform proposals. However, because plea agreements provide benefits to all of the primary participants in the process, we can expect that plea bargaining will continue to have a widespread impact on the vast majority of cases despite any efforts at reform.

SUMMARY

The past twenty-five years have brought a broader recognition of the importance of pretrial processes in determining what will happen to defendants and their cases in the criminal justice system. Discretionary decisions by prosecutors, judges, and even bail bondsmen help to determine which suspects will go free and which will lose their liberty while their cases proceed through the system. Because defendants must risk forfeiture of money or property in order to obtain bail, poor defendants are most likely to suffer the consequences of failing to gain pretrial release. These consequences are not limited to their loss of freedom. They also endure various hardships, including disintegration of family stability, loss of jobs, and confinement with dangerous cellmates as they wait for their cases to be processed.

Defendants' lives are also deeply affected by plea bargaining because negotiated outcomes determine the guilt and punishment of most people charged with crimes. As in bail decision making, the plea-bargaining process is determined by discretionary decisions. The prosecutor can establish the basis for plea discussions by deciding the specific charges and number of counts to be pressed against the defendant. The defendant's fate is ultimately determined by the interactions of the prosecutor and defense attorney. The attorneys for each side negotiate compromises concerning the charges and punishments to be imposed or, more commonly, engage in discussions to settle the facts of the case and apply the local going rate of punishment for particular offenses. The discretionary decisions made in bail setting and plea bargaining have the most significant impact on the lives of defendants in most cases.

These decisions, unlike verdicts rendered by juries after trials, are not subject to public attention. Bail setting and plea bargaining are relatively invisible administrative decisions that are made as a result of interactions among the interested parties. They are among the most crucial elements in determining the quality of justice achieved in the criminal justice process.

QUESTIONS FOR REVIEW

1. Why is the prosecutor considered the most powerful figure in the pretrial stage of the criminal justice system?
2. What is the bail-setting process?
3. What are the purposes of pretrial detention? Does pretrial detention violate American beliefs in individual liberty and the presumption of innocence?
4. What tactics do prosecutors and defense attorneys use in plea bargaining?
5. What are the criticisms and problems generated by plea bargaining?

NOTES

1. James G. Carr, "Bail Bondsmen and the Federal Courts," *Federal Probation* 57 (March 1993), pp. 9–14.
2. Frederic Suffet, "Bail Setting: A Study of Courtroom Interaction," *Crime and Delinquency* 12 (1988), p. 318.
3. Roy B. Flemming, *Punishment Before Trial* (New York: Longman, 1982), pp. 136–138.
4. Malcolm M. Feeley, *Court Reform on Trial* (New York: Basic Books, 1983), pp. 40–79.
5. *Schall* v. *Martin*, 467 U.S. 253 (1984).
6. *United States* v. *Salerno*, 481 U.S. 739 (1987).
7. Eric W. Single, "The Consequence of Pretrial Detention," paper presented at the Annual Meeting of the American Sociological Association, New Orleans, 1973.
8. John Goldkamp, *Two Classes of Accused* (Cambridge, MA: Ballinger, 1979).

9. *Santobello* v. *New York*, 404 U.S. 260 (1971).

10. Ibid., p. 261.

11. *Blackledge* v. *Allison*, 431 U.S. 71 (1976).

12. Candace McCoy, *Politics and Plea Bargaining: Victims' Rights in California* (Philadelphia: University of Pennsylvania Press, 1993).

13. *Boykin* v. *Alabama*, 395 U.S. 238 (1969).

14. *Ricketts* v. *Adamson*, 481 U.S. 1 (1987).

15. *Alford* v. *North Carolina*, 400 U.S. 25 (1970).

16. *Bordenkircher* v. *Hayes*, 343 U.S. 357 (1978).

CHAPTER 9
Courts and the Criminal Trial

THE TRIAL OF DAMIAN WILLIAMS
AND HENRY WATSON

In March 1991, the nation's attention was captured by a horrifying videotape shown over and over again on television news programs. Without being aware that they were being filmed from a nearby window, three Los Angeles police officers repeatedly beat motorist Rodney King with nightsticks. In April 1992, the white police officers were acquitted of state criminal charges for their videotaped assault on the African-American motorist. The verdict was rendered by a jury that contained no African-American jurors. Immediately, the city of Los Angeles erupted in a fiery frenzy of rioting and looting that left fifty-three people dead.

During the riot, the nation found itself again confronted with videotaped horror. A helicopter news crew filmed an innocent truck driver named Reginald Denny being pulled from his truck and beaten unconscious. On television screens, viewers saw Denny's crumpled, bleeding body lying in the street as his attackers viciously assaulted him and then jubilantly celebrated their actions for the helicopter news camera. The fact that Denny was white and his attackers were African-Americans heightened racial tensions that had boiled over from the Rodney King case.

Denny was rescued by African-American bystanders and slowly made a miraculous recovery in the hospital. The police used the news footage to identify Denny's attackers, and L.A. Police Chief Darryl Gates personally led a televised raid to arrest suspect Damian Williams. Williams and Henry Watson were charged with twelve felony counts, including attempted murder.

In November 1993, after a combative two-month trial in which five jurors were dismissed and replaced by alternates, a diverse jury containing whites, African-Americans, Hispanics, and Asian-Americans stunned the nation by acquitting the defendants of most charges. Although both defendants faced the possibility of life in prison for attempted murder and aggravated mayhem, Watson was convicted only of misdemeanor assault and Williams was convicted only of simple mayhem, a lesser felony. Watson was released immediately because his seventeen months in pretrial detention exceeded the six-month sentence for his misdemeanor and Williams was given a short sentence.

How could the jury acquit Watson and Williams of serious charges when the entire nation had witnessed the horrifying and brutal assault on Denny? Although many people were angered and perplexed by the verdicts, the cases of Watson and Williams clearly illustrated that trials are complex, human proceedings shaped by many unpredictable forces and events.

Courts are responsible for processing criminal cases and, through the use of fair procedures, deciding on blameworthiness and punishment for criminal offenders. In this chapter, we will focus on judges and juries and their interactions with prosecutors and defense attorneys. We will see how trials and other courtroom processes are affected by the decisions and discretionary powers of these various actors in the system. ★

THE STRUCTURE AND MANAGEMENT OF AMERICAN COURTS

The word *court* can refer to a variety of types of buildings, functions, and processes. At the top of the American system is the U.S. Supreme Court, which hears only about one hundred selected cases each year that have already been heard in as many as three or four different lower courts. At the bottom may be a simple large room where a judicial officer sits at a desk facing two nearby tables with several rows of chairs behind them. Such a modest court setting may be used for handling traffic, misdemeanor, or juvenile matters. In between these two extremes are innumerable varieties of courts, each with its own specific management structure and **jurisdiction**—the legal and geographical range of a court's authority.

The vast differences among American courts stem, in large part, from the decentralized nature of our judicial system. As we learned in Chapter 2, the United States has a dual system of both federal and state courts. One result is that each state has designed and operates its own system, often with distinctive subunits operated by and within individual cities. Despite the differences in design and function, courts have many things in common. They are all forums presided over by judges who interact with attorneys and other participants in the judicial process to reach decisions. They also typically have in common problems such as burdensome caseloads, fragmented administrative structures, and inadequate resources.

Since the beginning of the twentieth century, reformers have sought to improve the organization and efficiency of courts, focusing on four main goals:

1. Eliminating overlapping and conflicting jurisdictional boundaries (of both subject matter and geography)
2. Creating a hierarchical and centralized court structure, with administrative responsibility vested in a chief justice and court of last resort
3. Financing the courts by state governments
4. Creating a separate personnel system, centrally run by a state court administrator

From this list of objectives, you can see the nature of weaknesses and problems that reformers seek to change. Decentralized state judicial systems create overlapping responsibilities for their various courts. Also, courts tend to be administered by judges within each individual courthouse. This reliance on busy people trained in law, rather than on specialists trained in administration and finance, leads to significant problems in resource management, record keeping, and efficiency. In addition, courts are generally funded locally, at the city or county level. This creates great disparities in the judicial resources available from city to city within a state.

COURT STRUCTURE

The U.S. Supreme Court oversees both the federal and state systems because the Constitution protects the rights of defendants in all criminal cases. Most criminal behavior violates state law and is processed in state court systems, primarily in the trial courts of county and city governments. The federal

CHAPTER QUESTIONS

What is the structure of American courts?

How are judges selected?

What influences affect decisions that occur in the courtroom?

What are the unique features of jury trials?

How does the appeals process operate for criminal cases?

jurisdiction
The legal and geographical range of a court's authority.

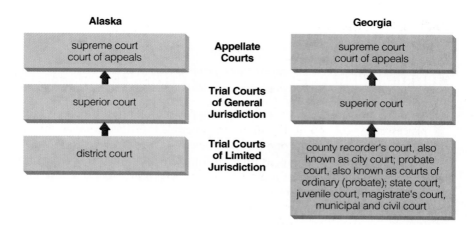

FIGURE 9.1

Court Structures of Alaska (reformed) and Georgia (unreformed) Reformers have pushed for states to reduce the number of courts, to standardize court names, and to demarcate their jurisdictions clearly.

SOURCE: National Center for State Courts, *State Court Caseload Statistics: Annual Report* (Williamsburg, VA: National Center for State Courts, 1989), pp. 184, 194.

appellate court

A court that does not try criminal cases but hears appeals of decisions of lower courts.

trial courts of general jurisdiction

Criminal courts that have primary responsibility for felony cases and that, in some states, may also hear appeals.

trial courts of limited jurisdiction

Criminal courts that generally have responsibility for misdemeanor cases, as well as arraignments, probable cause hearings in felony cases, and, sometimes, felony trials that may result in penalties below a specified limit.

courts deal with those accused of violating the criminal laws of the national government.

The courts of all fifty states are organized into three tiers: (1) appellate courts, (2) trial courts of general jurisdiction, and (3) trial courts of limited jurisdiction. Within this framework, the number of courts, their names, and their specific functions vary widely. As discussed previously, court reformers have advocated changes that would consolidate and simplify court systems in order to improve judicial efficiency and effectiveness. Figure 9.1 contrasts the court stucture of Alaska, a reformed state, with that of Georgia, where the court structure has not been reformed. Both are organized according to the three-tier model, but Georgia has more courts and greater jurisdictional complexity, with multiple courts of limited jurisdiction.

At the top of each system are **appellate courts**, which do not try criminal cases but hear appeals of decisions in lower courts. Each state has an appellate court (court of last resort), usually called the supreme court, and most states have intermediate appellate courts. The sole responsibility of these courts is to consider and decide questions of law and procedure that are claimed to have arisen through errors made by trial court judges. Intermediate appellate courts are usually obligated to hear appeals brought to them by lawyers after the conclusion of trial court proceedings. However, supreme courts usually have the discretion to pick and choose which decisions they will review.

At the core of the criminal court system are **trial courts of general jurisdiction**. These courts have primary responsibility for felony cases and are the location for most criminal trials. In various states, these courts are called superior court, circuit court, court of common pleas, and, in the federal system, district court.

At the bottom of the structural hierarchy are **trial courts of limited jurisdiction**. These courts are generally responsible for misdemeanor cases and can usually sentence offenders only to terms of one year or less of prison. They also handle arraignments, probable cause hearings, bail hearings in felony cases before those cases are transferred to the general jurisdiction trial courts, and, sometimes, felony trials that may result in penalties below a specified limit. Their powers may be limited to a specific geographic area (for example, municipal court) or to a specific category of cases (for example, traffic court, juvenile court). It is among the limited-jurisdiction courts that overlapping jurisdictional and geographic boundaries can cause great confusion.

In addition to hearing cases, many judges are in charge of the administration of their own courthouses. However, most lack the time and expertise to effectively supervise such problems as record keeping, case management, and personnel disputes. During the past two decades, there has been a steady trend toward having trained court administrators take charge of management issues within courts. Judges are still likely to be the most influential figures within each courthouse, but the court administrators can improve the efficiency of case processing and record keeping.

States have also centralized some aspects of court administration by appointing a state court administrator to oversee the distribution of judicial resources and keep state court systems current with the newest management techniques and computer technologies. Although state supreme courts appoint these state court administrators, local judges, court clerks, and administrators are often able to resist new procedures that they oppose.

State funding is a crucial element in any plan to create unified state court systems. It is difficult to provide new management techniques and computer technologies to courts throughout a state if those courts have varying abilities to pay for innovations. When courts are funded by each city or county, judicial administration depends on budgets made by local officials. Equitable funding is difficult to achieve unless all of the courts are funded from a common source, namely, the state budget. Although all states provide some funding for their courts, the levels of support range from 13 percent to 100 percent of local courts' budgets. Fewer than half of the states provide a substantial portion of the funding for their courts. Usually, courts must use a combination of state and local funding. Many of the courts that process large numbers of criminal cases must operate without the necessary resources.[1]

Reformers have also sought to create a centralized civil service personnel system for judicial employees. Personnel reforms have met opposition in those states with a tradition of political patronage in courthouse positions. Political parties compete with each other to win judgeships and court clerk positions in order to provide jobs to their loyalists. Even relatively low-level judicial positions may control significant numbers of jobs. For example, the elected clerk of court for the limited-jurisdiction municipal court in Akron, Ohio, controls fifty-three patronage positions through the appointment of deputy court clerks and other personnel. Even when a civil service plan overcomes political resistance and is enacted into law, difficulties remain in identifying exactly who should be part of the system. Probation officers, bailiffs, social workers, and other court personnel are sometimes supervised through the offices of a prosecutor, a sheriff, or a children's services department, so decisions have to be made about which personnel will be regarded as "court employees."

The decentralized nature of American court systems and the historical connections between courts and local politics have raised a number of issues that have led to reform efforts. Even if the reformers fulfill all of their objectives of administrative centralization, however, there is no guarantee that such reforms will improve the quality of justice produced by the courts. The creation of court systems that fit neat organizational charts may improve the funding for and resources of courts, but it will not change the nature of the criminal justice process and the manner in which decisions are made.

bench trial
Trial conducted by a judge who acts as both fact finder and determiner of issues of law; no jury participates.

Among the actors in the criminal justice system, judges possess the greatest formal power. Judges make rulings on bail, the issuance of search and arrest warrants, the admissibility of evidence, the selection of jurors, and the sentences to be imposed. In **bench trials**, in which judges act as both fact finder and determiner of issues of law, they even decide the guilt or innocence of defendants; no jury participates.

Judges are expected to *embody* the ideals of justice in their work by ensuring that court procedures are fair and by adopting a neutral stance when making decisions. By contrast, other actors in the system are not expected to be neutral but to further certain interests. The prosecutor seeks to obtain convictions, and the defense attorney seeks to avoid or limit the consequences of a criminal conviction for the defendant. In actuality, however, as human beings, judges bring their attitudes and values to the court. Because many of them were previously prosecutors or defense attorneys, their views about cases are influenced by their experiences and their beliefs about the nature of crime and justice. Moreover, judges' professional interests may influence their behavior and decisions. Judges' cooperation with and approval of plea bargaining can reflect their interest in minimizing the number of time-consuming trials and keeping the flow of cases moving steadily through the court.

In order to understand judges' role in the criminal justice process and the factors that influence their decisions, we must explore certain basic questions. What do trial court judges do? How are judges selected? What kinds of people become judges? As with other important participants in the criminal justice system, judges' impact on criminal cases stems from both the formal powers granted to them by the law and their cooperative interactions with other actors in the system.

A QUESTION OF ETHICS

Judge Harold Abrams of the Euclid District Court was angry. He had been sitting on the bench all Monday morning, arraigning, setting bail, and taking pleas from a steady stream of people who had been arrested over the weekend. Most of the people appearing before him were charged with such offenses as possession of a controlled substance, solicitation for the purpose of prostitution, drunk and disorderly conduct—samples of the range of behaviors that had attracted police attention on Saturday night. He had seen many of the accused before, and so he bantered with them as their cases proceeded.

"So it's you again, Lucille. When are you girls going to learn that you can't walk up and down First Avenue? In that eight-inch skirt, you're a menace to traffic. We can't have every Tom, Dick, and Harry—and I mean mostly Dick—screwing his eyes on you and not on the road. Get what I mean?"

"But this time I was just going to the store to buy a loaf of bread."

"Sure. You mean you were walking to make some bread! In fact you don't do much walking, do you Lucille: you're mainly on your back! How do you plead?"

"Guilty, but I didn't do no soliciting."

"Fifty dollars and costs. Now, I suppose you'll be back on the Avenue to earn the fine. See you again Lucille."

Throughout this exchange the courtroom regulars grinned. You could really see quite a show in Judge Abrams's courtroom.

Is this the way justice should be allocated? Are Judge Abrams's banter and manner appropriate? What are the defendants learning about the administration of justice? Should the judge be removed from the bench?

FUNCTIONS OF THE JUDGE

Contrary to popular conceptions, judges spend only part of each day presiding over their courtrooms. They have many formal courtroom responsibilities during hearings and trials, but they also have less formal, behind-the-scenes contacts with prosecutors and defense attorneys in discussing plea agreements and possible sentences. In addition, judges must spend time "off the bench" preparing rulings on pretrial motions, crafting jury instructions, and dealing with other issues that cannot be decided "on the spot" during the course of an adversarial hearing. In preparing rulings, judges may need to research the

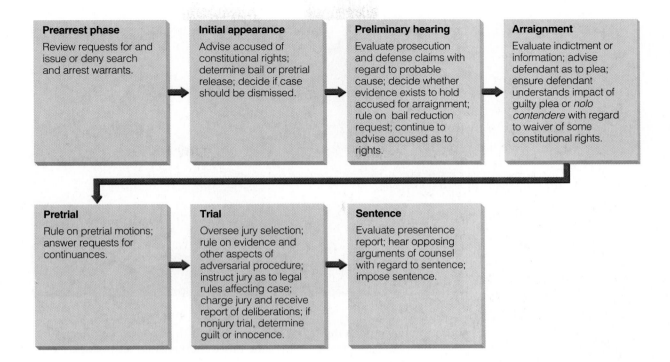

Prearrest phase	Initial appearance	Preliminary hearing	Arraignment
Review requests for and issue or deny search and arrest warrants.	Advise accused of constitutional rights; determine bail or pretrial release; decide if case should be dismissed.	Evaluate prosecution and defense claims with regard to probable cause; decide whether evidence exists to hold accused for arraignment; rule on bail reduction request; continue to advise accused as to rights.	Evaluate indictment or information; advise defendant as to plea; ensure defendant understands impact of guilty plea or *nolo contendere* with regard to waiver of some constitutional rights.

Pretrial	Trial	Sentence
Rule on pretrial motions; answer requests for continuances.	Oversee jury selection; rule on evidence and other aspects of adversarial procedure; instruct jury as to legal rules affecting case; charge jury and receive report of deliberations; if nonjury trial, determine guilt or innocence.	Evaluate presentence report; hear opposing arguments of counsel with regard to sentence; impose sentence.

law and draft written judicial orders. As Figure 9.2 shows, judges have a variety of responsibilities associated with several stages of the criminal justice process. In undertaking these responsibilities, judges perform three basic roles: adjudicators, negotiators, and administrators.

1. *Adjudicator.* Judges are assigned the role of neutral decision makers who must issue rulings after considering the competing arguments and evidence presented by the prosecution and defense. Judges must apply the law in a manner that upholds the due process rights of defendants while also accomplishing the societal goal of identifying criminals and imposing punishments. Judges apply discretion in their decisions as adjudicators. Decisions about bail, motions, evidence, and sentencing are guided by statutory and case law, but judges normally must use their values and judgments in reaching a precise conclusion about any of these issues. For example, state legislatures guide judges' bail decisions by setting forth the factual conditions that must exist for preventive detention (for example, dangerousness, risk of flight). It is the judge, however, who must determine whether these conditions exist and if they justify denying pretrial release. In making important decisions, judges hope to be as neutral as possible both to make fair decisions and to uphold the image of judges as the protectors of law and justice.

2. *Negotiator.* Most of the important decisions in the criminal justice process are made through interactions and negotiations. Such activities are obviously characteristic of plea bargaining, but they can also influence bail, jury selection, and other decisions. Judges must spend time in their chambers attempting to facilitate communication and compromise between prosecutors and defense attorneys. In misdemeanor cases, judges may informally mediate from the bench to seek a voluntary resolution of a dispute that has led one person to file charges against another. Some minor disputes over property damage, for example, may be filtered out of the criminal justice process if the

FIGURE 9.2
Typical Actions of a Trial Court Judge in Processing a Felony Case
Throughout the entire process, judges ensure that legal standards are upheld; they maintain courtroom decorum, protect rights of the accused, uphold trial rules, and ensure proper maintenance of court records.

A judge is expected to "embody justice." This neutral role means primarily seeing that due process is observed and the defendant is treated fairly.

judge can encourage the disputants to work out their own solution through the payment of compensation or some other alternative to legal sanctions. In some states, legal rules limit the participation of judges in plea bargaining and other forms of negotiation, but in many others, such informal practices can significantly affect the outcomes of cases.

3. *Administrator.* Judges often have significant administrative responsibilities, especially if their courts do not have court administrators. Thus, on top of their courtroom and negotiation duties, judges must worry about the hiring and firing of courthouse staff, the physical condition of the courthouse, the effectiveness of the court's record-keeping procedures, and various financial matters. In this role, the judge has to maintain good relationships with various elected officials, such as county commissioners and state legislators, in order to seek adequate resources for the court.

THE SELECTION OF JUDGES

Many lawyers consider judgeships to be desirable, prestigious positions. Judges generally have respect and status within their communities, as well as the power to make important decisions. The attributes of status and power make the position very attractive, but some lawyers would never be interested in being judges because the salaries, which vary by state and range from approximately $60,000 to $100,000 per year, are far less than what many lawyers earn in private practice. Because criminal court judges, especially in lower-level courts, often have the lowest status among all judges and work in the most difficult conditions, some lawyers would view being a criminal court judge as merely a temporary stepping-stone to more attractive civil or appellate court judgeships.

The particular individuals who will don the black robes and perform the functions of judge are selected by different methods in different states. As shown in Table 9.1, there are five principal methods of selecting judges: (1) appointment, (2) merit selection (Missouri plan), (3) nonpartisan election, (4) partisan election, and (5) hybrid. Except for the few states that use a hybrid of various

TABLE 9.1

Methods Used by States for Selection of Trial Judges
States use different methods to select their judges. Many judges, however, are initially appointed to fill a vacancy, which gives them an advantage if they subsequently must run for election.

SOURCE: *The Book of the States, 1992–1993 Edition* (Lexington, KY: Council of State Governments, 1992), pp. 233–235.

Partisan Election	Nonpartisan Election	Appointment	Missouri Plan	Hybrid
Alabama	Georgia	Delaware	Alaska	Arizona
Arkansas	Idaho	Maine	Colorado	California
Illinois	Kentucky	Maryland	Connecticut	Florida
Mississippi	Louisiana	Massachusetts	Hawaii	Indiana
North Carolina	Michigan	New Hampshire	Iowa	Kansas
Pennsylvania	Minnesota	New Jersey	Nebraska	Missouri
Texas	Montana	South Carolina	New Mexico	New York
West Virginia	Nevada	Virginia	Utah	Oklahoma
	North Dakota		Vermont	Rhode Island
	Ohio		Wyoming	South Dakota
	Oregon			Tennessee
	Washington			
	Wisconsin			

methods for selecting their judges depending on the jurisdiction, states are basically divided between those that appoint judges and those that elect judges.[2]

Selection by the electorate, as occurs in more than half the states, has long been part of our nation's tradition that judges must "feel the pulse of the people" in order to render justice. If judges' decisions go against public opinion, they may be voted out of office. However, many voters pay little attention to judicial elections, and candidates are barred by rules of judicial ethics from debating legal issues. When voters attempt to choose a judge on the basis of qualifications, there is very little that differentiates candidates since nearly all can claim to have legal experience and respectable educational backgrounds. One result is that elections are often won or lost on the basis of name recognition.

Judicial elections tend to give political parties significant influence over the selection of judges. In **partisan elections**, political parties mount open political campaigns to secure judgeships for lawyers who have been loyal party activists. These are nominees who have not only served their parties but also are viewed by party leaders as electable because they can raise campaign funds and are known in the community. However, political parties may be just as active and influential in **nonpartisan elections**. In many states, the parties actively recruit candidates and informally organize campaigns even though the "nonpartisan" ballot does not indicate the party affiliations of the competing candidates.

The selection of judges in election systems is complicated by the fact that significant percentages of judges in such systems initially gain office through a midterm appointment when a judge dies or retires from office. The interim appointment permits the judge to gain name recognition, run as the "incumbent" in the next election, and place the title "Judge" before his or her name in campaign literature. Thus, even in nonpartisan election states, political connections are important for the many judges who first gained office through an interim appointment by the governor or legislature.

By contrast, merit selection systems are usually modeled on the "Missouri plan," which was implemented in that state in 1940 and is designed to eliminate politics from the process. Under merit selection, the governor appoints a committee, primarily composed of lawyers, to evaluate possible

partisan election
An election in which candidates endorsed by political parties are presented to the voters for selection.

nonpartisan election
An election in which candidates who are not endorsed by political parties are presented to the voters for selection.

Judges are elected in about half the states. Does that compromise the principle that the judiciary should be removed from politics? Or does it rightfully make judges more responsive to their community?

appointees and submit a list of three final nominees to the governor. The governor selects the judge from among the recommended finalists. After one year and periodically thereafter, the judge stands before the voters in a retention election in which there is no opponent and the voters simply decide whether to retain the judge. Judges are rarely ousted from office in retention elections, so merit selection creates the equivalent of a lifetime job for most judges in these states.

What are the results of judicial selection? Most judges throughout the country are middle-aged, white, and male. Women and members of minority groups are significantly underrepresented. Female and minority judges may have a better chance of gaining office through election systems because political parties want to produce judicial candidates who will appeal to specific voting constituencies, especially in large cities.

The lack of diversity within the judiciary raises questions about whether judges who are drawn from the elite sectors of society can understand the social conditions and personal characteristics of the largely poor young people who face these judges, especially in urban courts. For example, Martin Levin's now classic study comparing judges in Minneapolis and Pittsburgh found that the Minneapolis judges, who generally came from business-oriented law firms, imposed much more severe sentences than the Pittsburgh judges. Unlike the elite Minneapolis judges, the Pittsburgh judges worked their way up through neighborhood political organizations to gain judgeships in partisan elections.[3] Their closer contacts and identification with lower-status residents from city neighborhoods may have contributed to their increased use of individualized sentences of probation and brief incarceration. Such studies raise interesting questions about how case outcomes in the criminal justice system might be different if judicial selection processes produced judges with different characteristics, values, and experiences.

CASE PROCESSING IN THE CRIMINAL COURT

The traditional image of the criminal courtroom highlights the adversarial posturing of the prosecution and defense under the neutral and watchful eyes of the judge. However, as noted in Chapter 8, most criminal cases are decided as a result of plea bargaining that is shaped by the local legal culture and the going rate for sentences. When imagining this plea-bargaining scene played out throughout the country, we need to remind ourselves that the key players in the courtroom are organized in workgroups.

THE COURTROOM WORKGROUP

workgroup
A collective of individuals who interact in the workplace on a continuing basis, share goals, develop norms as to how activities should be carried out, and eventually establish a network of roles that serves to differentiate the group from others.

grouping
A collective of individuals who interact in the workplace but, because of shifting membership, do not develop into a workgroup.

The concept of a courtroom workgroup helps us to analyze the relationships of the judge, prosecutor, and defense attorney, as well as those of the supporting cast (clerk, reporter, and bailiff), as they seek to complete the group's basic task: the disposition of cases. A **workgroup** is a collective of individuals who interact in the workplace on a continuing basis, share goals, develop norms as to how activities should be carried out, and eventually establish a network of roles that serves to differentiate the group from others. The workgroup concept seems especially important in the analysis of urban courts—where there are many separate courtrooms in the same system, where the number of judicial actors is large, and where the caseload is heavy. Figure 9.3 outlines criminal court decision making using the concept of the workgroup.

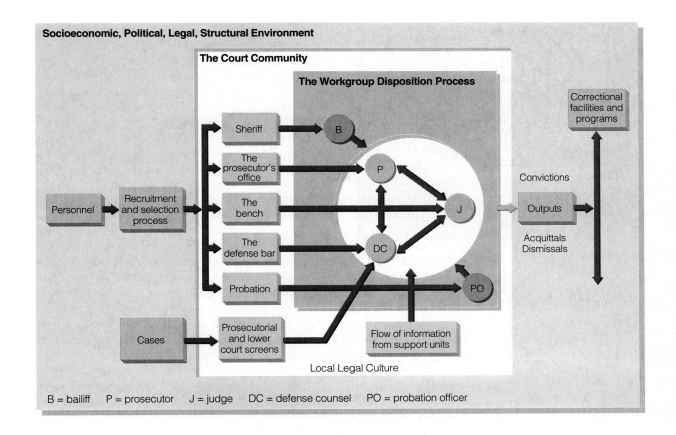

Socioeconomic, Political, Legal, Structural Environment

The Court Community

The Workgroup Disposition Process

Personnel → Recruitment and selection process → Sheriff, The prosecutor's office, The bench, The defense bar, Probation

Cases → Prosecutorial and lower court screens

Flow of information from support units

Correctional facilities and programs

Convictions

Outputs

Acquittals
Dismissals

Local Legal Culture

B = bailiff   P = prosecutor   J = judge   DC = defense counsel   PO = probation officer

Merely placing the major actors in the courtroom does not instantly make them into a workgroup. A **grouping** is a collective of individuals who interact in the workplace but, because of shifting membership, do not develop into a workgroup. Thrust together in a temporary grouping for a single case, the judge, prosecutor, and defense attorney may have trouble interacting and arriving at a plea agreement. If, however, this same group of participants interacts together regularly in seeking to dispose of cases, they will undoubtedly begin to work more quickly and easily. Repeated interactions let the individuals get to know one another and form prior understandings about the appropriate punishment for particular cases. Over time, the grouping becomes a workgroup in which the members share the norms and expectations that make case processing more efficient.

In some courthouses, the same judges, assistant prosecutors, and public defenders work out dozens of plea agreements together day after day. As they learn one another's preferences and values, they may become quite efficient in recognizing immediately how every other member of the workgroup will evaluate each defendant's case. No single member of the workgroup can dictate the plea agreement. The prosecutor's desire for a quick conviction requires that he or she give the defense attorney some kind of compromise or benefit that can be used to persuade the defendant to plead guilty. The defense attorney's goal of obtaining a favorable agreement quickly depends on cooperation from the prosecutor. Both the prosecutor and the defense attorney need to anticipate the judge's views on appropriate sentences. And the judge needs to avoid taking strict, absolutist positions with respect to acceptable sentencing recommendations in order to avoid the prospect of a larger number of cases going to trial.

FIGURE 9.3

Model of Criminal Court Decision Making
This model ties together the elements of the courtroom workgroup, sponsoring organizations, and the local legal culture. Note the influences on decision making. Are there other factors that should be considered?

SOURCE: Adapted from Peter Nardulli, James Eisenstein, and Roy Flemming, *Tenor of Justice: Criminal Courts and the Guilty Plea Process* (Urbana: University of Illinois Press, 1988). Copyright © 1988 by the Board of Trustees of the University of Illinois. Used with permission of the University of Illinois Press.

Behind the formally adversarial system, courtroom workgroup participants must constantly interact, negotiate, and cooperate.

Other officials may influence the smooth operation of the workgroup. For example, depending on the organization of the courthouse, a chief judge, prosecuting attorney, or chief public defender may limit the range of discretionary decision making undertaken by subordinates in the workgroup. Probation officers may work closely with the workgroup as they prepare presentence reports on which sentencing decisions may be based.

As the members of the workgroup interact, they must also ensure that their decisions and agreements do not harm their important relationships with actors outside the workgroup. The prosecutor, for example, needs to maintain good relations with the police in order to ensure cooperation during criminal investigations. This may limit the prosecutor's ability to "go easy" on a particular defendant, even if the prosecutor believes that the young first-offender deserves a break. Judges must be careful about how their sentencing decisions will be received and reported by news media, especially in states in which they will eventually face political opposition in a re-election campaign. Defense attorneys know that defendants and their families expect to see a vigorous defense, so they may take care to give the appearance that they are not too friendly with the prosecutor, even if they engage in highly cooperative plea bargaining. Indeed, the members of the workgroup may even cooperate with one another in "staging" an adversarial hearing to give the audience of police, defendants and their families, and the news media the impression that members of the workgroup are *not* cooperating with one another but are playing their stereotypical roles in an adversarial process.

Judges can be leaders in the courtroom context both for workgroups and for groupings that may never develop into workgroups. Judges who are passive or detached may find themselves confronted with messy personal conflicts between prosecutors and defense attorneys that hamper the efficiency of criminal case processing. Judges who actively take the lead in setting the tone for cooperative plea negotiations, establishing expectations for professional behavior, and facilitating the development of a consensus can anticipate problems and thereby increase the effectiveness of the courtroom actors in resolving cases.

THE IMPACT OF COURTROOM WORKGROUPS

James Eisenstein and Herbert Jacob studied the influence of courtroom workgroups on felony cases in Baltimore, Chicago, and Detroit.[4] In Chicago and Detroit, stable workgroups increased the efficiency of case processing. The shared understandings of these groups permitted prosecutors to screen cases effectively in order to dismiss those that should not be brought forward and to reach prompt plea agreements in other cases. By contrast, unstable workgroups in Baltimore produced fewer guilty pleas and caused more cases to be forwarded to the grand jury and ultimately to the trial courts.

Workgroups are more or less effective depending on other procedures employed in each jurisdiction and changes that occur within particular courthouses. For example, in Chicago and Detroit, most defendants had a preliminary hearing before they went to the trial court, while in Baltimore this stage was usually omitted. This reduced the opportunity in Baltimore for interactions, negotiated agreements, screening decisions, and other activities that might have completed cases earlier in the justice process.

Organizational changes implemented by prosecutors' and public defenders' offices or the court itself can upset the efficiency of the workgroup. They can also require participants to adapt to new conditions. If a prosecutor decides to screen cases less rigorously or a chief public defender decides to rotate assistants between courtrooms, the judges, prosecutors, and defense attorneys must adjust their interactions to cope with new kinds of cases or to reach agreements with new, unfamiliar participants.

The development of effective courtroom workgroups depends on many factors, including the organizational policies of the court, the prosecutor's office, and the public defender's office. Whether or not workgroups exist, negotiation and compromise between the courtroom participants determine the outcomes in all but a small percentage of cases.

TRIAL: THE EXCEPTIONAL CASE

Only 9 percent of felony cases go to trial. Of these, 5 percent are jury trials and 4 percent bench trials.[5] Trials take a lot of time and resources. Attorneys frequently spend weeks or months preparing—gathering evidence, responding to their opponents' motions, planning trial strategy, and setting aside anywhere from one day to several weeks for presenting the case in court. From the perspective of judges, prosecutors, and defense attorneys, plea bargaining is obviously an attractive alternative for purposes of efficiency. Some cases, however, simply cannot be resolved through plea bargaining. Think back to the discussion of the "wedding cake" model in Chapter 2. Prominent or wealthy defendants can afford to pay their attorneys to fight a case to the very end and therefore can demand trials even if they do not face especially serious charges. In addition, defendants who face harsh penalties such as death or life in prison may feel little incentive to plead guilty. At least with a trial, there is a chance that the jury will find that the prosecutor did not present enough evidence to prove guilt "beyond a reasonable doubt." The Close-Up recounts the trial of Robert Chambers, which had all of the elements expected of a courtroom drama.

As we have mentioned, there are two types of trials, bench and jury. Sometimes, defendants may choose to have a bench trial if the charges are so shocking or complicated that they fear juries may be biased against them or incapable of understanding the evidence. The alternative is trial by **jury**—a panel of citizens selected according to law and sworn to weigh testimony in a criminal case and to render a verdict of guilty or not guilty. By serving on juries, citizens are able to participate in judicial decision making and speak for the community.

jury
A panel of citizens selected according to law and sworn to weigh testimony in a criminal case and to render a verdict of guilty or not guilty.

THE JURY

The criminal jury is a traditional legal institution in the United States as well as other common law countries such as England, Canada, and Australia. In civil law countries, responsibility for making decisions about guilt and innocence is placed in the hands of judges, who may be assisted by several lay assessors. Jury trials are used more frequently in the United States than in any other common law country; 80 percent of all jury trials worldwide take place

From the time Robert Chambers was indicted by a New York City grand jury on murder charges in the death of Jennifer Levin until he plea-bargained as the jury deliberated his fate, the national media provided almost continuous coverage of the activities surrounding the case. All the elements for a gripping drama were there in what became known as "The Preppie Murder Case." It had Robert Chambers and Jennifer Levin, two privileged young people; their preppie friends and the milieu of Manhattan's nightclubs, money, drugs, alcohol, and sex; and the defendant's claim that he had accidentally killed the victim during an incident of "rough sex" when he tried to stop Jennifer from squeezing his genitals. With the *New York Post* and the *Daily News* headlines screaming "Jenny Killed in Wild Sex" and "Sex Got Rough," the public was ready for the story to be played out in the courtroom.

At Chambers's trial, Assistant District Attorney Linda Fairstein, chief of Manhattan's Sex Crimes Unit, entered into evidence blowups of the photographs of Jennifer Levin's face and body as she lay dead in Central Park. Chambers's attorney, Jack Litman, objected to the use of the photos with their depiction of the gory details of the victim's death. When the judge allowed use of the photos, Litman shifted his tactics to emphasize Levin's promiscuity.

When the prosecution entered a videotape of Chambers's confession, Litman and others felt that the defendant came across to the jurors as a frightened, candid teenager.

After a trial that lasted nearly three months, the jury retired to determine the fate of Robert Chambers. On the ninth day of their deliberations—longer than any other case for a single defendant in New York's history—the tensions among the jurors became apparent not only to the media but also to the judge. With the possibility of a mistrial looming, the attorneys met with the judge in his chambers and began to work out the details of a plea bargain.

Later in the day, Robert Chambers faced the judge and changed his plea to guilty to a reduced charge of first-degree manslaughter. The charge carried a sentence of five to fifteen years versus the possibility of life imprisonment for the charge of murder. As required by law to ensure that Chambers understood the plea, the judge questioned him. In response, Chambers initially said that he did not mean to hurt Jennifer. Assistant District Attorney Fairstein demanded that the question be phrased more directly. The judge asked, "Mr. Chambers, is it true that on August 26, 1986, you intended to cause serious physical injury to Jennifer Levin and thereby caused the death of Jennifer Levin?" Chambers answered, "Yes, Your Honor," yet he shook his head and his body language said no.

SOURCE: Adapted from Linda Wolfe, *Wasted: The Preppie Murder* (New York: Simon & Schuster, 1989).

in the United States.[6] In the United States, the jury is an ingrained feature of the American ideology and is mentioned in the Declaration of Independence, the Constitution, and numerous Supreme Court opinions.

Juries perform six vital functions in the criminal justice system:

1. Prevent government oppression by safeguarding citizens against arbitrary law enforcement.
2. Determine the guilt or innocence of the accused on the basis of the evidence presented.
3. Represent diverse community interests so that no one set of values or biases dominates decision making.
4. Serve as a buffer between the accused and the accuser.
5. Educate citizens selected for jury duty about the criminal justice system.
6. Symbolize the rule of law and the community foundation that supports the criminal justice system.

The adversarial legal process is based on the assumption that the best and fairest means of determining the truth is through the clash of competing advocates. The jurors are spectators in the unfolding courtroom drama and are expected to determine whether the defendant is guilty by sifting through the competing evidence and arguments presented by the prosecution and defense. They are the fact finders who must decide what happened. The prosecution presents evidence and the defense attempts to refute that evidence, but the final determination about what happened rests with the jury. The jury is free to reject evidence presented in court by disbelieving statements by witnesses, favoring the views of one side's experts in evaluating physical evidence, and even imposing its own perceptions and sympathies into the decision about the defendant's blameworthiness. There is little to stop a juror from voting to acquit or convict based on a "hunch" or some other basis unrelated to the formal evidence.

The primary impediment to arbitrary decisions by a jury is the fact that it is a *body of citizens* rather than a single individual making the decision. Even if one juror leans toward a decision based on bias or emotion, the other jurors can persuade or counterbalance this juror so that the outcome to the case is not determined by a single individual's irrational reaction. Thus, the selection, size, and composition of juries are important factors in the jury trial process.

Many people are surprised to learn that not all juries are comprised of twelve members. Twelve is the traditional size for juries, and such juries are employed for felony trials in most states. However, a few states permit smaller juries to render verdicts in criminal cases. For felony cases, seven states use juries of eight or six members, while for misdemeanor cases, nineteen states use juries with fewer than twelve members. In the case of **Williams v. Florida (1970)**, the Supreme Court approved the use of smaller juries in cases other than capital cases.[7] The use of small juries has raised questions about how the size of juries affects the quality of their deliberations. In small juries, fewer viewpoints are represented and one dominant juror is more likely to influence the other jurors. In addition, there are fewer individuals' memories at work in the jury room when jurors must recall, piece together, and interpret the evidence that was presented in court.

Williams v. Florida **(1970)**
Juries of fewer than
twelve members in
noncapital cases are
constitutional.

A related issue concerns whether the jury's decision must be unanimous. In most states, twelve-member juries must render unanimous verdicts in order to convict defendants. In a few states, however, juries are permitted to make nonunanimous decisions. This means that defendants who would not be convicted in most states could be convicted in the nonunanimous states even if one or two jurors were not convinced about the defendant's guilt. The Supreme Court has endorsed the use of nonunanimous verdicts for twelve-member juries, provided there are significant majorities in favor of conviction. A simple majority, such as a 7 to 5 vote, would not be adequate. However, the Supreme Court also requires that small juries achieve unanimity in order to convict a defendant.

JURY SELECTION

The selection of the jury as outlined in Figure 9.4 is a crucial first step in the trial process. Because people inevitably apply their experiences, values, and biases in their decision making, prosecutors and defense attorneys actively seek to identify potential jurors who may be automatically sympathetic or hostile to their side. When they believe they have identified such potential jurors, they try to find ways to exclude the jurors who may sympathize with the other side while striving to keep the jurors who may favor their side. Lawyers do not

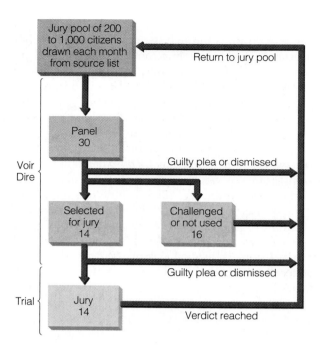

FIGURE 9.4

Jury Selection Process, Twelve-Member Jury Potential jurors are drawn at random from a source list. From this pool, a panel is selected and presented for duty. The *voir dire* examination may remove some jurors, while others will be seated.

necessarily succeed in this objective, because the selection of jurors involves the decisions and interactions of prosecutors, defense attorneys, and judges, each of whom has different objectives in the selection process.

Jurors are selected from among the citizens whose names have been placed in the jury pool. Thus, the composition of the jury pool has a critical impact on the ultimate composition of the trial jury. In most states, the jury pool is drawn from lists of registered voters, but research has shown that non-whites, the poor, and young people register to vote at much lower rates than the rest of the population. As a result, members of these groups are under-represented on juries. In many cases, the presence or absence of these groups may make no difference in the ultimate verdict. In some contexts, however, members of these groups may interpret evidence differently than their older, white, middle-class counterparts who dominate the composition of juries. For example, the poor, nonwhites, and young people may be more likely to have had unpleasant experiences with police officers and therefore be more skeptical when listening to testimony from police officers. While a middle-class juror may infer criminal intent from the fact that a defendant was carry-ing a pocketknife, a poor juror may disagree and simply view the carrying of pocketknives as normal, expected behavior among people in a rough neighbor-hood.[8] Such differences in viewpoints can influence the outcomes of cases.

Some jurisdictions have addressed the problem of unrepresentative jury pools by seeking to broaden the sources from which jurors' names are drawn. They have supplemented the lists of registered voters with other lists, such as those for driver's licenses, hunting licenses, and utility bills, so as to broaden the pool.

People in specific occupations, such as doctors, lawyers, and police offi-cers, are usually not called for jury duty. Other potential jurors may be ex-cused from duty if service would cause an economic or physical hardship. As a result, only about 15 percent of adult Americans have ever been called for jury duty. Because of the exclusions from service, retired people and home-makers with grown children tend to be overrepresented on juries because

they are less inconvenienced by serving. To make jury duty less onerous, many states have moved to a system of one-day-one-trial, as described in the Ideas in Practice on the next page.

In the courtroom, the process of ***voir dire*** (literally "to speak the truth") is used to question prospective jurors in order to screen out those who might be biased or incapable of rendering a fair verdict. Attorneys for each side, as well as the judge, may question jurors about their background, knowledge of the case, and acquaintance with any participants in the case. Jurors will also be asked whether they or their immediate family members have been crime victims or otherwise involved in a criminal case in a manner that may prevent them from making objective decisions about the evidence and the defendant. If it appears from a juror's responses that he or she will not be able to make fair decisions, the juror may be **challenged for cause**. The judge must rule on the challenge, but if the judge agrees with the attorney, then the juror is excused from that specific case. There is usually no limit to the number of jurors that the attorneys may challenge for cause.

Although challenges for cause are ultimately under the judge's control, the prosecution and defense can exert their own control over the jury's composition through the use of **peremptory challenges**. Using these challenges, the prosecution and the defense can exclude prospective jurors without the necessity of providing specific reasons. Attorneys use peremptory challenges to exclude those jurors that they think will be unsympathetic to their arguments. Normally, the defense is allowed eight to ten peremptory challenges, and the prosecution six to eight.

Use of peremptory challenges has raised concerns that attorneys can use them to exclude, for example, African-American jurors when an African-American is on trial. In a series of decisions in the late 1980s and early 1990s, the Supreme Court barred the systematic use of peremptory challenges to exclude potential jurors because of their race or gender. This does not mean that prosecutors cannot use a peremptory challenge to exclude a nonwhite or

voir dire
The process of questioning prospective jurors by the prosecution and defense to screen out persons who might be biased or incapable of rendering a fair verdict.

challenge for cause
Removal of a prospective juror due to bias or some other factor contributing to an inability to make fair decisions.

peremptory challenge
Removal of a prospective juror by the prosecution or defense without providing specific reasons.

female juror. It merely means that they cannot use challenges to *systematically* exclude such jurors. Attorneys must be prepared to give the judge a nondiscriminatory reason for such exclusions.

The jury selection process sets the stage for the trial by putting into place the decision makers who will decide the defendant's fate. Although *voir dire* takes place before the trial formally begins, it would be more accurate to view jury selection as the first step in the trial since both sides use the process to introduce themselves and their cases to the jurors. Lawyers know that, with jury selection, they have begun the process of strategic persuasion and performance that will determine the outcome in the case.

THE TRIAL PROCESS

After jury selection, the trial proceeds through several specific steps in which the attorneys challenge each other's arguments and evidence.

Opening Statements

When the trial formally begins, the clerk reads the complaint (indictment or information) containing the charges against the defendant. The prosecutor and defense attorney then each make an opening argument to the jury. In the opening statements, each side usually tries to provide a preview of what it expects to demonstrate during the trial in order to plant its arguments in the jurors' minds. The judge needs to keep tight control over opening statements by reminding the jurors that the attorneys' statements do not constitute evidence and therefore cannot be considered as proof of the defendant's guilt or innocence.

Presentation of the Prosecution's Evidence

Because the defendant is presumed to be innocent until proven guilty, the prosecution bears the burden of proving the defendant's guilt. The prosecution must make its presentation of evidence while observing legal rules about the kinds of evidence that can be introduced. For example, evidence that has been obtained through an illegal search and seizure may be excluded even though it is relevant to the case. The prosecution's objective is to convince the jurors that the defendant's guilt has been proven "beyond a reasonable doubt," the highest standard of proof under the law. By contrast, in a civil case, one side can prevail merely by convincing the jury that "a preponderance of evidence" weighs in its favor.

Several types of evidence may be presented to the jury. **Real evidence** includes physical objects such as a weapon, records, fingerprints, blood samples, or stolen property. Most evidence in a criminal trial, however, consists of the **testimony**—or oral evidence—of legally competent witnesses. Here, the judge may be required to determine whether the witness has the intelligence to tell the truth and the ability to recall what was seen. **Direct evidence** refers to eyewitness accounts from someone who saw the defendant

real evidence
Physical evidence such as a weapon, records, fingerprints, blood samples, and stolen property.

testimony
Oral evidence provided by a legally competent witness.

direct evidence
Eyewitness accounts.

commit the criminal act. By contrast, **circumstantial evidence** requires that the jury infer a fact. For example, testimony that someone saw the defendant with a gun moments before a shot was heard on the other side of the building is circumstantial evidence. The prosecution wants the jury to infer that the defendant fired the shot from his having been seen in the vicinity with a gun.

Presentation of the Defense's Evidence

After the prosecution has presented its evidence, it is the defense attorney's turn. Several strategies are available to the defense. It may attempt to cast doubt on the prosecution's evidence and presentation by presenting its own witnesses and experts. It may also offer an alibi by presenting testimony or other evidence to show that the defendant could not have committed the crime. Or it may present one of the affirmative defenses that we discussed in Chapter 3, such as self-defense or insanity.

In addition to choosing one of these three strategies, the defense must also decide whether to have the defendant provide sworn testimony from the witness stand. The Fifth Amendment's prohibition against compelled self-incrimination protects the defendant from having the prosecution seek to require him or her to testify. The jury is not permitted to infer the defendant's guilt from the fact that the defendant did not testify. If the defendant does choose to testify, however, he or she will be subject to cross-examination, or questioning by the opposing attorney. Just as the defense attorney can cross-examine the prosecution's witnesses, the prosecution can cross-examine the defendant if he or she testifies. Good lawyers may be able to use careful, strategic questioning in cross-examination to poke holes in the testimony of witnesses, including the defendant. Moreover, cross-examination sometimes creates opportunities for the prosecution to elicit information about the defendant's prior criminal record that otherwise might not be admitted into evidence. Thus, many defense attorneys choose not to have their clients testify because the risks are simply too great.

Presentation of Rebuttal Witnesses

On completion of the defense's case, the prosecution may present witnesses whose testimony is designed to discredit that of preceding witnesses. New evidence may be presented, but the defense has the opportunity to cross-examine the witnesses and to present its own rebuttal witnesses thereafter.

Closing Arguments by Each Side

The attorneys for each side use the closing arguments as an opportunity to appeal directly to the jury. This is the moment in the trial when lawyers attempt to use emotional or spellbinding summations to draw the jurors into their camp. The prosecution generally attempts to use the closing argument to retrace the case and tie the evidence together with the elements of the crime that it had set out to prove in the first place. The defense generally reviews and emphasizes what it claims are the weaknesses in the prosecution's case.

Judge's Instructions to the Jury

The jury decides the facts of the case, but the judge determines the law. Thus, the judge's decisions about appropriate jury instructions provide crucial guidelines that will shape the jury's deliberations and verdict. The prosecution and defense submit suggested jury instructions to the judge. The process of formulating instructions and persuading the judge about which instructions to

circumstantial evidence
Evidence provided by a witness from which a jury must infer a fact.

present to the jury can be a key to the trial's ultimate outcome. The presentation of instructions to the jury may take several hours, and jurors often become bored and detached while listening to the judge give lengthy, detailed instructions. As a result, many jurors may not clearly understand and follow the judge's precise instructions on how they should evaluate the evidence.

Decision by the Jury

Throughout the trial process, the jurors have passively received information. Although a few courts have begun to experiment with permitting jurors to submit written questions to the judge that the judge may direct to a witness, most courts forbid jurors from speaking or participating in the trial process in any way. Many courts even forbid the jurors from taking notes during the trial. They are expected to rely on their collective memories when re-creating the evidence during discussions in the jury room. The conclusion of the closing arguments suddenly thrusts responsibility for the case into the hands of a group of strangers who, until this point in the trial, have been forbidden from discussing any aspect of the case.

The jury must focus on whether the prosecution has proven the case beyond a reasonable doubt. Being "beyond a reasonable doubt" does not mean having no doubts at all. What it means is that if a juror is satisfied "to a moral certainty that this defendant . . . is guilty of any one of the crimes charged here, you may safely say that you have been convinced beyond a **reasonable doubt**. If your mind is wavering, or if you are uncertain . . . you have not been convinced beyond a reasonable doubt and you must render a verdict of not guilty."[9] In order to determine their verdict, the jurors retire to a room where their discussions and deliberations can be kept secret. The jurors elect a foreman to guide their deliberations and announce the eventual verdict, but the foreman may not necessarily lead the deliberations.

The dynamics of jury deliberations are such that there may be a mix of personalities and varying degrees of assertiveness among the members. Because jury deliberations are secret, scholars study juries by interviewing jury members after a trial or by holding mock trials in front of simulated juries. Research indicates that in the small-group deliberation context of juries, men are frequently more active than women, whites are more active than minority group members, and jurors' participation in the deliberation process is related to education level and social status. Although juries can often quickly agree on verdicts, in cases of disagreement, individual jurors may sway their colleagues through their persuasiveness, social status, or knowledge. Because jury decision making is fundamentally a very human process that can produce unpredictable results, many lawyers may urge their clients to accept the certainty of plea bargaining rather than risk the results of a jury trial.

Let us now return to the Los Angeles trial of two men charged in the beating of truck driver Reginald Denny that opened this chapter. Why did the jury acquit Watson and Williams of most charges, including attempted murder, when virtually everyone in the nation who had seen the videotape expected them to be convicted on serious felony charges?

Many people believe that the prosecutors made a mistake by overcharging the defendants. Conviction on a charge of attempted murder required that the prosecution prove intent to kill, which was difficult to do in the context of the spontaneous violence of the riot. The prosecution also neglected to charge Williams with the lesser included offense of assault with a deadly weapon. Williams's attorney, Edi Faal, seized on this error and succeeded in getting the judge to give a jury instruction that did not permit the jury to convict on lesser included offenses that were not part of the formal charges.

reasonable doubt
The standard used by jurors to decide if the prosecution has proved to a moral certainty that the defendant is guilty as charged; if jurors are uncertain, they should vote for acquittal.

Thus, when the jury rejected the attempted murder charge, they did not have the option of convicting for assault with a deadly weapon. The prosecution's strategic errors may have helped the defense.

In addition, the jury deliberated with the knowledge that some segments of the Los Angeles community believed that Watson and Williams were being cast as scapegoats for the riots, which caused millions of dollars in damage and took fifty-three lives. Comments by jurors after the trial indicated that they believed that there was a risk of renewed rioting if they convicted the two men on the serious felony charges.[10] Did the jurors' fears about possible community reactions affect their deliberations? We cannot know for certain, but it is possible.

In any event, a very human decision-making process produced an unexpected result. That is the inherently unpredictable nature of criminal trials. Although the prosecution gains its objective of securing the desired conviction in most trials, there is always the possibility that the jury will acquit or convict on lesser charges.

Just as the plea-bargaining process creates risks that innocent people may, in some circumstances, feel pressured to plead guilty, the trial process contains the risk that an innocent person may be convicted. Witnesses may make mistakes in their testimony, jurors may believe witnesses who are actually lying, and, in some unfortunate circumstances, law enforcement officers may manufacture phony evidence in an effort to solve a crime. Although some scholars have estimated that only about 1 percent of felony convictions are erroneous,[11] when these errors are made in death penalty cases they loom very large indeed. The adversarial trial process is regarded as the best method for seeking the truth about criminal cases, but it can never be perfect because its operations depend on perceptions, judgments, and reactions from a variety of human decision makers in the criminal justice system.

Sentencing

If the jury finds the defendant guilty, then the judge must determine the appropriate sentence. Many judges say that sentencing is their most difficult responsibility. Prior to sentencing, a probation officer usually prepares a **presentence report** to help the judge select the appropriate punishment that will reflect the seriousness of the crime and the background and characteristics of the defendant. In some states, probation officers conclude their reports by making a formal recommendation about the appropriate sentence.

In Chapter 10, we will examine more closely judges' sentencing decisions and the punishment options available in the criminal justice system. For now, suffice it to say, sentencing is an especially important stage in the trial process. Its outcome frequently reflects the values and discretionary judgments of both the probation officers who prepare presentence reports and the judges who must determine the sentences.

presentence report
A report prepared by a probation officer after an investigation into the background and characteristics of a convicted offender, which is designed to help the judge determine an appropriate sentence.

APPEALS

After being convicted and sentenced, defendants have a right to **appeal** the verdict to a higher court and request that it review actions taken in the trial. An appeal is based on a contention that one or more errors of law were made during the criminal proceedings that led to the conviction. The defendant may claim, for example, that improperly obtained evidence should not have been admitted at the trial or that the judge gave improper instructions to the jury.

appeal
A request to a higher court that it review actions taken in a completed trial.

THE APPEALS PROCESS

The appellate court does not reconsider the evidence in the case; rather, it considers only written and oral arguments narrowly focused on the question of law that was the basis for the asserted error in the lower court. If a defendant wins on appeal, he or she does not necessarily go free. Normally, the appellate court will simply order a new trial, which must be conducted without the contested evidence or with the judge making different jury instructions.

Judges hate to have their decisions overturned by a higher court. Correcting errors through the appeals process serves to encourage them to be careful in making trial decisions. Appellate courts also encourage uniform application of the law within a jurisdiction. If judges in different parts of a state are interpreting a provision of the criminal code differently, the appellate court can issue a decision to clarify the issue and ensure consistent application of the law.

There has been an increase in the number of appeals in both the state and federal courts during the past decade. A five-state study by Joy Chapper and Roger Hanson showed that (1) although a majority of appeals relate to trial convictions, about a quarter relate to nontrial proceedings such as guilty pleas and probation revocations; (2) homicides and other serious crimes make up over 50 percent of appeals; (3) most appeals come from cases in which the sentence is five years or less; and (4) the issues raised on appeal tend to concern the introduction of evidence, the sufficiency of evidence, and the jury instructions.[12]

Most appeals are unsuccessful. Chapper and Hanson found that in almost 80 percent of the cases they examined, the decision of the trial court was affirmed. Most of the other cases produced new trials or resentencing; relatively few decisions (1.9 percent) actually produced acquittals on appeal.[13] The appellate process rarely provides a ticket to freedom for someone convicted of a crime.

HABEAS CORPUS

habeas corpus
A writ or judicial order requesting that a person holding another person produce the prisoner and give reasons to justify continued confinement.

After people exhaust their avenues of appeal, they may pursue a writ of habeas corpus if they claim that their federal constitutional rights were violated during the lower-court processes. Known as "the great writ" from its traditional role in English law and its enshrinement in the U.S. Constitution, **habeas corpus** is a judicial order requesting that a person holding another person prisoner produce the prisoner and give reasons to justify continued confinement. This procedure permits the judge to decide whether the person is being legally held. Technically, this legal action is not limited to convicted offenders but can also be used by people confined to mental hospitals or any other restrictive governmental setting. Statutes permit offenders convicted in both state and federal courts to pursue habeas corpus actions in the federal courts. After first seeking favorable decisions by state appellate courts, convicted offenders can start their constitutional claims anew in the federal trial-level district courts and subsequently pursue their habeas cases in the federal circuit courts of appeal and the U.S. Supreme Court.

Only about 3 percent of habeas corpus petitions are successful. One reason may be that an individual has no right to be represented by counsel when pursuing a habeas corpus petition. Few offenders have sufficient knowledge of law and legal procedures to identify and present constitutional claims effectively in the federal courts.

SUMMARY

Courts provide the institutional setting in which interactions occur and decisions are made that determine the outcomes of criminal cases. Although various states structure, fund, and manage their courts differently, courts throughout the country depend on interactions among judges, prosecutors, and defense attorneys in developing plea agreements that resolve most criminal cases. The courtroom workgroup can be especially influential in allowing cases to be processed quickly and efficiently.

Judges are key participants in case processing, including the trial stage. Judges bring their own values and experiences to their decisions affecting dismissals, plea bargaining, and sentencing. These values may reflect the political context of judicial selection that brought the judges to the bench. Judges in various states may gain judgeships through different judicial selection systems. Elected judges may feel greater pressures to remain in contact with and more accountable to the local community.

In the trial stage, the jury plays a particularly important role in deciding the outcome of the case. The jury's ultimate verdict will reflect a complex mixture of factors during the trial sequence, including the strategic actions of the competing attorneys during jury selection, the presentation of evidence, and closing arguments. After a conviction, defendants have the opportunity to pursue direct appeals and habeas corpus petitions, but relatively few such efforts lead to the release of convicted individuals. Thus, the reality facing most people convicted of crimes is the inevitability of punishment. In the remaining chapters, we will look more closely at sentencing and punishment.

QUESTIONS FOR REVIEW

1. Why have reformers sought to centralize the administration of courts through unified court systems?
2. Can any judicial selection method expect to remove politics from the process of selecting judges? Is it necessarily harmful to have political aspects in the judicial selection process?
3. What roles do judges play? Do any of these roles conflict?
4. What kinds of cases are likely to result in trials?
5. What factors ultimately influence jury verdicts?
6. Why do we have appeals courts? How do they benefit society?

NOTES

1. Marcia Lim, "A Status Report on State Court Financing," *State Court Journal* 11 (Summer 1987), p. 7.
2. Christopher E. Smith, *Courts, Politics, and the Judicial Process* (Chicago: Nelson-Hall, 1993), p. 99.
3. Martin Levin, "Urban Politics and Policy Outcomes: The Criminal Courts," *Criminal Justice: Law and Politics*, 5th ed., ed. G. F. Cole (Pacific Grove, CA: Brooks/Cole, 1988), pp. 330–336.
4. Herbert Jacob and James Eisenstein, *Felony Justice: An Organizational Analysis of Criminal Courts* (Boston: Little, Brown, 1977).
5. U.S. Bureau of Justice Statistics, *Sourcebook of Criminal Justice Statistics— 1991* (Washington, DC: Government Printing Office, 1992), p. 545.

6. Valerie P. Hans and Neil Vidmar, *Judging the Jury* (New York: Plenum, 1986), p. 109; Stephen J. Adler, *The Jury* (New York: Times Books, 1994).

7. *Williams* v. *Florida*, 399 U.S. 78 (1970).

8. Claudia C. Cowan, William C. Thompson, and Phoebe C. Ellsworth, "The Effects of Death Qualification on Juror's Predisposition to Convict and on the Quality of Deliberation," *Law and Human Behavior* 8 (1984), p. 60.

9. Steven Phillips, *No Heroes, No Villains* (New York: Random House, 1977), p. 214.

10. Richard Lacayo, "A Slap for a Broken Head," *Time*, 1 November 1993, pp. 46–47.

11. C. Ronald Huff and Arye Rattner, "Convicted but Innocent: False Positives and the Criminal Justice Process," in *Controversial Issues in Crime and Justice*, ed. Joseph E. Scott and Travis Hirschi (Newbury Park, CA: Sage, 1988), p. 130.

12. Joy A. Chapper and Roger A. Hanson, *Understanding Reversible Error in Criminal Appeals* (Williamsburg, VA: National Center for State Courts, 1989), p. 4.

13. Ibid.

CHAPTER 10
Sentencing

SENT TO PRISON FOR FEEDING HIS PIGS

Ernest Krikava, a seventy-year-old farmer in Pawnee City, Nebraska, was in serious financial trouble. After working for fifty years to build up his farm, Krikava fell behind in making payments on a bank loan. He did not have enough money to buy feed for his pigs, and they were beginning to die of starvation. Because his livestock and farm served as collateral for his loan, he could not sell anything in order to get the money he needed to feed his pigs. From the bank's perspective, if Krikava sold anything, there would be fewer assets available for them to seize in order to satisfy the loan if the farmer defaulted. In violation of his agreement, Krikava sold $30,000 worth of livestock under the name of his sister-in-law. He used the money to buy feed for his pigs. When he later filed for bankruptcy, he denied that he had ever sold any of his property, an untruth. By lying under oath in a federal court proceeding, he violated the criminal law against perjury.

When it was revealed that the farmer had lied, Thomas Monaghan, the U.S. attorney in Omaha, filed criminal charges against Krikava, his son, Kevin, and his wife, Carol, who all participated in deceiving the court. Kevin and Carol agreed to plea bargains by admitting their guilt to the perjury charges and were sentenced to probation. Ernest Krikava, however, insisted that he had done nothing wrong since he had to keep his hogs from starving. According to Krikava, "It would have been a crime to let [the pigs] starve."[1]

The farmer insisted on his right to have a full trial, which resulted in his conviction of perjury. Under the federal sentencing guidelines enacted by Congress, Judge Warren Urbom was obligated to sentence Krikava to at least five months in prison. Only people who admitted their guilt and entered guilty pleas were eligible for probation under the guidelines.

The farmer's world had crumbled. His farm was auctioned off to pay his debts, and his wife died because they could not afford treatment for a respiratory ailment. Then, on July 3, 1994, Krikava's son drove him to the federal prison at Leavenworth, Kansas, to begin serving his sentence. Krikava had never before been away from his farm for more than two nights, and now he was facing five months behind bars for, in his view, merely trying to keep his pigs from starving.

The unique feature of criminal law is that the government imposes punishments on people who break a special set of societal rules. As you consider Krikava's case, ask yourself: Are we teaching him a lesson so he will never repeat such behavior again? Are we making an example of him so others will know that they should tell the truth in court? Are we hoping to make him a better person by imprisoning him? In this chapter, we will examine the various forms and goals of punishment. Forms of punishments imposed for different criminal acts should depend on the particular goal or mix of goals that society has in mind. ★

THE GOALS OF PUNISHMENT

There are four primary goals of criminal punishment: retribution, deterrence, incapacitation, and rehabilitation. Throughout the history of Western civilization, the design of criminal punishments has been shaped by the dominant philosophical and moral orientations of the time. Ultimately, all criminal punishment is aimed at maintaining social order. However, each goal represents a different approach to advancing society's interests.

Punishments reflect the dominant values at a particular moment in history. By the end of the 1960s, for example, decreasing numbers of Americans were sentenced to imprisonment because of a widespread belief in and commitment to rehabilitating offenders through counseling, education, and other forms of assistance. By contrast, record numbers of offenders were sentenced to prison in the early 1990s because of an emphasis on imposing strong punishments for the purposes of retribution and deterrence.

RETRIBUTION, OR DESERVED PUNISHMENT

Retribution refers to punishment inflicted on a person who has infringed on the rights of others and so deserves to be penalized. The biblical expression "An eye for an eye, a tooth for a tooth" illustrates the underlying philosophy. Retribution means that those who commit a particular crime should be punished alike, in proportion to the gravity of the offense or to the extent to which others have been made to suffer.

Some scholars claim that if the state does not provide retributive sanctions to reflect community revulsion at offensive acts, citizens will take the law into their own hands. Under this view, the failure of the government to satisfy the people's desire for retribution could produce social chaos.

This argument may not be valid for all crimes, however. If the criminal justice system inadequately punishes a rapist, then the victim's friends, family, and other members of the community may be tempted to exact their own retribution. But what about the pig farmer, Ernest Krikava? If the government failed to impose retribution on the pig farmer convicted of perjury, would the community really care? The same apathy may hold true with respect to offenders who commit other nonviolent crimes that have a modest impact on society. In these seemingly trivial situations, however, retribution may be useful and necessary to remind the public of the general rules of law and the important values being protected.

In recent years, there has been a resurgence of interest in retribution as a primary goal of the criminal sanction. This has occurred in large part due to dissatisfaction with the philosophical basis and practical results of rehabilitation, deterrence, and incapacitation. Using the concept of "just deserts," or deserved punishment, some theorists argue that one who infringes on the rights of others deserves to be punished.[2] This approach is based on the philosophical view that punishment is a moral response to harms inflicted on society. In effect, these theorists believe that basic morality demands that wrongdoers be punished. Andrew von Hirsch, a leading contemporary writer on punishment, has said that "the sanctioning authority is entitled to choose a response that expresses moral disapproval: namely, punishment."[3] According

CHAPTER QUESTIONS

What is the purpose of the criminal sanction, and how is it carried out?

What forms does the criminal sanction take?

What are the various types of sentences that judges may impose?

How effective are criminal punishments?

retribution
Punishment inflicted on a person who has infringed on the rights of others and so deserves to be penalized; the severity of the sanction should fit the gravity of the offense.

to von Hirsch and others, punishment should be applied only for the wrong inflicted and not primarily to achieve other goals such as deterrence, incapacitation, or rehabilitation. Underlying this emphasis on "just deserts" or earned punishment are the ideals of fairness and justice.

This theory could provide a basis for the criminal punishment imposed on the pig farmer, although one might argue that the actual sentence was too severe. By lying at a judicial proceeding and thereby violating the criminal law of perjury, Krikava had, in effect, earned society's punishment.

DETERRENCE

Many people think of criminal punishment as providing a basis for affecting the future choices and behavior of individuals. Politicians frequently talk about being tough on crime in order to send a message to would-be criminals. This deterrence approach has its roots in eighteenth-century England among the followers of social philosopher Jeremy Bentham.

Bentham was struck by what seemed to be the pointlessness of retribution. His fellow reformers adopted Bentham's theory of utilitarianism, which holds that human behavior is governed by the individual calculation of the benefits versus the costs of one's acts. Bentham argued that punishment should make it clear that the costs of committing a crime outweigh its benefits. Before stealing money or property, for example, potential offenders would consider the punishment that others had received for similar acts and would thereby be deterred.

general deterrence
Punishment of criminals intended to serve as an example to the general public and thus to discourage the commission of offenses.

special deterrence
Punishment inflicted on criminals with the intent to discourage them from committing crimes in the future.

What is the reason for sentencing a person to punishment? How well will the punishment serve retribution, deterrence, incapacitation, rehabilitation, or some other clear purpose?

There are two approaches to deterrence. **General deterrence** presumes that members of the general public will be deterred by observing the punishments of others and concluding that the costs of crime outweigh the benefits. For general deterrence to be effective, the public must be reminded constantly about the likelihood and severity of punishment for various acts. They must believe that they will be caught, prosecuted, and given a specific punishment if they commit a particular crime. Moreover, the punishment must be severe enough that they will be impressed by the consequences of committing crimes. For example, public hanging was once considered to be an effective general deterrent.

By contrast, **special deterrence**, also called *specific* or *individual deterrence*, targets the decisions and behavior of offenders who have already been

apprehended. Under this approach, the amount and kind of punishment are calculated to discourage the criminal from repeating the offense. The punishment must be sufficiently severe to cause the criminal to say, "The consequences of my crime were too painful. I will not commit that crime again because I do not want to risk being punished again."

There are some obvious difficulties with the concept of deterrence. Deterrence presumes that all people act rationally and think before they act. Deterrence does not account for the many people who commit crimes while under the influence of drugs or alcohol, or those whose harmful behavior stems from psychological problems or mental illness. Deterrence also does not account for people who act impulsively in stealing or damaging property. In other cases, the low probability of being caught defeats general or special deterrence. In order to be generally deterrent, punishment must be perceived as relatively fast, certain, and severe. That is, of course, not always the case.

Social science is unable to measure the effects of general deterrence; only those who are *not* deterred come to the attention of researchers. A study of the deterrent effects of punishment would have to examine the impact of different forms of the criminal sanction on various potential lawbreakers. How can we ever know how many people—or even if any people—stopped themselves from committing a crime because they were deterred by the prospect of prosecution and punishment? Therefore, while legislators often cite deterrence as a rationale for certain sanctions, we do not really know the extent to which sentencing policies based on deterrence achieve their objectives. Because contemporary American society has shown little ability to reduce crime through the imposition of increasingly severe sanctions, there is strong reason to question the effectiveness of deterrence for many crimes and criminals.

INCAPACITATION

The assumption of **incapacitation** is that society can remove a criminal's capacity to commit further crimes by detention in prison. Many people express such sentiments when arguing that we should "lock 'em up and throw away the key." In primitive societies, banishment from the community was the usual measure taken to prevent a recurrence of forbidden behavior. In the contemporary United States, imprisonment is the typical method of incapacitation. Offenders can be confined within secure institutions and effectively prevented from committing any additional harm against society during the duration of their sentences. Capital punishment is the ultimate method of incapacitation.

Any sentence that physically restricts an offender can have an incapacitative effect, even when the underlying purpose of the sentence is retribution, deterrence, or rehabilitation. Sentences based on incapacitation are future-oriented. Whereas retribution requires focusing on the past harmful act of the offender, incapacitation looks at the offender's potential future actions. If a particular offender is not likely to commit future crimes, then the sentence might be light. If an offender is likely to commit future crimes, then a severe sentence may be imposed—even for a relatively minor crime.

For example, under the incapacitation theory, a woman who kills her abusive husband as an emotional reaction to his verbal insults and physical assaults could receive a light sentence. As a one-time impulse killer who felt driven to kill by unique circumstances, she is not likely to commit additional crimes. By contrast, someone who shoplifts merchandise from a store and has been convicted of the offense on ten previous occasions may receive a severe sentence. The criminal record and type of crime indicate that he or she will commit additional crimes if released. Thus, incapacitation focuses on offenders rather than offenses.

Does it offend our sense of justice that a person could receive a more severe sentence for shoplifting than for manslaughter? That is one basis for criticizing incapacitation. In addition, there are questions about how to determine the length of sentences. Presumably, offenders will not be released until the state is reasonably sure that they will no longer commit crimes. However, can we accurately predict any person's behavior? Moreover, if we can accurately predict that a shoplifter will commit future crimes, does it fulfill our sense of justice to lock such an offender in prison forever?[4] On what

incapacitation
Deprivation of a criminal's capacity to commit further crimes by detention in prison.

grounds can we punish people for anticipated future behavior that we cannot accurately predict?

In recent years, greater attention has been paid to the concept of **selective incapacitation**, whereby offenders who repeatedly commit certain kinds of crimes are sentenced to long prison terms. Research has suggested that a relatively small number of offenders are responsible for a large number of violent and property crimes. Burglars, for example, tend to commit many offenses before they are caught. Thus, it is argued that career criminals should be locked up for long periods.[5] Such policies could be costly, however. Not only would correctional facilities have to be expanded, but the number of expensive, time-consuming trials might increase if more severe sentences caused fewer repeat offenders to plead guilty. In addition, we are unable to accurately predict which offenders will, in fact, commit more crimes upon release.

selective incapacitation
The strategy whereby offenders who repeatedly commit certain kinds of crimes are sentenced to long prison terms.

REHABILITATION

rehabilitation
The goal of restoring a convicted offender to a constructive place in society through some form of vocational, educational, or therapeutic treatment.

Rehabilitation refers to the goal of restoring a convicted offender to a constructive place in society through some form of vocational, educational, or therapeutic treatment. Rehabilitation is undoubtedly the most appealing modern justification for use of the criminal sanction. Americans want to believe that offenders can be treated and resocialized. During the twentieth century, many people have argued that techniques are available to identify and treat the causes of criminal behavior. If the offender's behavior is assumed to result from some social, psychological, or biological imperfection, the treatment of the disorder becomes the primary goal of corrections. The goal of rehabilitation is oriented solely toward the offender and does not imply any consistent relationship between the severity of the punishment and the gravity of the crime. People who commit lesser offenses can receive long prison sentences if experts believe that a long period of time will be required to rehabilitate them. By contrast, a murderer might win early release by showing signs that the psychological or emotional problems that led to the killing have been corrected.

According to the concept of rehabilitation, offenders are being treated rather than punished, and will return to society when they are "cured." Consequently, judges should set not fixed sentences but rather ones with maximum and minimum terms so that parole boards may release inmates when they have been rehabilitated. Such sentences are known as "indeterminate sentences" because no fixed release date is set by the judge. The indeterminate sentence is justified by the belief that if prisoners know when they are going to be released, they will not make an effort to engage in the treatment programs prescribed for their cure. If, however, they know that they will be held until they are cured, they will cooperate with counselors, psychologists, and other professionals seeking to treat their problems.

From the 1940s until the 1970s, the goal of rehabilitation was so widely shared that treatment and reform of offenders were generally regarded as the only issues worthy of serious attention. The assumption was that crime was caused by problems affecting individuals and that modern social sciences had given us the tools to address those problems. During the past twenty years, however, the assumptions of the rehabilitation model have been questioned. Studies of the results of rehabilitation programs have challenged the idea that we really know how to cure criminal offenders. Moreover, it is no longer taken for granted that crime is caused by identifiable, curable problems such as poverty, lack of job skills, low self-esteem, and hostility toward authority.

TABLE 10.1

The Goals of Punishment
At sentencing, the judge usually gives reasons for the punishment imposed. Here are possible statements that Judge Warren Urbom might have given to Ernest Krikava depending on the goal of the sanction that he wanted to promote.

Goal	Judge's Statement
Retribution	I am imposing this sentence because you deserve to be punished for committing perjury in this court. Your criminal behavior in this case is the basis of the punishment. Justice requires that I impose a sanction at a level that illustrates the importance that the community places on truthfulness in legal matters.
Deterrence	I am imposing this sentence so that your punishment for committing perjury in this court will serve as an example and deter others who may contemplate similar actions. In addition, I hope that this sentence will deter you from repeating such an illegal act.
Incapacitation	I am imposing this sentence so that you will be incapacitated and hence unable to commit perjury during the length of this term. Since you have not committed prior offenses, selective incapacitation is not warranted.
Rehabilitation	The trial testimony and information contained in the presentence report make me believe that there are aspects of your personality that led you to commit perjury. I am therefore imposing this sentence so that you can receive treatment that will rectify your behavior so that you will not commit another criminal act. With proper treatment, you should be able to return to society and lead a crime-free life.

Instead, some scholars argue that we cannot expect to identify the causes of criminal behavior for individual offenders. Clearly, many legislatures, prosecutors, and judges have abandoned the rehabilitation goal in favor of retribution, deterrence, or incapacitation. The various goals of punishment are summarized in Table 10.1.

Although the four goals of criminal sanctions are often discussed as if they were distinct, they overlap to a great extent. A sentence of life imprisonment can be philosophically justified in terms of its primary goal of incapacitation, but the secondary functions of retribution and deterrence are also present. Deterrence is such a broad concept that it mixes well with all the other purposes, with the possible exception of rehabilitation. As we explore the various forms of punishment, keep in mind the underlying goal or mix of punishment goals that justifies each form of sanction.

APPLICATION OF THE CRIMINAL SANCTION

Incarceration, intermediate sanctions, probation, and death are the basic forms of criminal sanction in the United States. Most people think of incarceration as the usual punishment. As a consequence, much of the public equates using alternatives to incarceration, such as probation, with allowing offenders to "get off." However, community-based punishments such as probation and intermediate sanctions are imposed almost three times as often as prison sentences. The death penalty, although rarely imposed, is, of course, the harshest punishment.

INCARCERATION

Imprisonment is the most visible penalty imposed by U.S. courts. Fewer than 30 percent of persons under correctional supervision are in prisons and jails, but incarceration remains the standard punishment for serious crimes. It is

Short of death, incarceration is the greatest restriction on freedom. Less than a third of persons under sentence are in prison, but the number of people in prison has more than doubled since 1980.

also used widely against people convicted of misdemeanors, who serve short terms in county jails. Imprisonment is believed to have a significant effect in deterring potential offenders. However, incarceration is extremely expensive for the state to carry out, and it raises problems of reintegrating offenders into society after release from prison.

In the criminal code, legislatures stipulate the type of sentences and the amount of prison time that may be imposed for each crime. Three basic sentencing schemes are used—(1) indeterminate sentences, (2) determinate sentences, and (3) mandatory sentences—each of which provides judges with varying degrees of discretion.

Indeterminate Sentences

When the goal of rehabilitation dominated corrections, legislatures enacted **indeterminate** (or *indefinite*) **sentences**. In keeping with the goal of treatment, indeterminate sentences give corrections officials and parole boards significant control over the amount of time a prisoner serves. Penal codes with indeterminate sentences stipulate a spread between a minimum date for a decision on parole eligibility and a maximum date for completion of the sentence (for example, 1–5 years, 3–10 years, 10–20 years, 5 years to life, and so on). At the time of sentencing, the offender is informed by the judge of the range of the sentence. The offender also learns that he or she will probably be eligible for parole at some point after the minimum term (minus "good time") has been served. The actual release date is decided by the parole board.

Determinate Sentences

Growing doubts about the effectiveness of rehabilitation led to the imposition of **determinate sentences** based on the assumption of deserved punishment. With a determinate sentence, a convicted offender is imprisoned for a specified period of time (for example, two years, five years, ten years). At the end of this term, again minus credited "good time," the prisoner is automatically freed without any decision by a parole board. The offender's release does not depend on participation in counseling, education, or other rehabilitative programs that would be used under indeterminate sentencing.

Some states have adopted determinate-sentence codes that stipulate a specific term for each crime category. In some states, the legislature or a sentencing commission specifies a presumptive determinate sentence, allowing judges to deviate only in special circumstances. In any of these schemes, the offender theoretically knows at sentencing the amount of time to be served. With determinate sentencing, the discretion of the judiciary is limited and sentencing disparities are reduced.

Mandatory Sentences

Politicians and the public have continued to complain that offenders are released before serving long enough terms, and legislatures have responded. Currently, all but two states have **mandatory sentences**, requiring that some minimum period of incarceration be served by persons convicted of selected crimes. No consideration may be given by the judge to the circumstances of the offense or the background of the offender, and nonincarcerative sentences may not be imposed.

indeterminate sentence
A period set by a judge in which there is a spread between the minimum date for a decision on parole eligibility and a maximum date for completion of the sentence.

determinate sentence
A sentence that fixes the term of imprisonment at a specified period of time.

mandatory sentence
Requirement that some minimum period of incarceration be served by persons convicted of selected crimes, regardless of the circumstances of the offense or the background of the offender.

CLOSE-UP
A Three-Strike Penal Law Shows It's Not As Simple As It Seems

In the fight against violent crime, perhaps no idea is more popular than "three strikes and you're out"—locking up repeat offenders for life without parole. . . . But only one state, Washington, has any experience with it. Two months after a law went on the books requiring criminals to spend life in prison without parole if they are convicted of three felonies, the first cases of "three strikes" are emerging. And they present a more complicated picture than does the baseball slogan that inspired 76 percent of Washington State voters to back the measure.

Prosecutors and police officers say the law has had some unintended side effects. With nothing to lose, some criminals are showing a tendency to be more violent or desperate when officers try to arrest them. And prosecutors say first- and second-time felony offenders are less willing to plea bargain, when it means pleading guilty, to a first or second "strike." These offenders are instead forcing full trials in a court system that has neither the manpower nor the space to take on the extra load.

Among the first candidates for life in prison under the three-strikes law, several seem to fit the profile of violent predators with long criminal histories. But other cases may not be what voters here had in mind. One man has led a life of small-time crime. His third-strike offense was robbing a sandwich shop of $151 while pretending a concealed finger was a gun. . . .

The case most troubling to the law's critics is that of Larry Lee Fisher, 35, who has been in and out of jail since he was a teenager. His first strike was in 1986 when he was convicted of robbery in the second degree—pushing his grandfather down and taking $390 from him. Mr. Fisher served four months in jail. Two years later came his second strike, a $100 robbery of a pizza parlor in which he concealed his finger and said it was a gun. He served 17 months on a work farm.

Last month Mr. Fisher was arrested for holding up a sandwich shop in Everett, again without a gun but pretending he had one by pointing a finger inside his coat pocket. The police found him an hour after the holdup drinking beer in a nearby tavern. Normally, he would face about 22 months in jail. But now, if convicted, he will spend the rest of his life in prison. . . .

Dave LaCourse, a leader of the three-strikes initiative, said Mr. Fisher's case was unusual but not unintended. "Here's a guy with 10 misdemeanors on his record, he's 35 years old and he hasn't learned his lesson yet," Mr. LaCourse said. "What's it going to take? He seems to be one of those people who's making crime a career." . . .

Washington prosecutors said states now considering three-strikes laws would do well not to put too many crimes in the mix of what qualifies. Because of cases like Larry Lee Fisher's, Washington's law may have to be refined, they said.

"Don't assume this will have a dramatic effect on crime," said John Ladenburg, Pierce County Prosecutor. "This is not a cure-all. This is not going to fix crime. What it will do is get some of the worst offenders off of the street forever."

SOURCE: Adapted from Timothy Egan, "A 3-Strike Penal Law Shows It's Not as Simple as It Seems," *New York Times*, 15 February 1994, p. 1

However, the intent of such legislation may still be thwarted by the decisions of judges and prosecutors. For example, the Massachusetts gun law decrees that anyone convicted of possessing an unregistered firearm *must* spend one year in jail. This law has had no deterrent or incapacitative effects because prosecutors and judges simply reduce charges when they do not believe justice would be served by punishing a particular individual.[6] When New York had tough, mandatory punishments for drug dealers, the draconian sentences prescribed by the law merely raised the stakes for the defendant so high that the prosecution had to reduce charges in order to obtain guilty pleas. Experience with a "three-strikes" law in the state of Washington is discussed in the Close-Up.

good time

A reduction of a convict's prison sentence awarded for good behavior at the discretion of the prison administrator.

FIGURE 10.1

Average Time Served by State Prison Inmates, by Offense Type

The data indicate that the average felony offender spends about two years in prison. What would be the public's reaction to this fact?

SOURCE: Adapted from U.S. Department of Justice, Bureau of Justice Statistics, *Report to the Nation on Crime and Justice*, 2d ed. (Washington, DC: Government Printing Office, 1988), p. 100.

Although many criminologists believe that mandatory sentences do not achieve their purpose, such sentencing schemes are not doomed to failure if the actors within the criminal justice system agree with and abide by the legislatures' intentions. Research conducted on Florida's mandatory minimum sentences supports the possibility that mandatory sentences can be effective.[7] The Florida law is designed to ensure that offenders in certain categories are not released early through good time and other provisions before a certain portion of their sentence has been served. Eleven categories of offenders—for example, those convicted of capital offenses and of certain drug and firearms offenses, and those designated habitual offenders—come under the mandatory provisions. These laws have been cited as a major cause of longer prison sentences and a growing Florida prison population.

The Sentence versus Actual Time Served

Regardless of judges' discretion, prison sentences imposed may bear little relation to the amount of time actually served. In reality, parole boards in indeterminate-sentence states have broad discretion in release decisions once the offender has served a minimum portion of the sentence. In addition, convicts can have their prison sentences reduced by earning "**good time**" for good behavior, at the discretion of the prison administrator.

Good-time policies are practiced in all but four states. Days are subtracted from prisoners' minimum or maximum term for good behavior or for participation in various types of vocational, educational, and treatment programs. Correctional officials consider these sentence-reduction policies necessary for maintaining institutional order and reducing overcrowding. The possibility of receiving good-time credit provides an incentive for prisoners to follow institutional rules. Good time is also taken into consideration by prosecutors and defense attorneys during plea bargaining. In other words, they think about the actual amount of time a particular offender is likely to serve.

The amount of good time that one can earn varies among the states, from five to ten days a month. In some states, once ninety days of good time are earned, they are vested; that is, the credits cannot be taken away as a punishment for misbehavior. Prisoners who violate rules in such systems may lose only recently earned and future good-time credits.

Judges in the United States often prescribe long periods of incarceration for serious crimes, but good time and parole serve to reduce the amount of time spent in prison. As shown in Figure 10.1, the average felony offender spends about two years in prison.

Because of variation in sentencing and release laws, it is difficult to compare the amount of time served with the length of sentence imposed from state to state. It is possible, however, to make comparisons in regard to different offenses in the same state. The Bureau of Justice Statistics has brought to light an interesting phenomenon: the more serious the offense, the smaller the proportion of the sentence served. An auto thief, for example, may be

Offense	Months
All offenses	26
Violent offenses	38
Murder	90
Manslaughter	36
Rape	54
Other sexual assault	34
Robbery	36
Assault	29
Kidnapping	41
Other violent offenses	19
Property offenses	19
Burglary	21
Arson	25
Auto theft	17
Forgery/fraud	19
Larceny	16
Stolen property	18
Other property	16
Drug offenses	19
Public order offenses	13
Other crimes	18

sentenced to twenty-four months in prison but actually serve twenty months, or 83.3 percent of the sentence. By contrast, a murderer may be sentenced to
thirty years but be released after fifteen years, or 50
percent of the sentence.[8] The more serious offense
draws the stiffer sentence, but the mechanisms for
sentence reduction and release operate to reduce
greater proportions of the longer sentences.

INTERMEDIATE SANCTIONS

In recent years, there has been increased interest in
creating **intermediate sanctions** that are more restrictive than traditional probation but less strin-
gent and costly than incarceration. Thus, they would not increase prison
crowding but would provide greater supervision of offenders serving their
sentences in the community than does probation.[9] Intermediate sanctions
provide a variety of restrictions on freedom such as fines, house arrest,
intensive-supervision probation, restitution, boot camp, forfeiture, and community service.

*Intermediate sanctions can
involve various types of supervision. They may include
some form of community service that may help offenders
recognize responsibilities for
their own acts.*

intermediate sanctions
A variety of punishments
that are more restrictive
than traditional probation
but less stringent and less
costly than incarceration.

In advocating increased use of intermediate sanctions, Norval Morris and
Michael Tonry argue that these sanctions should be combined with other
sanctions rather than applied individually. By mixing two or more intermediate sanctions, sentences can be designed to reflect the severity of the offense,
the characteristics of the offender, and the needs of the community.[10]

For intermediate sanctions to be effective, they must be backed up by
mechanisms that take seriously any breach of the conditions of the sentence.
For example, offenders should know that any violations of rules will lead to
automatic transfer to prison. If they fail a drug test, miss an appointment
with a probation officer, or violate a rule at boot camp, the infraction cannot
be overlooked. Offenders cannot be allowed to believe that they have "beaten"
the system. Likewise, citizens' confidence in the corrections system depends
on the fulfillment of the rules that restrict, supervise, and punish offenders.
Intermediate sanctions will be discussed more fully in Chapter 12.

PROBATION

The most frequently applied criminal sanction is **probation**, whereby an offender serves a sentence in the community under supervision. Nearly 65 percent of adults under correctional supervision are on probation. Designed to
serve multiple purposes, probation allows offenders to remain in the community under supervision while they attempt to straighten out their lives.
Probation is a judicial act, granted by the grace of the state rather than extended as a right, and conditions are imposed specifying how an offender will
behave throughout the length of the sentence. Probationers may be ordered
to undergo regular drug tests, abide by curfews, enroll in educational programs or remain employed, stay away from certain parts of town, and meet
regularly with probation officers. If the conditions are not met, the supervising officer may recommend to the court that the probation be revoked and
the remainder of the sentence be served in prison. Probation may also be revoked for commission of a new crime.

probation
A sentence served in
the community under
supervision.

Although probationers serve their sentences in the community, the sanction is often tied to incarceration. In some jurisdictions, the court is authorized to modify an offender's prison sentence after a portion is served by

changing it to probation. This is often referred to as **shock probation** (or *split probation* in California): An offender is released after a period of incarceration (the "shock") and resentenced to probation.

It is hard to assess how well probation prevents recidivism. Most studies indicate that from one-fifth to one-third of probationers fail to fulfill the conditions of their probation. A Rand Corporation study has cast doubt on other, more optimistic reports of probation effectiveness.[11] A sample of offenders from two urban California counties who had been placed on probation for FBI index crimes was followed up after forty months. The researchers found that 65 percent of the sample had been arrested for another felony or misdemeanor, 51 percent had been convicted of another crime, and 34 percent had been reincarcerated for technical violations of their probation or for new offenses. It should be noted, however, that the California study looked at offenders who had committed serious crimes. Most probationers are first-time offenders who have been convicted of misdemeanors or lesser felonies. For these offenders, probation may be more likely to work.

DEATH

Although other industrialized democracies abolished the death penalty years ago, the United States continues to use it. Capital punishment was imposed and carried out regularly prior to the late 1960s. Amid debates about the constitutionality of capital punishment, and with public opinion polls increasingly showing opposition to it, the U.S. Supreme Court suspended its use from 1968 to 1976. Eventually, after examining a series of cases, the Court decided that capital punishment does not violate the Eighth Amendment's prohibition on cruel and unusual punishment. Executions resumed in 1977 as a majority of states began, once again, to sentence murderers to death.

The number of persons facing the death penalty has increased dramatically in the past decade, as Figure 10.2 reveals. In 1994, 2,976 persons were

FIGURE 10.2
Persons Under Sentence of Death and Persons Executed, 1953–1994
Since 1976, approximately 250 new offenders have been added to death row each year, yet the number of executions has never been greater than 38. What explains this discrepancy?
SOURCE: NAACP Legal Defense and Education Fund, *Death Row, USA* (Dec. 1994).

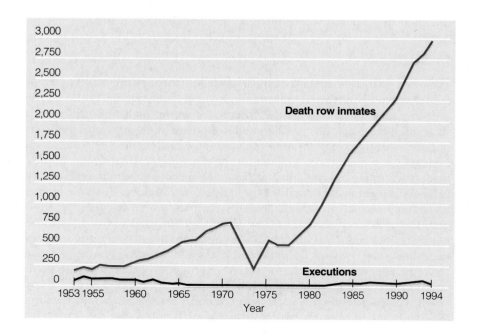

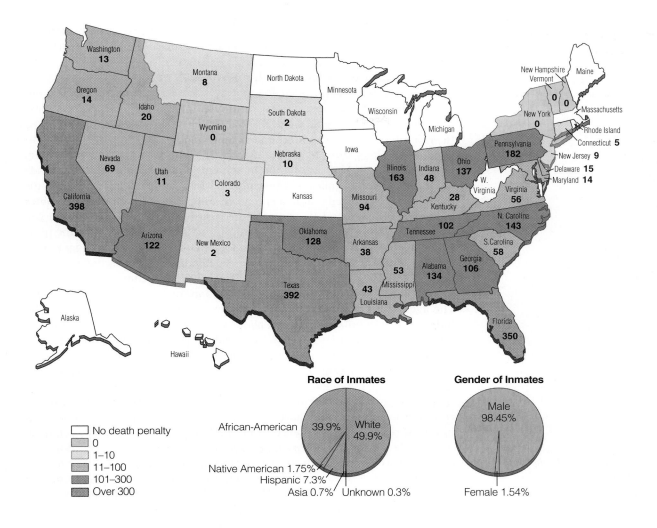

Race of Inmates

White 49.9%
African-American 39.9%
Native American 1.75%
Hispanic 7.3%
Asia 0.7%
Unknown 0.3%

Gender of Inmates

Male 98.45%
Female 1.54%

No death penalty
0
1–10
11–100
101–300
Over 300

awaiting execution in thirty-six of the death penalty states and in the federal jurisdiction. As Figure 10.3 shows, two-thirds of those on death row are in the South, with the greatest number concentrated in Florida, Georgia, and Texas.

The Death Penalty and the Constitution

Death obviously differs from other punishments in that it is final. As a result, the Supreme Court has examined the decision-making process in capital cases to ensure that the Constitution's requirements regarding due process, equal protection, and cruel and unusual punishments are fulfilled. Because life hangs in the balance, capital cases must be conducted according to higher standards of fairness and more careful procedures than other kinds of cases. Several important Supreme Court cases illustrate this fact.

Key Supreme Court Decisions. In ***Furman v. Georgia (1972)***, the Supreme Court ruled that the death penalty, as administered, constituted cruel and unusual punishment. The decision invalidated the death penalty laws in thirty-nine states and the District of Columbia.[12] Although a majority of justices objected to the way in which the death penalty was applied, they could not agree on the reasons that it was unconstitutional. Two justices argued that the death penalty always violates the Eighth Amendment's prohibition

FIGURE 10.3
Death Row Census, Winter 1994
As can be seen, inmates on death row are concentrated mainly in certain states. African-Americans comprise about 13 percent of the U.S. population yet comprise about 40 percent of death row inmates. How might you explain this discrepancy?

SOURCE: NAACP Legal Defense and Education Fund, *Death Row, USA* (Dec. 1994).

Furman v. Georgia (1972)
The death penalty, as administered, constituted cruel and unusual treatment.

on cruel and unusual punishment, but other members of the majority emphasized that the procedures used to impose death sentences were arbitrary and unfair.

Over the next several years, thirty-five states enacted new capital punishment statutes that provided for more careful decision making and more modern methods of execution, such as lethal injection. The new laws were tested before the Supreme Court in June 1976 in the case of *Gregg* v. *Georgia,* in which the Court upheld those laws that required the sentencing judge or jury to consider specific aggravating and mitigating circumstances in deciding which convicted murderers should be sentenced to death.[13] Instead of deciding the defendant's guilt and imposing the death sentence in the same proceeding, states created "bifurcated" proceedings in which a trial determines guilt or innocence and then a separate hearing focuses exclusively on the issue of punishment. Under the *Gregg* decision, the prosecution uses the punishment-phase hearing to focus attention on the existence of "aggravating factors," such as excessive cruelty or a defendant's prior record of violent crimes. The decision makers must also focus on "mitigating factors," such as the offender's youthfulness, mental retardation, or lack of a criminal record. The aggravating and mitigating factors must be weighed together before the judge or jury can make a decision about whether to impose a death sentence. The purpose of the two-stage decision-making process is to ensure thorough deliberation before someone is given the ultimate punishment.

Despite the Supreme Court's endorsement of the constitutionality of capital punishment, opponents of the death penalty continued to challenge it with new cases. Instead of making the broad claim that capital punishment is unconstitutional, these cases challenged aspects of it such as racial discrimination in capital sentencing and the execution of minors and the mentally retarded.

The U.S. Supreme Court may have dealt a fatal blow to the hopes of death penalty opponents in April 1987. In the case of **McCleskey v. Kemp**, the Court rejected a constitutional challenge to Georgia's death penalty on the grounds of racial discrimination.[14] Warren McCleskey, an African-American, was sentenced to death for the killing of a white police officer during a furniture store robbery. In the U.S. Supreme Court, McCleskey's attorneys cited research that showed a disparity in the imposition of the death sentence in Georgia based on the race of the murder victim and, to a lesser extent, the race of the defendant. Researchers had examined over two thousand Georgia murder cases and found that defendants convicted of killing whites had received the death penalty eleven times more often than had those convicted of killing African-Americans. Even after adjusting for 230 factors that might affect the results of capital cases, such as viciousness of the crime or quality of the evidence, the study showed that the death sentence was four times more likely to be imposed when the victim was white. Although 60 percent of Georgia homicide victims are African-American, all seven people put to death in that state since 1976 had been convicted of killing white people, and six of the seven murderers were African-American.

By a 5–4 vote, the justices rejected McCleskey's assertion that Georgia's capital sentencing practices violated the equal protection clause of the Constitution by producing racial discrimination. A slim majority of justices declared that McCleskey would have to prove that the decision makers acted with a discriminatory purpose in deciding his case. The Court also concluded that statistical evidence showing discrimination throughout the Georgia courts did not provide adequate proof. McCleskey was executed in 1991.

McCleskey v. *Kemp* **(1987)**
Rejected a constitutional challenge to Georgia's death penalty on the grounds of racial discrimination.

The *McCleskey* case was the most recent opportunity for opponents of capital punishment to seek its abolition. Other cases continue to challenge specific aspects of capital punishment, such as the execution of minors and the retarded and the length of the appeals process.

Execution of Minors and the Retarded. The laws of thirteen states do not specify a minimum age for offenders receiving capital punishment. Since 1642, when the Plymouth colony in Massachusetts hanged a teenage boy for bestiality, 281 juveniles have been executed in the United States.[15] Death penalty opponents have argued that adolescents do not possess the same capacity as adults to understand the consequences of their actions. In two cases, *Stanford* v. *Kentucky* (1989) and *Wilkins* v. *Missouri* (1989), the justices upheld the death sentences imposed on offenders who were sixteen and seventeen years old at the time of their crime.[16] Because they had previously rejected execution for a boy who committed a murder at age fifteen, their *Stanford* decision effectively set the minimum age for execution at sixteen. There are currently thirty-one males on death rows who were younger than the age of eighteen when they committed their offense.[17]

An estimated 250 offenders on the nation's death rows are classified as retarded. It is argued that retarded people have difficulty defending themselves in court since they have problems remembering details, locating witnesses, and testifying credibly on their own behalf. In 1989, the Supreme Court decided that the Eighth Amendment does not prohibit execution of the mentally retarded. The case involved Johnny Paul Penry, a convicted killer with an IQ of about 70 and the mental capacity of a seven-year-old.[18] The court noted that only Georgia and Maryland prohibited execution of the mentally retarded. Now, years after the Supreme Court decision, Penry is still on death row in Texas, in part because of the lengthy appeals process.

Appeals. A continuing controversy concerns the long appeals process for death penalty cases. Many critics argue that the goals of deterrence and retribution are defeated by the long delays between sentencing and execution. The average length of time from sentencing by a trial court to execution is between seven and eight years, during which time sentences are reviewed by various courts. Chief Justice Rehnquist has actively sought to reduce the opportunities for capital offenders to have their cases reviewed by multiple courts. Although Rehnquist was unsuccessful in persuading Congress to reform the statute governing postconviction reviews, the Supreme Court moved ahead and issued decisions that effectively accomplished his objective. In a series of decisions, the Court made it more difficult for death row inmates to raise constitutional claims. The Court limited each offender to one petition for federal court review, mandated forfeiture of federal claims if state court procedures are not followed precisely during earlier appeals, and limited the applicability of new evidence purporting to show the innocence of the offender.

The philosophical and legal arguments over capital punishment continue. More than 250 new death sentences are now being given out each year, yet the number of executions remains low. Despite a lack of evidence indicating that the death penalty has any impact on crime, many politicians and members of the public claim that increased executions would decrease the crime rate. Because the death penalty is applied to so few offenders each year, it is primarily a symbolic issue, disconnected from the great mass of violent and nonviolent crimes.

THE SENTENCING PROCESS

Now that we have reviewed the goals and forms of the criminal sanction, let us take a closer look at the process for deciding the punishment to be imposed. Regardless of how and where the decision has been made—misdemeanor court or felony court, plea bargain or adversarial contest, bench or jury trial—judges have the responsibility for imposing sentence.

Sentencing is often difficult and is frequently not merely a matter of applying clear-cut principles to individual cases. In one case, a judge may decide to sentence a forger to prison as an example to others despite his being no threat to community safety and probably not in need of correctional treatment. In another case, the judge may impose a light sentence on a youthful offender who, although he has committed a serious crime, may be a good risk for rehabilitation if he can be moved quickly back into society.

Judges have wide powers of discretion with regard to sentencing and may combine various forms of punishment to tailor the sanction to the offender. The judge may stipulate, for example, that the prison terms for two charges are to run either concurrently or consecutively or that all or part of the period of imprisonment is to be suspended. In other situations, the offender may be given a combination of a suspended prison term, probation, and a fine. Judges may also suspend a sentence as long as the offender stays out of trouble, makes restitution, or seeks medical treatment. The judge may also delay imposing any sentence but retain power to set penalties at a later date if the offender misbehaves. Table 10.2 provides data on the types of sanctions imposed.

Legislatures establish the penal codes that set forth the sentences that judges may impose. Within the discretion allowed by each code, various elements in the sentencing process influence the decisions of judges. Let us look at several of the factors that social scientists believe influence the sentencing process: (1) the administrative context of the courts, (2) the attitudes and values of judges, (3) the presentence report, and (4) sentencing guidelines.

A QUESTION OF ETHICS

Seated in her chambers, Judge Ruth Carroll read the presentence investigation report of the two young men she would sentence when court resumed. She had not heard these cases. As often happens in this overworked courthouse, the cases had been given to her only for sentencing. Judge Harold Krisch had handled the arraignment, plea, and trial.

The codefendants had held up a convenience store in the early morning hours, terrorizing the young manager and taking $47.50 from the till.

As she read the reports, Judge Carroll noticed that they looked pretty similar. Each offender had dropped out of high school, had held a series of low-wage jobs, and had one prior conviction for which probation was imposed. Each had been convicted of Burglary l, robbery at night with a gun.

Then she noticed the difference. David Bukowski had pled guilty to the charge in exchange for a promise of leniency. Richard Leach had been convicted on the same charge after a one-week trial. Judge Carroll pondered the decisions that she would soon have to make. Should Leach receive a stiffer sentence because he took up the court's time and resources? Was she obliged to impose the light sentence recommended for Bukowski by the prosecutor and defender?

There was a knock on the door. The bailiff stuck his head in. "Everything's ready, Your Honor." "OK Ben, let's go."

How would you decide? What factors would weigh in your decision? How would you explain your decision?

THE ADMINISTRATIVE CONTEXT OF SENTENCING

Judges are very much influenced by the administrative context within which they impose sentences. As a result, we can see differences between, say, the assembly-line type of justice allocated by misdemeanor courts and the more formal proceedings found in felony court.

Misdemeanor Court: Assembly-Line Justice

Misdemeanor or lower courts possess limited jurisdiction and cannot normally impose prison sentences of more than one year. These courts hear about 90 percent of criminal cases. While felony cases are processed in lower courts only for arraignments and preliminary hearings, misdemeanor cases are processed completely in the lower courts, normally through dismissals or guilty pleas. Only a minority of cases adjudicated in lower courts end in jail sentences; most cases result in fines, probation, community service, and/or restitution.

Most lower courts are overloaded and allot minimal time to each case. Judicial decisions are mass-produced because actors in the system share three assumptions. First, any person appearing before the court likely is guilty because doubtful cases have presumably been filtered by the police and prosecution through discretionary dismissals. Second, the vast majority of defendants will plead guilty. Third, those charged with minor offenses will be processed in volume, with dozens of cases being decided in rapid succession within a single hour. The citation will be read by the clerk, a guilty plea entered, and the sentence pronounced by the judge for one defendant after another.

Although lower criminal courts have been criticized for their assembly-line characteristics, social scientists are now beginning to see redeeming features in this style of justice. Susan Silbey argues, for example, that the informality, availability, and diversity of the lower courts are their most valuable qualities. As she points out, the lower courts have a unique capacity to resolve cases effectively because they are placed at the entry point of the criminal justice system, are dispersed throughout the nation, and are embedded within local communities.[19] Lower-court judges appear to be more interested in responding to "problems" than to formally defined "crimes." Thus, they seek to use their discretion to impose sentences that will fit the needs of the offender and the community rather than simply imposing the sentences provided by law.

Defendants whose cases are processed through the lower court assembly-line may appear to receive little or no punishment. However, people who get caught in the criminal justice system experience other punishments whether or not they are ultimately convicted. A person who is arrested but then released at some point in the process still incurs various tangible and intangible costs. Time spent in jail awaiting trial, the cost of a bail bond, and days of work lost have an immediate tangible impact. Poor people may even lose their jobs or be evicted from their homes if they fail to work and pay their bills for even a few days. For most people, simply being arrested is a devastating experience. It is impossible to measure the psychic and social price of being stigmatized, separated from family, and deprived of freedom.

As Malcolm Feeley has noted, pretrial costs not only have a detrimental impact on unconvicted arrestees but also encourage perfunctory practices in the courtroom and accelerated guilty pleas.[20] In order to get out of jail quickly

Most Serious Conviction Offense	Percent of Felons Sentenced to		
	Prison	Jail	Probation
All offenses	44%	26%	30%
Violent offenses	60	21	19
Murder	93	4	3
Rape	68	19	13
Robbery	74	14	12
Aggravated assault	44	28	28
Other violent	39	29	32
Property offenses	42	24	34
Burglary	52	23	25
Larceny	38	27	35
Fraud	31	21	48
Drug offenses	42	28	30
Possession	33	29	38
Trafficking	48	27	25
Weapons offenses	40	26	34
Other offenses	35	30	35

TABLE 10.2

Types of Felony Sentences Imposed by State Courts, 1992 Note that although we often equate a felony conviction with a sentence to prison, almost a third of felony offenders receive probation.

SOURCE: U.S. Department of Justice, Bureau of Justice Statistics, *Bulletin* (January 1995).

NOTE: For persons receiving a combination of sanctions, the sentence designation came from the most severe penalty imposed—prison being the most severe, followed by jail and then probation.

on probation and back to their jobs and families, defendants plead guilty as quickly as possible, whether or not they are in fact guilty. People who insist that they are innocent incur additional costs to their lives and families as they sit in jail or return to court repeatedly for various proceedings.[21]

Felony Court

Felony cases are processed and offenders are sentenced in courts of general jurisdiction. Because of the seriousness of the crimes, the atmosphere is more formal and generally lacks the chaotic, assembly-line environment of misdemeanor courts. Here, too, however, judges are influenced by the administrative context of the court. Caseload burdens can affect how much time is devoted to individual cases. Exchange relationships between courtroom actors can facilitate plea bargains and shape the content of prosecutors' sentencing recommendations. Sentencing decisions are ultimately shaped, in part, by the relationships, negotiations, and agreements among the prosecutor, defense attorney, and judge.

ATTITUDES AND VALUES OF JUDGES

All lawyers recognize that judges differ from one another in their sentencing decisions. The differences can be explained in part by the conflicting goals of criminal justice, administrative pressures, and the influence of community values. Judges' sentencing decisions also depend on their own attitudes toward the law, toward a particular crime, or toward a type of offender.

Judges are products of different backgrounds and have different social values. As discussed in Chapter 9, Martin A. Levin's study of the criminal courts of Pittsburgh and Minneapolis showed the influence of judges' values on sentencing behavior. He found that Pittsburgh judges, who came from humble backgrounds, exhibited a greater empathy toward defendants than did their colleagues in Minneapolis, who tended to come from upper-class backgrounds. While the Pittsburgh judges tried to make decisions that they believed would help straighten out the troubled defendants' lives, the Minneapolis judges were more inclined to follow the law precisely and to emphasize society's need for protection from crime.[22]

PRESENTENCE REPORTS

Even though sentencing is the judge's responsibility, the presentence report has become an important ingredient in the judicial mix. Usually, a probation officer investigates the convicted person's background, criminal record, job status, and mental condition in order to suggest a sentence that is in the best interests of both the offender and society. Although the primary purpose of the presentence report is to help the judge select the sentence, it also assists in the classification of probationers, prisoners, and parolees with respect to treatment planning and risk assessment. In the reports, the probation officer makes judgments about what information to include and what conclusions to draw from that information. In some states, however, probation officers present only factual material to the judge and make no sentencing recommendation. The probation officer need not follow evidentiary rules and may include hearsay statements as well as firsthand information. The Close-Up gives an example of a presentence report.

STATE OF NEW MEXICO

Corrections Department
Field Service Division
Santa Fe, New Mexico 87501

Date: January 4, 1994
To: The Honorable Manuel Baca
From: Presentence Unit, Officer Brian Gaines
RE: Richard Knight

Evaluation

Appearing before Your Honor for sentencing is 20-year-old Richard Knight who on November 10, 1993, pursuant to a Plea and Disposition Agreement, entered a plea of guilty to Aggravated Assault Upon a Peace Officer (Deadly Weapon) (Firearm Enhancement), as charged in Information No. 89-5736900. The terms of the agreement stipulate that the maximum period of incarceration be limited to l year, that restitution be made on all counts and charges whether dismissed or not, and that all remaining charges in the Indictment and DA Files 39780 be dismissed.

The defendant is an only child, born and raised in Albuquerque. He attended West Mesa High School until the 11th grade at which time he dropped out. Richard declared that he felt school was "too difficult" and that he decided that it would be more beneficial for him to obtain steady employment rather than complete his education. The defendant further stated that he felt it was "too late for vocational training" because of the impending l-year prison sentence he faces, due to the Firearm Enhancement penalty for his offense.

The longest period of time the defendant has held a job has been for 6 months with Frank's Concrete Company. He has been employed with the Madrid Construction Company since August 1993 (verified). Richard lives with his parents who provide most of his financial support. Conflicts between his mother and himself, the defendant claimed, precipitated his recent lawless actions by causing him to "not care about anything." He stressed the fact that he is now once again "getting along" with his mother. Although the defendant contends that he doesn't abuse drugs, he later contradicted himself by declaring that he "gets drunk every weekend." He noted that he was inebriated when he committed the present offense.

In regard to the present offense, the defendant recalled that other individuals at the party attempted to stab his friend, he and his companion left and returned with a gun in order to settle the score. Richard claimed remorse for his offense, and stated that his past family problems led him to spend most of his time on the streets, where he became more prone to violent conduct. The defendant admitted being a member of the 18th Street Gang.

Recommendation

It is respectfully recommended that the defendant be sentenced to 3 years incarceration, on Information No. 89-5736900, and that the sentence be suspended. It is further recommended that the defendant be incarcerated for l year as to the mandatory Firearm Enhancement and then placed on 3 years probation under the following special conditions:

1. That restitution be made to Juan Lopez in the amount of $622.40.
2. That the defendant either maintain full-time employment or obtain his GED, and:
3. That the defendant discontinue fraternizing with the 18th Street Gang members and terminate his own membership in the gang.

The impression that the presentence report conveys about the offender is very important. The language is crucial. Summary statements may be written in a totally noncommittal style or may convey the notion that the defendant is either well behaved and worth favoring or unruly and worth punishing. Judges say that they read the report to get an understanding of the defendant's

Severity Levels of Conviction Offense	Criminal History Score						
	0	1	2	3	4	5	6 or More
Unauthorized use of motor vehicle	12	12	12	15	18	21	24
Possession of marijuana							*23–25*
Theft-related crimes ($150–$2,500)	12	12	14	17	20	23	27
Sale of marijuana							*25–29*
Theft crimes ($150–$2,500)	12	13	16	19	22	27	32
					21–23	*25–29*	*30–34*
Burglary—felony intent	12	15	18	21	25	32	41
Receiving stolen goods ($150–$2,500)					*24–26*	*30–34*	*37–45*
Simple robbery	18	23	27	30	38	36	54
				29–31	*36–40*	*43–49*	*50–58*
Assault, second degree	21	26	30	34	44	54	65
				33–35	*42–46*	*50–58*	*60–70*
Aggravated robbery	24	32	41	49	65	81	97
	23–25	*30–34*	*38–44*	*45–53*	*60–70*	*75–87*	*90–104*
Assault, first degree	43	54	65	76	95	113	132
Criminal sexual conduct, first degree	*41–45*	*50–58*	*60–70*	*71–81*	*89–101*	*106–120*	*124–140*
Murder, third degree	97	119	127	149	176	205	230
	91–100	*116–122*	*124–130*	*143–155*	*168–184*	*195–215*	*218–242*
Murder, second degree	116	140	162	203	243	284	324
	111–121	*144–147*	*153–171*	*192–214*	*231–255*	*270–298*	*309–339*

TABLE 10.3

Minnesota Sentencing Guidelines Grid (presumptive sentence length in months) The italicized numbers within the grid denote the range within which a judge may sentence without the sentence being deemed a departure. The criminal history score is found by adding one point for each prior felony conviction, one-half point for each prior gross misdemeanor conviction, and one-quarter point for each prior misdemeanor conviction.

SOURCE: Minnesota Sentencing Guidelines Commission, *Report to the Legislature* (1983).

attitude. A comment such as "the defendant appears unrepentant" can send a person to prison.

Given the crucial role of the presentence report and the manner in which the information it contains is collected, one might expect that the offender would have a right to examine it and to challenge the contents. In fact, the Supreme Court has ruled that while a convicted person does not have a right to cross-examine persons who supplied the information in the report, he or she must be given the opportunity to deny or explain the information.[23]

The presentence report is one means by which judges ease the strain of decision making. The report lets judges shift partial responsibility to the probation department. Because a substantial number of sentencing alternatives are open to judges, they often rely on the report for guidance. After studying sentencing decisions in California, Robert Carter and Leslie Wilkins found a high correlation (96 percent) between a recommendation for probation in presentence reports and the court's disposition of the cases.[24] When the probation officer recommended incarceration, there was a slight weakening of this relationship, an indication that the officers were more punitive than the judges.

SENTENCING GUIDELINES

In recent years, **sentencing guidelines** have been established in the federal courts, throughout several states, and in selected jurisdictions in other states to indicate to judges the expected sanction for particular types of offenses.

These guidelines are intended to limit the sentencing discretion of judges and to reduce the disparity among sentences given for similar offenses. Although statutes provide a variety of sentencing options for particular crimes, guidelines attempt to direct the judge to more specific actions that *should* be taken. For most offenses, sentence ranges are based on the seriousness of the crime and the criminal history of the offender.

Legislatures construct sentencing guidelines as a grid of two scores. As shown in Table 10.3, one dimension relates to the seriousness of the offense, and the other to the likelihood of offender recidivism. The offender score is obtained by totaling the points allocated to such factors as the number of juvenile, adult misdemeanor, and adult felony convictions; the number of times incarcerated; the status of the accused at the time of the last offense, whether on probation or parole or escaped from confinement; and employment status or educational achievement. Judges look at the grid to see what sentence should be imposed on a particular offender who has committed a specific offense. Judges are expected to provide a written explanation when they depart from the guidelines.

Although the use of guidelines has been found to make sentences more uniform, many judges object to having their discretion limited in this manner. For example, many senior federal judges have rebelled against sentencing guidelines by refusing to accept criminal cases as part of the caseloads that they voluntarily handle after reaching retirement age.

sentencing guidelines
An instrument developed to indicate to judges the expected sanction for particular types of offenses.

IS PUNISHMENT IMPOSED FAIRLY?

The prison populations of most states contain a higher proportion of African-Americans and Hispanic-Americans than is found in the general population. In addition, poor people are more likely to be convicted of crimes than those with higher incomes. Is this situation a result of the prejudicial attitudes of judges, police officers, and prosecutors? Are poor people more liable to commit crimes that elicit a strong response from society? Are enforcement resources distributed so that certain groups are subject to closer scrutiny than other groups? The research evidence on these and similar questions is inconclusive. Some studies have shown that members of racial minorities and the poor are treated more harshly by the system; other research has been unable to demonstrate a direct link between harshness of sentence and race or social class.[25]

For example, one study of sentencing in Texas found that African-Americans received longer prison terms than whites for most offenses but shorter terms than whites for others. African-Americans received longer sentences than whites when they were convicted of burglary (largely an interracial offense) but shorter sentences than whites when they were convicted of murder (a predominantly intraracial offense) or of intraracial rape.[26] Other studies have found links between race and social class that create disadvantages for members of minority groups who are also poor and therefore less able to hire their own attorneys or gain release on bail. In one study, for example, researchers found that the incarceration rate for African-American males was 20 percent higher than that for white males. Whites were more likely to receive long periods of probation, and African-Americans were more likely to receive short prison terms.[27]

James Richardson is released from Florida's death row after his murder conviction was overturned. Is capital punishment justifiable in a system that sometimes puts the innocent to death?

Another serious criminal justice issue concerns individuals who are falsely convicted and sentenced. While many people express concerns about those who "beat the system" and go free, comparatively little attention is paid to those who are innocent yet convicted. Each year, several such cases of innocent persons convicted come to national attention. For example, Randall Dale Adams, whose story was told in the film *The Thin Blue Line*, had his murder conviction overturned in 1989 after spending twelve years on death row. Likewise, James Richardson was freed after twenty-one years in Florida prisons when it was revealed that prosecutors had hidden evidence of his innocence in the poisoning deaths of seven children. How prevalent are miscarriages of justice such as these? C. Ronald Huff and Arye Rattner estimate that about 1 percent of felony convictions are in error.[28] They attribute wrongful convictions to eyewitness errors, unethical conduct by police and prosecutors, community pressures, false accusations, inadequate counsel, and plea-bargaining pressures. Society is hurt by such erroneous convictions because our ideals of justice are violated and because the real perpetrator remains free and unpunished.

SUMMARY

Sentencing—the specification of the criminal sanction—can be viewed as both the beginning and the end of the criminal justice system. With guilt established, a decision must be made about what to do with the person who has been convicted. Much of the efforts of the defendant, prosecutor, and defense attorney during the presentencing phase are based on assumptions about the sanction that may follow conviction. Various justifications for the criminal sanctions have been given in succeeding eras. Although the goals of retribution, deterrence, incapacitation, and rehabilitation can be viewed as distinct, there is a great deal of overlap among the first three goals.

Incarceration, intermediate sanctions, probation, and death are the major forms of criminal sanction. Sentences of incarceration may be either indeterminate, determinate, or mandatory. Good-time provisions allow for a reduction in the amount of time actually served in prison. Intermediate sanctions provide judges with a range of options so that offenders receive a punishment that is commensurate with their crime. Probation is the most widely used criminal sanction, and death the least widely used.

Various influences are brought to bear on judges in the sentencing process. The administrative context, especially the differences between misdemeanor and felony courts; the attitudes and values of the judges; the presentence report; and sentencing guidelines—all are factors that influence judges' decisions.

Criminal sentences have an impact not only on the offender but also on officials and the general public. The effectiveness of the system, as judged by the police, attorneys, and the public, is frequently assessed according to the sentences that are imposed. Sentences that are perceived as too lenient may generate public criticism and give police a disincentive to vigorously investigate and apprehend perpetrators of certain types of crime.

Many observers also judge the effectiveness of the system by the extent of injustice that appears at sentencing. As long as judges are given discretion in sentencing, however, there will be disparities in the punishments of similarly situated offenders. When sentencing disparities produce racial and social-class discrimination, or when innocent people are convicted and sentenced, there are strong reasons to seek improvements in the courts.

QUESTIONS FOR REVIEW

1. What are the purposes of criminal sanctions?
2. What are the forms of criminal sanctions?
3. What intermediate sanctions are currently in use?
4. What has been the Supreme Court's position with regard to the constitutionality of the death penalty?
5. What factors are found to influence the sentencing behavior of judges?

NOTES

1. Dirk Johnson, "A Farmer, 70, Saw No Choice, nor Did the Sentencing Judge," *New York Times*, 20 July 1994, p. A10.
2. Twentieth Century Fund, Task Force on Criminal Sentencing, *Fair and Certain Punishment* (New York: McGraw-Hill, 1976).
3. Andrew von Hirsch, *Doing Justice* (New York: Hill & Wang, 1976), p. 49.
4. Herbert L. Packer, *The Limits of the Criminal Sanction* (Stanford, CA: Stanford University Press, 1968), p. 51.
5. Peter Greenwood, "Controlling the Crime Rate Through Imprisonment," in *Crime and Public Policy*, ed. James Q. Wilson (San Francisco: ICS Press, 1983), p. 258.
6. U.S. Department of Justice, "Mandatory Sentencing: The Experience of Two States," *Policy Briefs* (Washington, DC: Government Printing Office, 1982).
7. Florida Department of Corrections, "Mandatory Minimum Sentences in Florida: Past Trends and Future Implications," 11 February 1991.
8. U.S. Department of Justice, Bureau of Justice Statistics, *Bulletin* (January 1988).
9. Norval Morris and Michael Tonry, *Between Prison and Probation: Intermediate Punishments in a Rational Sentencing System* (New York: Oxford University Press, 1990).
10. Ibid., p. 37.
11. Joan Petersilia, Susan Turner, James Kahan, and Joyce Peterson, *Granting Felons Probation: Public Risks and Alternatives* (Santa Monica, CA: Rand Corporation, 1985).
12. *Furman* v. *Georgia*, 408 U.S. 238 (1972).
13. *Gregg* v. *Georgia*, 428 U.S. 153 (1976).
14. *McCleskey* v. *Kemp*, 478 U.S. 1019 (1987).
15. Ron Rosenbaum, "Too Young to Die?" *The New York Times Magazine*, 12 March 1989, p. 60.
16. 492 U.S. 361 (1989).
17. NAACP Legal Defense and Educational Fund, *Death Row USA* (Fall 1993).
18. *Penry* v. *Lynaugh*, 492 U.S. 302 (1989).

19. Susan S. Silbey, "Making Sense of the Lower Courts," *Justice System Journal* 6 (Spring 1981), p. 20.

20. Malcolm Feeley, *The Process Is the Punishment* (New York: Russell Sage Foundation, 1979).

21. Ibid., p. 200.

22. Martin A. Levin, "Urban Politics and Policy Outcomes: The Criminal Courts, " in *Criminal Justice: Law and Politics*, 6th ed., ed. George F. Cole (Belmont, CA: Wadsworth, 1993), p. 348.

23. *Williams* v. *New York*, 337 U.S. 241 (1949); *Gardner* v. *Florida*, 430 U.S. 349 (1977).

24. Robert M. Carter and Leslie T. Wilkins, "Some Factors in Sentencing Policy," *Journal of Criminal Law, Criminology, and Police Science* 58 (1967), p. 503.

25. Michael Tonry, *Malign Neglect* (New York: Oxford University Press, 1994).

26. Henry A. Bullock, "Significance of the Racial Factor in the Length of Prison Sentences," *Journal of Criminal Law, Criminology, and Police Science* 52 (1961), p. 411.

27. Cassia Spohn, John Gruhl, and Susan Welch, "The Effect of Race on Sentencing: A Reexamination of an Unsettled Question," *Law and Society Review* 16 (1981–82), p. 85.

28. C. Ronald Huff and Arye Rattner, "Convicted but Innocent: False Positives and the Criminal Justice Process," in *Controversial Issues in Crime and Justice*, ed. Joseph E. Scott and Travis Hirschi (Newbury Park, CA: Sage, 1988), p. 130.

PART IV *Corrections*

Historically, there has been no consensus about the best sanctions to use against lawbreakers. Unfortunately, over the course of time, the corrections system has risen to peaks of excited reform, only to drop to valleys of despairing failure. In Part IV, we look at the various ways in which the American system of criminal justice now deals with offenders. Chapters 11–14 will discuss how offenders are punished and how various influences have structured our correctional system. As these chapters unfold, recall the processes that have occurred before the imposition of the sentence, especially as they determine the goals of the correctional portion of the criminal justice system.

CHAPTER 11
Corrections

TEENS BANISHED TO ISLAND AFTER ROBBERY CONVICTION

Two teen-aged Native Americans, convicted of robbing and beating a pizza delivery driver in Everett, Washington, were sentenced by the Tlingit Tribal Court to spend twelve to eighteen months on separate uninhabited islands off the Alaskan coast. Such a banishment was not an option according to the Washington State penal code, which required that the Superior Court of Snohomish County sentence first-time robbery offenders to three to five years in prison. With the court's approval, however, the alternative punishment was arranged by Rudy James, a Tlingit tribal elder. The Tlingit offenders, Adrian Guthrie and Simon Roberts, were given only sleeping bags, forks for digging clams, axes, and enough food to carry them through the first few days. They will be expected to live alone without modern conveniences.[1]

Banishment is an ancient punishment that has not been formally imposed by a U.S. court since the beginning of the republic. As the punishment of these two young offenders makes us aware, prisons are not the only form of corrections. Given folklore, films, and songs about prison life, most Americans understandably think of incarceration when they think of corrections. It must be emphasized, however, that only about one-third of persons under correctional supervision are incarcerated; the remainder live in the community.

The corrections subsystem of the American system of criminal justice is composed of a great number of programs, services, facilities, and organizations responsible for the management of people who have been accused or convicted of criminal offenses. In addition to prisons and jails, corrections also includes probation, alternative incarceration centers, education and work release programs, parole, and community service. These programs are operated in halfway houses, in forest camp sites, in Goodwill thrift stores, in prisons owned by private corporations, and in YMCA buildings. Corrections is authorized by all levels of government and employs more than 500,000 officers, counselors, psychologists, and others. It supervises more than 4 million adults (1 out of every 43) at an annual cost of over $25 billion.[2]

In this chapter, we will trace the history of corrections so as to understand how contemporary institutions and programs evolved. We will then examine the organization of corrections in the United States. Finally, we will look at incarceration trends and the characteristics of inmates. ★

THE HISTORICAL DEVELOPMENT OF CORRECTIONS

As we look at corrections today, we may wonder how we got here. Why are offenders now placed on probation or incarcerated rather than being whipped or burned as they were in colonial times? Over the past two hundred years, society's ideas about appropriate punishment have moved first in one direction and then another. As we consider the evolution of present policies, consider also how future societal change may lead to new forms of corrections.

THE INVENTION OF THE PENITENTIARY

The latter part of the eighteenth century was a remarkable period. During this "Age of Enlightenment," as it is called, scholars and social reformers in Europe and America rethought the nature of society and the place of the individual in the world. Philosophers and writers challenged tradition with new ideas about the individual, limitations on government, and rationalism. Such thinking was the major intellectual force behind the American Revolution and also affected developing views about law and criminal justice. During this period, reformers began to raise questions about the nature of criminality and the methods of punishment.

Prior to 1800, Americans copied the European practice of using physical punishment as the main criminal sanction. Fines, stocks, flogging, branding, and maiming were used to control deviance and to maintain public safety. For more serious crimes, offenders were regularly sent to the gallows. In the state of New York, for example, about 20 percent of all crimes were capital offenses, and criminals were regularly hanged for picking pockets, committing burglaries and robberies, and stealing horses.[3] The early American state governments did not use incarceration as a means of punishment. Jails served only the limited purpose of holding people awaiting trial or punishment or those unable to pay their debts.

The French scholar Michel Foucault has chronicled the spread of Enlightenment ideas during the latter portion of the eighteenth century. Before the French Revolution of 1789, European governments tried to control crime by making punishments such as torture and hanging into public spectacles. Practices included literally branding criminals for life or displaying their dismembered bodies. In the early nineteenth century, such practices gradually were replaced by "modern" penal systems that emphasized fitting the punishment to the individual offender. The new goal was not to inflict pain on the offender's body but to change the individual and set him or her on the right path.[4]

Obviously, this constituted a major shift in punishment policy. The change from physical (corporal) punishment to correction of the deviant individual reflected new ideas about the causes of crime and the possibility of reforming human behavior.

Many people promoted the reform of correctional practices, but John Howard (1726–1790), the sheriff of Bedfordshire, England, was particularly influential. His book, *The State of Prisons in England and Wales*, was an unsentimental, factual account of his observations of the prisons that he visited.[5] Among generally horrible conditions, he was particularly concerned about the lack of discipline in the prisons. Public response to the book resulted in

the passage by the English Parliament of the Penitentiary Act of 1779. The act called for the creation of a house of hard labor in which people convicted of crimes would be imprisoned for up to two years. The institution would be based on four principles:

1. A secure and sanitary structure
2. Systematic inspection (to ensure that offenders followed the rules)
3. The abolition of fees (offenders were not to pay for their food)
4. A reformatory regime

During the night, prisoners were to be confined to solitary cells, and during the day, they were to labor silently in common rooms. The regimen was to be strict and ordered. Perhaps influenced by his Quaker friends, Howard believed that the new institution should be not merely a place of industry but also one for contrition and penance. In the silent environment of discipline and order, the wrongdoer could seek spiritual forgiveness and divine guidance to become a proper and productive member of society. In short, the purposes of the penitentiary were to punish and to reform.

The penitentiary legislation was enacted during Howard's lifetime but was not implemented until 1842, a half-century after his death. However, although Great Britain was slow to act, the United States applied Howard's theories much more quickly.

REFORM IN THE UNITED STATES

From 1776 to around 1830, a revolution occurred in the American conception of criminal punishment. Although based on the ideas of the English reformers, the new correctional philosophy reflected many ideas expressed in the Declaration of Independence, such as an optimistic view of human nature and the concept of individual perfectibility. Emphasis shifted from the assumption that deviance was part of human nature to a belief that crime was a result of environmental forces. The new nation's humane and optimistic ideals were to be focused on reforming the criminal.

In the first decades of the nineteenth century, the creation of penitentiaries in Pennsylvania and New York attracted the attention of legislators in other states as well as investigators from Europe. Even travelers from abroad with no special interest in penology made it a point to include a penitentiary on their itinerary, much as they planned visits to a southern plantation, a textile mill, or a frontier town. By the middle of the nineteenth century, the U.S. penitentiary had become famous around the world.

The Pennsylvania System

A number of groups in the United States dedicated themselves to reforming the institutions and practices of criminal punishment. The first of these groups was the Philadelphia Society for Alleviating the Miseries of Public Prisons, formed in 1787. This group, which included many Quakers and was inspired by Howard's ideas, argued that criminals could best be reformed if they were placed in **penitentiaries**—isolated from one another and from society so that they could reflect on their misdeeds, repent, and reform themselves. In fact, the word *penitentiary* is rooted in the Quaker idea that criminals need an opportunity for penitence (sorrow and shame for their wrongs) and repentance (willingness to change their ways).

In a series of legislative acts in 1790, Pennsylvania authorized penitentiaries for the solitary confinement of "hardened and atrocious offenders." The first such facility, created out of an existing three-story stone structure in Philadelphia, was the Walnut Street Jail. This twenty-five-by-forty-foot building contained eight cells on each floor, each dark cell measuring six by eight by nine feet, and had an attached yard. Only one inmate occupied each cell, and from a small, grated window high on the outside wall, the inmate "could perceive neither heaven nor earth." No communication of any kind was allowed.

It was from this limited beginning in the Walnut Street Jail that the Pennsylvania penitentiary system of **separate confinement** developed, based on five basic principles:

1. Prisoners would not be treated vengefully but would be convinced through hard and selective forms of suffering that they could change their lives.
2. Solitary confinement would prevent further corruption inside prison.
3. In isolation, offenders would reflect on their transgressions and repent.
4. Solitary confinement would be punishment because humans are by nature social animals.
5. Solitary confinement would be economical, because prisoners would not need long periods of time to repent, fewer keepers would be needed, and the costs of clothing would be lower.[6]

penitentiary
An institution intended to isolate prisoners from society and from one another so that they could reflect on their past misdeeds, repent, and thus reform.

separate confinement
A penitentiary system, developed in Pennsylvania, in which each inmate was held in isolation from other inmates and in which all activities, including craft work, were carried on in the cells.

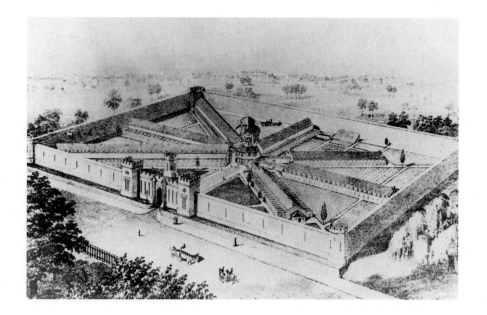

The opening of Eastern Penitentiary near Philadelphia in 1829 culminated forty-two years of reform activity by the Philadelphia Society. The first prisoner was an eighteen-year-old sentenced to a two-year term for larceny. He was assigned to a cell twelve by eight by ten feet that had an individual eighteen-foot exercise yard. In each cell was a fold-up steel bedstead, a simple toilet, a wooden stool, a workbench, and eating utensils. Light came from an eight-inch window in the ceiling. Solitary labor, Bible reading, and reflection were the keys to the moral rehabilitation that was supposed to occur within the prison walls. Although the cell was larger than most in use today, it was the only world the prisoner would see throughout the entire sentence. The only other human voice the prisoner heard would be that of a clergyman who would visit on Sundays. Nothing was to distract the penitent prisoner from the path toward reform.

Unfortunately for the reformers, their theories were not given the opportunity to be practiced under ideal conditions. The Walnut Street Jail became overcrowded as more and more offenders were held for longer periods of time, eventually becoming a "warehouse of humanity" controlled by Philadelphia politicians, who took over its operation. A second Pennsylvania penitentiary located near Pittsburgh was soon declared outmoded because isolation was not complete and the cells were too small for solitary labor. Like the other institutions, it became overcrowded and was recommended for demolition in 1833.

The New York System

In 1819, New York opened a penitentiary in Auburn that evolved as a rival to Pennsylvania's concept of separate confinement. Under the Auburn **congregate system**, prisoners were held in isolation at night but worked with fellow prisoners during the day under a rule of silence; in fact, they were forbidden even to exchange glances while on the job or at meals. Auburn reflected some of the growing emphases of the Industrial Revolution. The men were to have the benefits of labor as well as meditation. They lived under

congregate system
A penitentiary system, developed in Auburn, New York, in which each inmate was held in isolation at night but worked with fellow prisoners during the day under a rule of silence.

tight control, on a simple diet, and according to an undeviating routine, and they worked to pay for a portion of their keep.

American reformers saw the New York approach as a great advance in penology, and it was copied throughout the Northeast. At an 1826 meeting of prison reformers in Boston, the New York system was described in glowing terms:

> At Auburn, we have a more beautiful example still, of what may be done by proper discipline, in a Prison well constructed. . . . The unremitted industry, the entire subordination, and subdued feeling among the convicts, has probably no parallel among any equal number of convicts. In their solitary cells, they spend the night with no other book than the Bible, and at sunrise they proceed in military order, under the eye of the turnkey in solid columns, with the lock march to the workshops.[7]

During this period of reform, advocates of both the Pennsylvania and New York plans debated on public platforms and in the nation's periodicals. Often, the two systems have been contrasted by noting that the Pennsylvania (Quaker) method aimed to produce honest persons whereas the New York system sought to mold obedient citizens. Advocates of both systems agreed, however, that the prisoner must be isolated from society and placed in a disciplined routine. They believed that deviance was a result of corrupting influences from society that institutions like the family and church did not sufficiently counterbalance. Only when offenders were removed from the temptations and influences of society and subjected to a silent, disciplined environment could they see the error of their ways and become useful citizens.

THE REFORMATORY MOVEMENT

By the middle of the nineteenth century, reformers had become disillusioned with the results of the penitentiary movement. Neither the New York or Pennsylvania systems nor any of their imitators had achieved rehabilitation or deterrence. This failure was seen as the result of poor administration rather than as a sign of weakness in the basic concept. Within forty years of their being built, the penitentiaries had become overcrowded, understaffed, and minimally financed. Discipline was lax, brutality was common, and administrators were viewed as corrupt. At Sing Sing penitentiary in Ossining, New York, in 1870, for example, investigators discovered that "dealers were publicly supplying prisoners with almost anything they would pay for" and that convicts were "playing all sorts of games, reading, scheming, trafficking."[8] As with so many other institutions in human society, the ideals that had spurred the penitentiary movement were difficult for government to carry out.

In 1870, the newly formed National Prison Association (the predecessor of today's American Correctional Association) issued a Declaration of Principles that called for a new round of penal reform. Progressive penologists advocated a new design for **penology**—the branch of criminology dealing with the management of prisons and treatment of offenders—according to which the goal of criminal punishment should still be the moral regeneration of criminals, but the means to achieve this goal should be changed. Like the Quakers, these reformers also believed that rehabilitation should be done behind walls. However, the Cincinnati Declaration stated that prisons should

penology
A branch of criminology dealing with the management of prisons and treatment of offenders.

reward prisoner reformation with release. Fixed sentences should be replaced by sentences of indeterminate length, and proof of reformation should replace the "mere lapse of time" in decisions about when to release a prisoner. Thus, instead of being released automatically after two or more years of silent reflection and discipline, inmates would remain imprisoned until they clearly had changed their ways. This program of reformation required a progressive classification of prisoners based on improvements in character.

The first major test of these ideas began in 1876. According to Zebulon Brockway, superintendent of the new model reformatory at Elmira, New York, the key to reform and rehabilitation was in education:

> The effect of education is reformatory, for it tends to dissipate poverty by imparting intelligence sufficient to conduct ordinary affairs, and puts into the mind, necessarily, habits of punctuality, method and perseverance. . . . If culture, then, has a refining influence, it is only necessary to carry it far enough, in combination always with due religious agencies, to cultivate the criminal out of his criminality, and to constitute him a reformed man.[9]

In support of this approach, the New York legislature passed laws allowing indeterminate sentences and permitting the release of reformed inmates on parole. At Elmira, attempts were made to create a school-like atmosphere with courses in both academic and moral subjects. Inmates who performed well in the courses and who obeyed the rules progressed to a point where they were eligible for parole. Poor grades and misconduct extended the inmates' terms of incarceration. Society could reform criminals, Enoch Wines said, only "by placing the prisoner's fate, as far as possible, in his own hands, by enabling him, through industry and good conduct, to raise himself, step by step, to a position of less restraint; while idleness and bad conduct, on the other hand, keep him in a state of coercion and restraint."[10]

By 1900, the reformatory movement had spread throughout the nation; less than two decades later, however, it was already in decline. In most institutions, the architecture, attitudes of the guards, and emphasis on discipline differed little from orientations of the past. Too often, the educational and rehabilitative efforts took a back seat to the traditional emphasis on punishment. Moreover, even Brockway admitted that it was difficult to distinguish between inmates whose attitudes had changed and those who superficially conformed to prison rules. Being a good prisoner became the way to win parole, but this did not guarantee that the prisoner had truly changed.

REFORMS OF THE PROGRESSIVES

In the first two decades of the twentieth century, reformers focused on questions concerning such modern developments as industrialization, urbanization, and scientific advancement. This was the era of the Progressives, who attacked the excesses of urban society, in particular those of big business, and advocated state action against the problems of slums, vice, and crime. The Progressives believed that science could help solve social problems. Concepts from the social and behavioral sciences thus replaced religious and traditional moral wisdom as the guiding ideas for criminal rehabilitation. The Progressives' two main goals were to improve conditions in the social environments thought to be breeding grounds of crime and to improve ways of rehabilitating individual deviants.

Group therapy and counseling programs are part of the rehabilitation model in prisons.

By the 1920s, such Progressive reforms as probation, indeterminate sentences, parole, and treatment programs were being espoused as part of a more scientific approach to criminality. All of these components remain in corrections today, although they are not necessarily used strictly in accordance with the Progressives' goals and methods.

THE REHABILITATION MODEL

Although the Progressives advanced new penal ideas, it was not until the 1930s that attempts were made to implement fully what became known as the *rehabilitation model* of corrections. Taking advantage of the new prestige of the social sciences, penologists helped shift the emphasis of corrections. The new approach took the social, intellectual, or biological deficiencies of criminals to be the causes of their crimes. With the essential structural elements of parole, probation, and the indeterminate sentence already in place in most states, incorporation of the rehabilitation model required only the addition of classification systems and scientific theories for diagnosing offenders and creating rehabilitative treatment programs.

Because penologists likened the new correctional methods to those used by physicians in hospitals, this approach was often referred to as the *medical model*. Under this approach, correctional institutions were to be staffed with persons who could diagnose the causes of an individual's criminal behavior, prescribe a treatment program, and determine when the defender was cured and could be safely released to the community.

Following World War II, rehabilitation won new adherents. Group therapy, behavior modification, counseling, and numerous other treatment approaches became part of the "new penology." Yet even during the 1950s, when the medical model was at its zenith, only a small proportion of state correctional budgets was allocated for rehabilitation. What frustrated many persons committed to treatment was that, even while states adopted the rhetoric of the rehabilitation model, the institutions were still being run with custody as an overriding goal.

The rehabilitation model failed to achieve its goals, and although its rhetoric still survives in the statements of some judges and social workers, it became discredited in the 1970s. The rehabilitation model incorrectly presumed that corrections officials and psychologists could make consistent, accurate judgments about when particular prisoners had been rehabilitated. Studies of rehabilitation programs showed that some prisoners successfully reentered mainstream society, while others committed additional crimes. Corrections officials apparently did not know precisely which techniques would be effective or whether every prisoner had the potential to be rehabilitated. As a result of dissatisfaction with the rehabilitation model, new reforms emerged.

THE COMMUNITY MODEL

As we have seen, correctional goals and methods have been greatly influenced by changing social and political values. During the 1960s and early 1970s, U.S. society experienced the civil rights movement, the war on poverty, and resistance to the war in Vietnam. It was a time in which the traditional ways of government were challenged. In 1967, the President's Commission on Law Enforcement and Administration of Justice reported that "crime and delinquency are symptoms of failures and disorganization of the community. . . . The task of corrections, therefore, includes building or rebuilding social ties, obtaining employment and education, securing in the larger sense a place for the offender in the routine functioning of society."[11] This model of **community corrections** was based on the assumption that the goal of corrections should be to reintegrate the offender into the community. It did not represent a complete break with the Progressives' original emphasis on rehabilitation, but it embodied new thinking about the context in which offenders could best be reintegrated.

Proponents of the community corrections model advocated rehabilitating offenders in the community rather than in prisons. Prisons were viewed as artificial environments that hindered offenders from finding a crime-free lifestyle. The emphasis was on increasing the opportunities for offenders to be successful citizens rather than on providing psychological treatment. Programs were supposed to help offenders find jobs and remain connected to their families and the community. Imprisonment was to be avoided, if possible, in favor of probation, so that offenders could seek educational and vocational training that would help their adjustment. The small proportion of offenders who had to be incarcerated would spend a minimal amount of time in prison before release on parole. To promote reintegration, correctional workers were to serve as advocates for offenders. Instead of watching the offender to make sure that all rules were followed, they were to act on the offenders' behalf in dealing with governmental agencies providing employment counseling, medical treatment, and financial assistance.

This community model did not last long as the dominant emphasis of corrections. Significant numbers

community corrections
A model of corrections based on the assumption that the reintegration of the offender into the community should be the goal of the criminal justice system.

While serving his prison term, David E. Johnson (left) participated in a volunteer program under which he worked with patients at the Fernald School in Waltham, Massachusetts. His participation in the project helped win his parole from prison. Such programs promote the goals of community corrections, which are focused on helping offenders become productive members of the community.

CLOSE-UP
Corrections Is More Than Prison

The blue van passes through a small town and then veers off the highway onto a secondary road where only occasional houses punctuate the fields and woods. We are heading toward a looming fortress. As we approach it we see gray stone walls, barbed-wire fences, gun towers, steel bars. The van passes through opened gates and comes to a stop. Blue-uniformed guards move briskly to the rear doors, and in a moment four men, linked by wrist bracelets on a chain, stand on the asphalt and look about nervously.

For most Americans, prison comes to mind when they think of corrections. This is perhaps understandable, given the history of corrections in this country, the folklore, films, and songs about prison life, and the fact that incarceration is the most visible aspect of the process. But corrections is much more than prisons. Consider the following.

It is 11:00 A.M. in New York City. A five-man crew of convicted offenders has been removing trash from a park in the Bronx for several hours. Across town in Rikers Island, the view down a corridor of jail cells is of the hands of the incarcerated, gesturing through the bars as they converse, play cards, share cigarettes—the hands of people doing time. About a thousand miles to the south, over two hundred inmates sit on Florida's death row. In the same state, a woman on probation reports to a "community-control officer." She is wearing an electronic monitoring device on her ankle; it signals the officer if she leaves her home at night without permission. On the other side of the Gulf of Mexico, crops are tended by sunburned Texas prisoners dressed in stained work clothes. Almost due north in Kansas, an inmate grievance committee in a maximum security prison reviews complaints of guard harassment. Beside the Pacific, in San Francisco, a young man leaves a center-city office building on his way to work after dropping off a urine sample and talking with his parole officer. All of these activities are part of corrections. And all of the central actors are offenders.

of offenders continued to commit additional crimes, the crime rate did not fall, and critics complained that lawbreakers were not being adequately punished. By the end of the 1970s, many penologists despaired over their inability to develop and implement effective programs.

CORRECTIONS IN THE 1990S

The political climate of the United States changed after the turbulent 1960s. Critics attacked rehabilitation and its constituent elements, including indeterminate sentences, treatment programs, and discretionary release on parole. Legislators and judges sought to impose longer sentences, especially on repeat offenders and violent criminals. In general, incarceration was used more extensively as punishment, rather than as a means of treatment.

The doubling of the probation and prison populations during the 1980s put such great pressure on correctional systems that most states were able to provide only minimal services. Probation departments emphasized *risk assessment* as a means of supervising those offenders with the greatest propensity to commit new offenses. Officers worked as watchdogs of probationers rather than as advocates for offenders. Even so, given their limited resources, they were able to supervise only selected offenders. Officials running crowded correctional institutions had to de-emphasize treatment programs because of limited space and money and place greater emphasis on the goals of custody and security.

To a great extent, corrections in the 1990s is being driven by the public's demand for crime control, the war on drugs, and the financial resources of the states. Although the National Crime Victimization Survey data suggest that levels of crime have remained fairly stable since the mid-1970s, the public continues to demand greater efforts to control it. In response, legislators have increased penalties, especially for crimes involving drugs and violence.

The 1994 federal crime bill provided funds to hire thousands of new police officers across the nation. As these officers begin to patrol the streets, they will feed additional defendants into the already clogged courts and corrections systems. In turn, the courts can be expected to respond with stiffer penalties, and corrections will have to deal with even more prisoners and probationers. The system is strained, yet politicians and the public continue to insist that we should incarcerate more offenders for longer periods of time.

Corrections is at a crossroads. In some states, more money is being spent on corrections than on higher education. At some point, the public may begin to question these expenditures, especially if there does not appear to be any reduction in criminality, and the "corrections pendulum" may swing back toward less expensive intermediate sanctions. Whatever the future holds, as the accompanying Close-Up box shows, we must remember that corrections consists of much more than impersonal fortresses.

ORGANIZATION OF CORRECTIONS IN THE UNITED STATES

The corrections part of the criminal justice system includes a wide variety of programs and facilities. In chapters 12–15, you will learn not only about prisons but also about probation, boot camps, halfway houses, parole, and other corrections programs. The administration of corrections is fragmented because each level of government bears responsibility for its own programs. The federal government, the fifty states, the District of Columbia, the 3,047 counties, and most cities each operate at least one corrections facility and many programs. Table 11.1 gives an example of how this fragmentation is reflected in one American city. Typically, only a small portion of offenders are under federal correctional supervision. Because most lawbreakers violate state laws, state and local governments pay about 95 percent of the cost of all U.S. correctional activities.[12]

THE FEDERAL CORRECTIONS SYSTEM

The U.S. Bureau of Prisons, created by Congress in 1930, currently holds over 80,000 inmates in its integrated system of prisons. Facilities and inmates are classified by security level, ranging from Level 1 (the least secure, camp-type settings) through Level 6 (the maximum security U.S. Penitentiary in Marion, Illinois). The four intermediate levels include other U.S. penitentiaries, administrative institutions, medical facilities, and several other specialized institutions for women and juveniles. Because of the nature of federal criminal law, federal prisoners are quite different from those in state institutions. For example, they include a larger proportion of inmates who have been convicted of white-collar crimes. However, drug offenders are becoming more numerous in the federal population.

Probation and parole supervision for federal offenders is provided by the Division of Probation, a branch of the Administrative Office of the United

	Correctional Function	Level and Branch of Government	Responsible Agency
Adult Corrections	Pretrial detention	Municipal/executive	Department of Human Services
	Probation supervision	County/courts	Court of Common Pleas
	Halfway houses	Municipal/executive	Department of Human Services
	Houses of corrections	Municipal/executive	Department of Human Services
	County prisons	Municipal/executive	Department of Human Services
	State prisons	State/executive	Department of Corrections
	County parole	County/executive	Court of Common Pleas
	State parole	State/executive	Board of Probation and Parole
Juvenile Corrections	Detention	Municipal/executive	Department of Public Welfare
	Probation supervision	County/courts	Court of Common Pleas
	Dependent/neglected	State/executive	Department of Human Services
	Training schools	State/executive	Department of Public Welfare
	Private placements	Private	Many
	Juvenile aftercare	State/executive	Department of Public Welfare
Federal Corrections	Probation/parole	Federal/courts	U.S. Courts
	Incarceration	Federal/executive	Bureau of Prisons

TABLE 11.1
Distribution of Correctional Responsibilities in Philadelphia County, Pennsylvania
Note the various correction functions performed by different governmental agencies.
SOURCE: Taken from the annual reports of the responsible agencies.

States Courts. The officers responsible for these programs are appointed by the federal judiciary.

THE STATE CORRECTIONS SYSTEMS

Every state has a centralized department of its executive branch that administers corrections, although departments' responsibilities may vary. In some states, they operate probation and parole programs; in other states probation is handled by the judiciary, and parole by a separate organization. Wide variation also exists in how responsibilities are divided between the state and local governments. For example, in Connecticut, Rhode Island, and Vermont, all correctional workers are state employees while in California more than half (53 percent) are employed by local governments.

For adult felons, state correctional institutions include a great range of facilities and programs, including prisons, reformatories, industrial institutions, prison farms, conservation and forestry camps, and halfway houses. However, most institutionalized offenders are in prisons. These facilities generally are old and large—over half of the nation's inmates are in institutions with populations of more than 1,000, and about 35 percent are in prisons built more than fifty years ago. Even more inmates are in very large "mega-prisons" that have many of the maintenance and operational deficiencies associated with other old, intensively used buildings. Some states have created facilities that are small and are designed to meet individual offender needs, but these are the exception.

The security level of a correctional institution is often fairly easy to see. While the massive stone walls of maximum security prisons are topped by barbed wire and strategically placed guard towers, the campus-type setting of many minimum security institutions permits relative freedom of movement within the boundaries of the institution.

Twenty-six percent of state prison inmates live in maximum security institutions—fortress-like structures designed to prevent escapes. Inmates live in cells that have plumbing and sanitary facilities. The barred doors may be operated electronically so that an officer can lock all prisoners within their cells by merely flipping a switch. The purpose of the maximum security facility is custody and discipline. Some of the most famous prisons, such as Stateville, Attica, Yuma, and Sing Sing, are maximum security facilities.

Medium security institutions house 49 percent of state prison inmates. Physically, they resemble the maximum security prison, but they may be organized differently. Prisoners have more privileges and more contact with the outside world through visitors and mail, and they usually have more access to rehabilitative programs. Although in most states the inmates of this type of facility have probably committed serious crimes, they are not perceived as hardened criminals by correctional officials.

Minimum security institutions hold 25 percent of state prison inmates. These are normally the least violent offenders or those preparing for release to parole. The minimum security prison does not have guard towers and high walls. Prisoners usually live in dormitories and may even have small private rooms rather than cells. There is a relatively high level of personal freedom: Inmates may have television sets, choose their own clothes, and move about casually within the buildings. These institutions are most likely to emphasize treatment programs and provide opportunities for education and work release. Although outsiders may sometimes feel that little punishment is associated with the minimum security facility, it is still a prison. Even minimum security inmates must endure loss of freedom and the life-long stigma of a criminal record.

JAILS: LOCAL CORRECTIONAL FACILITIES

The U.S. jail has been called the "poorhouse of the twentieth century."[13] It is a strange correctional hybrid: part detention center for people awaiting trial, part penal institution for persons convicted of misdemeanors, and part holding facility for social misfits of one kind or another taken off the street. There are approximately 3,300 locally administered jails in the United States with the authority to detain individuals for more than forty-eight hours. The most recent one-day census of the jail population found 426,479 inmates (one out of every 430 adult residents of the United States), a 61 percent increase in five years. The ten largest jails hold 20 percent of the nation's jailed inmates, with the Los Angeles County Men's Central Jail alone containing more than eight thousand inmates. While 63 percent of all jails hold fewer than fifty persons, the number of jails are decreasing as more regional, multicounty prisons are built.

The turnover rate is so great that more than 20 million Americans are jailed in any given year. Generally, about 50 percent of jail inmates are pretrial detainees. Many people are held for less than twenty-four hours, but a few may be held for more than a year awaiting trial. A high proportion (87 percent) of the sentenced population stays in jail for less than one month; others may reside in jail as sentenced inmates for up to one year. In some states, convicted felons may serve terms of more than one year in jail rather than in prison.

Jails are usually locally administered by elected officials (sheriffs or county administrators). Only in Alaska, Connecticut, Delaware, Hawaii, Rhode Island, and Vermont are they run by the state. Traditionally, jails have been run by law enforcement agencies despite the fact that about half of the inmates are sentenced offenders under correctional authority. It seems reasonable that the agency that arrests and transports defendants to court should also administer the facility that holds them, but neither sheriffs nor their deputies generally have much interest in corrections. They think of themselves as police officers and regard the jail as merely an extension of law enforcement. Because jails are under local control and frequently under the control of officials who are not focused on corrections issues, the quality of their administration can suffer. For example, when the state of Maryland took over control of the Baltimore City Jail, which had previously been administered by city officials, it was discovered that some inmates had languished in jail for over a year without being formally charged with a crime because their paperwork had been lost. Without any relatives to complain on their behalf and with no one on the inside believing their claims of unjust incarceration, they had simply been locked away and forgotten.

Increasingly, jails are housing sentenced felons awaiting transportation to prison and those convicted of parole or probation violations. As a result of this backup, judges must often put misdemeanants on probation for lack of jail space.

Jails and police lockups shoulder responsibility for housing not only criminal defendants and offenders but also other "problem" people. Here we can see how the criminal justice system is linked to other government agencies. In recent decades, many states have closed their mental hospitals and released the patients, many of whom ended up living on the streets. Together with the rise in homelessness, this has served to shift new populations into the criminal justice system. Many such people are unable to cope with urban living and are reported to the police for various deviant behaviors. In response, the police often use temporary confinement in the lockup or jail if appropriate social services are not immediately available. In Denver, for example, the situation has been described as a revolving door. First, these "street people" are picked up by police and taken to the station. From there, they are transported to the wing of the jail designated for psychiatric cases. After an appearance in court, they often are released to the streets to start their cycle through the system all over again.

The national concern about drunk driving has also placed an additional burden on jails. In response to MADD (Mothers Against Drunk Driving) and other citizen groups, legislators have enacted mandatory jail sentences for persons convicted of driving while intoxicated. These campaigns encourage the police to devote additional resources to catching drunk drivers and may result in jail overcrowding. In some counties, people convicted of drunk driving must wait for months or even more than a year before they can spend their required three days or one week in jail.

Jails usually lack correctional services. This stems from the rapid inmate turnover, which prevents the development of sustained education, counseling, and other programs, as well as from the local control of jails, which makes cost-conscious local governments reluctant to devote scarce resources to suspects and convicted offenders. Such conditions contribute to the idleness, tension, and emotional pain associated with jail incarceration. High levels of violence and suicides are a hallmark of many jails. Many sentenced felons are glad to leave the jail setting because the living conditions and programs in state prisons are often much better.

As criminal justice policy has become more punitive, jails, like prisons, have become more crowded. Surveys show annual increases in jail populations averaging 6 percent since 1990. Even with new construction, release on recognizance programs, diversion, intensive probation supervision, and house arrest with electronic monitoring, the jail population continues to rise. With new facilities costing as much as $100,000 per cell and incarceration of an inmate costing about $15,000 per year, the $4.5 billion cost of operating jails is a great burden for local governments.

INSTITUTIONS FOR WOMEN

Because only 6 percent of the incarcerated population are women, there are relatively few women's facilities. Although the ratio of arrests is approximately six men to one woman, the ratio of admissions to correctional institutions is eighteen men to one woman. A higher proportion of women defendants are sentenced to probation and other intermediate punishments, partly as a result of male offenders' tendency to commit the large majority of violent crimes.[14]

Until the beginning of the nineteenth century, women offenders in Europe and North America were treated no differently than men, and the sexes were not separated in prisons. Attention to the needs of female offenders began with John Howard's exposé of prison conditions in England in 1777. Among the English reformers, Elizabeth Gurney Fry, a middle-class Quaker, was the first person to press for changes in the treatment of female offenders. She and fellow Quakers were shocked by the conditions in which the female prisoners and their children were living in London's Newgate Prison in 1813. The Quakers' visit to the prison helped to spur them to call for reforms.

News of Fry's efforts spread to the United States, and reform efforts were mounted in a number of states. The first organization devoted to improving the treatment of female prisoners, the Women's Prison Association, was formed in New York in 1844. It was not until 1873, however, that Indiana built the first U.S. prison intended exclusively for women. Thirteen other states followed suit in the subsequent decades. There are now forty-five state and two federal institutions for women. In some states with no separate facilities, women offenders are assigned to a section of the state prison for men; other states pay to have their women transferred to prisons in other states.

Conditions in correctional facilities for women are more attractive than in similar institutions for men since there usually are not gun towers and barbed wire. However, because of the smaller numbers of women in prisons, many of these institutions do not offer the full range of programs and facilities available to male offenders. In addition, a state's lone institution for female offenders typically is located in a remote rural setting and therefore far from the inmates' families.

PRIVATE PRISONS

In response to prison crowding, businesspeople have argued that they can build and run prisons more inexpensively, safely, and humanely than can government. It is not a new idea to contract out parts of correctional services. Food and medical care, educational and vocational training, maintenance, security, and industrial programs often are provided by private businesses. What is new is the idea of running entire institutions for adult felons under private contract.

In January 1985, the U.S. Corrections Corporation opened Kentucky's Marion Adjustment Center, the first privately owned and operated minimum security facility for the incarceration of adult felons. By mid-1989, sociologist Charles Logan counted about a dozen companies in as many states, running about two dozen adult confinement institutions with a total capacity of

Privately constructed and operated correctional institutions arrived on the scene in the 1980s. Advocates say that private prisons provide the same levels of security and care but at less cost.

about seven thousand beds. Logan notes that it is difficult to count such facilities because it is not always clear how to classify them and because they can spring so rapidly into and out of existence.[15] Currently, privately operated adult institutions include jails, state and county prisons, prerelease facilities, lockups for parole violators being returned to custody, and detention centers for the U.S. Immigration and Naturalization Service.

The major advantage cited by advocates of privately operated prisons is that these institutions provide the same level of care but at a lower cost. They also point out that prison space requirements rise and fall and that private entrepreneurs are more flexible in meeting changing needs. However, Logan's study highlights the difficulties of measuring private prisons' costs and quality.[16] One problem is that many of the "true costs" of prison administration (employee benefits, contract supervision, federal grants) are not taken into consideration when businesses make their claims about superior service at a lower price. Labor unions have opposed these incursions into the public sector, pointing out that the salaries, benefits, and pensions of workers in private businesses are often lower than those of public workers.

Before corrections can become too heavily committed to the private ownership and operation of prisons, a number of political, fiscal, and administrative issues must be resolved. The most difficult issues are the ethical and political problems of placing social control functions in private hands. Some people believe that the administration of justice is one of the basic functions of government and that it should not be delegated. There is also concern that correctional policy would be skewed because contractors would use their political influence to lobby for the continuation of programs not in the public interest. They might, for example, press for the maintenance of high incarceration rates in order to support their business activities and profitability, even during periods when the crime rate dropped due to changes in demographic patterns. Finally, there are questions about quality of services, accountability of service providers to corrections officials, and contract supervision. In other cases of privately contracted services, such as group homes, day-care centers, hospitals, and schools, there have been scandals revolving around corruption, brutality, and poor services.

The idea of privately run correctional facilities has stimulated much interest among the general public and among criminal justice professionals. Further privatization may happen, or privatization may be a passing phenomenon spawned at a time of prison crowding, fiscal constraints on governments, and revival of the free-enterprise ideology. The controversy over privatization has, however, forced corrections officials and observers to rethink some strongly held beliefs. Whether private prisons fade away or flourish, the re-examination that they have spurred appears to benefit the system.

PRISON POPULATIONS: TRENDS AND CHARACTERISTICS

From the mid-1940s through the early 1970s, both the incarceration rate and the characteristics of incarcerated individuals in the United States remained fairly stable. During the 1940s and 1950s, the rate held at about

120 prisoners per 100,000 population—primarily poor whites convicted of nonviolent crimes in most regions. For a brief period in the late 1960s, when community corrections became a new focus, the incarceration rate actually decreased.

Since the mid-1970s, however, the size of the prison population has more than doubled, and the characteristics of inmates have changed. Increasing numbers of African-Americans and Hispanics were sent to prison, and a larger number of offenders of all races were sentenced for violent offenses. By 1995, the demographic and numerical makeup of the typical American prison was much different than it had been a few decades before.

INCARCERATION TRENDS

The U.S. Bureau of Justice Statistics conducts an annual census of the prison population. As Figure 11.1 shows, since 1980, each of these surveys has reported a new record-high number of men and women incarcerated—with no end in sight to this dramatic rise. In 1994, the number of prisoners topped one million. Because of this explosive growth, many institutions have become overcrowded, and federal judges have ordered that measures be taken to prevent conditions that violate the Eighth Amendment's prohibition on cruel and unusual punishment. As a result, massive amounts of public money are being spent to build new facilities that fill as soon as they open.

Why has the prison population increased so much in the past two decades? Several answers have been suggested.

Public Attitudes

Beginning in the 1980s, the American public began vigorously to demand that something be done about crime. As pointed out by Alfred Blumstein, public pressure to "do something" about the crime problem resulted in legislators increasing punishments without really questioning whether that approach would be effective in reducing crime.[17]

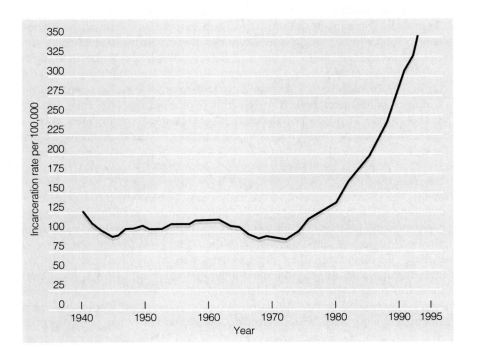

FIGURE 11.1

Incarceration per 100,000 Population, 1940–1993

From 1940 through the mid-1970s, the incarceration rate remained fairly steady. Since 1975, there has been a continuing increase, with today's rate more than double what it was in 1980.

SOURCE: U.S. Department of Justice, Bureau of Justice Statistics, *Bulletin* (June 1994).

The hardening of public attitudes has led to longer sentences, a smaller proportion of offenders being granted probation, and fewer offenders being released at the time of their first parole hearing. Judges may feel obligated to follow the tough state-mandated sentences rather than use their own discretion. In addition, the shift to determinate sentences has removed the safety valve of discretionary parole release in many states.

Better Police and Prosecution

A second explanation for the increase in the prison population is that the billions of dollars spent on the nation's crime problems, especially with regard to the war on drugs, may be producing positive results. Although crime rates overall have been fairly steady during the past decade, arrest and prosecution rates have increased for drug offenses and violent crimes. Thus, successful law enforcement efforts may simply have caught more criminals.

War on Drugs

The appearance of crack cocaine in the 1980s pushed the problem of drugs onto the public agenda. On reaching office in 1988, President Bush pressed Congress to appropriate $7.9 billion in the first year for enforcement of drug laws, to build new prisons, to extend criminal penalties, to give military aid to drug source countries, and to create additional treatment and education programs.

The war on drugs had an immediate impact on the size of the prison population. In 1986, drug offenders constituted only 8.6 percent of state prisoners. By 1994, over 60 percent of federal prisoners and about 25 percent of those in state prisons were there on a drug charge. Some states have experienced a sharp increase in the percentage of new commitments to prison for drug offenses. For example, 45 percent of those sent to prison in New York in 1991 were drug offenders.[18]

Regional Attitudes

Some people point to the high incarceration rates in the states of the "Old Confederacy" to explain the prison population increase. Some of the highest ratios of prisoners to civilians are found in these states. Those favoring this regional perspective point to the high levels of violence in the South, the long sentences provided for by the penal codes, and a long history of racial conflict. They suggest that African-American men in these states are prime candidates for incarceration. However, this hypothesis does not fully account for the growth in prison populations, since high incarceration rates also are found in Alaska, Arizona, Delaware, the District of Columbia, Michigan, and Nevada (see Figure 11.2).

Construction

Finally, the increased rate of incarceration may be related to the creation of additional space in the nation's prisons. Public attitudes in favor of more punitive sentencing policies may have influenced legislators to build more prisons, but the existence of additional cells may better account for the actual rate of increase. Scholars who study organizations have contended that when the government creates new facilities and programs, they will be used. For corrections, this means that "beds will be filled"—after new cells are constructed, judges may not hesitate to fill them. When the crime rate diminishes, non-violent offenders may be sentenced to incarceration. When the crime rate

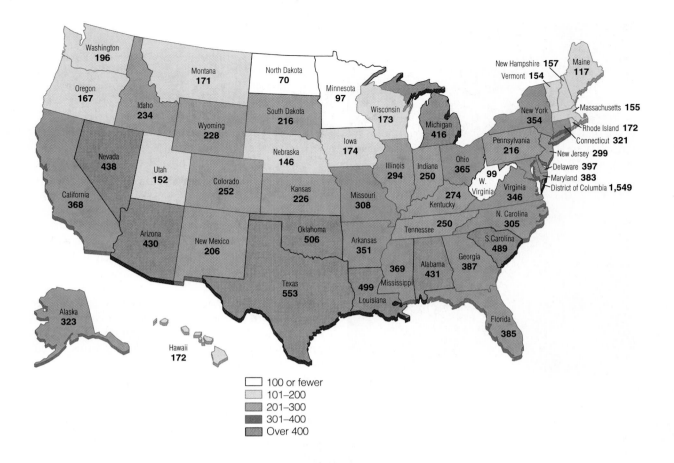

100 or fewer	
101–200	
201–300	
301–400	
Over 400	

increases, the cells may be occupied primarily by those who commit violent or other serious offenses. In short, the escalating incarceration rates in some states may primarily reflect the impact of these states' prison expansions.

The high cost of building new prisons may deter some state and local governments from acting on their desire to imprison larger numbers of offenders. Legislatures typically estimate costs of new construction at $25,000–$125,000 per cell, but recent analyses suggest that these figures are very low. One study computed the true cost of constructing and operating a hypothetical five-hundred-bed medium security prison, using real designs and construction estimates. In addition to the base cost of $61,015 per bed or $31 million for the facility, hidden (but expected) costs such as architects' fees, furnishings, site preparation expenses, and so on pushed the estimate to $82,246 per bed for a total of $41 million. At a conservative estimate of $14,000 per inmate per year, the annual operating cost would be $7 million. Thus, the thirty-year bill to the taxpayers for construction and operation would be $250 million versus the $31 million originally described.[19]

Given current public attitudes on crime and punishment, continued high crime rates, and the expansion of prison space, incarceration rates will most likely stay high. However, the high costs involved may eventually lead to a search for less expensive methods of punishment. Alternatively, changes in societal values or theories about punishment may shift the emphasis toward intermediate punishments or other approaches to corrections.

FIGURE 11.2

Sentenced Prisoners in State Institutions per 100,000 Civilian Population, 1994
What can be said about the differences in incarceration rates among the states? In addition to regional differences, there are differences between contiguous states that would seem to have similar socioeconomic and crime characteristics.

SOURCE: U.S. Department of Justice, Bureau of Justice Statistics, *Bulletin* (May 1995).

271

The prison population is composed predominantly of poor, young males. What might the future be like for this California inmate?

WHO IS IN PRISON?

On the basis of a national survey of state prisons, the Bureau of Justice Statistics claimed in 1982, and later confirmed in 1991, that the U.S. prison population is predominantly

> poor young adult males with less than a high school education. Prison is not a new experience for them; they have been incarcerated before, many first as juveniles. The offense that brought them to prison was a violent crime or burglary. On the average they already served $1\frac{1}{2}$ years on a maximum sentence of $8\frac{1}{2}$ years. Along with a criminal history, they have a history of drug abuse and are also likely to have a history of alcohol abuse.[20]

Figure 11.3 provides more data. Note that most prisoners are in their late twenties to early thirties, have less than a high school education, and are disproportionately members of minority groups. In addition, more than half are incarcerated because of a violent crime.

FIGURE 11.3

Sociodemographic and Offense Characteristics of State Prison Inmates Do these data support the contention that many offenders do not "need" to be incarcerated?

SOURCE: U.S. Department of Justice, Bureau of Justice Statistics, *Survey of State Prison Inmates* (Washington, DC: Government Printing Office, 1993), p. 4.

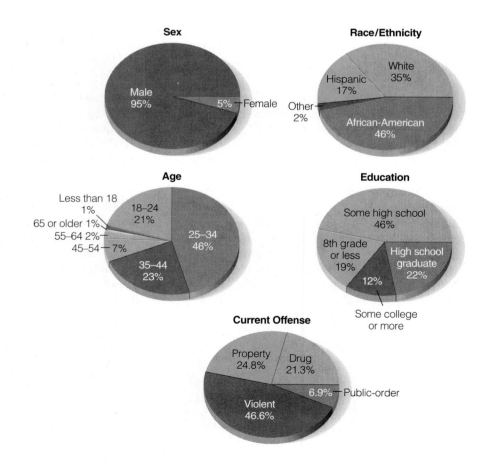

Recent studies show that recidivist inmates and those convicted of a violent crime make up an overwhelming proportion of the populations. Nationally, more than 60 percent of inmates have been either incarcerated or placed on probation at least twice; 45 percent of them, three or more times; and nearly 20 percent, six or more times. Two-thirds of inmates were serving a sentence for a violent crime or had previously been convicted of a violent crime.[21] These are major shifts from the prison populations of earlier decades, when only about 40 percent of all inmates had committed such offenses. Today's typical prisoner has a history of persistent criminality.

Correctional officials have recently become aware of the increasing number of prison inmates who are older than age fifty-five. Nationally, that number is now more than 20,000, with about 400 over age eighty-five. About half of these inmates are serving long sentences, while the other half committed crimes late in life. Older inmates still comprise a small proportion of the total inmate population, but their numbers are doubling every four years. The increase is significant because elderly prisoners have special security and medical needs. In a number of states, they have been placed in special sections of institutions so that they will not have to mix with the younger, tougher inmates. Chronic illnesses such as heart disease, stroke, and cancer, which develop in any aging population, raise prison medical costs. The average yearly maintenance and medical costs for inmates over fifty-five is about $69,000, triple that for other prisoners. The care of elderly prisoners will be a growing and costly concern for corrections officials in the foreseeable future.[22]

AIDS AND OFFENDERS

Elderly prisoners do not pose the only new challenge for corrections. Correctional staff must now deal with offenders who have the human immunodeficiency virus (HIV) and who may develop or already have contracted full-blown AIDS while incarcerated or under supervision in the community. Probation, parole, jail, and prison populations contain a high concentration of individuals at particular risk for the disease—those with histories of intravenous drug use and those who have engaged in unsafe heterosexual or homosexual behavior. Not surprisingly, studies have shown that offenders with AIDS tend to be concentrated in those areas of the country where drug use is highest (District of Columbia, New York, New Jersey).

A QUESTION OF ETHICS

The policy directive was precise:

All inmates will be tested for HIV. All inmates found to be positive will be placed in Wing A, regardless of their physical condition, conviction offense, or time remaining in their sentence.

Testing for the deadly virus began at Elmwood State Prison soon after Warden True's directive was posted. All of the 753 inmates were tested over a three-week period, as was every new prisoner entering the institution.

Six weeks later, the test results were known. For most of the inmates, there was relief in the knowledge that they had not contracted the virus. For a few, however, the news that they had tested positive was traumatic. Most responded with an expletive, others burst into tears, and still others sat in stunned silence.

Word of the new policy at the prison was leaked to the press. There was an immediate response from the state chapter of the American Civil Liberties Union and the Howard Association for Prisoners' Rights. These groups protested the "state's invasion of privacy" and the "discriminatory act of segregating gays and drug users, most of the latter being African-American and Hispanic." They emphasized that it would be years before most of the infected would come down with a "full" case of AIDS; compassion, not stigmatization, should be the response of corrections to the disease.

Warden True told reporters that he had a responsibility for the health of all inmates and that the policy has been developed to prevent transmission of the disease. He said that although the HIV inmates would be segregated, they would have access to all of the facilities available to the general population, but at separate times. He denied that he intended to stigmatize the twenty prisoners who had thus far tested positive.

What do you suppose Warden True considered in developing this policy? Is his policy likely to do harm or good? Is it ethical to segregate the prison population? Is it ethical to add conditions to parole for prisoners who test HIV positive?

Offenders with HIV or AIDS present correctional personnel with a number of problems and policy issues. Administrators have been developing policies covering such matters as methods to prevent transmission of the disease, the housing of those infected, and medical care for inmates who have the full range of symptoms. In doing so, they face a host of difficult legal, political, medical, budgetary, and attitudinal factors.

SUMMARY

At various times in U.S. history, different approaches to punishment have been considered appropriate. With the development of the penitentiary at the beginning of the nineteenth century, incarceration became the primary means of punishing serious offenders. Although keeping offenders in custody has been a dominant goal, rehabilitation and reintegration into the community were major alternative objectives from the end of World War II to the early 1970s. After a return to an emphasis on incarceration as deserved punishment, prison populations expanded rapidly as the public demanded and legislatures mandated tougher sentences. As a result of higher incarceration rates, new prisons were constructed throughout the country to alleviate overcrowding.

Corrections in the United States is organized along several lines: The Federal Bureau of Prisons, state prison systems, and local (mainly county-run) jails are the three major instruments of incarceration. The characteristics of the inmate populations differ for each. There are also separate prison facilities for women in most states. The number and type of inmates in an institution greatly influence the character of that facility and the problems faced by administrators. For example, the extent to which wardens must deal with prison gangs, racial tensions, elderly offenders, and AIDS in prison will depend on the prison population.

QUESTIONS FOR REVIEW

1. What were the major differences between the New York and Pennsylvania corrections systems in the nineteenth century?
2. Why did rehabilitation go out of favor with corrections officials and legislators?
3. Who was Elizabeth Fry, and what role did she play in correctional reform?
4. What problems are involved in the use of private prisons?
5. What explanations have been advanced for the rise in prison populations?
6. What are some of the management problems associated with special offenders populations, such as those who are elderly or who have contracted AIDS?

NOTES

1. *New York Times*, 4 September 1994, p. 1.
2. U.S. Department of Justice, Bureau of Justice Statistics, *Sourcebook of Criminal Justice Statistics* (Washington, D.C.: Government Printing Office, 1991), p. 19; U.S. Department of Justice, Bureau of Justice Statistics, *National Update* (Washington, DC: Government Printing Office, January 1992), p. 4.

3. David J. Rothman, *The Discovery of the Asylum: Social Order and Disorder in the New Republic* (Boston: Little, Brown, 1971), p. 49.

4. Michel Foucault, *Discipline and Punish*, trans. Alan Sheridan (New York: Pantheon, 1977), pp. 8, 16.

5. John Howard, *The State of Prisons in England and Wales* (London: J. M. Dent, 1977/1929).

6. Thorsten Sellin, "The Origin of the Pennsylvania System of Prison Discipline," *Prison Journal* 50 (Spring-Summer 1970), pp. 15–17.

7. Ronald L. Goldfarb and Linda R. Singer, *After Conviction* (New York: Simon & Schuster, 1973), p. 30.

8. David J. Rothman, *Conscience and Convenience* (Boston: Little, Brown, 1980), p. 18.

9. Goldfarb and Singer, *After Conviction*, p. 40.

10. As quoted Goldfarb and Singer, *After Conviction*, p. 41.

11. President's Commission on Law Enforcement and the Administration of Justice, *The Challenge of Crime in a Free Society* (Washington, DC: Government Printing Office, 1967), p. 7.

12. U.S Department of Justice, Bureau of Justice Statistics, *Report to the Nation on Crime and Justice*, 2d ed. (Washington, DC: Government Printing Office, 1988), p. 117.

13. Ronald Goldfarb, *Jails: The Ultimate Ghetto* (Garden City, NY: Doubleday, 1975), p. 29.

14. U.S. Department of Justice, Bureau of Justice Statistics *Bulletin* (May 1993).

15. Charles Logan, *Private Prisons: Cons and Pros* (New York: Oxford University Press, 1990), p. 16.

16. Charles H. Logan, "Well Kept: Comparing Quality of Confinement in Private and Public Prisons, *The Journal of Criminal Law and Criminology* 83 (Fall 1992), pp. 577–613.

17. Alfred Blumstein, "Prisons," in *Crime*, ed. James Q. Wilson and Joan Petersilia (San Francisco: Institute for Contemporary Studies, 1995), p. 399.

18. U.S. Department of Justice, Bureau of Justice Statistics, *Survey of State Prison Inmates: 1991* (Washington, DC: Government Printing Office, 1993), p. 4.

19. *Time to Build?* (New York: Edna McConnell Clark Foundation, 1984), pp. 18–19.

20. U.S. Department of Justice, Bureau of Justice Statistics, *Bulletin* (December 1982), p. 1; U.S. Department of Justice, *Survey of State Prison Inmates*, p. 3.

21. Ibid.

22. *Newsweek*, 20 November 1989, p. 70.

CHAPTER 12
Community Corrections: Probation and Intermediate Sanctions

CRIMINALS SENT HOME: THEY MAY BE OUT OF SIGHT BUT ARE WE OUT OF OUR MINDS?

Judge Stanley Goldstein presides over the drug court in Miami, Florida. Although the trend nationally is to send drug offenders to prison for a long time, Judge Goldstein sentences drug offenders with no history of violence to live at home or to enter residential treatment programs. Those living at home must agree to participate in a year-long drug treatment program. Periodically, they must submit to drug urine tests and appear before Judge Goldstein to report on their progress. Those who fail the tests may be sent briefly to jail or to residential drug treatment programs. When one offender appeared before the court, the Judge said, "You dropped 15 urines—all dirty. I am going to take you in and clean you up, put you in a residential program."

The offender protested, "I'm going to lose my job [if I am sent away]."

"It's a choice between your life or your job," the judge replied. "It's going to be all right, Albert. Don't worry about it. All you gotta worry about today is you."[1]

Scenes like the one in the Miami court are becoming more common across the United States. During the past few years, there has been a shift in American corrections from a focus on crime control through incarceration to a renewed interest in community corrections. In this chapter, we discuss the assumptions underlying the community corrections alternative and examine specific strategies such as probation and electronic monitoring. ★

FIGURE 12.1
Percentage of Persons Under Correctional Supervision in All Categories
Although most people think of corrections as prisons and jails, almost three-quarters of offenders actually are supervised within the community.
SOURCE: U.S. Department of Justice, Bureau of Justice Statistics, *Bulletin* (September 1994), p. 4.

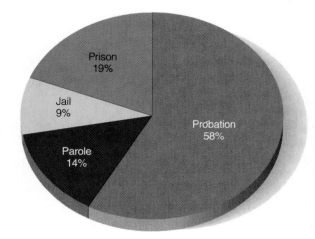

COMMUNITY CORRECTIONS: ASSUMPTIONS

Since the early nineteenth century, supervision in the community has been recognized as an appropriate punishment for some offenders. Although probation had been developed in the 1840s and was widely used by the 1920s, incarceration remained the usual sentence for serious crimes until the 1950s. Beginning in the 1960s, a range of community alternatives was developed. As a result, incarceration rates fell as probation was viewed as the "punishment of choice" for most first-time offenders.

However, as Americans wearied of crime in the 1980s, many legislatures passed tough sentencing laws and stipulated that incarceration should be the new priority punishment. The so-called war on drugs further increased the number of offenders incarcerated as well as added to probation supervision. By the late 1980s, criminal justice scholars recognized that many imprisoned offenders, if properly supervised, could be punished more cheaply in the community. At the same time, probation clearly was inappropriate for some offenders since supervision is impossible when officers carry caseloads of three hundred. The answer to this problem has been to create a set of intermediate sanctions such as intensive probation supervision, home confinement, and electronic monitoring. As Figure 12.1 shows, today more than three-quarters of persons under correctional supervision are living in their communities.

With the increased use of community sanctions, many offenders who have committed relatively serious crimes are walking the streets under various forms of correctional supervision. Because many of these criminals are not first-time, minor offenders, community corrections faces more difficult challenges than in the past. Rehabilitation and reintegration formerly were the primary elements of community corrections, but today the primary elements are more often surveillance and control.

Community corrections seeks to maintain offenders in the community by building ties to family, employment, and other normal sources of stability and success. It seeks to restore family links, provide employment placement and education programs, and develop offenders' confidence in their ability to succeed as law-abiding citizens. This model of corrections assumes that the offender must change, but it also recognizes that factors within the community that might encourage criminal behavior (unemployment, for example) must also change.

Four justifications are usually given for community corrections. First, many offenders' criminal record and current offense are not serious enough to warrant incarceration. Second, community supervision is cheaper than incarceration. Third, recidivism rates for those who serve prison time are no lower than for those under community supervision. In fact, some studies show that just being in prison raises the offender's potential for recidivism, perhaps by hardening attitudes toward society or transmitting criminal skills and behaviors. Fourth, when compared to alternative sentences and their consequences, incarceration is more destructive to both the offender and society. In addition to the pains of imprisonment and the harmful effects of prison life, incarceration enhances the suffering of family members, particularly the children of women offenders.

Central to the community corrections approach is a belief in the "least restrictive alternative"—the notion that the criminal sanction should be applied only to the minimum extent necessary for the community's protection, the gravity of the offense, and society's need for deserved punishment. If these goals can be fulfilled without incarceration, so much the better. Supporters of community corrections call for expanding such postincarceration programs as halfway houses, work release and furlough programs, and parole services. They believe that such programs give offenders more opportunities to succeed in law-abiding activities and reduce their contact with the criminal world.

PROBATION: CORRECTION WITHOUT INCARCERATION

As explained in Chapter 10, probation refers to the conditional release of the offender into the community under the supervision of corrections officials. Probationers are not under constant supervision. They live at home with their families and work in regular jobs, but they must report regularly to their probation officers and abide by certain conditions such as submitting to drug tests, obeying curfews, and staying away from certain people or parts of town.

Probation may be combined with other sanctions, such as fines, restitution, and community service. Fulfillment of these other sanctions may, in effect, become a condition for successful completion of probation. The sentencing court retains authority over the probationer, and if he or she violates the conditions or commits another crime, the judge may order the entire sentence to be served inside a prison.

Often, the judge imposes a prison term but then suspends serving of that sentence and instead places the offender on probation. Increasingly, however, judges in some states are using the tactics of split sentences or shock incarceration, in which a short period of imprisonment is followed by probation. This reflects a theory that a taste of imprisonment will jar some offenders sufficiently to change their lives and obey the conditions of their probation.

Much has been written about overcrowded prisons, yet many observers do not recognize that the adult probation population has also been increasing—at a rate of 154 percent since 1980.[2] Today, over 2.5 million offenders (60 percent of all offenders) are on probation. At the same time, the social and political climate has supported harsher correctional policies, and as a result, probation practices now stress punishment of the offender and protection of the community more than rehabilitation. Probation budgets in many states have been cut and caseloads increased as greater resources are diverted to prisons. However, the reality of overflowing prisons will undoubtedly mean that judges will continue to be forced to place more offenders convicted of serious crimes, especially drug crimes, on probation. This means that probation officers will continue to deal with more and more clients at high risk of failing to fulfill the conditions of probation.

ORIGINS AND EVOLUTION OF PROBATION

The historical roots of probation lie in the procedures for reprieves and pardons of early English courts. The actual development of probation itself, however, occurred in the United States. John Augustus, a prosperous Bostonian, has become known as the world's first probation officer. He persuaded a judge in the Boston Police Court in the 1840s to place a convicted but not yet sentenced offender in his custody for a brief period and succeeded in helping the man to appear rehabilitated by the time of sentencing.

Massachusetts developed the first statewide probation system in 1880, and by 1920, twenty-one other states had followed suit. In 1925, the federal courts were authorized to hire probation officers. By the beginning of World War II, forty-four states had probation systems.

Probation began as a humanitarian effort to give first-time and minor offenders a second chance. Probation officers attempted to act like modern social workers by intervening in clients' lives and guiding them toward law-abiding and successful lives. Early probationers were not only required to obey the law but expected to behave in a morally acceptable fashion. Officers sought to provide moral leadership so as to shape probationers' attitudes and behavior with respect to family, religion, employment, and free time.

By the 1920s, the development of psychology led probation officers to shift their emphasis from moral leadership to therapeutic counseling. This shift brought several important changes. First, the officer no longer primarily acted as a community supervisor charged with enforcing a particular morality. Second, the officer became more of a clinical counselor whose goal was to help the offender solve psychological and social problems. Third, the offender was expected to become actively involved in the treatment. The pursuit of rehabilitation as the primary goal of probation gave the officer extensive discretion in defining and treating the offender's problems. Officers used their own judgment to evaluate each offender and develop a treatment approach to the personal problems that presumably had led to crime.

During the 1960s, a new shift occurred in probation techniques. Rather than counseling offenders, probation officers provided them with concrete social services, such as assistance with employment, housing, finances, and education. This emphasis on reintegrating offenders and remedying the social problems they faced was consistent with federal efforts to conduct a "war on poverty." Instead of being a counselor or therapist, the probation officer became an advocate, dealing with employers, school officials, and government agencies in an effort to create new opportunities for the probationer.

In the late 1970s, the orientation of probation changed yet again as the goals of rehabilitation and reintegration gave way to risk control. This approach, still dominant today, attempts to minimize the probability that an offender will commit a new offense. Risk control reflects two basic goals. First, based on the deserved-punishment ideal, the punishment should match the offense, and correctional intervention should neither raise nor lower the level of punishment. Second, according to the community protection criterion, the amount and type of supervision provided are determined according to the risk that the probationer will return to crime.

ORGANIZATION OF PROBATION

Although probation is viewed as a form of corrections, in many states it is administered locally by the judiciary. In other words, the punishment program that affects the largest number of offenders is not handled by the state department of corrections. The state may set standards, provide financial support, and conduct training courses, but about two-thirds of all persons under probation supervision are actually handled by locally administered programs.[3]

This seemingly odd arrangement produces benefits as well as problems. On the positive side, keeping probationers under the supervision of the courts permits judges to keep closer tabs on them and to order incarceration if the conditions of probation are violated. On the negative side, some judges know little about the goals and methods of corrections, and probation increases the administrative duties of the already overworked courts.

One strong reason for judicial control is that probation works best when the judge and the supervising officer have a close relationship. Proponents of this system say that judges need to work with probation officers whom they can trust, whose presentence reports they can accurately evaluate, and on whom they can rely to report on the success or failure of individual cases.

For the sake of their clients and the goals of the system, probation officers need direct access to corrections and other human services agencies. However, these agencies are located in the executive branch of government. As a result, a number of states have considered combining probation and parole services in the same agency in order to increase the coordination of resources and efforts. Others point out, however, that probationers are quite different from parolees. Parolees already have served terms in prison, frequently have been involved in more serious crimes, and often have become more disconnected from mainstream society. By contrast, most probationers have not developed criminal lifestyles to the same degree and do not have the same problems of reintegration into the community.

PROBATION SERVICES

As we have seen, probation officers are expected to act as both police personnel and social workers. In our examination of sentencing in earlier chapters, we saw their importance in providing the judiciary with presentence investigations and reports. After a sentence of probation is imposed, officers supervise clients in order to keep them out of trouble and assist them in the community. In addition, they must monitor the client's behavior and enforce the conditions

Probation officers have the dual responsibilities of providing assistance to, and supervision of, their clients.

of the sentence. This law enforcement role involves discretionary decisions about whether to report violations of probation conditions. Not surprisingly, individual officers may emphasize one role over another, and the potential for conflict is great. Studies have shown, however, that most probation officers have backgrounds in social service and are more partial to that role than to the law enforcement role.

One continuing issue for probation officers is the size of their caseloads. How many clients can an officer effectively handle? In the 1930s, the National Probation Association recommended a 50-unit caseload, and in 1967, the President's Commission reduced it to 35. However, the national average is currently about 115, and some caseloads exceed 300. The oversized caseload is usually identified as one of the major obstacles to successful operation of probation. Recent evidence indicates, however, that the size of the caseload is less significant than the nature of the supervision experience, the classification of offenders, the professionalism of the officer, and the services available from the agencies of correction. In other words, the number of offenders handled by each probation officer is less important than the quality of the services and supervision applied to the probationers.

During the past decade, probation officials have developed methods of classifying clients according to their service needs, the element of risk that they pose to the community, and the predicted likelihood of recidivism. Through this process, probationers may be supervised less as they continue to live within the conditions of their sentence. Risk classification schemes fit the deserved-punishment model of the criminal sanction in that the most serious cases receive the greatest restrictions and supervision.[4]

Whether serious cases actually receive more supervision is influenced by a number of factors. Consider the war on drugs. It has significantly increased probation caseloads in urban areas because large numbers of drug dealers and people convicted of possession are placed on probation.[5] Many of these offenders have committed violent acts and live in inner-city areas marked by drug dealing and turf battles to control drug markets. Under these conditions, direct supervision can be a dangerous task for the probation officer. In some urban areas, probationers are merely required to telephone or mail reports of their current residence and employment. In such cases, it is hard to see how any goals of the sanctions—deserved punishment, rehabilitation, deterrence, or incapacitation—are actually being realized.

REVOCATION OF PROBATION

Probationers who violate the provisions of their sentences may have their probation revoked by a judge. Since probation is usually granted in conjunction with a suspended jail or prison sentence, incarceration may follow revocation. Revocation can also result from a new arrest. Violating curfew, failing a drug test, or using alcohol are among the violations that may lead to incarceration.

Probation officers and judges have widely varying notions of what constitutes grounds for revoking probation. Once the officer has decided to call a violation to the attention of the court, the probationer may be arrested or summoned for a revocation hearing. Since the contemporary emphasis is on avoiding incarceration except for flagrant and continual violation of the conditions of probation, most revocations today occur because of a new arrest or conviction.

In 1967, the U.S. Supreme Court gave its first opinion concerning the due process rights of probationers at a revocation hearing. In *Mempa v. Rhay*, the justices determined that a state probationer had the right to counsel at a combined revocation and sentencing hearing, but the Court did not refer to any requirement for a hearing.[6] This issue was addressed by the Court in *Gagnon v. Scarpelli (1973)*, in which the justices ruled that before probation or parole may be revoked, the offender is entitled to a preliminary and a final hearing and to specific elements of due process.[7] When a probationer is taken into custody for violating the conditions of probation, a preliminary hearing must be held to determine whether probable cause exists to believe that the incident occurred. If there is a finding of probable cause, a final hearing, where the revocation decision is made, is mandatory. At these hearings, the probationer has the right to cross-examine witnesses and to be given notice of the alleged violations and a written report of the proceedings. The Court ruled, however, that probationers have no automatic right to counsel—this decision is to be made on a case-by-case basis. At the final hearing, the judge decides whether to continue probation or to impose tougher restrictions, such as incarceration.

Mempa v. *Rhay* (1967)
Probationers have the right to counsel at a hearing considering revocation of a suspended sentence.

Gagnon v. *Scarpelli* (1973)
Before probation or parole may be revoked, the offender is entitled to a preliminary and a final hearing and to specific elements of due process.

ASSESSING PROBATION

Probation is at a crossroads. Some critics see probation as nothing more than a slap on the hand, an absence of punishment. Given the huge caseloads of many officers, probationers are given very little guidance, supervision, or assistance. A Philadelphia criminal court judge, Lois Forer, has remarked: "Probation is not a penalty. The offender continues with his life style. . . . If he is a wealthy doctor, he continues with his practice; if he is an unemployed youth, he continues to be unemployed. Probation is a meaningless rite; it is a sop to the conscience of the court."[8] In the context of the Miami drug court described at the beginning of the chapter, one must wonder whether probationers are beating the system when they are not sent back to prison after repeatedly flunking drug tests.

How effective can probation be? Studies indicate that from one-fifth to one-third of probationers fail to fulfill the conditions of their sentence. Although this recidivism rate is less than that for offenders who have been incarcerated, researchers question whether this is a direct result of supervision or an indirect result of the aging process. Most offenders placed on probation do not become career criminals, their criminal activity is short-lived, and they become stable citizens as they obtain jobs and get married. Even most of those who are arrested a second time do not repeat their mistake.

What rallies support for probation is its relatively low cost: Keeping an offender on probation rather than behind bars costs roughly $700 a year, a savings of more than $17,000.

In recent years, as prisons have become overcrowded, increasing numbers of felony offenders have been placed on probation. Over one-third of today's probationers have been convicted on felony charges. In addition, upwards of 75 percent of probationers are addicted to drugs or alcohol. These factors present new challenges for probation, since officers can no longer assume that their clients pose little threat to society and that they possess the skills and motivation to live productive lives in the community.

The new demands on probation have given rise to calls for increased electronic monitoring and for risk management systems that will differentiate the levels of supervision required for different offenders. If probation is to be a viable alternative to incarceration, however, additional resources will be needed.

INTERMEDIATE SANCTIONS

Dissatisfaction with traditional probation supervision, coupled with the crowding of American prisons, has resulted in a call for intermediate sanctions within the community that are more restrictive than simple probation and constitute actual punishment for serious offenders. The case for intermediate sanctions can be made on several grounds, but Norval Morris and Michael Tonry have put it best in saying, "Prison is used excessively; probation is used even more excessively; between the two is a near vacuum of purposive and enforced punishments."[9]

Intermediate sanctions may be viewed as a continuum of punishments reflecting different degrees of intrusiveness and control. Probation plus a fine or community service may be appropriate for minor offenses, while six weeks of boot camp followed by intensive probation supervision may be right for more serious crimes. But will offenders be able to fulfill conditions added to probation? Moreover, if prisons are overcrowded, does incarceration pose a believable threat if offenders fail to comply?

Across the country, many different types of intermediate sanctions are being used. Let us divide them into (1) those that are administered primarily by the judiciary (fines, restitution, and forfeiture), (2) those that are primarily administered in the community with a supervision component (home confinement, community service, day reporting centers, and intensive probation supervision), and (3) those that are administered inside institutions followed by community supervision. We should emphasize that sanctions may be imposed in combinations—for example, a fine in conjunction with probation, or boot camp with community service and probation.

INTERMEDIATE SANCTIONS ADMINISTERED PRIMARILY BY THE JUDICIARY

Fines

Typically, fines are the only criminal sanction administered directly by the court. A **fine** is simply a sum of money to be paid to the state by a convicted person as punishment for an offense. Fines are routinely imposed for offenses ranging from traffic violations to felonies. Studies have shown that the fine is used widely as a criminal sanction and that courts annually collect well over $1 billion in fines.[10] Fines are rarely used as the *sole* punishment for crimes more serious than motor vehicle violations, however. Typically, fines are used in conjunction with other sanctions, such as probation and incarceration. For example, a judge may impose two years of probation and a $500 fine for larceny, minor assaults, or other offenses.

Many judges cite the difficulty of collecting fines as the reason that they do not impose them more often.[11] They report that fine enforcement receives a low priority among their various duties. Unless courts have developed administrative procedures to seek collection of fines, enforcement will inevitably take a back seat to the demanding flow of criminal prosecutions,

fine
A sum of money to be paid to the state by a convicted person as punishment for an offense.

sentencing decisions, and probation revocations. However, the judiciary also may have little incentive to expend its own resources collecting fines since the proceeds are not earmarked for the courts.

In addition, because so many criminal offenders are poor, not only is it difficult for them to pay fines, but they might commit additional illegal acts to acquire the necessary funds. Furthermore, reliance on fines as an alternative to incarceration might enable the affluent to "buy" their way out of jail with little discomfort while the poor would have to serve time. Finally, in cases in which a poor offender actually can pay, payment might be most burdensome to his or her family, who would suffer the loss of bare necessities.

Unlike in the United States, in Europe fines are extensively imposed and strongly enforced. They are normally the sole sanction for a wide range of crimes, with amounts geared to the severity of the offense and the resources of the offender. To deal with the concern that fines exact a heavier toll on the poor than on the wealthy, Sweden and the former West Germany developed the "day fine." Under this system, the fines levied are adjusted to take into account the differing economic circumstances of offenders who have committed the same crime.

Currently, Arizona, Connecticut, Iowa, and Oregon are experimenting with the day fine concept, but it is too early to judge whether the system will work in the United States. To some critics, the system may punish wealthy people more severely than poorer people by imposing larger fines for the same offense. From this perspective, affluent people are receiving extra punishment simply because they and their families have been more successful in the American economic system. The debate over which system of fines is fairest—equal or adjusted amounts of money—is new and still developing.

Installment plans are increasingly being used to insure the payment of fines.

Restitution

In its simplest form, **restitution** is repayment by an offender to a victim who has suffered financial loss or physical harm from the crime. In the Middle Ages, restitution was a common way to settle a criminal case: The offender was ordered to pay the victim or do the victim's work. The growth of the modern state saw the decline of such punishments based on "private" arrangements between offender and victim. Instead, the state prosecuted offenders, and punishments focused on the wrong the offender had done to society.

Yet victim restitution has remained a part of the U.S. criminal justice system, though largely unpublicized. In many instances, restitution derives from informal agreements between law enforcement officials and offenders developed at the police station, during plea bargaining, or in the prosecutor's sentence recommendations. Only since the late 1970s, however, has restitution been institutionalized in many jurisdictions, usually as one of the conditions of probation. As with fines, convicted offenders have differing abilities to pay restitution, and the conditions inevitably fall more harshly on less affluent offenders who cannot easily pay. Someone who has the "good fortune" to be victimized by an affluent criminal offender may receive full compensation while someone victimized by a poor offender may never receive a penny.

restitution
Repayment by an offender to a victim who has suffered financial loss or physical harm from the crime.

forfeiture
Seizure by the government of property and other assets derived from or used in criminal activity.

Forfeiture

With the passage of two acts in 1970—the Racketeer Influence and Corrupt Organizations Act (RICO) and the Continuing Criminal Enterprise Act (CCE), Congress resurrected forfeiture, a criminal sanction not used in the United States since the American Revolution. By amending these laws in 1984 and 1986, Congress improved procedures for implementing forfeitures.[12] Similar laws are now found in most states, particularly with respect to controlled substances and organized crime.

Basically, **forfeiture** entails seizure by the government of property and other assets derived from or used in criminal activity. Forfeiture proceedings take civil or criminal forms. Under civil forfeiture, property utilized in criminal activity (contraband, equipment to manufacture illegal drugs, automobiles) can be seized without a finding of guilt. Criminal forfeiture is a punishment imposed as a result of conviction that requires the offender to relinquish various assets related to the crime.

From 1985 to 1990, an estimated $1 billion worth of assets was confiscated from drug dealers by state and federal officials.[13] Since then, concern has been raised about the excessive use of this sanction. In a 1993 opinion, the Supreme Court ruled that the Eighth Amendment's ban on excessive fines requires that a relationship exist between the seriousness of the offense and the value of the property that is forfeited.[14] Such a decision places limits on the government's ability to seize property and invites the judiciary to monitor the government's forfeiture activities when they are challenged by convicted offenders.

INTERMEDIATE SANCTIONS ADMINISTERED IN THE COMMUNITY

Home Confinement

home confinement
A sentence requiring the convicted offender to remain at home during specified periods.

With the increase in prison crowding and advances in technological innovations that provide for electronic monitoring, **home confinement**, whereby convicted offenders must remain at home during specified periods, has gained new attention. Offenders may also face other restrictions, such as the usual probation rules against alcohol and drugs, as well as strictly monitored curfews and check-in times. Some offenders are allowed to go to a place of employment, education, or treatment during the day but must return home by a certain hour. The supervising community corrections personnel may telephone offenders' homes at various times of the day and night to speak personally with offenders to ensure that they are complying. Home confinement has the advantage of flexibility, since it can be used as a sole sanction or in combination with other penalties, at almost any point in the criminal justice process: during the pretrial period, after a short term in jail or prison, or as a condition of probation or parole.[15] In addition, home confinement relieves the government of responsibility for providing food, clothing, and housing for the offender, as it must do in prisons.

The development of electronic monitoring equipment makes home confinement a viable sentencing option.[16] Two basic types of electronic devices are now in use. The first is a continuously signaling transmitter that is attached to the probationer, along with a receiver-dialer that is attached to the probationer's home telephone. When the signal stops, the dialer notifies a central monitoring station that the offender is not in the house. The second device is a computer programmed to telephone the probationer randomly or at specific times. The offender has a certain number of minutes to answer the phone and to verify that he or she is indeed the person under supervision.[17]

Electronic monitoring is obviously much less expensive than imprisonment. Moreover, the state can reduce its expenses by charging the offender a daily fee to defray the cost. However, electronic monitoring has not yet been as widely adopted as might be expected. Probation departments have found that the devices are expensive and far from foolproof. Thirty-three states now have some type of permanent or experimental electronic monitoring, but only about 12,000 offenders are being monitored.[18] Of interest is the type of offender under electronic monitoring. As Figure 12.2 shows, major traffic and property crime offenders are the main groups being monitored, but a few probationers who have committed serious crimes are also included. Presumably, these offenders might otherwise have been costing the state much more as inmates.

Some critics claim that home confinement has merely widened the net of social control. In other words, offenders who in the past would not have been sent to prison but placed on "regular" probation are now placed under house arrest with its greater restrictions. As a result, rather than saving money and resources, home confinement actually applies more expensive corrections techniques to people who formerly would merely have been on probation. Other observers have pointed out, however, that with prisons full and increased numbers of high-risk offenders on probation, home confinement is a necessary shift in correctional policy to ensure that society is protected.

Despite favorable publicity, certain legal, technical, and correctional issues must be addressed before home confinement with electronic monitoring can become a standard sanction. First, some criminal justice scholars question its constitutionality, suggesting that it may violate the Fourth Amendment's protection against unreasonable searches and seizures. Here, the issue is the clash between the constitutional protection for reasonable expectations of privacy and the invasion of one's home by surveillance devices. Second, technical problems are still extensive. Third, failure rates may prove to be high. Being one's own warden is difficult, and visits by former crime associates and

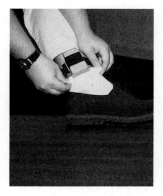

One type of electronic monitoring uses a transmitter attached to the offender. How might offenders "trick" this device?

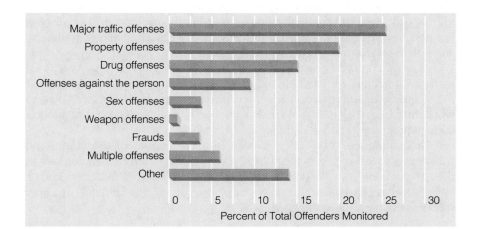

Major traffic offenses
Property offenses
Drug offenses
Offenses against the person
Sex offenses
Weapon offenses
Frauds
Multiple offenses
Other

0   5   10   15   20   25   30

Percent of Total Offenders Monitored

FIGURE 12.2
Electronically Monitored Offenders Categorized by Offense
Although most offenders currently being monitored have committed offenses for which prison is not the normal sanction, there are a few who have committed crimes that might have resulted in their incarceration.

SOURCE: Annesley K. Schmidt, "Electronic Monitoring of Offenders Increases," *Research in Action* (Washington, DC: National Institute of Justice, 1989), p. 2.

other enticements may become problematic for many offenders.[19] Because home monitoring keeps offenders in the same environment from where their crimes emerged, it may be difficult for some offenders to shake free from old values as they remain in daily contact with family members, neighbors, and friends. Tolerance levels for home confinement have not yet been researched, but some observers believe that four months of full-time monitoring is about the outside limit before a violation will occur. And because corrections personnel do not control the daily lives of offenders but merely check periodically on the offender's location during the day and night, offenders must face the temptations to drink, take drugs, or commit new crimes on their own.

Community Service

community service

A sentence requiring the offender to perform a certain amount of labor in the community.

In general terms, a **community service** sentence requires the offender to perform a certain amount of labor in the community. Community service may take many forms, such as working in a social service agency, cleaning up parks and roadsides, or assisting the poor. The sentence specifies the number of hours to be worked and usually requires supervision by a probation officer. Community service can be tailored to the skills and abilities of offenders. For example, less educated offenders may pick up litter along the highway while those with more schooling may teach reading in evening literacy programs. There is also symbolic value in the offender's effort to make reparation to the community offended by the crime.

Although community service has many supporters, some labor unions and workers criticize it for possibly taking jobs away from law-abiding citizens. In addition, some experts believe that if community service is the only sanction, it may represent too mild a punishment, especially for upper-class and white-collar criminals. Moreover, experts note that community service is appropriate only for those who have committed modest property crimes. It is not appropriate for violent offenders or others whose crimes deserve a more significant sanction.

Day Reporting Centers

day reporting center

Community correctional center to which the offender must report each day to carry out elements of the sentence.

Another option in a number of states are **day reporting centers**—community correctional centers to which the offender must report each day to carry out elements of the sentence.[20] They are designed to ensure that sentence employment and treatment requirements are followed and to increase the likelihood that probation supervision will be considered credible by offenders and the general public. Originally developed in Great Britain, the day reporting concept has been applied more extensively in the United States during the past five years. The Close-Up describes a day reporting center (called an alternative incarceration center) in Connecticut.

Most day reporting centers incorporate a variety of common correctional methods. In some, for example, offenders are required to spend eight hours in the facility or to report to the center for drug urine checks before going to work. In others with a rehabilitation component, drug and alcohol treatment, literacy programs, and job searches are carried out.

These programs have not yet been formally evaluated. In determining their success with regard to recidivism, it will be important to examine whom they are treating. If such centers are used only for selected offenders with a low risk of recidivism in the first place, then it will be difficult to know whether the centers are effective.

When it comes to working with criminal offenders, Peter Roesing doesn't have much use for pop psychology. Give him a convicted felon and he won't try to hypnotize him or lie him down on a leather couch to cure his errant behavior. He'll put him to work, put him in Alcoholics Anonymous, put him on a straight track. And if his client waivers off that track, Roesing will put him back in prison.

As case manager for the Torrington, Connecticut, Alternative Incarceration Center, Roesing is primarily responsible for offering people who would otherwise be serving prison time a chance at a new start.

"We're going to work on what got you here," he said recently, discussing the center's philosophy. "I don't care when a guy was potty trained, I don't care what his first words were. . . . That's chasing the rainbow. . . . What happens to these people here is they tip their lives upside down, and we provide them with some structure."

The clientele consists mostly of people charged with crimes serious enough to land them in prison but focuses on those either in pretrial stages or at the start of their sentence. That allows prisons to keep the most serious offenders who are serving long sentences.

Instead of lying in a prison cell or lifting weights—activities that have little chance of bringing about reform—clients at the center are given job and substance abuse counseling and required to find a place to live, maintain daily contact with center staff, submit to regular drug testing, and contribute a minimum of twenty-five hours to community service projects.

The center's yearly cost, per client, runs around $3,000. It is contracted through the state and is operated by Connecticut Halfway Houses, Inc., a private nonprofit organization, making it even more cost-effective to strained state coffers. Because the numbers are kept low (thirty-six clients) and terms are held to six months, a more personal approach in dealing with the clients is possible.

Clients are not treated at the center as if they were at a summer camp. One offender asked to go to Niagara Falls to get married, and his request was quickly rejected.

"I told him, 'You wouldn't ask the warden to do that if you were in jail,'" Roesing said. "You can't give them too many breaks. It may seem hardhearted, but that's what this is all about. I firmly believe that the attitude has to be positive."

"The atmosphere in prison is punitive; it's not correctional at all," Roesing said. " I firmly believe that the attitude has to be positive. They have to believe that something good can happen to them."

SOURCE: Adapted from David Howard, "Reform Is Key in Structuring Lives of Criminals," *Register Citizen* (Litchfield, CT), 17 August 1991.

Intensive Probation Supervision (IPS)

Research findings indicate that a small core of high-risk offenders commits a disproportionate amount of crime. Various localities have developed probation programs to intensively supervise such offenders.[21] **Intensive probation supervision** uses probation as an intermediate form of punishment by imposing conditions of strict reporting to a probation officer with a limited caseload. The theory is that daily contact between the probationer and officer may cut rearrest rates and permit offenders who might otherwise go to prison to live in the community. Offenders have incentives to obey rules knowing that they must meet with their probation officer daily and in some cases must speak with officers even more often. Additional restrictions often are imposed on offenders, as shown in Table 12.1.

IPS programs have been called "old-style" probation, because each officer has only twenty clients and has frequent face-to-face contact. The goal is to place high-risk offenders in the community instead of in prison and thereby

intensive probation supervision
Probation granted under conditions of strict reporting to a probation officer with a limited caseload.

TABLE 12.1

Key Features of Selected IPS Programs in Thirty-One States IPS entails more than daily contacts with a probation officer; twenty-three other restrictions are often imposed. Given a choice, would you prefer IPS or a short prison term?

SOURCE: James M. Byrne, Arthur I. Lurigio, and Christopher Baird, "The Effectiveness of the New Intensive Supervision Programs," *Research in Corrections* 2 (September 1989), p. 16.

Program Feature	Number of States Using Feature	Percentage of IPS Programs with Feature
Curfew/house arrest	25	80.6%
Electronic monitoring	6	19.3
Mandatory (high needs) referrals/special conditions	22	70.9
Team supervision	18	58.1
Drug monitoring	27	87.1
Alcohol monitoring	27	87.1
Community service	21	67.7
Probation fees	13	41.9
Split sentence/shock incarceration	22	70.9
Community sponsors	4	12.9
Restitution	21	67.7
Objective risk assessment	30	96.7
Objective needs assessment	29	93.5

save money. Questions have been raised, however, about how much difference constant surveillance can make to probationers with numerous problems. Such offenders frequently need help to secure employment, counseling to deal with emotional and family situations, and a variety of supports to avoid drug or alcohol problems that may have contributed to their criminal behavior. Frequent IPS contacts is no magic wand against everyday problems.

A Georgia program requires probationers to meet with a probation officer five times a week, to provide 132 hours of community service work, and (except in unusual cases) to abide by a 10 P.M. curfew. The standards are enforced by pairs of probation and surveillance officers, supervising twenty-five probationers. Evaluation of the Georgia program suggests that it has reduced the flow of offenders to prison and that the cost of intensive supervision, although higher than that of regular probation, is much less than the cost of prison. Recidivism rates are lower for those under intensive supervision than for either regular probationers or those released from prison on parole.[22] However, IPS might make little difference for people who are driven by their addictions to procure and use illegal drugs—such as the individual appearing before the Miami drug court, as described at the beginning of the chapter.

IPS has become popular among probation administrators, judges, and prosecutors, and many states have instituted programs. Most require a specific number of monthly contacts with officers, performance of community service, curfews, drug and alcohol abuse testing, and referral to appropriate job training, education, or treatment programs.

Observers have warned that IPS is not a "cure" for the rising costs and other problems facing corrections systems. IPS can also increase the number of offenders sent to prison. Preliminary evidence suggests that as caseloads were reduced, recidivism increased. A larger number of probationers were sent to prison because officers were in a position to more easily detect violations.[23] The fewer the probationers assigned to a particular officer, the more time that officer has to check up on each offender.

Interestingly, given the option of serving prison terms or participating in IPS, many offenders have chosen prison. In New Jersey, 15 percent of offenders withdrew their applications for IPS once they learned the conditions and requirements. Similarly, when offenders in Marion County, Oregon, were asked if they would participate in IPS, one-third chose prison.[24] Apparently, some offenders would rather spend a short time in prison, where conditions differ little from their accustomed life, than spend a longer period under demanding restrictions in the community. IPS does not represent freedom to these offenders since it is so intrusive and the risk of revocation is perceived as high.

Despite problems and continuing questions about its effectiveness, IPS has rejuvenated probation. Some of the most effective offender supervision is being carried out by these programs.[25] As we noted in our discussion of regular probation, within reasonable limits, the size of a probation officer's caseload is often less important for preventing recidivism than the quality of supervision and assistance provided to probationers. If IPS is properly implemented, it may improve the quality of supervision and services that foster success for more kinds of offenders.

INTERMEDIATE SANCTIONS ADMINISTERED IN INSTITUTIONS FOLLOWED BY COMMUNITY SUPERVISION

Boot Camps

Among the most publicized intermediate sanctions are the boot camps now operating in thirty states[26] (see Figure 12.3). Those programs vary, but all are based on the belief that young offenders can be "shocked" out of their criminal ways. **Boot camps** put offenders through a physical regimen designed to develop discipline and respect for authority. Like the Marine Corps, most programs emphasize a spit-and-polish environment and keep the offenders in a disciplined and demanding routine that seeks ultimately to build self-esteem. Most camps also include education, job training programs, and other rehabilitative services. On successful completion of the program, offenders are released to the community and remain under some form of probation supervision.

Based on initial evaluations of boot camp programs, the initial optimism about such approaches has begun to fade. Critics suggest that the emphasis on physical training ignores young offenders' real problems. Some also point

boot camp

Program that puts offenders through a physical regimen designed to develop discipline and respect for authority.

FIGURE 12.3
Boot Camp Programs in the United States
Boot camps for young offenders have rapidly spread across the country. The concept has attracted much public and legislative support even though research suggests it may not be as successful as the public imagines.
SOURCE: U.S. Department of Justice, *National Institute of Justice Journal* (November 1993), p. 21.

States with programs
States planning or considering programs
States with no programs

Boot camps for young offenders have received much publicity since they were first introduced in the 1980s. Advocates believe that boot camps build self-esteem and discipline. Skeptics wonder if this is another correctional panacea.

out that, like the military, shock incarceration builds esprit de corps and solidarity, characteristics that have the potential for improving the leadership qualities of the young offender and therefore actually enhancing a criminal career.[27] In addition, a study of offenders released from Louisiana boot camps revealed that 37 percent were arrested at least once during their first year of freedom, compared to 25.7 percent of parolees.[28] Some advocates counter that boot camps build the self-esteem among offenders necessary to keep them out of future trouble. This point of view is supported by a study of shock incarceration in Louisiana in which it was determined that those completing the course left the boot camp with more positive attitudes about their experience and society in general than those who were incarcerated in prison.[29] Defenders of the boot camps argue that the camps are accomplishing their goals, but that education and job training services are lacking back in their communities. Because boot camps are very popular with members of the public who imagine that strict discipline and harsh conditions will instill young offenders with positive attributes, such camps are likely to continue operating whether or not they are more effective than probation.

IMPLEMENTING INTERMEDIATE SANCTIONS

Although the use of intermediate sanctions is spreading rapidly across the country, three major questions have emerged. First, which agencies should implement the sanctions? Second, which offenders should be admitted to these programs? And third, will the "community corrections net" widen as a result of these policies so that intermediate sanctions are applied to those who would receive simple probation rather than those who would otherwise be sent to prison?

Administrative politics is an ongoing factor in any public service organization, and corrections is no exception. In many states, agencies compete for the additional funding needed to run the programs. It remains to be seen whether the traditional agencies of community corrections, such as probation offices, will receive the funding, or whether the new programs will be contracted out to nonprofit organizations. Probation organizations argue that they know the field, have the experienced staff, and—given the additional resources—could do an excellent job. They correctly point out that a large proportion of offenders sentenced to intermediate sanctions are also on probation. Critics of probation argue that these state agencies are stuck in a traditional mindset and are unreceptive to innovation. They claim that probation agencies give too much attention to traditional supervision and will not become sufficiently involved in helping clients solve problems.

Regarding the type of offender who should be given an intermediate sanction, one school of thought emphasizes the seriousness of the offense, another the problems of the offender. If offenders are categorized by offense seriousness, they may be given such close supervision that they are unable to abide by the sentence. For example, sanctions for serious offenders may accumulate to include probation, drug testing, addiction treatment, and home confinement.[30] As the number of conditions is increased, even the most willing probationer finds it hard to fulfill every one of them.

Some agencies want to accept into their intermediate sanctions program only those offenders who *will* succeed. These agencies are concerned about their success ratio, especially because of threats to future funding if the agencies do not reduce recidivism. Critics point out that this strategy leads to "creaming"—taking the most promising offenders and leaving those with worse problems to traditional sanctions.

"Net widening" describes a process in which the new sanction increases rather than reduces the control over offenders' lives. This can occur when a judge imposes a *more* intrusive sanction than usual. For example, rather than merely giving an offender probation, the judge might also require that the offender perform community service. Critics of intermediate sanctions argue that they have created several types of such "nets":

- *Wider nets.* Reforms increase the proportion of individuals in society whose behavior is regulated or controlled by the state.
- *Stronger nets.* Reforms augment the state's capacity to control individuals with more intensive interventions.
- *Different nets.* Reforms transfer jurisdictional authority from one agency or control system to another.[31]

If these are indeed the effects, intermediate sanctions will not achieve the goal of reducing prison overcrowding.

COMMUNITY CORRECTIONS IN THE 1990S

In 1980, 1.4 million Americans were under community corrections; by 1990, this figure had grown to 3.2 million, an increase of more than 130 percent. Yet, despite its tremendous growth, community corrections often lacks public support. Intermediate sanctions and other forms of community corrections suffer from an image of being "soft on crime." As a result, some localities provide resources not for community corrections, but for traditional criminal justice and human services agencies.

Community corrections is also faced with the reality that offenders today require closer supervision than those formerly placed on probation.[32] The crimes, criminal records, and drug problems of contemporary offenders are often worse than those of lawbreakers in earlier eras. In New York, for example,

77 percent of probationers are convicted felons, and about a third have been found guilty of violent crimes. Yet, as Joan Petersilia points out, these people are supervised by officials whose caseloads number in the hundreds.[33] Obviously, such officials cannot provide effective supervision and services to all of their probationers.

Greater caseload pressures are being placed on community corrections during this last decade of the twentieth century. With responsibility for about three-fourths of all offenders under correctional supervision, probation and community corrections need an infusion of resources. Public support is essential, but it will be forthcoming only if citizens believe that offenders are being given appropriate punishments. Citizens must recognize that policies designed to punish offenders in the community yield not mere "slaps on the wrists" but meaningful sanctions, even while these policies allow offenders to retain and reforge their ties to their families and society. As indicated by the fact that many offenders would rather go to prison than be assigned to intensive probation supervision, community corrections can be serious punishment. Yet it can also simultaneously promote mechanisms for reintegration, education programs, and other tools to combat recidivism.

SUMMARY

Community supervision has long been a major element of U.S. corrections. Its basic forms are probation, intermediate sanctions, and parole. During the 1960s and 1970s, the concept of community corrections attracted the attention of penologists and policymakers. This model emphasizes the reintegration of the offender into society. In the more conservative 1980s, much of the fervor over community corrections waned. Today, community corrections focuses less on the provision of services to offenders and more on surveillance. Because of prison overcrowding and the high costs of incarceration, however, there is renewed interest in less expensive approaches to punishment.

Intermediate sanctions, which incorporate one or more punishments, are more restrictive than probation but less restrictive than prison. Some intermediate sanctions are implemented by the courts, while others are administered by probation offices or by correctional agencies. The main forms of intermediate sanctions are shock incarceration, fines, restitution, community service, forfeiture, day reporting centers, home confinement, intensive supervision, and boot camps. Electronic monitoring is used as a part of many of these sanctions. Ongoing evaluation research has not yet proven the effectiveness of intermediate sanctions. However, the number of programs to implement these punishments is expanding throughout the country as the criminal justice system seeks to cope with the overall increase in the number of offenders.

Think back to the example of the Miami drug court at the beginning of the chapter. The initial description of the court may have made it appear that criminals were simply being released to community without being punished. If we think of corrections as having multiple goals, including punishment *and* reintegration into the community, then probation and other forms of community sanctions make sense. Alternatively, even if we think of criminal sanctions as entirely for retribution, the existence of community-based options permit us to consider whether this goal can be achieved without the great expense of incarceration. The debate as to whether it is desirable to keep offenders among us in the community or whether this approach makes the most sense for certain categories of offenders will undoubtedly continue.

QUESTIONS FOR REVIEW

1. What is the nature of probation, and how is it organized?
2. What is the purpose of intermediate sanctions?
3. What are the primary forms of intermediate sanctions?
4. Why do some offenders prefer imprisonment to intensive probation supervision?
5. What problems do policymakers continue to face as they consider the possibility of expanding intermediate sanctions?

NOTES

1. Melinda Buck, "Kicking the Prison Habit," *Newsweek*, 14 June 1993, pp. 32, 36.
2. U.S. Department of Justice, Bureau of Justice Statistics, *Bulletin* (September 1994), p. 4.
3. Randall Guynes, "Difficult Clients, Large Caseloads, Plague Probation, Parole Agencies," *Research in Action* (Washington, DC: National Institute of Justice, 1988).
4. Todd Clear and Vincent O'Leary, *Controlling the Offender in the Community* (Lexington, MA: Lexington Books, 1983), pp. 77–100.
5. *New York Times*, 19 June 1990, p. A16.
6. *Mempa* v. *Rhay*, 389 U.S. 128 (1967).
7. *Gagnon* v. *Scarpelli*, 411 U.S. 778 (1973).
8. Quoted in Kevin Krajick, "Probation: The Original Community Program," *Corrections Magazine* 6 (December 1980), p. 7.
9. Norval Morris and Michael Tonry, *Between Prison and Probation: Intermediate Punishments in a Rational Sentencing System* (New York: Oxford University Press, 1990), p. 3.
10. Sally T. Hillsman, Joyce L. Sichel, and Barry Mahoney, *Fines in Sentencing* (New York: Vera Institute of Justice, 1983).
11. George F. Cole, Barry Mahoney, Roger Hanson, and Marlene Thornton, *Attitudes and Practices of Trial-Court Judges Toward the Use of Fines* (Denver: Institute for Court Management, 1987).
12. Karla R. Spaulding, "'Hit Them Where It Hurts': RICO Criminal Forfeitures and White Collar Crime," *Journal of Criminal Law and Criminology* 80 (1989), p. 197.
13. *New York Times*, 16 July, 1990.
14. *Austin* v. *U.S.*, 61 USLW 4811 (1993).
15. Marc Renzema, "Home Confinement Programs: Development, Implementation, and Impact," *Smart Sentencing: The Emergence of Intermediate Sanctions*, ed. James M. Byrne, Arthur J. Lurigio, and Joan Petersilia (Newbury Park, CA: Sage, 1992), p. 41.
16. Terry L. Baumer and Robert I. Mendelsohn, "Electronically Monitoring Home Confinement: Does It Work," in *Smart Sentencing*, p. 54.
17. Annesley K. Schmidt, "Electronic Monitoring of Offenders Increases," *Research in Action* (Washington, DC: National Institute of Justice, 1989).
18. Renzema, "Home Confinement Programs," p. 41.
19. Terry L. Baumer, Michael G. Maxfield, and Robert I. Mendelsohn, "A Comparative Analysis of Three Electronically Monitored Home Detention Programs," *Justice Quarterly* 10 (March 1993), p. 121.
20. Jack McDevitt and Robyn Miliano, "Day Reporting Centers: An Innovative Concept in Intermediate Sanctions," in *Smart Sentencing*, p. 152. Day

reporting centers are often called "probation centers" or "alternative incarceration centers."

21. See *Crime and Delinquency* 36 (January 1990), an entire issue devoted to intensive probation supervision.

22. Billie S. Erwin and Lawrence A. Bennett, "New Dimensions in Probation: Georgia's Experience with Intensive Probation Supervision," *Research in Brief*, National Institute of Justice (Washington, DC: Government Printing Office, 1987); Joan Petersilia, *Expanding Options for Criminal Sentences* (Santa Monica, CA: Rand Corporation, 1987), pp. 10–32.

23. Joan Petersilia and Susan Turner, *Intensive Supervision for High-Risk Probationers: Findings from Three California Experiments* (Santa Monica, CA: Rand Corporation, 1990).

24. Joan Petersilia, "When Probation Becomes More Dreaded Than Prison," *Federal Probation* (March 1990), p. 24.

25. Todd Clear and Patricia L. Hardyman, "The New Intensive Supervision Movement," *Crime and Delinquency* 36 (January 1990), p. 42.

26. U.S. Department of Justice, National Institute of Justice, *Boot Camp for Adult & Juvenile Offenders* (Washington, DC: Government Printing Office, 1994).

27. *New York Times*, 4 March 1988, pp. B1, B4.

28. *Newsweek*, 21 February 1994, p. 26.

29. Doris Layton MacKenzie and James W. Shaw, "Inmate Adjustment and Change During Shock Incarceration: The Impact of Correctional Boot Camp Programs," *Justice Quarterly* 7 (March 1990), pp. 125–150.

30. Thomas Blomberg and Karen Lucken, "Intermediate Punishment and the Piling Up of Sanctions," *Criminal Justice: Law and Politics*, 6th ed., ed. George F. Cole (Belmont, CA: Wadsworth, 1993), p. 470.

31. James Austin and Barry Krisberg, "The Unmet Promise of Alternatives to Incarceration," *Crime and Delinquency* 28 (1982), pp. 374–409.

32. Petersilia and Turner, *Intensive Supervision Probation for High-Risk Offenders*.

33. Joan Petersilia, "Measuring the Performance of Community Corrections," *Performance Measures for the Criminal Justice System* (Washington, DC: Bureau of Justice Statistics, 1993), p. 61.

CHAPTER 13
Incarceration and Prison Society

PRISONERS AND GUARDS: CAPTIVES IN THE POWDERKEG

On Easter Sunday in 1993, a fight broke out in the recreation yard at the Southern Ohio Correctional Facility in Lucasville, a "supermax" prison reserved for the most violent and incorrigible offenders. Within minutes, the fight grew into a full-scale riot. Eight corrections officers were taken hostage by the 450 prisoners who barricaded themselves inside Cellblock L. The prisoners held their ground—and their hostages—for more than a week. During the uprising, prisoners murdered others whom they regarded as "snitches," and six inmate bodies were dumped into the recreation yard.

When the prisoners threatened to kill one of the hostages, a spokesperson for the state said it was "a standard threat they've been issuing." Shortly thereafter, correctional officer Robert Vallandingham was murdered. Another hostage told the media that the officer was murdered because the prisoners were angry that their threats were not being taken seriously. According to George Skatzes, an inmate who negotiated with authorities on behalf of his fel-low prisoners, "We are going to remain no matter what they put on us. . . . If we die, we die."[1] Eventually, the prisoners negotiated their surrender, the remaining hostages were released, and the state began prosecuting various prisoners on criminal charges stemming from the riot and murders.

Life behind bars receives brief public attention when prisons periodically erupt. However, prisons like Lucasville share many of the same problems and circumstances as many or even most other correctional institutions: racial conflict, gangs, allegations of brutality, restrictive policies, and inmate violence. The reason that outbursts are relatively infrequent is simply that most institutions manage to keep the lid on the cauldron.

In this chapter, we examine incarceration and prison society. We focus on such issues as the inmate's experience while living in prison and the corrections officer's experience while working in prison. We also discuss violence in prison and the structures, policies, and programs that may keep corrections institutions from boiling over. ★

GOALS OF INCARCERATION

CHAPTER QUESTIONS

What is the formal organization of a prison?

What is the role of correctional officers?

What are the rights of prisoners?

What is it like to be in prison?

What programs are available to prisoners?

American correctional institutions have always been more varied than one would gather from movies or novels. Typically, fictional depictions of prison life are set in the fortress "big house"—those maximum security prisons where the prisoners are tough and the guards are just as tough or tougher. Although big houses predominated in much of the country during the first half of the twentieth century, many prisons, especially in the South, did not conform to this model. There, racial segregation was maintained, prisoners were involved in farm labor, and the massive walled structures were not so common.

The typical big house of the 1940s and 1950s was a walled prison with large, tiered cell blocks, a yard, and shops and industries. The prisoners, averaging about 2,500 per institution, came from both urban and rural areas, were usually poor, and, outside the South, were predominantly white. The prison society was essentially isolated; access to visitors, mail, and other kinds of communication were restricted. Prisoners' days were strictly structured, with rules enforced by the guards. There was a basic division between inmates and staff; rank was observed and discipline maintained. In the big house, little in the way of treatment programs existed; custody was the primary goal.

During the 1960s and early 1970s, most penologists accepted the rehabilitation model of corrections. Many states built new facilities and converted others into "correctional institutions." Treatment programs administered by counselors and teachers became a major part of prison life, although the institutions actually continued to place their greatest emphasis on the custody goals of security, discipline, and order.

Since the 1970s, American prisons have undergone many changes. It is now difficult to find an institution that conforms exactly to the big-house model depicted in films and analyzed by such social scientists as Donald Clemmer and Gresham Sykes.[2] The characteristics of the inmate population has changed, with a major increase in the proportion of African-American and Hispanic inmates. There are more inmates from urban areas and more who have been convicted of drug-related and violent offenses. Former street gangs, often organized along racial lines, today regroup inside prisons and have raised the levels of violence in many institutions. Finally, with the rise of public employee unions, correctional officers have used collective bargaining to influence working conditions, safety procedures, and training.

As discussed in Chapter 11, the last two decades have produced a doubling of the number of persons held in prisons. This increase has led to greater tensions within overcrowded institutions. Although contemporary correctional administrators seek to provide humane incarceration, they must struggle with limited resources and cell space. Thus, the modern prison faces many of the difficult problems that confront other components of the criminal justice system: racial conflicts, legal issues, limited resources, and increasing populations. Despite these challenges, can prisons still achieve their objectives? The answer to this question depends, in part, on how we define the goals of incarceration.

It is natural to regard security as the dominant purpose of a prison, and the high walls, barbed-wire fences, searches, checkpoints, and inmate counts clearly serve this function. At the same time, modern correctional administrators pursue additional goals that shape prison policies and activities and help set the tone for prison life.

custodial model
A model of corrections that emphasizes security, discipline, and order.

Three models of incarceration have been prominent since the early 1940s: custodial, rehabilitation, and reintegration. Each summarizes the assumptions and characteristics associated with one style of institutional organization.

1. The **custodial model** is based on the assumption that prisoners have been incarcerated for the purposes of incapacitation, deterrence, or retribution. It emphasizes security, discipline, and order, subordinating the prisoner to the authority of the warden. Discipline is strict, and most aspects of behavior are regulated. This model was prevalent within corrections prior to World War II, and it dominates most maximum security institutions today.

rehabilitation model
A model of corrections that emphasizes the provision of treatment programs designed to reform offenders.

2. The **rehabilitation model**, developed in the 1950s, emphasizes the provision of treatment programs designed to reform the offender. According to this model, security and housekeeping activities are viewed primarily as preconditions for rehabilitative efforts. In line with the idea that all aspects of the organization should be directed toward rehabilitation, professional treatment specialists enjoy higher status than other employees. Since the rethinking of the rehabilitation goal in the 1970s, treatment programs still exist in most institutions, but very few prisons conform to this model.

reintegration model
A model of corrections that emphasizes the maintenance of offenders' ties to family and community as a method of reform, in recognition of the fact that they will be returning to the community.

3. The **reintegration model** is linked to the structures and goals of community corrections. This model emphasizes the maintenance of offenders' ties to family and community as a method of reform, in recognition of the fact that they will be returning to the community. Thus, incarceration is directed toward later reintegration into society. Prisons that have adopted the reintegration model gradually give inmates greater freedom and responsibility during their confinement, moving them to halfway houses or work release programs before releasing them to community supervision.

Although specific correctional institutions conform to each of these models, most prisons are mainly custodial. Nevertheless, treatment programs do exist, and because almost all inmates return to society at some point, even the most custodial institutions cannot neglect to prepare them for that move. In many correctional systems, regardless of the basic model, inmates spend the last portion of their sentence in a prerelease facility.

We ask a lot of our prisons. As Charles Logan notes, "We ask them to correct the incorrigible, rehabilitate the wretched, deter the determined, restrain the dangerous, and punish the wicked."[3] In light of such high and incompatible goals, not surprisingly, most prisons seem doomed to limited success.

PRISON ORGANIZATION

total institution
An institution that completely encapsulates the lives of those who work and live there, with one group controlling the lives of the other.

Some years ago, sociologist Erving Goffman argued that, like mental hospitals and monasteries, prisons are **total institutions**: They completely encapsulate the lives of those who work and live there, with one group controlling the lives of the other.[4] Whatever prisoners do or do not do begins and ends in the prison; every minute behind bars must be lived according to the institution's rules as enforced by the staff. Adding to the totality of the prison is a basic split between the large group of inmates who have very limited contact with the outside world and the small group of staff who supervise inmates within the prison walls. Staff members view inmates as secretive and untrustworthy, while inmates view staff as condescending and mean.

Although the total institution may have characterized the custodial big-house prison of the past, the contemporary prison is permeated by outside influences. Today's inmates have greater access to the outside world through television, radio, and telephone. The presence of racial and ethnic cliques discourages the development of a sense of inmate solidarity in opposition to the staff. Community advocacy groups and the courts have dented the total power of administrators by initiating reforms and forcing officials to respect prisoners' civil rights. All of these factors have limited the ability of wardens to completely control institutions.

The prison differs from almost every other institution or organization in modern society. Not only are its physical features different from those of most institutions, but it is a place where a group of persons devotes itself to managing a group of captives. Prisoners are required to live according to the dictates of their keepers, and their movements are sharply restricted. Unlike managers of other governmental agencies, prison managers must operate under several unique limitations:

- They cannot select their clients.
- They have little or no control over the release of their clients.
- They must deal with clients who are there involuntarily.
- They must rely on clients to do most of the work in the daily operation of the institution and to do so by coercion and without fair compensation for their work.
- They must depend on the maintenance of satisfactory relationships between clients and staff.

Given these unique characteristics, how should a prison be run? What rules should guide administrators? As we have seen, wardens and other key personnel are asked to perform a difficult task, one that requires skilled and dedicated managers.

THREE LINES OF COMMAND

Most prisons are expected to carry out a number of goals related to keeping (custody), using (employment), and serving (treatment) inmates. Because individual staff members are not equipped to perform all these functions, there are separate organizational lines of command for the groups of employees that fulfill these different tasks. One group is charged with maintaining custody over the prisoners, another group supervises them in their work activities, and a third group attempts to treat them.

The custodial employees are the most numerous. They are normally organized along military lines, from warden to captain to officer, with corresponding pay differentials down the chain of command. The professional personnel associated with the employment and treatment functions, such as industry supervisors, clinicians, and teachers, are not part of the custodial structure and have little in common with its staff. All employees are responsible to the warden, but the treatment personnel and the civilian supervisors of the workshops have their own salary scales and titles. The formal organization of staff responsibilities in a typical prison for adults is shown in Figure 13.1.

As a result of multiple goals and separate employee lines of command, the administration of correctional institutions often is filled with conflict and ambiguity. Conflicts between different segments of staff as well as between inmates and staff provide administrators with significant challenges.

FIGURE 13.1

Formal Organization of a Prison for Adult Felons
Prison staff are divided into various sections consistent with the goals of the organization; however, employees associated with custody are the most numerous.

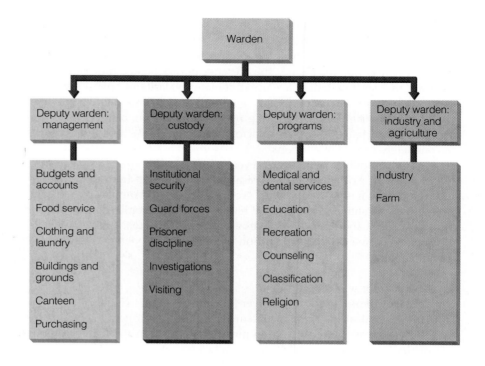

THE LIMITS OF POWER

Much of the public believes that prisons are operated in an authoritarian manner in which correctional officers *give* orders and inmates *follow* orders. The officers have a monopoly on the legal means of coercion and can be backed up by the state police and National Guard if necessary. Why, then, should questions arise about how prisons are run?

Imagine a prison society made up of hostile and uncooperative captives ruled by force, in which prisoners could be legally isolated from one another, physically abused until they cooperate, and put under continuous surveillance. Theoretically, such a society is possible. In reality, however, officers have limited power, because many prisoners have little to lose by misbehaving and unarmed officers have only limited ability to force compliance with rules. Thus, officers must cultivate the inmate's cooperation by developing rapport with the offenders and by offering incentives, such as overlooking minor infractions of rules.

MAINTAINING CONTROL

As Gresham Sykes has noted, physical coercion is an inefficient way to make people carry out complex tasks.[5] Prison efficiency is further diminished by the realities of the usual one-to-forty officer-to-inmate ratio and the potential danger of the situation. Such ratios increase the potential for inmate retaliation against officers who inspire their distrust. Thus, correctional officers' ability to threaten the use of physical force is limited. Physical force normally can be applied only for self-defense or the protection of officers' and inmates' safety, and not simply to make prisoners shut up and obey orders.

Because there are few permissible situations for the use of physical coercion, corrections officials must gain compliance and maintain control through the use of limited rewards and punishments. For example, privileges such as good-time allowances, choice job assignments, and favorable parole reports may be offered in exchange for obedience. The reward system is defective, however, because most privileges are given to the inmate at the start of the sentence and are taken away only if rules are broken. Few additional rewards can be granted for progress or exceptional behavior, although a desired work assignment or transfer to the honor cell block will induce some prisoners to maintain good behavior.

Punishments include denial of future good-time credits, loss of television or other privileges, and transfer to "administrative segregation" cells for major infractions or consistent misbehavior. One problem is that the punishments for breaking rules do not represent a great departure from the prisoners' usual status. Because they are already deprived of many freedoms and valued goods—heterosexual relations, money, choice of clothing, and so on—inmates have little else left to lose. The punishment of not being allowed to attend a recreational period may not carry much weight. Moreover, there are legal limitations on what types of punishments can be imposed.

One way that correctional officers obtain inmates' cooperation is through the types of exchange relationships described in earlier chapters. The key officials in these exchanges are the housing unit officers, who work closely with the prisoners throughout the day in the cell block, workshop, or recreation area. Although the formal rules require a social distance between officers and inmates, physical closeness makes them aware that each is dependent on the other. The officers need the cooperation of the prisoners so that they will look good to their superiors, and the inmates depend on the guards to relax the rules or occasionally look the other way. However, such relationships pose risks of blackmail to careless officers. For example, prisoners may solicit favors from officers in exchange for cooperation and then threaten to report the officer for overlooking small infractions if the officer does not now agree to overlook larger ones. In some institutions, officers have even been induced into smuggling drugs and weapons into the prison.

Some officials also try to use inmate leaders to control other convicts. Inmate leaders have been "tested" over time so that they are neither pushed around by other inmates nor distrusted as stool pigeons. Because staff can also rely on them, they serve as the essential communications link between the staff and inmates. By being able to acquire inside information and access to higher officials, they command respect from other prisoners and are granted special privileges and jobs by officials. In turn, they distribute these benefits to other prisoners, thus bolstering their own influence within the society. In practice, however, prison administrators of the big-house era were more successful at using inmate leaders to maintain order than are today's administrators.

A QUESTION OF ETHICS

After three years of daily contact, correctional officer Bill MacLeod and inmate Jack Douglas knew each other very well. They were both devoted to the Red Sox and the Celtics. Throughout the year, they would chat about their teams' fortunes and futures. MacLeod got to know and like Douglas, who was serving a three- to five-year sentence. They were about the same age and had come from similar backgrounds. Why they were now on opposite sides of the bars was something that MacLeod could not figure out.

One day Douglas told MacLeod he needed money because he had lost a bet gambling on the Celtics. Douglas said that his wife would send him the money. The problem was that it couldn't come through the prison mail to him in cash. A check or money order would have to go into his commissary account.

"The guy wants cash. If he doesn't get it I'm dead," said Douglas. "Could you bring it in for me? She'll mail the money to you at home. You could just drop the envelope on my bed."

"You know the rules. No gambling and no money," said MacLeod.

"But I'm scared shitless," said Douglas. "It won't be any big deal for you and it will make all the difference for me. Come on, we've gotten along well all these years. You're different from those other officers."

What should MacLeod do? Is it likely to be a one-time occurrence with Douglas? What if MacLeod's sergeant finds out? What if other inmates learn about it?

Prison wardens are often viewed as aloof. However, a "hands-on" style of management is the most effective way of learning what concerns inmates and staff so as to nip problems in the bud.

In most of today's institutions, prisoners are divided by race, ethnicity, age, and gang affiliation, so that no single leadership structure exists.

DOES MANAGEMENT MATTER?

One of the amazing facts about prisons is that most of the time they work. Order is maintained and activities are carried out, despite the fact that the administrative policies and practices at various prisons can differ widely. Although the organizational structure of most prisons takes a similar bureaucratic form, management styles vary.

John DiIulio studied the management of selected prisons in Texas, California, and Michigan.[6] He found differences that were related to the leadership philosophy, political environment, and administrative style of individual wardens. DiIulio argues that the quality of prison life as measured by levels of order, amenity, and service is mainly a function of the management. He believes that prisons can be governed, violence can be minimized, and services can be provided to the inmates if proper leadership is provided by correctional managers.

DiIulio suggests that prison systems perform well if managers work competently with the political and other pressures that make for administrative uncertainty and instability. In particular, he points to the success of those wardens whose management style has been characterized as "management by walking around." This means that wardens must be "hands-on" and proactive, paying close attention to details and not waiting for problems to arise. They must know what is going on inside, yet also recognize the need for outside support. In short, they are strangers neither in the cell blocks nor in the aisles of the state legislature.[7]

CORRECTIONAL OFFICERS

As discussed previously, a prison is supposed to simultaneously keep, use, and serve its inmates. The achievement of these goals depends heavily on the performance of its correctional officers. Their job isn't easy. Not only do they work long, difficult hours with a hostile client population, but their superiors expect them to do so with few resources or punishments at their disposal. Most of what they are expected to do must be accomplished by gaining and keeping the cooperation of the prisoners.

The role of the correctional officer has changed since the 1960s. No longer merely responsible for "guarding," today's officers must carry out a variety of tasks including counseling, supervising, protecting, and processing those under their care. The range of tasks creates conflict about their roles: Are they law enforcers or counselors? Does their relationship with prisoners in one role defeat their ability to perform effectively in the other role? Officers are held responsible both for maintaining order and for cooperating with treatment personnel by counseling inmates and assuming an understanding attitude. They are expected to use discretion, yet somehow to behave in both a custodial and therapeutic manner. As Donald Cressey notes, "If they enforce the rules, they risk being evaluated as 'rigid'; on the other hand, if they do not enforce the rules and so jeopardize institutional security or order, they are not 'doing their job.'"[8]

Few people start out intending to become corrections officers. The work generally is regarded as boring, the pay as low, and advancement as unusual. However, as studies have shown, people are attracted to the job because it is part of the civil service and is therefore secure. In addition, prisons offer better employment options than other employers in the rural areas where most prisons are located. Because officers are recruited locally, most are rural and white, whereas the majority of prisoners frequently come from urban areas, and many are African-American or Hispanic.

As the prison population has grown, so has the number of correctional officers. Salaries have increased as well, so that now the average annual entry-level pay runs between $15,000 in some southern and rural states to $30,000 in states such as New York, Minnesota, and California.[9] Special efforts have been made to recruit women and minorities. Women are no longer restricted to working with female offenders, and the number of correctional officers from minority groups has increased dramatically.

Increasing numbers of women have become correctional officers in prisons for males. What are the pluses and minuses of having women in these roles?

PRISON SOCIETY

In many ways, an American maximum security prison hosts a world and culture unto itself. As the Close-Up box reveals, prisoners form a society with its own traditions, norms, and leadership structure. Some members may choose to associate with only a few close friends while others form cliques along racial or "professional" lines. Still others may be the politicians of the convict society, attempting to represent convict interests and distribute valued goods in return for support.

As in any society, the convict world has certain norms and values. Often described as the **inmate code**, the values and norms of prison society help to define the inmate's image of the model prisoner and to emphasize the solidarity of inmates against the staff. For example, inmates should never inform on one another, pry into one another's affairs, run off at the mouth, or put another inmate on the spot. They must be tough and not trust the officers or the principles for which the guards stand. Further, guards are "hacks" or "screws"; the officials are wrong and the prisoners are right.

Some sociologists believe that the code emerges from within the institution as a way to lessen the pain of imprisonment; others believe that it is part of the criminal subculture that prisoners bring with them. The inmate who follows the code can be expected to enjoy a certain amount of admiration from other inmates as a "right guy" or a "real man." Those who break the code are labeled "rat" or "punk" and will probably spend their prison life at the bottom of the convict social structure, alienated from the rest of the population and targeted for abuse.[10]

inmate code
The values and norms of prison society that define the inmate's image of the model prisoner and emphasize the solidarity of inmates against the staff.

305

One Man's Walk Through Atlanta's Jungle

Michael G. Santos

I was not expecting to receive the Southern hospitality for which Atlanta is famous when the bus turned into the penitentiary's large, circular drive, but neither did I expect to see a dozen uniformed prison guards—all carrying machine guns—surround the bus when it stopped. A month in transit already had passed by the time we made it to the U.S. Penitentiary in Atlanta, the institution that would hold me (along with over 2,000 other felons) until either we were transferred to other prisons, we were released, or we were dead.

I left the jail in Tacoma, Washington on the first of August, but I didn't see the huge gray walls that surround USP Atlanta until the first of September. That month was spent in a bus operated by the U.S. Marshal Service as it moved across the country, picking up federal prisoners in local jails and dropping them off at various Bureau of Prison facilities.

As I crossed the country, I listened to tales from numerous prisoners who sat beside me on the bus. There wasn't much to discuss except what was to come. Each of us was chained at the hands and feet. There were neither magazines to read nor was there music playing. Mostly people spoke about a riot that had taken place behind USP Atlanta's walls a few months earlier. A lot of the men had been to prison before, and Atlanta would be nothing new. Those prisoners either were talking about reuniting with old friends, explaining prison routine, or sitting like stone-cold statues waiting for what was to come. I'd never been confined before, so it was hard to tune out the stories that others were telling. While I was listening, though, I re-member telling myself that I *would* survive this sentence. No matter what it took, I *would* survive.

I was in my early 20s, younger than perhaps every other prisoner on the bus. Pimples spotted my face as I began my term, but I was certain my black hair would be white by the time I finished. I had been sentenced to 45 years by a U.S. District Court Judge in Tacoma on charges related to cocaine trafficking. I was expected to serve close to 30 years before release. It was hard then—just as it is hard now—to believe the sentence is real. The best thing I could do, I reasoned, was to stay to myself. I'd heard the same rumors that every suburban kid hears about prison. I was anxious about what was to come, but I was determined to make it out alive and with my mind intact. It was now time to *begin*!

After the bus stopped, the guards began calling us off by last name and prison number. It is not easy walking with a 12-inch chain connected to each ankle, and wrists bound to a chain that runs around the waist, but when my name was called, I managed to wobble through the bus's aisle, hop down the steps, then begin the long march up the stairs leading to the fortress. As I was moving to the prison's doors, I remember glancing over my shoulder, knowing it would be the last time I'd see the world from the outside of prison walls for a long time.

Once inside the institution, the guards began unlocking my chains. About fifty other prisoners arrived with me that day, so the guards had plenty of chains to unlock, but their work didn't stop there. They also had to squeeze us through the dehumanizing admissions machine. The machine begins with photographs, fingerprints, and interrogations. Then comes the worst part, the strip search, where each prisoner stands before a prison official, naked, and responds to the scream: "Lift up your arms in the air! Let me see the back of your hands! Run your fingers through your hair! Open

A single, overriding inmate code may not exist in contemporary institutions. Instead, race has become a key variable dividing convict society. In an apparent reflection of tensions throughout American society, many prisons now have racially motivated violence, organizations based on race, and voluntary segregation of inmates by race whenever possible (for example, in recreation areas and dining halls).

In the absence of a single code accepted by the entire population, administrators find their task more difficult. They must be aware of the varia-

your mouth! Stick your tongue out! Lift your balls! Turn around! Bend over! Spread your ass! Wider! Lift the bottom of your feet! Move on!" The strip search, I later learned, is a ritual Atlanta's officers inflict on prisoners every time there is contact with anyone from outside the walls, and sometimes randomly as prisoners walk down the corridor.

There was a lot of hatred behind those walls. Walking through the prison must be something like walking through a jungle, I imagined, not knowing whether others perceive you as predator or prey, knowing that you must remain alert always, watching every step, knowing that the wrong step may be the one that sucks you into the quicksand. The tension is ever present; I felt it wrapped all over, under and around me. I remember it bothering me that I didn't have enough hatred, because not hating in the jungle is a weakness. As the serpents slither, they spot that lack of hatred and salivate over a potential target.

Every prisoner despises confinement, but each must decide how he or she is going to do the time. Most of the men run in packs. They want the other prisoners either to run with them or run away from them. I wasn't interested in doing either. Instead of scheming on how I could become king of the jungle, I thought about ways that I could advance my release date. Earning academic credentials, keeping a clean record, and initiating projects that would benefit the communities both inside and outside of prison walls seemed the most promising goals for me to achieve. Yet working toward such goals was more dangerous than running with the pack; it didn't take me long to learn that prisoners running in herds will put forth more energy to cause others to lose than they will to win themselves. Prison is a twisted world, a menagerie.

I found that a highly-structured schedule would not only move me closer to my goals, but also would limit potential conflicts inside the prison. There is a pecking order in every prison, and prisoners vying for attention don't want to see others who are cutting their own path. I saw that bullies generally look for weaker targets, so I began an exercise routine that would keep me physically strong. If I was strong, I figured, others would be more reluctant to try me. Through discipline, I found, I could develop physical strength. Yet I've never figured out how to develop the look of a killer, or the hatred off which that look feeds.

I don't know whether the strategies I have developed for doing time are right for everyone. But they are working for me. Still, I know that I may spend many more years in prison. The only fear I have—and as I'm working on my eighth year, it's still here—is that someone will try me and drag me into an altercation that may jeopardize my spotless disciplinary record. I've been successful in avoiding the ever-present quicksand on my walk through the jungle so far, but I know that on any given day, something may throw me off balance, or I may take a wrong step. And one wrong step in this jungle can drown me in quicksand, sucking me into the abysmal world of prison forever. That wrong step also could mean the loss of life, mine or someone else's.

In prison, more than anywhere else I know, it is vital to understand that some things are beyond an individual's sphere of control. No matter how much preparation is made, the steel and concrete jungle is a dangerous place in which to live.

SOURCE: This Close-Up by Michael G. Santos was written especially for *Criminal Justice in America*. All rights reserved. Mr. Santos is now incarcerated in the Federal Correctional Institution—McKean in Bradford, Pennsylvania. While in prison he has completed a B.A. and is working on a master's degree.

tions that exist among the groups, recognize the norms and rules that members hold, and deal with the leaders of many cliques rather than with a few inmates who have risen to top positions in the inmate society.

ADAPTIVE ROLES

On entering prison, a newcomer ("fish") is confronted by the question, How am I going to do my time? Some may decide to withdraw into their own

world and isolate themselves from their fellow prisoners. Others may decide to become full participants in the convict social system. While some choose to orient themselves toward the outside world, others identify primarily with the convict world. The choice is influenced by prisoners' values and, in turn, will help to determine strategies for survival and success that they will follow in prison.

Three terms describe basic role orientations that most male inmates use to adapt to prison: "doing time," "gleaning," and "jailing."[11] "Doing time" and "gleaning" are the choices of those who try to maintain their links with and the perspective of the free world. Those who are "doing time" view their term as a brief, inevitable break in their criminal careers, as merely a cost of doing business. These inmates tend to avoid trouble, serve their time quietly, and work for release as soon as possible. Inmates who are "gleaning" try to take advantage of prison programs in order to better themselves and improve their prospects for success after release. "Jailing" is the choice of those who cut themselves off from the outside and try to construct a life within the prison. These are often "state-raised" youths who have spent much of their lives in institutional settings and who identify little with the values of free society. A fourth role orientation—the "disorganized criminal"—describes inmates who are unable to develop any of the other three role orientations. They may be psychologically or physically handicapped and therefore targets of exploitation by other prisoners.

As these roles suggest, prisoners are not members of an undifferentiated mass. Individual convicts choose to play specific roles in the convict society. The roles they choose reflect the physical and social environment and contribute to their relationships and interactions in prison.

THE PRISON ECONOMY

In prison, as in the outside world, individuals desire goods and services that are not freely provided by authorities. Although the state feeds, clothes, and houses all prisoners, amenities are scarce. Since the mid-1960s, the items that a prisoner may purchase or receive through legitimate channels have increased. In some institutions, for example, inmates may own television sets, civilian clothing, and hot plates. However, these few luxuries are not enjoyed by all prisoners, nor do they satisfy lingering desires for a variety of other goods, including extra food.

Recognizing that prisoners do have some needs that are not met, all prisons have a commissary or "store" in which inmates may, on a scheduled basis, purchase a limited number of items—toilet articles, tobacco, snacks, and other food items—in exchange for credits drawn on their "bank accounts." The size of a bank account depends on the amount of money deposited on the inmate's entrance, gifts sent by relatives, and amounts earned in low-paying prison industries.

However, the peanut butter, soap, and cigarettes of the typical prison store do not satisfy the consumer needs and desires of most prisoners. Consequently, an informal, underground economy is a major element in prison society. Many items taken for granted on the outside are inordinately valued on the inside. For example, talcum power and deodorant take on added importance because of the limited bathing facilities. Goods and services not consumed at all outside prison can have exaggerated importance inside prison. For example, unable to enjoy their accustomed alcoholic beverages, offenders will seek the same effect by sniffing glue. Or, to distinguish themselves from others, offenders may pay laundry workers to iron a shirt in a particular way, a modest version of conspicuous consumption.[12]

David Kalinich has documented the prison economy at the Southern Michigan State Prison in Jackson.[13] He learned that the market economy provides goods and services not available or allowed by prison authorities. As a principal feature of the prison culture, this informal economy reinforces the norms and roles of the social system and influences the nature of interpersonal relationships. The extent of the economy and its ability to produce desired goods and services—food, drugs, alcohol, sex, preferred living conditions— vary from prison to prison according to the extent of official surveillance, the demands of the consumers, and the opportunities for entrepreneurship. Inmates' success as "hustlers" will determine the luxuries and power that they can enjoy.

The standard currency in the prison economy is cigarettes. Because possession of real money is prohibited and a barter system is somewhat restrictive, "cigarette money" is a useful substitute. Cigarettes are not contraband, are easily transferable, have a stable and well-known standard of value, and come in denominations of singles, packs, and cartons. Furthermore, they are in demand by smokers. Even prisoners who do not smoke keep cigarettes for prison currency.

Certain positions in prison society enhance opportunities for entrepreneurs. For example, inmates assigned to work in the kitchen, warehouse, and administrative office steal food, clothing, building materials, and even information to sell or trade to other prisoners. The goods may then become part of other market transactions. Thus, the exchange of a dozen eggs for two packs of cigarettes may result in the reselling of the eggs in the form of egg sandwiches made on a hot plate for five cigarettes each. Meanwhile, the kitchen worker who stole the eggs may use the income to get a laundry worker to starch his shirts or a hospital orderly to provide drugs or to pay a "punk" for sexual favors. The transactions wind on and on.

Economic transactions may lead to violence when goods are stolen, debts not paid, or agreements violated. Disruptions of the economy may occur when officials conduct periodic "lockdowns" and inspections. Confiscation of contraband may result in temporary shortages and price readjustments, but gradually hustling returns.

PRISON PROGRAMS

Modern correctional institutions differ from those of the past in the number and variety of programs for inmates. Prison industries were a part of early penitentiaries such as Auburn; educational, vocational, and treatment programs were added when rehabilitation goals became prominent. Programs are important to administrators in dealing with the problem of time. They know that the more programs available, the less likely that inmate idleness will turn into hostility—the less cell time, the fewer tensions.

Deciding on the appropriate program for an individual prisoner usually involves a **classification** process whereby a committee of department heads for security, treatment, education, and industry determines the inmate's security level, treatment needs, work assignments, and, eventually, readiness for release. Unfortunately, classification decisions are often made on the basis of administrative rather than inmate needs. Certain programs are limited, and the demand for them is great. Thus, inmates may find that the few places in the electrician's course are filled and that there is a long waiting list. Another problem is that inmates may be excluded from programs because prison housekeeping work must be done. Also, inmates from the city may be assigned to farm work because that is where they are needed. Prisoners are often angry and frustrated by the classification process and the limited availability of treatment programs. Release on parole often depends on a good record of participation in these programs, yet entrance for some inmates is blocked.

Education programs provide a range of opportunities to take academic courses. Frequently, all prisoners who have not completed eighth grade are assigned full-time to an education program. Education programs may provide remedial assistance with basic reading and math skills. They also permit prisoners to earn high school equivalency diplomas. Many institutions offer college courses in cooperation with a local college or university, although funding for such programs has come under attack from people who oppose tax dollars funding prisoners' college tuition when law-abiding students must pay for their own education. Studies have shown that prisoners assigned to education programs are good risks to avoid committing crimes after release. However, it is not clear whether education helps to rehabilitate these offenders or whether the types of prisoners who are assigned to education programs tend to be those motivated to avoid further crimes.

Vocational programs are designed to teach skills like plumbing, automobile mechanics, printing, and computer programming. Unfortunately, most such programs are unable to keep abreast of technological advances and needs of the free market. Too many programs train inmates for trades that already have an adequate labor supply or in which the skills being taught are already obsolete.

Prison industries trace their roots to the early prison workshops of Auburn, New York. These programs are intended to teach good work habits and skills that will assist prisoners' re-entry into the outside work force. In

classification

A process by which a committee of prison department heads determine an inmate's security level, treatment needs, work assignments, and eventually readiness for release.

practice, institutions rely on prison labor to provide basic food, custodial, secretarial, and other services. In addition, many prisons contain manufacturing facilities that produce goods, such as office furniture and clothing, to be used in correctional and other state institutions. Most states and the federal government have restrictions on the sale of prison-made goods in the outside economy.

Although the idea of employing inmates sounds attractive, the economic value may be offset by the inefficiencies of prison industries. The turnover rate among prisoners is high because many spend less than two years incarcerated and often are transferred during that period. Supervisors have found that, because of inmates' low education levels and lack of good work habits, it is difficult for prisoners to perform at the levels of modern production.

Rehabilitative programs seek to treat the personal defects thought to have brought about the inmate's criminality. In most correctional systems, a range of psychological, behavioral, and social services is available. The extent of their use seems to vary according to the goals of the institution and the attitudes of the administrators. Nationally, very little money is spent for treatment services, and these programs reach only 5 percent of the inmate population.[14] Rehabilitation programs remain a part of correctional institutions, but their emphasis has diminished. Indeed, incarceration's current goal of humane custody implies no effort to change inmates.

Although the supporters of each type of program argue that their particular approach contributes to reforming inmates, debates continue about whether offenders can be rehabilitated through treatment and education or reintegrated through vocational training and work experience. Each type of program may benefit certain offenders. However, we are largely unable to predict the extent to which any specific prisoner will benefit from a program. Moreover, few resources are devoted to the programs because most contemporary corrections systems and state legislatures have fallen back on custodial goals.

WOMEN IN PRISON

Most scholarship on prisons has been based on institutions for males. We now examine prisons for women to see how they differ from prisons for men and to focus on the special problems of female inmates.

Women constitute only 6 percent (about 50,000) of the entire U.S. prison population. This figure is slightly higher than in past years, due in part to increased drug convictions. However, since 1980, the rate of growth in the number of incarcerated women has been greater than that of men: Between 1980 and 1992, the number of men behind bars rose 163 percent while the number of women rose 276 percent.

Men's and women's prisons differ in a number of ways. Women's prisons are smaller and less security-conscious, and the relationships between inmates and staff are less structured. Women inmates are less committed to the inmate code, and physical aggression and violence seem to be less common in women's institutions. The hidden economy is not so well developed. And because women serve shorter sentences, there is perhaps more fluidity in the prison society as new members join and others leave.

Research has shown that incarcerated women are young (average age twenty-nine), are poorly educated (less than half have finished high school),

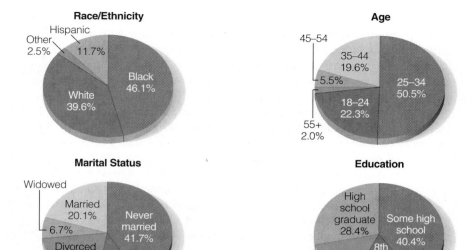

Race/Ethnicity
Other 2.5%
Hispanic 11.7%
Black 46.1%
White 39.6%

Age
45–54 5.5%
35–44 19.6%
25–34 50.5%
18–24 22.3%
55+ 2.0%

Marital Status
Widowed 6.7%
Married 20.1%
Never married 41.7%
Divorced 20.5%
Separated 11.0%

Education
High school graduate 28.4%
Some high school 40.4%
8th grade or less 16.5%
Some college or more 14.8%

and were employed at unskilled jobs. In addition, nonwhite women make up a higher percentage of the prison population than in the general population (see Figure 13.2). Nearly half of women inmates were caring for dependents at the time they were incarcerated, yet few had a husband or boyfriend at home. Prisoners who used drugs were more common than those with alcohol problems.[15]

Because only a few states operate more than one prison for women and some operate none, inmates are generally far removed from their families, friends, and attorneys. In addition, because the number of inmates is small, there is less political pressure on administrators to design programs to meet individual offenders' security and treatment needs. Women's prisons frequently lack the rehabilitation, education, and vocational programs available to male offenders. In addition, the lack of facilities hinders effective classification and assignment of offenders. Thus, dangerous women offenders are often mixed in with the general population of female offenders.

SOCIAL RELATIONSHIPS

Esther Heffernan discovered that three terms of prison slang—"square," "cool," and "in the life"—correspond to the real-world identities of noncriminal, professional, and habitual offenders in women's correctional institutions. "Square" is used, as in the larger community, to describe a person who holds conventional norms and values. For example, a woman who killed her husband in a moment of rage is likely to be "square." She attempts to maintain a conventional life while incarcerated, strives to gain the respect of officers and fellow inmates, and seeks to be a "good Christian woman." "Cool" prisoners are professional criminals who "keep busy, play around, stay out of trouble, and get out." They attempt to manipulate others and get through their incarceration on "easy time," seeking to gain as many amenities as they can without risking a longer stay.

By contrast, to be "in the life" is to be antisocial in prison, just as one was on the outside. Those who are "in the life"—about 50 percent of women in prison—are the habitual offenders who have been involved in prostitution, drugs, gambling, and shoplifting. Because they have frequently served previous prison terms, they interact with others with similar experiences and find community within the prison. It is important to them to stand firm against authority.[16]

What types of social relationships do women prisoners maintain, and how do these differ from those that men maintain in prison? As in all types of penal institutions, homosexual relationships are found. Among women prisoners, these relationships are more likely to be voluntary rather than coerced. More importantly, female inmates tend to form pseudofamilies in which they adopt various roles—father, mother, daughter, sister—and interact as a unit. Heffernan views these "play" families as a "direct, conscious substitution for the family relationships broken by imprisonment, or . . . the development of roles that perhaps were not fulfilled in the actual home environment."[17] Such links help to relieve the tensions of prison life, to assist the socialization of the new inmate, and to allow individuals to act according to clearly defined roles and rules.

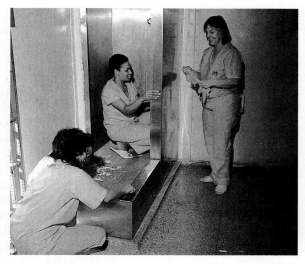

Compared with the convict society in prisons for males, many female prisoners form pseudofamilies, developing strong bonds with family members.

The principal difference between men's and women's prisons lies in such interpersonal relations. In a comparative study of four prisons for men and one for women, James Fox noted that male prisoners have their gangs or cliques but not the network of "family" relationships that has been found in prisons for women. In the men's prisons, Fox found little sharing. Men are expected to do their *own* time. Their norms stress autonomy, self-sufficiency, and the ability to cope with one's own problems.[18]

Some researchers have ascribed the distinctive female prison subculture to the nurturing, maternal qualities of women. Others have criticized this analysis as gender-role stereotyping.

PROGRAMS AND THE FEMALE ROLE

There are two major criticisms of programs in women's prisons. First, they do not have the variety of vocational and educational programs available in men's institutions. Second, existing programs tend to conform to gender stereotypes of "female" occupations: cosmetology, food service, housekeeping, sewing. Although such activities reflect the roles of women in past decades, they do not correspond with the employment opportunities and needs of women today, especially those who must support their households as single parents. Vocational and educational programs are crucial means for passing time in prison and for improving life after prison, yet women often have few opportunities. Gradually, however, many states are increasing the number and kinds of women's educational, vocational, and other programs.

Many critics have also noted a lack of medical, nutritional, and recreational services in women's prisons. In particular, most female institutions share physicians and hospital facilities with male prisons because officials believe there are too few women to justify separate medical staffs.

MOTHERS AND CHILDREN

Incarcerated mothers worry a great deal about their children. The best available data indicate that about 75 percent of women inmates are mothers, with an average of two dependent children. On a typical day, an estimated

167,000 children in the United States—two-thirds of them under age ten—have mothers who are in jail or prison.[19] One study found that roughly half of these children do not see their mothers while they are in prison.[20]

Few of these mothers have husbands or male partners who are able or willing to maintain a home for the children. In a study of the effects of separation on 133 inmates and their children, Phyllis Jo Baunach found that the children were most often cared for by their maternal grandmothers and that the knowledge of this arrangement gave the inmates some peace of mind.[21] When an inmate had no relative who would care for the children, they were often put up for adoption or placed in state-funded foster care. This development can obviously be a source of lingering emotional pain and distress for both the mother and her children.

Mothers frequently have difficulty maintaining contact with their children because of the distance of prisons from the children's homes, intermittent telephone privileges, and the conditions under which they interact with their offspring during visits. In some correctional institutions, child visitors must abide by the rules governing visits by adults: Physical contact is not allowed and visiting time is strictly limited.

Increasingly, programs are being developed to deal with these problems. In some states, children may meet with their mothers at almost any time, for extended periods, and in playrooms or nurseries where physical contact is possible. Some states arrange transportation for visits. In some institutions, children can even stay overnight. In both South Dakota and Nebraska, for example, children may stay with their mothers for up to five days each month. A few prisons have family visiting programs that allow the inmate, her legal husband, and her children to be together, often in a mobile home or apartment, for up to seventy-two hours.[22]

In most states, a baby born in prison must be placed with a family member or social agency within three weeks, to the detriment of the early mother–child bonding thought to be important for the development of a baby. Some innovative programs make longer placement periods possible. The emphasis on community corrections as it developed in the 1970s gave rise to programs that permitted mothers and their children to live together in halfway houses. These programs have not expanded as much as it was first thought they might, in part because the presence of children upsets the routine of the facility.

It is difficult to predict the future of women's correctional institutions. More women are being sent to prison now, and more have committed violent crimes and drug offenses that used to be more typical of male offenders. Will these changes affect the adaptive roles and social relationships that differentiate women's prisons from men's? Will women's prisons need to become more security-conscious and to enforce rules through more formal relationships between inmates and staff? These are important research issues.

VIOLENCE IN PRISON

A major challenge facing administrators is the control of prison violence. As illustrated by the description of the Lucasville riot at the beginning of the chapter, prisons provide a perfect recipe for violence. Frequently, they confine in cramped quarters a thousand men, some with histories of violent behavior. For an indefinite period of time, they are not allowed contact with women and live under highly restrictive conditions. Sometimes, these conditions spark collective violence, as in the riots at Attica (1971), Santa Fe (1980), Atlanta (1987), and Lucasville (1993). Although such events are widely reported in the news media, few people are aware of the level of everyday interpersonal violence in U.S. prisons. Each year, hundreds of prisoners die violent deaths and countless others are assaulted. For example, in 1990, 98 prisoners committed suicide, 49 deaths were "caused by another," and 261 died in ways that left it unclear as to whether the death was natural, self-inflicted, accidental, or homicidal.[23] Great numbers of prisoners live in a state of constant uneasiness, always on the lookout for persons who might subject them to homosexual demands, steal their few possessions, or otherwise make their lives more difficult.

AGE, RACE, AND VIOLENCE

Violence in prison is associated with three particular factors: age, attitude, and race. Studies have shown that young males, both inside and outside prison, are more prone to violence than their elders. Prisoners incarcerated for violent crimes are generally a year or two younger than the average inmate. Not only do the young have greater physical strength, they lack those commitments to career and family that are thought to restrict antisocial behavior. In addition, many young men have difficulty defining their status in society. As a result, they often interpret the actions of others as challenges. Machismo, the concept of male honor and the sacredness of one's reputation as a man, has a bearing on violence among the young in that it requires physical retaliation against those who insult one's honor. The potential for violence among prisoners who value machismo is obvious.

One of the sociological theories advanced to explain crime is that a subculture of violence exists among members of low-income groups and that, in its value system, violence is "tolerable, expected, or required."[24] Arguments are settled and decisions are made by violence rather than by verbal persuasion. These attitudes are brought into the prison as part of an inmate's heritage.

Race has become a major source of division in prison populations. In most institutions, racist attitudes have become part of the convict code. The fact of forced association with persons with whom one would not be likely to associate on the outside amplifies racial conflict. Violence against members of another race may be how some inmates deal with the frustrations of their lives both inside and outside of prison. In addition, the presence of gangs organized along racial lines contributes to violence in prison.

PRISONER–PRISONER VIOLENCE

Although prison folklore may attribute violence to brutal guards, most of the violence occurs among inmates. A study of four Virginia institutions recorded 9.96 prisoner–prisoner attacks per 100 inmates per year.[25] These levels of violence are not necessarily related to the size of the prisoner population in a particular facility. The sad fact is that uncounted inmates are injured by assaults. As Hans Toch has observed, the climate of violence in prisons has no free-world counterpart: "Inmates are terrorized by other inmates, and spend years in fear of harm. Some inmates request segregation, others lock themselves in, and some are hermits by choice."[26] However, for some prisoners, this situation parallels life in their old neighborhoods, particularly where the local murder victimization rates for young men are high.

Racial or ethnic gangs are now linked to violence in many prison systems, and these gangs make certain prisons more dangerous than any American neighborhoods. In essence, the gang wars of the streets are often continued in close quarters within the prison. Gangs are organized primarily with the intention of controlling an institution's drug, gambling, loan-sharking, prostitution, extortion, and debt collection rackets. In addition, gangs provide protection for their members from other gangs and instill a sense of macho camaraderie.

Contributing to prison violence is the fact that gang membership is often based on "blood-in, blood-out": A would-be member must stab a gang's enemy to be admitted, and once admitted, he cannot drop out without endangering his own life. Given the racial and ethnic foundation of the gangs, violence between them can easily spill over into the general prison population.

PRISONER–OFFICER VIOLENCE

The mass media have focused on riots in which guards are taken hostage, injured, and killed. However, violence against officers typically occurs in specific situations and against certain individuals. Officers do not carry weapons within the institution because a prisoner may seize them. In the course of a workday, an officer may encounter situations that require the use of physical force against an inmate—for instance, breaking up a fight or moving a prisoner to segregation. Officers know that such situations are especially dangerous and may enlist the assistance of others to minimize the risk of violence. The officer's greatest concern is unexpected attacks. These may take the form of a missile thrown from an upper tier, verbal threats and taunts, or an officer's "accidental" fall down a flight of stairs. The fact that the officer must be constantly watchful against personal attacks adds to the stress and keeps many officers distant from inmates.

OFFICER–PRISONER VIOLENCE

A fact of life in many institutions is unauthorized physical violence by officers against inmates. Stories abound of guards giving individual prisoners "the treatment" when supervisors are not looking. Many guards view physical force as an everyday, legitimate procedure.

Correctional officers are expected to follow departmental rules in their dealings with prisoners, yet supervisors are usually unable to observe directly the face-to-face confrontations between staff and prisoners that may produce violence. Prisoner complaints about officer brutality are often given little credence until an officer gains a reputation for harshness. In addition, wardens may feel that they must uphold the actions of their officers in order to maintain morale. Moreover, it is often difficult to judge whether excessive force has been used, based on competing stories from an officer and an inmate. Without corroborating evidence, an inmate's complaint is unlikely to be taken seriously.

COMBATTING VIOLENCE

In analyzing prison violence, Lee Bowker lists five contributing factors: (1) inadequate supervision by staff members, (2) architectural design that promotes rather than inhibits victimization, (3) the easy availability of deadly weapons, (4) the housing of violence-prone prisoners near relatively defenseless persons, and (5) a general high level of tension produced by close quarters.[27]

Effective prison management may decrease the level of assaultive behavior by limiting opportunities for attacks. To do so, wardens and correctional officers must recognize the types of people with whom they are dealing, the role of prison gangs, and the structure of institutions. John DiIulio argues that no group of inmates is "unmanageable [and] no combination of political, social, budgetary, architectural, or other factors makes good management impossible."[28] He points to such varied institutions as the California Men's Colony, New York City's Tombs and Rikers Island, the Federal Bureau of Prisons, and the Texas Department of Corrections under the leadership of George Beto, where good management practices resulted in prisons and jails where inmates can "do time" without fearing for their personal safety. Failures of prison organization and management were the most important determinants of the violence that occurred in the major prison riots from 1971 to 1986.[29] Wardens who exert leadership and effectively manage their prisons maintain an environment of governance so that problems do not fester and erupt into violent confrontations.

PRISONERS' RIGHTS

Prior to the 1960s, the judiciary maintained a "hands-off" policy with respect to prisons: Prisoners did not possess protected rights, and courts deferred to the expertise of corrections officials in deciding how to run prisons. Since the 1960s, however, the courts have limited the management freedoms of correctional administrators. Judicial decisions have recognized and defined the constitutional rights of incarcerated offenders and the need for correctional policies and procedures that respect these rights.

The most far-reaching departure from the hands-off policy occurred in 1964 when the Supreme Court ruled in **Cooper v. Pate** that prisoners are entitled to the protection of the Civil Rights Act of 1871 and may challenge conditions of their confinement in the federal courts.[30] This ruling imposes civil liability on any person who deprives another of constitutional rights. Because of the decision in *Cooper* v. *Pate*, the federal courts now permit prisoners to sue state officials for such things as brutality by guards, inadequate nutritional and medical care, theft of personal property, and the denial of basic constitutional rights.

The first successful prisoners' rights cases involved the most excessive of prison abuses: brutality and inhuman physical conditions. Gradually, however, prison litigation has focused more directly on the daily activities of the institution, especially on the administrative rules that regulate inmates' conduct. The result has been a series of court decisions concerning the First, Fourth, Eighth, and Fourteenth Amendments to the Constitution.

The 1960s growth of the Black Muslim religion within prisons holding large numbers of urban African-Americans set the stage for litigation demanding that this group be granted the same privileges as other faiths (for example, special diets, access to clergy and religious publications, opportunities for group worship). Attorneys for the Muslims succeeded in winning several important cases that helped to establish for prisoners the First Amendment right to free exercise of religion. These decisions also have helped Native Americans and other minority groups to practice their religions while incarcerated. Additional First Amendment cases by Muslims and others clarified the permissible scope of corrections officials' censorship of mail and reading materials.

Cooper v. *Pate* (1964) Prisoners are entitled to the protection of the Civil Rights Act of 1871 and may challenge conditions of their confinement in the federal courts.

Prisoners now have access to law libraries to do research on their own cases. In fact, knowing one's way around the law library has become such a marketable skill that some inmates "charge" other inmates for legal advice.

The Fourth Amendment prohibits "unreasonable" searches and seizures, but the courts have not been active in extending these protections to prisoners. Courts place great emphasis on the need for correctional officers to conduct searches in order to prevent weapons and other contraband in prisoners' possession from disrupting safety and security.

The Eighth Amendment prohibition against cruel and unusual punishment has been interpreted by the courts to mean that prisons must maintain decent living conditions and minimum health standards. When widespread conditions of brutality, unsanitary facilities, overcrowding, and inadequate food have been found, judges have used the Eighth Amendment to order sweeping changes and, in some cases, even to take over administration of entire prisons or corrections systems. In these cases, judges have directed wardens to institute specific internal procedures and to spend money on specific improvements, thus limiting wardens' discretion.

Many conditions that violate the rights of prisoners may be corrected by administrative action, training programs, or a minimal expenditure of funds, but others are simply beyond the control of prison managers. For example, overcrowding requires an expansion of facilities or a dropping of the intake rate, yet prison officials by themselves have no way to increase the capacities of their institutions or to reduce the number of offenders sent to them by the courts. These decisions ultimately lie with the courts, legislatures, and voters.

Two clauses of the Fourteenth Amendment are relevant to the question of prisoners' rights—those requiring procedural due process and equal protection. In the 1970s, the Supreme Court began to insist that procedural fairness be observed in two of the most sensitive of institutional decisions: the process by which inmates are sent to solitary confinement and the method by which good-time credit may be lost because of misconduct. In the 1974 case of ***Wolff* v. *McDonnell***, the Court ruled that basic elements of procedural due process must be present when decisions are made concerning the disciplining of an inmate. Specifically, inmates are entitled to receive notice of the complaint, to have a fair hearing, to confront witnesses, to be assisted in preparing for the hearing, and to be given a written statement of the decision.[31] Yet the Court also ruled that inmates have no right to counsel at a disciplinary hearing.[32] The courts have emphasized the need to balance the rights of the prisoner against the interests of the state. In effect, however, the courts have reduced the freedom of prison officials to punish offenders as they please.

As a result of the Supreme Court decisions, most prisons have established rules that provide some elements of due process in disciplinary proceedings. In many institutions, a disciplinary committee receives the charges, conducts hearings, makes a ruling, and decides on appropriate punishment. Such committees are usually made up of administrative personnel, but sometimes inmates or citizens are included. Even with these protections, prisoners essentially are powerless and may fear further punishment if they challenge too strenuously the disciplinary decisions of the warden.

In recent years, the Supreme Court has been less inclined to support the expansion of prisoners' rights, and a few decisions in the 1990s reflect a retreat from earlier decisions. Lower courts continue to monitor the policies and practices at various correctional institutions, but the Supreme Court has

***Wolff* v. *McDonnell* (1974)** Basic elements of procedural due process must be present when decisions are made concerning the disciplining of an inmate.

made it clear that courts should respect the need for officials to maintain internal safety and security.

The prisoners' rights movement has brought about numerous court orders and can probably be credited with some general changes in American corrections since the late 1970s.[33] The most obvious are concrete improvements in institutional living conditions and administrative practices. Law libraries and legal assistance are now generally available, communication with the outside is easier, religious practices are protected, inmate complaint procedures have been developed, and due process requirements are emphasized. Today's prisoners in solitary confinement undoubtedly suffer less neglect than those so punished before the 1970s. Although overcrowding is still a major problem in many institutions, many conditions are much improved, and the more brutalizing elements of prison life have been diminished. These changes were not entirely the result of court orders, however. They also coincide with the growth in influence of college-educated corrections professionals who have sought on their own to improve prisons.

SUMMARY

Incarceration takes place in a variety of correctional institutions, each with its own traditions, organization, and environment. Because the nature of American prisons and prisoners has changed over the years, corrections officials face a variety of challenges in seeking to run safe, secure, and successful institutions. Factors like racial polarization, prison gangs, overcrowding, and limited resources all make prison administration more difficult. The public belief that wardens and officers have total power over inmates is outdated. The relationship between the managers and the prisoners is much more fragile and interconnected than any organizational chart would indicate.

The correctional officers are the real linchpins to the prison system. They are in constant close contact with prisoners and are the first to become aware of their problems and needs. The effective functioning of the institution weighs heavily on their shoulders. They work in a complex environment with inmates who pursue adaptive roles within their own special culture.

Some prisoners seek to take advantage of the education, vocational, and rehabilitation programs offered within institutions, but programs are limited. Moreover, other prisoners' values may lead them to focus on success within the prison social structure of gangs or the hidden economy.

Women's prisons present their own problems. Although women inmates tend to be more collectivist in forming social groupings and engaging less often in assaultive behavior, women's facilities often have fewer available programs. In addition, women inmates feel special pressures, especially stemming from their separation from children and other relatives who are likely to be located a significant distance from the prison.

Violence in prison is a fact of life in most institutions. Although the public knows about prison riots, most violence is between prisoners. Factors such as the age, attitude, and race contribute to prison violence. Effective management is probably the most important factor in limiting violence.

The prisoners' rights movement has brought about many changes in the administration and conditions of American prisons. Through litigation in the federal courts, prisoners have challenged the conditions of their confinement. In many cases, judges have responded by ordering that unconstitutional procedures and conditions be changed.

QUESTIONS FOR REVIEW

1. Why do prison managers have difficulty governing the society of captives?
2. What is meant by an adaptive role? Which roles have been found in male prison society? In female prison society? How do these roles compare?
3. How does the prison economy operate?
4. In what ways is the convict society in institutions for women different from that found in prisons for men?
5. What factors are associated with prison violence?
6. What was the impact of the prisoners' rights movement?

NOTES

1. Bill Turque, "Deadly Showdown in Lucasville," *Newsweek*, 26 April 1993, pp. 52–53.
2. Donald Clemmer, *The Prison Community* (New York: Holt, Rinehart & Winston, 1940); Gresham M. Sykes, *The Society of Captives* (Princeton, NJ: Princeton University Press, 1958).
3. Charles H. Logan, "Criminal Justice Performance Measures in Prisons," U.S. Department of Justice, Bureau of Justice Statistics (Washington, DC: Government Printing Office, 1993), p. 5.
4. Erving Goffman, *Asylums* (Garden City, NY: Anchor Books, 1961).
5. Sykes, *Society of Captives*, p. 49.
6. John DiIulio, Jr., *Governing Prisons* (New York: Free Press, 1987).
7. Ibid., p. 242.
8. Donald R. Cressey, "Limitations on Organization of Treatment in the Modern Prison," in *Theoretical Studies in Social Organization of the Prison*, ed. Richard A. Cloward, Donald R. Cressey, George H. Grosser, Richard McCleery, Lloyd E. Ohlin, Gresham M. Sykes, and Sheldon L. Messinger (New York: Social Science Research Council, 1960), p. 103.
9. U.S. Department of Justice, Bureau of Justice Statistics, *Sourcebook of Criminal Justice Statistics* (Washington, DC: Government Printing Office, 1992), p. 112.
10. Sykes, *Society of Captives*, pp. 84–90.
11. Ibid., pp. 67–79.
12. Vergil L. Williams and Mary Fish, *Convicts, Codes, and Contraband* (Cambridge, MA: Ballinger, 1974), p. 50.
13. David B. Kalinich, *Power, Stability, and Contraband* (Prospect Heights, IL: Waveland Press, 1980).
14. Paul Gendreau and Robert R. Ross, "Effective Correctional Treatment: Bibliotherapy for Cynics," in *Effective Correctional Treatment*, ed. Robert R. Ross and Paul Gendreau (Toronto: Butterworths, 1980), p. 25.
15. Joycelyn M. Pollock-Byrne, *Women, Prison, and Crime* (Pacific Grove, CA: Brooks/Cole, 1990), p. 57.
16. Esther Heffernan, *Making It in Prison* (New York: Wiley, 1972), p. 88.
17. Ibid., pp. 41–42.
18. James G. Fox, *Organizational and Racial Conflict in Maximum-Security Prisons* (Lexington, MA: Lexington Books, 1982).
19. *New York Times*, 30 November 1992, p. A10.
20. *New York Times*, 27 December 1992, p. D3.

21. Phyllis J. Baunach, "You Can't Be a Mother and Be in Prison. Can You? Impacts of the Mother-Child Separation," in *The Criminal Justice System and Women*, ed. Barbara Rafel Price and Natalie J. Sokoloff (New York: Clark Boardman, 1982), pp. 155–169.

22. Virginia V. Neto and LaNelle Marie Bainer, "Mother and Wife Locked Up: A Day in the Family," *Prison Journal* 63 (Autumn-Winter 1983), p. 124.

23. U.S. Department of Justice, *Sourcebook*, p. 701.

24. Marvin Wolfgang and Franco Ferracuti, *The Subculture of Violence* (London: Tavistock, 1967), p. 263.

25. Lee H. Bowker, *Prison Victimization* (New York: Elsevier, 1980), p. 25.

26. Hans Toch, *Peacekeeping: Police, Prisons, and Violence* (Lexington, MA: Lexington Books, 1976), pp. 47–48.

27. Lee Bowker, "Victimizers and Victims in American Correctional Institutions," in *Pains of Imprisonment*, ed. Robert Johnson and Hans Toch (Newbury Park, CA: Sage, 1982), p. 62.

28. John J. DiIulio, Jr., *No Escape: The Future of American Corrections* (New York: Basic Books, 1990), p. 12.

29. Bert Useem and Peter Kimball, *States of Siege: U.S. Prison Riots 1971–1986* (New York: Oxford University Press, 1989).

30. *Cooper* v. *Pate*, 378 U.S. 546 (1964).

31. *Wolff* v. *McDonnell*, 94 S.Ct. 2963 (1974).

32. *Baxter* v. *Palmiagiano*, 425 U.S. 308 (1976).

33. Malcolm M. Feeley and Roger A. Hanson, "The Impact of Judicial Intervention on Prisons and Jails: A Framework of Analysis and a Review of the Literature," in *Courts, Corrections and the Constitution*, ed. John J. DiIulio, Jr. (New York: Oxford University Press, 1990), pp. 12–46.

CHAPTER 14
Release and Community Supervision

PAROLE: FIRST STEP TO NEW LIFE OR DANGER TO THE COMMUNITY?

Leslie Allen Williams was released from a Michigan prison on parole in 1972 after serving one year of a one- to five-year sentence for breaking into a store. While on parole, he broke into a home and attempted to strangle a teen-age girl. He received a new sentence of eighteen months to ten years after pleading guilty to breaking and entering. Within weeks of his release on parole in 1975, he abducted and raped another teenager. He was given a sentence of fourteen to twenty-five years, yet he was released after serving less than eight years. Within two weeks, he kidnapped a woman. Sentenced to seven to thirty years for this new crime, he was released on parole for a fourth time after serving seven years. While out on parole, he raped and murdered four women over the course of two years and was not caught until he attempted to kidnap a fifth woman. During this period, his parole officer reported that he was having "no problems," so authorities had no clue that this parolee was responsible for the murder spree. In 1992, Williams was given multiple life sentences for the murders.[1]

How many people would be spared from criminal victimization if Williams and other parolees were forced to serve their full sentences? On the one hand, mistakes clearly can be made in deciding that certain offenders pose little risk to the community. On the other hand, if we make every offender serve a maximum sentence, will we be wasting scarce prison space on some people who have straightened themselves out when we need those cells to hold incoming violent offenders? Although Leslie Allen Williams's case reflects a series of disastrous parole decisions, all parolees are not like Williams. Can we afford to design our prison release policies based on our fears about the worst-case examples? These are difficult and haunting questions.

Society cannot avoid the hazards of releasing offenders back into the community. Most prisoners have limited-term sentences, which means they will return to society even if they serve out their maximum terms. In this chapter, we will examine the release of convicted offenders from prison and their reintegration into the community. ★

parole

The conditional release of an inmate from incarceration under the legal custody and supervision of the state.

PAROLE: RE-ENTRY INTO SOCIETY

O
ffenders placed on **parole** are released from prison, but they remain under the legal custody and supervision of the state. The term *parole* refers to both a releasing mechanism and a method of community supervision. Although releasing mechanisms have changed in many states, most former prisoners are still required to serve a period of time under supervision, abiding by specified conditions and reporting regularly to a parole officer. Failure to comply may result in parolees being sent back to prison to complete their full terms of incarceration.

Each year, almost 400,000 convicted felons are released from prison and allowed to live in the community. Only felons are released on parole. Adult misdemeanants are usually released directly from jail when they complete their sentences. Until the advent of determinate sentencing and parole decision-making guidelines, upwards of 85 percent of the persons serving prison sentences were returned to society through the discretionary decision of the parole board. However, as shown in Figure 14.1, currently, only about 40 percent of releases from state prisons come about as a result of a discretionary parole board decision. Instead, an increasing majority of felons are returned to society through mandatory release as specified by the terms of their sentences.

THE ORIGINS OF PAROLE

Parole in the United States evolved during the nineteenth century from the English, Australian, and Irish practices of conditional pardon, apprenticeship by indenture, transportation of criminals from one country to another, and the issuance of "tickets-of-leave." The common denominator of all these methods was the movement of criminals out of prison. These practices generally were not developed as part of any coherent theory of punishment or as a means to advance any particular goal of the criminal sanction. Instead, they emerged in response to such problems as prison overcrowding, unemployment, and the cost of incarceration.

The practice of punishing offenders by keeping them under the authority of the state, yet not confined to an institution, developed in conjunction with Britain's efforts to establish colonies. In the sixteenth century, England's Act of Banishment provided for the movement of criminals and "rogues" to the colonies as laborers for the king in exchange for a pardon. The pardons initially were unconditional, but they evolved to become conditional on the completion of a period of service. In later times, especially during the eighteenth century, English convicts were released and indentured to private persons to work in the colonies until they were freed at the end of a set term.

After the American colonies gained independence, Australia became the major colonial destination for offenders banished from England. The governor of Australia was granted the power to pardon felons. Initially, unconditional pardons were given to offenders with good work records and good behavior. As problems arose with the behavior of some pardoned offenders, the pardons became conditional. The essential condition was a requirement that prisoners support themselves and remain within a specific district. This method of parole, known as a "ticket-of-leave," was similar to the modern concept of parole, except that the released prisoner was not under government supervision.

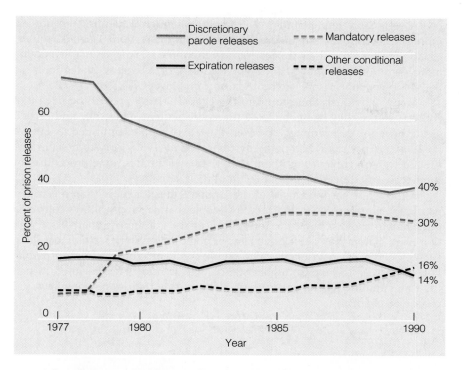

FIGURE 14.1

Percentage of State Prisoners Released by Various Methods, 1977–1990
With the increase in determinate sentences and mandatory release, fewer prisoners are released by parole boards.

SOURCE: U.S. Department of Justice, Bureau of Justice Statistics, *Bulletin* (November 1991), p. 5.

A key figure in developing the concept of parole in the nineteenth century was Captain Alexander Maconochie, who served as an administrator of British penal colonies in Tasmania and elsewhere in the South Pacific and later as a prison governor in England. Maconochie criticized definite prison terms and devised a system of rewards for good conduct, labor, and study. He developed a classification procedure by which prisoners could pass through five stages of increasing responsibility and freedom: (1) strict imprisonment, (2) labor on government chain gangs, (3) freedom within a limited area, (4) a ticket-of-leave or parole resulting in a conditional pardon, and (5) full restoration of liberty. Like modern correctional practices, this procedure assumed that prisoners should be prepared gradually for release. In the transition from imprisonment to conditional release to full freedom, we can see the roots of the American system of parole.

Maconochie's idea of requiring prisoners to earn their early release caught on first in Ireland. There, Sir Walter Crofton built on Maconochie's idea that an offender's progress in prison and a ticket-of-leave were linked. Prisoners who graduated through Crofton's three successive levels of treatment were released on parole with a series of conditions. Most importantly, parolees were required to submit monthly reports to the police. In Dublin, a special civilian inspector helped releasees find jobs, visited them periodically, and supervised their activities.

Alexander Maconochie

THE DEVELOPMENT OF PAROLE IN THE UNITED STATES

In the United States, parole developed during the prison reform movement of the latter half of the nineteenth century. Relying on the ideas of Maconochie and Crofton, such American reformers as Zebulon Brockway of the Elmira State Reformatory in New York began to experiment with the concept. Following New York's adoption of indeterminate sentences in 1876, Brockway started to release prisoners on parole.

mandatory release
The required release of an inmate from incarceration upon the expiration of a certain time period, as stipulated by a determinate sentencing law or parole guidelines.

discretionary release
The release of an inmate from incarceration at the discretion of the parole board within the boundaries set by the sentence and the penal law.

Members of the Massachusetts Board of Parole discuss the possibility of release with a prisoner and his attorney. What factors would you consider if the offender had committed murder? What if the crime was sexual abuse?

As originally implemented, the parole system in New York did not require supervision by the police. Instead, volunteers from citizens' reform groups assisted with the parolee's reintegration into society. As parole became more common and applied to larger numbers of offenders, states replaced the volunteer supervisors with correctional employees.

Many individuals and groups in the United States opposed the release of convicts before they had completed the entire sentence that they had earned as the price for their crimes. However, the use of parole continued to spread. By 1900, twenty states had parole systems, and by 1932, forty-four states and the federal government had them. Today, every state has some procedure for the release of offenders before the end of their sentences.

Although it has been used in the United States for more than a century, parole remains controversial. To many people, parole simply allows convicted offenders to avoid serving the full sentences they deserve. Public dissatisfaction with parole has been fueled by periodic news stories about parolees, such as Leslie Allen Williams, who commit violent crimes while on parole. Public pressure to take a tougher stance with criminals has resulted in half the states and the federal government restructuring their sentencing laws and release mechanisms.

RELEASE MECHANISMS

In states using **mandatory release** systems, determinate sentences and parole guidelines set the length of a prisoner's incarceration (see Chapter 10). Such systems give correctional authorities little discretion in deciding whether the offender is ready to return to society. With determinate sentencing, the judge is responsible for fixing the amount of time to be served. Thus, with mandatory release, the prisoner is automatically discharged to community supervision at the end of the term, less credited good time.

In states retaining indeterminate sentences, **discretionary release** by the parole board, within the boundaries set by the sentence and the penal law, is the step by which most felons leave prison. This approach is tied to the rehabilitation model and the idea that the parole board should assess the prisoner's readiness for release. In reviewing the prisoner's file and asking questions about the prisoner, the parole board focuses on the nature of the offense committed, the inmate's behavior and participation in rehabilitative programs, and the prognosis for a crime-free future. This process effectively places great faith in the ability of parole board members to make accurate predictions about the future behavior of offenders.

THE ORGANIZATION OF RELEASING AUTHORITIES

Parole boards tend to be organized either as part of a department of corrections or as independent government agencies. Some commentators have argued that a parole board must be independent so that members can be insulated from the activities and influence of staff in correctional departments. According to this viewpoint, an independent parole board is less likely to be influenced by such staff considerations as reducing the size of the prison population and punishing inmates who do not conform to institutional rules. Theoretically, members of an autonomous board make independent judgments about readiness for release based on the prisoner's rehabilitation.

Whether a parole board is independent or a component of a corrections department, it cannot exist in a vacuum. Board members cannot ignore the public's attitudes and fears about crime. If a parolee commits a crime and public indignation is aroused, the board members inevitably will make decisions more cautiously in order to avoid public condemnation and embarrassment. For example, members of one parole board said that they had to be very cautious in releasing prisoners because, if parolees committed additional crimes, the news media always blamed the board for improperly releasing unworthy offenders.

Parole boards also are susceptible to influence from departments of corrections and must maintain good working relations with them. For example, if even an autonomous board develops a conflict with the department, the department may not cooperate in providing the board with information it needs. Information about particular offenders may become "unavailable," or the state may provide biased information about particular offenders that officials wish to see punished. By contrast, a board that is closely tied to corrections officials may have access to information and receive complete cooperation. However, such a board runs the risk of being viewed by prisoners and the general public as merely the rubber stamp of the department.

Most people assume that parole boards are comprised of experts on human behavior who can accurately evaluate whether an offender is ready for release. In some states, this view is reasonably accurate. However, no one can predict human behavior with complete accuracy, especially when dealing with offenders, many of whom have histories of substance abuse or irrational behavior or are unable to function well in society due to illiteracy and other problems.

In other states, political considerations dictate membership on the parole board. Governors seek to appoint citizens to the board who fit specific racial, geographic, occupational, and other demographic criteria. In the recent past, for example, the Mississippi board consisted of a contractor, a businessman, a farmer, and a clerk; the Florida board included a

A QUESTION OF ETHICS

The five members of the parole board questioned Jim Allen, an offender with a long history of sex offenses involving teenage boys. Now approaching forty-five and having met the eligibility requirement for a hearing, Allen respectfully answered the board members.

Toward the end of the hearing, Richard Edwards, a dentist who had recently been appointed to the board, spoke up: "Your institutional record is good, you have a parole plan, a job has been promised, and your sister says she will help you. All of that looks good, but I just can't vote for your parole. You haven't attended the behavior modification program for sex offenders. I think you're going to repeat your crime. I have a thirteen-year-old son, and I don't want him or other boys to run the risk of meeting your kind."

Allen looked shocked. The other members had seemed ready to grant his release. "But I'm ready for parole. I won't do that stuff again. I didn't go to that program because electroshock to my private area is not going to help me. I've been here five years of the seven-year max and have stayed out of trouble. The judge didn't say I was to be further punished in prison by therapy."

After Jim Allen left the room, the board discussed his case. "You know, Rich, he has a point. He has been a model prisoner and has served a good portion of his sentence," said Brian Lynch, a long-term board member. "Besides, we don't know if Dr. Hankin's program works."

"I know, but can we really let someone like that out on the streets?"

Are the results of the behavior modification program for sex offenders relevant to the parole board's decision? Is the purpose of the sentence to punish Allen for what he did or for what he might do in the future? If you were on the board, would you vote for his release on parole? Would your vote be the same if his case had received media attention?

After three years, three months, and four days in Stanhope Correctional Facility, Ben Brooks was ready to go before the Board of Parole. He woke with butterflies in his stomach, realizing that at nine o'clock he was to walk into the hearing room to confront what he knew was a "roomful of strangers." As he lay in his bunk, he rehearsed the answers to the questions he thought the board members might ask. "How do you feel about the person you assaulted?" "What have you done with your time while incarcerated?" "Do you think you have learned anything here that will convince the board that you will be able to live a crime-free life in the community?" "What are your plans for employment and housing?" Prison scuttlebutt had it that these were the types of questions, and you had to be prepared to tell that you were sorry for your past mistakes, had taken advantage of the prison programs, had a job waiting for you, and that you planned to live with your family. You had to "ring bells" with the board.

At breakfast, friends dropped by Ben's table to reassure him that he "had it made." As one said, "Ben, you've done everything they've said to do. What else can they expect?" That was the problem: What did they expect?

At eight thirty, Officer Kearney came by the cell. "Time to go, Ben." They walked out of the housing unit and down the long corridors of the prison to a group of chairs outside the hearing room. Other prisoners were already seated there. "Sit here, Ben. They'll call when they're ready. Good luck."

At ten past nine, the door opened and an officer called, "First case, Brooks." Ben got up and walked into the room. "Please take a seat, Mr. Brooks," said the black man seated in the center of the table. Ben knew that this was Reverend Perry, a man known as being tough but fair. To his left was a white man and to his right a Hispanic woman.

The white man (his name card said Nelson

newspaperman, an attorney, and a man with experience in both business and probation; the state of Washington board included persons with training and experience in sociology, government, law, the ministry, and juvenile rehabilitation. Parole boards act much like a jury in that they can apply the community's values in determining whether particular offenders deserve to be released.

THE DECISION TO RELEASE

An inmate's eligibility for parole depends on requirements set by law and the sentence imposed by the court. As we have noted, in the states with determinate sentences or parole guidelines, release from prison to community supervision is mandatory once the offender has served the required amount of time. In these states, the release procedure becomes a matter of bookkeeping to ensure that the correct amount of good time and other credits have been recorded and that the court's sentence has been accurately interpreted. In nearly half the states, however, the decision is discretionary, and the parole board has the authority to establish a date based on the sufficiency of rehabilitation and the individual's characteristics as an inmate.

Discretionary Release
Based on the assumptions of indeterminate sentences and rehabilitative programs, discretionary release is designed to allow the parole board to release inmates when they are deemed "ready" to re-enter the community as law-

MacDonald) led the questioning. "Mr. Brooks. You were convicted of armed robbery and sentenced to a term of five to ten years. Please tell the board what you have learned during your incarceration."

Ben paused and in a hesitant voice answered, "Well, I learned that to commit such a stupid act was a mistake. I was under a lot of pressure when I pulled the robbery and now am sorry for what I did."

"You severely injured the woman you held up. What might you tell her if she was sitting in this room today?"

"I would just have to say, I'm sorry. It will never happen again."

"But this is not the first time you have been convicted. What makes you think it will never happen again?"

"Well this is the first time I was sent to prison. You see things a lot differently from here."

Ms. Lopes, the other board member, spoke up. "You have a good prison record—member of the Toastmaster's Club, passed your GED, have kept your nose clean. Tell the board about your plans for the future should you be released."

"My brother says I can live with him until I get on my feet, and there is a letter in my file telling you that I have a job waiting at a meat processing plant. I will be living in my hometown, but I don't intend to see my old buddies again. You can be sure that I am now on the straight and narrow."

"But you committed a heinous crime. That woman suffered a lot. Why should the board believe that you won't do it again?"

"All I can say is that I'm different now."

"Thank you, Mr. Brooks," said Reverend Perry. "You will hear from us by this evening." Ben got up and walked out of the room. It had taken only eight minutes, yet it seemed like hours. Eight minutes during which his future was being decided. Would it be back to the cell or out on the street? It would be about ten hours before he would receive word from the board as to his fate.

abiding citizens. What criteria guide the decision? A formal statement of standards may list such elements as inmates' attitudes toward their families, their insights into the causes of their past conduct, and the adequacy of their parole plan. Additional considerations might include whether offenders have accepted responsibility for their actions and whether they have a plan for steady employment after release. These are important and relevant issues, but the discretionary decision to release a prisoner typically is based on various other kinds of information as well as fundamental moral judgments about the severity of the crime, the prisoner's culpability, and the adequacy of the term served as punishment for the crime. It is frequently said that parole boards release only good risks, but as one parole board member has said, "There are no good-risk men in prison. Parole is really a decision of when to release bad-risk persons."[2]

Other considerations also weigh heavily on the board members. If parole is not regularly awarded to most prisoners who gain eligibility, morale among all inmates may suffer as they fear that they will not gain release at the anticipated date. The prospect of gaining parole is a major incentive for many prisoners to follow rules and cooperate with corrections officials. The Close-Up box traces the parole hearing of one inmate.

Parole board members are also concerned about public sentiments. They do not wish to receive public criticism for making controversial decisions. Thus, notorious offenders, such as Sirhan Sirhan, the man convicted of assassinating presidential candidate Robert Kennedy in 1968, are unlikely ever to gain parole release even if they behave well in prison.

The Prisoner's Perspective: How to Win Parole

"If you want to get paroled, you've got to be in a program." This statement reflects one of the most controversial aspects of the rehabilitation model: the link between treatment and discretionary release. Many experts argue that therapy and other programs cannot succeed in a coercive atmosphere, yet some parole boards clearly do link release to participation in rehabilitative programs. In addition, although penologists frequently say that prison programs should be voluntary, some corrections officials use parole to pressure prisoners to participate in self-improvement programs. For example, a prisoner whose reading and other academic skills are below the high school level may be told that he will never be eligible for parole unless he attends basic education classes. Technically, the prisoner's participation in the classes is voluntary because he or she could decline to enroll. In reality, however, few prisoners would knowingly prolong their incarceration by refusing to participate when parole eligibility is at stake.

Although some people may reject the idea that program participation should be a consideration for release, the fact remains that inmates believe that program participation helps them to build a good record for the board. Most parole boards stipulate that an inmate's institutional adjustment, including participation and progress in self-improvement programs, is one of the criteria to be considered in a release decision. A Connecticut inmate noted, "The last time I went before the board they wanted to know why I hadn't taken advantage of the programs. Now I go to A.A. and group therapy. I hope they will be satisfied." The "parole board game" may be the main reason many inmates participate in prison programs.

In some states, inmates convicted of drug or sex offenses may be expected to participate in substance abuse or sex abuse treatment programs. However, the state correctional system may not have enough treatment programs to serve all of them. Offenders may wait long periods before gaining admission to a particular program, or they may be in an institution that does not have the program they need. Because they cannot force the prison system to transfer them to the appropriate institution, they may become frustrated hearing about other people gaining parole while they remain stuck inside without an opportunity to prove themselves to the board. Moreover, some kinds of treatment programs, especially for sex offenders, may involve intrusive counseling therapies or medications that have lingering physical effects and a limited likelihood of success. Yet, faced with the threat of denial of parole if they refuse to participate, prisoners may not feel able to decline such treatments.

Structuring Parole Decisions

In response to the criticism that parole boards' release decisions are somewhat arbitrary, many states have adopted guidelines to ensure proper and consistent decisions. As in sentencing guidelines, a "salient factor" score measures the offender's criminal history (drug arrests, prior record, age at first conviction, and so on) and risk factors regarded as being relevant to successful completion of parole (see Table 14.1), and a "severity scale" ranks crimes according to their seriousness (see Table 14.2). By placing the offender's salient factors score next to his or her particular offense on the severity scale, the board, the inmate, and correctional officials are able to identify the **presumptive parole date** soon after the offender enters prison. This is the date by which the inmate can expect to be released if there are no disciplinary or

presumptive parole date

The presumed release date stipulated by parole guidelines for an offender who serves time without disciplinary or other problems.

Criminal History/Risk Factor	Points	Score
A No prior felony convictions as an adult or juvenile:	3	
One prior felony conviction:	2	
Two or three prior felony convictions:	1	
Four or more prior felony convictions:	0	_____
B No prior felony or misdemeanor incarcerations (that is, executed sentences of ninety days or more) as an adult or juvenile:	2	
One or two prior incarcerations:	1	
Three or more prior incarcerations:	0	_____
C Verified period of three years conviction-free in the community prior to the present commitment:	1	
Otherwise:	0	_____
D Age at commencement of behavior leading to this incarceration was _____ :		
Date of birth was _____ / _____ / _____ .		
Twenty-six or older and at least one point received in A, B, or C:	2	
Twenty-six or older and no points received in A, B, or C:	1	
Twenty-one to under twenty-six and at least one point received in A, B, or C:	1	
Twenty-one to under twenty-six and no points received in A, B, or C:	0	
Under twenty-one:	0	_____
E Present commitment does not include parole, probation, failure to appear, release agreement, escape, or custody violation:	2	
Present commitment involves probation, release, agreement, or failure to appear violation:	1	
Present commitment involves parole, escape, or custody violation:	0	_____
F Has no admitted or documented substance abuse problem within a three-year period in the community immediately preceding the commission of the crime conviction:	1	
Otherwise:	0	
Total history risk assessment score:		_____

TABLE 14.1
Criminal History/Risk Assessment under the Oregon Guidelines for Adult Offenders
The amount of time to be served is related to the severity of the offense and the criminal history/risk assessment of the inmate. The criminal history score is determined by adding the points assigned each factor in this table. Based on that total, the presumptive release date can be determined (see Table 14.2).

SOURCE: Adapted from State of Oregon, Board of Parole, ORS Chapter 144, Rule 255-75-026 and Rule 255-75-035.

other problems during incarceration. The presumptive release date may be modified on a scheduled basis. The date of release may be advanced because of good conduct, superior achievement in programs, and other factors that demonstrate rehabilitation. Alternatively, the presumptive release date may be postponed if there are disciplinary infractions or if a suitable community supervision plan has not been developed.

THE IMPACT OF RELEASE MECHANISMS

The release mechanisms employed by states do more than simply determine the date at which a particular prisoner will be sent back into the community. Parole release also has an enormous impact on other parts of the system, including sentencing, plea bargaining, and the size of prison populations.

One important result of discretionary release is that an administrative body—the parole board—can shorten a judge's sentence. Even in states that have determinate sentencing or parole guidelines designed to limit discretion,

TABLE 14.2

Number of Months to Be Served Before Release (presumptive parole date) under the Oregon Guidelines
The presumptive release date is determined by finding the criminal history score (Table 14.1) and the category of the offense. Thus, an offender with an assessment score between 6 and 8, convicted of a category 3 offense, can expect to serve 10–14 months.

SOURCE: Adapted from State of Oregon, Board of Parole, ORS Chapter 144, Rule 255-75-026 and Rule 255-75-035.

Offense Severity	Criminal History/Risk Assessment Score			
	11–9 Excellent	8–6 Good	5–3 Fair	2–0 Poor
Category 1: Bigamy, criminal mischief I, dogfighting, incest, possession of stolen vehicle	6	6	6–10	12–18
Category 2: Abandonment of a child, bribing a witness, criminal homicide, perjury, possession of controlled substance	6	6–10	10–14	16–24
Category 3: Assault III, forgery I, sexual abuse, trafficking in stolen vehicles	6–10	10–14	14–20	22–32
Category 4: Aggravated theft, assault II, coercion, criminally negligent homicide, robbery II	10–16	16–22	22–30	32–44
Category 5: Burglary I, escape I, manslaughter II, racketeering, rape I	16–24	24–36	40–52	56–72
Category 6: Arson I, kidnapping I, rape II, sodomy I	30–40	44–56	60–80	90–130
Category 7: Aggravated murder, treason	96–120	120–156	156–192	192–240
Category 8: Aggravated murder (stranger-stranger, cruelty to victim, prior murder conviction)	20–168	168–228	228–288	288–life

various potential reductions built into the sentence mean that the full sentence is rarely served. "Good time," for example, can reduce punishment even if there is no parole eligibility.

To understand the impact of discretionary release on criminal punishment, we need to compare the amount of time actually served in prison with the sentence specified by the judge. In some jurisdictions, up to 80 percent of felons sentenced to prison are released to the community after their first appearance before the parole board. Eligibility for discretionary release is ordinarily determined by the minimum term of the sentence minus good time and jail time. As we have seen, good time allows the minimum sentence to be reduced for good behavior during incarceration or for exceptional performance of assigned tasks or personal achievement. Jail time—credit given for time spent in jail while the offender awaited trial and sentencing—also shortens the period that must be served before the inmate's first appearance before the parole board.

There is considerable variation among the states, but according to estimates, felony inmates nationwide serve an average of less than two years before release. The amount of time served in prison varies with the nature of the offense. However, even offenders who commit serious, violent offenses may serve relatively short prison terms. In fact, most people would probably be shocked to learn that the actual time served is so much less than the sentences announced in court and reported in the media.

Figure 14.2 helps us understand how indeterminate sentences, good-time provisions, and discretionary release on parole shortened the amount of time that inmates were incarcerated in federal prisons. Although offenders who received longer sentences remained in prison for longer periods of time, the proportion of the sentence actually served dropped rapidly as the length of the sentence increased. For example, the robbery offenders who were sen-

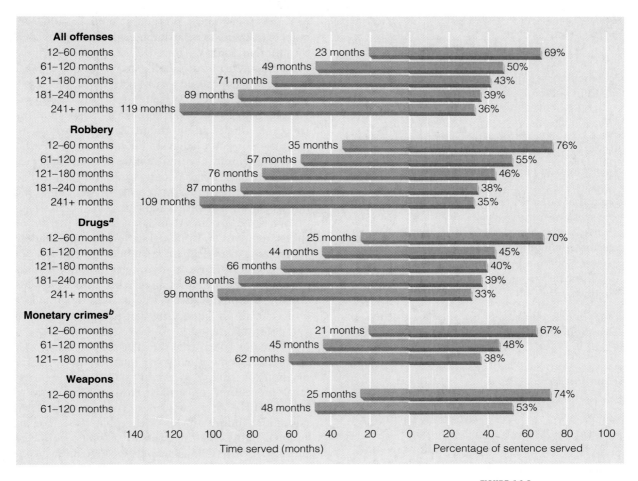

All offenses
	Time served (months)	Percentage of sentence served
12–60 months	23 months	69%
61–120 months	49 months	50%
121–180 months	71 months	43%
181–240 months	89 months	39%
241+ months	119 months	36%

Robbery
	Time served (months)	Percentage of sentence served
12–60 months	35 months	76%
61–120 months	57 months	55%
121–180 months	76 months	46%
181–240 months	87 months	38%
241+ months	109 months	35%

Drugs[a]
	Time served (months)	Percentage of sentence served
12–60 months	25 months	70%
61–120 months	44 months	45%
121–180 months	66 months	40%
181–240 months	88 months	39%
241+ months	99 months	33%

Monetary crimes[b]
	Time served (months)	Percentage of sentence served
12–60 months	21 months	67%
61–120 months	45 months	48%
121–180 months	62 months	38%

Weapons
	Time served (months)	Percentage of sentence served
12–60 months	25 months	74%
61–120 months	48 months	53%

Time served (months) — 140 120 100 80 60 40 20 0

Percentage of sentence served — 0 20 40 60 80 100

tenced to terms of 12–60 months actually served 76 percent of their terms. By contrast, offenders sentenced to terms of 181–240 months actually served only 38 percent of their terms.

The probability of release well before the end of the formal sentence encourages plea bargaining by both prosecutors and defendants. Prosecutors can receive the benefits of quick, cooperative plea bargains that look tough in the eyes of the public. Meanwhile, the defendant agrees to plead guilty and accept the sentence because of the high likelihood of early release through parole.

Beyond the benefits of parole to prosecutors, supporters of discretion for the paroling authority argue that it has invaluable benefits for the overall system. Discretionary release mitigates the harshness of the penal code. If the legislature must establish exceptionally strict punishments as a means to convey a "tough-on-crime" image to frustrated and angry voters, parole can effectively permit sentence adjustments that make the punishment fit the crime. Everyone convicted of larceny may not have caused equivalent harm, yet some legislatively mandated sentencing schemes may impose equally strict sentences. Early release on parole can be granted to an offender who is less deserving of strict punishment, such as someone who voluntarily makes restitution, cooperates with law enforcement officials, or shows genuine regret.

Parole has benefits in other contexts, too. In states that place extensive discretionary authority for sentencing in the hands of judges, parole may

FIGURE 14.2

Average Time Served by Adults Convicted of Selected Federal Offenses

This figure includes adult offenders who had initial hearings between 1 July 1979 and 30 June 1980 and who were released prior to 1 January 1987 or had a release scheduled by the Parole Commission for a later date. Offenders sentenced to one year or less are excluded.

SOURCE: Adapted from U.S. Department of Justice, Bureau of Justice Statistics, *Special Report*, (June 1987), p. 4.

[a]Includes marijuana, drug, and controlled substance offenses.

[b]Includes counterfeiting, forgery, mail theft, embezzlement, interstate transportation of stolen securities, and receiving stolen property with intent to sell. Excludes burglary and theft.

At the time of sentencing, Ben Brooks had been held in jail for six months awaiting trial and disposition of his case. He was given a sentence of five to ten years for robbery with violence. Brooks did well at Stanhope, the maximum security prison to which he was sent. He did not get into trouble and was thus able to amass good-time credit at the rate of one day for every four that he spent on good behavior. In addition, he was given thirty days' meritorious credit when he completed his high school equivalency test after attending the prison school for two years. Computation of Ben's eligibility for an appearance before the Board of Parole is shown below:

Maximum sentence	3,650 days (10 years)
Minimum sentence	1,825 days (5 years)
"Jail time"	-180
	1,645
Meritorious good time	-30
	1,615
Good time (1 for 4)	-404
Actual time served	1,211 days
	(3 years, 4 months)

After serving three years, three months, and four days of his sentence, he appeared before the Board of Parole and was granted release into the community.

What factors were considered in computing parole eligibility? Does the use of these factors make sentences too short? Are you surprised by the gap between the minimum sentence and the actual time served?

be used to equalize sentences between similarly culpable offenders who happened to be sentenced by different judges. Thus, the excessively punitive judge's sentence can be mitigated by parole so that offenders who caused equivalent harm can serve equivalent sentences. In addition, as discussed previously, parole is necessary to assist prison administrators in maintaining order. Parole provides an incentive for good behavior for many inmates who otherwise would have no reason to cooperate with prison officials. Some people argue that parole also is beneficial because the parole stage offers the opportunity for a more detached evaluation of an offender and a crime than is possible in the atmosphere of a trial. Unlike trial judges who handle sentencing, parole board members usually do not make decisions in the glare of television news lights or in a courtroom full of angry citizens. Parole benefits the criminal justice system as well by providing a mechanism for alleviating the substantial financial costs of incarceration.

A major criticism of the effect of parole is that it has shifted responsibility for many of the primary decisions of criminal justice from a judge, who holds legal procedures uppermost, to an administrative board, where discretion rules. Through their legal education, judges are knowledgeable about constitutional rights and the need to provide basic legal protections to criminal defendants. By contrast, parole board members may not have knowledge about and sensitivity to these constitutional values. In most states that allow discretion, parole decisions are made in secret hearings, with only the board members, the inmate, and correctional officers present. Often, no published criteria exist to guide decisions, and the prisoners are given no reason for either the denial or granting of their release. Should we place such significant discretionary power in the hands of parole boards? Because there is so little oversight over their decision making and so few constraints on their decisions, some parole board members will make arbitrary or discriminatory decisions that are inconsistent with the values underlying our constitutional system of government and civil rights. Generally, our legal system seeks to avoid determining people's fates through such methods.

SUPERVISION IN THE COMMUNITY

Parolees must abide by certain conditions when they are released from prison. If they violate these conditions, they may be returned to prison to serve out their complete sentence behind bars. They cannot commit additional crimes, and they must live according to rules designed both to help them readjust to society and to control their movements. These rules may require them to abstain from alcoholic beverages, keep away from former associates, maintain good work habits, and not leave the state without permission. The restrictions are justified on the ground that people who have been incarcerated must gradually readjust to the community. Presumably, this will make them less susceptible to the negative temptations of a free society and less likely to fall back into their preconviction habits and associations. However, the enforcement of strict rules for parolees creates problems not only for the parolee but also for the administration of this type of community treatment program. In addition, it raises questions about the appropriateness of attempting to impose standards of conduct on parolees that are not imposed on law-abiding citizens.

When they first come out of prison, parolees face a staggering array of problems. In most states, they are given only clothes, a token amount of money, the list of rules governing their conditional release, and the name and address of the parole supervisor to whom they must report within twenty-four hours. Although a promised job is often a condition for release, actually becoming employed may be another matter. Most ex-convicts are unskilled or semiskilled, and the conditions of parole may restrict their movements. Thus, they may not be permitted to move to areas where jobs are most plentiful. If the parolee is African-American, male, and under thirty, he joins the largest group of unemployed people in the country. Moreover, in most states, laws prevent former prisoners from being employed in certain types of establishments—where alcohol is sold, for example—thus ruling out many jobs. In many trades, union affiliation is a requirement for employment, and there are restrictions on the admission of new members. Finally, many parolees, as well as other ex-convicts, face a significant dilemma. If they are truthful about their backgrounds, many employers will never hire them. If they are not truthful, however, they can be fired for lying if the employer ever learns about their conviction.

The situation of the newly released parolee has been described as follows:

> He arrives without a job in an urban area, after years in prison, with perhaps $20 or $30 in his pocket. Surviving is a trick, even if he's a frugal person, not inclined to blow his few dollars on drinks and women. The parole agents—with some remarkable exceptions—don't give a damn. He's deposited in the very middle of the city, where all he can find is a fleabag hotel in the Tenderloin. He has an aching determination to make it on the outside, but there are hustlers all over him; gambling con games, dollar poker.[3]

Other re-entry problems may plague parolees. For many, the transition from the highly structured life in prison to the open society proves too difficult to manage. Many just do not have the social, psychological, and material resources to manage the temptations and complications of modern life. For these parolees, freedom may be short-lived as they fall back into forbidden activities such as drinking, abusing drugs, and stealing.

IDEAS IN PRACTICE

Carl DeFlumer has spent 42 of his 62 years in prison for killing a boy when he was fourteen and sodomizing another 29 years later. In September 1994, the New York State Board of Parole granted his release to live with his sister. Word of DeFlumer's impending release caused a howl of protest in Bethlehem, the rural community where his sister lives. Residents expressed fear for the safety of their children. As one said, "You need a building permit to put a fence in your yard. But they can put one of these guys next door and not even tell you."

Should residents be allowed to determine if parolees can live in their community? What should happen to offenders who complete their sentence and have no place to reside?

Finally, offenders must adjust not only to the challenges and temptations of living in a free society but also to changes that have taken place in society itself while they were in prison. This transitional period is believed to be the critical time that will determine whether the offender can avoid returning to a life of crime.

COMMUNITY PROGRAMS FOLLOWING RELEASE

Various programs have been developed to assist parolees re-entering society. Some programs help prepare inmates for release; other programs provide employment and housing assistance after release. Together, the programs are intended to help the offender progress steadily toward reintegration into the community.

Programs of partial confinement prior to parole are used to test the readiness of the offender for full release. While the prisoner is still confined, correctional staff members must evaluate a variety of issues. Community-based corrections assumes that there are several alternatives to incarceration and that the goal is to choose the least restrictive alternative that will lead to eventual reintegration. Thus, staff members must first consider whether a particular offender needs to be in maximum security custody or whether he or she is ready for a less structured environment. If a less structured environment is appropriate, then the staff must decide whether the offender should be moved to a halfway house within the community. The staff must also consider whether the offender has the necessary skills to obtain employment and become self-sufficient.

Among the many programs developed to assist offenders in their return to the community, three are especially important: work and educational release, furloughs, and residential programs. Although they are similar in many ways, each offers a specific approach to helping formerly incarcerated individuals re-enter the community.

Work and Educational Release

work and educational release
The release of inmates from correctional institutions during the day so that they may work or attend school.

Programs of **work and educational release**, whereby inmates are released from correctional institutions during the day so that they may work or attend school, were first established in Vermont in 1906. However, the Huber Act, passed by the Wisconsin legislature in 1913, is usually cited as the model on which such programs are based. By 1972, most states and the federal government had instituted them.

Although most work and educational release programs are justifiable in terms of rehabilitation, many correctional administrators and legislators like them because they cost relatively little. In some states, a portion of the inmate's employment earnings may even be deducted for room and board. One of the problems of administering the programs is that the person on release is often viewed by other inmates as being privileged, and such perceptions can lead to resentment and conflict within the prison. Another problem is that in some states, organized labor complains that jobs are being taken from free citizens. Furthermore, the releasee's contact with the community increases the chances of contraband being brought into the institution. To deal with such bootlegging and to assist in the reintegration process, some states and counties have built special work and educational release units in urban areas.

Furlough

Isolation from loved ones is one of the pains of imprisonment. Although conjugal visits have been a part of correctional programs in many countries, they have been used in only a few U.S. correctional systems. Many penologists view the **furlough**—the temporary release of an inmate from a correctional institution for a visit home—as a meaningful alternative. Consistent with the focus of community corrections, brief home furloughs are being used more frequently in the United States. In some states, an effort is made to ensure that all eligible inmates are able to use the furlough privilege on Thanksgiving and Christmas. In other states, however, the program has been much more restrictive, and often only those about to be released are given furloughs.

Furloughs are thought to offer an excellent means of testing an inmate's ability to cope with the larger society. Through home visits, family ties can be renewed and the tensions of confinement can be reduced. Most administrators also feel that furloughs are good for prisoners' morale. The general public, however, does not always support the concept. Public outrage is inevitable if an offender on furlough commits another crime or fails to return. In the 1988 presidential campaign, Democratic candidate Michael Dukakis, the governor of Massachusetts, lost voter support because the opposition publicized the fact that a prisoner named Willie Horton had committed a horrible rape while on furlough from a Massachusetts prison. Correctional authorities are often nervous about using furloughs because they fear being blamed for a "Willie Horton" incident.

Residential Programs

The **community correctional center** is an institution that houses soon-to-be-released inmates and that connects them to community services, resources, and support. It may take a number of forms and serve a variety of offender clients. Throughout the country, halfway houses, prerelease centers, and correctional service centers can be found. Most programs require offenders to reside at the facility while they work in the community or visit with their families. Other facilities are designed primarily to provide services and programs for parolees. Often, these facilities are established in former private homes or small hotels, which helps create a homey, less institutional environment. Individual rooms, group dining rooms, and other homelike features are maintained whenever possible.

The term **halfway house** has been applied to a variety of community correctional facilities and programs whereby felons work in the community but reside in the halfway house during nonworking hours. Halfway houses range from secure institutions in the community with programs designed to assist inmates preparing for release on parole to group homes where parolees, probationers, or persons diverted from the system are able to live with minimal supervision and direction. Some halfway houses are organized to deliver special treatment services, such as programs designed to deal with alcohol, drug, or mental problems.

There is no recent data on the number of halfway houses in the United States or on the number of clients housed in them. In the early 1980s, there were an estimated eight hundred halfway houses, most operated under contract by private organizations. Their average capacity was twenty-five residents, who generally stayed eight to sixteen weeks.[4] There are three models of release or transfer to halfway houses. In one model, halfway houses serve as a preparation station for offenders who will soon be released on parole. In this setting, they can

furlough
The temporary release of an inmate from a correctional institution for a brief period, usually one to three days, for a visit home.

community correctional center
An institution housing soon-to-be-released inmates and connecting them with community services, resources, and support.

halfway house
Term applied to a variety of community correctional facilities and programs whereby felons may work in the community but reside in the halfway house during nonworking hours.

The halfway house provides a supportive atmosphere for parolees, probationers, and those diverted from the system. In this San Francisco halfway house a prospective new resident is interviewed by the director and present residents.

prepare for the challenges of returning to life in free society. In the second model, offenders are paroled from prison directly to a halfway house, where officials can monitor their adjustment and help them reintegrate. The third model involves paroling offenders directly into the community and making the halfway house available as a resource for parolees who need support or assistance.[5]

Residential programs have problems. Not unexpectedly, few neighborhoods want to host halfway houses or treatment centers for convicts. Community resistance has been a significant impediment to the development of community-based corrections facilities and even has forced some successful facilities to close. Community corrections has become a major political issue, as have programs for the mentally disabled and the retarded. Many communities, often wealthier ones, have succeeded in blocking placement of halfway houses or treatment centers within their boundaries. One result of this "not in my backyard" attitude is that centers are established in deteriorating neighborhoods inhabited by poor people, who lack the political power and resources to block unpopular programs.

The future of residential programs is unclear. Originally advocated for both rehabilitative and financial reasons, they do not seem to be saving as much money for the correctional system as officials had hoped. Medical care, education, vocational rehabilitation, and therapy are expensive. Thus, the costs of quality community programs likely differ little from the costs of incarceration. Effective programs require the services of teachers, counselors, and other professional personnel. Moreover, in order to be truly effective, these officials must work with small numbers of offenders. The savings from having fewer custodial personnel in community programs may be offset by the costs of providing needed counseling and other professional services.

If recidivism rates of offenders who have been involved in community treatment were proven to be lower, the expenditures might more readily be justified. However, the available data are discouraging. For example, one evaluation of a federally administered prerelease guidance center found a recidivism rate of 37 percent among its clients versus a 32 percent rate among a control group. Apparently, the excitement and optimism associated with the community correctional movement may have been unwarranted.

PAROLE OFFICER: COP OR SOCIAL WORKER?

After release, a parolee's principal contact with the criminal justice system is through the parole officer, who is responsible for seeing that the conditions imposed by the parole board are followed. The conditions imposed by Connecticut's Board of Parole are quite substantial and not atypical. Consider how difficult it must be for a parole officer to monitor the following twelve conditions, especially when the officer is responsible for many parolees at once.

1. Upon release from the institution, you must follow the instructions of the institutional parole officer (or other designated authority of the Division of Parole) with regard to reporting to your supervising parole officer and/or fulfilling any other obligations.
2. You must report to your parole officer when instructed to do so and must permit your parole officer or any parole officer to visit you at your home and place of employment at any time.
3. You must work steadily, and you must secure the permission of your parole officer before changing your residence or your employment, and

you must report any change of residence or employment to your parole officer within twenty-four hours of such change.

4. You must submit written reports as instructed by your parole officer.
5. You must not leave the state of Connecticut without first obtaining permission from your parole officer.
6. You must not apply for a motor vehicle operator's license, or own, purchase, or operate any motor vehicle without first obtaining permission from your parole officer.
7. You must not marry without first obtaining written permission from your parole officer.
8. You must not own, possess, use, sell, or have under your control at any time any deadly weapons or firearms.
9. You must not possess, use, or traffic in any narcotic, hallucinatory, or other harmful drugs in violation of the law.
10. You must support your dependents, if any, and assume toward them all moral and legal obligations.
11. (a) You shall not consume alcoholic beverages to excess. (b) You shall totally abstain from the use of alcoholic beverages or liquors. (Strike out either a or b, leaving whichever clause is applicable.)
12. You must comply with all laws and conduct yourself as a good citizen. You must show by your attitude, cooperation, choice of associates, and places of amusement and recreation that you are a proper person to remain on parole.

Huge caseloads make effective supervision practically impossible in some states. A national survey has shown that parole caseloads range from fifty to seventy. Although this is smaller than probation caseloads, offenders who have just been released from prison require more extensive services. For one thing, parolees, by the very fact of their incarceration, have generally committed much more serious crimes than probationers. For another, probationers continue their lives in the community while living under a set of restrictive conditions, whereas parolees are making a very difficult transition from the highly structured prison environment back into a society in which they have previously failed to live as law-abiding citizens. It is exceptionally difficult for a parole officer to monitor, control, and assist clients who may have little knowledge of or experience with living successfully within society's rules.

Parole officers are asked to play two different roles: cop and social worker. In their role as police officer, they are given the power to restrict many aspects of the parolee's life, to enforce the conditions of release, and to initiate revocation proceedings if parole conditions are violated. Like other officials in the criminal justice system, the parole officer has extensive discretion in low-visibility situations. In many states, parole officers have the authority to search the parolee's house without warning, to arrest him or her without the possibility of bail for suspected violations, and to suspend parole pending a hearing before the board. This authoritative component of the parole officer's role can produce a sense of insecurity in the ex-offender and hamper the development of mutual trust. The law enforcement powers granted to parole officers are justified on the grounds that the community must be protected from offenders who are coming

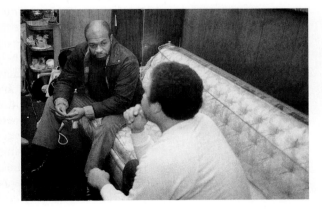

Parole officers are responsible for both supervising the activities of ex-offenders and helping them find the resources they need to successfully establish their lives outside of prison.

out of prison. However, because these powers diminish the possibility for the officer to develop a close relationship with the client, they may weaken the officer's other role of assisting the parolee's readjustment to the community.

In addition to their policing responsibilities, parole officers must act as social workers by helping the parolee to find a job and restore family ties. Officers must be prepared to serve as agent-mediators between parolees and the organizations with which they deal and to channel them to social agencies, such as psychiatric clinics, where they can obtain help. As caseworkers, officers must try to develop a relationship that allows parolees to feel free to confide their frustrations and concerns. Since parolees are not likely to do this if they are constantly aware of the parole officer's ability to send them back to prison, some researchers have suggested that parole officers' conflicting responsibilities of cop and social worker should be separated. Parole officers could maintain the supervisory aspects of the position, and other personnel, such as a separate parole counselor, could perform the casework functions. Alternatively, parole officers could be charged solely with social work duties while local police check for violations.

The parole officer works within a bureaucratic environment. The difficulties faced by many parolees are so complex that the officer's job is almost impossible. At the same time, like most other human services organizations, parole agencies are short on resources and expertise. As a result, they frequently must classify parolees and give priority to those most in need. To serve those with the greatest need, most parole officers spend more time with the newly released. As the officer gains greater confidence in the parolee, the level of supervision can be adjusted to "active" or "reduced" surveillance. Depending on how the parolee has functioned in the community, he or she eventually may be required only to check in with the officer periodically rather than submit to regular home visits, searches, and other intrusive monitoring.

ADJUSTMENT TO LIFE OUTSIDE PRISON

With little preparation, the ex-offender moves from the highly structured, authoritarian life of the institution into a world that is filled with temptations and complicated problems. Suddenly, ex-convicts who are not even accustomed to undertaking such simple tasks as going to the store for groceries are expected to assume pressing, complex responsibilities. Problems are not limited to finding a job and a place to live. The parolee must also make significant social and psychological role adjustments. A male ex-convict, for example, is suddenly required to become not only a parolee but also an employee, neighbor, father, husband, and son. The expectations, norms, and social relations in the free world are quite different from those learned in prison. The inmate code is replaced by society's often nebulous rules of behavior—rules that the offender had failed to cope with during his or her previous life in free society.

The re-entry problems of parolees are reflected in their rearrest rates. As shown in Figure 14.3 about 25 percent are arrested during the first six months, almost 40 percent within the first year, and 62 percent within three years.[6] About 40 percent of those rearrested will be reincarcerated.

It is not surprising that the recidivism rate is so high, given that today's average ex-convict has been convicted of serious crimes (83 percent for violent or property offenses), has a criminal record of multiple arrests (8.4 prior arrests), and has been incarcerated before (67 percent).[7] Few can be characterized as situational offenders who have run afoul of the law only once when they made a bad decision or acted impulsively. Instead, most prisoners have committed serious crimes and have a long history of difficulties with the criminal justice system. The numbers indicate that a large percentage of today's inmates are career criminals who will resort to their old habits upon release. In addition, the experience of spending time in prison is essentially designed to punish people for their harmful acts. By itself, the experience of incarceration is unlikely to teach anyone how to succeed in the community. In fact, the artificial environment of prisons moves people farther away from the atmosphere, attitudes, habits, and responsibilities that make for success in American society.

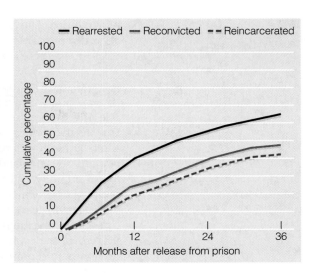

REVOCATION OF PAROLE

Always hanging over the ex-inmate's head is the potential revocation of parole for committing a new crime or failing to adhere to the parole contract. Since parolees still have the status of inmate, some corrections experts believe that parole should be easily revoked without the use of formal procedures, hearings, or rules of evidence. In some states, liberal parole policies have been justified to the public on the grounds that revocation is swift and can be imposed before a crime is committed. For example, some state statutes provide that if the parole officer has reasonable cause to believe that the parolee has lapsed or is about to lapse into criminal ways or has otherwise violated the conditions of parole, a report of these suspicions should be made to the parole board so that the parolee can be apprehended. Statutes may also permit parole officers to take the parolee into custody and call for a revocation hearing. The parolee who leaves the state or has been charged with a new offense is usually arrested and detained until a revocation hearing or a criminal trial is held.

If the parole officer alleges that a technical (noncriminal) violation of the parole contract has occurred, a revocation proceeding will be held before the parolee is sent back to prison. In the case of ***Morrissey v. Brewer (1972)***, the U.S. Supreme Court held that a parolee who faces parole revocation must be accorded due process rights and a prompt, informal inquiry before an impartial hearing officer. However, the Court distinguished the requirements of such a proceeding from the normal requirements of the criminal trial.[8] The Court has required a two-step hearing process whereby the parole board determines whether the contract has been violated. Parolees have the right to be notified of the charges against them, to know the evidence against them, to be allowed to speak on their own behalf, to present witnesses, and to confront the witnesses against them.

The number of parole revocations is difficult to determine since the published data do not distinguish between parolees returned to prison for technical violations and those sent back for new criminal offenses. Because prisons are so overcrowded, most revocations occur only when the parolee has been arrested on a serious charge or cannot be located by the parole officer. Given the normal caseload, most parole officers are unable to monitor parolees closely and thus may be unaware of technical violations. Under the

FIGURE 14.3
Cumulative Percentage of State Prisoners Rearrested, Reconvicted, and Reincarcerated Thirty-Six Months After Release
The first year after release is the period of greatest probability for recidivism. What factors separate those who successfully complete parole from those who return to prison?
SOURCE: U.S. Department of Justice, Bureau of Justice Statistics, *Special Report* (April 1989).

Morrissey v. *Brewer* (1972)

A parolee who faces parole revocation must be accorded due process rights and a prompt, informal inquiry before an impartial hearing officer.

341

new requirements for prompt and fair hearings, some parole boards discourage officers from issuing violation warrants following infractions of parole rules unless there is evidence of new crimes.

THE FUTURE OF PAROLE

The effectiveness of corrections is usually measured by the recidivism rate. Despite the modest success of parole and various release methods as measured by recidivism rates, these programs are likely to expand. As prison populations rise, demands that felons be allowed to serve part of their time in the community will undoubtedly mount. These demands will not come from the public, which typically believes that all offenders should serve their full sentences. Instead, they will come from the legislators and corrections officials who recognize that we lack the money and facilities to incarcerate all offenders for the complete terms of their sentences. In states with discretionary release, parole provides one of the few ways for correctional officials to relieve institutional pressures. In many states where mandatory release is the way out of prison, offenders nearing expiration of their terms are being moved to community facilities so that they can begin the reintegration process. Although many offenders are not successfully integrated into the community, we must recognize that most offenders will end up back in free society whether or not they serve their full sentences. Parole and community programs represent an effort to address the inevitability of their return. Even if such programs do not prevent all offenders from leaving the life of crime, they do help some to turn their lives around.

CIVIL DISABILITIES

In theory, once a person has been released from prison, paid a fine, or completed parole or probation, the debt to society has been paid and the punishment has ended. For many offenders, however, a criminal conviction is a lifetime burden. In most states, certain civil rights are forfeited forever, some fields of employment are closed, and some insurance or pension benefits may be denied. It does not matter if an ex-convict successfully obtains steady employment, raises a family, and contributes time to community organizations.

The extent of civil disabilities varies greatly among the states. In some states, persons who have been convicted of certain crimes are subjected to specific restrictions. A conviction for forgery, for example, prevents employment in the banking or stock-trading fields. In other states, blanket restrictions are placed on all felons regardless of the circumstances of the crime. These restrictions are removed only upon completion of the sentence, after a period subsequent to completion of the sentence, or upon action of a board of pardons. The forfeiture of rights can be traced to Greek and Roman times, and American courts have generally upheld the constitutionality of such restrictions.

The civil rights to vote and hold public office are generally limited upon conviction. Three-fourths of the states return the right to vote after varying lengths of time, while the remainder keep felons off of the voting lists unless they are pardoned or apply for the restoration of full citizenship. Nineteen states permanently restrict the right to hold public office to felony offenders unless pardoned or given back their full citizenship, and twenty-one states return the right following discharge from probation, parole, or prison. Other civil rights such as eligibility to serve on juries and access to public employment are denied felons in many states.[9]

Although most former felons may not believe that restrictions on their civil rights will make it difficult for them to lead normal lives, barriers to certain fields of employment are a problem. Ironically, many prison vocational programs lead to occupations from which former inmates may be barred. In various states, restricted occupations include nurse, beautician, barber, real estate salesperson, chauffeur, employee in a place where alcoholic beverages are served, cashier, stenographer, and insurance agent. According to Richard Singer, "In all, nearly six thousand occupations are licensed in one or more states; the convicted offender may find the presumption against him either difficult or impossible to overcome."[10] Many observers assert that the restrictions push offenders toward menial jobs at low pay and may lead them back to crime.

Critics of civil disability laws point out that, upon fulfilling the penalty imposed for a crime, the former offender should be assisted to full reintegration into society. They argue that it is counterproductive for the government to promote rehabilitation with the goal of reintegration while at the same time preventing offenders from fully achieving that goal. Supporters counter that the possibility of recidivism and the community's need for protection justify these restrictions. Between these two extremes is the belief that not all persons convicted of felonies should be treated equally and that society can be protected adequately by the placement of restrictions on only certain individuals.

SUMMARY

The primary method by which inmates return to society is release on parole. Parolees receive a conditional release from incarceration but remain under correctional supervision. The mechanism may be based on state guidelines involving mandated calculations concerning the offense, offender, and time served, or it may be based on the discretionary decisions of a parole board. Because parole boards cannot accurately predict the future behavior of convicted offenders, public controversies inevitably arise when parolees commit new crimes. If ex-offenders are arrested or violate the rules of their parole, they may be returned to prison after a revocation hearing. The parole officer is often a key figure in determining whether a parolee will be returned to prison. Because parole officers are responsible for enforcing rules for parolees, they cannot always work effectively in counseling and assisting parolees in the reintegration process.

Upon release, offenders face a number of problems: They must find housing and employment and renew relationships with family and friends. Community corrections assumes that re-entry should be a gradual process and that parolees should be assisted in it. Halfway houses, work and educational release, furloughs, and community correctional centers are geared to ease the transition. In some states, prerelease counseling programs help prisoners prepare to cope with the situations that they will face on the street. Despite the efforts of these programs, many offenders inevitably return to prison. Even those who succeed in staying away from further criminal activities bear the burdens of civil disabilities whereby various states restrict their employment options and civil rights. Like other aspects of the criminal justice system, the release and reintegration of offenders presents daunting challenges that are not easily solved.

QUESTIONS FOR REVIEW

1. What are the basic assumptions of parole?
2. What are the historical roots of parole? How did the system evolve?
3. What is the difference between mandatory release and discretionary release?
4. What is the role of the parole officer?
5. What problems confront parolees upon their release?

NOTES

1. Robert James Bidinotto, "Revolving-Door Justice: Plague on America," *Reader's Digest*, February 1994, pp. 35–36.
2. As quoted in Donald J. Newman, "Legal Models for Parole: Future Developments," in *Contemporary Corrections*, ed. Benjamin Frank (Reston, VA: Reston, 1973), p. 246.
3. As quoted in Jessica Mitford, *Kind and Usual Punishment* (New York: Knopf, 1973), p. 217.
4. Edward Latessa and Harry Allen, "Halfway Houses and Parole: A National Assessment," *Journal of Criminal Justice* 10 (1982): 156. See also Edward J. Latessa and Lawrence F. Travis, III, "Residential Community Correctional Programs," in *Smart Sentencing*, ed. James M. Byrne, Arthur J. Lurigio, and Joan Petersilia (Newbury Park, CA: Sage, 1992), p. 166.
5. Latessa and Allen, "Halfway Houses and Parole," p. 156.
6. U.S. Department of Justice, Bureau of Justice Statistics, *Special Report* (April 1989).
7. Ibid.
8. *Morrissey* v. *Brewer*, 408 U.S. 471 (1972).
9. Velmer S. Burton, Jr., Francis T. Cullen, and Lawrence F. Travis, III, "The Collateral Consequences of a Felony Conviction: A National Study of State Statutes," *Federal Probation* 51 (September 1987), pp. 52–60.
10. Richard Singer, "Conviction: Civil Disabilities," in *Encyclopedia of Crime and Justice*, ed. Sanford H. Kadish (New York: Free Press, 1983), p. 246.

PART V *The Juvenile Justice System*

15 *Juvenile Justice*

Crimes committed by juveniles have become a serious national problem. The *Uniform Crime Reports* show that just over a third of the people arrested for an index crime are under eighteen years of age. Children who are charged with crimes, who have been neglected by their parents, or whose behavior is deemed to require official action come in contact with the juvenile justice system, an independent process that is interrelated with the adult system. As Chapter 15 will demonstrate, many of the procedures used in the handling of juvenile problems are similar to those used with adults, but the overriding philosophy of juvenile justice is somewhat different, and the extent to which the state may intrude into the lives of children is much greater.

CHAPTER 15
Juvenile Justice

HE WANTED A MOUNTAIN BIKE

During the summer of 1993, Gregory Morris, a fourteen-year-old from Brooklyn, New York, decided that he wanted a mountain bike. He and his friends went looking for one in Brooklyn's Prospect Park. They spotted Allyn Winslow, a forty-two-year-old drama teacher, riding past on a blue bike, and Morris decided he had found what he wanted. He handed his .22-caliber revolver to a friend and shouted, "Get him! Get him!" Winslow was shot in the back, but he managed to pedal away before dying. The youngsters were unable to steal the bike.

At trial, Jerome Nisbett, codefendant with Gregory Morris, was prosecuted as an adult, because New York law permits sixteen-year-olds to be treated as adults when they commit serious crimes. He received the maximum sentence for felony murder: twenty-five years to life. Fourteen-year-old Morris also received the maximum sentence. However, his was only for five years with the possibility of release after two and one-half years. Morris participated in a felony murder, a charge that could garner the death penalty for adults in some states, even if they, like Morris, did not actually pull the trigger. The lighter sentence given to Morris was the result of his age and the fact that New York law provides lesser felony murder sentences when those under sixteen do not

actually complete the robbery in the course of committing the homicide.[1]

Did Morris receive a fair sentence? Are the vast differences in the sentences given to Morris and Nisbett justified? If a fourteen-year-old and a sixteen-year-old participate in the same felony murder, why shouldn't they receive the same sentence?

The case of Gregory Morris illustrates several important issues of concern for American society. Crimes committed by juveniles are no longer limited to vandalism, theft, and drag-racing. The 1950s images of tough teenage hoodlums who fight each other with fists and occasionally with knives has been displaced by a more frightening image of 1990s gang members who kill each other—and innocent bystanders—with automatic weapons. Moreover, well-armed juvenile offenders do not just target each other. They may commit precisely the same crimes as the worst adult offenders, including vicious homicides in the course of small-time robberies involving items such as team jackets and basketball shoes. At the same time that society confronts the frightening recognition that young offenders can commit terrible acts, there is no agreement on a solution for the problem. Should we continue to treat juveniles differently than adults when they commit crimes because we assume that juveniles can be taught to change their ways? Or should we treat all criminals alike by being tough on everyone who commits violent crimes? As we will see in this chapter, separate institutions and processes have developed to handle crimes by juveniles. ★

YOUTH CRIME IN THE UNITED STATES

To a great extent, crime in the United States is a phenomenon of youth. Fewer than 12 percent of Americans are aged fifteen to twenty-one, yet this group accounts for 31.3 percent of all arrests for violent index crimes and 46.9 percent of all arrests for property index crimes (see Figure 15.1). Almost 2 million juveniles under age eighteen are arrested each year; nearly a million are processed by juvenile courts. Most juvenile crimes are committed by males; only 24 percent of arrestees under age eighteen are females. The youthfulness of persons prone to crime is illuminated by other facts: About one-third of those arrested each year are under twenty-one, and about half are under twenty-five.[2] Some researchers have estimated that one boy in three will be arrested by the police at some point before his eighteenth birthday. More tragic is the fact that homicide is now the leading cause of death for African-American males aged fourteen to forty-four, and juvenile murder arrest rates rose 332 percent from 1965 to 1990.[3]

Many youthful offenders are intimately connected to the contemporary problems of drugs and violence in American society. Data supplied by the National Council of Juvenile and Family Court Judges show that drug abuse is a problem in between 60 and 90 percent of the cases referred to them.[4] A study of four hundred detained juveniles in Florida showed that 41 percent tested positive for drug use. Of those who tested positive for cocaine, 51 percent were arrested or referred to juvenile authorities for a property misdemeanor within eighteen months of the testing.[5] In addition, the presence of youth gangs in most large American cities has brought new attention to the problem of juvenile crime. Many of the same gangs that now exist in the adult correctional system have their younger counterparts on the streets. Today's gangs have become a major element in the drug trade and its crimes of violence.

FIGURE 15.1

Percentage of Arrests of Persons under Age Twenty-One for Index Crimes
Although they make up less than 12 percent of the population, persons aged fifteen to twenty-one are arrested out of proportion to their numbers. Property offenses are the crimes most often committed by young people yet the number of violent crimes committed by this group is rising.

SOURCE: U.S. Department of Justice, *Crime in the United States* (Washington, DC: Government Printing Office, 1993), p. 233.

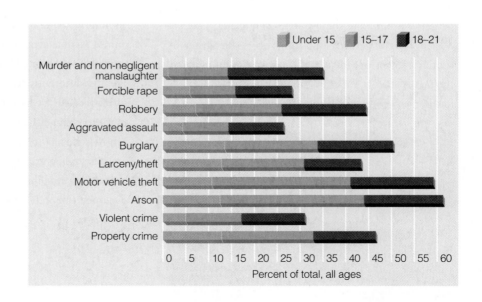

The idea that children should be treated differently from adults has its roots in the common law and the chancery courts of England. Under the common law, children under seven years of age were regarded as incapable of felonious intent and were therefore not criminally responsible for their actions. Children aged seven to fourteen could be held accountable only if it could be shown that they understood the consequences of their actions. This long-standing legal treatment of children's harmful acts as being different from similar acts committed by adults provided a basis for the different approaches to the processing and punishment of young offenders.

Under the doctrine of ***parens patriae***—the state as "parent" or guardian and protector of all citizens unable to protect themselves—the chancery courts exercised protective jurisdiction over all children, particularly those involved in questions of dependency, neglect, and property. The doctrine legitimized the intervention of the state on behalf of the child and provided a basis for placing juvenile crime into a different context than other kinds of criminal cases.

In the American colonies, the earliest attempt to deal with problem children was passage of the Massachusetts Stubborn Child Law in 1646. Based on the colony's religious principles, the law assumed that disobedient children were evil and that those who were not controlled by their families would be punished by the law. From this beginning point, as outlined in Table 15.l, there have been shifts in the ways that the United States has dealt with the problems of youth. Each era is characterized by changes in the juvenile justice arena that reflect the social conditions and political values of the time. Over almost two hundred years, population shifts from rural to urban areas, massive immigration, developments in the social sciences, political reform movements, and the continuing problem of youth crime have all had their impact on the ways Americans have treated juveniles. As the nature of youth crime and American viewpoints about juveniles have changed, so have the processes and institutions of juvenile justice.

parens patriae
The state as "parent" or guardian and protector of all citizens (such as juveniles) who are unable to protect themselves.

THE REFUGE PERIOD (1824–1899)

As the population of American cities began to grow, reformers became concerned with the problem of youth crime and neglect. The reformers focused their efforts primarily on the urban immigrant poor and sought to have parents declared "unfit" if their children roamed the streets and were apparently "out of control." The state's power was to be used to prevent delinquency. The solution was to create institutions for these children where they could learn good work and study habits, live in a disciplined and healthy environment, and develop "character."

The first of these institutions was the House of Refuge of New York, which opened in 1825. Over time, various states also created "reform schools" and facilitated the placement of children in private homes, often in rural settings to remove children from the bad influences of the city. Children were placed in these schools and homes by court order, usually because of neglect or vagrancy. They often stayed there until they were old enough to be legally regarded as adults.

Period	Major Developments	Causes and Influences	Juvenile Justice System
Puritan 1646–1824	Massachusetts Stubborn Child Law (1646)	A Puritan view of child as evil B Economically marginal agrarian society	Law provides: A Symbolic standard of maturity B Support for family as economic unit
Refuge 1824–1899	Institutionalization of deviants; House of Refuge in New York established (1825) for delinquent and dependent children	A Enlightenment B Immigration and industrialization	Child seen as helpless, in need of state intervention.
Juvenile court 1899–1960	Establishment of separate legal system for juveniles; Illinois Juvenile Court Act (1899)	A Reformism and rehabilitative ideology B Increased immigration, urbanization, large-scale industrialization	Juvenile court institutionalized legal irresponsibility of child.
Juvenile rights 1960–1980	Increased "legalization" of juvenile law; *Gault* decision (1967); Juvenile Justice and Delinquency Prevention Act (1974) calls for deinstitutionalization of status offenders	A Criticism of juvenile justice system on humane grounds B Civil rights movement by disadvantaged groups	Movement to define and protect rights as well as to provide services to children.
Crime control 1980–present	Concern for victims, punishment for serious offenders, transfer to adult court of serious offenders, protection of children from physical and sexual abuse	A More conservative public attitudes and policies B Focus on serious crimes by repeat offenders	System more formal, restrictive, punitive; increased percentage of police referrals to court; incarcerated youths stay longer periods.

TABLE 15.1

Juvenile Justice Developments in the United States

The nature of juvenile justice evolved in conjunction with changes affecting American society.

SOURCE: Adapted from U.S. Department of Justice, *A Preliminary National Assessment of the Status Offender and the Juvenile Justice System* (Washington, DC: Government Printing Office, 1980), p. 29; Barry Krisberg, Ira M. Schwartz, Paul Litsky, and James Austin, "The Watershed of Juvenile Justice Reform," *Crime and Delinquency* 32 (January 1986), pp. 5–38.

THE JUVENILE COURT PERIOD (1900–1959)

With services for neglected youth widely established in most states by the end of the nineteenth century, the problem of juvenile criminality became the focus of attention. Reformers in the Progressive movement pushed for adoption of probation, treatment, indeterminate sentences, and parole for adult offenders and were successful in establishing similar programs for juveniles. Referred to as the "child savers," these upper-middle-class reformers sought to use the power of the state to "save" children from a life of crime.[6] They were motivated by concern over the influence of environmental factors on children's behavior and their belief that the developing social sciences provided the means for the government to cure social problems.[7]

Reformers believed that a separate juvenile court system was needed so that the problems of individual youths could be addressed using flexible procedures. They put this belief into action with the creation of the juvenile court. The first comprehensive system of juvenile justice was established through passage of the Illinois Juvenile Court Act in 1899. The act brought together under one jurisdiction cases of dependency, neglect, and delinquency for children under age sixteen. By 1904, ten states had implemented procedures similar to those of Illinois, and by 1920, all but three states had a juvenile court.

The philosophy of the juvenile court derived from the idea that the state should deal with a child who broke the law much as a wise parent would deal with a wayward child. The doctrine of *parens patriae* again helped legitimize the system. Procedures were to be informal and private, records were to be confidential, children were to be detained apart from adults, and probation and social worker staffs were to be appointed. Even the terminology and physical setting of the juvenile system were changed to emphasize diagnosis and treatment rather than findings of guilt. The term *criminal behavior* was replaced by *delinquent behavior* as it pertained to the acts of children. Moreover, delinquency was regarded as including behaviors such as smoking and running away from home, which are not criminal offenses if committed by adults. The terminology reflected the underlying belief that these children could be "cured" and returned to society as law-abiding citizens.

Because juvenile court procedures were not to be adversarial, lawyers were regarded as unnecessary. Thus, psychologists and social workers, who could determine the juvenile's underlying behavior problem, were the key professionals attached to the system.

THE JUVENILE RIGHTS PERIOD (1960–1979)

Few people questioned the necessity for the sweeping powers given to juvenile justice officials. Then, in the early 1960s, with the "due process revolution" in full sway with regard to the rights of adult defendants, lawyers and scholars began to criticize the extensive discretion exercised by juvenile justice officials, and a number of juvenile court decisions were appealed to the U.S. Supreme Court. In *Kent* v. *United States* (1966), the Court extended due process rights to children. In this case, a sixteen-year-old boy was remanded from the juvenile to the adult court without his lawyer present. He was convicted of rape and robbery in the adult court and sentenced to a thirty- to ninety-year prison term. The Supreme Court found the procedure of transferring the case to the adult court wanting and ruled that juveniles had the right to counsel at a waiver hearing.

Kent was followed by ***In re Gault (1967)***, which extended due process rights to juveniles. Gault had been sentenced to six years in a state training school for making a prank phone call. He was convicted and sentenced in an informal proceeding without being represented by counsel. The justices held that a child in a delinquency hearing must be afforded certain procedural rights, including notice of charges, right to counsel, right to confront and cross-examine witnesses, and protection against self-incrimination. Writing for the majority, Justice Abe Fortas emphasized that due process rights and procedures adhere to juvenile justice: "Under our Constitution the condition of being a boy does not justify a kangaroo court."[8]

Although these and other court decisions would seem to have placed the rights of juveniles on a par with those of adults, critics have charged that the states have not fully implemented these rights. The law on the books is different from the law in action. Most notably, writes Barry Feld, "In many states half or less of all juveniles receive the assistance of counsel to which they are constitutionally entitled."[9]

Another reform concerned status offenders—juveniles who committed **status offenses**, or acts that were not illegal when they were committed by an adult, such as skipping school or running away from home. In 1974, Congress passed the Juvenile Justice and Delinquency Prevention Act, which included provisions for the deinstitutionalization of status offenders. Since then, efforts have been made to divert such children out of the system, to reduce the possibility of incarceration, and to rewrite the laws with regard to status offenses.

***In re Gault* (1967)**
Juveniles have the right to counsel, to confront and examine accusers, and to have adequate notice of charges when there is the possibility of confinement as a punishment.

status offense
Any act committed by a juvenile that would not be a crime if it were committed by an adult, such as skipping school or running away from home.

As juvenile crime rates continued to rise during the 1970s, the public began to demand tougher approaches in dealing with delinquents. In the 1980s, at the same time that stricter sanctions were imposed on adult offenders, juvenile justice policies shifted more directly to crime control.

THE CRIME CONTROL PERIOD (1980–PRESENT)

The recognition that juvenile crime continues to be a serious problem has produced another revolution in the way the United States has dealt with juvenile offenders since 1980. With the public demanding that there be a "crackdown on crime," legislators have responded with changing the system. Greater attention is now being focused on repeat offenders, with policymakers calling for harsher punishment for juveniles who commit crimes.

In *Schall* v. *Martin* (1984), the Supreme Court significantly departed from the trend toward increased juvenile rights.[10] Noting that any attempt to structure such rights "must be qualified by the recognition that juveniles, unlike adults, are always in some form of custody," the Court confirmed the general notion of *parens patriae* as a primary basis for the juvenile court, equal in importance to the Court's desire to protect the community from crime. Thus, juveniles may be held in preventive detention before trial if they are deemed a "risk" to the community.

The *Schall* decision reflects the ambivalence permeating the juvenile justice system. On one side are the liberal reformers, who call for increased procedural and substantive legal protections for juveniles accused of crime. On the other side are conservatives devoted to crime control policies and alarmed by the rise in juvenile crime. The present crime control policy has resulted in many more juveniles being tried in adult courts.

Transfer to adult courts is accomplished either through a judicial waiver or by legislative exclusion.[11] **Judicial waiver** is the procedure by which the juvenile court waives its jurisdiction and transfers the case to the adult criminal court. In the past, during a waiver hearing, the state had to make a case that the youth was not amenable to rehabilitation in the juvenile system before a transfer to the adult court. Now, many states place on the youth the burden of proof of amenability to treatment.[12] In **legislative exclusion**, many states' criminal statutes exclude only murder charges from juvenile court, but others have extended the range of offenses automatically transferred to adult court to include rape, armed robbery, and other violent crimes.[13]

judicial waiver
Procedure by which the juvenile court waives its jurisdiction and transfers the case to the adult criminal court.

legislative exclusion
Provision of criminal statutes whereby certain offenses automatically are transferred to adult court, possibly including rape, armed robbery, and other violent crimes.

The juvenile justice system deals with those who are neglected or dependent as well as those who are delinquent.

In spite of the increasingly tough policies directed at juvenile offenders, changes that occurred during the juvenile rights period continue to have a profound impact. These changes have been referred to as the "Big Ds" of juvenile justice: diversion, decriminalization, deinstitutionalization, and due process.[14] Lawyers are routinely present at court hearings and other stages of the process, adding a note of formality that was simply not present twenty years ago. Status offenders seldom end up in secure, punitive environments such as training schools. The juvenile justice system looks more like the adult justice system than it did, but it still is less formal. Its stated intention is also less harsh: to keep juveniles in the community whenever possible.

Juvenile justice is handled by state and local governments, and processes therefore vary from state to state and county to county. In general, the juvenile justice system functions through many of the existing organizations of the state adult criminal justice system, but often with specialized structures for activities having to do with juveniles. Despite the differences among and within states with respect to the institutions and processes designed to handle juveniles' cases, two basic factors characterize the jurisdiction of the juvenile justice system: (1) the ages of the clients, and (2) the categories of cases under juvenile court jurisdiction.

AGE OF CLIENTS

Age normally determines whether a person is processed through the juvenile or adult justice system. The upper age limit for a juvenile varies from sixteen to eighteen. In thirty-eight states and the District of Columbia, it is the eighteenth birthday; in eight states, the seventeenth; and in the remainder, the sixteenth. In most states, judges have the discretion to transfer juveniles to adult courts through a waiver hearing as discussed previously.

CATEGORIES OF CASES UNDER JUVENILE COURT JURISDICTION

Four types of cases enter the juvenile justice system: delinquency, status offenses, neglect, and dependency. A **delinquent** is a child who has committed a criminal or status offense such as auto theft, robbery, or assault. As we have seen, acts that are illegal only if they are committed by juveniles are known as status offenses. Rather than having committed a violation of the penal code, status offenders have been designated as ungovernable or incorrigible: as runaways, truants, or **PINS/CINS/JINS** (persons/children/juveniles in need of supervision). The accompanying Close-Up traces the case of Fernando, a JIN whose total environment revolves around crime.

Some states do not distinguish between delinquent offenders and status offenders and label both as "juvenile delinquents." Those judged to be ungovernable and those judged to be robbers may find themselves sent to the same correctional institution. Beginning in the early 1960s, many state legislatures attempted to distinguish status offenders and to exempt them from compiling a criminal record. The 1974 Juvenile Justice and Delinquency Prevention Act required states to remove noncriminal offenders from secure detention and correctional facilities.

Juvenile justice also deals with problems of neglect and dependency—situations in which children are viewed as being hurt through no fault of their own because their parents have failed to provide a proper environment for them. Such situations have been the concern of most juvenile justice systems since the turn of the century, when the idea that the state should act as a parent to a child whose own parents are unable or unwilling to provide proper care gained currency. A **neglected child** is classified as one who is not receiving proper care because of some action or inaction of his or her parent(s). A **dependent child** is classified as one whose parent(s) or guardian(s) is not able to give proper care because of some physical or mental disability. The jurisdiction here is broad and includes a variety of situations in which the child can be viewed as a victim of adult behavior.

delinquent
A child who has committed a criminal or status offense.

PINS/CINS/JINS
Acronyms for "person in need of supervision," "child in need of supervision," and "juvenile in need of supervision"; used to designate juveniles who either are status offenders or are thought to be on the verge of getting into trouble.

neglected child
A child who is not receiving proper care because of some action or inaction of his or her parent(s).

dependent child
A child whose parent(s) or guardian(s) is unable to give proper care because of some physical or mental disability.

CLOSE-UP
Fernando, 16, Finds a Sanctuary in Crime

Fernando Morales was glad to discuss his life as a sixteen-year-old drug dealer, but he had one stipulation owing to his status as a fugitive. He explained that he had recently escaped from Long Lane School, a state correctional institution that became his home after he was caught with $1,100 worth of heroin known as P.

"The Five-O caught me right here with the bundles of P," he said, referring to a police officer, as he stood in front of a boarded-up house on Bridgeport's East Side. "They sentenced me to 18 months, but I jetted after four. Three of us got out a bathroom window. We ran through the woods and stole a car. Then we got back here and the Five-O's came to my apartment, and I had to jump out the side window on the second floor."

What Future?

Since his escape in December, Fernando had been on the run for weeks. He still went to the weekly meetings of his gang, but he was afraid to go back to his apartment, afraid even to go to a friend's place to pick up the three guns he had stashed away. "I would love to get my baby, Uzi, but it's too hot now."

"Could you bring a photographer here?" he asked. "I want my picture in the newspaper. I'd love to have me holding a bundle right there on the front page so the cops can see it. They['re] going to bug out."

The other dealers on the corner looked on with a certain admiration. They realized that a publicity campaign might not be the smartest long-term career move for a fugitive drug dealer—"Man, you be the one bugging out," another dealer told him—but they also recognized the logic in Fernando's attitude. He was living his life according to a common assumption on these streets: There is no future.

When you ask the Hispanic teenagers selling drugs here what they expect to be doing in five years, you tend to get a lot of bored shrugs. Occa-

sionally they'll talk about being back in school or being a retired drug dealer in a Porsche. But the most common answer is the one that Fernando gave without hesitation or emotion: "Dead or in jail."

The story of how Fernando got that way is a particularly sad one, but the basic elements are fairly typical in the lives of drug dealers and gang members in any urban ghetto. He has grown up amid tenements, housing projects, torched buildings and abandoned factories. His role models have been adults who use "the city" and "the state" primarily as terms for the different types of welfare checks. His neighborhood is a place where 13-year-olds know by heart the visiting hours at local prisons.

The Family: A Mother Leaves, A Father Drinks

Fernando Morales was born in Bridgeport, Connecticut, on September 16, 1976, and his mother moved out a few months later. Since then he has occasionally run into her on the street. Neither he nor his relatives can say exactly why she left—or why she didn't take Fernando and her other son with her—but the general assumption is that she was tired of being hit by their father.

The father, Bernabe Morales, who was 24 years old and had emigrated from Puerto Rico as a teenager, moved the two boys in with his mother at the P. T. Barnum public housing project. Fernando lived there until the age of eight, when his grandmother died. . . .

After that Fernando and his brother Bernard lived sometimes with their father and his current girlfriend, sometimes with relatives in Bridgeport or Puerto Rico. They eventually settled with their father's cousin, Monserrate Bruno, who already had 10 children living in her two-bedroom apartment. . . .

His father, by all accounts, was a charming, generous man when sober but something else altogether when drinking or doing drugs. He was arrested more than two dozen times, usually for fighting or drugs, and spent five years in jail while Fernando was growing up. He lived on welfare, odd jobs, and money from selling drugs, a trade that was taken up by both of his sons.

The "Industry": Moving Up in the Drug Trade

Fernando's school days ended two years ago, when he dropped out of ninth grade. "School was corny," he explained. "I was smart, I learned quick, but I got bored. I was just learning things when I could be out making money."

Fernando might have found other opportunities. He had relatives working in fast-food restaurants and repair shops, and one cousin tried to interest him in a job distributing bread that might pay $700 a week—but nothing with such quick rewards as the drug business flourishing on the East Side.

He had friends and relatives in the business, and he started as one of the runners on the street corner making sales or directing buyers to another runner holding the marijuana, cocaine, crack, or heroin. The runners on each block buy their drugs—paying, for instance, $200 for 50 bags of crack that sell for $250—from the block's lieutenant, who supervises them and takes the money to the absentee dealer called the owner of the block.

By this winter Fernando had moved up slightly on the corporate ladder. "I'm not the block lieutenant yet, but I have some runners selling for me," he explained as he sat in a bar near the block. Another teenager came in with money for him, which he proudly added to a thick wad in his pocket. "You see? I make money while they work for me."

Fernando still worked the block himself, too, standing on the corner watching for cars slowing down, shouting "You want P?" or responding to veteran customers for crack who asked, "Got any slab, man?" Fernando said he usually made between $100 and $300 a day, and that the money usually went as quickly as it came.

He had recently bought a car for $500 and wrecked it making a fast turn into a telephone pole. He spent money on gold chains with crucifixes, rings, Nike sneakers, Timberland boots, an assortment of Russell hooded sweatshirts called *hoodies*, gang dues, trips to New York City and his 23-year-old girlfriend.

His dream was to get out of Bridgeport. "I'd be living fat somewhere. I'd go to somewhere hot, Florida or Puerto Rico or somewhere, buy me a house, get six blazing girls with dope bodies." In the meantime, he tried not to think about what his product was doing to his customers.

"Sometimes it bothers me. But see, I'm a hustler. I got to look out for myself. I got to be making money. Forget them. If you put that in your head, you're going to be caught out. You going to be a sucker. You going to be like them." He said he had used marijuana, cocaine and angel dust himself, but made a point of never using crack or heroin, the drugs that plagued the last years of his father's life. . . .

The Gangs: "Like a Family" of Drug Dealers

"I cried a little, that's it," was all that Fernando would say about his father's death. But he did allow that it had something to do with his subsequent decision to join a Hispanic gang named *Neta*. He went with friends to a meeting, answered questions during an initiation ceremony, and began wearing its colors, a necklace of red, white, and blue beads.

"It's like a family, and you need that if you've lost your own family," he said. "At the meetings we talk about having heart, trust, and all that. We don't disrespect nobody. If we need money, we get it. If I need anything they're right there to help me."

Neta is allied with Bridgeport's most notorious gang, the Latin Kings, and both claim to be peaceful Hispanic cultural organizations opposed to drug use. But they are financed at least indirectly by the drug trade, because many members like Fernando work independently in drug operations, and the drug dealers' disputes can turn into gang wars. . . .

"I like guns, I like stealing cars, I like selling drugs, and I like money," he said. "I got to go to the block. That's where I get my spirit at. When I die, my spirit's going to be at the block, still making money. Booming." . . .

"I'll be selling till I get my act together. I'm just a little kid. Nothing runs through my head. All I think about is doing crazy things. But when I be big, I know I need education. If I get caught and do a couple of years, I'll come out and go back to school. But I don't have that in my head yet. I'll have my little fun while I'm out."

SOURCE: John Tierney, *New York Times*, 13 April 1993, pp. Al, B6. Copyright © 1993 by The New York Times Company. Reprinted by permission.

Percentage of Total Cases Referred			
11% Crimes Against Persons		**5% Drug Offenses**	100%
Criminal homicide	1%	**1% Offenses Against Public Order**	
Forcible rape	2	Weapons offenses	6%
Robbery	17	Sex offenses	6
Aggravated assault	20	Drunkenness and disorderly conduct	23
Simple assault	59	Contempt, probation, and parole violations	21
	100%	Other	44
			100%
46% Crimes Against Property		**17% Status Offenses**	
Burglary	25%	Running away	28%
Larceny	47	Truancy and curfew violations	21
Motor vehicle theft	5	Ungovernability	28
Arson	1	Liquor violations	23
Vandalism and trespassing	19		100%
Stolen property offenses	3		
	100%		

TABLE 15.2
Delinquency and Status Offenses Referred to Juvenile Court
The juvenile courts deal with cases of delinquency, status offenses, and such noncriminal matters as neglect, adoption, and dependency. Note the distribution of delinquency and status offenses in this table. Do you think that these figures will change in the future?

SOURCE: U.S. Department of Justice, Bureau of Justice Statistics, *Report to the Nation on Crime and Justice*, 2d ed. (Washington, DC: Government Printing Office, 1988), p. 78.

Nationally, about 75 percent of the cases referred to the juvenile courts are delinquency cases. Of these, some 20 percent are concerned with status offenses, about 20 percent are dependency and neglect cases, and about 5 percent involve special proceedings, such as adoption. Because the system deals with both criminal and noncriminal cases, some observers have expressed concern that juveniles who have done nothing wrong are categorized either officially or in the public mind as delinquents. In some states, little effort is made in pre-judicial detention facilities or in social service agencies to keep the classes of juveniles separate. Table 15.2 shows the types of delinquency and status offenses that are referred to juvenile court.

JUVENILE JUSTICE OPERATIONS

Underlying the juvenile justice system is the philosophy that the police, judges, and correctional officials should be concerned primarily with the interests of the child. Prevention of delinquency is the system's justification for intervening in the lives of juveniles who are involved in either status or criminal offenses.

In theory at least, the juvenile system proceedings are to be conducted in a nonadversarial environment, and the juvenile court is a place where the judge, social workers, clinicians, and probation officers work together to diagnose the child's problem and select a rehabilitative program to attack this problem. Juvenile justice is a particular type of bureaucracy that is based on an ideology of social work and is staffed primarily by persons who think of themselves as members of the helping professions. Even the recent emphasis on crime control and punishment has not removed the philosophy of rehabilitation from most juvenile justice systems. In order to rehabilitate offenders, officials need to apply substantial powers of discretion, but this is hard to do when resources are scarce. The rhetoric of rehabilitation may be overcome by political pressures and resource constraints that focus attention on punishing the most serious offenders rather than working to prevent delinquency in the complete range of troubled children who come into contact with the system.

Like the adult criminal justice system, juvenile justice functions within a context of exchange relationships between officials of various agencies that influence decisions. The juvenile court must deal not only with children and their parents but also with patrol officers, probation officers, welfare officials, social workers, psychologists, and the heads of treatment institutions—all of whom have their own goals, their own perceptions of delinquency, and their own concepts of treatment.

POLICE INTERFACE

Many police departments, especially in cities and larger towns, have special juvenile units. The juvenile officer often is carefully selected and trained to relate to youths, is knowledgeable about relevant legal issues, and is sensitive to the special needs of young offenders. The juvenile officer is also viewed as an important link between the police and other community institutions, such as the schools, recreation facilities, and organizations serving young people.

Most complaints against juveniles are brought by the police, although they may be initiated by an injured party, school officials, or even the parents. The police must make three major decisions with regard to the processing of juveniles: (1) whether to take the child into custody, (2) whether to request that the child be detained following apprehension, and (3) whether to refer the child to court.[15]

As might be expected, the police exercise enormous discretion with regard to these decisions. They do extensive screening and make informal adjustments in the street and at the station house. In communities and neighborhoods where law enforcement officials have developed close relationships with the residents or where law enforcement policy dictates, the police may deal with violations by giving warnings to the juveniles and notifying their parents. As Figure 15.2 shows, 64.2 percent of those taken into police custody have their cases referred to the juvenile court, 28.1 percent are handled within the department and then released, and 7.7 percent are referred to other agencies or to an adult court.

Officers in many communities are trained to work with juveniles in their neighborhoods.

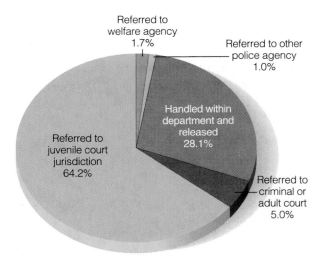

FIGURE 15.2

Disposition of Juveniles Taken into Police Custody

The police have discretion with regard to the disposition of juvenile arrest cases. What factors may explain the different ways in which cases are handled?

SOURCE: U.S. Department of Justice, Bureau of Justice Statistics, *Sourcebook of Criminal Justice Statistics* (Washington, DC: Government Printing Office, 1993), p. 455.

Initial decisions about what to do with each suspected offender are influenced by such factors as the officer's attitude toward the juvenile, the juvenile's family, the offense, and the court; the predominant attitude of the community; and the officer's conception of his or her own role.

A study of the police in a metropolitan industrial city of 450,000 revealed that the choice of disposition of juvenile cases at the stage of arrest depended very much on the prior record of the child, but second in importance was the offender's demeanor.[16] Juveniles who had committed minor offenses but were respectful and contrite were defined by the officers as worthy candidates for rehabilitation and were given an informal reprimand. Those who were argumentative or surly were defined as "punks" who needed to be taught a lesson through arrest. The researchers found that only 4 percent of the cooperative youths were arrested, in comparison with 67 percent of those who were uncooperative.

INTAKE

When the police believe that formal actions should be taken by the juvenile justice system, a complaint is filed with a special division of the juvenile probation department for preliminary screening and evaluation. During this intake stage, an officer reviews the case to determine whether the alleged facts are sufficient to cause the juvenile court to take jurisdiction or whether some other action would be in the child's interest. The intake officer thus has considerable discretion and power. Nationally, between 40 and 50 percent of all referrals from the police are disposed of at this stage, without formal processing by a judge.[17]

For cases sent to court, the actions of the juvenile court judge must be consistent with local values. Acts of delinquency that outrage the community will inspire pressures on the court to deal severely with transgressors. Normally, however, a variety of lenient dispositions are available, including probation, outpatient care at a psychiatric clinic, and incarceration in a therapeutic community. Not all juvenile offenders end up in the reform school or industrial school.

In most juvenile justice systems, the probation officer plays a crucial role during the intake phase. Because intake is essentially a screening process to determine whether a case should be referred to the court or to a social agency, it often takes place without judicial supervision. Informal discussions among the probation officer, the parents, and the child are important means of learning about the child's social situation, of diagnosing behavioral problems, and of recommending treatment possibilities. An estimated half of all delinquency cases nationwide each year are settled informally and unofficially during this pre-judicial stage.[18]

DIVERSION

Although informal ways of diverting alleged delinquents away from the courts and toward community agencies have always existed, the number and types of diversion programs have greatly expanded during the past two decades. In keeping with the philosophy of the juvenile court, many people believe that diversion should be promoted as much as possible. When behavioral problems can be identified early, the child should be given access to the necessary remedial education and counseling programs without being taken before a judge and labeled delinquent. However, the increased availability of diversion programs has apparently widened the reach of juvenile courts by drawing into the system children who formerly would have been dealt with through informal means.[19]

DETENTION

After it has been decided that some formal action should be taken against a juvenile, the question arises of whether to place the youth in **detention**, or temporary custody, until disposition of the case. This decision is usually made by an intake officer of the juvenile court.

    One of the early reforms of the juvenile justice system was to ensure that children were not held in jails in the company of adults who were also awaiting trial or sentencing. To mix juveniles—some of whom are status offenders or under the protection of the court because they are neglected—in the same public facility with adults accused of crimes has long been thought unjust, but in many areas, separate detention facilities for juveniles do not exist.

    Although much attention is focused on the adjudication processes of the juvenile court and the sanctions imposed by judges, many more children are punished through confinement in detention centers and jails before any court action has taken place than are punished by the courts. An estimated half-million juveniles are detained each year, sometimes for several months; however, only about 15 percent are eventually confined to a group home, training school, or halfway house. These figures seem to indicate that detention and intake decisions have a greater impact than do the decisions of the court. A widespread belief seems to be that a brief period of detention is a good device to "shake up the kid and set him straight," even for children who have not yet been convicted of any crime.

detention
A period of temporary custody of a juvenile before disposition of his or her case.

ADJUDICATION

The primary questions before the court are whether to attach the label "delinquent" to a juvenile and what sanctions to apply. The Supreme Court's decision in *Gault* (1967) and other due process rulings mandated changes in criminal proceedings that have brought about shifts in the philosophy and actions of the juvenile court. Contemporary proceedings are more formal than those of the past, although juvenile courts are still more informal than adult courts. Copies of formal petitions with specific charges must be given to the parents and child; counsel may be present and free counsel appointed if the juvenile is indigent; witnesses may be cross-examined; and a transcript of the proceedings must be kept. In about thirteen states, juveniles have a right to a jury trial.

    As with other Supreme Court decisions, the reality of local practice may differ sharply from the

A disposition in keeping with the needs of the offender holds a high priority in the juvenile justice system.

procedures spelled out in the high court's rulings. Juveniles and their parents often waive their rights in response to suggestions made by the judge or probation officer. The lower social status of the offender's parents, the intimidating atmosphere of the court, and judicial hints that the outcome will be more favorable if a lawyer is not present are reasons the procedures outlined in *Gault* may not be followed. The litany of "getting treatment," "doing what's right for the child," and "working out a just solution" may sound enticing, especially to people who are unfamiliar with the intricacies of formal legal procedures. In practice, then, juveniles still lack many of the protections accorded adult offenders. Some of the differences between the juvenile and adult criminal justice systems are listed in Table 15.3.

TABLE 15.3

Adult versus Juvenile Criminal Justice
Compare the basic elements of the adult and juvenile systems. To what extent does a juvenile have the same rights as an adult? Are the different decision-making processes necessary because of the fact that a juvenile is involved?

The Adjudicatory Process

In some jurisdictions, the adjudication process is more adversarial than it was before the *Gault* decision. Like adult cases, however, juvenile cases tend to be adjudicated in a style that conforms to the Crime Control (administrative) Model: Most are settled in preliminary hearings by a plea agreement, and few go on to formal trial. At the preliminary hearing, the youth is notified of the charges and his or her rights, and counsel may be present. Because in most cases the juvenile has already admitted guilt to the arresting or intake officer, the focus of the hearing is on the disposition. In contested cases, a prosecutor presents the state's case, and the judge oversees the proceedings, ruling on the admission of evidence and the testimony of witnesses. Because juries are used only sparingly, even in states where they are authorized, guilt

Element	Adult System	Juvenile System
Philosophical assumptions	Decisions made as result of adversarial system in context of due process rights	Decisions made as result of inquiry into needs of juvenile within context of some due process elements
Jurisdiction	Violations of criminal law	Violations of criminal law, status offenses, neglect, dependency
Primary sanctioning goals	Retribution, deterrence, rehabilitation	Retribution, rehabilitation
Official discretion	Widespread	Widespread
Entrance	Official action of arrest, summons, or citation	Official action, plus referral by school, parents, other sources
Role of prosecuting and defense attorneys	Required and formalized	Sometimes required; less structured; poor role definition
Adjudication	Procedural rules of evidence in public jury trial required	Less formal structure to rules of evidence and conduct of trial; no right to public jury in most states
Treatment programs	Run primarily by public agencies	Broad use of private and public agencies
Application of Bill of Rights amendments		
Fourth: Unreasonable searches and seizures	Applicable	Applicable
Fifth: Double jeopardy	Applicable	Applicable (re waiver to adult court)
Self-incrimination	Applicable (*Miranda* warnings)	Applicable
Sixth: Right to counsel	Applicable	Applicable
Public trial	Applicable	Applicable in less than half of states
Trial by jury	Applicable	Applicable in less than half of states
Eighth: Right to bail	Applicable	Applicable in half of states
Fourteenth: Right to treatment	Not applicable	Applicable

or innocence is determined by the judge, who then passes sentence.

With the increased concern about crime, prosecuting attorneys are taking a more prominent part in the system. In keeping with the traditional child-saver philosophy, prosecuting attorneys rarely appeared in juvenile court prior to the *Gault* decision. Now, given the presence of a defense attorney, the state often is represented by legal counsel as well. In many jurisdictions, prosecutors are assigned to deal specifically with juvenile cases by advising the intake officer, administering diversion programs, negotiating pleas, and acting as an advocate during judicial proceedings.

Juvenile proceedings have traditionally been closed to public scrutiny in the interest of protecting the child's privacy and rehabilitative potential. It has been pointed out, however, that the unavailability of juvenile court records to judges in the adult courts means that persons who have already served time on probation and in juvenile institutions are erroneously perceived to be first offenders when they are processed for crimes as adults. Some people argue that juvenile records should be made available to adult courts and that efforts should be made to treat young criminals more severely in order to deter them from future illegal activity.

Disposition

If the court makes a finding of delinquency, a dispositional hearing is required, either immediately following the entry of a plea or at a later date. Typically, the judge receives a social history or predispositional report before passing sentence. Few juveniles are found by the court to be not delinquent at trial, since the intake and pretrial processes normally filter out cases in which a law violation cannot be proved. In addition to dismissal of a petition, five other choices are available: (1) suspended judgment, (2) probation, (3) community treatment, (4) institutional care, and (5) waiver to an adult court.

The traditional belief of juvenile court advocates was that rehabilitation through treatment was the only goal of the sanction imposed on young people. For most of this century, judges have sentenced juveniles to indeterminate sentences so that correctional administrators would have the discretion to determine when release was appropriate. As with the adult criminal justice system, indeterminate sentences and unbridled discretion have been under attack during the past decade. A number of states have tightened the sentencing discretion of judges, especially with regard to serious offenses. The state of Washington, for example, has adopted a determinate sentencing law for juveniles. In other states, a youth may be transferred more readily to the adult court for adjudication and sentencing. Jurisdictions such as the District of Columbia, Colorado, Florida, and Virginia have passed laws requiring mandatory sentences for certain offenses committed by juveniles.

CORRECTIONS

Many aspects of juvenile corrections are similar if not identical to those of adult corrections. Both systems, for example, mix rehabilitative and retributive sanctions. However, juvenile corrections differs in many respects from the adult system. Some of the differences flow from the *parens patriae* concept and the youthful, seemingly innocent persons with whom the system deals. At times, the differences are expressed in formal operational policies, such as contracting for residential treatment; at other times, the differences are apparent only in the style and culture of an operation, as in juvenile probation.

One predominant aim of juvenile corrections is to avoid unnecessary incarceration. When children are removed from their homes, they are inevitably damaged emotionally, even when the home life is harsh and abusive, for they are forced to abandon the only environment they know. Further, placing children in institutions has labeling effects; the children begin to perceive themselves as "bad" because they have received punitive treatment, and children who see themselves as bad are likely to behave that way. Finally, treatment is believed to be more effective when the child is living in a normal, supportive home environment. For these reasons, noninstitutional forms of corrections are seen as highly desirable in juvenile justice and have proliferated in recent years.

Alternative Dispositions

Although probation and commitment to an institution are the major dispositional alternatives, judges have wide discretion to warn, to fine, to arrange for restitution, to refer a juvenile for treatment at either a public or a private community agency, or to withhold judgment. In making this decision, the judge relies on a social background report, developed by the probation department and often including reports from others in the community, such as school officials or a psychiatrist. When psychological issues are involved, a disposition may be delayed pending further diagnosis.

Judges sometimes suspend judgment, or continue cases without a finding, when they wish to put a youth under supervision but are reluctant to apply the label "delinquent." Judgment may be suspended for a definite or indefinite period of time. The court thus holds a definitive judgment in abeyance for possible use should a youth misbehave while under the informal supervision of a probation officer or parents.

Probation

By far the most common method of handling juvenile offenders is to place them on probation. Juvenile probation operates in much the same way as adult probation, and it is sometimes carried out by the same agency. In two respects, however, juvenile probation can differ markedly from adult probation. Traditionally, juvenile probation has been better funded, so that officers have had smaller caseloads. Second, the juvenile probation officer is often infused with the sense that the offender is worthwhile and can change and that the job is valuable and enjoyable. Such attitudes make for greater creativity than is possible with adult probation—for example, pairing the offender with a "big brother" or "big sister" from the community.

Community Treatment

In the past decade, treatment in community-based facilities has become much more common. In particular, there are more private, nonprofit agencies that contract with the states to provide services for troubled youths. Community-based options include foster homes in which juvenile offenders live with families, usually for a short period of time, and group homes, often privately run facilities for groups of twelve to twenty juvenile offenders. Each group home has several staff personnel who work as counselors or houseparents on eight- or twenty-four-hour shifts. Group home placements can allow juveniles to attend local schools, can provide individual and group counseling, and can otherwise offer a more structured life than most of the residents received in their own homes. However, critics suggest that group homes often are mismanaged and may do little more than "warehouse" youths.

Institutional Care

Incarceration of juveniles has traditionally meant commitment to a state institution, often called a training school, reform school, or industrial school. Large custodial training schools located in outlying areas remain the typical institutions to which juveniles are committed, although in the past decade an increasing number of privately maintained facilities accepted residents sent by the courts. The last census revealed that more than 92,000 juveniles were housed in 3,200 public and private centers, with 62 percent of these youths in public facilities.[20] Unknown numbers of children under the care of the juvenile court have been placed in noncorrectional private facilities such as schools for the emotionally disturbed, military academies, and even preparatory schools. Although courts usually maintain jurisdiction over delinquents until they attain legal adulthood, data from the training schools indicate that nationally the average length of stay is approximately ten months.

Results from a national survey of public custodial institutions showed that 40.7 percent of juveniles were incarcerated for violent offenses, 60 percent used drugs regularly, and 50 percent said that a family member had been in prison at some time in the past. Also, 88 percent of the residents were male, only 30 percent had grown up in a household with both parents, and the percentage of African-American (42.8 percent) and Hispanic (15.5 percent) were greater than the percentage of those groups in the general population.[21] Figure 15.3 shows the types of offenses and nondelinquency reasons for the placement of juveniles in correctional facilities.

A QUESTION OF ETHICS

Residents of the Lovelock Home had been committed by the juvenile court because they were either delinquent or neglected. All twenty-five boys, aged seven to fifteen, were streetwise, tough, and interested only in getting out. The institution had a staff of social services professionals who tried to deal with the residents' educational and psychological needs. Since state funding was short, these services looked better in the annual report than to an observer who might visit Lovelock. Most of the time, the residents watched TV, played basketball in the backyard, or just hung out in one another's rooms.

Joe Klegg, the night supervisor, was tired from the eight-hour shift that he had just completed on his "second job" as a daytime convenience store manager. The boys were watching television when he arrived at seven. Everything seemed calm. It should have been, since Joe had placed a tough fifteen-year-old, Randy Marshall, in charge. Joe had told Randy to keep the younger boys in line. Randy used his muscle and physical presence to intimidate the other residents. He knew that if the home was quiet and there was no trouble, he would be rewarded with special privileges such as a "pass" to go see his girlfriend. Joe wanted no hassles and a quiet house so that he could doze off when the boys went to sleep.

Does the situation at Lovelock Home raise ethical questions, or does it merely raise questions of poor management practices? What are the potential consequences for the residents? For Joe Klegg? What is the state's responsibility?

By contrast, the private agencies select "motivated" and high-status clients and pass on to public agencies the harder-to-work-with, resistant clients. In return for opening their doors to court referrals, the treatment centers expect to be able to transfer their troublesome cases to state institutions.[22]

Institutional Programs

Because of the emphasis on rehabilitation that has dominated juvenile justice for much of the past fifty years, a wide variety of treatment programs has been used. Counseling, education, vocational training, and an assortment of psychotherapy methods have been incorporated into the juvenile correctional programs of most states. Unfortunately, for many offenders, incarceration in a juvenile training institution primarily seems to prepare them for entry into

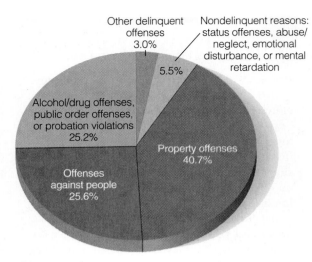

Other delinquent offenses
3.0%

Nondelinquent reasons: status offenses, abuse/ neglect, emotional disturbance, or mental retardation
5.5%

Alcohol/drug offenses, public order offenses, or probation violations
25.2%

Offenses against people
25.6%

Property offenses
40.7%

FIGURE 15.3
Juveniles in Public Facilities: Types of Offenses and Nondelinquency Reasons for the Placement
A significant proportion of juveniles in detention facilities are held for property and status offenses that would not lead to the incarceration of adult offenders.

SOURCE: U.S. Department of Justice, Office of Juvenile Justice and Delinquency Prevention, *OJJDP Update on Statistics* (January 1991), p. 4.

adult corrections. Research has raised many questions about the effectiveness of rehabilitation programs in the juvenile corrections setting. John Irwin's concept of the state-raised youth is a useful way of looking at children who come in contact with institutional life at an early age, lack family relationships and structure, become accustomed to living in a correctional environment, and are unable to function in other environments.[23]

One continual problem for the treatment of juvenile offenders is the range of theories that have been advanced to explain delinquency. Where one generation looked to slum conditions as the cause of juvenile crime, another now points to the affluence of the suburbs. Psychologists may stress masculine insecurity in a matriarchal family structure, and some sociologists note the peer group pressures of the gang. The array of theories has occasioned an array of proposed—and often contradictory—treatments. With this type of confusion, those interested in the problems of youth may well throw up their hands in despair. What is clear is that additional research is needed to give insights into the causes of delinquency and the treatment of juvenile offenders.

SUMMARY

Crimes committed by youths are a major problem in the United States. While the amount of crime reported to the police or measured by victimization surveys has remained fairly stable since the early 1980s, crimes committed by juveniles have increased.

Each development period in juvenile justice history was characterized by social and political developments that had an impact on the criminal justice system. The creation of the juvenile court in 1899 and its extension throughout the nation brought into being a separate juvenile justice system. This system was based on assumptions concerning the causes of delinquent behavior and the justice processes that should be used to deal with that behavior. Until 1960, juvenile justice officials were given wide discretion to fashion processes and sanctions that would serve the best interests of the child. With the Supreme Court's decisions in *In re Gault* and other cases, the due process revolution reformed many informal practices and provided specific protections for juveniles brought to court—although these protections are not always provided in the manner required by the Court. In recent years, legislatures have adopted more of a crime control focus to deal with juvenile delinquency in the 1990s.

Decisions by police officers and intake workers of the juvenile justice system dispose of a large portion of cases without their being referred to the court for formal processing. Diversion is a major aspect of this process. Institutional and noninstitutional programs for those judged to be offenders are available in great numbers and variety. The predominant aim of juvenile corrections is to avoid unnecessary incarceration, yet there is no consensus about which treatment programs or other mechanisms can prevent troubled children from slipping into criminal careers.

QUESTIONS FOR REVIEW

1. What are the major historical periods in the development of juvenile justice in the United States?
2. What is the jurisdiction of the juvenile court?
3. What are the major components of the juvenile justice system?
4. What are the sentencing alternatives for juveniles judged to be delinquent?
5. What due process rights do juveniles possess?

NOTES

1. Jan Hoffman, "Quirks in the Juvenile Offender Law Stir Calls for Change?" *New York Times*, 12 July 1994, p. B1.
2. Clifford Krauss, "No Crystal Ball Needed on Crime," *New York Times*, 13 November 1994, p. 4.
3. James D. Wright, Joseph F. Sheley, and M. Dwayne Smith, "Kids, Guns, and Killing Fields," *Society* 30 (November/December, 1992): 84; Michel Marriott, "Young, Angry, and Lethal," *Newsweek*, 26 December 1994–2 January 1995, p. 122.
4. Metropolitan Court Judges Committee Report, "Drugs—The American Family in Crisis" (Reno: University of Nevada, National Council on Juvenile and Family Court Judges, 1988).
5. U.S. Department of Justice, National Institute of Justice, *Research in Brief* (May 1990).
6. Anthony Platt, *The Child Savers*, 2d ed. (Chicago: University of Chicago Press, 1977).
7. John Sutton, *Stubborn Children: Controlling Delinquency in the United States* (Berkeley: University of California Press, 1988).
8. *In re Gault*, 387 U.S. 9 (1967).
9. Barry C. Feld, "Criminalizing the Juvenile Court," in *Crime and Justice: A Review of Research*, vol. 17, ed. Michael Tonry (Chicago: University of Chicago Press, 1993), p. 222.
10. *Schall* v. *Martin*, 467 U.S. 253 (1984).
11. Dean J. Champion and G. Larry Mays, *Transferring Juveniles to Criminal Courts* (New York: Praeger, 1991), pp. 59–82.
12. Franklin Zimring, "The Treatment of Hard Cases in American Juvenile Justice: In Defense of Discretionary Waiver," *Notre Dame Journal of Law, Ethics, and Public Policy* 5 (1991): 267; Barry C. Feld, "Bad Law Makes Hard Cases: Reflections on Teen Aged Axe Murderers, Judicial Activism, and Legislative Default," *Journal of Law and Inequality* 8 (1990), p. 1.
13. Feld, "Criminalizing the American Juvenile Court," p. 239.
14. James O. Finckenauer, *Juvenile Delinquency and Corrections: The Gap Between Theory and Practice* (Orlando: Academic Press, 1984), p. 190.
15. H. Ted Rubin, *Juvenile Justice: Policy, Practice, and Law*, 2d ed. (New York: Newbury Award Records, 1985), p. 87.
16. Irving Piliavin and Scott Briar, "Police Encounters with Juveniles," in *Back on the Street*, ed. Robert M. Carter and Malcolm W. Klein (Englewood Cliffs, NJ: Prentice-Hall, 1976), pp. 197–206.
17. U.S. Department of Justice, Bureau of Justice Statistics, *Report to the Nation on Crime and Justice*, 2d ed. (Washington, DC: Government Printing Office, 1988), p. 79.

18. Mark Creekmore, "Case Processing: Intake, Adjudication, and Disposition," in *Brought to Justice?: Juveniles, The Court, and The Law*, ed. Rosemary C. Saari and Yeheskel Hasenfeld (Ann Arbor: University of Michigan, National Assessment of Juvenile Corrections, 1976), p. 126.

19. Scott H. Decker, "A Systematic Analysis of Diversion: Net Widening and Beyond," *Journal of Criminal Justice* 13 (1985), pp. 206–216.

20. U.S. Department of Justice, Office of Juvenile Justice and Delinquency Prevention, *OJJDP Update on Statistics* (January 1991), p. 1.

21. Ibid., p. 2.

22. Richard A. Cloward and Irwin Epstein, "Private Social Welfare's Disengagement from the Poor: The Case of the Family Adjustment Agencies," in *Social Welfare Institutions: A Sociological Reader*, ed. Mayer N. Zald (New York: Wiley, 1965), p. 626.

23. John Irwin, *The Felon* (Englewood Cliffs, NJ: Prentice-Hall, 1970).

APPENDIX

Constitution of the United States: Criminal Justice Amendments

The first ten amendments to the Constitution, known as the Bill of Rights, became effective on December 15, 1791.

IV   The right of the people to be secure in their persons, houses, papers, and effects, against unreasonable searches and seizures, shall not be violated, and no warrants shall issue but upon probable cause, supported by oath or affirmation, and particularly describing the place to be searched, and the persons or things to be seized.

V   No person shall be held to answer for a capital or otherwise infamous crime, unless on a presentment or indictment of a grand jury, except in cases arising in the land or naval forces or in the militia when in actual service in time of war or public danger; nor shall any person be subject for the same offence to be twice put in jeopardy of life or limb; nor shall be compelled in any criminal case to be a witness against himself, nor be deprived of life, liberty, or property, without due process of law; nor shall private property be taken for public use without just compensation.

VI   In all criminal prosecutions the accused shall enjoy the right to a speedy and public trial, by an impartial jury of the State and district wherein the crime shall have been committed, which district shall have been previously ascertained by law, and to be informed of the nature and cause of the accusation; to be confronted with the witnesses against him; to have compulsory process for obtaining witnesses in his favor, and to have the assistance of counsel for his defense.

VIII   Excessive bail shall not be required, nor excessive fines imposed, nor cruel and unusual punishments inflicted.

The Fourteenth Amendment became effective on July 28, 1868.

XIV   Section 1. All persons born or naturalized in the United States, and subject to the jurisdiction thereof, are citizens of the United States and of the State wherein they reside. No State shall make or enforce any law which shall abridge the privileges or immunities of citizens of the United States; nor shall any State deprive any person of life, liberty, or property, without due process of law; nor deny to any person within its jurisdiction the equal protection of the laws.

CREDITS

PART ONE
1, © Dick Frank/The Stock Market

CHAPTER 1
2, Bob Riha, Jr./Gamma Liaison. 4 (left), © Eugene Richards/ Magnum Photos; (right), UPI/Bettmann Newsphotos. 8, Michael Newman/PhotoEdit. 15, © Mary Kate Denny/PhotoEdit. 19, © Billy E. Barnes/ Stock.Boston. 22, © 1991 Phil Huber/Black Star.

CHAPTER 2
25, © Michael Fernandez/The Gamma Liaison Network. 26, Bob Daemmrich/Stock.Boston. 33, © 91 David Portnox/Black Star. 36, © Larry Downing/Woodfin Camp & Assoc. 39, Cary Wolinsky/Stock.Boston. 47, © L.A. Daily News/Sygma.

CHAPTER 3
51, © John Neubauer/PhotoEdit. 59, The Illustrated London News Picture Library. 61, UPI/Bettmann. 65, UPI/Bettmann. 68, © Nubar Alexanian/Woodfin Camp & Assoc. 71, AP/Wide World Photos.

PART TWO
75, Bob Daemmrich Photography/Stock.Boston.

CHAPTER 4
76, © 1993 Alon Reininger/Contact Press Images. 80, Culver Pictures, Inc. 83, © Free Press/Black Star. 85, © S. Elbaz/Sygma. 90 (top), Misha Erwitt/Magnum; (center), Rene Burri/Magnum; (bottom), © David R. Frazier/Photolibrary. 93, © Eugene Richards/Magnum Photos.

CHAPTER 5
97, Alex Webb/Magnum Photos Inc. 111, © Cynthia Johnson/The Gamma Liaison Network. 114, © Frank Siteman 1989/Stock.Boston. 117, © Stephen Ferry/The Gamma Liaison Network. 121, © Craig Filipacchi/Gamma Liaison.

CHAPTER 6
128, © Mark Richards/PhotoEdit. 129, © Craig Filipacchi/ Gamma Liaison. 133, © Bob Daemmrich/Stock.Boston. 141, © Bob Daemmrich/Stock.Boston. 145, © Frances M. Roberts. 148, © Ron Grishaber/PhotoEdit.

PART THREE
153, Michael Patrick/Folio, Inc.

CHAPTER 7
154, Reuters/Bettmann. 155, AP/Wide World Photos. 159, © 1989 David Lissy/Leo de Wys, Inc. 161, © Jean Marc Giboux/Gamma Liaison. 168, © Billy E. Barnes.

CHAPTER 8
179 (top), John Running/Stock.Boston; (bottom), Ellis Herwig/Stock.Boston. 184, © Cheyenne Rouse/ Photophile. 186, © 1991 Frank Fournier/Contact Press Images. 192, © David Burnett/Woodfin Camp & Assoc. 193, © Jim Pickerell 1985/Stock.Boston. 195, © John Neubauer/PhotoEdit.

CHAPTER 9
203, © Jim Pickerell/Tony Stone Worldwide. 204, © Evan Agostini/The Gamma Liaison Network. 210, © Zephyer. 212, © Granitsas/The Image Works. 214, © Frank Fournier/Woodfin Camp & Assoc. 219, © Frank Fournier/Woodfin Camp & Assoc.

CHAPTER 10
227, The Bettmann Archive. 230, Wide World Photos, Inc. 234, © Steve Lehman/SABA. 237, Adam Zetter/Leo de Wys Inc. 247, AP/Wide World Photos.

PART FOUR
251, © Bill Swersey/The Gamma Liaison Network.

CHAPTER 11
252, © Bob Daemmrich. 255, Library of Congress. 257, American Correctional Association. 260, The Bettmann Archive. 261, AP/Wide World Photos.

CHAPTER 12
276, © Jacques Chenet 1990. 281, American Correctional Association. 285, SZABO Photography. 287, Courtesy of Sensing Alternatives, Anaheim, California. 292, © Gerd Ludwig.

CHAPTER 13
297, Ed Kashi © 1989. 304, © John Chiasson/The Gamma Liaison Network. 305, © Alan Levenson. 308, Bob Daemmrich/Stock.Boston. 313, Bob Daemmrich. 318, AP/Wide World Photos.

CHAPTER 14
322, David Woo/Stock.Boston. 325, Mary Evans Picture Library. 326, © John Curtis. 337, Bruce Kleine/Jeroboam Inc. 339, AP/Wide World Photos.

PART FIVE
345, Betsy Herzog/AP/Wide World Photos.

CHAPTER 15
346, © 1994 Alon Reininger/Woodfin Camp & Assoc. 347, Fritz Hoffmann/NYT Pictures. 352, © Renato Rotolo/Gamma Liaison. 357, © Alon Reininger/Woodfin Camp & Assoc. 359, © Billy E. Barnes.

INDEX/GLOSSARY

C

Capital punishment, 238–241
  and constitutional rights, 239–241
  and Eighth Amendment, 71–72, 238, 241
  and incapacitation, 231
Carter, Robert, 246
Case evolution, 164–165
Causation, 54–55
Challenge for cause Removal of a prospective juror due to bias or some other factor contributing to an inability to make fair decisions. 219
Chambers, Robert, 216
Chapper, Joy, 224
Charging, 39
Chimel v. *California*, 119–120
Cincinnati Declaration, 258–259
Circumstantial evidence Evidence provided by a witness from which a jury must infer a fact. 220
Citation A written order issued by a law enforcement officer directing those accused of committing a minor offense to appear in court at a specified time rather than place them under arrest. 188
Civil disabilities, 342–343
Civilian review boards, 143–144
Civil law, 53
Civil liability suits, 144–145
Civil Rights Act (1871), 144, 317
Civil rights movements, 83
Clark, Marcia, 155, 157, 158
Class discrimination
  and bail, 190–191
  and incarceration, 247, 270
  by police, 83
  and visible crime, 7–8
Classification A process by which a committee of prison department heads determine an inmate's security level, treatment needs, work assignments, and eventually readiness for release. 310
Clearance rate The percentage of crimes known to the police that they believe they have solved through an arrest; a statistic used a measure of a police department's productivity. 103–104
Clemmer, Donald, 299
Clinton, Bill, 5–6, 9, 68
Coast Guard, 86
Coercion defense, 59
Commission on Accreditation for Law Enforcement Agencies (CALEA), 144
Community correctional center An institution housing soon-

to-be-released inmates and connecting them with community services, resources, and support. 337
Community corrections A model of corrections based on the assumption that the reintegration of the offender into the community should be the goal of the criminal justice system. 261–262, 277–294
  intermediate sanctions, 41, 237, 284–293
  juvenile, 362–363
  and parole, 336–338
  probation, 41, 237–238, 279–284
Community-oriented policing, 84–85, 111–112
Community service A sentence requiring the offender to perform a certain amount of labor in the community. 288
Comprehensive Crime Control Act (1984), 62–63
Congregate system A penitentiary system, developed in Auburn, New York, in which each inmate was held in isolation at night but worked with fellow prisoners during the day under a rule of silence. 257–258
Constitutional rights, 63, 64–72
  and capital punishment, 238, 239–241
  and civil disabilities, 342
  and defense, 166–167
  and federalism, 28–29
  and forfeiture, 286
  and habeas corpus, 224
  and incarceration, 269
  and juvenile justice, 351, 359–360
  and parole, 341
  and plea bargaining, 198–200
  and police, 119–124
  prisoners, 317–319
  and probation, 283
  See also specific cases
Continuing Criminal Enterprise Act (CCE), 286
Contract system of indigent defense, 171
Cooper v. *Pate* Prisoners are entitled to the protection of the Civil Rights Act of 1871 and may challenge conditions of their confinement in the federal courts. 317
"Copping out" Courtroom procedure in which the judge asks the defendant a series of questions to determine whether a guilty plea is accurate and voluntary. 199

Corrections, 36, 41, 253–274
  community model, 261–262
  current trends, 262–263
  English penitentiary development, 254–255
  juvenile, 361–364
  organization of, 263–268
  Pennsylvania system, 256–257
  Progressive reforms, 259–260
  reformatory movement, 258–259
  rehabilitation model, 260–261
  See also Incarceration; Prisons
Corruption, 185, 258. *See also* Police corruption
Count Each separate offense of which a person is accused in an indictment or an information. 160
County police agencies, 87
Courts, 204–207
  administration, 207
  appeals, 41, 223–224
  juvenile justice, 359–361
  and probation, 280–281
  structure, 205–206
  workgroups in, 212–215
  See also Judges; Trials
Crime A specific act of commission or omission in violation of the law, for which punishment is prescribed.
  defined, 5–6
  elements of, 56
  extent of, 3–4, 8–12
  impact of, 17–19
  statutory definitions, 56–57
  trends in, 13–15
  types of, 6–8
  See also specific topics
Crime Control Model A model of the criminal justice system that assumes that freedom is so important that every effort must be made to repress crime; it emphasizes efficiency and the capacity to apprehend, try, convict, and dispose of a high proportion of offenders; and it also stresses speed and finality. 27–28, 48
  juvenile justice, 352, 360
  police, 35
Crime prevention, 28, 35
Criminal justice system
  crime control vs. due process models, 47–49
  decision making in, 37–41
  discretion in, 32–33
  elements of, 35–36
  as filtering process, 34, 35
  goals of, 27–28
  parallel systems, 28–31, 70
  resource dependence of, 33

Ewing, Jack, 190

Exchange A mutual transfer of resources among individual decision makers, each of whom has interests and goals that he or she cannot readily accomplish alone. 31–32, 303

Exclusionary rule The principle that illegally obtained evidence must be excluded from a trial. 67–68, 69–70, 122–124

Expert witnesses, 62–63

Explicit plea bargaining Direct negotiations between the prosecution and defense, sometimes with the participation of judges, in which a defendant agrees to plead guilty in exchange for reduced charges or the recommendation of a lighter-than-maximum sentence. 194

Ex post facto laws, 54

F

Faal, Edi, 222
Fairstein, Linda, 216
Fear of crime, 18–19, 110
Federal Bureau of Investigation (FBI), 26, 29, 86. *See also Uniform Crime Reports*
Federalism A system of government in which power is divided between a central (national) government and regional (state) governments. 28–29
and corrections, 263–267
and courts, 36, 205–206
and police, 85–87
Federal marshals, 81–82
Federal Trade Commission, 7
Feeley, Malcolm, 243
Feld, Barry, 351
Felony A serious crime punishable by one year or more of imprisonment or by death. 6, 244
Fielding, Henry, 78
Fielding, Sir John, 78
Fifth Amendment, 64, 68–70, 122
Filtering process A screening operation in which some defendants are sent on to the next stage of decision making while others are either released or processed under changed conditions. 34, 35
Fine A sum of money to be paid to the state by a convicted person as punishment for an offense. 284–285
First Amendment, 317
Flemming, Roy, 187–188
Foot patrols, 80, 82–83, 109–110

Forensic techniques, 116
Forer, Lois, 283
Forfeiture Seizure by the government of property and other assets derived from or used in criminal activity. 286
Fortas, Abe, 351
Fosdic, Raymond, 82
Foucault, Michel, 254
Fourteenth Amendment Constitutional amendment forbidding states from violating people's right to due process of law and thereby nationalizing the application of many provisions of the Bill of Rights. *See* Due Process Model
Fourth Amendment, 64, 66–68, 119–122, 318
Fox, James, 313
Frankpledge system A system in medieval England whereby members of a tithing, a group of ten families, agreed to maintain order, uphold the law, and commit violators to a court. 78
Fraud, 7
Fry, Elizabeth Gurney, 267
Fuld, Leonhard, 82
Funding, 33, 207
Furlough The temporary release of an inmate from a correctional institution for a brief period, usually one to three days, for a visit home. 336–337
Furman v. Georgia The death penalty, as administered, constituted cruel and unusual punishment. 70, 71, 239–240
Fyfe, James, 136, 138

G

Gacy, John Wayne, 60
Gagnon v. Scarpelli Before probation or parole may be revoked, the offender is entitled to a preliminary and a final hearing and to specific elements of due process. 283
Gambling, 8. *See also* Victimless crime
Gangs, 316
Garcetti, Gil, 156, 157
Gates, Daryl, 204
Gault. See In re Gault
Gender
discrimination, 133, 212
and jury selection, 219
victims, 16–17
and youth crime, 348
See also Women

General deterrence Punishment of criminals intended to serve as an example to the general public and thus to discourage the commission of offenses. 230
Gideon v. Wainwright Defendants have a right to counsel in felony cases, and the state must provide attorneys for defendants who are too poor to hire their own. 70
"Gleaning," 308
Goetz, Bernhard, 58
Goffman, Erving, 300
"Going rate" Local view of the appropriate punishments for specific crimes based on the seriousness of offense and offender's prior record. 195
Goldstein, Stanley, 277
Good-faith exception, 123–124
"Good time" A reduction of a convict's prison sentence awarded for good behavior at the discretion of the prison administrator. 234, 236–237, 303, 332. *See also* Parole
Gram, Lawrence, Jr., 61
Grand jury, 39–40
Gregg v. Georgia Capital punishment statutes are permissible if they provide careful procedures to guide decision making by judges and juries. 71, 240
Grouping A collective of individuals who interact in the workplace but, because of shifting membership, do not develop into a workgroup. 213
Guthrie, Adrian, 253

H

Habeas corpus A writ or judicial order requesting that a person holding another person produce the prisoner and give reasons to justify continued confinement. 224
Halfway house Term applied to a variety of community correctional facilities and programs whereby felons may work in the community but reside in the halfway house during nonworking hours. 337–338
Hall, Jerome, 54
Hamlin, Charles, 180, 184, 185
Hanson, Roger, 224
Hearst, Patty, 59, 167
Heffernan, Esther, 312, 313
Hickock, Bill, 81
Hinckley, John, 46, 60, 61

Knapp Commission, 140
Krikava, Ernest, 228, 229

L

Law enforcement The police function of determining the identity or whereabouts of the violator and apprehending the suspect. 91. *See also specific topics*

Legalistic style A style of policing that emphasizes professionalism and law enforcement whereby officers are expected to act against all infractions of the law and to employ a single standard of community conduct treating all groups the same. 89

Legal sufficiency model Prosecution policy that asks whether sufficient evidence exists to provide a basis for prosecution of a case. 163–164

Legislative exclusion Provision of criminal statutes whereby certain offenses automatically are transferred to adult court, possibly including rape, armed robbery, and other violent crimes. 352

Levin, Jennifer, 216

Levin, Martin A., 212, 244

Line functions Police actions that directly involve field operations such as patrol, investigation, traffic control, vice and juvenile crimes, and so on. 104

Local legal culture Norms shared by members of a court community as to case handling and participants' behavior in the judicial process. 195

Logan, Charles, 267–268

Lorenzano, Tracy, 103

Lucasville riot, 298

M

Machismo, 315

Maconochie, Alexander, 325

MADD (Mothers Against Drunk Driving), 266

Magna Carta, 78

Mandatory release The required release of an inmate from incarceration upon the expiration of a certain time period, as stipulated by a determinate sentencing law or parole guidelines. 326, 328

Mandatory sentence Requirement that some minimum period of incarceration be served by persons convicted of selected crimes, regardless of the circumstances of

the offense or the background of the offender. 234–236, 266, 270

Manson, Charles, 46, 60

Mapp v. Ohio Evidence obtained through unreasonable searches and seizures by state and local law enforcement officers must be excluded. 67, 119, 122, 123

Marshall, Thurgood, 71

Massachusetts Stubborn Child Law (1646), 349

Masterson, Bat, 81

McCleskey v. Kemp Rejected a constitutional challenge to Georgia's death penalty on the grounds of racial discrimination. 72, 240–241

McCoy, Candace, 194

Medical model, 260. *See also* Rehabilitation

Mempa v. Rhay Probationers have the right to counsel at a hearing considering revocation of a suspended sentence. 283

Men. *See* Gender

Mens rea "Guilty mind," or blameworthy state of mind, necessary to be held responsible for a criminal offense. 55, 56, 60

Mentally retarded people, 241

Metcalf, Eric, 37

Midnight Run, 186

Minorities
careers, 132, 305
and jury selection, 218
victimization, 17
See also Race; Racial discrimination

Minors. *See* Juvenile justice system

Miranda v. Arizona Confessions made by suspects who have not been informed by police about their due process rights cannot be admitted as evidence. 68, 70, 122, 123

Misdemeanor An offense less serious than a felony and usually punishable by one year or less of imprisonment or by probation, fines, and/or community service. 6, 243–244

"Missouri plan," 211–212

Mistake defense, 59–60

M'Naghten Rule, 61

Model A representation of something that cannot be visualized, permitting generalized statements to be made about it and evaluations of its strengths and weaknesses. 47

Model Penal Code, 62

Mollen Commission, 129, 140

Monell v. Department of Social Services for the City of New York, 144

Moore, Mark, 83

Moore v. *Dempsey*, 65

Moran, Richard, 61

Morris, Gregory, 347

Morris, Norval, 237, 284

Morrissey v. Brewer A parolee who faces parole revocation must be accorded due process rights and a prompt, informal inquiry before an impartial hearing officer. 341

Motion An application to a court requesting that an order be issued to bring about a specified action. 182

Municipal police agencies, 87

Murphy, Cristina, 134

N

National Crime Victimization Surveys (NCVS) Interviews of samples of the U.S. population conducted for the Bureau of Justice Statistics to determine the number and types of criminal victimization and thus the extent of unreported as well as reported crime. 9–10, 11–12, 13, 16, 263

National Incident-Based Reporting System (NIBRS) System in which the police will report each offense in a crime incident as well as data on offenders, victims, and the environments in which they interact. 11

National Organization of Black Law Enforcement Executives (NOBLE), 144

National Parks Service, 86

National Prison Association, 258

National Probation Association, 282

National Sheriffs Association (NSA), 144

National Stolen Property Act, 29

Necessarily included offense An offense committed for the purpose of committing another offense, such as weapons possession for the purpose of committing robbery. 160

Necessity defense, 58–59

Neglected child A child who is not receiving proper care because of some action or inaction of his or her parent(s). 353

"Net widening," 293

New York system, 257–258

New York v. *Class*, 121

New York v. *Quarles*, 70, 123

911 procedure, 102, 103

Nix v. *Williams*, 123

some form of vocational, educational, or therapeutic treatment. 232–233, 260–261, 300
and community corrections, 261
and parole, 326
and penitentiaries, 254, 255, 256–257
prison programs, 311
and Progressive corrections reform, 259–260
and reformatory movement, 258–259

Rehabilitation model A model of corrections that emphasizes the provision of treatment programs designed to reform offenders. 300

Rehnquist, William, 67, 68, 71, 241

Reintegration model A model of corrections that emphasizes the maintenance of offenders' ties to family and community as a method of reform, in recognition of the fact that they will be returning to the community. 300

Release, 41
and civil disabilities, 342–343
See also Parole; Pretrial processes

Release on own recognizance (ROR) Pretrial release without bail granted on the defendant's promise to appear in court. 188

Responsibility, 57–63

Restitution Repayment by an offender to a victim who has suffered financial loss or physical harm from the crime. 285–286

Retribution Punishment inflicted on a person who has infringed on the rights of others and so deserves to be penalized; the severity of the sanction should fit the gravity of the offense. 229–230

Richardson, James, 248

Ricketts **v.** *Adamson* Defendants must uphold plea agreements or suffer the consequences. 200

Right-from-wrong test, 61

Risk assessment, 262

Rizzo, Frank, 143

Roberts, Simon, 253

Robinson v. *California*, 54

Rostenkowski, Dan, 196

S

Sandifur, Robert, 77

Santobello **v.** *New York* Prosecutors are obligated to fulfill promises made during plea negotiations. 193

Santos, Michael, 306–307

Savage, Edward H., 80, 81

Schall **v.** *Martin* Pretrial detention of a juvenile is constitutional to protect the welfare of the minor and the community. 189, 352

Search and seizure, 64, 66–68, 119–122, 318

Search warrant An order issued by a judge that allows a police officer to search a designated place for specific persons or items to be seized. 119

Secret Service Division, 86

Securities and Exchange Commission, 7

Sedition Act (1789), 8

Selective incapacitation The strategy whereby offenders who repeatedly commit certain kinds of crimes are sentenced to long prison terms. 232

Self-defense, 58

Self-incrimination Provision of the Fifth Amendment that one cannot be forced to answer questions that may tend to incriminate oneself. 64, 68–70, 122

Sentencing, 40, 223, 228–248
capital punishment, 238–241
fairness, 247–248
guidelines, 246–247
incarceration, 233–237
intermediate sanctions, 237
probation, 237–238
process, 242–247
and punishment goals, 229–233

Sentencing guidelines An instrument developed to indicate to judges the expected sanction for particular types of offenses. 246–247

Separate confinement A penitentiary system, developed in Pennsylvania, in which each inmate was held in isolation from other inmates and in which all activities, including craft work, were carried on in the cells. 256

Service The police function of providing assistance to the public, usually in matters unrelated to crime. 36, 80, 92

Service style A style of policing that emphasizes the provision of services to the community and individualized treatment at the hands of the police. 89

Sexism. *See* Gender

Shapiro, Robert, 155, 158, 165, 175

Sheriffs, 81

Sherman, Lawrence W., 110

Shock incarceration. *See* Shock probation

Shock probation A sentence during which an offender is released after a period of incarceration and resentenced to probation. 237–238, 279

Silbey, Susan, 243

Simpson, O.J., 46, 155, 156, 157, 158, 165, 167, 175

Sirhan Sirhan, 329

Sixth Amendment, 64, 70–71, 176

Skatzes, George, 298

Skolnick, Jerome, 136, 138

Slavery, 80–81

Smith, Bruce, 82

Socialization The process by which the rules, symbols, and values of a group or subculture are learned by its members. 131

Social services. *See* Service

Special deterrence Punishment inflicted on criminals with the intent to discourage them from committing crimes in the future. 230

Spelman, William G., 108

Split sentences. *See* Shock probation

Staff functions Police actions that supplement or support the line functions, based in the chief's office and the auxiliary services and staff inspection bureaus. 104

Stanford v. *Kentucky,* 241

State corrections system, 264–265

State of Prisons in England and Wales, The (Howard), 254–255

State police agencies, 86–87

Status offense Any act committed by a juvenile that would not be a crime if it were committed by an adult, such as skipping school or running away from home. 351

Statute of Winchester, 78

Stewart, Potter, 193

Stoddard, Ellwyn, 141

Stress, 136–137, 316

Strickland v. *Washington,* 176

Strict liability Offenses involving health and safety in which no demonstration of *mens rea* is required. 55

Subculture The aggregate of symbols, beliefs, values, and attitudes shared by members of a subgroup within the larger society. 132, 134–137

Substantial Capacity Test, 62

Substantive criminal law Law defining the behaviors that are subject to punishment by the government and the sanctions for such offenses. 53, 54–63
principles of, 54–56
and responsibility, 57–63
statutory definitions, 56–57
Suffet, Frederic, 187
Sworn officers Police employees who have taken an oath and been given powers by the state to make arrests, apply necessary force, and so on in accordance with their duties. 104
Sykes, Gresham, 299, 302
System A complex whole consisting of interdependent parts whose operations are directed toward goals and are influenced by the environment within which they function. 31
System efficiency model Operation of the prosecutor's office that encourages speedy and early disposition of cases in response to caseload pressures in the system. 164

T

Tax evasion, 7
Tennessee v. Garner Deadly force may not be used against an unarmed and fleeing suspect "unless it is necessary to prevent the escape and the officer has probable cause to believe that the suspect poses a significant threat of death or serious physical injury to the officer or others." 139
Terry v. Ohio A police officer may stop and frisk an individual if it is reasonable to suspect that a crime has been or will be committed. 120
Testimony Oral evidence provided by a legally competent witness. 220
Thin Blue Line, The, 248
"Three-strikes" laws, 235
Threshold inquiries, 120
Ticket-of-leave, 325
Tierney, John, 354–355
Tlingit Tribal Court, 253
Toch, Hans, 315
Tonry, Michael, 237, 284
Total institution An institution that completely encapsulates the lives of those who work and live there,

with one group controlling the lives of the other. 300–301
Traffic policing, 117–118
Trial courts of general jurisdiction Criminal courts that have primary responsibility for felony cases and that, in some states, may also hear appeals. 206
Trial courts of limited jurisdiction Criminal courts that generally have responsibility for misdemeanor cases, as well as arraignments, probable cause hearings in felony cases, and, sometimes, felony trials that may result in penalties below a specified limit. 206
Trial sufficiency model Prosecution policy that asks whether sufficient legal elements exist to ensure successful prosecution of a case. 164
Trials, 40, 215–223
juries, 215–220
process of, 220–223
See also Courts
Trop v. *Dulles*, 71
Tyson, Mike, 167

U

Uniform Crime Reports (UCR) An annually published statistical summary of crimes reported to the police based on voluntary reports to the FBI by individual police departments. 9, 10–11, 13, 14, 56, 57, 88, 94
Unions, 145–146, 268
United States attorneys Officials appointed by the president and responsible for the prosecution of crimes that violate federal laws; members of the Department of Justice. 156
U.S. Corrections Corporation, 267
United States v. *Cronic*, 176
United States **v. Leon** Evidence seized using a warrant later found to be defective is valid if the officer was acting in good faith. 67, 123–124
United States **v. Salerno** Preventive detention provisions of the Bail Reform Act of 1984 upheld as a legitimate use of governmental power to prevent people from committing crimes while out on bail. 71, 189
Urbanization, 17, 82
Urbom, Warren, 228

V

Vice operations, 118, 141
Victimless crime Offenses involving a willing and private exchange of illegal goods or services for which there is a strong demand. Although participants do not feel that they are being harmed, prosecution is justified on the grounds that society as a whole is being injured by the act. 8, 101, 118, 141
Victimology A subfield of criminology that examines the role played by the victim in precipitating a criminal incident. 15–16
Victim precipitation, 20
Victims, 15–17, 19–20
and prosecution, 161–162
Vietnam War, 8
Violent Crime Control and Law Enforcement Act (1994), 8–9
Visible crime Offenses against persons and property committed primarily by members of the lower class. Often referred to as "street crimes" or "ordinary crimes," these are the offenses most upsetting to the public. 7–8
Voir dire The process of questioning prospective jurors by the prosecution and defense to screen out persons who might be biased or incapable of rendering a fair verdict. 219
Vollmer, August, 82
von Hirsch, Andrew, 229–230

W

Waco incident, 26
Walker, Samuel, 132
Walnut Street Jail, 256
War on drugs. *See* Drug enforcement
Warrant A court order issued by a judge authorizing police officers to take certain actions, such as arresting suspects or searching premises. 39
Warren, Earl, 65, 69, 70, 71, 124
Watchman style A style of policing that emphasizes order maintenance whereby officers exercise discretion and deal informally with many infractions. 89
Watson, Henry, 204, 222
Weeks v. *United States*, 67
White, Byron, 67–68
White-collar crime. *See* Occupational crime